THE END OF RECIPROCITY

Why should America restrain itself in detaining, interrogating, and targeting terrorists when they show it no similar forbearance? Is it fair to expect one side to fight by more stringent rules than the other, placing itself at disadvantage? Is the disadvantaged side then permitted to use the tactics and strategies of its opponent? If so, then America's most controversial counterterrorism practices are justified as commensurate responses to indiscriminate terror. Yet different ethical standards prove entirely fitting, the author contends, in a conflict between a network of suicidal terrorists seeking mass atrocity at any cost and a constitutional democracy committed to respecting human dignity and the rule of law. The most important reciprocity involves neither uniform application of fair rules nor their enforcement by a simple-minded approach. Real reciprocity instead entails contributing to an emergent global contract that encompasses the law of war and from which all peoples may mutually benefit.

Mark Osiel has written five books on the law of war, most recently *Making Sense of Mass Atrocity* (Cambridge University Press, 2009) and *Mass Atrocity, Ordinary Evil, and Hannah Arendt: Criminal Consciousness in Argentina's Dirty War* (2001). He has lectured at the International Criminal Tribunal for the former Yugoslavia and advised on the prosecution of General Augusto Pinochet and the perpetrators of the Rwandan genocide. He regularly consults to international organizations and governments in postconflict societies on issues of transitional justice. Osiel has been a Visiting Fellow at Cambridge University, Harvard's Kennedy School of Government, the London School of Economics, and universities in Argentina, Brazil, France, and India. He teaches law at the University of Iowa and is director of International Criminal and Humanitarian Law at the T. M. C. Asser Institute, a think-tank in The Hague devoted to international law and part of the University of Amsterdam.

The End of Reciprocity

TERROR, TORTURE, AND THE LAW OF WAR

MARK OSIEL

College of Law, University of Iowa
Director of International Criminal and Humanitarian Law
T. M. C. Asser Institute, The Hague

CAMBRIDGE
UNIVERSITY PRESS

CAMBRIDGE UNIVERSITY PRESS
Cambridge, New York, Melbourne, Madrid, Cape Town, Singapore, São Paulo, Delhi

Cambridge University Press
32 Avenue of the Americas, New York, NY 10013-2473, USA

www.cambridge.org
Information on this title: www.cambridge.org/9780521730143

First published 2009

Printed in the United States of America

A catalog record for this publication is available from the British Library

Library of Congress Cataloging in Publication data

Osiel, Mark.
The end of reciprocity : terror, torture, and the law of war / Mark Osiel.
    p.   cm.
Includes bibliographical references and index.
ISBN   978-0-521-51351-7 (hardback) – ISBN   978-0-521-73014-3 (pbk.)
1. Humanitarian law.   2. War on Terrorism, 2001 – Law and legislation   3. Lex
talionis.   4. Reciprocity (Psychology)   I. Title.
KZ6471.O845   2009
341.6′7 – dc22   2008034560

ISBN   978-0-521-51351-7 hardback
ISBN   978-0-521-73014-3 paperback

For my recent international students:
Khaliq, Mohit, Rohit, Sergei,
Elvana, Jon, and David

We acquire attachments to persons and institutions according to how we perceive our good to be affected by them. The basic idea is one of reciprocity, a tendency to answer in kind. Now this tendency is a deep psychological fact. Without it our nature would be very different.

John Rawls, A Theory of Justice, 1971

International humanitarian law texts rarely admit it, yet without reciprocity in practice those texts may be of little avail, for not all belligerents will be so saintly as to observe restraint and to honour humanitarian obligations in the face of an enemy's persistent refusal to do so. The most effective actual working engine of international humanitarian law observance, far from being established or even mentioned in the Geneva Conventions . . . works in fact in apparent defiance of them. Reciprocity is its name. Reciprocity may roughly back humanitarian principle, whether humanitarians or principle ask it to or not.

Geoffrey Best, War and Law since 1945, 1994

Since we have reacted in kind, your description of us as terrorists . . . necessarily means that you and your actions must be defined likewise. . . . If killing those that kill our sons is terrorism, then let history witness that we are terrorists. . . . We treat others like they treat us. . . . The Americans started it, and retaliation . . . should be carried out following the principle of reciprocity, especially when women and children are involved. . . . If we don't have security, neither will the Americans. . . . We swore that America could never dream of safety, until safety becomes a reality for us living in Palestine. . . . Terror for Terror . . . Blood for blood, destruction for destruction . . . Stop spilling our blood in order to save your own.

Osama bin Laden, Messages to the World: The Statements of Osama bin Laden (2005), and 2007 fatwa

Whoever fights monsters should see to it that in the process he does not become a monster. And when you look long into an abyss, the abyss also looks into you.

Friedrich Nietzsche, Beyond Good and Evil, 1886

Contents

Introduction

What treatment is fitting for high-ranking Al Qaeda suspects who can be detained or located, who repudiate humanitarian law,[1] and who qualify as neither prisoners of war nor protected civilians under the Geneva Conventions?[2] Such persons undoubtedly have information about terrorist organizations and plans[3] that could be useful in preventing mass atrocity. If militant jihadists continue to threaten the United States with attacks on the scale of 9/11, is it defensible to detain hundreds of such individuals indefinitely? And may such groups' leaders be killed at any time, even when far from any combat?[4] More generally, when may a country at war expect the enemy to reciprocate its own restraint in following the law of armed conflict?[5] And if the enemy will not exercise a similar forbearance, at what point (and in what ways) is the law-abiding state released from its normal legal duties, to restore a tactical and moral symmetry in confrontation?

The law of war rests on certain assumptions not immediately applicable to America's conflict with Al Qaeda and kindred groups.[6] Within such law, for instance, the justice of a country's cause is irrelevant to how enemies should treat that country's soldiers.[7] Conscripts are often the innocent means by which unjust rulers pursue their ignoble ends. Even enlistees in a wrongful cause are generally misguided dupes of well-intentioned nationalist ardor, aroused by powerful leaders employing state censorship and propaganda. Such leaders remain the true culprits, behind the scenes. The lowly "grunt" or "doughboy" acts from duty, not from passion, except perhaps the understandable passion to protect immediate combat "buddies." Belligerent forces consist of modern armies that, as formal bureaucracies, are committed to a means-end rationality. The Geneva Conventions, in their protections for prisoners of war (POWs) and other detainees, are predicated on all these assumptions.

But what happens to the law of war when these assumptions cannot be made? Has traditional humanitarian law become today's conceptual "iron cage," preventing fresh thinking about the novelties of the West's strategic predicament and the legal challenges it poses?

Some will reply that the answers to most such questions are now clear from the U.S. Supreme Court's 2006 opinion in *Hamdan v. Rumsfeld*.[8] All captives enjoy the considerable protections afforded by Common Article 3 of the Conventions. That provision prohibits treatment of detainees amounting to "outrages upon human dignity, in particular, humiliating and degrading treatment."[9] It permits a detainee's prosecution only by "a regularly constituted court, affording all the judicial guarantees which are recognized as indispensable by civilized peoples."[10] Assassination has long been banned by executive order,[11] thereby eliminating it from the American arsenal of lawful fighting methods. Positive law is thus clear, to this extent.

Yet this is not the proper endpoint of legal, much less of moral or sociological analysis. The principle of reciprocity continues to infuse much of international law, including humanitarian law, both customary and treaties, particularly those governing the conduct of hostilities and prohibiting certain weapons. The United States has also "persistently objected" to the development of a customary rule prohibiting "reprisals" against civilians, and so America is not bound by such an emergent rule.[12] As a moral principle with deep roots throughout international law and in the U.S. law of foreign relations, reciprocity has a strong gravitational force. It could be understood to justify forcible countermeasures through targeted killing of Al Qaeda leaders, for instance, and perhaps also their sustained, preventive detention and coercive interrogation.[13]

Insofar as they may be justified by the reciprocity principle, the three practices here in question would entail a qualified relaxation of normal rules of humanitarian law in response to its complete repudiation by the belligerent whose fighters would be so treated. Retaliation directed only against those in positions of responsibility within Al Qaeda would withstand the perennial criticism that reprisals punish the innocent.[14] Such reprisals would be, in fact, highly discriminating and hence respect humanitarian law's most central principle. On this understanding of reprisal, leaders – whether combatant or civilian – of a fighting force dedicated to mass attacks on civilians may be subjected to degrading measures insofar as these practices are directed toward protecting civilian populations, through incapacitation and intelligence gathering.[15]

Answering the legal questions does not entirely resolve, in any event, the more basic moral question: In this type of conflict, what should the law permit, prohibit, and require concerning Al Qaeda leaders whose where-abouts can be identified or who have been detained? In offering an answer, this book aims to move existing discussion beyond the tired opposition between a crude "utilitarianism" (the ends justify the means) and "Kantian" absolutism (torture and extrajudicial killing are always impermissible, though the heavens may fall).

There is also the question of why states do or do not comply with their duties. We lack, and urgently need, what might be called a sociology of restraint: an account of the forces within and between societies that lead them to honor or to stray beyond the law's bounds when engaged in war. The demands of positive law in this area have not always been sufficient to motivate full adherence, even for constitutional democracies committed to the "rule of law."[16] In international relations, knowing the formalities of positive law "on the books" is rarely enough to know what will actually happen "in action."

American practice regarding detained Al Qaeda suspects is widely and rightly regarded as troubling. Yet it is notable how broad the range of American support has been for only the most minimal restraint. More than half of Americans report to survey researchers that they find it "convincing" that "given what we learned from the 9/11 attacks, we cannot afford to tie our hands by declaring off limits any method for getting information that could be useful in the war on terrorism."[17]

Six of seven 2008 Republican presidential hopefuls, in their second public debate, expressly condoned the use of "aggressive interrogation techniques" on terrorist suspects.[18] In June 2007, only two of the party's enlarged group of ten announced candidates favored closing the Guantánamo detention facility.[19] Its closure would, in any event, have entailed sending many of its denizens home to countries more likely to mistreat them seriously than has the United States. And in a public lecture, Supreme Court Justice Antonin Scalia even praised the television program *24*, announcing that there should be no "absolute" prohibitions on torture.[20] Memoranda by Steven Bradbury, acting head of the Justice Department's Office of Legal Counsel, continued to authorize harsh interrogation methods well after the Bush administration publicly claimed to have abandoned them.[21] In February 2008, Republican presidential nominee John McCain voted against a bill that would have barred the CIA from waterboarding detainees and encouraged President Bush to veto the legislation.[22] In her electoral campaign, Senator Hillary Clinton expressly countenanced the presidential authorization of torture in a "ticking time-bomb" situation.[23]

The illegality of such methods hence cannot be the end of the conversation. The more pressing question is: What forces might restrain a state tempted to employ such methods? More specifically, what is to stop the United States from indefinitely detaining Al Qaeda leaders and other militant jihadists who appear to pose a significant threat? In fact, why should the U.S. *not* coercively interrogate such people whenever it has good reason to believe they possess valuable information about terrorist groups' internal operations, personnel, and plans? Some influential voices would indeed like to see current law changed, by domestic statute or international agreement, thereby permitting more aggressive tactics for fighting terrorist networks whose members do not honor humanitarian norms.[24]

That international law itself often tells us so little about what actually will be done in war paradoxically renders the purely moral questions even more salient. The normative question this book examines is whether humanitarian law should operate reciprocally, so that Al Qaeda's disregard for noncombatant rights would authorize the United States to do targeted killings of jihadist leaders – a policy accepted by all major presidential hopefuls in the 2008 primaries[25] – and relax presumptive standards for detention and treatment of Al Qaeda suspects.[26] Or should humanitarian law be understood as largely nonreciprocal, in which case its consistent violation by Al Qaeda would in no way diminish American legal duties toward detained Al Qaeda members or its leaders still at large?

Our intuitive, unschooled reaction to this question is likely to be mixed. On the one hand, most agree that basic principles of humanity (and perhaps also considerations of national self-interest) limit what may be done to even the most egregious violators of fundamental humanitarian norms.[27] No one seriously argues, for instance, that "these terrorists do not deserve any better treatment than the treatment they have displayed toward their victims."[28]

On the other hand, fairness has often been thought to require that each side to an armed conflict be subject to the same restrictions and that neither should be permitted to seek unfair advantage by violating them. Reciprocity in the sense of tit-for-tat also makes possible self-policing,[29] which is often necessary in the absence of effective international enforcement.[30] Self-help is always the ultimate remedy when the "social contract" and its normal method of execution completely break down. "Gated communities" arose in response to rapidly rising crime rates, after all. In war, self-enforcement offers a practical form of corrective justice and a means of deterring future violations.[31] For these reasons, as Sir Hersch Lauterpacht wrote, "It is impossible to visualize the conduct of hostilities in which one side would be bound by rules of warfare without benefiting from them and the other side would benefit from rules of warfare without being bound by them."[32] Hans Kelsen, an equally distinguished jurist, said much the same.[33]

What legal rules, then, should mark the meeting point between our contending intuitions here? Today, both reciprocal and nonreciprocal impulses find expression in different parts of the Geneva and Hague Conventions. This creates some vexing ambiguities.

America's greatest military and political leaders have long felt pulled in both directions. During the Revolutionary War, General George Washington often reminded his troops that they were fighting for liberties and freedoms that, as rights of all humanity, extended even to their enemies. When the British treated captive American "rebels" so poorly that more died in captivity than on the battlefield,[34] Washington nonetheless informed the British General Lord Howe that, in retaliation, he intended to conduct reprisals.[35] Yet Washington ultimately refrained from exercising that right, instead ordering subordinates in charge of 221 British troops captured at Princeton to "treat them with humanity, and let them have no reason to complain of our copying the brutal example of the British army in their treatment of our unfortunate brethren."[36] That Washington both avowed his right of reprisal and ultimately declined to exercise it begins to capture the ambivalence that the doctrine evoked even then, an ambivalence that has only deepened over time.

History casts a long shadow over current controversies. Since the mid-nineteenth century, the Geneva Conventions – treaties today ratified by virtually all states – have chiefly regulated the treatment of noncombatants and prisoners of war. The Hague treaties, beginning in 1899, do so as well, but they and their many progeny also govern the conduct of hostilities (e.g., weapons and their permissible uses).[37] The more recent agreements seek, for instance, to ban the manufacture or international trade in particular armaments, from small arms and antipersonnel land mines to biological and chemical weapons or small arms.[38] The law of Geneva and that of weapons prohibitions share a concern with eliminating unnecessary human suffering caused by war. Yet they often diverge in their stance toward reciprocity.[39]

Several aspects of the West's conflict with Al Qaeda have longstanding precedents that may serve as guidance. Others have none. Those who drafted The Hague and Geneva Conventions did not foresee, in particular, conflicts combining elements of war, criminal law enforcement, and domestic national emergency. The drafters mainly contemplated war between states.[40] To a lesser extent, they anticipated conflicts involving entities closely resembling states, such as armed militias fighting alongside a state's army and subject to its effective control.[41] They did not anticipate, or write rules regarding, armed conflict with multinational terrorist networks.

Because international law has traditionally focused on states, the international law of war focuses on armies. When championing the cause of human rights against state oppression, we are today likely to condemn the state-centric nature of international law, the pride of place it gives to national sovereignty. Yet the key conceptual distinctions of humanitarian law, such as that between a state's combatants and its civilians, rest on this very state-centrism, on a stark dichotomy between those whom the state authorizes to kill on its behalf (and who may hence be targeted in war) versus those who may not be deliberately killed because they have not been so authorized (i.e., noncombatants).[42] Without any inkling of possible inconsistency, we decry in the first breath a state-centrism that we find inviolable, even sacred, in the next.

The Third Geneva Convention, for instance, clearly embodies these statist assumptions in its provisions regarding POWs. It refers to belligerents who employ regular armed forces, display identifying insignia, have formal chains of command, and generally adhere to the laws of war governing states.[43] The treaties also assume belligerents who seek only the traditional goal of territorial control (to enhance their national power), rather than belligerents who harbor more amorphous aspirations[44] and fight on no particular battlefield. We can no longer make any of these assumptions about belligerents and must therefore reassess the law's main categories. Little of the considerable debate, public or scholarly, has directly engaged the question of reciprocity, though that question has always hovered ominously in the background.

The questions dominating public debate have often been poorly formulated. What most laypeople regard as the key question was reportedly never even asked by those at the highest levels of law enforcement. In fact, the State Department's Legal Adviser following 9/11 maintains that "no serious analysis of the advantages and disadvantages of adhering to Geneva rules regarding interrogation methods was undertaken before it was decided that because the Conventions did not apply as a matter of law, they should not guide our conduct."[45]

The operative answer became, We should do whatever the law allows and we should interpret the law, where ambiguities so permit, to allow as much force as possible.[46] This is the almost the antithesis of the stance adopted by the Judge Advocate Generals (JAGs). Even in public statements, the president left no doubt about his central priority: "My most important job as your president is to defend the homeland; it is to protect the American people from further attacks."[47] The JAGs differed here only in that they understood this aim to be fully compatible with other vital national objectives; this is a story told in Chapter 12.

THE ARGUMENT

This book argues that the reciprocity principle is well embedded in the law and, as generally understood, cannot support a policy of restraint in fighting Al Qaeda or similar militant jihadists. The Geneva Conventions and other relevant treaties, as well as the recent U.S. Detainee Treatment Act and Military Commissions Act, do not provide satisfactory answers to the central questions. These legal materials lack a coherent, principled view of when compliance by one party to a conflict should be contingent on compliance by its opponents.

This book first argues against a common version of Kantian ethical theory, which posits that fairness generally requires the shared commitment by all parties to common rules, ensuring like treatment of like conduct. From behind a Rawlsian veil of ignorance, no prospective belligerent would accept a law of war that put it at unfair disadvantage by affording its adversary less onerous constraints. Other theories also based on Kant's ethics similarly conclude that fairness demands a symmetry in the risks that each party may impose on its counterpart; it involves a balance of benefits and burdens reflected in rules equally binding on all. The law thereby establishes a moral parity that demands restoration when one party's wrongs effectively disrupt it. Al Qaeda violates humanitarian law in ways that disrupt this symmetry: Jihadist terror takes unfair advantage of the liberal state's continued adherence to humanitarian law. As an U.S. Air Force officer writes, "The basic strategy is that one party fights by the rules, whereas another does not. Moreover, a state's . . . compliance with the law of armed conflict is essential to the effective execution of an adversary's strategy to exploit it."[48]

Though this statement is more straightforward than what one finds in scholarly writing on these issues, it is only by turning to Internet chit-chat that we may come to appreciate the full depth and intensity of such thinking, concealed behind the veil – now not of Rawlsian ignorance – but rather authorial anonymity. One such blogger, for instance, unburdens himself of this intentional *reductio ad absurdem*:

> Let's say you could fight a war very humanely. We're talking super-surgically, with a Human Rights Watch liaison and a lawyer attached to every squad. Any enemy caught alive would have to be proven to be an enemy (i.e., chain of evidence, etc.) . . . by a neutral party. Your army

would be willing to lose man after man attacking a fortified house that might have civilians in it rather than risk an airstrike. Whatever, you get the drift. Now, say I'm on the other side. I know that if I decide to make war on you, my losses among my women and children will be very low. I risk only my men and even then it won't be so bad. I have a sort of advantage in that I can kick sand and bite, but you won't. That's a bit of a moral hazard in some ways.[49]

Quickly retreating from his own suggestion, however, even the anonymous blogger feels curiously compelled to add, in conclusion, "The above is a thought experiment only." Still, the blogger's point about moral hazard, in particular, is compelling and goes entirely unremarked in the scholarly literature on terrorism. A situation of moral hazard is one in which someone engages in harmful conduct because he or she is insured against its costly consequences.[50] International law, for instance, prohibits the United States from targeting terrorists in a country that, though itself "unable" to prosecute, denies permission to attack them on its territory.[51] The *ex ante* effect of such a rule is to ensure that terrorists seek refuge in precisely such a country. For that is where they can escape the costs of their criminal activity. It insures them against the risks of such conduct. The result is both inefficient and unfair, insofar as "people should bear the consequences of the risky choices they make," theorists of many persuasions agree.[52]

The upshot of such thinking, whether or not restrained by scholarly decorum, is that restoring symmetry and the fairness ideal on which it rests may sometimes require rules that release the victim of material breach from the very duties the victimizer has violated. The basic idea is familiar from domestic contract law,[53] in that "flagrant breach by one side of a bargain generally releases the other side from the obligation to observe its end of the bargain."[54] The question, then, is whether Al Qaeda's consistent breach of the most basic rules of humanitarian law authorizes the United States to respond with methods also at odds with such standards to reestablish symmetry in the risks that belligerents may lawfully impose on one another. In a word, this view concludes that fairness requires reciprocity.

"Realist" views of international relations, focused on power politics, differ greatly from such moral thinking. Yet they reach a similar conclusion: Effective restraint in war demands reciprocity. Such views are this book's other primary antagonist. Realists anticipate that successful enforcement of humanitarian law will prove impossible without granting a right of retaliation for war crimes. If humanitarian law is to work at all, each belligerent's duties must remain contingent on continued adherence to like duties by adversaries. In this way, reprisal becomes indispensable for punishing and preventing violations.[55]

This second rationale for reciprocity, unlike the previous one, is concerned with the practical consequences of response in kind. How well has reciprocity actually worked to restrain warfare's illicit methods? Modern military history offers extensive materials for answering this question. Recent social science employs this historical record to incisive effect, finding that forbearance in treatment of an enemy is almost never unidirectional, nonreciprocal. And reciprocal restraint occurs only when fighting takes place between certain kinds of states and military organizations, adversaries of a sort not faced in the conflicts with Al Qaeda or even with Iran and North Korea.

These studies suggest that a belligerent should be "nice," as game theorists use the term, only with adversaries prepared to play tit-for-tat. That game requires the players to accept modest punishment for their prior defection from cooperative rules, rather than interpreting such sanction as a new and independent wrong against them, providing legitimate grounds for retaliation – specifically, for increased use of the forbidden practice. There are few exceptions to the statistical regularity: no restraint without reciprocal forbearance.

These anomalies nonetheless suggest an entirely different way to view the matter. They indicate that the argument for forbearance in U.S. treatment of Al Qaeda detainees should be sought neither in liberal theories of morality nor in realist/rationalist tit-for-tat, but in a professional ethic of honor derived from military culture and an attendant account of individual and collective self-respect. These anomalies begin on the vocational plane, but extend potentially to the national.

The point of departure for this approach lies in the JAGs' argument for unqualified adherence to Geneva norms. That argument, reflected in their 2006 congressional testimony and internal memoranda preceding it, appealed to "who we are" and "what we stand for." These sources and related interviews also suggest a novel pathway for enhancing future U.S. adherence to international humanitarian law and perhaps to international law more generally.

To what extent can identity – national and professional – provide a major basis of foreign policy? That question preoccupies the last part of this book. The "realist" preoccupation with American power nevertheless receives sympathetic attention. The question of whether to employ coercive interrogation is submitted to cost-benefit analysis.[56] Realists' use of such methods has been unduly selective, leading them to miss considerations essential to the effective projection of positive U.S. influence abroad.

Even most realists today are concerned with enhancing "soft power," which may be described as the "summation of economic leverage, cultural pull, and intellectual clout that has made the U.S. the preeminent force in the world."[57] Rightly understood, realist (and related rationalist) approaches to international relations support a policy of self-restraint in fighting Al Qaeda, despite the apparent impossibility of reciprocity from this antagonist. Those concerned chiefly with enhancing American global influence should therefore favor forbearance in U.S. detention and interrogation policies.

This conclusion begins to suggest a third type of reciprocity – as neither fairness in fighting nor as an enforcement device – based rather on U.S. gains from preserving world confidence in an international legal system to which the Geneva Conventions are now integral. That system provides a public good in which the United States is heavily invested and from which it greatly profits. This argument highlights the advantages of contributing to an effective international legal system in exchange for its current and future benefits. Only this last conception of reciprocity can convincingly support American restraint in fighting Al Qaeda and its affiliates. This view appreciates that a state at war is at once involved both with its immediate antagonists and also with a much larger group of states with whom reciprocal relations must be maintained throughout the conflict and thereafter. In the notion of *erga omnes*, these states – though not party to the war – today find a legal basis for concern about how each side treats the other's civilians and detained fighters.

This variety of reciprocity is diffuse rather than specific.[58] In specific reciprocity, two parties sequentially exchange actions of equivalent value. A breach of humanitarian law by one belligerent might immediately permit its antagonist an act of reprisal, according to this logic. With diffuse reciprocity, by contrast, the value equivalence is less precise, and the exchange of value is not immediate. The crucial difference between these types of reciprocity is that the diffuse variety can become the basis for a general system of rules, such as that of free trade. Specific reciprocity cannot, except for the rule, if it may even be so called, that every concession must elicit a concession of equal value by the other side. In international trade, specific reciprocity would mean that, as under early GATT rules, that each state must make comparable accommodation to every other state from which it sought a given trade arrangement. We may contrast this to today's World Trade Organization rules, under which a multilateral organization decides whether and to what extent international law permits the victim of a trade law violation to retaliate with national sanctions against the violator.[59] The practice of specific or bilateral reciprocity is mediated through a multilateral organization employing a systemwide set of rules.

The international law of copyright, by contrast, still heavily relies on a more strictly specific reciprocity in that states enter bilateral treaties affording "national treatment" to intellectual property claims by each other's citizens (i.e., promising that they will treat the other state's nationals no worse than their own).[60] Similarly, states enter bilateral treaties of "Friendship, Commerce, and Navigation" by which they agree to accord equal treatment to each other's citizens. These treaties are based on each state's appreciation that its nationals can expect to be treated only as well as it treats the other's.

Diffuse reciprocity operates in many situations, large and small. It is the variety to which Piaget refers when describing the moral development of children as they begin to acquire the first intuition of being party to a social contract:

> The child begins by simply practicing reciprocity, in itself not so easy a thing as one might think. Then, once one has grown accustomed to this form of equilibrium in his action, his behavior is altered from within, its form reacting, as it were, upon its content. What is regarded as just is no longer mere reciprocal action, but primarily behavior that admits of indefinitely sustained reciprocity. The motto, "do as you would be done by," thus comes to replace the conception of crude equality. The child sets forgiveness above revenge, not out of weakness, but because "there is no end" to revenge.[61]

This stage of moral development finally transcends the schoolyard variety – with its impulsive, undeferred gratification – that the young C. S. Lewis had not yet reached when he writes, "My brother and I, as very small boys, were drawing pictures at the same table, I jerked his elbow and caused him to make an irrelevant line across the middle of his work; the matter was amicably settled by my allowing him to draw a line of equal length across mine."[62]

THIS BOOK'S ORGANIZATION

This study has four parts. The first examines the place of reciprocity within international humanitarian law and the U.S. law pertaining to it.[63] These chapters reveal the widespread and growing ambivalence that exists about the practical utility and moral defensibility of reciprocity, an ambivalence that has left the law rather incoherent and lacking principled justification.

The second part explores the moral questions that lie beneath the current legal and policy debate regarding acceptable methods of fighting Al Qaeda. These chapters engage a number of leading liberal thinkers, primarily in the Kantian tradition, showing how their arguments are receptive to the possibility that coercive interrogation, indefinite detention, and targeted killing are defensible in terrorist war.

The third part assesses the contribution of social thought to this question. Its chapters employ ideas respectively from postcolonialism, cultural sociology, political economy, and anthropology to assess key dimensions of U.S. counterterrorism law and policy. The book's final part identifies several factors pointing toward what may be described, with only slight hyperbole, as "the end of reciprocity." This term refers to the increasing questioning, qualifying, and even rejection of traditional forms of reciprocity within humanitarian law and the conduct of war. Thus, whereas the volume's first part focuses on the relevant law, the next three parts shift, respectively, toward ethics, social science, and public policy.

A brief argument in favor of the third or diffuse variety of reciprocity is sketched, with reservations about whether its rationale for restraint in terrorist war really counts as reciprocity at all. In speaking of the "end" of reciprocity, the intention is also to raise the question of what the law's primary objective should be in seeking to establish or restore relations of reciprocity in the international arena during and following war. Is the primary goal to create short-term, bilateral wartime cooperation with enemies – a cooperation that is necessarily precarious – or longer term, multilateral relationships with third parties, relations of the sort approximating a social contract?

The reader uninterested in legal aspects of current debate may wish to skim Chapter 3 quickly and skip Chapter 2 entirely. Still, it would be worth some effort to give these pages a try, if only because, unlike the Bush administration at times, they offer a sustained argument for some of its key positions that takes international law very seriously, rather than viewing it as merely an annoying obstacle to untrammeled U.S. discretion.[64] Early readers have described these two chapters as offering a more convincing defense of key Bush administration positions than the administration itself provided.[65] The upshot is indeed to suggest the strength of certain untapped resources within humanitarian law that would permit a stronger case for several of the administration's key policies than it publicly offered. Yet by no means is this book a partisan intervention, much less one in defense of torture. It is an argument for careful assessment of one key issue in the larger discussion: the proper place of reciprocity within war and the law governing it. In this connection, the study is no less critical of the administration and its intellectual defenders than of their opponents.

The book's first half (Parts One and Two) stresses the value of bilateral reciprocity within humanitarian law, whereas the second half (Parts Three and Four) focuses on such reciprocity's limits and liabilities, identifying areas where it should give way to competing concerns or be entirely reconceived. In particular, an honorable soldier or self-respecting liberal society finds little guidance in the notion of reciprocity because a strong sense of character already governs their conduct. A preoccupation with bilateral reciprocity is also harmful to America's global soft power, which requires maintaining the country's reputation as a guardian of human rights and the rule of law, regardless of what its enemies may do. But though many have casually invoked the notion of soft power in recent years, particularly when criticizing the Bush administration's counterterrorism policies, this book seeks to identify the social mechanisms underlying this species of power, with a view to discovering how they might be reinforced.

PROS AND CONS OF RECIPROCITY

The pros and cons of building reciprocity into humanitarian law, as it bears on the conflict with Al Qaeda, have only begun to receive serious discussion.[66] Public talk about reciprocity came into prominence during the congressional debate over the Military Commissions Act of 2006.[67] In that forum, leading active-duty American military lawyers broke ranks with their civilian superiors in the Defense Department.[68] They joined retired officers in vigorously arguing that, in U.S. treatment of accused terrorists, the country must apply and adhere to Geneva standards without qualification, regardless of differences between adversaries and whether adversaries themselves adhere to like norms.[69]

One rationale for this view, as the *New York Times* voiced in a critique of the new law, is that "by repudiating key protections of the Geneva Conventions, [the legislation] needlessly increases the danger to any American soldier captured in battle."[70] Our enemies will reciprocate, good and ill: They will treat our soldiers as we threat theirs. Paul Rieckhoff, head of a major veterans' organization, added in a *Times* op-ed piece: "It's not hard to imagine that one of our Special Forces soldiers might one day be captured by Iranian forces while investigating a potential nuclear weapons program. What is to stop that soldier from being waterboarded, locked in a cold room for days without sleep as Iranian pop music blares all around him – finally sentenced to die without a fair trial or the right to see the evidence against him?"[71] Senator and Republican presidential nominee John McCain, as well as former Secretary of State Colin Powell, prominently voiced similar views.[72]

Who can argue with the Golden Rule: the notion that we should treat others as we ourselves would like to be treated? The rule is sometimes formulated as an affirmative exhortation, sometimes as a prohibition. The prohibition (i.e., "what is hateful to you, do not do unto your neighbor") is often preferred in the Hindu, Jewish, and Confucian traditions.[73] The Christian tradition adopts the affirmative exhortation: Do unto others as you would have them do unto you.[74] This is how American military lawyers have trained U.S. troops for a generation, exhorting that they ask themselves, "Would it bother you if it was done to one of your own soldiers?"[75]

The Golden Rule is an endorsement of what may be called positive reciprocity, but not of negative. Thus, it does not authorize, much less demand, that you punish your neighbor for the wrongs he or she has committed against you. Jesus even exhorts one to "love your enemies,"[76] which is the opposite of reciprocating their mistreatment. It is hence a mistake to equate the Golden Rule with reciprocity *tout court,* as some do.[77] The fear of negative reciprocation is indeed one to be reckoned with: Will American troops face retaliatory misconduct for U.S. mistreatment of Al Qaeda suspects? This is a fear that resonates strongly with many Americans and surely has at least an initial plausibility. Thus, both national self-interest in protecting U.S. troops and justice itself – roughly equated for the moment with the Golden Rule – seem to speak unequivocally for forbearance in the U.S. treatment of terror suspects.

Neither of these arguments turns out to hold up especially well, however, as we shall see. For instance, the fear for the fate of U.S. troops, on closer inspection, proves to be based on insufficient attention to the dynamics of warfare. Norms of restraint develop during particular wars in light of the antagonists' specific ends and means of combat and evolve in ways to which the formalities of Geneva law do not closely correspond. The Geneva Conventions, though relevant, are neither necessary nor sufficient to such forbearance. The JAGs' empirical claim in this regard is weak – certainly overconfident, at the very least. This fact must lead us to wonder whether they may actually have been prompted by something quite different, perhaps more compelling. Their interventions combine a modern humanitarianism with a much older notion of martial honor. The latter concept, in particular, is more difficult to articulate and defend in public, democratic discussion. This book contends that, when reformulated in a more modern idiom, the

JAGs' way of thinking ultimately offers a better guide to action than the international law assayed in Part One, the liberal normative theory in Part Two, or the cost-benefit analysis employed in Chapters 10 and 11.

RECIPROCITY AS A THEME IN PUBLIC DEBATE

The administration's critics dwell on parts of the Geneva Conventions that reject reciprocity. They point, for instance, to provisions in the Fourth Convention that may accord certain protections even to unprivileged belligerents if they meet certain nationality requirements.[78] Such critics contend, moreover, that POW status makes little difference to the rights of detainees (i.e., that once captured, their rights to humane treatment are largely unaffected by whether they or their comrades-in-arms have honored legal duties when fighting).[79] No reciprocity required, in other words.

The administration's supporters, however, stress the ways in which relevant law embraces the reciprocity norm, as where reprisals and forcible countermeasures are permitted.[80] Such authors also interpret Geneva Common Article 3 more narrowly, leaving those subject to it with weaker safeguards than POWs or protected civilians under the Third and Fourth Conventions, respectively. Yet proponents of this position often reject – or offer labored interpretations of – Geneva provisions that clearly repudiate reciprocity, arguing that these provisions are in any case often also impractical. They are correct, however, that the actual experience of warfare suggests that these provisions may have fallen into desuetude and are thus at odds with currently accepted state practice, a crucial component of customary international law.[81]

A more impartial view of the matter is surely necessary at this point. Perhaps the only thing that may be said with certainty here is that, if one believes that humanitarian law largely accepts the reciprocity norm, one will then interpret several key (and opaque) provisions in ways antithetical to how one would understand them from a standpoint opposed to reciprocity. This is true whether that opposition is based on drafting history or on more straightforwardly moral considerations. Much of the contemporary debate, in Guantánamo litigation no less than in the larger public rhetoric, turns on this underlying issue. Yet it rarely receives explicit treatment of any sort and never in any sustained fashion. The tension between reciprocity and antireciprocity thus identifies a central axis of disagreement over much of the Bush administration's counterterrorism policy, even when not explicitly couched in these terms. What one thinks about the morality and efficacy of reciprocity in general closely corresponds to where one comes out on a wide range of legal questions that initially appear rather technical and unrelated to one another.

Consider treaty interpretation, for instance. Wherever evidence of the Geneva drafters' intent is unclear and their resulting text ambiguous, the most careful critic of the administration's approach, Derek Jinks, invariably repudiates reciprocity as a basis for interpreting these agreements.[82] Yet nowhere does he directly confront the moral defensibility of the principle itself or the question of its legitimate scope. A French legal scholar at McGill, Frederic Mégret, is more forthright in heralding the "abandonment of the requirement of reciprocity" in recent humanitarian law "as a capital development, because it meant at least that Western powers could not argue that the incapacity of 'savages' to reciprocate justified their own refusal to apply the laws of war."[83] Both authors, whether implicitly (Jinks) or explicitly (Mégret), view reciprocity as standing in opposition to justice as they understand it,[84] rather than as its expression. That view is often compelling, as when belligerent reprisals, a common expression of reciprocity,[85] victimize the innocent – they generally do – even when successful in ending an adversary's violations, as they regularly have been.[86]

The problem with reprisals, as with such other retaliation for wrong as "retorsion," is that it is often impossible to correct injustice without also foreseeably causing it, albeit perhaps in lesser measure. This paradox is by no means confined to humanitarian law.[87] Legal systems acknowledge this dilemma's inevitability and struggle with it every day.[88] The law of civil remedies, for instance, seeks to minimize and manage such "collateral damage," keeping it within acceptable, unavoidable limits. It cannot be entirely banished, however. If the law's limitations in this regard are common in peacetime, we should not be surprised to find them even more prevalent in war, where the deployment of state power and lawful violence is necessarily less precise.

RECIPROCITY AS A "QUASI-SOCIAL" NORM

What kind of principle or norm is reciprocity? Elster calls it a "quasi-moral" norm, a fruitful notion. As a quasi-moral norm, reciprocity differs from genuinely "moral" norms, such as that of "equal sharing," which demand that one "do what would be best if everyone did the same" (i.e., regardless of what others actually do). True moral norms embody a sort of "everyday Kantianism," as he puts it.[89] Quasi-moral norms, by contrast, are only "triggered by the presence or behavior of others."[90] They resemble "social norms" in this regard, like those of etiquette or rules of the road (e.g., whether one must drive on the right or left side in a given country).

Elster is initially uncertain about whether conduct guided by quasi-moral norms can be described as altruistic. He decides against that characterization. For as he observes, "The norm of reciprocity allows you *not* to help others in distress unless they have helped you previously.[91] A typical moral norm is to help others in distress unconditionally, even if there is no prior history of assistance.... Moral norms, one might say, are *proactive*, quasi-moral norms are *reactive*."[92] These are useful distinctions, for the social nature of the reciprocity norm helps underline the sociological dimensions of reciprocity within international relations, even in war, on which this study focuses in Part Three. The norm's nature as merely "quasi" moral also helpfully keeps in view the fact that Kantian-inspired conduct is not a prominent feature of international politics, even in peace.

Tit-for-tat is far more common. As Keohane noted soon after 9/11, "The attacks have made the U.S. more dependent on other states for assistance in its 'war against terrorism.' Normally, when a state asks others for assistance, some form of reciprocity is to be anticipated. Not surprisingly, therefore, the U.S. is being more solicitous of Pakistan's request for economic aid than before September 11."[93] Such aid indeed has exceeded ten billion dollars since 9/11.[94] Reciprocity of this sort may be entirely defensible, but because it arises from the likelihood of mutual benefit rather than from the disinterested respect for moral principle (and because Pakistan is not a democratic republic), such an exchange is decidedly not of Kantian inspiration.

DIFFERING CONCEPTIONS OF RECIPROCITY

Reciprocity is a concept that admits of several conceptions. Four of these are useful in grappling with moral restraint in war and in the U.S. conflict with Al Qaeda in particular. Each sheds some light on different dimensions of current concerns. One of these usages, however, will concern us much more than the rest. This is the sense in which reciprocity describes the common tendency for one to behave toward another as one perceives the other behaving toward oneself.[95] In other words, you will treat me well only as long as, and to the extent that, you believe that I treat you well. Adam Smith observed this long ago in his *Theory of Moral Sentiments*:

> As every man doeth, so it shall be done to him, and retaliation seems to be the great law which is dictated to us by nature. Beneficence and generosity we think due to the generous and beneficent. Those whose hearts never open to the feelings of humanity, should, we think, be shut out in the

same manner. . . . The man who is barely innocent, who only observes the laws of justice with regard to others, and merely abstains from hurting his neighbors, can merit only that his neighbors in turn should respect his innocence.[96]

This conception of reciprocity has an empirical side, describing an observable feature of social life. We may readily observe, for instance, that country A's decision to grant copyright to authors from country B will generally be reciprocated by B's like concession to A's authors, and that when country C expels eleven of country D's embassy personnel as spies, that D will expel precisely eleven of C's personnel.

This sort of reciprocity is sometimes also taken as normative, insofar as one has a duty to repay good deeds and at least a right to reciprocate bad ones. Malinowski, in his study of the Trobriand Islanders, thus called it the "give-and-take *principle*."[97] One might be initially inclined, for simplicity's sake, to call this "reciprocity as retaliation." Reprisals in war, for instance, are retaliatory. So are many other violent responses by one belligerent to another in wartime.

Retaliation should perhaps be distinguished here, conceptually at least, from simple vengeance,[98] even if it is often all but impossible to tell them apart. Ricoeur distinguishes the two in these terms: Whereas "vengeance is limitless; retaliation has an element of *measure* provided by the very principle of equivalence . . . a sense of measure characteristic of justice."[99] In acts of vengeance, moreover, the vengeful party takes acknowledged pleasure,[100] as Al Qaeda members unabashedly do in jihadist violence against the West,[101] whereas a calculated retaliation may be conducted dispassionately, *sine ire et studio*. As in aristocratic warfare, one need not hate the adversary against whom one retaliates, as long as it fights by professional rules shared across the lines of battle.

Still, to retaliate denotes a negative response to unfavorable treatment, whereas our concern here will also be with the positive response to favorable treatment, as in the use of "confidence-building" methods during diplomatic negotiations, such as those designed to end armed conflict. Tit-for-tat is hence a more useful shorthand for this first variety of reciprocity, for it is as concerned with rewarding good behavior as with punishing bad.[102] Retaliation is also purely reactive, whereas we are sometimes concerned as well with proactive initiatives to establish cooperation where none exists. Tit-for-tat has proven highly conducive to sustained cooperation in many venues. A violent act of reprisal in war must be consistent with the ground rules of tit-for-tat, though the accompanying mental state must also be of a particular sort for the action to count as lawful.

It is an empirical datum that people tend to respond to others with an implicit policy of like for like and that this facilitates cooperation between them. This elementary fact has profound implications for the effective design of law and institutions. One may infer, in particular, that social institutions are most practicable if organized in light of it. In this way, the empirical observation becomes a foundation or parameter for public policy and the drafting of legal rules to implement such policy.[103] Many writers on international relations, especially those of an economic bent, deduce a clear lesson from this first conception of reciprocity: Where there is no independent adjudicator to execute governing rules, the parties themselves must enforce them by punishing each other's violations.

In the theory of international relations, tit-for-tat permits equilibrium through the proportionate sanctioning of rule violations. Despite anarchy, cooperation becomes possible. Reciprocity therefore here concerns not only law and high politics but also the military strategy and tactics governed by such law. If international law ignores such practicalities, they will govern events rather than the law.[104] The question then becomes how best to accommodate these considerations, what role to afford them, and how to channel the forces they embody so as to vindicate law's purposes.

A second meaning of reciprocity involves rules applied equally to all parties in a conflict because these rules reflect an acceptable balance of benefit and burden among those so governed,[105] a balance to which they will often have agreed, whether expressly or tacitly (by their conduct). This conception is normative.[106] Just as fairness requires that individual citizens be treated equally before the law, so too with sovereign states. Keohane illustrates the workings of this idea within international relations:

> The norm of reciprocity is implied by that of sovereignty, and respect for reciprocity is therefore part of the practice of sovereign statehood: "It would be impossible to have a society of sovereign states unless each . . . recognized that every other . . . had the right to claim and enjoy its own sovereignty as well. This reciprocity is inherent in the Western conception of sovereignty."[107]

In this example, each state owes every other the rights entailed by sovereignty in international law regardless of other differences between them, differences admittedly central to other matters. Before the legal defense of Western colonialism reached its "positivist" apogee in the modern era, Renaissance and early modern international lawyers applied this principle of intersovereign reciprocity – often expressly described in such terms – to relations even with non-Western peoples, at least in Asia.[108] The principle is egalitarian in a key respect. As Byers comments, "Reciprocity is a legal consequence of the formal equality of States."[109] The appealing implications of this stance for customary international law are especially noteworthy: "By ensuring that any State claiming a right . . . accords that same right to all other States, the principle of reciprocity qualifies the application of power. . . . This is because a generalized right subjects the state to corresponding obligations *vis-à-vis* all other States," Byers concludes.

The prospect of such generalization limits the imposition of new customary rules,[110] for it reflects within international relations Kant's first version of the categorical imperative: "Act only according to that maxim by which you can at the same time will that it should become a universal law."[111] A century earlier, Pufendorf similarly described reciprocity, both within and between societies, as "only a Corollary of that Law which obliges us to hold all Men equal with our selves, and therefore may be demonstrated *a priori*."[112]

To justify the uniform application of a set of rules to all, the rules must establish an acceptable balance of benefits and burdens between parties to an interaction – including interaction between military antagonists, in the case of rules for war. This balance makes possible a symmetry of the relevant risks each side may impose on the other.[113] As long as one follows the rules, and as long as the rules themselves enshrine the terms of an acceptable risk allocation, one need not consciously stop to consider whether one is keeping up one's side of the bargain with others – day to day, from one interaction to the next. When one party breaks the rules, putting its victim to unfair disadvantage, justice requires that the balance be restored in some way, according to this view. In war, fairness thus requires that shared rules of humanitarian law be equally binding on all belligerents and that the law provide in some way for redress of their violation.

The first and second conceptions of reciprocity are linked in the following way: Any set of rules establishing an acceptable benefit-burden balance would have to authorize those governed by them to interact through tit-for-tat when no other means of rule enforcement was available.[114] In other words, tit-for-tat provides the best method yet discovered for restoring the symmetry of risk in such circumstances. The second conception of reciprocity must therefore accommodate for the first.

A third conception of reciprocity disrupts this natural convergence, this easy intimacy of the first and second conceptions. It involves the sharing of burdens and benefits in society at large through what is often called a social contract, establishing a governing entity, perhaps only over limited issues, with effective powers of implementation. Unlike the first conception (and sometimes the second as well), the third conception of reciprocity always adds parties who are not subject to the given dispute, as well as institutions for the collective enforcement of rules. Tit-for-tat is no longer necessary to preserve a cooperative equilibrium. As within a functioning nation-state, the prospect of justice presented by a criminal trial "diverts the victim and his sympathizers from taking the matter into their own hands," as John Gardner notes.[115] Examples spring readily to mind. For many, a major appeal of the new International Criminal Court is precisely its promise to eliminate any justification for interstate retaliation in the face of an adversary's war crimes. Once effective – a large leap of faith, to be sure – the court would show states that such wrongdoing will be prosecuted and punished by a neutral third party, obviating any need for reprisal or "victor's justice" in biased, home-controlled courts.[116]

Finally, a fourth conception of reciprocity describes the process by which participants in public discussion seek, through reasoned and respectful efforts at persuasion, to reach agreement.[117] Let us call this type of reciprocity "deliberative." It might be seen as simply a special case of the second, in that the fair rules of discursive interaction establish a mutually acceptable balance between the benefits of speaking and the burdens of listening to those one may not initially care to hear. But since speaking can prove a burden and listening a benefit, it is better to approach this fourth variety of reciprocity on its own terms.

It is the first of these four meanings that is chiefly at stake, unless otherwise specified. For this is the meaning of reciprocity with which international relations, especially in war, has been most immediately concerned.[118] Whenever the second conception is implicated, the first will be as well, because the rules by which all are governed must accommodate tit-for-tat to restore the balance of benefit and burden wherever third-party enforcement is lacking.

EXAMPLES OF RECIPROCITY IN WAR

To conclude this introduction, let us consider two brief illustrations – one historical, one contemporary – of reciprocity at work in humanitarian law. These are designed to elicit the reader's ambivalence toward the principle itself and toward the notion that it should occupy a superior place within such law. Both stories are morally unsettling, not simply because they involve blood and death – hardly unusual in war – but also because they make it difficult to identify the law's proper response. These examples should hence help us begin, pretheoretically, to unearth and sort out our rough moral intuitions, reciprocal and antireciprocal, and also help us decide where humanitarian law should fix the line between their respective spheres of operation.

1. *German Reprisals against French Civilians in World War II*

The reciprocity principle could have produced an appealing result in a leading Nuremberg case, had the International Military Tribunal embraced it. Prosecutors argued that indiscriminate Nazi reprisals against French civilians violated Germany's 1929 Geneva Convention duties as a military occupier, thereby excusing – as community self-defense – partisan attacks on German soldiers. Reprisal is, among other things, a means of self-defense,[119] and self-defense has long been regarded as a natural right – inherent first in personhood or individual sovereignty, later also in state sovereignty. Earlier attacks by French partisans had elicited the German reprisals in the first place. If the partisans' violence were thereafter justified as self-defense, however, they could not be convicted and punished. Because they were in fact punished by extrajudicial execution, the German Nuremberg defendants – in ordering such killings – were guilty of war crimes, on this view.

Consistent with this reasoning, international law had long held that

> [military] occupation created a contract between citizen and occupier. The citizen was required to cease resistance and give obedience to the occupier; in exchange the occupier gave up its belligerent rights . . . and assumed responsibility for the protection of the population. In other words, as [Gen. Henry W. Halleck in his 1861 treatise, International Law] summarized it, "the duty of allegiance is reciprocal to the duty of protection." Forceful resistance to the occupation was permissible only . . . if the occupier failed to live up to its legal obligations to the point that its conduct became "so injurious to the conquered people as to render submission intolerable."[120]

That Nazi reprisals against innocent French civilians were rightly "intolerable" might seem an easy conclusion. Yet the Nuremberg Tribunal was unpersuaded by such reasoning. It held that the Nazi policy of terrorizing French society through indiscriminate reprisals against civilians did not release the general population of an occupied country from its Geneva Convention duty to refrain from hostile activities.[121] The partisans' punishment would therefore have been lawful had some measure of criminal process been afforded.

But what if the tribunal had here embraced the reciprocity principle? Then the partisans' duty to respect humanitarian law would have been contingent on general adherence to it by the German occupiers of their country. In that case, Nazi collective punishment of French civilians would have discharged such civilians from their duties of nonresistance. Nazi punishment of the partisans for lawfully defending their communities would then have been criminal and the Nuremberg defendants guilty as charged.[122] Rejecting reciprocity, as the tribunal here elected, foreclosed this appealing result.

The judges had their reasons. If reciprocity had been the governing rule across the board, then the German defendants could have credibly argued that they themselves had been released from *prima facie* duties as occupiers on account of the French population's consistent failure to honor its corresponding Geneva duties of nonresistance (i.e., once military occupation had been established). It had been only such illegal French resistance, after all, that had prompted the German reprisals to begin with.

How should this case have been decided? In particular, is there a principled basis for a rule that would excuse the French from their Hague and Geneva duties in response to German violations,[123] without also excusing the Germans from their own like duties once French civilians took up arms? (Most German victims, one might add, were young conscripts.) In a word, should the respective Geneva duties of the French and Germans be regarded as interdependent, so that material breach of such obligations by either side freed the other from its own?

Any rule derived from such a case could easily have far-reaching ramifications. Thus, like civilians dwelling in occupied territory, prisoners of war similarly acquire their legal protections in exchange for agreeing not to fight. Once captured, they may therefore no longer lawfully employ force against the enemy detaining them.[124] When one belligerent breaches the law's bargain of benefit and burden, the opposing belligerent generally abandons it too. In World War II, for instance, after Japanese POWs repeatedly tried to sabotage American submarines that had taken them captive, the submarines largely ceased rescuing Japanese sailors at all (i.e., those surviving U.S. destruction of their vessels).[125]

2. *Targeted Killing of Al Qaeda Leaders*

Like French partisans fighting their Nazi occupiers, Al Qaeda members are not entitled under international law to engage in acts of combatancy and can hence be criminally prosecuted for doing so. While they are "taking direct part in hostilities,"[126] they may also lawfully be killed. As the term has come to be commonly employed, a targeted or extrajudicial killing is something slightly different, however. It is a lethal attack on someone thought to pose serious violent threat, but who is not at the moment necessarily engaged in hostilities and who is not a "combatant" because he is part of neither a state's "armed force" nor its associated "militias."[127] Terrorists resemble pirates here, in key respects. International law historically permitted the killing of pirates wherever they might be found, particularly when they could not be captured and prosecuted. The law regarded them as *hostis humani generis*, the enemies of all humankind.[128] The analogy between pirates and today's terrorists is sometimes drawn, with certain plausibility.[129] But the international law of human rights now bans killing a person "arbitrarily"[130] (i.e., without due process).

In assessing their response to Al Qaeda after 9/11, Bush administration attorneys concluded that international law allows the killing of unprivileged belligerents,[131] not merely their detention and prosecution,[132] wherever discovered. The United States could take such action at any time, not only while the targeted individuals were actively engaged in attack or its imminent preparation.[133] On September 17, 2001, President Bush issued a secret directive authorizing the CIA to capture or kill a number of people designated as terrorists.[134] Pursuant to this authority, one Al Qaeda leader was killed in Yemen along with several followers.[135] Others have since been successfully targeted within Pakistan. In 1998 President Clinton had already issued such a "presidential finding" initiating covert action of this sort against Al Qaeda and Osama bin Laden.[136]

The contemporary impulse to target terrorist leaders with military force, rather than to seek their criminal prosecution, can be largely explained, and is sometimes expressly justified, in terms of reciprocity: Because terrorist leaders target enemy populations with impunity and display no capacity for, or interest in prosecuting enemy leaders, the states they target in turn become reluctant to put terrorists on trial, even where this could be practicable. The impulse to rely on martial reciprocation regularly tends to displace any hope of employing criminal law.

Reciprocity of this sort permits both sides to "play by the same rules," one could say, once one of them firmly resolves to depart from the law. Reprisals, in particular, are designed, as one legal specialist writes, "to equalize the position of the belligerents by releasing the one from obedience to the law which the other has flouted."[137] According to this logic, the United States may attack civilians who take up arms against it by serving in Al Qaeda, because Al Qaeda directly attacks U.S. civilians and civilian property.[138] The country's remedies are not confined to those modestly afforded by the Fourth Geneva Convention.[139] As Richard Baxter noted during the Vietnam War, "If combatants disguise themselves as civilians, then civilians will become suspect," and treated accordingly.[140] Two prominent Bush administration defenders put the point more forcefully: "Combatants cannot fairly be told to refrain from using force against civilians if they regularly suffer attacks from such groups."[141] This is especially true with respect to the civilian leaders of these groups. The point is compelling, and skeptics of reciprocity in humanitarian law are hard pressed to deny either its moral or legal force.[142] Few do, in fact, apart from the most minor quibbles.[143]

Yet how much should we properly infer from this conclusion? How far afield does its underlying principle extend? For Bush administration supporters, it became the edge of a wedge for pressing the reciprocity principle into more controversial territory. John Yoo and a coauthor, for instance, argued that the Third Geneva Convention denies POW status not only to unprivileged belligerents (i.e., civilians who take up arms) but also to soldiers of a state's regular armed forces, such as Afghanistan's Taliban in 2001–02, if these forces do not generally adhere to the law of war.[144] The Taliban often did not.[145]

Yoo relies on a plausible basis in the pertinent text for this interpretation,[146] though it remains unclear just how widespread one side's nonadherence must become before the other would be released from its duties to accord POW status to enemy soldiers. The more common view today opposes to Yoo's and holds that soldiers "who commit war crimes should be punished, but their crimes should not be used as an excuse to deprive others of the protections due POWs."[147] Textual support for this position within the Convention itself or its drafting history is difficult to discern, however. Those rejecting a reciprocity requirement simply cite back and forth to one another here, with each scholar, NGO activist, and judge resting claims on bald assertions by the others, in a circular, self-confirmatory ritual of mutual back slapping.

The deeper rationale for Yoo's proffered rule – making the POW status and Article 3 rights of a state's soldiers contingent on its humanitarian law compliance – is clearly the reciprocity principle. Both the first and second conceptions of reciprocity are implicated here, as we would expect: a set of common rules binding on all, rules legitimating the proclivity to respond like for like in the absence of effective third-party enforcement. In short, one must fight lawfully to enjoy the lawful rights of a combatant. To enjoy the rights of a lawful combatant, in short, one must fight lawfully.[148] Accepting this line of thinking, the U.S. Supreme Court in *Ex Parte Quirin* permitted the execution of German saboteurs during World War II on the grounds that, in violating key Geneva rules, they had forfeited their right to treatment as POWs.[149]

A recent critic of such thinking, in struggling to understand its appeal to many in current circumstances, offers this elaboration: "The intuition that aggressive questioning of detainees would be inappropriate in conventional warfare may be acceptable – even necessary – in asymmetric conflict – i.e., where others make no effort to respect basic rules of humanitarian law – is widely shared, even where it goes unrecognized by the law. In circumstances where detainees are thought to possess information that may have a direct impact on military security, soldiers may feel that laws protecting the rights of irregular fighters express a perverse set of values. . . . The distinction between legitimate and illegitimate opponents . . . has traditionally been at the centre of the military understanding of war."[150]

That centrality has not been confined to the military's understanding, one might add. It is shared by many civilians who rightly understand themselves to be the chief beneficiary of this distinction between them and belligerents. On this point, Vice President Dick Cheney surely expressed the views of many when he said, "Terrorists don't deserve the same guarantees and safeguards that would be used for American citizens going through the normal judicial process."[151]

The centrality of the reciprocity norm to the current conflict is apparent even in the way Osama bin Laden seeks to throw it back in America's face. In statements like his epigraph to the present book, he is evidently responding to those charging that forbearance toward Al Qaeda detainees is unwarranted. They charge that this organization will not reciprocate any such restraint. Bin Laden's reply is, in essence,

> We do *too* reciprocate, but we respond to your real behavior not your rhetoric: for every Muslim woman and child you have killed, we will kill one of yours, since we do not accept your professed distinction between intentional and inadvertent killing, which is meaningless to your victims, our religious brethren. We have a long way to go before we catch up to you, the United States, in the violence we may rightfully inflict. We are only seeking to restore the balance of burden and benefit that humanitarian law enshrines. For now, we will reciprocate your violence – not your restraint, of which we see very little in any event.

Reciprocity ramifies still further afield. Even the impulse to deny *habeas corpus* to detained Al Qaeda suspects would be much weaker if that organization accorded some comparable process to the Western civilians it captured, rather than summarily beheading them. One JAG officer puts the point with unusual candor. In the current conflict with militant jihadists, he writes in an Army journal of opinion, "The notion that opposing forces will ever make these unique legal privileges" (i.e., that the U.S. affords Al Qaeda suspects) "reciprocally available to the US armed forces simply doesn't warrant serious consideration."[152] If a concern with reciprocity lies somewhere behind Bush administration policy, it finds no express reference in the Solicitor General's learned oral argument before the U.S. Supreme Court in *Boumediene*,[153] which addressed the *habeas* issue through recondite issues of statutory and constitutional interpretation. Yet beneath many arguments – moral, political, legal – there often lies a psychic genealogy that never rises to the surface because it is only semi-conscious, sits uneasily with acceptable terms of public discourse, or can find no formal legal footing – often, all three. The law of *habeas*, unlike the Third Geneva Convention, provides no textual basis for an argument from reciprocity. In the *habeas* context, then, reciprocity is a norm that dare not speak its name.

It is unlikely, however, that the two sides of *Boumediene*'s refined legal debate just happen to have lined up, jot for jot, along this unstated moral divide. It can scarcely be accidental that, on the question of whether the Constitution allows Congress to substitute its military commisions for federal court *habeas* rights, both Congress and the president take a view that ultimately denies such rights to suspected members of organizations that do not themselves provide Westerners any such protections. Neither can it be sheer happenstance that lawyers for these detainees propose constitutional interpretations that make reciprocity wholly immaterial to the availability of *habeas corpus*.

The principle of reciprocity is thus clearly implicated, directly or indirectly, in most if not all of the more technical, doctrinal disputes. For this reason, the Bush administration's critics, such as Jeremy Waldron, were wrong to denounce its stance on these disputes as formalistic, legalistic, "narrowly textual,"[154] looking for "loopholes."[155] On the contrary, the stance was quite principled. In fact, the so-called torture memoranda, beneath the surface of their doctrinal details, virtually wrap themselves in the principled flag of reciprocity. The problem is not then one of an eroding commitment to principle in preference for technicalities, but of tension between competing principles. The pressing question becomes, What place should we accord this principle within our law?

Even Yoo acknowledges certain limits to reciprocity. He does not contend, for instance, that a belligerent's criminal *resort* to armed conflict should permit denial of POW status to its soldiers.[156] All agree, in fact, that humanitarian law does not and should not extend reciprocity *that* far. This is a useful illustration of humanitarian law's commitment to confining the reciprocity principle within a certain orbit.[157] In a debate where there has been so little agreement about almost anything, it is valuable to identify points of clear consensus. We may then infer the principles for which such fixed points stand and ask what these principles might further entail for other situations as we encounter them, case by case, real or hypothetical. Reciprocity is not the only principle within humanitarian law, after all; where and when it must cede to others is the key question.

We should not be content with complacent compromise here. Reciprocity clearly has an indispensable but limited place in law and international relations. Yet this tells us almost nothing about where the line should be drawn on particular legal issues, much less in disputed cases. To say, for instance, that law here somehow "mediates" (as some sententiously intone)[158] between our competing impulses toward and against reciprocity, is, without more, to say virtually nothing of significance. Still less is a convincing answer likely to be found in any single, coherent account of morality or society that we might pluck from the theoretical shelf.

Let us begin then, more modestly, almost casuistically, by locating places within international law where reciprocity has found a footing and where it has not, seeking to discern what may distinguish the two and whether such distinctions are defensible or in need of revision. In this first effort and beyond, we will employ the approach that Dennis Thompson calls "institutional political theory,"[159] in seeking at once to (1) discern the meaning of pertinent principles – reciprocity, in this case – within a particular institutional setting (here, war); (2) seriously engage the arguments and self-understandings of those working therein (here, military lawyers and human rights advocates); and hence (3) operate at a level of analysis intermediate between the most comprehensive general theory and the highly specialized world of policy wonkery (counterterrorism legal policy, in the present instance). The objective, in short, is "to seek principles informed enough by actual practice to connect to political agents, but detached enough to provide a critical perspective on their actions."[160]

PART ONE

RECIPROCITY IN HUMANITARIAN LAW

Reciprocity in the Law of War:
Ambient Sightings, Ambivalent Soundings

RECIPROCITY AS PRIMITIVISM

The earliest references to reciprocity in Western literature are very old, and many arise in the context of war. Xenophon wrote of King Cyrus that he "prayed that he might live long enough to be able to repay with interest both those who had helped him and those who had injured him."[1] Due in part to such ancient ancestry, several authors suggest that reciprocity as tit-for-tat appeals to our baser, more primitive nature, or at least to what we like to think of in such terms. We typically regard these sentiments as contemporary, but they were already regularly voiced as early as the eighteenth century. "At the beginning of the 19th century," writes one legal historian, "it was easy to suppose that reprisals were a thing of the past."[2]

Modern culture is reluctant to acknowledge that reciprocity of this variety has any but the most vestigial influence on us. William Ian Miller thus observes,

> We are supposed to believe that when we give a gift we are making no demand for a return, and that when we are victims of hostile actions we have not been obliged to pay back the wrongdoer. We tell ourselves that it would be childish, immoral, unchristian, irrational, barbaric, to do so. Yet despite this official ideology, the norm of reciprocity holds a remarkable grip on our beings. The law may outlaw revenge, but people hunger for movies, books, and tales of vengeful justice clearly invoking sympathy and admiration for the avengers. . . . If the recipients of our "free" gifts fail to make adequate requital we do not fail to subject them to social sanction. . . . The norm of reciprocity persists, almost with a vengeance. We still feel, even as we refuse to understand it or admit it, that gifts oblige us and that wrongs oblige us to make return and even up accounts. We, officially at least, prefer a culture in which debts both of positive and negative moral value do not make strong demands for

repayment. . . . [Yet] despite the claims of the law . . . we still live as if we were people of honor. . . . [Despite] the hegemony of modern institutions, we still manage to create space for ourselves within which we function rather preindustrially for all that. And it is in these spaces that we often find our deepest being engaged.[3]

The linkage to which Miller points has been further plumbed by evolutionary psychologists, who find that "gratitude and vengefulness . . . are two sides of one coin. It would be hard to evolve one without the other. An individual who had gratitude without vengefulness would be an easy mark for exploitation, and a vengeful and ungrateful individual would quickly alienate all potential . . . partners."[4]

If such scholars are correct in asserting that reciprocity is so primitive, perhaps even biologically hard-wired,[5] then it is scarcely surprising that war, one of humankind's earliest recorded and most violent activities, displays it in abundance – with a vengeance, as Miller says. Bin Laden himself even invokes, less plausibly, the language of physics: "You [in the West] should remember that every action has a reaction."[6] We shall later see that the impulse to reciprocate like for like has become highly refined, through the thought of Kant and Rawls, in a way that bears little relation to the variety of instinctual and primordial revenge that Miller has in mind. Still, even these more sophisticated moral rationales for reciprocity often turn out to justify human conduct that is, in the end, little different, apart perhaps from considerations of proportionality. What has changed in the course of such refinement remains an open question.[7]

There is no doubt that reciprocity as a social practice in war has a long history. As a normative principle, it has nearly as long a history within the law of war. Thucydides, for instance, discussed the legality of reprisals at some length in his account of the Spartan prosecution of the Plataeans.[8] Reprisal by a belligerent against foreigners in its midst was common during early periods of ancient Greek warfare.[9] On the basis of reciprocity, the Magna Carta sought to protect each side's merchants from wartime attack by the other.[10] In the Renaissance and early modern periods, retaliation for war crime – and its intellectual defense – knew few legal bounds. Alberico Gentili, a founder of international law in the late sixteenth century, endorsed it,[11] as did Emerich de Vattel, the most influential eighteenth-century writer in the field, albeit with qualifications.[12] David Hume was the first thinker to identify the precise psychological mechanism entailed in reciprocity, which he immediately applied to the ethics of warfare:

> I learn to do service to another, without bearing him any real kindness, because I foresee that he will return my service, in expectation of another of

the same kind, and in order to maintain the same correspondence of good offices with me or others. And accordingly, after I have served him and he is in possession of the advantage arising from my action, he is induced to perform his part, as foreseeing the consequences of his refusal.[13]

Hume had no doubts about the ramifications of such reciprocity for the law of war: "Were a civilized nation engaged with barbarians who observed no rules even of war, the former must also suspend their observation of them, where they no longer serve to any purpose."[14]

In the nineteenth century, the Lieber Code, governing conduct of the Union Army in the American Civil War, provided that a belligerent who refused to grant quarter – that is, to accept surrender – was not entitled to receive it.[15] Even in the early twentieth century, humanitarian law treaties often contained *si omnes* clauses,[16] providing that all belligerents in a given conflict were released from treaty duties if *any* of its belligerents had not ratified.[17] Certain multilateral treaties today are understood to allow all affected parties to suspend or withdraw in the event of material breach by a single crucial member, on whose adherence the entire agreement effectively rests.[18]

Normally, the rule is different, to be sure: When state A violates a multilateral treaty, other states remain bound under it to one another, though it no longer binds them in their relations with A. This normal rule makes no sense, it was soon discovered, when the treaty prohibits the development of chemical weapons, for instance. If state B responds to A's breach by itself developing the prohibited weapon in order to protect itself from A, B would violate its duties to states C, D, and E. The treaty prohibits possession, not merely use, and such possession is not a relational property.

Let us say that the treaty prohibits the testing of new weapons in a certain category. States A and B are now the Soviet Union and the United States at the height of the Cold War. Here, the rationale for continuing to hold America to its treaty duties upon Soviet breach quickly begins to dissolve. The United States must be released from its treaty relations not only to the Soviet Union but also to China, France, and the United Kingdom. Testing, like possession, is not a relational activity. The United States could not begin testing the prohibited new weapon vis-à-vis the Soviet Union in response to the latter's breach without at once violating its treaty duties vis-à-vis, say, China.[19] So the whole regime essentially collapses once one central party breaches.

Within the law of war, reciprocity was long considered a crucial method of deterring war crime.[20] Its defenders view the doctrine of reprisal – still legally acknowledged but now greatly limited by treaty – as offering something of a middle ground. That ground lies between the extremes of, on the one hand, allowing one party's breach to release entirely the victim state from its treaty duties and, on the other, authorizing no practical remedy whatever for such breach, other than the slim reed of appeal to multilateral organizations.[21] To be lawful, reprisals must meet stringent conditions, rarely satisfied in practice.

The effort to prohibit belligerent reprisals partook of the same heady optimism about public international law that suffused the world community for the first four years after World War II. This period witnessed the creation of many new international institutions. The project for what became the 1949 Geneva Conventions was very much an expression of this *zeitgeist*, which proved fleeting as the Cold War emerged. During that brief, hopeful period, many anticipated the advent of true collective security through the new United Nations. It was widely thought that this organization would soon be joined by an international criminal court. With the power to punish war criminals from all countries, this court was expected to dispense with any need of belligerent reprisals for enforcing humanitarian law. But the failure of these noble hopes ensured that reprisals – in all their heartbreaking destructiveness – remained on military commanders' tables in ensuing conflicts.

REPRISAL AS JUSTIFICATION

Like self-defense, reprisal is not – in legal terms – a mere excuse. An excuse is a wrongful act for which the defendant lacks blameworthiness. Rather, reprisal is a full justification. Because it is a lesser evil, the law does not consider it even wrongful. Defending this view, Antonio Cassese invokes the example of reprisal for the use of prohibited weapons:[22]

> Society and the law make a positive appraisal of what would otherwise be misconduct. Society and the law want the person [i.e., the initial offender] to behave, because in weighing up the two conflicting values (the need not to use prohibited weapons and the necessity to impose on the enemy belligerent compliance with law) they give pride of place to one of them, although this entails the exceptional infringement of the legal rules designed to satisfy the other need.[23]

The schoolyard platitude that "two wrongs don't make a right" is therefore inapt, because the second "wrong" – initial appearances to the contrary – is not really wrongful. There is an exchange of bad for bad, but not of wrong for wrong. The party engaged in lawful reprisal does not really "stoop to the same low level," as is sometimes said,[24] when resorting to prohibited methods first employed by its foe. As in any other justified form of defense, one does not "become just like the enemy" when engaged in lawful reprisal. By this logic, America does not "lose the moral high ground" when it coercively interrogates suspected Al Qaeda operatives or detains them for extended periods without charging them with a crime. This is the response to the claim that America's very use of sustained detention and coercive interrogation destroys any seeming justification for their use: the fact that "we are not like them." Such claims were made frequently in the U.S. torture debate, as when Col. Morris Davis, former chief prosecutor for the Guantánamo military commissions, remarked, "We can never retake the moral high ground when we claim the right to do unto others that which we would vehemently condemn if done to us."[25]

The action involved in a lawful reprisal may admittedly be the same as the act eliciting it, but the intention – the mental state – is entirely distinct, *ex hypothesi*. The two are thus quite different from a moral point of view. Whether U.S. conduct in these respects is truly defensible by the law of reprisal (Chapter 2) and its underlying morality of reciprocity (Chapters 5 through 7) are possibilities later examined. Even if its conduct proves acceptable on these terms, however, there remains the fact, confronted in Chapters 11 through 13, that "by making calculated attacks on civilians a badge of the terrorism they opposed, Americans reinforced the expectation that they would abstain from similar methods,"[26] as writes an historian of U.S. thinking about collateral damage since World War II.

The longstanding traditional view contends that banning reprisals is counterproductive. However objectionable reprisals are in punishing the innocent,[27] the increasing legal restrictions on such actions are misguided even from a humanitarian perspective. The United States still officially upholds this position, and partly for this reason, it refused to ratify Additional Protocol I to the Geneva Conventions.[28] Yet since 1929, the Conventions themselves have set increasingly stringent limits on reprisals, reflecting growing doubts about both their practical efficacy and their moral defensibility.[29] Typical today is the position of the 1958 British Manual of Military Law in disavowing a very broad, unencumbered right of reprisal: "A belligerent is not justified in declaring himself freed altogether from the obligation to observe the laws of war . . . on account of their suspected or ascertained violation by his adversary."[30] Since the seventeenth century, in fact, international law has sought to impose increasing limits on the scope of permissible reprisals, beginning modestly with a prohibition on retaliation against foreign ambassadors.[31]

Reprisal is the most explicit recognition of the reciprocity principle within humanitarian law.[32] The history of reprisal is therefore helpful in understanding the workings of reciprocity in war. Even today, humanitarian law does not reject reprisal entirely. As World Court judge Stephen Schwebel writes,[33] the Geneva Conventions and their Protocols "prohibit reprisals not generally, but in specific cases."[34] The 1949 treaties do not bar reprisal, for instance, against enemy civilians and civilian property unprotected by the Fourth Convention, such as those within territory under enemy control.[35] This can be a large group of people, as was the case during the war between Iran and Iraq.[36]

Also permissible are certain "countermeasures," which sometimes involve force.[37] Material breach of the Geneva Conventions does not entitle a victimized state to suspend or terminate such treaties in its relations with the breaching state, as we will see. No state has ever openly argued its legal right to suspend the Geneva Conventions, even in part, on the basis of an adversary's prior breach of them. However, the victim state may take countermeasures in response to such "internationally wrongful acts" as war crimes, if these measures do not themselves violate humanitarian law – as many forms of violent reprisal would now do.[38] There is no gainsaying the ineliminable primitivism of reprisal (and the conception of reciprocity on which it relies), despite the sophisticated arguments defending it, including those in this book.

NORMAL EMERGENCY AND ABNORMAL EMERGENCY AS THE ABSENCE OF RECIPROCITY

There may exist a difference between ordinary armed conflicts, in which reciprocity enforces legal norms, and extraordinary wars, in which it cannot. In reaction to the 9/11 attacks, there has been much debate about how democratic constitutions should address situations of national emergency.[39] The criteria by which true emergencies should be distinguished from false, large from small, are the primary issues in contention. Also controversial are the grounds by which we decide who may make such judgments. In times of emergency, authority over vital matters – even at the most local level – can become centralized in the national executive.[40]

The notion of the "state of exception"[41] has recently captured the imagination even of literary intellectuals. The clergy was long fascinated with the miracle as the divine suspension of natural law; so too a portion of the literary clerisy is today enthralled – through Walter Benjamin's and Giorgio Agamben's work – by the notion of the emergency as an executive suspension of man-made law. One such littérateur playfully proffers this definition: a situation "where law is 'in force in the form of a suspension,' where what was outside and external to the law was indistinguishable from what was internal to the law, where there was no difference between following and transgressing a norm."[42] In such fanciful formulations, there is even a sly insinuation that the culturati,[43] despite their customary preference for elliptical allusion over more prosaic precision, have caught us logical lawyers in a contradiction. For the notion of "a juridical rule that decides the fact that decides on its application"[44] seems no mere paradox.

The "rule of law" exists only at the sufferance, the indulgence, of whoever has the constitutional authority to suspend it. Liberal legality could therefore be effectively abolished overnight by executive fact-finding of the existence of a putative "emergency." Noble invocation of the rule of law and the urgency of preserving it in the face of countervailing pressures is thus a shibboleth. "The problem with the 'rule of law' response to the war on terrorism," one author thus infers, "is that it ignores the way that the law is fundamentally implicated in the project of sovereignty with its corollary logic of exception."[45] Whereas an executive finding of emergency is not subject to prompt judicial review under many constitutions, which often also permit the dissolution of parliament, the rule of law has always really been, on this view, something of a fig leaf for the powers that be – a façade readily discarded whenever those who *really* rule may deem necessary.[46] In other words, let the workers rise up in general strike and create a political crisis. The capitalist state will promptly respond by declaring a national emergency, overriding all contrary claims of right, individual and collective, in a manner perfectly consistent with its vaunted rule of law. Such liberal legality has always been, of course, only a cover for power, never truly about justice. Workers of the world, do not be misled! You have nothing to lose but your pointless bourgeois rights![47]

Such are the veiled insinuations of this line of analysis, more guardedly couched in today's political climate perhaps than when Walter Benjamin first articulated them, at a time when the hope of socialist revolution still stirred many hearts. Yet the fact that a legal doctrine is subject to potential abuse – many are, after all – is not an argument for its repudiation, but only for its careful limitation and circumspect application. As Michael Walzer remarks, "Supreme emergency is not in fact a permissive doctrine. It can be put to ideological and apologetic uses, but that is true of every moral argument, including the argument for individual rights,"[48] and of the rule of law itself. That authoritarian rule may be effected consistently with most features of the rule of law, even without recourse to declaration of a state of emergency, will come as no surprise to anyone who has seriously examined the question.[49]

The rationale for legal recognition of supreme emergency is not in any event liberal. It is communitarian. "If the political community were nothing more than a neutral framework within which individuals pursued their own versions of the good life, as some liberal political philosophers suggest, the doctrine of supreme emergency would have no purchase," Walzer correctly observes.[50] Despite their self-understanding, left litterateurs critical of emergency doctrine have hence delivered no meaningful indictment of liberalism or its law. These critics are themselves often quick to invoke the language of emergency in justifying humanitarian interventions, as for Rwanda in 1993 or Kosovo in 1999.

Yet such interventions amount to "exceptions" from rules of international law prohibiting resort to force without UN Security Council authorization, which proved impossible to obtain in both cases. Invocations of "national emergency," within the meaning of the Trade Related Aspects of Intellectual Property Rights treaty and WTO Doha Declaration, were also prominent in the successful effort by human rights groups to lobby for compulsory patent licenses on AIDS pharmaceuticals; these licenses permitted countries like Brazil and India to begin manufacturing antiretroviral medications for parallel export to still poorer countries. "Something must be done," the critics clamor in such situations. But one can't have it both ways: Either there are genuine conditions of necessity, requiring departure from normal international rules, or there aren't. And if there are, then the law must confront the paradoxical challenge of establishing their defensible scope.

The 9/11 attacks created an abnormal climate of emergency. Many began to assert that, though reciprocity is possible in normal times and even in normal wars, it is impossible in the conflict with a far-flung, loosely connected terrorist network of suicidal ideological zealots. Normal humanitarian law is fine for normal wars, in which reciprocation (or its ever-present possibility) engenders self-restraint. But abnormal wars against this new type of enemy are different, it was suggested. Sterner methods are demanded against an adversary that rejects standard, means-end rationality. Within the broad genus of war, there are different species, some relatively amenable to normalization through law, others much less so.

Those who endorse targeted killing, coercive interrogation, and sustained detention argue that predictable emergencies created by interstate conflicts may involve conventional methods of fighting. But then there are abnormal emergencies – abnormal abnormalities, if you will – that are not susceptible to cooperative equilibrium of any sort, much less to effective international legal regulation. A key difference between the two would lie precisely in whether reciprocity, as an instrument of law enforcement, can actually deter atrocity. Abnormal international emergencies are defined as those in which it would not. Whether America's conflict with Al Qaeda and kindred groups presents such a situation, where reciprocation of restraint cannot be anticipated, is a question that should not be cavalierly dismissed. Under Secretary of Defense Douglas Feith, a key policymaker on these issues, had no doubts about the answer: "You are not really in the same world as the rest of us if you are worried about reciprocity from Al-Qaeda."[51]

True enough – at least, for now.[52] But talk of national emergency and its legal requirements quickly offers a serious hypothesis for inquiry, at least, and cannot be cavalierly dismissed.

Even so, talk of emergency and its legal requirements quickly threatens to pile exception on exception. First, the law of war exempts a country from certain normal requirements of human rights law. The war then leads to a state of national emergency that exempts the executive from normal constitutional restrictions in relation to other branches of government. Finally, when one belligerent adopts methods barred by humanitarian law, its adversary's executive – now released from constraints of both domestic and international human rights law – insists on exempting itself from even the law of war (i.e., from that law's already modest restrictions on violence) by reciprocating the enemy's martial misdeeds. With each exceptional empowerment built on the preceding action, one must begin to doubt whether the rule of law retains much meaning or intelligibility. As a practical matter, apart from the law's internal, rule-like structuring, the exception/exemption becomes the rule, as in Walter Benjamin's dark premonition of 1940.[53] A regime for which "everything is possible," because permitted by law, was Hannah Arendt's definition of totalitarianism.

An ancient maxim holds that *necessitas legem non habet* – necessity knows no law. This has never been a legal rule, however. The law itself – domestic and international – limits claims of necessity in many ways.[54] Whether such limits are respected in practice is another matter. The question that the law faces is whether and in what ways to accommodate the fact that exigent circumstances will sometimes genuinely require departures from normal procedures. The answer must deal effectively with the danger that exceptional powers, once formally authorized, will tend to be abused. Should we incorporate the normlessness of true necessity into the law itself, so that the law will never be subordinated to it from without? Or is it worse to be subjected to it from within, where principles of emergency governance may begin to infect the legal system even in more normal times?

Perhaps, it is better that a liberal constitution should be broken, rather than bent or slowly twisted into its opposite, so that at least the extent of the rupture will be transparent to the citizenry and others whose rights are thereby taken from them. This question arises independently of the perennial theoretical one of whether securing moral ends sometimes requires employing immoral means.[55] For even if the answer is yes, there remains the further, practical query of whether this answer ought to find its way into the law; that is, whether it should receive express public acknowledgment in such a way.

In their cold, clear-eyed disillusionment about the law's potential, at least the left litterateurs here do not make a mistake that is common among many liberal critics of emergency doctrine. The latter often talk as if the alternative to providing a legal route to exceptional governance (including torture, extrajudicial killing, etc.) is to prevent such governance entirely by legally foreclosing its possibility. Yet too often, history suggests, the alternative to legal cabining of the exception has been the uncabined exception; that is, a more overt executive (even military) usurpation of other branches' constitutional powers,[56] often with apparent public support and/or legislative acquiescence.[57] It is a much mooted query today among constitutional lawyers which of these unpalatable alternatives is preferable.[58] This is a hard question that should concern anyone of liberal political proclivities and one that the left literary critique studiously avoids.

WHEN RECIPROCITY THROUGH RETALIATION IS IMPOSSIBLE: ATTRACTIONS OF ANTICIPATORY SELF-DEFENSE

The Bush administration's invocation of the need for anticipatory self-defense, even "preventive war"[59] – as used to justify its 2003 Iraq invasion – was as controversial as its use of coercive interrogation. Administration defenders claimed that, when terrorists wield weapons of mass destruction, their intended victim cannot afford to wait until attacked, nor even until attack is imminent – the law of war's normal requirements for resorting to force in self-defense. "The smoking gun may be a mushroom cloud," Secretary of State Condoleezza Rice famously announced.[60] The United States must therefore seek out and destroy key sites of terrorist activity wherever they may be found, before the risk they represent can fully materialize, by which point averting it will be much more difficult.

This view assumes that reciprocity in war cannot be established with most militant jihadist groups. Suicide bombers do not value their own lives in secular ways that would deter them by threat of death.[61] Even more important is that effective retaliation for terrorist attack will often be impossible because the parties most responsible simply cannot thereafter be located. They are likely to be highly dispersed and ensconced in the world's most inaccessible areas. No tit-for-tat equilibrium is possible with an adversary that cannot credibly be threatened with prompt and effective retaliation on its home ground for violations of humanitarian law.

In response to this sort of problem, arms control negotiations between the United States and the Soviet Union sought to ensure that both sides would retain the capacity to retaliate if victimized by a first strike.[62] This notion invariably appears perverse at the outset to the uninitiated. Yet mere parity in the number of Soviet and American missiles would not establish a stable equilibrium, strategists came to realize, unless those missiles were designed and deployed in ways that denied both sides a good chance at victory by striking first. Without some punitive capability, "the fear of being a poor second" at the draw would induce both to be too quick on the trigger, argued Schelling, Brodie, and Wohlstetter influentially.[63] Granting the Soviets a *second*-strike capacity was eventually recognized as essential to U.S. interests in preventing a Soviet *first* strike. Legal mechanisms embodying these dynamics were then built into the arms control treaties themselves. With all its undoubted perils, this was how the nuclear peace was preserved for a half-century.

The appeal of anticipatory self-defense against terrorist groups relies on the same logic, only the facts are flipped on their head. The elusiveness of militant jihadist leaders and the impenetrability of their financial operations[64] mean that the United States lacks the capacity to retaliate promptly and effectively against well-conceived attacks. Because it cannot deter such attacks through threat of *ex post* response, America is tempted instead to act preventively against these organizations and individuals, wherever and in whatever manner possible (i.e., without waiting for them to attack). The perceived impossibility of restraint through reciprocity with current foes again lies at the root of the problem – and becomes a major source of American policy.

Many today repudiate the Bush administration's strategic doctrine of preventive war, particularly for its extensions beyond any hitherto accepted notion of preemptive self-defense. To reject that theory persuasively, however, one would need to refute its conclusions about the impossibility of playing tit-for-tat with militant jihadists, especially those over whom Al Qaeda itself has little control.[65] Yale Law professor W. Michael Reisman is right to acknowledge that, when fighting terrorists who are "impervious to the controls of reciprocity and retaliation that operate on territorial elites . . . a government in a functioning democracy whose population faces such violence will not last long if . . . it tells its electorate that international law prevents it from taking anticipatory or preemptive action."[66] A compelling critique of preventive war doctrine would require an alternative solution to the impossibility of deterrence in such circumstances.

As with the previous section of this chapter, the purpose here is simply to underline yet another manifestation of reciprocity's centrality to current counterterrorism policy and hence also to any law that would seek to govern such policy.

ASYMMETRICAL WARFARE: IMPETUS TO ANTIRECIPROCITY

What is unique about current jihadist terrorism is its melding of a now perennial mode of warfare – avoidance of direct, battlefield confrontation – to suicide bombing with the most advanced technologies.[67] Also unusual, though not unprecedented, are the unclear objectives on both sides, making it difficult to know when the conflict has ended.[68] If we are to discover the changes that humanitarian law today requires, we must carefully distinguish the novel features of the current predicament and opponents from longstanding practices that the law of war has already addressed.

As a weapon of the weak, asymmetrical warfare and the legal challenges it presents have been around for some time.[69] The British faced such asymmetry from early American Revolutionary forces,[70] as did France in its Napoleonic wars.[71] It is therefore not unique to the Western encounter with non-Western antagonists. Nor is it any more brutal than other longstanding forms of Western warfare.[72] Neither is the absence of a single "battlefield" truly a distinguishing feature of the conflict with Al Qaeda. The same could be said of the Cold War.[73] And like the current conflict, the Cold War was also fought as much by diplomatic pressure, positive incentives given to third parties to elicit cooperation, and strategic alliances based on overlapping interests as by force of arms.

It is now harder to identify the exact shape of today's antagonists than when opposing the Soviet Union, given their apparent amorphousness. But even in the Cold War, there often arose the question of whether a particular country's civil war or leftist opposition was a manifestation of the larger Soviet threat. Whether local Islamists and jihadists in certain countries pertinently resemble Al Qaeda today presents a similar question for U.S. policymakers. It is especially vexing where such political forces seek to operate simultaneously through liberal electoral methods, however illiberal their ultimate ends.

The more recent recognition has been that, when the methods of asymmetrical warfare are harnessed to the West's own, most modern technology, "the strong are weaker than anyone imagined,"[74] as John Gray observes. Like any other body of law, the Geneva Conventions have been regularly revised in light of novel challenges in warfare. In fact, major revisions have occurred about every twenty-five to thirty years.[75] By that standard, the world is now due for another such reassessment. To recommend their partial reconsideration is not to suggest that – in devising norms for a type of conflict that is neither "crime" nor "war" in the normal sense of either term – we must start from ground zero.[76]

The Bush administration's critics, in fact, are among the first to demand new rules for regulating private military contractors,[77] and they are right to do so.[78] The U.S. military's increased reliance on such contracting is no simple, lingering legacy of Reagan-era privatization. Rather, it is a more recent reaction to post-Cold War military contingencies that require a faster and more flexible response to conflict situations and missions – some of which are humanitarian in nature.[79] Military privatization has been primarily a means to this end. The challenge now faced by humanitarian law is then not merely that the West faces new, irregular enemies; it is that new enemies always stimulate the development of a new type of "regular" military force to fight them. This challenge resembles how contemporary architecture – especially for embassies and international financial institutions – has already creatively evolved to incorporate post-9/11 security concerns.[80]

Private contractors are simply the current expression of this perennial process, abundantly evidenced throughout military history. Nor are they entirely novel, as they resemble the "letters of marquee and reprisal" process commonly employed by most early modern states and embraced by the U.S. Constitution.[81] That these new organizational forms currently escape the reach of much military law is likely no coincidence, as critics stress.[82] But neither do they arise in isolation from some very real changes – strategic, operational, and tactical – in the security environment.[83]

Terror, too, will again morph in response to such novel forms of counterterrorism, as it has before.[84] The deeper roots of terrorist movements may lie in some amalgam of religious and secular political experience. But their operative methods are more fruitfully analogized to tax avoidance stratagems, drafted by each generation of lawyers to overcome regulatory obstacles. Methods of terror, like other forms of armed conflict, mutate and evolve in reaction to legal change. If they elude its categories, this is partly a consequence of exploring and exploiting the law's own limits and loopholes, including those of tax regulation itself (on charitable contributions to religious organizations, for example), as well as other financial regulation. For this reason, it is not hard to give some credence to reports that, when captured in Pakistan, among Khalid Sheikh Mohammed's first words reportedly were, "I'll see you in New York with my lawyers."[85]

THE LAW OF WAR AS OXYMORON?

Most who write on humanitarian law are drawn to it by a commitment to reducing human suffering by subordinating war to law. Yet the very idea of a "law of war" once struck most people as oxymoronic. For many, it still does. Any book on the subject that is intended partly for nonspecialists must therefore offer some justification for the effort. To some, it may even seem that to theorize the law of war is to adopt the most abstruse of standpoints toward the most quixotic of legal endeavors. To show that this need not be so is one of this book's aspirations.

Still, what could be more absurd, one might fairly ask, than lawyers' efforts to ensure the recognition of human dignity in situations that essentially amount to suspensions of it?[86] At its best, law is clean, transparent, logical, neat, orderly, civilized, and peaceful, whereas war is dirty, opaquely foggy, irrational, emotional, unkempt, disorderly, and savagely violent. How could the messy experience of the latter ever be made to fit the concepts of the former? On these understandings of law and war, at least, how could there ever really exist a law of war; that is, as more than an elusive apparition? This common view is well captured by historian Geoffrey Best. Describing elite attitudes at the outset of World War II, he writes,

> Among the major military powers, professions of legal good intention were not lacking. They were, however, chiefly designed to serve the ends of political and public relations; they coexisted in at least some of the most influential minds, civilian and military alike . . . with predictable *arrières-pensées* that reciprocity was after all the master-rule – that arguments of necessity and reprisals could be relied on to excuse almost any excess – and in any case that, in desperate last resorts, anything was permissible.[87]

In a similar spirit, some who write on the law of war are lured by the very paradox of any such effort, often with a view to counseling against undue reliance on the high hopes the endeavor today inspires.[88] According to this second view, war is simply too blunt a policy "instrument" – if so delicate a term may even be used[89] – to submit to fine-grained legal regulation. This is because war necessarily involves forcing another to submit to one's brute will,[90] a sort of coercion to which the rule of law – almost by definition – is seemingly antithetical. And this is true not only at the beginning of one's inquiry, one should add, but at the end as well. Admittedly, it may be true, as Descartes wittily remarked, that the main point of finesse is our frequent unwillingness to use it[91] (i.e., when cruder concepts better suit our baser purposes). But it is also unfair for the law to expect most people – on pain of serious criminal liability, facing the most exigent circumstances and excruciating choices – to act in conscious recognition of the most refined and subtle of legal distinctions barely intelligible to the average attorney. On this view, well reflected in General Sherman's famous lamentation, "War is cruelty, and you cannot refine it."[92] More precisely (though less pungently), because victory in war requires some measure of ruthlessness, a humanitarian law that banishes any place for ruthlessness is – as long as war continues to exist – doomed from the start.

This objection to the very enterprise of humanitarian law should be sobering and cautionary, but it ultimately proves too much, for the law is always an instrument of violence, no less than a means of civilizing it, as Robert Cover observed.[93] That the law of war at once limits and legitimates great violence hardly distinguishes it from much other law, even if the measure of force it authorizes does represent something of a *ne plus ultra*. The law of war, in its authorization of controlled uses of force, is on the same continuum as the law of policing. It is true that the law here indirectly legitimates war itself by expressly authorizing certain ends and means for fighting it. This is the unremarkable insight of much postmodernist writing on the subject.[94]

A deeper paradox is that, although war is obviously an "antisocial" activity, the relations between belligerents display aspects that could only be described as social in nature, as intensely social to their core. The antagonists must view each other through the shared concept of "enemy." In other words, they must share the idea that they *are* at war, with the many implicit social understandings this entails. "War is a form of collective intentionality," Wendt argues, "and as such it is only war if both sides *think* it is war." Otherwise, as in Cambodia under the Khmer Rouge, "killing there may be aplenty, but it is akin to the slaughtering of animals, not war."[95]

"In order to be fighting at one level we have to be cooperating in having a fight at another level,"[96] observes John Searle. This is to say that war, like chess, is a "game," the rules for which are constitutive, in the sense that war itself is constituted and so distinguished from simple conquest and enslavement, for instance – by acting in accord with these rules, even as they may change over time. Without sharing the concept of reprisal, in particular, such retaliation by one side for the other's war crimes would be unintelligible as punishment and indistinguishable from a new violation. There is ample evidence of Searle's insight in that reciprocity – a social phenomenon *par excellence* – has been so salient an issue in war and in the law governing it. "The reciprocal activity of injuring"[97] is how Elaine Scarry defines war's essence.

The parties' self-understanding is relevant even to the definition of war. If neither side believes itself to be at war with the other, this fact alone speaks against the legal characterization of a violent confrontation in these terms. A conflict that jihadist militants insist is a war might be regarded by their adversaries as simply a matter for international police cooperation[98] or a state of emergency. And if the leaders of both sides see themselves as being at war with each other, this shared self-awareness contributes to the legal conclusion that this is indeed the case.[99] The fact that both Osama bin Laden and President George W. Bush, with congressional acquiescence if not express endorsement,[100] have characterized the conflict as a war would therefore suggest *ipso facto* that it is and may be so treated for purposes of international law.[101] We may call this the element of *opinio juris* in war's definition – how the parties view their legal circumstance – though it is also a verbal component of the relevant state practice.[102] This element of war's legal definition is especially helpful in uncertain cases. When accompanied by overt expressions of hostile intent, violent "acts which would otherwise have been equivocal may be treated as 'offensive,' if the state which perpetrates them considers itself to be in a state of war,"[103] writes a leading authority.

A third reason for interest in the law of war – the author's, for instance – is simply the moral richness of the questions it poses and the vital human stakes these entail. This source of interest does not require any precommitment to or against a belief in the necessary efficacy of this body of law and so enables one to remain agnostic on whether heavy reliance on it is most likely to advance human interests and liberal purposes in a given circumstance. In assessing the empirical evidence of military activity, one is then predisposed neither for nor against the hypothesis that humanitarian law has made any nontrivial difference in combat conduct. Neither is one prepared to assume even that any such difference has necessarily served the cause of justice, because unreciprocated adherence to humanitarian norms may sometimes prejudice the success of the aggrieved belligerent against the aggressor.

This third approach does not require one to decide, before immersing oneself in a given problem, that its principal solution must lie primarily within international law,[104] as opposed to diplomacy, moral suasion, socialization,[105] foreign aid, cross-border interagency cooperation and other "soft" governance, or even force. International law then remains an instrument or means, not an end, much less the spiritual touchstone – or, less generously, surrogate religion – it may occupy in the imagination of many who choose public international law and its study as a vocation. Such apotheosis is tempting to many, for "with the collapse of the certainties of Marxism, liberal progressivism and the Cold War, 'universal human rights' has become the only surviving meta-narrative," observes Stanley Cohen.[106]

This third stance toward the subject will be the most congenial to anyone seriously influenced by pragmatism, by Oliver Wendell Holmes, or by the intellectual movement known as legal realism.[107] Though humanitarian law and international human rights often seem the most hopeful of endeavors, it is wise to recall that their late-twentieth-century revival was driven less by faith in humankind than by fear of its worst tendencies, abundantly evidenced during World War II.[108] The field would do better to draw more from those who fear the worst of their fellow human beings than from those who perennially insist on imagining the best.[109] This is not to say that it needs those who believe the task of thought, as of Sophoclean tragedy, is simply to help us contemplate and resign ourselves to history's horrors. But neither should humanitarian and human rights law become "the creed of those who have given up an irrational belief in God for an irrational belief in mankind,"[110] as John Gray contends it has. At its best, international humanitarian law seeks to remain sensitive to warfare's unsavory political realities – which it aims to govern – without simply subordinating itself to them. Scholarship in this field, alas, has too much feared the latter fate to make much progress toward the former aim.

This third standpoint toward humanitarian law is willfully *ad hoc*, in search of no grand *a priori* theory of the field's scope, purpose, or methods. It is brazen in its modesty, content to let grand theory fly – with the night owl of Minerva – well behind the day's expedient temporizing. Only through a process of trial and error, of experiment and reflection on it, may we learn when international law is likely to prove preferable to other modalities of influencing the conduct of war.[111] Oxford's Andrew Hurrell retorts that "the ethical claims of international law rest on the contention that it is the only set of globally institutionalized processes by which norms can be negotiated on the basis of dialogue and consent, rather than simply imposed by the most powerful."[112] Yet that statement is mistaken twice over: in its view of lawmaking and adjudication as implicitly operating above the battle for political power, and also of nonlaw or nonlegal interaction between peoples as involving nothing but a simple choice between domination or submission.

The standpoint of this book is very different. In its last three chapters, in fact, it therefore turns away from the law almost entirely, finding the most compelling sources of martial forbearance in other precincts altogether. The chief point here is simply that, in regard to the American conflict with Al Qaeda, international law proves less important than other legitimate considerations in counseling national restraint in counterterrorism policy. From this avowedly pragmatic perspective, the central question becomes, When is it best to expect either international law or the logic of reciprocity, alone or in conjunction, to do the normative work we want them to, and when should we turn elsewhere, to other modes of assessing and advancing our aims and ideals?[113]

A corollary question is: If humanitarian law is to reject reciprocity in key places, how may it do so without discrediting only itself – that is, through its likely failure effectively to discipline actual conduct between belligerents?[114] "The law of war should not be a nice façade of impracticable rules but a solid construction which will withstand the rigors of war,"[115] wrote a Swiss lawyer following World War II. The challenge, however, is to choose rules that will not merely "withstand" or accommodate such rigors but will also exercise some major mitigating influence over them. The next chapter begins to address these questions through attention to the legal materials.

2

Reciprocity in Humanitarian Law:
Acceptance and Repudiation

This chapter examines the changing place of the reciprocity principle within humanitarian law, as this legal field bears on America's conflict with Al Qaeda and kindred groups. The conclusion is that reciprocity occupies a more prominent place within such law, especially as it has been adopted by the United States and the U.K., than is generally acknowledged. This prominence has implications for assessing the legality of America's most controversial counterterrorism policies. It requires us to view these policies in a more favorable light than permitted by other accounts of the pertinent law, even those offered by the Bush administration itself. This is the case even if – for quite different reasons that are elaborated on in Chapters 10 through 12 – the United States should ultimately forswear some of these methods.

Let us begin by identifying various places where humanitarian law accepts and rejects reciprocity. I then ask whether the line between the two makes sense – logically or morally. The main contention here is that humanitarian law is incoherent in its treatment of reciprocation as a remedy for breach, yet is nonetheless correct in rejecting both the stark extremes of perfect reciprocity, on one hand, and its total repudiation, on the other. Given the complexity of combat's novel forms and the moral issues they present, it is inadvisable for the law to fix the boundary between these rival domains with any principled bright line. The incoherence of humanitarian law is not fatal to the enterprise, I conclude. However, such incoherence does suggest that humanitarian law provides only the most uncertain guidance in answering key questions of U.S. counterterrorism policy. Those answers, later chapters will show, are to be found not principally in the rules of humanitarian law, but rather in other considerations altogether.

If the administration had wanted to defend its most contested policies on grounds of legal principle, this chapter is roughly what its argument would have looked like. The objective here is not a supercilious exercise in devil's advocacy, but rather – in a spirit of moral seriousness, joined to a willful intellectual "naiveté" – an effort to raise the level of public discussion by looking afresh at the most fundamental questions, as if no rivers of blood – physical and metaphorical/political – had yet been spilled over them. These vexing public issues will not disappear with the presidency of George W. Bush, after all. Thus more blood – of one sort or the other – remains likely to run, at some point, especially with respect to targeted killing and almost certainly a legal regime employing preventive detention, the most pressing topic in counterterrorism law at the moment.[1]

The present enterprise will require excavating and reconstructing the intellectual edifice of reciprocity within the law of war, thereby establishing its continuing doctrinal, practical, and moral importance. The field of humanitarian law is defined by the principal purpose of preventing superfluous suffering in war. This purpose is advanced by both Geneva law and Hague-type, weapons-restriction treaties. The latter branch of humanitarian law largely endorses the principle of reciprocity as a way of ensuring that both sides may play by the same rules. But the Geneva Conventions increasingly reject reciprocity by greatly restricting a belligerent's right of reprisal.[2] When both of its branches are examined *in pari materia*, it is clear that humanitarian law as a whole, like public international law generally, accords the reciprocity principle broad sway, with a few notable exceptions. Identifying the contours of and rationales for these exceptions is the chief concern here and in the next chapter.

We will see that it is a considerable exaggeration to claim, as does the International Criminal Tribunal for the former Yugoslavia (ICTY) in one case, that "the defining feature of modern international humanitarian law is . . . the obligation to uphold key tenets of this body of law regardless of the conduct of enemy combatants."[3] This chapter is less concerned with arguing about exactly how the law might be modified to deal with current conundrums and longstanding internal inconsistencies than simply with the preliminary groundwork of clarifying the intellectual landscape. Laying this groundwork requires explicating a number of treaty provisions, as well as the relevant customary international law, to see how the question of reciprocity resolves itself somewhat differently on each of several legal issues and factual circumstances. The reader should therefore approach the ensuing discussion less as a single linear argument than, by musical analogy, as a series of variations on a theme.

Nonetheless, this analysis makes the following contentions about the current state of legal doctrine, contentions that are straightforward enough in themselves, though rendered more complex by being sometimes cast in the alternative. First, when interpreted in light of enduring state practice, the pertinent treaties do not fully outlaw civilian reprisal, as they purport to do on their face. Second, even insofar as these treaties ban civilian reprisal, they are at odds with customary law, which does not do so. Third, to the extent that customary law has moved in the direction of prohibiting civilian reprisals, the United States has been a persistent objector to that trend and therefore is not bound by it.[4] The same goes for *jus cogens* norms, a concept that the United States has never officially endorsed in any dispute.

If there is an armed conflict with Al Qaeda, then America does not need a right of reprisal to kill that organization's leaders and detain its members for the duration of the conflict. Both leaders and followers could then be considered combatants and as such may lawfully be treated in these ways. But if there is no armed conflict, then even a right of belligerent reprisal would not permit torture, other inhumane treatment, and arbitrary detention, insofar as the United States may have accepted the *jus cogens* status of these prohibitions. Any legal argument in favor of such practices would then have to be consistent with the international law of peacetime countermeasures, which is even more restrictive of force than the rules on belligerent reprisals. Applying this view of the law to pertinent facts, reprisals and countermeasures – the chief expression of the reciprocity principle within relevant law – were therefore either unnecessary or insufficient to authorize the Bush administration's most controversial counterterrorism practices.

Yet, this is only because current humanitarian law, as the United States and key allies endorse it, relies on distinctions that are logically incoherent or morally indefensible, we will see. These countries insist that international law respect the reciprocity principle to such an extent that remaining doctrinal obstacles to justifying all Bush administration policies as lawful reprisal become entirely arbitrary. Moreover, most legal specialists hold the view that members of terrorist groups are not "directly participating in hostilities" except when immediately or imminently perpetrating violence against others.[5] If so, then they generally remain protected as civilians at other times, and the reprisal right then becomes necessary to justify America's attacking them.

INTERNATIONAL LAW

The Geneva Conventions today accord little place to reciprocity – as in-kind retaliation – when governing the permissible response to their breach. It is therefore not surprising that the Bush administration, in seeking maximal latitude for its counterterrorism policy, sought legal support for the conclusion that these treaties did not apply to the conflict with Al Qaeda. There were several steps in the analysis leading to this conclusion.

First, the conflict was not between states and therefore not covered by Common Article 2 on all accounts.[6] Second, most of the Guantánamo detainees (i.e., all but Iraqis, Afghans, and Westerners from countries with troops in Iraq or Afghanistan) were citizens of states not party to the conflict and so did not qualify by their nationality as "protected persons" under the Fourth Geneva Convention, designed only for civilians of this sort.[7] Third, Al Qaeda members are unprivileged belligerents because they took up arms without joining an organization constituting an "armed force," defined by international law as the military of a sovereign state.[8] They were therefore not entitled to prisoner of war (POW) status and treatment, according to Article 4 of the Third Convention,[9] which in this way relies on an expectation of reciprocity.[10] Fourth, Al Qaeda had declined to "accept and apply" the Conventions, which might arguably have afforded its members the rights corresponding to the acknowledgment of such duties.[11] Fifth, even Taliban soldiers were not POWs because the Taliban had routinely flouted the requirements for such status imposed by this same provision.[12] Both Taliban and Al Qaeda fighters thus fell into a third category – neither POWs nor protected persons under the Geneva Convention concerning civilians. This category was not a novel creation of Bush administration lawyers, since mercenaries, saboteurs, and spies occupy it as well and all have a long history. Sixth, the conflict with Al Qaeda was not a civil war, because it is not exclusively "occurring in the territory of one of the High Contracting Parties" – the pertinent wording of Common Article 3. In a closely related argument, given the multinational reach of Al Qaeda, the conflict could hardly be considered "not of an international character" by any ordinary reading of that term, a reading long entertained by certain leading scholars of international law; this further suggested Article 3's inapplicability.[13]

None of these contentions was preposterous (i.e., beyond accepted ethical standards of lawyerly contention); in fact, some were virtually beyond cavil. To be sure, when counseling the president before he acts, rather than defending his conduct *post facto*, his legal advisers in the Office of Legal Counsel must adopt a more demanding test than nonfrivolousness. But few contend that the standard they should employ is as pristinely impartial as that of judicial neutrality.[14] In any event, it was on questions of domestic constitutional and statutory law where the administration occupied much weaker ground. On international law, the questions were much closer. For instance, the view that Common Article 3 "applies automatically to [non-international] armed conflict is simply not accepted in practice,"[15] wrote one disinterested scholar some years before the *Hamdan* litigation. In that case, the U.S. Supreme Court saw fit to resolve ambiguities over Common Article 3 by reference to Article 75 of Geneva Additional Protocol II. However, America has not ratified this treaty, and though the United States regards portions of Article 75 as reflective of customary law, this concession is not dispositive of the matter where evidence of state practice indicates otherwise.[16]

In any event, this Additional Protocol confers its rights only contingently, upon a display of some reciprocity by nonstate actors. The protocol requires that nonstate forces be capable of implementing the treaty, which reintroduces an expectation of reciprocity. For the treaty applies and confers its rights only when nonstate antagonists are able, on account of the extent of their organization (and control of territory, on some accounts) to reciprocate the martial restraint of their governmental adversary.[17]

Nonetheless, the Supreme Court was ultimately unconvinced by the administration's final two arguments above (though these were persuasive to the Court of Appeals), and therefore found the detainees to be protected by Common Article 3, with its prohibition against cruel and degrading treatment.[18] Yet even as legitimate doubts about the application of this provision were thereby resolved for present purposes, there remain other sources of humanitarian law that offered some support for the administration's policies and must be addressed in a more comprehensive analysis of pertinent authorities.

The wide scope of operation or field of maneuver granted to the reciprocity principle springs from the law's recognition that fairness in any contest generally requires common rules for all participants and that much of warfare's internal dynamics are those of tit-for-tat. This latter fact remains true whether each side's methods of fighting are lawful or unlawful. Thus, for instance, one belligerent is likely to respond to the other's lawful offensive with a counteroffensive. And the victim of a legal violation in warfare has generally sought its redress by way of a like action in retaliation, as the historical evidence presented in Chapter 10 establishes. Such reciprocation is a very prominent feature of state practice within war, and state practice is a key component of customary international law. The preeminent place of reciprocity in both Hague law and state practice means that this principle enjoys strong gravitational force and hence warrants weighty consideration when legal ambiguities arise.[19]

Recently, notable ambiguities of this sort have included the meaning of Geneva Common Article 3[20] and Article 4 of the POW Convention. "The failure of Common Article 3 to mention reprisals," for instance, as one scholar observes, "could be taken to mean that they are permitted during internal armed conflict, especially since certain types of reprisal are explicitly prohibited elsewhere in the Conventions."[21] Internal armed conflict is shorthand for "armed conflict not of an international character," and the U.S. Supreme Court has classified America's confrontations with Al Qaeda in just this manner. Carried to its logical conclusion, such an argument would view violations of Geneva Common Article 3 as establishing a *prima facie* case against the accused that is rebuttable – like any *prima facie* case – by a cognizable defense of excuse or justification, in this case, the defense of reprisal. This position allows us to reject the Bush administration's initial stance that Article 3 does not apply at all, even presumptively, to detained Al Qaeda suspects.

The law of treaties itself expressly counsels that their interpretation be informed by subsequent state practice reflecting the parties' understandings of the norms enshrined therein.[22] Several respected scholars contend, for instance, that the increasing state practice of "humanitarian intervention" without UN Security Council approval "has drastically altered the meaning and content of [Charter] Article 2(4),"[23] a treaty purporting to bar the resort to force except in national self-defense against armed attack. The relevant norms and associated state practice in the present context are those concerning civilian reprisal, the prohibition of which is no less settled and ostensibly absolute within Geneva Additional Protocol I than are the protections afforded *hors de combat* in Geneva Common Article 3. The pervasive state practice of reprisal and professed reprisal therefore remains legally relevant, even as the Geneva Conventions,[24] on their face, increasingly sought to retire this practice for good, understandably viewing it as a barbarity. Virtually all states engaging in such practice of retaliation have been party to both the 1949 and 1977 Geneva Conventions.

Treaty and customary law are equally applicable in evaluating American conduct in the conflict with Al Qaeda and like-minded groups.[25] If customary law permits a much broader range of violent acts as belligerent reprisal than does treaty law,[26] then the law of war's two chief sources may here prove to be at war with one another. This is not uncommon in international law concerning mass atrocity.[27] The predicament cannot be comfortable for anyone commited to increasing the coherence and practical relevance of public international law. Historian Geoffrey Best ably captures the paradox in this book's epigraphs. In a passage clearly targeted at international lawyers and, in particular, at human rights advocates, he quips tauntingly,

> International humanitarian law texts rarely admit it, yet without reciprocity in practice those texts may be of little avail, for not all belligerents

will be so saintly as to observe restraint and to honour humanitarian obligations in the face of an enemy's persistent refusal to do so. The most effective actual working engine of international humanitarian law observance, far from being established or even mentioned in the Geneva Conventions . . . works in fact in apparent defiance of them. Reciprocity is its name. Reciprocity may roughly back humanitarian principle, whether humanitarians or principle ask it to or not.[28]

The reciprocity widely reflected in state practice, however, is insufficient to create customary law, on the subject of reprisal or any other. State practice must be accompanied by widespread *opinio juris* – the consistent legal opinion of relevant states – endorsing such practice as lawful. Some accounts of customary international law, however, accord less weight to such opinion than do other theories.[29] Hans Kelsen (and several others since) concluded that this "subjective element" of custom was wholly unworkable.[30] If the problem of ascertaining *opinio juris* does not often arise, this is because legal opinion may often fairly be inferred directly from consistent practice, unless such practice is deliberately concealed, as with police torture.[31] The International Law Association hence adopts the view that states "usually do not look specifically for evidence of *opinio juris* unless there is reason to believe . . . that consistent state practice . . . does not 'count' towards . . . customary law."[32] *Opino juris* may also sometimes be inferred from silence. Most states decline to condemn the successful targeting of terrorist leaders,[33] thereby indicating their view that the practice is permissible. Even Human Rights Watch declined to condemn the 2002 U.S. killing of an Al Qaeda leader and his associates in Yemen.[34]

Independent of state practice, evidence concerning states' opinions about the legitimacy of belligerent reprisal (i.e., broader than the Geneva Conventions themselves afford) is mixed. There clearly exists no settled legal opinion *against* civilian reprisal, as leading specialists in humanitarian law reluctantly acknowledge. The United States, like the United Kingdom, has in any event expressly objected to tendencies within customary law formation that would narrow permissible reprisals to those allowed by Geneva law, especially by Additional Protocol I, which bars them altogether.[35] Having "persistently objected" to these developments, such states would not be bound by them, according to standard doctrine on customary law's creation.[36] Both France and the United Kingdom also entered formal reservations to this effect when ratifying the provision. Treaty rules do not become customary law, moreover, in the face of such major-state objections to this development.[37] It is true that, in reserving a right of civilian reprisal, France, Britain, and the United States have never expressly affirmed an intention to exercise that right by way of extrajudicial execution, sustained detention, or coercive interrogation. But the law of reprisal has never required states exercising it to specify in advance, when claiming such a right in the abstract, the particular means by which they may later wish to exercise it.

The pervasive practice of reprisal – real and professed – hence differs importantly in its accompanying *opinio juris* from the pervasiveness of police torture and of interstate aggression throughout the world. No state affirms a legal right to torture or to aggress against its neighbors, whereas major military powers do assert a right of belligerent reprisal and many states invoke this right when retaliating against their enemies' perceived violations of humanitarian law. The prohibition of civilian reprisals does not rise to the stature of *jus cogens*, moreover, because it does not meet the Vienna Convention's requirement that such a norm be "accepted and recognized by the international community of states *as a whole*."[38]

Where states avow that a given prohibition – like the treaty provisions banning most forms of reprisal – does not precisely pertain to the facts of their conduct, one should not assume that these states still affirm the rule's continuing validity.[39] When engaged in acts of reprisal, if states believe themselves – even if incorrectly – to be acting consistently with current law, then their actions would not supersede existing custom.[40] But if they are right about current customary law (or about how state practice should influence treaty interpretation), then there can be no legal objection to their reprisals, provided such actions meet reprisal's own requirements (i.e., last resort, advance warning, proportionality of response). Every act of retaliation for war crime, including retorsion (lawful but unfriendly acts) and retaliatory actions not meeting all formal requirements of reprisal, helps establish the centrality of the reciprocity principle to state practice. Also relevant to such practice, of course, are violent acts squarely satisfying reprisal doctrine's requirements – admittedly, a small subset of total retaliatory violence in war. All such retaliatory acts that states widely regard as consistent with reprisal contribute to the *opinio juris* necessary to the crystallization and consolidation of pertinent customary law.

All authorities agree that – for better or worse – states are not "created equal" in the making of customary international law. When determining customary norms governing the use of force, in particular, states with greater military capability exercise greater influence by way of their greater "practice" of arms. And it is no surprise that the world's major military powers (and the states facing the greatest prospects of war) have been the most reluctant about accepting international restrictions on a state's exercise of force. This is the case not only with respect to hoary rules of reprisal but also, more conspicuously, in the nonratification of the recent International Criminal Court statute by China, Russia, the United States, India, Pakistan, Indonesia, and Israel.

It is true that a few countries like Switzerland, through its ICRC, do seek to influence customary humanitarian law in measure greatly disproportionate to their military commitments. But because they are detached from any significant state practice of armed conflict, the *opinio juris* of such a state and its semi-private spin-offs do not contribute significantly *per se* to binding international custom.[41]

In the conflict between the United States and Al Qaeda, the ultimate question today would be whether coercive interrogation, sustained detention, and extrajudicial killing of "civilian" terrorist leaders could be justified either under customary law or a persistent objection to it, as forms of reprisal for Al Qaeda's myriad violations of humanitarian law.[42] A Dworkinian would say that the state practice of reprisal, like any social practice, should be interpreted and its rules applied in light of its best overall meaning and purpose (i.e., the values it should be understood to serve).[43] The deterrent purpose of reprisal suggests that leaders of a fighting force committed to attacks on civilian populations may be legally vulnerable to degrading measures insofar as these acts are calculated to elicit intelligence necessary to protecting such civilians. If targeted killings are done in reprisal, then they too would be defensible insofar as they are designed to protect innocent civilians from future attack, rather than simply as retribution or for strategic advantage.[44]

The workings of deterrence implicit in these conclusions differ somewhat from conventional understandings of the concept. Yet the underlying purpose remains the same: crime prevention. It is immaterial that this enduring aim may today be advanced less by the threat of future punishment than by present incapacitation and intelligence collection. When it is impossible to appeal to the self-interest of potential offenders by altering their incentives, prevention must be pursued by these other methods. Sustained detention, coercive interrogation, and targeted killings of terrorist leaders are justified insofar as they are reasonably designed to reduce the likelihood of prohibited attacks on civilian populations. That purpose – long thought to bar reprisals – is here nonetheless served by employing them in these several ways.

If the first purpose of reprisal is to punish and thereby deter humanitarian law breaches, the second aim is to restore parity between belligerents in the methods lawfully available to them.[45] This rationale turns out to justify the same species of retaliatory actions in most circumstances. That is because it is only by restoring the possibility of parity through common rules that rights of reprisal may effectively discourage continued violations. The deterrent value of reprisal rights derives precisely from the prospective violator's recognition that it will gain little by such violation, for it knows that its victim will thereby be permitted to respond in kind, in otherwise unlawful ways. Kant's account of law as establishing a reciprocal balance of benefit and burden yields a defense of criminal punishment generally characterized as retributive, whereas the purpose adduced today for belligerent reprisals is often said to be primarily deterrent. Such hairsplitting, however, is here misplaced. When reprisals deter at all, they do so only by retrospective sanctioning of past wrong. They are proportionate or "fitting" precisely to the extent necessary to restore the risk symmetry that the law establishes, a symmetry disrupted by such wrong.

Generally, the law – including humanitarian law – restores the balance both to reverse a past injustice and to preclude unfair prospective advantage (i.e., where a continuing relationship exists, even if only that between belligerents). During an ongoing armed conflict, a belligerent's response to war crime necessarily looks both backward and forward. The traditional rationales for punishment – the relative merits of which moral theorists heatedly dispute – are often in practice virtually coterminous in the conduct they authorize. Reprisal may therefore take its measure from either. As John Gardner observes, "The link between the blameworthiness of an offender and what irks the victim and her sympathizers is . . . intimate. . . . Thus the starting point of the blameworthiness inquiry – the action which was wrongful – is also the normal trigger for the retaliatory responses on behalf of the victim."

Such retaliation by the victim-state for war crimes and crimes against humanity must often – given the gaps in global governance – serve at once as self-defense, deterrence, corrective compensation, expressive affirmation of law's values, and perhaps even retribution (i.e., if these aims are to be advanced at all). This will remain the case until more effective international institutions of criminal and civil justice develop. Only less primitive institutions than currently exist could dispense with such an undifferentiated fusion of purposes in a single act. And it is not chiefly the continued availability of the state practice of retaliation, moreover, that impedes the development of such global institutions.

There are admittedly many situations where egregious wrongdoing produces only the most trivial advantage. But the fact that such wrong often fails to gain for the offender the measure of superiority he sought from it is irrelevant, insofar as the wrong consists in the act itself and how it disrupts the law's established moral balance, not in the fortuity of whether the act achieves its dastardly ends. Deterrence too would fail if belligerents knew that breaches of humanitarian law yielding them no significant advantage would enjoy impunity.

If an ongoing state of international armed conflict exists between the United States and Al Qaeda, then leaders and other members of terrorist groups would be belligerents and could lawfully be detained or targeted. There would be no need to justify their killing by way of a right to reprisal.[46] The same would be true of sustained detention, because the Geneva Conventions allow holding combatants and unprivileged belligerents until the termination of hostilities. Because the prohibition of torture is peremptory, the practice is unlawful in war no less than in peace, whether as a method of interrogation or otherwise. So even during armed conflict – international or noninternational – reprisal could not be used to justify torture. This would not be true, however, of coercive measures short of "torture."[47] Many critics of the Bush administration contend that, in international armed conflicts, participants who do not honor humanitarian law and therefore do not satisfy the requirements for POW status under Article 4 of the Third Geneva Convention are *ipso facto* civilians under the Fourth Geneva Convention. There is no third or intermediate category, according to this view, and no gap between the first two.[48] In that case, a doctrine of belligerent reprisal would be necessary to justify attacking any such civilians, including terrorist leaders, outside any theater of conflict while they were taking an active part in hostilities.

With a view to finding detained terror suspects protected by Geneva Common Article 3, the U.S. Supreme Court saw fit to classify the conflict between the United States and Al Qaeda as a noninternational armed conflict, on the grounds that it is not a war between states. In a conflict of this variety, nonstate fighters are unprivileged belligerents and, as belligerents, may be attacked. If they are detained, they must be treated consistent with the requirements of Common Article 3. That provision would preclude most forms of coercive interrogation unless the right of belligerent reprisal were extended beyond the scope asserted even by most defenders.

One might first think that no continuing state of armed conflict – international or otherwise – would exist, however, if terrorist attacks are only intermittent, punctuating the international landscape periodically but not continually and unremittingly.[49] This view is mistaken. Terror attacks should be viewed in conjunction with one another if there exist legally pertinent links between those undertaking them (i.e., if these ties consist of more than mere mutual identification with a common cause). An armed conflict may also exist because the state or states chiefly targeted by such groups are now engaged in sustained efforts to thwart these attacks on their populations. The

United States and the U.K., as well as several other states, devote considerable resources to identifying and targeting terrorist leaders and cells whenever and wherever they can be found, after all. There is nothing intermittent about their commitment to this endeavor, nor that of their opponents in concocting future attacks. Such planning is much different in its level of resource commitment and deployment from garden-variety "war gaming," in which peacetime armed forces spin out a variety of hypothetical scenarios for possible future conflict. The persistent character of these efforts, by both Al Qaeda and its Western target states, speaks to the level of organization they betray, and degree of organization is one factor in the legal test for finding an armed conflict. Thus, the episodic nature of terror attacks does not foreclose their legal treatment as a single armed conflict or small set of related armed conflicts. As for organization, Al Qaeda is "a kind of virtual state,"[50] observes Philip Bobbitt, for it displays a division of labor involving an intelligence cadre, civil service, treasury, standing "army," and even (like Hamas) welfare programs. Members of its sleeper cells describe themselves as "awaiting orders,"[51] prepared to obey instructions from superiors.

But for purposes of determining whether there exists a state of war, a belligerent's "level of organization" should not be equated with its degree of reliance on formal, ideal-typical bureaucracy. This is because "command responsibility" is no longer the chief doctrinal vehicle by which to hold "big fish" responsible for the criminal acts of "small fry." No less than many real-world bureaucracies (with all their *de facto* departures from formal procedures), a social network like Al Qaeda – though more informal in operation – may prove well organized indeed. Such networks in different countries share more than a generic anti-Western agenda. They share such operational objectives as the targeting of Western civilian interests and certain methods for pursuing those targets. These groups might even be said to form a "joint criminal enterprise,"[52] an increasingly influential concept within international criminal law. This doctrine allows every member of such an undertaking – defined by its common purpose – to be held liable for the criminal actions of every other. The upshot is to permit conviction of a top leader for war crimes even though the people directly committing the violent acts are not within his effective control. This legal approach is consistent with social science findings that "when a common purpose is shared, loosely tied groups can function better than strongly bonded ones when it comes to containing dissent or bickering," as long as there are "individual group members who can circulate through disparate parts of the team, reduce conflict, and help generate collective spirit when it is needed.[53] A single, central leader is also unnecessary to organizational efficacy, these studies find.

Only because such control was considered necessary to convicting superiors for their subordinates' actions was the legal definition of armed conflict thought to require evidence of a formal organizational link between the two echelons. Today, by contrast, all Al Qaeda members above a certain level might plausibly be legally treated as members of the same enterprise, one responsible for war crimes.[54] The rationale for requiring a certain "level of organization" among belligerent forces before finding an armed conflict to exist is therefore satisfied.

There are other organizational forms, apart from bureaucracy and enterprise, through which mass atrocity may be conducted. One such form is the franchise. Some have used this term to fairly describe Al Qaeda's relation to certain other jihadist groups in the Muslim world as they have come increasingly under its influence and even adopted its "brand."[55] A franchise involves "the sole right granted by the owner of a trademark or trade name to engage in business or to sell a good or service in a certain area," generally "using local capital and management."[56] In exchange for training and other material support from bin Laden, an Algerian jihadist group recently changed its name to Al Qaeda in the Maghreb. In this way, the name Al Qaeda begins to approximate a trademark.

Franchising has been a major legal vehicle for expanding the global reach of many organizations, after all.[57] A *de facto* relation of franchise might be judicially determined to exist and the legal relationship then implied at law. This would be much like the legal fiction of a constructive trust.[58] Such a trust is created by courts *post facto* to allow the imposition of shared legal responsibility where justice so requires. International criminal law already does something similar in looking to a superior's *de facto* control over subordinates where there is no formal, *de jure* relation of hierarchy between them.[59]

Most importantly, franchisors can sometimes be held liable for the misconduct of franchisees.[60] War conducted through the legal instrumentality of franchise or criminal enterprise might even be described as no less "organized" than that conducted through bureaucracy. In any event, bureaucracy is only an ideal-type that real armies in combat often do not approximate. These other forms of fighting are simply organized along alternative lines, modeled on different legal templates. To judge from its multiple successes throughout the world, Al Qaeda's various organizational avatars have been quite effective. Such efficacy might itself be counted among the indicia of "organization" for purposes of determining whether an armed conflict exists.

If there is no armed conflict, however, then international human rights law would apply and bar all three disputed practices, including sustained detention without charge insofar as it was "arbitrary" (i.e., effected without due process). In such circumstances, only a doctrine of forcible counter-measures would permit targeted killing, sustained detention, and/or coercive interrogation.[61] That doctrine was widely thought to have died with the UN Charter's prohibition of force for purposes of resolving disputes between states. Several scholars nonetheless contend that forcible counter-measures remain implicit within the "inherent right to self-defense" granted by Charter Article 51 to any state suffering "armed attack" or simply remain valid as customary international law, antedating and independent of the UN Charter.[62] (The Charter's Article 103 exempts that treaty from super-session by later treaties, not by subsequent customary norms.)[63] The upshot of such arguments is to recognize and reintroduce the reciprocity principle in circumstances where other provisions of the UN Charter seem to foreclose it.[64]

These urgent, contemporary concerns are best approached, however, in light of a broader and longer term assessment of the place of reciprocity and antireciprocity within humanitarian law.

DEMARCATING THE RIVAL DOMAINS

Within humanitarian law, some rights are reciprocal, whereas others are not.[65] What explains the difference? And are the legal lines between the domains of reciprocity and of its repudiation defensible – logically or morally? When the law rejects reciprocity, it does so not always in service of human rights, we will see. Other purposes are sometimes more central, such as preserving peace – though justice requires common rules – or favoring belligerents for a just cause over unjust adversaries. Consider a few quick examples falling on each side of the line.[66]

1. *The Realm of Antireciprocity*

First, there are places where the law repudiates reciprocity. States must release enemy POWs at the end of active hostilities, regardless of whether the enemy has yet done so.[67] A state may not target an enemy's protected cultural property despite its enemy's targeting of its own such property.[68] When one state unlawfully employs civilians as "shields," for instance by surrounding its vulnerable targets with noncombatants, its adversary does not thereby gain the right to deploy civilian shields. Geneva Additional Protocol I provides more broadly that "any violation of these prohibitions shall not release the Parties to the conflict from their legal obligations with respect to the civilian population and civilians, including the obligation to take the precautionary measures provided for" elsewhere in the Protocol.[69]

Hospitals and religious institutions enjoy immunity from attack; though particular facilities forfeit this immunity by surreptitiously shielding military objectives – a form of perfidy – other such facilities belonging to that belligerent remain immune and its opponent does not become entitled to conceal military matériel within its own churches and medical facilities. Even when the members of an armed organization are not entitled to POW status, they often retain many of the same rights under the Civilian Convention and Additional Protocol I.[70] Protected civilians who take up arms and are captured, for instance, must still be treated with "humanity" and, when prosecuted for unlawful combatance, accorded the due process rights granted by the Fourth Convention.[71]

The *jus ad bellum*, governing a state's first resort to force, sets further limits on reciprocity. Thus, a state suffering violent force at its neighbor's hands may not itself respond with force unless it has been the victim of "armed attack,"[72] as defined quite narrowly by the International Court of Justice.[73] Border skirmishes and provision of weapons plus financial and logistical assistance to rebels usually fall short of armed attack, in this sense. The rationale for rejecting a perfect reciprocity of rights here is the belief that allowing it would often lead to a conflict's escalation.[74] The UN Charter regards keeping the peace as more important than a justice that can be achieved only through a jot-for-jot reciprocity in violence. In any event, such justice was to be ensured by the UN's own collective security organs, to which states were to contribute their armed forces under Charter Article 43 – a plan that never materialized and has no present prospect of doing so.[75]

Finally, under Geneva Additional Protocol I, the armed forces of nation-states must wear identifying insignia to distinguish their members from civilians at all times,[76] and may be attacked at any time. Yet "national liberation movements,"[77] a prominent feature of international political life when that treaty was drafted, need not visibly distinguish their fighters much before launching violent assaults and may be targeted only when actually fighting or visibly on the verge of initiating attack.[78] They are thus permitted to engage in conduct resembling pirates, who hoisted the Jolly Roger at the last minute before laying siege to a victim ship.[79] This dispensation approximates an exception to the rule against perfidy.[80] Thus, the two sides effectively fight by different rules, because the first cannot lawfully reciprocate the second's stratagems of self-concealment.[81]

The proffered rationale for this approach to revolutionary, anti-imperial movements was widely shared within educated opinion at the time. I vividly recall this from my undergraduate days as a resident of University of California-Berkeley's International House in the mid-1970s. The climate of opinion suggested that "whatever atrocities they ["Third

World" insurgencies] might have committed were well within their rights, considering the magnitude of the atrocity that had been committed against them" by Western colonizers, as Clive James recently put it.[82]

The first efforts to accord rights of belligerency to nonstate actors did not begin with national liberation movements and Geneva Additional Protocol 1. They began in the mid-nineteenth century with repeated efforts in a number of humanitarian law treaties to strengthen smaller states against bigger ones feared likely to aggress against them.[83] The aim was to protect members of civilian militias who might seek to resist foreign invaders of a more powerful state after their country's armed forces had been routed. In the Brussels Conference of 1874, for instance, a declaration by the recently unified Italy – supported by other small states – sought to establish the right of partisans to POW status. Only a century later in the 1970s did organized armed groups like the PLO and still more radical Palestinian factions realize (and persuade global sympathizers) that strengthening such rules might prove advantageous not only for nonstate victims of state violence but also for nonstate initiators of violence against civilians. The historical rationale to create these special dispensations – for irregulars, acting on behalf of their nation-state, resisting massive external aggression against it, targeting only other combatants – was all but turned on its head.

In all the ways just indicated, the treaties governing war seek to limit the scope of the reciprocity principle.

2. *The Realm of Reciprocity*

On other issues, by contrast, humanitarian law embraces reciprocity as essential or at least unavoidable, whether on grounds of fairness or as an effective means of law enforcement. To start with a simple example, any serious violation of an armistice permits the victimized state to recommence hostilities immediately.[84] As early as 1907, the Fourth Hague Convention established that "the inhabitants of a territory which has not been occupied who, on the approach of the enemy, spontaneously take up arms to resist the invading troops without having had time to organize themselves in accordance with Article 1," requiring that commanders have effective control over subordinates, "shall be regarded as belligerents *if* they carry arms openly and *if* they respect the laws and customs of war."[85] The consequence is that today, as indicated, combatants are only entitled to POW status if the party for which they fight generally adheres to central tenets of humanitarian law.[86] In a discussion where little agreement exists, few deny that the highest level of protection, that to be afforded POWs, is contingent on lawful combatancy and is therefore predicated on reciprocity. It follows that if Taliban and Al Qaeda detainees are not POWs, then the Geneva Convention bar on reprisals against POWs does not protect them.

For similar reasons, the ban on reprisals against civilians is immaterial to Al Qaeda members if they are not "civilians." Whether Al Qaeda members and especially its leaders remain "civilians," rather than becoming only unprivileged combatants (at least when captured while taking direct part in hostilities), is open to serious question, as the pertinent legal authorities offer no clear definition of this key term.[87] If such fighters forfeit their civilian status in this way or were never "protected persons" under the Fourth Convention (covering civilians) because they are nationals of states not party to the conflict, then the bar against civilian reprisal would not pertain to them.[88] In any event, the ban on civilian reprisals in Geneva Additional Protocol I does not reflect customary law, on most accounts, as it is opposed by several major military powers and the United States has not ratified this treaty. The result – reached rather circuitously, to be sure – is a tacit requirement of reciprocity in exchange for favorable treatment as a civilian.

Most treaties banning particular weapons permit "reprisal" for their violation.[89] In fact, suspension or withdrawal has been the standard remedy for the breach of such agreements. In this respect, though humanitarian in purpose, they resemble most other treaties.[90] The Vienna Convention on the Law of Treaties provides that continued duties under an international agreement remain contingent on their mutual respect by other ratifying states. Some early humanitarian treaties even contain provisions expressly making themselves, or parts thereof, subject to reciprocity.[91] As mentioned, state practice suggests that retaliation for perceived humanitarian law violations is anticipated, common,[92] and often regarded as legitimate by the retaliator and neutral third parties, even when it does not meet the more stringent treaty criteria for lawful reprisal. A belligerent state may not lawfully withdraw from the Geneva Conventions when a war is still in progress.[93] This step is hence unavailable as a remedy for its enemy's consistent breach of these agreements, which increases the danger that a party violating humanitarian law will gain unfair advantage from its misconduct. It is particularly important that such law be interpreted to afford some alternative remedy in the near-present (i.e., in addition to the chance of later criminal prosecution).

Customary humanitarian law may here introduce a crucial caveat to the Geneva Conventions. The question of whether customary international law now prohibits civilian reprisals, in particular, is a delicate and uncomfortable one among scholars of international law. Theodor Meron is correct that, "given the scarcity of practice and the diverse views of states and commentators," an affirmative answer cannot confidently be offered. In fact, he admits that a negative answer would credibly be voiced by many experts in military law.[94] The 1977 Geneva Additional Protocol seeking to bar such reprisals did not purport to declare existing custom. The Protocol itself was not ratified – or ratified only with reservations on this very issue – by many leading military powers. As the ICTY's president, Meron now concludes, in diplomatic understatement, "In reality, of course, reciprocity and reprisals, or the fear of reprisals, remain more significant than acknowledged in the treaty text."[95] And "since then, a body of state practice transforming this prohibition into general rules of international law has not emerged," he acknowledges, concurring here with Antonio Cassese, the ICTY's first president.[96]

Reciprocity has still further ramifications within humanitarian law. If a state enters a "reservation" when ratifying a treaty – including a human rights treaty – other states receive the benefit of that reservation in their relations with the reserving state.[97] Certain reservations to the Geneva Conventions, like those of North Vietnam, were morally grave: Enemy combatants who commit war crimes do not receive POW status.[98] This is reciprocity with a vengeance. And reservations to many multilateral treaties expressly make the ratifying state's duties to another contingent on the second's fully honoring its treaty duties to the first, where the treaty itself has not already so provided. For instance, the prohibition against civilian reprisals in Geneva Additional Protocol I has been subject to reservation by several Western powers, including the U.K., France, Germany, and Italy.[99] These states, along with the United States (which did not ratify at all), claim the right to engage in such reprisals where they deem these measures necessary. The U.K. expressly acknowledges that, in so reserving, its adversaries may therefore claim this same right against it.[100] Reservations and persistent objections of this sort by major military powers mean that the 1977 treaty norm against civilian reprisals has not attained the degree of consistent and uniform state practice necessary to render it binding as custom.

With reprisals partly in mind, the World Court in its Advisory Opinion on nuclear weapons rejected the argument that humanitarian law prohibits the use of such arms in all circumstances.[101] One judge, and several states in their *amicus* briefs, offered conditions – involving a response to the first use of prohibited chemical or biological weapons – for the lawful resort to tactical nuclear arms in reprisal.[102] The United States threatened precisely this step in late 1990 during the conflict with Saddam Hussein over his invasion of Iraq,[103] as did Israel at the same time. President Bill Clinton reiterated this U.S. stance vis-à-vis Iraq in 1996.[104] Reciprocity through reprisal is also relevant to the targeted killing of Al Qaeda leaders, assuming that they remain civilians when not directly employing force against their professed enemy. This practice could be legally permissible as reprisal where the targeted civilians are not in U.S. custody, especially if located in areas under enemy control.[105] Such is the case, for instance, of certain mountainous, tribal areas in northwestern Pakistan,[106] where several U.S. missile strikes have recently been directed.

Humanitarian law here relies heavily, however, on a distinction that may be irrelevant or at least unable to bear such a moral burden. This is the distinction between civilians in areas under enemy control, who may be targeted in reprisal, and those elsewhere, who may not. Coercive interrogation of Al Qaeda suspects in U.S. detention would be more difficult to justify through a right of civilian reprisals, on account of Common Article 3 of the 1949 Conventions, which the United States ratified without reservation.

From a moral point of view, however, why should custody vs. noncustody determine the legal availability of reprisal? The upshot of this distinction, after all, is that thousands of innocent civilians may be intentionally killed in reprisal for like conduct through direct targeting of enemy population centers. Yet reprisal does not justify subjecting Al Qaeda leaders to challenging conditions of detention and interrogation because these persons have been captured and are hence "in the power of the enemy,"[107] within the meaning of the Third Geneva Convention. This result is rather counterintuitive, to say the least. If the chief objection to reprisals is that they are indiscriminate, punishing the innocent for the guilty's conduct, then reprisal against clearly culpable parties does not succumb to this objection, and the fact that they are in custody greatly increases the ability to be discriminating (i.e., to ensure that innocents are not harmed).

Surely, customary humanitarian law, through its rules on reprisal, should justify targeting or coercive interrogation of terrorist leaders and sustained detention of members without charge before it justifies the incineration of entire cities.[108] The legal line in both instances appears not merely arbitrary, but unintelligibly perverse. The missing link in what would be a compelling legal argument for the Bush administration's most controversial counter-terrorism practices arises from a distinction without moral merit. Here, as Dickens might say, "The law is an ass – an idiot."[109] If one were looking for evidence that humanitarian law had grown wildly out of touch with the moral reality of the contemporary warfare it strives to govern, this would surely be a good place to begin.

This is not to suggest that humanitarian law need invariably respond unreflectively to all claims of immediate victims, for often there are competing considerations – long-term consequences for both sides and future conflicts, the absence of state consensus over potential rules, and the preservation of martial honor – that are equally weighty in influencing how the legal lines are drawn and the resulting rules interpreted. Some of these concerns, explored in Chapters 10 through 13, weigh as heavily against the use of coercive methods in a given situation (where the law arguably allows them) as does the suffering of potential victims. At such times, the law's apparent moral inadequacies are checked by these further considerations, some partly at work within the law itself, others external to it.

BILATERAL RECIPROCITY IN MULTISTATE WAR?

Let us consider how the Geneva Conventions handle the reciprocity question in other respects. A recurring theme throughout this study is the ramifications of reciprocity as the number of parties involved increases beyond two.

We begin with two key sentences in Article 2, common to all the 1949 treaties. The third paragraph of this Article provides, "Although one of the Powers in conflict may not be a party to the present Convention, the Powers who are parties thereto shall remain bound by it in their mutual relations. They shall furthermore be bound by the Convention in relation to the said Power, if the latter accepts and applies the provisions thereof." The first of these two sentences is striking in that it endorses bilateral reciprocity even within a multilateral, interstate war. Hence, if country A has ratified the Conventions and is fighting an alliance of countries B and C, where B has also ratified the Conventions but C has not, then A must honor its treaty duties vis-à-vis B, but not C. This move reflects hard-fought progress from earlier Geneva Conventions in which all parties to a conflict were released from treaty duties if any of them had not ratified.

Yet notice the anomaly introduced by the change. Because B and C are allies, they *both* profit from the fact that A remains treaty-bound in its military engagements with B. That profit – which may be considerable – accrues to C, even though C itself is not bound by treaty norms. Though it is true that A would likewise have no direct treaty duties to C, A must nonetheless establish different rules of engagement for targeting, and different detention procedures for treatment of fighters from B and C; that is, if it wishes to exercise its full rights vis-à-vis each of its antagonists. On most readings, B could even assist C in its mistreatment of A's captured combatants (and perhaps C's illicit attacks on A's civilians), without releasing A from its Geneva duties toward B.

The possibility of significant unfairness to A thus arises, in the sense that A must now choose between fighting the B-C alliance by the higher standard it owes to B alone or incur the costs of trying to play by different rules with each national component of its united enemy, however intermingled their operations. Moreover, whereas A made its decision to ratify the Conventions before the conflict (i.e., before it could know of the later alliance between B and C), these latter states gain the advantage of knowing about A's ratification before choosing to ally with each other. A variation on this hypothetical arises whenever the United States fights in joint operations alongside military allies who have ratified the 1977 Geneva Additional Protocols, holding them to higher standards than the 1949 Conventions to which America adheres. The practical demands of interoperability effectively compel America to honor rules that it has never ratified.[110] This issue arose most recently concerning cluster munitions, a type of weapon that nearly all America's allies have legally forsworn, though the United States has not.[111]

Now consider the second sentence of the quoted paragraph in Article 2. It provides that if a belligerent not party to the Conventions nonetheless "accepts and applies" them, then enemies who have ratified are also bound (i.e., notwithstanding the contrary inference that the first sentence would otherwise allow). The purpose of this wording is to create incentives for nonparties to embrace humanitarian norms in practice.[112] Hence, at the outset of World War II, though Japan was not party to the 1929 Geneva Conventions, it formally notified the International Committee for the Red Cross (ICRC) that it would respect these norms as long as its adversaries did so.[113] In this light, reciprocity almost begins to appear ethically farsighted, and no mere antediluvian *lex talionis*.

Yet here too, curious anomalies quickly emerge. Let us say that A is again fighting against both B and C. This time, B has ratified the Conventions, and C again has not, but has nonetheless pledged to apply them. If C does not honor its pledge and instead violates Geneva norms, then A is no longer bound to respect these norms vis-à-vis C. By contrast, if B does not in practice honor its treaty duties to A, then A nonetheless remains bound to these duties in relation to B. The treaties by terms do not make most such duties contingent on B's actual compliance in relation to A.

Again, what possible rationale could there be for imposing differential obligations on A, depending on the mere formality of whether its Geneva-violating adversary has officially ratified the Conventions or merely pledged to honor them? The effect on A is the same in both cases. This legal arrangement even creates perverse incentives for B to ratify without any intention of complying with the corresponding duties. Thus, with both the first and second sentences of the quoted provision, it is by no means clear why the lines lie where they do. In practice, the disparity can often be resolved only by finding both B and C subject to Geneva norms as they are reflected in customary law (i.e., to the extent neither state has been a persistent objector to the development of the particular rule that has allegedly been violated).

The law's conflicted treatment of reciprocity, as thus briefly outlined, reflects a perfectly reasonable ambivalence based on the desire finally to transcend such primitive methods[114] in favor of more mature institutions of collective security in which states threatened by violent neighbors might realistically place their trust.[115] Such institutions would aim to ensure a fair fight,[116] at the very least, if not also a just result. Until these reliable institutions actually exist, however, the law has to rely on encouraging cooperation in other ways, some less pretty than the UN Charter drafters desired.

THE LAW OF TREATIES AND REMEDIES FOR BREACH

The Vienna Convention on the Law of Treaties provides that a state victimized by a treaty breach may suspend its duties toward the breaching state.[117] The rationale is that, because there is no world police, interstate agreements tend to work only if they are self-enforcing. The parties' incentives must therefore be aligned. To this end, each side must be able to retaliate against the other's infractions. Treaties prohibiting or controlling the permissible number of particular weapons, for instance, operate according to this background or "default" principle, unless by their terms they specifically provide otherwise, which they rarely do.

Consider how this default principle would apply to the treatment and interrogation of detainees. Restraint would be self-enforcing as long as each belligerent gains more from the humane treatment of its prisoners by the enemy than it loses from not interrogating enemy prisoners coercively, provided each party can monitor the other. Such monitoring can be done through intermediaries like the ICRC that, by conveying credible information between the parties (and so reducing transaction costs), restrain temptations toward opportunistic behavior.[118] In war, historian Geoffrey Best observes,

> Good deeds by one side are likely to be reciprocated by the other. In such matters as releases and exchanges of prisoners, they very often are, and the ICRC preeminently is accustomed to be their benevolent godfather and go-between. What international humanitarian law expects states to

do, and what they would do if they voluntarily obeyed the law, will usually only get done if some experienced neutral body . . . succeeds in assuring each side that the other won't cheat.[119]

The rationale for authorizing reciprocation is essentially tit-for-tat: Defection from cooperation must be punished, then forgiven, and not so severely punished as to preclude return to cooperative "play" thereafter.[120] The underlying morality is candidly consequentialist[121]: One may violate a *prima facie* norm, despite its moral validity and legal applicability, in order to restore cooperation, because doing so will have better overall consequences, thereafter inducing greater law abidingness by all.[122] In its preferred rationale, the international law of countermeasures here closely tracks this hopeful view of tit-for-tat's prevalence within international relations. "Countermeasures . . . should be a wager on the wisdom, not on the weakness of the other Party," one major arbitration panel concludes.[123] As the intermediary between such parties, the ICRC allows each belligerent to assess the extent of its opponent's compliance.

The law of treaties then makes an exception to the reciprocity principle, however, for agreements "relating to protection of the human person contained in treaties of a humanitarian character."[124] Here, breach by one state does *not* release the other from its duties. There are two rationales for the exception. The first is that human rights treaties aim to protect persons against abuse by their own state of nationality, not to protect one state against abuse by another.[125] For instance, state A must respect its citizens' international human rights regardless of how much neighboring state B abuses the like rights of its own citizens. Reciprocity between states is largely irrelevant here.[126]

To be sure, people in country A may nonetheless be concerned about the plight of B's citizens. But this concern need not be reciprocated and often runs heavily in one direction. Legal economist Alan Sykes thus observes,

> Citizens of the United States may care about the fate of repressed minorities in Serbia, Iraq or Afghanistan, but there is little reason to think that citizens of those countries simultaneously worry about human rights violations in the United States. Thus, human rights agreements do not fit well within the standard model of international agreements under which each signatory gains from the elimination of a reciprocal externality.[127]

In the standard model, such externalities are negative, as when human rights abuse forces citizens of country A to flee as refugees across the border to B. The externality in question here, by contrast, is of the positive variety, referring to the "external" projection of disinterested concern by

A's enlightened citizenry to those suffering political oppression in B. The economic terminology is incongruous, but the point is well taken: Human rights treaties are not particularly concerned with preserving any form of reciprocity between ratifying states.

Yet the Vienna Convention's exception to reciprocity, though pertinent to human rights treaties (like the International Covenant on Civil and Political Rights), does not make nearly so much sense with certain humanitarian law treaties – and the Convention language, quoted earlier, appears to lump the two together.[128] With humanitarian law, where state B is A's adversary in armed conflict, what A does in violating its international duties can *greatly* affect state B's legitimate interests. State B ratified the Geneva Conventions because its leaders concluded that what it gained by acquiring the right to impose certain risks on adversaries such as A in future warfare would exceed the loss to its security from having to bear exposure to like risks. There was hence always a *quid pro quo,* even if the treaties themselves speak on their face only of rights that the ratifying state accords to others, rather than of the rights it thereby acquires. Because tacit exchange occurs, reciprocity has often received more sympathetic legal treatment in humanitarian law than in human rights treaties.[129]

This sympathy is particularly evident in treaties prohibiting weapons systems. Here, each side forswears the weapon with the understanding that its potential adversaries will do the same. The benefit is bargained for and won in exchange for assuming the burden of abandoning a particular technology. The suitable remedy for A's material breach is formal suspension or withdrawal by B. The treaty then no longer restricts B's interactions with A for that weapon.

Yet weapons-prohibition protocols might plausibly be described as "treaties of a humanitarian character . . . relating to the protection of the human person." This language from the Vienna Convention forecloses reciprocity as a remedy for breach, unless customary law was to the contrary and was found to be weightier. The Convention language here is overinclusive, however, vis-à-vis its chief underlying purpose, which is to acknowledge that human rights commitments are nonreciprocal because they do not follow the logic of *quid pro quo* bargaining between the states that ratify them.

Though weapons-prohibition treaties are "of a humanitarian character," they do not actually "relat[e] to protection of the human person," certainly not as directly and clearly as do human rights conventions of the sort squarely contemplated by the Convention drafters.[130] Human rights treaties create individual rights for such "human protection," rights justiciable either directly or through national implementing legislation. In contrast, weapons-prohibition treaties do not create or recognize any rights for human persons, certainly none justiciable in any court, national or international. These treaties directly address only matters of interstate relations and establish rights that states may assert against one another. Though humanitarian in underlying purpose, they do not aim to vindicate that purpose by way of legal protections afforded to any human beings as such.

On this view, weapons treaties do not fall within the exception provided by Article 60(5) of the Vienna Convention and therefore remain subject to the principle of reciprocity, which thereby retains its central place within humanitarian law, exercising broad gravitational force. The drafting history of the provision makes clear that it was not intended to cover weapons treaties,[131] but it was to include the Geneva Conventions.[132] Yet the exception itself was somewhat controversial even concerning Geneva law, with the second Special Rapporteur seeking to exclude it entirely for fear of weakening a victim state's ability to react effectively to its enemy's Geneva breaches.[133]

The second and deeper rationale for the exception to reciprocity in humanitarian treaties is nonconsequentialist: the notion that certain misconduct cannot be excused, regardless of its positive consequences in restoring interstate cooperation. Not all forms of such cooperation are even desirable. The military elites of warring states should not be able tacitly to agree, for instance, to target each other's cities, excusing their crimes thereafter on the basis of a right to reprisal in response to their enemy's prior misconduct. Military leaders may not, in this way, simply contract out of duties that seek to protect the rights of potential victims.[134] This is also the reason why certain international human rights may not be "derogated" even during periods of "national emergency."[135]

The Fourth Geneva Convention thus demands that "no party shall be allowed to absolve itself or any other party of any liability incurred by itself or by another . . . party with respect to alleged grave breaches of humanitarian law."[136] A bilateral "agreement" of mutual amnesty, of the sort implicitly imposed by Nazi Germany on Vichy France, is thereby foreclosed. It is immaterial, when one's own violations are judged, that one's military opponent committed the same breaches. The world says simply, a plague on both your houses! Here, it is simply wrong to release either side from its humanitarian duties on grounds of reciprocity.

Yet on what normative basis, we must ask, are any of the preceding distinctions drawn? How high, precisely, should be the minimum standard of acceptable treatment for detainees who themselves breach the most basic

Geneva norms and fight for a belligerent who regularly does so?[137] More generally, when should a state's wartime duties be contingent on compliance with like duties by its adversaries? Whenever the adversary obtains unfair advantage by its unrequited breach? Or should unfair advantage not necessarily be enough to excuse like conduct by the victimized state? And does every form of unreciprocated breach by one side necessarily create unfair advantage over the other, or only a subset of such violations?

To all these insistent questions, practical and theoretical, international humanitarian law now does not provide any straightforward answers. At most, it offers some enduring principles that will remain useful in rethinking the relevant distinctions. But these distinctions are often ethically extraneous. For example, they sometimes condition detainees' treatment on their nationality,[138] though they fight for a multinational network. In this context, the preceding discussion will suffice for a description of current law.

HUMANITARIAN LAW AS STATUTE OR CONTRACT?

Lawyerly readers, at least, if unfamiliar with international humanitarian law, may find it reassuring to sidle up to such large and professionally unfamiliar issues of war, mass atrocity, and international human rights by way of the more comfortable terrain of contract and statute, even if we must move beyond these concepts soon thereafter. Hence, let us begin to address the question of reciprocity's proper scope within humanitarian law by asking whether such law is better understood as a contract or statute. Methods for interpreting statutes, and especially for answering questions about the scope of duties they impose, differ from those employed to interpret contracts. They do so in ways that bear on whether one party's duties are contingent on another's like adherence. Contractual duties are often contingent; statutory ones, especially in criminal law, usually are not. What sort of law is humanitarian law in this respect? Should it be seen as more like a contract or a statute?

Reciprocity's defenders in the "war on terrorism" predictably invoke a comparison to contract.[139] John Yoo even extends the metaphor of private contract – treating it quite literally, unmetaphorically – to the matter of the UN's promise to provide collective security in exchange for agreement by states to give up their unrestricted right to resort to force in self-defense, however they might understand this right. Because of the UN's failure to honor its security vows, Yoo contends, "states are not receiving the full benefits of their bargains. . . . It is time," he concludes, that "states demand a better bargain."[140]

Yet even contracts sometimes have noncontingent duties, whether negotiated by the parties themselves or implied at law, from a statute or constitutional provision reflecting policy or principle. Statutes now regularly require
fathers, for instance, to pay child support to custodial mothers even when
the mother violates her duty to permit paternal visitation, as provided in the
divorce settlement agreement, which is a kind of contract. This is because
the true beneficiary of the contract is not the mother, but the child.

Though bilateral treaties closely resemble contracts, multilateral treaties
adopted by most of the world – like the Geneva Conventions – more
closely resemble legislation and are often interpreted accordingly. The different treatment of bilateral and multilateral treaties in this respect is often
explained by the fact that the former (like contracts) seek to benefit only the
immediate parties, whereas the latter (like statutes) aim to benefit society
at large – international society, in the case of multilateral conventions. The
duties that legislation imposes are not reciprocal: That A seeks (and fails)
to murder B, for instance, does not free B thereafter to attempt A's murder.

Yet even legislation itself can be analogized to a contract, according to
"public choice" analysis. On this view, a statute may be seen as a transaction among the various interests involved in negotiating its drafting
and enactment.[141] This view suggests that disputes over the application of
statutes – and multilateral treaties, by analogy – might be resolved by the
same interpretive methods employed in contractual contests. In the latter
disputes, everything in the agreement resulted from *quid pro quo* exchange,
it is assumed. Unfairness would therefore result whenever one side breaches
a promise without excusing the other from whatever it agreed to give up
in exchange for that promise. The legal result is often to excuse the victim
from the duty it would have assumed, in remedy for the duty a counterpart
has breached.

Different in this regard, however, are peremptory duties, like the torture prohibition, which are derived from human rights law. These duties
more closely resemble "bill of rights" provisions in national constitutions,
overriding all inconsistent law and certainly any agreement among military
antagonists – for instance, to mistreat one another's civilians.[142] Even public choice theories of statutory interpretation acknowledge that enactments
imposing negative externalities on third parties must be viewed through
a more "public interested" interpretive lens. They should be applied differently from those fairly characterized as a deal struck among all affected
parties, knowledgeably acting in their own interests. The contract metaphor
might here seem to break down entirely. Yet if the contract is truly between
a given state and the international community at large (as the *erga omnes*

doctrine entails), rather than simply between opposing belligerents in a particular war, then there can *be* no externalities for nonparties, because all affected states are conceived as party to the agreement. Since no one is external to the transaction, all costs it may impose are distributed among the transacting parties, hence internalized.

The conception of treaties as contracts finds further support in the fact that several countries, including major military powers, have introduced reservations, declarations, and understandings designed to qualify their acceptance of such treaty duties. Most Muslim countries and the Vatican reserve against all human rights treaties granting equality to women.[143] In any event, some of the key duties in the Convention Against Torture are so vaguely defined, if at all,[144] that they may not bar certain forms of coercive interrogation. As in some contracts, terms are deliberately left ambiguous, because the parties could not concur on their definition, but wish to proceed with some form of binding agreement nonetheless.

For all these reasons, humanitarian law remains as much a matter of contract as of peremptory norm. Its interpretation must therefore afford considerable sway to the reciprocity principle. Even so, there are features of international humanitarian law, particularly its customary and peremptory components, that depart in significant ways from both the models of statute and contract, as we later see. These departures further complicate the effort to locate reciprocity's role within this body of law.

DUTIES OWED TO ALL THE WORLD:
ERGA OMNES OBLIGATIONS

Through its use of humanitarian law, the world at large sometimes condemns both belligerents equally for their wartime violations, rather than releasing one from its duties on account of the other's prior breaches. One may ask, however, on what basis does "the world" presume to have anything to say in the matter? This question is especially vexing if the agreement resembles a contract as much as or more than a statute.

The answer is that some legal norms, like the ban on torture and crimes against humanity, are not only *jus cogens* but also *erga omnes*. According to the International Court of Justice, all humankind – not just a given adversary – has a "legal interest" in their enforcement, "in view of the importance of the rights involved."[145] This interest is not of the material sort implicated by, for instance, depletion of the earth's ozone layer or the accumulation of greenhouse gases in the stratosphere. It confessedly rests only on "solidarity"[146] with the victims based on indignation at the violation of their rights and concomitant suffering. The "legal interest" in the question thus derives from moral ideals and their impact on the self-understanding of states, statesmen, and ordinary people everywhere as "citizens of the world." The notion of *erga omnes* underlies, for instance, any defensible resort to military force for humanitarian purposes; the proffered justification for such intervention is always that the target state's rulers have violated the human rights of their own nationals in ways with which the rest of the world is legitimately concerned. In other words, not only does the immediate victim have a human right against *jus cogens* violators, but the rest of us have the right to demand that it be respected.

From the standpoint of international law, then, others' expressions of concern about U.S. treatment of Al Qaeda suspects are not mere officious intermeddling in matters of American national security. Others have a legal right to demand the discontinuation of practices outlawed by *erga omnes* duties.[147] Indeed, they may do so even if a given detainee's state of nationality does not intercede on his behalf,[148] as some have not.

As indicated, the rejection of reciprocity for certain legal duties rests on the argument that the principles underlying them are universally and uniformly binding.[149] The mutual recognition by states of these principles essentially defines "the international community" as such. To be sure, there is some circularity in defining the international community by reference to its members' commitment to prosecuting violations of certain humanitarian norms, while defining the class of such norms by way of the revulsion they uniformly elicit throughout the international community. But let us put such logical quibbles aside to focus on issues of law and morality.

The ICRC exhorts that the Geneva Conventions are best understood as "a series of unilateral engagements solemnly contracted before the world as represented by the other Contracting Parties." Thus, they are "not merely concluded . . . on the basis of reciprocity."[150] (That organization's authority to make such pronouncements, however, is more questionable than most appreciate.[151]) If there exists a contract and not a statute, the contract is nonetheless with the international community at large, not with any particular potential enemy. The duties that a state assumes by ratification therefore do not dissolve when its adversaries violate their own "unilateral engagements." Each state has its own such agreement with the international community, which remains unaffected by others' violations of their own. The victim state (or nonstate actor) is simply the intended third-party beneficiary of the contract between the victimizer and the international community. Like most such intended beneficiaries, it has a legal claim against the wrongdoer, no less than would the international community itself and its other members. In sum, reciprocity may come to mean and demand something quite different as the number of parties with a legal interest in a dispute expands beyond the immediate belligerents. (Chapter 12 develops this position.)

As formal analysis, this argument is plausible enough and is certainly morally appealing on its face. Whether this sort of lovely lawyer talk has any real purchase on the reality of war, however, is another matter entirely. The same may be said of the question whether humanitarian law treaties should be read more as statutes or as contracts. The more practical questions regarding the real relevance in combat of such analytical acrobatics is examined later, particularly in Chapter 10.

TWO TYPES OF RECIPROCITY WITHIN TREATIES

For humanitarian law to apply to an interstate war at all, both sides must be bound by it. The Fourth Geneva Convention thus provides, for instance, that "Nationals of a State which is not bound by the Convention are not protected by it."[152] Reciprocity in this sense is required. It is easily satisfied in such a war, as all states have ratified the major Geneva Conventions and are also bound to most of the same rules by way of customary law. Call this "first-order" reciprocity, following Derek Jinks, who rightly regards it as uncontroversial, an obvious requirement of fairness.[153] This variety of treaty reciprocity means, for instance, that if one belligerent has ratified the more demanding 1977 Geneva Protocols but its antagonist has bound itself only to the less demanding 1949 Conventions, the first state need not adhere to the higher 1977 standard in its war with the second. To acknowledge a reciprocity requirement here is to concede nothing to Bush administration positions on any contested issues, especially if Al Qaeda members are bound to Geneva duties as nationals of ratifying states.[154]

But then the questions get harder. What happens to their legal relations when both belligerents are bound to Geneva norms, but one of them consistently violates these duties? Does the other side remain bound irrespective of resulting losses, even if its defeat is thereby rendered probable? Could the law possibly expect such saintliness? Even if it did, is there much chance such a rule would actually be honored when the chips are down? If not, why have such a rule at all? For "expressive" purposes? But why should the law undermine its own credibility by insisting on expressing values that we admit are too supererogatory actually to enforce against anyone?

As might be expected, the answers here are multiple, complex, full of qualification and even some deliberate equivocation. This book is devoted to finding those answers or at least deepening the analysis necessary to do so. Humanitarian law accepts notions of reciprocity in some places and rejects them in others, in ways that specialists strive to render both practical and principled. Many of the basic distinctions on which the law relies to that end are perfectly intelligible and largely defensible.[155] However, as we have begun to see, it is not at all obvious where the legal lines for answering the preceding questions are actually drawn, much less why they lie where they do.

Jinks contends that the Conventions reject the "second-order" reciprocity that would excuse one party from treaty requirements on the grounds that these had been consistently violated by the other. Second-order reciprocity might be defended in terms of a legal right to suspend or withdraw from the treaty as a whole, from particular duties within it that the counterparty has materially breached. Or reciprocity might find expression through a right of reprisal, arising not from within the particular convention but from background customary law. Each move in Jinks's argument is designed to foreclose these possibilities and to construe law's engagement with the reciprocity principle as binding the United States to upholding the highest standards of treatment toward detained jihadist suspects. To this end, Jinks must show both the applicability of first-order reciprocity (i.e., binding and therefore also protecting such detainees) and the inapplicability of second-order reciprocity (finding relinquishment of such protections upon the breach of correlative duties).

His interpretation is problematic in both respects. Its repudiation of second-order reciprocity ignores Article 4 of the POW Convention, which expressly conditions POW status for a party's soldiers on its compliance with several requirements of humanitarian law.[156] On this basis, the Bush administration rightly concludes, as confirmed by one federal court,[157] that Taliban detainees are not POWs, a view reluctantly accepted even by most critics. Moreover, states at war routinely engage in (otherwise illegal) retaliation, defending it as lawful "reprisal." This routine use of retaliation proves relevant to ascertaining and applying customary international law.

More important perhaps, the distinction between first-order and second-order reciprocity makes no sense normatively, in that each of the possible rationales for reciprocity – ensuring the rules' effective uniformity for all players or their self-enforceability – logically applies no less to the second than to the first type of reciprocity. If either or both of these considerations provide a reason for reciprocity on entry into a treaty, they would also justify reciprocity on exit as well. Yet Jinks offers no explanation for why the Geneva Conventions' drafters – or anyone else since – would want to uphold first-order reciprocity that would not logically carry over to second-order reciprocity (i.e., if the law is to have any principled coherence). The distinction makes little sense in practice, moreover. A state that did not wish to abide by the Conventions could then simply ratify, proceed to disregard the laws of war, and have its enemies still be bound.[158] An interpretation of the treaty texts that is so completely out of touch with their moral and political underpinnings, so indifferent to perverse incentives, cannot persuade.

Jinks further argues that first-order reciprocity – mutual adoption of a treaty as a condition of rights and duties under it – is germane to the current conflict. This assertion is counterintuitive. Though Al Qaeda cannot ratify the Conventions and indeed has expressly repudiated them, its members are nonetheless bound as nationals of ratifying states, Jinks argues. Al Qaeda members must honor the Conventions because they are protected by them. This is a corollary of first-order reciprocity. A state binds its nationals when it ratifies a treaty, on this view, whether or not they fight on behalf of that state.

This argument, though offered on behalf of individual "human rights," makes the necessary but incongruous move of anchoring these rights on the central place of states within international law. The argument ingeniously exploits such law's contradictions, invoking its very state-centrism against states, for humanitarian ends. That an individual detainee's rights to Geneva protection as a civilian could turn on his nationality underlines the Conventions' subordination of universalistic moral principles to preserving reciprocity between sovereign states. States thus accord protection to one another's nationals on the basis of mutual ratification. What determines the legal rules pertaining to individual detainees is not their simple humanity, as the name "humanitarian law" would seem to imply. States understandably regarded the nationals of their military adversaries as the only "civilians" whose wartime protection was pertinent and appropriate in the interstate conflicts that the Conventions chiefly contemplated.

When states ratify treaties, they normally bind themselves only in their relations with other states, incurring international state liability when they breach such duties. The Geneva Conventions, like most treaties, are devices by which states swap reciprocal rights and duties. States may then also proceed to bind their nationals by way of domestic law, implementing the state's international duties where the treaty and national constitutional law require. The simple fact that the state has ratified the Geneva Conventions, then, should not necessarily mean that its nationals are individually bound to honor such treaties in a civil war against its rulers.[159]

It is true, to be sure, that, since the 1949 Conventions, these treaties also confer certain rights directly on protected persons. Whether they can directly impose duties on such individuals is a harder question. The near-uniform consensus is that nonstate belligerents are bound and protected by Article 3 of the Geneva Protocol for noninternational armed conflicts. A contrary rule would clearly be unfair. For if such groups and their members were protected without being bound by this provision, the balance of benefit and burden would not be reciprocal. Their state antagonists would be held to rules to which such nonstate belligerents could blithely remain impervious.

Yet the basis for holding nonstate belligerents to Geneva law has been somewhat uncertain when they have not expressly consented to be bound, as Al Qaeda has not and as would be required in any international armed conflict. Geneva Protocol I, at least once implemented by national legislation (in countries requiring this), becomes part of such national law, binding on all within the country's territory. This move does not resolve all problems, however. First, it makes more sense when the conflict is a standard civil war, taking place "in the territory of one of the High Contracting Parties," than when it is waged simultaneously in several states, into which most of whose territories a given defendant will never have ventured. Even more important, the state attacked on 9/11 has not ratified Protocol I and does not accept the pertinent portions on protective parity as binding custom, entirely apart from its continued insistence on a right to reprisal.

If the treaty's application were based on the nationality of the attackers themselves, the further complication then arises that reservations and national legislation implementing the Geneva Conventions vary from one country to the next, sometimes quite significantly.[160] This variation means that jihadist detainees from different states may have disparate rights and duties vis-à-vis their American captors. The law would therefore require as many legal regimes of detainee treatment as there are states and nationalities represented among the hundreds of past, present, and future detainees. It is unlikely that the states drafting and ratifying the Geneva Conventions intended to assume the duties implicit in such a complex and burdensome regime.[161] A view of the 9/11 attackers as bound to the pertinent Geneva norms only by their individual nationalities is therefore dubious, as a matter of drafters' and ratifiers' intent.

Scarcely less than such critics of U.S. policy, the Bush administration itself sometimes gave undue weight to the formality of nationality. It did so in deciding whether a given terror suspect should be indefinitely detained as an enemy combatant (a route that has been reserved for noncitizens) or afforded a lawyer and criminally prosecuted, if he is a citizen. A detainee born in the United States but raised and residing abroad, such as Yaser Esam Hamdi, may have no morally relevant ties to America, whereas an "alien" detainee like Ali Saleh al-Marri will have much closer links to, and identification with, this country, in which he spent several years, accumulated meaningful ties, and sought to raise a family.[162] In a truly multinational struggle such as that between Al Qaeda and the West, for the law's response to rely so heavily on the vicissitudes of individuals' nationalities is incongruous and anachronistic, bordering on the preposterous.

CUSTOMARY LAW, PEREMPTORY NORMS, AND INDIVIDUAL DUTY

Perhaps rebels and terrorists are bound directly as individuals by many Geneva norms, rather than only indirectly by way of national implementing legislation. For most such duties, this binding could only be through customary international law. Since the Nuremberg judgment (confirmed in the *Tadić* case by the ICTY), international tribunals have concluded that individuals may have duties directly under such law (i.e., not merely as nationals of ratifying states). Both the text and drafting history of Geneva Common Article 3 suggest, moreover, that it was intended to apply to nonstate actors and individuals fighting on their behalf. Drafters and interpreters of humanitarian law could easily have decided to grant humane treatment rights to insurgents and terrorists without imposing any corresponding duties on them. But by all accounts, this is not what the law has done.

Yet we must wonder, as does one careful scholar, "how can Common Article 3 impose binding obligations upon nonstate parties who have never agreed to the Conventions and who, furthermore, have no capacity to become parties?"[163] In other words, how could such a result be consistent with the basic requirement of consent to be bound, a first principle of international law?[164] The question never arose when rights were at issue (i.e., rights granted by ratifying states to insurgents, their likely victims in civil wars and other noninternational armed conflicts). The controversy arises only when the possibility of corresponding duties is in question. Members of an internal insurgency who commit war crimes, if asked whether they agreed to be bound by Geneva rules, would likely decline the offer (i.e., as long as the rights they receive under these treaties are not conditional on accepting any correlative obligations). And "they are unlikely to feel a strong sense of duty towards international obligations agreed to by the very government to which they are so violently opposed,"[165] a British legal scholar wryly notes.

Such scholars rightly point to a disconcerting gap here in law's underlying rationale. One may first be tempted to say that the misconduct of terrorists, their violation of Geneva Common Article 3, resembles the breaking of a contract. The problem with this view is that these fighters never committed themselves to the Convention's terms in exchange for the rights they are said to have received under it.[166] We might wish to respond that the relation between insurgents and the international community established by Article 3 at least resembles a quasi-contract or *quantum meruit*,[167] in that they would unjustly profit from receiving the rights thereby bestowed on them without accepting equivalent duties toward others. But even those doctrines create only civil liability, not criminal, for they are modeled on the private law of contract, not the political theory of social contract.

A second approach would say that the humane treatment required by Geneva Article 3 had been extended to them as a matter of their human rights. Yet then it would have been entirely gratuitous and indefensible to demand in return that they respect the Article 3 rights of their enemies.

Many distinguished scholars dispute the ICRC Commentary to the Third Geneva Convention,[168] which asserts without argument that a belligerent force is bound by Common Article 3 simply on account of being a "Party" to the armed conflict, by participating in it, even though the belligerent is neither a signatory to the Convention nor "a legal entity capable of undertaking international obligations." The U.S. Supreme Court endorsed the ICRC's view in *Hamdan*.[169] So had the UN Secretary-General,[170] the UN Human Rights Commission,[171] and the Inter-American Commission on Human Rights.[172] But none of these are principal sources of international law,[173] and even the occasional judicial endorsement of this position does not amount to binding precedent, given the absence of *stare decisis* within international law.[174] The statements of these authorities on the matter are also entirely conclusory (i.e., providing neither normative nor positive-legal rationale for the result they wish to reach).[175] All are simply assertion.

The most plausible rationale for such a rule would surely be the reciprocity principle, in the sense of an equitable balance of benefit to burden for all whose conduct the rules govern. In other words, because states agree to accord rebel groups basic rights under Geneva Common Article 3 (and Protocol II), rights these groups never repudiate, the members of such groups must accept the corresponding burden of honoring the same rights in their adversaries. The standard requirement of actual consent before an entity's members may be bound by an international treaty is simply abandoned. This abandonment should be initially puzzling, at least.

Once the implicit reasoning at work here is laid out, however, it becomes immediately clear why no one would wish openly to articulate it. For *sub rosa*, such reasoning reintroduces the reciprocity principle into humanitarian law at the very point where human rights advocates, in particular, have so earnestly sought to expunge it.[176] Yet the question is inescapable: If humanitarian law can impose duties on belligerents simply by according them concomitant rights, then why shouldn't it expect these belligerents to honor those duties as a condition of continuing to enjoy such rights?

It would appear that Geneva rules can now bind not only through the consent of those obligated but also because the balance such rules establish – between benefit and burden – is simply fair, morally defensible on its own terms, like ordinary domestic legislation aspires to be. Yet if so, then this fair balance cannot thereafter simply be ignored once the rules reflecting it take effect. Without a world state to secure them, Geneva benefits remain conditional on assuming Geneva burdens – in action, no less than "on the books." If humanitarian law, like a private contract, is to insist on reciprocity between rights and duties when defining relations between belligerents, then logically it must do so – as with a contract, again – when the legal terms of that relationship are exercised and enforced.

The law cannot, consistent with its first principles, impose an involuntary obligation on insurgents (and terrorists) simply on the grounds that it accords them correlative rights to human treatment under Geneva Article 3. For such fighters have not consented to the terms of this arrangement. And when they repudiate these duties, as they generally do, their corresponding rights cannot remain unaffected, because the arrangement entailed a burden-benefit balance justified by the reciprocity principle in the first place. To keep these vexing and embarrassing questions from coming to the fore, international law has embraced an important new rule – binding insurgents and terrorists to Article 3 duties without their agreement to be bound – virtually without explanation, much less a sustained and satisfactory justification. This despite the fact that the new rule is strikingly at odds with international law's first principle: consent to such law, as a condition of being bound by it.[177]

In this respect, international law differs from domestic law, which routinely imposes duties without necessarily matching them at once with any corresponding rights of equal value. This is because when a democratic country adopts a law, the new legislation is understood to form part of a much broader social contract – establishing and sustaining the state and social order – within which the burden-benefit balance need not be perfectly re-equilibrated, jot for jot, with each new enactment.[178] In the international realm, however, the social contract – if one may be said to exist at all[179] – governs neither so broadly nor deeply. Hence the balance must be struck afresh, with the express consent (or at least tacit consensus) of all concerned in each new treaty, in relative isolation from preceding ones.

Greatly compounding the problem is that terrorist groups often operate apart from any such global social contract, beyond its reach almost altogether, believing that they have little stake in it. Humanitarian law must be concerned not only with finding a defensible normative basis for binding terrorists to its rules but also with convincing them that they are in fact bound. Yet in practice it is quite unlikely, as one prominent international lawyer admits, that "transnational armed groups – entities that oppose the whole of the interstate system and the values proclaimed . . . by the international community – [would] be impressed by alleged customary rules, which are based more upon aspirations of do-gooders and a new wind of natural law than upon what those who fight all over the world actually do."[180]

In cases historically litigated under Geneva law, moreover, defendants have fought on behalf, and subject to the authority, of the state whose nationality they bear; that is, a state belligerent (or state-affiliated paramilitary) involved in the armed conflict. Liability has therefore never rested entirely on a direct and unmediated link between customary international law and an accused individual. The facts of all prior cases are thus readily distinguishable from the circumstance in which the United States has recently found itself.[181]

The view that fighters, to be bound by and to enjoy rights under the Conventions, must fight for a state party to those treaties rests not merely on precedent. It is also grounded in a central purpose of international humanitarian law: to hold states responsible for the war crimes of their agents and hold these agents, in turn, responsible for their criminal abuse of state power. If a state were not involved in the criminality, there would be little reason to internationalize such wrongs in the first place, for the state's own courts, applying domestic law, could then provide adequate redress.

Yet on Jinks's reasoning, militant jihadists would be bound to (hence also entitled under) Geneva norms by their nationality even when the state against which they fought had engaged in no wrongdoing. Moreover, Article 4 expressly conditions one's rights to POW status, at least, on the features and behavior of the very organization for which one fights. A fighter's rights as an individual detainee are thus clearly contingent on compliance with humanitarian law by the larger entity for which he battles. It would be odd if his corresponding duties derived in a way and from a source entirely different from his rights – that is, rights from treaty, corresponding duties from custom – though this is conceivable. There is little evidence of such custom, however, especially where the war is "international," in the sense of surpassing the borders of a single state, as most wars do. For all these reasons, it is questionable whether Al Qaeda members are bound to Geneva norms on the basis of nationality or customary law and whether corresponding duties to them in turn derive from such first-order reciprocity.

The Bush administration could have argued that, where customary law gives out, there is a *jus cogens* rule – essentially, a "natural law"[182] – governing armed conflict and outlawing crimes against humanity, a rule extending to those not bound by either treaty or custom. However, this would require a large leap in that doctrine's current interpretive scope. Even with this doctrinal leap, the same rule would then apply to the United States. A peremptory norm prohibiting Al Qaeda members from employing torture, for instance (whether as a war crime, crime against humanity, or free-standing offense), would also bind the United States in relation to these antagonists. This follows from what was earlier called the second conception of reciprocity, which the law here adopts. Insofar as certain requirements of the Convention Against Torture are binding as *jus cogens*, any American treaty reservations encroaching on these would become invalid (assuming U.S. acceptance of the *jus cogens* idea itself). This is not a move the Bush administration, however, wished to make. Like duties *erga omnes*, the notion of *jus cogens* began to acquire significance scarcely two generations ago. The United States opposed the very concept of peremptory norms during negotiations leading to its inclusion within the Vienna Convention on the Law of Treaties.[183] In litigation, America has never made a *jus cogens* claim of its own, for that matter, and has resisted every application of the concept offered by others in all such disputes.[184] To reject – for all intents and purposes – the doctrine of *jus cogens* (with its denial of a reciprocity requirement)[185] is by implication to preserve a continuing place for that principle.

American hesitancy at embracing the very notion of *jus cogens* is best understood not as brazen *realpolitick*, an insistence that the United States stands blithely above even international law's deepest ethical concerns, but rather as a sincere belief that – as a matter of legal principle – the requirements of reciprocity in warfare extend, if not quite "all the way down," then damn near. Admittedly, for reasons of diplomatic delicacy, this view is almost never stated so boldly or bluntly. But it may nonetheless be readily inferred by induction from a large number of assembled official and semi-official statements implying it, statements often by the most intellectually inclined of America's recent foreign policy architects.[186]

In sum, Jinks's distinction between two types of treaty reciprocity rests on no basis in principle or practice, and when it is carefully applied to the conflict with Al Qaeda and kindred groups, it yields conclusions almost exactly opposite from those Jinks himself reaches. For it suggests that Al Qaeda members are not bound by their mere nationality to Geneva law or by international custom as individual persons.

A further possibility is that Al Qaeda members are bound and hence protected by Geneva law through ratification by the state on whose territory they fight. This is the only basis for personal jurisdiction asserted, for instance, by the Special Court for Sierra Leone.[187] International law deems us to have consented to the laws of the countries we choose to enter – all of which, including Afghanistan, have ratified the principal humanitarian treaties. Yet the Conventions expressly release belligerents from key duties at various points where an opponent consistently repudiates humanitarian law. Thus, it is likely that jihadist militants might be bound by Geneva norms, in virtue of fighting on Afghan soil, without enjoying POW rights, because their organizations failed to honor Article 4 duties. They would then only enjoy the more limited rights afforded by Common Article 3, at least after the 2006 *Hamdan* decision from the U.S. Supreme Court so finding.

In that litigation, Justice Thomas (in dissent) embraced the view, long articulated by certain leading scholars,[188] that a conflict is "international" not only if it is formally between sovereign states but also if its conduct and chief consequences involve peoples in more than one state. Thomas thus endorsed the Bush administration's initial view that, because the conflict with Al Qaeda and other jihadists was "international in scope," it thus was not "occurring in the territory of one of the High Contracting Parties," as required for Article 3 to apply.[189] It followed that jihadist detainees have no Common Article 3 rights. But if these detained fighters had no such Geneva rights, then on what basis could they have had any corresponding duties, violation of which would be necessary to permit their prosecution? One would think that the Convention ceases to operate altogether because jurisdiction simply no longer exists in such a case.

This question was especially vexing for the Bush administration and its supporters, who contend that the Conventions are predicated on the reciprocity principle. After all, that principle insists that there are no rights without corresponding duties establishing a balance of benefit and burden. But this formulation also demands that there be no duties without concomitant rights. It was perhaps only because the Bush administration gave so little priority to criminal prosecution for several years following 9/11 that this contradiction in its legal stance did not earlier come to public attention.

Those who fight in domestic insurgencies – in civil wars on a state's home territory – are bound to Article 3 simply through that state's ratification and implementing legislation (where required), just as they would be bound by the state's ordinary legislation. One is bound by such legislation, after all, whether or not one consents to it. Legislation may impose duties, rights, or both. Article 3 clearly accords humane treatment rights to insurgents, rights against the state they oppose. By its express terms, however, Article 3 does not directly impose any duties on such insurgents. Moreover, unlike Article 2 (for international wars), Article 3 (for noninternational conflicts) does not require the nonparty to the Conventions to agree to honor their requirements in order to receive their protections.

This would suggest that Article 3 abandons any demand for reciprocity. The drafting history does indicate that the provision was intended to serve as a temporary protective baseline until the parties could come to an agreement for greater safeguards, ideally those of the full Conventions. However, in reality this has rarely occurred, and if any agreement is made it concerns only a few protections. Further, such agreements have often been breached. Because there is no "second-order" reciprocity under Article 3, it follows that if Al Qaeda members are covered by the provision (notwithstanding Justice Thomas's objection), they enjoy the rights accorded there, regardless of whether the Conventions directly impose any duties on them.[190]

RIGHTS AND DUTIES OF AL QAEDA MEMBERS

On one side of the public debate, certain Bush administration support-ers claimed that the Geneva Conventions – which insist, for instance, on various privileges for officers among POWs – are quaintly irrelevant to the novel challenges presented by what they sometimes describe as "global jihad."[191] On the other side, the administration's fiercest critics, espe-cially some lawyers for Guantánamo detainees, insisted that Common Arti-cle 3, covering only conflicts "not of an international character," extended seamlessly to their clients.[192] Yet the current conflict does not "occur in the territory of [only] one of the High Contracting Parties" and is therefore "international" in all but the most recondite and anachronistic senses of the word. This did not deter some learned legal specialists from insisting that the number of countries in which a terrorist group operates and initiates attacks is irrelevant to whether the armed conflict in which it participates is "international."[193] All that matters, on their view, is the nature of the belligerents involved: For the conflict to be international, it must be one between states.

The demand that detained terror suspects must be accorded the rights of protected civilians, under the Fourth Geneva Convention, is still weaker in most cases (i.e., other than for Iraqi nationals captured in Iraq). For the pertinent Convention provides (in Article 4), "Nationals of a *neutral* State who find themselves in the territory of a belligerent State, and nationals of a co-belligerent State, *shall not be regarded as protected persons* while the State of which they are nationals has normal diplomatic representation in the State in whose hands they are."[194] That language excludes most Al Qaeda suspects from protection, as most of the detained are nationals of neutral states, such as Egypt, Saudi Arabia, and so forth.[195] Thus, for such purposes, it is immaterial whether these detainees are considered civilians,[196] for they are not civilian nationals of states that are party to the armed conflict.

The "unlawful enemy combatant," as the Bush administration has called him,[197] is a conceptual anomaly, neither fish nor fowl.[198] An anomaly in this sense is something that a regnant taxonomy is incapable of acknowledging because it escapes the confines of recognized categories. The Al Qaeda member is not a combatant under the Geneva Conventions, because the conflict in which he participates is "not of an international character." According to the Supreme Court, "international" means "interstate." This is consistent with the word's historical understanding within international law, which traditionally focused almost entirely on states. The conclusion that the Al Qaeda detainee is not a "combatant" finds further support in the fact that he does not fight with or alongside an "armed force," which humanitarian law defines as a state's military.[199]

Yet even if he is a civilian, he nonetheless is not a "protected person" under the Fourth Geneva Convention, which declines to cover nationals of states not party to the pertinent conflict. Here, the state-centrism of international law no longer rides to humanitarianism's rescue. Even nationals of belligerent states are protected only to the extent they are "taking no direct part in hostilities." If an Al Qaeda member takes part in hostilities, he is not protected as an ordinary civilian would be.

The transgression of such a person consists, one might say, not only in the wrongfulness of his acts but also in how he defies the law's typological scheme. His elusiveness apparently resides as much at the conceptual and discursive level as at the tactical and operational. Administration critics often insist that he must be one or the other, combatant or civilian (and entitled to the respective Geneva protections of each), as if that binary opposition necessarily exhausts the universe of relevant types. Yet his dangerousness at least partly resides in how artfully he eludes such legal categories, which either permit or forbid individuals to employ lethal force. David Luban accuses the Bush administration of inconsistency in opportunistically picking out the features of the two preexisting legal models – war and crime – that are most hospitable to its interests.[200] In this way, the administration selectively constructed its own "hybrid" model, he charges, giving itself the rights but not the duties of both criminal law enforcement and armed conflict. But what if it is not America, but its adversaries that have first chosen to efface the traditional line between law's two traditional models? What if it is the phenomenon in question, the very thing to be conceptualized, in other words, which has strategically elected to combine elements of both ancient archetypes?

The Al Qaeda supporter cannot readily be rendered an enemy combatant and so killed without legal qualm. Nor can he be accepted and respectfully treated as a fellow civilian altogether remote from acts of armed conflict. Like the Jewish *kapos* who helped administer Nazi death camps, the unprivileged belligerent occupies a "gray zone"[201] between two more comforting categories: the innocent civilian, who is always on the verge of becoming a victim – a result the law strives unequivocally to avoid – and the combatant, who is always poised as a potential killer and so may lawfully be treated as such. In their familiarity and seeming stability, these categories are reassuring to us: All danger can be confined to a single conceptual cubbyhole, each with its own rules.

The unprivileged belligerent evokes a kind of horror not only for his acts of terror but also for how the very possibility of his existence violates the purity of law's distinction between those who may and may not employ force and be directly subjected to it. As two anthropologists suggest, "With the terrorist menace we are at the very heart of the political darkness of danger and taboo."[202] His "profanity" consists in how he circumvents this inviolable marker, one on which international law and its system of states are predicated. Whenever we see constitutive, identity-defining principles at stake, we tend to expect – even crave – a bright line, as between just and unjust, combatant and civilian, war and peace.

In the face of such seemingly existential stakes, all but the most narrow minded and professionally blinded (i.e., us attorneys) would likely recoil when the law offers up only the paltry vicissitudes of a "multifactor test." For such tests attempt to finesse a line between the mundane and something approximating the sacred, or its functional equivalent within modern, secular society. Such tests shake the cognitive foundations of our world. Their complex legal standards will strike many laypeople as obtuse, if not obscene.

Either a war is just or it is not, they will say, and either an Al Qaeda member is a combatant or a civilian, etc. Any lawyerly equivocation here simply shows that the profession cannot be trusted with answering such vital questions.

Yet as Alan Dershowitz observes with his customary delicacy:

> The traditional sharp distinction between soldiers in uniform and civilians in nonmilitary garb has given way to a continuum. At the more civilian end are babies and true noncombatants; at the more military end are the religious leaders who incite mass murder; in the middle are ordinary citizens who facilitate, finance, or encourage terrorism. There are no hard and fast lines of demarcation, and mistakes are inevitable – as the terrorists well understand.... As more women and children are recruited by their mothers and their religious leaders to become suicide bombers, more women and children will be shot at – some mistakenly. That too is part of the grand plan of our enemies. They want us to kill their civilians, who[m] they also consider martyrs, because when we accidentally kill a civilian, they win in the court of public opinion. One Western diplomat called this the "harsh arithmetic of pain," whereby civilian casualties *on both sides* "play in their favor."[203]

For such reasons, the conflict with Al Qaeda may soon force us all to view the legal distinction between combatant and civilian much as Foucault taught us to think of that between heterosexuality and homosexuality[204]: an unduly binary opposition, unknown in such polar terms for much of human history, too restrictive of the true range of human possibility, and from which history's ruptures in prevailing *épistémès* will soon "liberate" us. Violent acts are no more logically connected to violent legal identities than are sexual acts necessarily connected to fixed sexual identities. This is a sobering and unwelcome thought, to be sure. It is one not much on the minds of the many who today decry national sovereignty and international law for their admittedly constricted – often binary – conceptual and moral universe.

To be sure, the state-centrism of public international law permeates many of its rules quite far afield. The doctrine of incidental or collateral damage, for instance, is implicitly state-centric in distinguishing between intended harm – which is always to the enemy's combatants – and unintended but foreseeable harm, which is generally to its civilians and civilian property. What distinguishes intended victims from unintended ones, like combatants from civilians, is their relationship to the state, their membership or nonmembership in its armed forces. Yet the difference between one who is harmed foreseeably versus one harmed intentionally has apparently lost its moral import for many today.[205] They reject it because what matters to them is the sheer fact of preventable civilian deaths in large numbers. Critics of collateral damage see themselves as seeking to strengthen the immunity of civilians from even unintended harm.

Yet this effort to afford greater protection to noncombatants – on the basis of their nonstate character – necessarily strengthens the state-centrism of international law by entrenching still more deeply the distinction between state and nonstate actors, an effect such critics would decry in any other context.[206] For a similar reason, the Bush administration nearly eviscerated the traditional legal distinction between combatants and civilians in its treatment of Al Qaeda members. It did not see the continued moral import of that distinction once significant numbers of civilians – viz, Al Qaeda members – chose to take up weapons and directly participate in armed confrontation. The administration's response therefore sought to efface the public-private distinction that critics of international law have long disparaged.[207]

In both criticisms, from the left and right, the concern has been that public purposes are often imperiled by nonstate actors; thus, vindicating such purposes requires more aggressive forms of state action vis-à-vis private parties. With its origins in medieval merchant guilds and Renaissance natural law theology, international law preceded the advent of the state system. This system's period of unchallenged ascendancy is no more, notwithstanding its healthy resilience in many respects. Therefore, international law will have to wean itself from conceptual dependence on that geopolitical system if it is to retain its future relevance.

One variety of unlawful belligerent – the child soldier – presents a still further classificatory conundrum. A significant number of jihadist suicide bombers have been minors.[208] Children have committed some of the very worst barbarities in conventional war,[209] especially in Africa – precisely because they are too young to appreciate the moral significance of their actions. Yet no one would deny that they are also, and more pertinently, victims of the still greater wrong done by the elders enlisting them for such ends. Hence, some of the first arrest warrants from the International Criminal Court have involved the recruiting of children to serve as soldiers,[210] an offense never before prosecuted internationally. The Convention on the Rights of the Child prohibits states from employing persons younger than age fifteen as soldiers in their armed forces.[211]

Because they are not lawfully soldiers, children younger than this age presumably do not enjoy the privileges of legal combatancy, and their every act of war-related violence would therefore be criminal.[212] As minors, however, they enjoy immunity from felony liability under many national legal systems. And no international criminal tribunal would give a moment's thought to prosecuting them, even if it had jurisidiction over them, which the International Criminal Court does not.[213] From the perspective of reciprocity, the problem presented by child soldiers is they are the very boys described earlier on Piaget's schoolyard: They can understand reciprocity only in terms of immediate bilateral exchange rather than of extended multilateral relations. So, when their enemy shows no forbearance, neither can such boys.[214] The fact that the domestic social contract has also often broken down through "state failure" makes the problem still harder, for these children will have had no environing exposure to a social order based in such a contract. But because of their age alone, they would find it difficult even to imagine one.

The anomalies abound: We consider terrorist leaders to be war criminals and insist on our right to to try or target them, even if they remain civilians, as many contend.[215] And we recoil from the thought of punishing child soldiers, though they directly commit the most violent and vicious criminal acts in war. Such incongruities – one could observe many more – between our legal categories and our settled moral convictions require that we pose a disconcerting question.[216]

IS THE COMBATANT/CIVILIAN DICHOTOMY OBSOLETE?

Legal critics of the Bush administration dismissed as "oxymoronic"[217] its designation of Al Qaeda members as "unlawful combatants." Yet it is only so if the binary pair of solid and liquid renders self-contradictory the concept of viscosity. Most people concur that the concept of "a battlefield" is singularly inapt in characterizing important features of the continuing conflict with militant jihadist groups, particularly its geographical diffuseness. Members of such groups, in preparing and conducting their attacks, act neither exclusively on nor off a battlefield. The word itself appears in no dictionaries of military law, for it is not a juridical term of art. Hence, whether a state of armed conflict exists cannot very well turn on the spatial co-presence of military antagonists on a territorial battlefield in any legal sense of the expression. An intermediate category between combatant and civilian may therefore be entirely apt here. As Pildes suggests, "The reasons a government may confine suspected terrorists do not parallel the reasons for confining domestic criminals or even prisoners of war."[218] The chief alternative, surely unsatisfactory, is to treat Al Qaeda members as civilians who lose their noncombatant immunity only intermittently, whenever exclusively participating in hostilities, promptly regaining it when they return to other activities – unless mere "membership" itself constitutes "direct participation." And it is unclear what membership would even mean within an informal social network.

As a matter of rhetoric, to describe as "a hole" – much less a black one – a situation that is not governed by law is hardly a neutral designation. By implication, a hole must be filled in, if one is not to trip and fall. Yet the law – national as well as international – leaves many situations substantially unregulated. The pertinent parties either cannot agree to mutually satisfactory terms or believe their problems are better resolved in other, more flexible ways than by simple rule-adherence. For both reasons apparently, the states negotiating Geneva Protocol II, for instance, declined to prohibit civilian reprisals.[219] During the drafting of Protocol II, the ICRC sought to include several such prohibitions, but states rejected them; "that a rebel force might be given the power to take reprisals against a government" – in a noninternational armed conflict – "was seen as out of the question."[220] This treaty governs "noninternational armed conflicts." America's confrontation with Al Qaeda must be so classified, according to the U.S. Supreme Court in *Hamdan*.

Pirates and slave traders had no legal rights, even as the international law against piracy and slave trading became quite developed.[221] Notwithstanding their undoubted "humanity," in the sense of their membership in the species, these two groups were not thought morally to merit the law's protection, as Yoo rightly observes.[222] By contrast, the legal regime governing treatment of the Guantánamo detainees is quite complex. Their predicament implicates multiple bodies of law, notably several treaties in the area of international human rights, including the Convention Against Torture, plus U.S. constitutional law (on due process and *habeas corpus*, in particular), as well as humanitarian law, both customary and treaty based. Even the Bush administration admitted early on that the Geneva Conventions "applied" to the Taliban, giving them the presumptive status of POWs – but for their failure to respect attendant duties under Article 4. In sum, the detainees were caught not in a black hole but in a set of intersecting spiders' webs. Few could seriously doubt that their legal circumstance was at least somewhat anomalous. The problem, however, is that when the line is unclear between peace and war, so too becomes the line between murder and lawful killing.

Anthropology suggests that it is often enough for anomalous entities to be isolated from society at large, locked safely away, rather than destroyed. They mostly threaten society's image of itself, secured through its conceptual apparatus. They normally present less serious a challenge to its material existence, however much the latter may rely on the former. Yet Al Qaeda's attacks are on the West's very material being, no less than on the coherence of its law.[223]

Elements of the country's officer corps would like to see "the U.S.... lead serious international initiatives to update and revise the Geneva Conventions"[224] to this end, enabling the law to identify and define these current adversaries with greater precision. But the critics' response to the suggestion that the administration "might have proposed negotiations on a new Geneva convention to cover the new situation," is a disdainful "Dream On."[225] In fact, certain discussions toward filling this legal gap have indeed taken place within the Bush administration,[226] and with British allies,[227] albeit with no result. Furthermore, the desirability of legally acknowledging a third or middle category of person, who may be subject to administrative detention for the direct and individualized threat he poses, is widely recognized by America's allies.[228] His detention on these grounds would then be possible regardless of criminal prosecution.

Drafting language agreeable to all pertinent parties, foreign and domestic, proves extremely difficult. Even America's closest allies have been skeptical – in fact, distrustful – of its efforts.[229] This distrust is not entirely caused by the U.S. abuse of captive terror suspects. Asks one European scholar: "Why reinvent the rules to make them applicable to groups and individuals who will never apply them, who cannot by definition apply them?"[230] And one wonders, with an international lawyer who served on Clinton's National Security Council, about "the possibly quixotic nature of applying a body of law premised in part on considerations of reciprocity to a conflict with terrorists whose principal aim is to kill civilians in violation of that body of law."[231] In any event, insofar as the prohibition on degrading treatment may now be *jus cogens*, a revision to the Geneva Conventions relaxing that prohibition for terrorists (presumably to allow such methods as sleep deprivation and truth serum in a true, "ticking time bomb" scenario), would probably be invalid. For the Vienna Convention on the Law of Treaties, some of which the United States accepts as customary law, provides that no treaty may derogate from a *jus cogens* norm.[232]

The revisions in Geneva law sought by the United States will also likely depart in key places from longstanding legal distinctions, such as that between combatant and noncombatant. The Military Commissions Act of 2006, for instance, effaces this distinction by classifying civilians who intentionally provide "material support" to terrorist activity as "unlawful enemy combatants"[233] and susceptible to targeting. Material support of this sort is not currently a war crime in international law. Revision of domestic law, such as noncriminal administrative detention[234] and regulations on CIA interrogation practices, holds greater promise to this end than the more remote possibility of change in international law.

WHAT GOES AROUND . . .

Imagine if the reciprocity principle were applied to the prohibition of "material support" and the United States successfully promoted international law's adoption of such a rule. Then, American civilians who intentionally assisted an American war effort – Halliburton's personnel and CEO, for instance – might become lawful "military objectives" for an enemy.[235] Perhaps even the act of buying a "war bond" would strip one of civilian immunity. In enacting the Military Commissions Act, Congress and the president did not wish to embrace the reciprocity principle to this extent, of course. Yet it is hard to see how any principled and coherent rule could avoid this unwelcome result.

   At present, civilians like Halliburton's CEO may lawfully be targeted only when directly involved in hostile activities, including armaments production, as on the shop floor of a tank factory.[236] Such facilities are, after all, "objects which by their nature, location, purpose or uses make an effective contribution to military action and whose . . . destruction . . . offers a definite military advantage."[237] Material assistance to the war effort, short of this quoted standard, does not subject a civilian to permissible targeting. Even if Halliburton's CEO and corporate headquarters could be said to satisfy that standard in some respects, the U.S. legislation speaks of material support to terrorist organizations, not to military action generally.

   To distinguish the CEO's contribution to the war from that of, say, an Al Qaeda sympathizer who sells arms to that organization, we would need an internationally accepted definition of "terrorism." This would distinguish it from ordinary acts of lawful combatancy, as well as from war crimes and crimes against humanity – to which the lawful response is criminal prosecution, not military attack. Such a definition has largely eluded the international community for more than thirty years.[238] It would be unacceptable not only to those few the United States regards as terrorists, whose views need not concern us; it would be dismissed as well by the many more who sympathize with some of their underlying aims. Thus, any hope of reciprocity in restraint becomes problematic. Though both are nonstate actors, Halliburton differs importantly from Al Qaeda, to be sure, in acting as the legal "agent" of a state, and thereby exercising by delegation that state's right under international law to initiate force in self-defense and employ it generally within a theater of armed conflict. This argumentative move traffics on such law's continuing state-centrism, however, which may be enough for predicting how courts will act but is no longer sufficient for deeper normative purposes.

The United States' strong demand for reciprocity in its Military Commissions Act of 2006 has a way of coming back to haunt. For instance, the Blackwater guards who protect traveling U.S. dignitaries outside Baghdad's Green Zone carry their arms openly, but do not usually wear identifying insignia, much less formal military or company uniforms. If captured, they would therefore not be entitled to POW status and its protections under current international law. They may employ lethal force only in self-defense, and they may not fire on enemy fighters unless they have good reason to believe their own lives are in danger. However, there have been strong indications that their use of force has sometimes extended further afield,[239] thereby turning them into unprivileged belligerents. Moreover, the U.K. and the United States are among the very few states still asserting a customary legal right to attack civilians by way of reprisal.[240] The reciprocity principle, as grounded in both custom and treaty, hence authorizes their adversaries in armed conflict to do the same; that is, to employ civilian reprisals against British and American civilians.[241] This inference has profound and far-reaching implications.

Having declared a state of war with the United States in 1996[242] (again in 1998 and thereafter),[243] and having broadly defined the geographical scope of armed conflict (to include Palestine, in particular),[244] Osama bin Laden would arguably have been within his rights to target U.S. civilians in proportionate reprisal for U.S. humanitarian law violations. He alleged that America's aiding and abetting of Israeli occupation policies and of several repressive Arab regimes constituted such breaches. Bin Laden might have sought to justify the 9/11 attacks on this basis, had he cared to offer a secular legal argument. He certainly gave plenty of advance notice of his intentions, as the law of reprisal requires.

"As a result of its persistent objection," writes one leading scholar of international law, "the objecting State remains governed by the old rule (or absence of a rule) in its relations with all other States. But as a result of the principle of reciprocity and despite the existence of the new, generalized rule, other States may also claim the same rights vis-à-vis the objecting State as they were previously able to claim."[245] Thus, because the United States has claimed a right to civilian reprisal under customary international law against its adversaries, they are entitled to exercise that right against the United States.

In its embrace of reciprocity, the Bush administration presumably did not have this in mind[246] – nor had its predecessors, for that matter, in retaining a right to reprisal against civilians, *in extremis*. Yet here as elsewhere, the sword of reciprocity is double-edged and so cuts both ways. What it gives, it also takes away or, more precisely, gives also to one's enemy. More collo- quially, with reciprocity, what goes around, comes around, as Elaine Scarry observed,[247] echoing many Bush administration critics. It may be only the "realist" constraint – the lack of countervailing power in a unipolar world – that today deters other states from torturing Americans in reciprocation for U.S. torture of their own, Noah Feldman suggests.[248] The legal principle of reciprocity is permitted little role here, but for reasons that have nothing to do with law or morality.

If the West should be free to discriminate between types of civilians – treating those culpable in atrocity as different from the rest – then the reciprocity principle would authorize militant jihadists to do the same. When they attack a Jerusalem yeshiva whose leaders are committed to expanding Israeli settlement of the West Bank,[249] the world's reaction need not be the same as when they detonate a bomb in the general student cafeteria of Hebrew University.[250] There is nothing in current humanitarian law, however, permitting such distinctions. So much the worse for such law.

OBSTACLES TO CHANGE, FORCES FOR LEGAL ANACHRONISM

Past experience discourages hope for rapid progress in legal change at the international level. Humanitarian conventions have almost invariably been reactive, lagging behind present and emergent problems. Hence, in the immediate wake of 9/11, international lawyers found no clear authority for the proposition that a nonstate entity could be legally responsible for an "armed attack," entitling the victim state to respond with force in its own defense.[251] Indeed, when Sheik Omar Abdel Rahman and nine others were tried for plotting to blow up the United Nations, the George Washington Bridge, and the Lincoln Tunnel,[252] prosecutors had to indict them under a Civil War-era statute for seditious conspiracy, which made it a crime to "levy war" on the United States.[253] Instead, legal reforms tend to follow major wars and are rarely drafted during an ongoing conflict.[254] Only then are states willing to take a long-term view, because they need not judge proposed new rules as benefiting either themselves or their current enemy. Yet the conflict with Al Qaeda and kindred groups shows no signs of ending soon. A moment of repose for disinterested legal thought is not on the horizon.

Apart from the partisanship of a passing moment, it is odd that Bush administration critics generally proved so reluctant to acknowledge the lim- itations of traditional rules of humanitarian law for governing terrorist war. Such critics are the first to point out, in other contexts, how international law operates with a conceptual template, derived from Western experience, that often does not closely correspond to the history and present reality of many non-Western societies. International law, and the law of war in particular, has been almost entirely a law of states, by states, and for states. Yet the state, as we understand the term, is a peculiarly Western creation, one that crystallized gradually over centuries in Europe and has been, in recent decades, adopted only with considerable difficulty and resistance in much of Africa, the Middle East, Asia, and even parts of Latin America.

This fact is sometimes invoked opportunistically. For instance, the Bush administration argued early on that Taliban fighters were not entitled to Geneva Convention protections because Afghanistan was a "failed state." Because it no longer controlled much of its prior territory and since few other countries recognized its government, Afghanistan simply no longer existed as a "High Contracting Party" to those treaties.[255] Its soldiers were therefore no longer protected by them. Yet the inescapable corollary of this analysis was that neither were such Taliban soldiers bound by such treaties.[256] At least, they were not bound as nationals of the former state of Afghanistan, and not as physically present on its territory, because there no longer existed a state to have a territory. This in turn meant that Taliban leaders could not readily be prosecuted criminally for violating the Geneva Conventions, a conclusion the Bush administration would not have welcomed.[257]

In any event, to speak of "failed states," as critics of international law thus correctly observe, is often merely an uncharitable way of saying that many people in many places remain loyal to longstanding forms of social and political organization, such as the "tribe" or ethnoreligious clan, in which they and those they love have successfully placed their trust for long periods, sometimes millennia. It is hence unreasonable to expect them readily to abandon a gift economy of reciprocal exchange, one that has traditionally extended into the political realm, to embrace novel forms of governance requiring that public officials act only on abstract principle (i.e., the rule of law).[258]

Yet much of humanitarian law as we know it is the product of this very system of states, initiated in the Peace of Westphalia. That its rules of warfare do not closely correspond to "the facts on the ground" of contemporary armed conflicts involving domestic insurgencies and transnational terrorist networks should scarcely surprise us. And just as Western thinkers have rightly grown somewhat more circumspect in recent years about deriding Africa for "state failure,"[259] so too we should become more wary of denouncing methods of war, employed effectively beyond (and often against) the West, simply on the basis of their failure to conform to Western, state-centric rules.

None of this is to defend jihadist terror, of course, but merely to suggest that the very features that make it so effective may require corresponding regulatory innovation.

Defense counsel for Guantánamo detainees often argue as if the Geneva Conventions were eternal, inalterable monuments to human dignity, when in fact they and other humanitarian law treaties have undergone several major revisions over a century and a half, evolving in light of problems posed by new forms of warfare.[260] Jihadist terror is simply the most recent such form. One could be forgiven for surmising that Bush administration critics cling to historic rules for regulating warfare much like doddering officers cleave to established technologies for fighting it. This inclination toward anachronism finds vivid expression in the Fourth Circuit's June 2007 *Al-Marri* ruling, holding that a person may not "be classified as an enemy combatant because of his criminal conduct on behalf of an enemy organization,"[261] but only on the basis of directly engaging in hostilities for a state at war with another state. It followed that the president may not designate anyone as such, much less an "unlawful" enemy combatant, and detain him indefinitely on that ground in the conflict with Al Qaeda. As a citizen of a friendly nation – Qatar, in this case – the detainee could not be treated as a combatant. Q.E.D. Nowhere did the court acknowledge that a nonstate group, though not an "armed force" according to applicable legal sources, might nonetheless be capable of committing unlawful acts of force "against the territorial integrity and political independence of a state," as prohibited by the UN Charter.[262]

A Dworkinian jurisprudent might say here that the court refused to accord sufficient gravitational force to the reciprocity principle, as reflected in the facts before it: the principle that noncombatants may not take up arms and may not participate in armed conflict against foreign states if they expect to enjoy the protections afforded civilians by humanitarian law. Jeremy Waldron and other administration critics, when forced to confront gaps in the detainee protections of Geneva's positive law, avow that courts must employ "analogy, inference, and reasoned elaboration" to extend the latent principle of nonbrutality, with a view to filling these holes. Yet the same could often be said of, and done with, the reciprocity principle. In *Al-Marri*, where is the Fourth Circuit's standard judicial practice of "analogy, inference, and reasoned elaboration" that administration critics demand for *their* preferred principles?[263] This is Waldron's avowed strategy, in particular, which is critically assessed in Chapter 4.

Conversely, easy evocations of "a new kind of unconventional war,"[264] warranting brutal methods long abjured, should be greeted with skepticism, for the law has heard such proclamations before, notably concerning the conquest of Native Americans and colonized peoples.[265] The view that today's militant jihadists are unwilling to play tit-for-tat, to behave "rationally" in that sense, may even appear a dusted-off, barely updated revision of the hoary claim that Orientals and Redskins fight in "savage" ways, befitting their lack of "civilization."[266] This criticism by way of historical analogy is examined in some detail (and largely rejected) in Chapter 8.

COHERENCE AND CONTRADICTION WITHIN HUMANITARIAN LAW

In an effort to find some coherence in the law's distinctions, it may help to observe that the exception to reciprocity for humanitarian treaties, mentioned before, clearly cannot sensibly apply to every provision in every such treaty and does not purport to do so. It applies to Geneva law on the treatment of war's victims much more than to Hague-type and weapons-prohibition law governing the more immediate conduct of hostilities,[267] as the ICTY has acknowledged.[268] Barring recourse to a prohibited weapon despite its first use by an enemy can readily permit unfair advantage, which would in turn encourage the weapon's use. The 1925 Geneva Gas Protocol, for instance, permits suspension of obligations as a remedy for its violation. Reciprocity has here been considered essential to limit possibilities for exploitation and thereby stabilize social relations insofar as possible, as sociologists have long noted.[269]

This rationale for reciprocity proves too much, however, in that it would logically extend beyond weapons prohibitions to many Geneva restrictions as well. One way to deter an adversary from torturing POWs or holding civilians hostage as "shields" would be to provide an in-kind reprisal remedy for these breaches. The same may be said of attacks against dams, dikes, or electricity-generating facilities,[270] the destruction of which may seriously degrade an enemy's capacity to wage war. For most of the twentieth century, influential theorists of air power regarded the direct targeting of population centers as highly advantageous, in that it undermined civilian morale and diminished the economic foundations of the enemy's war effort.[271] Conversely, it was the fear of retaliation in kind that led both British and German leaders to refrain from such civilian bombing during the first year of World War II.[272]

Yet despite the potential deterrent value of such measures, Geneva law now permits none of these actions, even in reprisal.[273] Where military advantage may be gained by violating these restrictions, as many belligerents have clearly believed, this advantage can be taken without fear of meeting lawful reprisal in kind. It may be that unfair advantage is more predictably gained, as a practical matter, by recourse to a prohibited weapon than to prohibited actions against *hors de combat*. Yet that conclusion is by no means obvious. Many weapons come to be prohibited by treaty only after their utility has been recognized as slight; for instance, expanding bullets after the Crimean War.[274] Moreover, even actions that only occasionally cause unfair advantage may sometimes have significant impact. The law ought therefore presumably to allow some means for their redress at such times.

This redress would serve both the goals of providing *post facto* fairness to victims and would deter potential perpetrators *ex ante*. When Germany used gas warfare in 1915, thereby violating the Hague Declaration of 1899 and the Conventions on Land Warfare, the Western states – also parties to these treaties – felt authorized, even compelled to retaliate in kind.[275] The next time round, Walzer argues, "Winston Churchill was entirely justified when he warned the German government, early in World War II, that the use of gas by its armies would bring an immediate Allied reprisal."[276] The United States and its Allies were ready and committed to using chemical and biological weapons in reprisal against any German first use.[277] The Germans did not use gas in World War II. The threat of reprisal effectively deterred them. In sum, Geneva norms, no less than Hague weapons norms, are susceptible to the logic of reciprocity; the law could logically choose to so treat them.

To similar effect, in ratifying the 1925 Gas Protocol, some forty states entered reservations providing that they would be bound only vis-à-vis adverse states that had similarly ratified and that, even against such co-ratifiers, all bets were off if the adversary breached its duties by first resorting to the prohibited weapon.[278] Other states, including the United States, took the position that a reservation was redundant.[279] Reciprocity was already the governing principle in the law of treaties,[280] and therefore part of the legal background against which any treaty is drafted, providing the default rule whenever a given treaty does not specify to the contrary. When one side breaches an agreement, the other may suspend or withdraw from it. The large number of reciprocity-reservations to the Gas Protocol also establishes state practice in a way that precludes crystallization of the treaty's prohibitions into customary law (i.e., without a reciprocity exception).

One might at first seek to distinguish the acceptance of reciprocity in Hague and several other weapons treaties from its rejection in Geneva law on the basis of the latter's close connection to human rights norms, particularly international *jus cogens* rules from which no derogation is possible even in exigent circumstances. This rationale proves too much, however. As treaties, full Geneva protections do not apply to all (or even most) conflicts in which basic human rights are violated. They apply only to those international armed conflicts in which both sides have ratified or, in the case of nonstates, "accepted and applied" them. This is a small subset of contemporary armed conflict. The *jus cogens* or human rights rationale for rejecting reciprocity would logically extend this repudiation to cover civil war (i.e., well beyond the point the law actually reaches). The rationale would logically lead, in other words, to much more stringent rules than we actually have, and so it cannot satisfactorily explain or justify current rules.[281]

THE RECIPROCITY OF *TU QUOQUE*

The legal defense of *tu quoque* – "my accusers did the same thing" – is based on reciprocity as common rules for all.[282] The term is fancy, lawyer's Latin for "Look who's talking!" or "That's the pot calling the kettle black!" The underlying intuition is endorsed by the longstanding equitable defenses of "unclean hands" and *in pari delicto,* according to which civil plaintiffs are barred from recovery if they shared with the defendant any measure of responsibility for the harm he suffered.

As a legal defense to a charge of war crimes, *tu quoque* differs from reprisal in its unconcern with chronology.[283] Understood in terms of tit-for-tat, at least,[284] reprisal succeeds as a defense only if the accused invoking it acted in response to an adversary's prior breach. By contrast, even the first violator of humanitarian law is not barred from offering a defense of *tu quoque* against the second violator (i.e., where the second is among those conducting the prosecution). It might initially seem that the *tu quoque* defense is necessarily available in a greater range of factual situations.[285] But *tu quoque*'s scope is also narrower insofar as it excuses only misconduct exactly like it, whereas reprisal admits that one type of breach may be met with an altogether different type (i.e., of comparable but no greater gravity).

Still, the belligerent who engages in reprisal can claim that it is seeking to deter recurrence of its enemy's demonstrable recent misconduct. However, a belligerent claiming *tu quoque* would find it difficult to convince judges of that intention if it had already breached the very norm without provocation by like behavior of its adversary. Yet its intentions here are legally irrelevant, one might argue, if the purpose of *tu quoque* is not to deter misconduct, but only to achieve fairness in the sense of common rules for all, regardless of whose breach came first. Reprisal serves both purposes, however. In any event, the chronological order of breach and response to breach – that is, who "started it" – is *highly* relevant to the fairness question. For these reasons, the doctrine of *tu quoque* is dispensable precisely because, and to the extent that, the right of reprisal already fills the function of fairness-restoration.

The *tu quoque* defense was nonetheless expressly accepted by Germany's Federal Constitutional Court in the 1995 espionage prosecution of former East German "spymaster" Markus Wolf. That court held that East Germans who spied domestically for their state could not be prosecuted after unification because West German officials had done the same. And "espionage for a power that seeks to oppress others is, in international law, seen as no different from espionage for a power whose aim is seen as preservation of freedom and the rule of law."[286]

At Nuremberg, however, the Tribunal formally rejected *tu quoque* as a defense to war crimes, as did the counterpart Tokyo court.[287] The Nuremberg judges then nonetheless quietly embraced it when sentencing Admirals Karl Dönitz and Erich Raeder, not punishing them at all for unrestricted submarine warfare against neutral merchant ships. The British also employed it in the Skagerrak and with the Americans in the Pacific, according to the testimony of defense witness Admiral Chester Nimitz.[288] Prosecutors did not even charge any Nazi defendants with planning and ordering the mass bombing of British cities, on account of similar Allied targeting of German and Japanese population centers. In his autobiography, the American judge at Nuremberg, Frances Biddle, later confessed the rationale for this decision: "We would have looked like fools"[289] if Germans were punished for conduct indistinguishable from what Americans and the British had likewise transparently done.

Still, formally endorsing a "you did it too" defense – even if only to punishment rather than liability – would have effectively shrunk all humanitarian law to a modest rule of "no first use."[290] Once a rule was violated by any belligerent, its application would be effectively suspended for the duration of hostilities,[291] unless – through negotiation, presumably – a rule-consistent equilibrium could be restored. This awful scenario is what game theorists aptly call the "grim trigger."[292] As Julius Stone said of reprisal, ready recourse to *tu quoque* could facilitate an implicit collusion of the most perverse sort between military leaders on both sides of the battle lines: a "mutual helpfulness . . . in reciprocally emancipating each other from irksome rules."[293]

International law therefore gives no formal recognition here to reciprocity in this form, as the ICTY has affirmed.[294] But *sub rosa*, the Dönitz and Raeder judgments suggest that the *de facto* rule is precisely the contrary. And because these judgments were not condemned by states, then or since, one could even say that, as a defense to punishment,[295] "the *tu quoque* argument can still be considered a valid principle of customary international law," as a Chinese scholar has recently argued.[296] The official rule for conduct, *ex ante*, and the unofficial rule for *ex post* judgment of such conduct appear distinct, in other words. It is unlikely, moreover, that they today remain "acoustically separated,"[297] such that the decision rule has no impact on relevant conduct, if only because the Doenitz case is itself so widely taught to military lawyers throughout the world. These are the lawyers who, in turn, train each new generation of their country's officers.

It was more sensible to allow such a *tu quoque* defense at Nuremberg than it would be today, before the International Criminal Court. The postwar International Military Tribunal was not a truly international court. Its judges were drawn exclusively from victor Allied nations, who were also the accusers. These nations, one could credibly say, were the judge, jury, prosecutor, and executioner. Because such states were unquestionably responsible for certain major offenses legally similar to those of the accused, a hypocritical redolence hung heavily in the courtroom air.

In contrast, as the International Criminal Court is truly international in composition and structure, the accuser becomes the international community at large, not the parties proximately victimized by the perpetrators' wrong. Because the relation between accuser and accused is no longer bilateral, the principle of reciprocity – as common rules for both sides – no longer stands in the way of prosecution. The charge of "victor's justice" entirely disappears once the law replaces bilateral with a genuinely systemic, multilateral reciprocity.[298]

In sum, humanitarian law follows an inconsistent path in its on-again, off-again relation to reciprocity. One might be tempted to say that such law is internally consistent in that Geneva law, because of its increasing resemblance to human rights law, rightly rejects reciprocity, whereas Hague-type weapons treaties understandably accept it. Though such weapons treaties aim to minimize unnecessary suffering, they still are chiefly concerned, in the remedy of withdrawal for their breach, with preventing unfair advantage through one side's use of the prohibited weapon against the other. They again resemble arms control treaties, limiting deployable numbers of a particular weapon, though the latter are concerned more with avoiding a fight – by preserving a balance of power – than with ensuring its fairness.[299] As a leading treatise on such conventions explains,

> In arms control law reciprocity is the dominant factor ... reciprocity in the form of a balance of mutual responsibilities and obligations is implied. ... The supervisory mechanisms in most arms control treaties, even when they contain elaborate rules for verification, generally offer little specific remedies after a case of non-compliance has been established. This means that, in general, reactions to situations of non-compliance in arms control law will be conditioned by the principle of reciprocity.[300]

The author adds that this conclusion reflects the general principle that any state victimized by another's treaty breach is entitled to suspend performance of its own treaty duties in relation to the violater.[301] In defense of this approach, he continues, "Though this ... may seem detrimental to the co-operation between States Parties, instead it may precisely have the effect of preserving the treaty regime because States Parties prefer to seek solutions to problems within the regime rather than facing the possibility of a state falling back on countermeasures or other unilateral remedies."[302]

MORAL CONFLICT WITHIN HUMANITARIAN LAW

Perhaps it is a mistake to dismiss humanitarian law as morally incoherent. Or maybe the mistake lies instead in assuming that there ever really existed a single body of law by that name at all. This is unconvincing, however. Geneva law and Hague-type weapons prohibitions have always been viewed as united in their common aim of minimizing the unnecessary suffering of war, a goal that sets them apart even from other law explicitly designed to foster human dignity. That these two bodies of law have been so closely linked throughout modern history is by no means gratuitous.

One thus cannot really banish the problem of moral incoherence by simply hiving off a portion of the pertinent field and calling it by a different name.[303] Arms control agreements are not entirely reciprocal, for that matter, any more than Geneva law is entirely nonreciprocal. Procedural violations of weapons treaties, in particular, are regarded differently from substantive breaches. If a party refuses access to its territory to teams of international inspectors, for instance, other parties do not have the right to refuse inspections on their territory in response.[304]

Assessing the relative scope afforded to reciprocity and antireciprocity, we may say that the law (especially state practice, Hague, and weapons law) gives much scope to reciprocity, with important side constraints. One could observe that the law here presents something of a patchwork or checkerboard quilt,[305] making distinctions for which no principled rationales are offered by drafters or readily apparent to contemporary inheritors of their efforts. Humanitarian law is not merely confusing, but confused and conflicted. It is therefore only natural that readers should by this point feel somewhat off balance as they finish surveiling the varied topography we have just reconnoitered. The sense of disorientation likely experienced in struggling through this dense doctrinal thicket renders this chapter itself something of a performative utterance. For it re-creates in the course of its reading the very state of perplexity and unsatisfied craving for consistency that this body of legal doctrine itself so lavishly reveals. If I have, to your satisfaction, lucidly and convincingly explicated each issue and the law's response to it along the way, then I will have failed, in a sense, adequately to convey the law's overall condition of randomness and disorder. (But be reassured, dear readers, that the book's final section, Part Four will, of course, set all aright!)

The law routinely tolerates such tensions where they are acknowledged as ineradicable. As with the line between individualism and altruism, or popular sovereignty and individual rights, their respective demarcation within a body of legal rules is likely impossible to locate on the basis of any fixed principles, honored consistently throughout modern history, grounded in any single coherent theory of self or society.[306] Humanitarian law is no more inconsistent in this regard than, say, a law of tort that tells defendants at once that they must pay only those damages reasonably foreseeable to them when acting *and* that they nonetheless "take the plaintiffs as they find them," with all their idiosyncratic vulnerabilities, however unforeseeable.

Anyone with domestic legislative experience will know that the negotiation and drafting of statutes (as with treaties) are often an unlovely process, requiring departure from first principles by all sides. If the results are morally compromised and hence analytically incoherent, such are the demands of political compromise in a democratic republic (and an international anarchy). The range of deeply held principles is even wider in the international arena than in the domestic one, making international law still less likely to cohere around any single, dominant principle, such as human rights, on the one hand, or state sovereignty on the other.

It is axiomatic that a liberal society must accommodate competing conceptions of the good life, based on conflicting ultimate values.[307] Its law will thus try to steer clear of taking sides on such questions,[308] concentrating instead on protecting those rights compatible with and required by processes of social cooperation. But differences arise over the right, hardly less than over the good, and they create conflicts over a liberal law's proper dispensations and duties. These moral conflicts find reflection within legal doctrine, especially where competing "principles are inevitable aspects of any decent response to the world's complexity,"[309] as Dworkin observes.

Such value conflict emerges in disagreements over whether a given legal duty, domestic or international, should be reciprocal or nonreciprocal. If humanitarian law displays no neat, fixed line of demarcation between its reciprocal and antireciprocal domains, this reflects the fact that we both see a valued place for reciprocity within social life and yet acknowledge the necessity of limiting its scope at certain times. We limit it in light of other values that will sometimes outweigh it, in circumstances that cannot always be anticipated and hence legally codified in advance.

Tensions of this sort within legal doctrine can be called "contradictions," as Duncan Kennedy insists, only if that term fairly describes the fact that a glass of wine makes one feel happy whereas an entire bottle makes one drunk and – the next morning – very unhappily hungover.[310] It was liberals like Isaiah Berlin who first announced the fact of value pluralism,[311] not liberalism's critics. Because law enshrines our deepest values, the fact of value plurality inevitably finds legal expression in indeterminacy. This occurs wherever claims by one such value, reflected for instance in a given treaty provision, begin to run up against those reflected in another provision, or in another treaty altogether, equally applicable to the facts. Jurisprudents of a pragmatist stripe will be untroubled by the presence of competing principles within a doctrinal area, as long as these compromises reflect a fair legislative process and the resulting rules are applied through a judicial process bound to reasoned argument.

Those who demand, by contrast, that all such compromises themselves be principled,[312] and the resulting statute or treaty morally coherent in that sense, will reject the seeming humility of this aspiration as "false modesty,"[313] inconsistent with the rule of law, properly understood.[314] Within humanitarian law, we have found clear traces of thesis and antithesis, but no real stable synthesis. To most people, a humanitarian law that entirely rejected reciprocity (of both the first and second order) would be no more appealing in moral or practical terms than one that embraced it without qualification.[315]

"Balancing" is the metaphor generally invoked for confronting such situations. The law often speaks of rebalancing when there arises a strong inclination to accord greater weight to a principle or policy hitherto subordinated within a longstanding paired opposition (e.g., order vs. law, security vs. liberty, efficiency vs. fairness). American courts have often engaged in such balancing when assessing the constitutional rights of criminal defendants under the Fourth and Fifth Amendments to the Constitution, as by increasing such protection as crime rates decline.[316] In the present context, a balancing test would presumably let the law accord more weight to reciprocity where it has a chance of achieving some deterrence and perhaps grant greater weight to human rights considerations where it does not.[317] (On this basis, the reader might even find it helpful to revisit each of the more specific doctrines and factual scenarios assayed in the preceding pages to see exactly how this species of balancing test would pertain.)

The present chapter has not been chiefly concerned, however, with defending the notion of balancing as a solution to the many problems and complexities identified herein. Most legal defenders of Bush administration counterterrorism policy, by contrast, have followed this route. For this reason, the admittedly wooly notion of balancing became the primary target for jurisprudential critics of the administration's legal approach.[318] These critics decline to conduct the fight on the enemy's intellectual terrain. They not merely resist the particular calculus employed in executive efforts at rebalancing (the approach adopted here in Chapters 10 through 12); they resist the very idea of balancing *per se*. They prefer a harder, sharper, simpler, and more uncompromising line of opposition.

This harder line is supported in turn by an altogether different theoretical stance (and concomitant methodological tools), one embracing an absolutism against coercive interrogation and indefinite detention under any circumstances.[319] Taking that line is also easier and more comforting, as it frees one of any need for messy qualifications and periodic recalibrations of cost and benefit. Alas, however, sometimes the world itself does not indulge so simple a response to its most vexing and persistent complexities. One common way to minimize the moral complexities of armed conflict is to argue that humanitarian law, with the latitude it has historically afforded to reciprocity, must today be subordinated to a very different legal vision: that of international human rights. The next chapter critically assesses this contention. As we will see, human rights advocate-activists are the first to invoke "balancing" when this interpretive method serves their purposes. This is the case when human rights law can be successfully applied to armed conflict only by contending that such law seeks merely to provide a balance to countervailing military considerations, rather than to subordinate them – a more extreme view that military leaders and courts would never accept.[320]

If humanitarian law rests on a foundation of reciprocity "all the way down," then any truly nonreciprocal situation threatens to render the law completely silent. At that point – but for a militantly antireciprocal law of human rights – there would remain nothing left with which to govern the conduct of war except military strategy and the political calculations underlying it. Hence the dilemma: If humanitarian law does its best work by facilitating the workings of bilateral reciprocity (as social science suggests, in Chapter 10), the wellsprings of which are often plenty strong without it, then such law borders on the superfluous.[321] Yet when humanitarian law ventures much beyond the domain where the dynamics of reciprocity effectively underwrite it, this legal endeavor quickly risks becoming inconsequential, the subject of the ridicule to which it is widely subject. Even the most dedicated scholars-advocates of humanitarian law hence periodically ask themselves, "Is humanity in war possible of itself, outside of any military advantage it might bring?"[322]

We must admit, as Geoffrey Best teased early on, that reciprocity is generally the *de facto* engine making humanitarian law effective in war (i.e., when it is so). This acknowledgment will lead us to deny the efforts of those – particularly human rights lawyers – who believe that today's most urgent task is to move humanitarian law beyond reciprocity altogether by identifying universal norms capable of restraining violence even in nonreciprocal circumstances. The answer to the puzzle will ultimately lie not there, but in a position that both realistically recognizes warfare's inherently reciprocal nature and venturously reimagines reciprocity itself in a way consistent with our ethical identity and geopolitical aspirations.

3

Humanitarian vs. Human Rights Law:
The Coming Clash

Many recent efforts to make belligerents more accountable for the needless suffering they cause take the form of attempts to infuse the law of human rights into that of warfare, sometimes virtually to the point of supplanting rather than merely supplementing the latter. That effort is largely misconceived, as this chapter shows. If bilateral reciprocity is the central fact about social relations, as theorists of widely different persuasions maintain,[1] then no society can afford entirely to contravene this principle within its law. This is especially true of international society, since it lacks the sort of multilateral social contract characteristic of any domestic society with a robust, well-functioning state. And if the effective governance of war, in particular, continues to depend heavily on bilateral reciprocity (as Chapter 10 shows), then it would be unwise for international law to rely heavily on rules affording that principle little place.

The international law of human rights accords it almost none. Indeed, this is one of the chief sources of appeal about human rights ideals to many: Such rights continue to protect people who are unable (or simply unwilling) to reciprocate *anything* vis-à-vis others who occupy the same society, national or international. One might even say that the very notion of a human right borne by all persons, simply as members of the species, is designed to minimize the importance of differences in our moral character and in the nature of relationships between us. One key such difference in these social relations is the presence or absence of reciprocity. And one key difference is our moral constitution is our relative willingness to reciprocate the forbearance of others, especially those who threaten us.

Since humanitarian law already chiefly seeks the preservation of humanity in war, the only rationale for supplementing it with human rights law – as many scholars now advocate[2] – would be to accord still greater weight to humanitarianism, when its claims begin to run up against strictly military factors that humanitarian law more amply accommodates. This is apparent from the World Court's decisions in *D.R.C. v. Uganda*[3] and the *Israeli Wall* judgments. In the latter case, human rights law was accorded pride of place, while lawful military considerations (of proportionality and necessity in self-defense) bearing on Israel's security were summarily dismissed without analysis.[4] This is symptomatic of the pervasive tendency for human rights law and its defenders to banish military contingencies rather than acknowledge and critically assess them.

Human rights and humanitarian law share a concern for preserving human dignity in political hard times. They offer quite different answers, however, to the question of how an unprivileged belligerent at liberty or a detained terror suspect may be treated. Humanitarian law treaties have set increasing limits on the scope of reciprocity, as the last chapter showed, even if state practice has lagged well behind. But human rights law goes still further in that direction, virtually abandoning reciprocity altogether. The result is that the particular portions of humanitarian law allowing reciprocity – such as the right of reprisal – are precisely those most likely to run afoul of human rights law.

Crucially, duties under human rights law bind only governments. Insurgent groups in noninternational armed conflict owe no duties under such law to state forces. A major rationale for this lack of reciprocity has been that nongovernment forces generally lack the capacity to respect many standard rights – as to due process, because these forces do not operate courts and legal systems of their own.[5] The impulse to subordinate humanitarian law to human rights standards thus turns out to be largely an effort to reduce the permissible scope of the reciprocity principle in warfare.

Although the Universal Declaration of Human Rights and the major Geneva Conventions were both negotiated in 1948, they were drafted separately and made slight effort to take account of each other.[6] Only in the 1950s and 1960s, with the European Convention on Human Rights and then the International Covenant on Civil and Political Rights, did human rights begin to take explicit cognizance of how war might affect such law's proper application.[7] The clash between these two bodies of law first emerged in the mid-1970s in drafting Geneva Additional Protocol I.[8] In those negotiations, the Palestine Liberation Organization and the ICRC "saw an opportunity to import more demanding human rights standards into the laws of war by rejecting Geneva's traditional reciprocity requirements, and by ensuring that there were 'no gaps' in the basic protections provided to even the most vicious and law-defying combatants,"[9] as one leading international lawyer observes. Most of the world, including

America's major military allies, accepted this change. The United States did not.

Soon thereafter, the end of the Cold War impelled two new leading human rights nongovernmental organizations (NGOs) – first Amnesty International, then Human Rights Watch – to enter the field of humanitarian law that they had previously consigned to the discretely private intercessions of the ICRC. These human rights groups did not share the Red Cross's longstanding commitment to preserving the confidentiality of its findings about states' legal breaches. In fact, their aim was precisely to publicize such violations, with a view to "naming, blaming, and shaming" offenders into compliance.

Current approaches to the relationship between human rights and humanitarian law "are divergent and oppose each other more passionately than ever," writes a legal scholar.[10] One reason why this relationship is now so vexing and complex is that Western armies find themselves engaged at once in peace-building operations, military occupation, neighborhood stabilization efforts, intense firefights, and humanitarian assistance, often side by side, with each activity employing both soldiers and civilian personnel. The upshot is a dizzying mélange defying standard legal classification:

> There are civilians all over the battlefield – not only insurgents dressed as refugees, but special forces operatives dressing like natives, private contractors dressing like Arnold Schwarzenegger, and all the civilians running the complex technology and logistical chains "behind" modern warfare.... Civil affairs officers run after the troops dispensing compensation and apologetic words in a campaign for hearts and minds, or where the military rebuilds what it has destroyed.... Is this a battlefield? How do we allocate the privilege to kill when combat blurs easily with stabilization and law enforcement?[11]

In other words, which set of legal rules – those for war or those for peace – apply when the reality to be governed inextricably mixes elements of both? During peace operations – to stop a genocide, for instance – humanitarian law applies to UN forces only "to the extent and for the duration of their engagement," according to the Secretary General.[12] One leading scholar, Mary Ellen O'Connell, interprets this to mean that the law of war pertains "only when peacekeepers are engaged in fighting and ceases to apply immediately after a particular engagement is over."[13] Presumably the very moment at which it "is over" will be perfectly clear, in real-time, to all concerned. So the eighteen-year-old Finnish conscript will recognize that those shooting at him a moment ago have not simply paused to change cartridges or await reinforcements. We are also assured that, despite the hundreds of significant military confrontations since World War II between rival states (and between states and armed insurgencies) and the many lives therein lost (five million in the Congo region alone), for legal purposes "armed conflict should be treated as a declining category of human conduct."[14] It would be wonderful indeed if war and all its attendant human suffering could be so readily banished from the repertoire of human conflict resolution by such lawyerly fiat.

ARE WE REALLY AT WAR?

When norms of positive law fail to anticipate novel situations, the law student is taught always to look beneath the codified rules to the principles underlying them. Whereas the rules of humanitarian law are found in conventions and custom, the two key principles to be discovered there are: 1) distinction – between fighters and non-fighters – and, 2) avoiding damage unnecessary to attaining military objectives. These legal principles would extend to new varieties of warfare even where the rules themselves do not, that is, insofar as such conflicts clearly implicate such norms. In line with this reasoning, the World Court held that both principles – discrimination and proportionality, as they are also called – apply to the use of nuclear weapons even though no treaty expressly so provides.[15] Wrongdoers in other, non-martial contexts – from tax fraud to racial discrimination – often modify their methods to accomplish the same malevolent purpose by novel means, with a view to eluding the law's prohibitions. When they do so, the law's standard response is to adapt, adjusting its terms – by reinterpretation or statutory revision – in light of the new challenge, meeting criminal creativity with conceptual innovation of its own. One would expect the same in legal definitions of war.[16]

Yet O'Connell moves in exactly the opposite direction, in order to enlarge the domain of human rights law, seeking to "conquer" war itself for this burgeoning moral empire. Leading military historians and international relations scholars, however, have generally defined the phenomenon in terms easily encompassing America's conflict with Al Qaeda: as "organized violence carried on by political units against each other," in Hedley Bull,[17] for instance, or "an act of force to compel our enemy to do our will," for Clausewitz.[18] Like proportionality and discrimination, the concept of war reflects concerns of policy and principle with a wider reach than any given incarnation within positive law at a particular time. No serious scholar or practitioner of military affairs would define war so narrowly as to be abruptly discontinuous in the way O'Connell suggests – to begin, end, and start up again every time a soldier picks up or puts down a rifle on a given street corner. One is almost embarrassed to have to mention such considerations since they may appear self-evident. Yet prominent legal critics of the Bush administration like O'Connell make no effort to anticipate and refute them.

Humanitarian law might admittedly choose to regard "armed conflict" as a legal term of art having little to do with the human experience of war as we know it. But the result would only be to detach such law still further from the social reality of violent, collective confrontation that it strives to govern. It is remote enough already. Terrorizing civilian populations by targeting them directly, moreover, has long been a regular – albeit unlawful – method of warfare in forms more conventional than today's militant jihad. Thus, terror is already a war crime.[19]

There is still further reason to afford war's legal definition some conceptual breathing room: The Martens clause in humanitarian treaties expressly encourages us to "fill gaps"[20] and resolve legal uncertainties – about whether we are at war, in this case – in light of considerations of humanity and public conscience. These considerations presumably encompass the inhumanity and unconscionability of terrorist methods and the attendant importance of holding accountable those employing these – as by authorizing the treatment of such persons as combatants, hence targeting or detaining them until the end of hostilities, and prosecuting them as war criminals.[21]

One might naively have expected that Bush administration critics like O'Connell, before concluding that the concept of war simply does not pertain, would give at least a quick nod to the advent of the Internet – "where jihadists recruit each other in chat rooms and can download bomb-making materials . . ."[22] – and how the Internet has, in the words of a leading scholar of jihadist movements, "enabled a new wave of terrorist wannabes," as much as Al Qaeda itself, "who now constitute the main . . . threat to the West."[23] Some explicit recognition would also seem warranted, at least in passing, that, as two prominent foreign policy analysts write,

> While it is a multi-dimensional conflict in which intelligence, ideas and diplomacy all loom large, in its military dimensions it is a violent conflict against a resilient enemy whose publicly declared goals are to wound the West as grievously as possible, to overturn governments across the Middle East, Africa and Central and Southeast Asia, to destroy Israel, and to cause an exhausted and demoralized American to withdraw from the Middle East.[24]

The acquisition of weapons of mass destruction should be added here to this list of Al Qaeda's stated aims. One would think that such features of an organization – its ruthless means (amply demonstrated in practice) and its apocalyptic ends (candidly proclaimed) – suggest that those it declares sworn enemies might find themselves confronted with something at least approximating an armed conflict. Not so, say several distinguished scholars of international law.

In assessing whether armed conflict exists today between the United States and Al Qaeda, O'Connell also sees fit to analogize that organization's several cumulating attacks throughout the world, causing thousands of deaths, with "precedents" – i.e., where no armed conflict was thought to exist – involving unintentional encounters between vessels at sea, humanitarian interventions, and minor border skirmishes.[25] She admits, however, that the Inter-American Commission on Human Rights' classification of a brief attack (lasting thirty hours, against an Argentine military facility by some forty aging, sixties-era civilian leftists) as an "armed conflict," rather than an "internal disturbance," is problematic to her position.[26]

The most natural inference from the Commission's finding here would surely be that the duration of a violent confrontation might be very brief for the law of armed conflict nonetheless to apply.[27] O'Connell states the holding quite differently: "The decision indicates that fighting less than thirty hours might not be 'protracted,'" and therefore not count toward establishing the existence of "armed conflict."[28] She makes no mention of legal authorities who suggest that the threshold of violence necessary to constitute "armed conflict" is greater for international war than noninternational ones[29] – the latter category encompassing America's conflict with Al Qaeda, according to the U.S. Supreme Court. O'Connell even concludes that Israel, during the height of the two Intifadas, had no international right of self-defense against Hamas or the PLO because its military occupied the Palestinian territories, making them effectively part of Israel, and a state cannot invoke the right of self-defense against itself.[30] Q.E.D.

O'Connell regards the control of territory by the nonstate belligerent to be a necessary condition for classifying its violent confrontations with a state adversary as an "armed conflict."[31] Yet there is nothing to this effect in Common Article 3 or Protocol II to the Geneva Conventions, the treaty provisions governing such conflicts. Her response: Learned European commentators nonetheless "mention this factor."[32]

No war. Hence no need for the law of war.

If one adopts O'Connell's definition of war, few of the many successful anticolonial insurgencies that gave rise to new states from 1945 through 1975 would have been involved in armed conflict. Their operational and tactical circumstances ensured that attacks on colonial forces were generally sporadic, and such insurgents often did not control territory for long periods, especially at the outset and sometimes thereafter. This would mean that such anticolonial and anti-apartheid fighters did not enjoy the rights and privileges of lawful combatants, a conclusion O'Connell would surely find unacceptable.

The legal questions of whether a state of armed conflict exists at a given place and time and whether humanitarian law therefore applies to it can today be answered only by reference to a complex multifactor test. Among the variables in this test is the demonstrated existence of "protracted armed violence," according to the ICTY in the *Tadić* and *Harandinaj* cases.[33] This court interprets the phrase "protracted armed violence" to refer more to the intensity of violence than to its duration. Of course, duration can be assessed only well after the violence has begun, not at its outset, when decisions must be made about what the law permits in response.

Yet intensity can only be measured in reference to the pertinent "zone of combat," which might be conceived broadly or narrowly, depending on one's view of the conflict's pertinent scope. This phrase, though presumably intended to enlarge the relevant geographical range beyond that implied by the term "battlefield," is itself unsettled in its temporal and spatial contours. It is therefore often uncertain whether the violent acts in dispute should be evaluated in relation to other such acts within the distance of a few city blocks, within a *de facto* national subdivision (e.g., Iraq's Sunni triangle), within the country as a whole, or – as perhaps during World War II – within a regional theater of operations covering a significant portion of the globe.

For the wars of the former Yugoslavia, the ICTY has sometimes held that a situation of armed conflict did not exist in the immediate locale because a lengthy period of calm preceded the violence that is the subject of a particular prosecution.[34] The ICTY hence classified such violence not as the conduct of war, but rather as acts of internal disturbance – to which human rights law, not humanitarian law, would hence apply. Yet what may be rightly seen in retrospect as a diminution in intensity might at the time have reasonably appeared simply a change in tactics or strategy; for example, from open confrontation to more surreptitious sniping and ambush. With so opaque and indeterminate a legal standard as that just described, the conscientious commander may frequently have little advance warning about whether his orders to troops would be later judged by the law of war or peace. "War is a volatile enterprise," writes one military historian. "Tactics, strategies, and commanders must be sorted out amid death and destruction before the proper combination is found to defeat the enemy."[35] This fact greatly complicates the real-time effort of soldiers to determine which body of law applies to them, from moment to moment.

One "solution" to the problem would be always to follow the more demanding of the two standards. And it is true that "any killing which is in breach of international humanitarian law is also in breach of non-derogable provisions in international human rights texts."[36] But the converse is decidedly untrue: Many breaches of human rights law would not violate humanitarian law. If there is anything that can be said with certainty here, it is that the jihadist terror suspect, far from being *homo sacer* – the exiled, rightless figure in Roman law who could be killed by anyone[37] – is today caught in a tangled web of cross-cutting legal governance. The problem, *pace* Agamben, is not the absence of applicable legal norms, but the overlay of so many.

When does each of the two pertinent bodies of law pertain? If there are situations where both apply, how are differences between their demands reconciled? A first cut at the answers would say that humanitarian law, as a branch of the law of war, governs only during a state of armed conflict, whereas human rights law applies only in peacetime. This view has been favored by many militaries,[38] including that of the United States.[39] The demands of the two legal domains cannot run afoul because their spheres of operations do not overlap, from this perspective. Consistent with this view, very few armed forces offer their officers any exposure to human rights law, in contrast to humanitarian law training, which virtually all countries provide, albeit in differing measure.

If the conflict with Al Qaeda is not really a war at all,[40] then human rights protections pertain,[41] with their much lesser dispensation for the use of force. Most of the world, including many of America's closest allies, has been unconvinced that the conflict with Al Qaeda can fairly be described as a war or legally treated as one. They avow that detention at Guantánamo is hence unlawful for all terror suspects, even the highest ranking, when not captured on an actual battlefield.[42] The law of human rights would then pertain, rather than the law of the battlefield. And as Anthony Dworkin observes, where human rights law applies, "the right not to be held in prolonged arbitrary detention appears to demand that all detained terrorist suspects be given a chance to appeal against the detention before a neutral tribunal, as well as regular review of the continued need for holding them."[43]

Even where violence is organized and intense, there may be no legal state of war under current rules. For instance, when the United States targets terrorist leaders in other countries (or renders detainees there), it often confidentially secures the consent of the other state involved.[44] But this very consent "offers a strong argument for . . . the human rights paradigm," notes a leading international lawyer. "For once the target state consents, one can claim that there is simply no armed conflict at all on its territory," since that state has ratified the actions involved and the law defines "armed conflict" as a confrontation between states, including their affiliated militias.

It follows that if no state of war exists, then "both the target state and the United States are necessarily bound by human rights law . . . for two states cannot simply consent to displace international human rights law with *jus in bello* by declaring that they are engaged in an armed conflict with a non-state actor on the territory of one of them."[45] Yet if this result indeed follows from current rules, strictly construed, then that may suggest the moral urgency of new rules or more capacious interpretation of existing ones. This is not to claim, of course, that states should be able simply to resolve and stipulate that they are at war without any material indicia of sustained, organized violence "on the ground."

Even if elements of the pertinent conflict might fairly be described as a war, it turns out that people may have certain human rights in war as well as in peace, so that both bodies of law apply. Certain aspects of the conflict with Al Qaeda can be analyzed in terms of the parties' human rights, many observe. Rendition of terror suspects to home countries where there are "substantial grounds for believing" they may be tortured,[46] for instance, probably runs afoul of the International Covenant on Civil and Political Rights and the Convention Against Torture, which prohibits complicity in the practice.[47] The regular rendition and extradition of ordinary criminal suspects often take place in peacetime and certainly bear no inherent relationship to armed conflict.[48] That the law of war should override conflicting claims of human rights is implausible here. And this is but one example.

Some go so far as to contend that international human rights law would now require the United States to provide judicial hearings and counsel for detainees (who assert civilian status) captured in a conventional war between states, though the Geneva Conventions themselves do not require this.[49] During the Second World War, the Allies held millions of POWs, each of whom would today enjoy such a human right to due process, on this reasoning. To enforce that right, active duty soldiers might need to be recalled from the battlefield in order to testify. The government might need to establish a chain of custody over all evidence, collected in combat, presented to justify continued detention of a given Al Qaeda suspect. This is precisely the parade of horribles often invoked by voices warning against the infusion of human rights principles into humanitarian law.[50]

The ICRC, like many human rights organizations, takes the view that human rights law is generally applicable in war no less than in peace, *mutatis mutandis.* The organization makes extensive use of human rights law in its interpretations of customary humanitarian law. This heroic view proves difficult to sustain in many places, however. As a human rights lawyer who "cross-trains" practitioners in both areas acknowledges, "A military officer schooled in the rules determining whom he has license to target might find discussion of the 'right to life' slightly vexing. A human rights professional is often equally baffled by the definition of a military objective, i.e., a lawful target. Communication breakdown in these situations can be rapid."[51] Human rights law, as one scholar writes, "is premised on near-zero tolerance for loss of human life, while humanitarian law operates within the context of conflict situations . . . in which the loss of (combatant) life is taken for granted, and allowance is made for the incidental loss of civilian life in . . . lawful military operations."[52] In short, during war a combatant may legally deprive an opposing combatant of his human right to life and liberty, albeit not "arbitrarily."

This is not to say that the two legal fields are mutually exclusive, as was long believed.[53] Peacekeeping operations, in particular, involve the armed forces in constabulary activities altogether different from those of high-intensity warfare. It is axiomatic today that human rights law applies to police work. Internal armed conflicts also concern the relations between the state and its nationals, which is the central concern of human rights law. There also exist interpretive methods for reconciling the two bodies of law at key points, as the World Court thoughtfully does in its Nuclear Weapons Advisory Opinion.[54] There, the majority employs humanitarian law to interpret an ambiguous term – "arbitrary" – within human rights law, even as Judge Weeramantry, in dissent, employs human rights law to interpret ambiguous terms within humanitarian law, invoking the latter's Martens clause as authorization for this move.[55] The Yugoslavia tribunal has since done much the same.[56]

In other contexts, the rationale for relying on the relevant *lex specialis* rather than more general legal rules, when the two diverge,[57] has always been that states are more likely to have contemplated application to the situation at hand of the more immediately pertinent body of law and so agreed to such application. The *lex specialis* rule therefore rests firmly on the very foundations of international law itself: state consent. Abandoning this rule for humanitarian law – the direction in which the World Court appears recently to have moved – consequently shakes the foundations of this larger legal edifice.

In these recent cases, the World Court has sought to apply humanitarian and human rights law simultaneously. The effect of this is to allow enhanced prominence for human rights norms than if they were rendered inapplicable once war begins, and to resolve any discoverable ambiguities within humanitarian law so that human rights goals may be advanced.[58] The likely effect will be to diminish still further the lawful scope of the reciprocity principle within armed conflict. This approach reaches its apotheosis – or nadir, depending on one's viewpoint – in the World Court's *Advisory Opinion on the Legal Consequences of a Wall in the Occupied Palestinian Territory*.[59] There, legitimate considerations of national security and their implications for how to apply rules of military necessity yield entirely to analysis of the duties of an occupying power in relation to the human rights of those residing in the occupied territory, particularly their right to freedom of movement.[60]

Some norms of human rights law may be straightforwardly applicable to situations of armed conflict despite its special vicissitudes. The particular circumstances of war, however, would surely require some reinterpretation of other human rights. In the middle of a military invasion, for instance, the right to freedom of assembly could not have exactly the same contours as before or after. So too the evidentiary protections, derived from the human right to due process, afforded those accused of war crimes where admissible evidence would have to be gathered on an active battlefield. Finally, in some cases, no interpretive method will be able to reconcile the prohibitions of human rights law with the allowances of humanitarian law (i.e., without subordinating one to the other). The task of legal scholarship today should be to discover the range of each of these three scenarios.[61]

Yet even this seemingly innocuous observation belies the extent of the obstacles. Applying two entirely distinct bodies of rules to the same situation necessarily increases the legal uncertainty faced by those occupying it. This is a practical drawback to any effort at implementing human rights law – however interpreted, stringently or indulgently – within a war zone. Enhanced uncertainty is an obvious and weighty consideration, though apparently undeserving even of mention in the extensive literature now endorsing the simultaneous application of both legal domains to armed conflict.[62]

TREATING COMBATANTS AS INDIVIDUALS, OR AS MEMBERS OF ARMED GROUPS?

On one hand, war at the macro-level is essentially a conflict between collectivities, not individual persons. It is perfectly defensible from this perspective to treat the individual members of a belligerent armed force on the basis of how its other members have behaved toward their common adversary: the other collectivity called – in the singular, not plural – "the enemy." Some have even inferred from this that targeted killing of enemy leaders (even terrorist leaders),[63] in its individualizing of response to a collectively organized threat, is based on a misunderstanding of war's very nature. This is so even as these same critics insist in the same breath that the "war on terror" is not really a war, which would presumably mean that the threat posed by terrorist leaders arises primarily from them as individuals, linked only informally to other individuals, the immediate perpetrators.[64]

On the other hand, at the micro-level, though no longer largely *mano a mano*, war still widely affords individual fighters at all organizational levels the opportunity to make important moral choices about the degree to which they will adhere to international humanitarian law. Given this fact, it seems unfair to treat one enemy captive on the basis of how his or her comrades in arms have behaved, especially when he or she has behaved much better than they. Human rights advocates like to decry the collective responsibility entailed in holding good soldiers responsible for what bad soldiers do, as lawful retaliation for war crimes permits. Yet it is at least equally true that collective responsibility is entailed in crediting bad soldiers with the conduct of their more scrupulous comrades.

With perfect information, of course, it would be easy to make the relevant distinctions and discriminations in their treatment. But perfect – or even good – information is almost invariably lacking in this regard.[65] And the particular individuals have generally served in any event as legal agents of a relevant collectivity – that is, the armed forces of their nation-state – even if this cannot so easily be said of some of the looser terrorist "networks."

Concerns with the human rights of individuals permeate key provisions of the Fourth Geneva Convention, which governs treatment of civilians who illegally take up arms, much more than the Third Geneva Convention, pertaining to soldiers who become POWs. Yet why should entitlement to POW status by particular soldiers, who may individually have committed no war crime, depend on whether their comrades have done so, whereas the rights of unprivileged belligerents are made entirely contingent on their individual comportment? Why does the law, in setting the scope of reciprocity, sometimes assimilate the individual to the group (as in the Third Convention), but sometimes not (the Fourth)?[66]

An individual soldier who regularly and flagrantly violates humanitarian law remains entitled to POW treatment and to combatant privilege as long as the armed force for which he fights is party to the Conventions and generally honors such law. (Only the question of whether he is actually a member of such a group must be individually assessed, in the fashion of human rights, i.e., whenever there is "any doubt" about this, according to Article 5.) But if that armed organization is not subject to the Conventions, then a civilian who takes up arms for it becomes an unprivileged combatant; despite otherwise adhering to the law, he appears to lose his protections as a civilian without gaining the rights of a combatant. He retains a treaty right to humane treatment under Common Article 3, if America's conflict with Al Qaeda is regarded as "noninternational," though this provision cannot be applied in isolation from relevant customary law.

The same distinction applies to the targeting of individual persons, though it ceases to have any moral basis in the current conflict. Combatants, as members of a belligerent armed force, may be targeted at any time, whereas civilians who take up arms may be targeted only "for such time as they take direct part in hostilities,"[67] as we have seen. Yet as a leading Canadian military lawyer writes,

> An individualist approach to targeting highlights the tension that arises between a human rights-based concentration on the individual and the traditional group-based concept of the combatant. Attempting to limit attacks based solely on individual conduct does not take fully into account the nature of modern warfare. While the lone actor armed with a weapon of mass destruction is a threat to society, it is the danger posed by well resourced, organized and technologically advanced groups with global reach such as al Qaeda that makes hostilities with private nonstate actors "warlike" in nature. As a result, these nonstate actors may pose the same type of group threat as members of armed forces who have the status of combatants. The "humanization" of humanitarian law with its emphasis on protecting the individual is an important endeavor, but the credibility of that effort will directly depend on the extent to which it fully accounts for the nature of warfare.[68]

A human rights approach, conceiving each Al Qaeda member as an isolated individual rather than in service of a larger armed group, does not "account for the nature of warfare" in this conflict, he concludes.

If there has been any consensus about global justice in general, it has been about the limited scope of the subject matter, as Thomas Nagel observes: "The international requirements of justice include standards governing the justification and conduct of war and standards that define the most basic human rights."[69] Yet even when the field's concern is delimited in this way (and "the most basic human rights" confined to the civil and political), disagreements quickly arise over the priority of such norms when they conflict.

We can organize and somewhat advance the current debate by casting it in terms of argumentative thrust and parry. The Bush administration's critics claim that the international law of human rights applies to wartime detention and treatment, citing the International Court of Justice, the International Committee of the Red Cross, the United Nations, and the European Union.[70] Human rights law purports to protect people as human beings, which we remain at all times, even in war. There could be few organized societal activities more inimical to basic human rights than warfare, after all, even when it is conducted lawfully. The official Commentary to the Third Geneva Convention proclaims, "With regard to the concept of humanity, the purpose of the Convention is none other than to define the correct way to behave towards a human being."[71]

The Bush administration responds that it is not human rights law, but rather humanitarian law – especially that governing the means and methods of warfare – that applies to the conflict with Al Qaeda and kindred groups. The more specifically applicable law always overrides any contrary general law.[72] We may all be *homo sapiens*, bearing basic rights as a matter of *lex generalis*,[73] but more to the point is that – when at war – we are also combatants and civilians, statuses unique to armed conflict. This view of the *lex specialis* doctrine is that, when the more specific requirement seems to conflict with the more general, the first simply overrides the second. But a second understanding of *lex specialis* is that the more specific rule should be understood, wherever possible, as an application of the general rule to a more particular context. The general rule then remains relevant in interpreting the specific, in resolving the latter's ambiguities. This second approach is widely applied to conflicting provisions within a single treaty, however, rather than to the conflicting demands of distinct treaties within different legal fields.[74]

When states are at war, the law of war is the applicable *lex specialis*.[75] Human rights treaties, the administration also argued, focus on protecting people from the abusive policies of their own state. When a state ratifies such treaties, it does not generally intend them to apply beyond its borders (except perhaps when it exercises complete control),[76] certainly not to interstate wars in which the given state is not even a belligerent. The deeper rationale here is that, though we may always be individual humans, reciprocity is equally a ubiquitous feature of the human condition within society, as Rawls observes,[77] one to which the law must therefore attend. A proclivity to reciprocity, for good or ill, is one of the traits that make us human. Attention to our common humanity, then, does not foreclose due regard for reciprocity in the design of social institutions, including that of humanitarian law.

That said, the impulse to reciprocate is shared by some advanced apes and so is not uniquely human.[78] Yet any doctrine of human rights based on the belief that humans are radically different from all other animals is likely to fail, in any event.[79] The reason is hinted at in the recent legislative efforts within Western Europe to extend certain human rights – hitherto understood as such – to the higher apes.[80] The inclination to treat terror suspects on the basis of their human rights rather than their (apparent rejection of) rationally self-interested reciprocation is also not exclusively human. It is their continued capacity for suffering that stirs this "humanistic" or "humanitarian" impulse in us, their captors. But the capacity for suffering is shared with most animals. So is the propensity to offer support to another in suffering,[81] as every dog owner seems quick to attest. And the avoidance of unnecessary war-related suffering has always been the principal aim of humanitarian law. If our chief concern is with avoiding the detainees' superfluous suffering, then both humanitarian and human rights doctrine prove too little, because we are also concerned with the superfluous suffering of certain nonhumans. Moreover, human rights law advances myriad social aims – such as religious and political freedom – other than preventing suffering. As a rationale for our legal rules, the concern with avoiding unnecessary suffering hence does not uniquely fit and justify either body of law, in isolation or combination.

The attempted infusion into humanitarian law of human rights law is much more recent. At Nuremberg and since, courts and legal scholars have debated whether the full measure of suffering experienced by war's victims in a given situation was actually necessary to achieving the desired military results. The key point is simply that there is nothing specifically human in the moral impulse to treat suspected terrorists according to their human rights. The humanity of human beings "proves too little" in explaining the scope of relevant law, which is aimed at preventing superfluous suffering and hence encompasses the law criminalizing cruelty to animals.[82]

We criminalize such cruelty because we think, for instance, that torturing animals is wrong, and not merely uncharitable. And we may feel this even if – as in the case of cows and pigs – we have no compunction about eating them, especially if they experience no unnecessary suffering in the course of their treatment. Hence America's Humane Slaughter Act,[83] requiring that cattle to be rendered senseless, as painlessly as possible, before any cutting of flesh. As Scruton writes, "Animals bred or kept for our [culinary] uses are not honorary members of the moral community, as pets are. Nevertheless the use we make of them imposes a reciprocal duty to look after them . . . To criticize battery pig farming as violating a duty of care is surely right and proper . . . Where there are conscientious carnivores, there is a motive to raise animals kindly."[84] But our duties to such creatures do not arise entirely from their ability to reciprocate, which after all is quite limited. The notion of reciprocity as mutual advantage therefore does not fully capture our considered judgments about what justice requires. For that matter, when we are born, none of us is able to reciprocate much of anything to anyone.[85] If social order were to require immediate reciprocity from everyone, the species would quickly come to an end.

What, then, *are* the moral limits of reciprocity, precisely? How should these limits figure within humanitarian law generally and U.S. counterterrorism policy specifically? That is a question to which we return in later chapters. The current discussion only suggests the limitations of human rights discourse as guidance to counterterrorism law.

Though we are admittedly human beings even in war – not exactly a deep insight – we could as easily observe that peacetime social relations regularly display highly conflictive, almost war-like features, as many prominent thinkers have stressed.[86] There is surely no more common characteristic of human behavior throughout history, moreover, than "man's inhumanity to man" (and to other species), leading John Gray to offer *homo rapiens* as more apt as a species-distinguishing moniker.[87] Our shared humanity, in other words, is neither confined to nor defined by our desire to be treated with dignity.

One may still object again that, if there is no actual state of war, then the law of armed conflict simply does not pertain. Its traditional deference toward the reciprocity principle is beside the point, for this principle occupies no comparable force within ordinary criminal law, much less in the law of human rights. Opponents of Bush administration policy, however, were the first to describe America's current political reality as one of permanent and ubiquitous war, albeit a state of war allegedly created by the United States itself.[88] The Bush administration might respond that the American public has clearly accepted the trope of a "war" on "terror" as the apt narrative framing of the political moment.[89] And humanitarian law is in key places even more protective of noncombatants than is human rights law,[90] which allows administrative detention even outside the context of criminal prosecution.[91]

President Bush's critics reply that humanitarian law is not material to the national circumstance, because there exists no general state of armed conflict against "terrorism" as such, only discrete attacks at specific times and places by distinct terrorist groups, as on 9/11 by Al Qaeda in Manhattan and Washington, D.C.[92] Though the ICRC strongly asserts this position, none of its many publications on the subject of armed conflict offer any real definition of the beast, much less the narrow definition the organization selectively chooses to employ here.[93] Defenders of the Bush administration also retort that individuals within many countries are committed to violent jihadist militance. They are admittedly far-flung but sometimes demonstrably linked. The law ignores this patent geopolitical fact only at the risk of becoming unable to confront key challenges presented by the world before us.

The president's opponents answer that, even if only humanitarian law applies, its principal goal – protecting human dignity, when politics severely threaten it – is essentially the same as that of human rights law.[94] Key legal doctrines therefore straddle both fields, such as the "necessity" defense and the prohibition on "excessive force" by public authorities.[95] Human rights law might hence set some desirable limits on humanitarian law's easier indulgence of violence. This might mean, as the Israeli Supreme Court concluded, that the human right to life does not allow targeting civilians participating in hostilities when arresting them for trial is equally possible, even if doing so may put those conducting the arrest at risk.[96] In this view, ambiguities in humanitarian law – and there are plenty – should be resolved by reference to human rights law, which has enjoyed much greater judicial attention and refinement in recent decades.[97]

Yet even when the two legal fields employ the same term, it often refers to entirely different matters. This creates the translator's perennial problem of "false friends." For instance, both human rights law and humanitarian law require "proportionality" in the use of force. In human rights law, the term refers to the degree of force that may lawfully be exercised on a person in the course of arrest. Therefore, the police must employ only the minimum degree of force necessary. In humanitarian law, by contrast, the targeted individual may be killed, so proportionality refers only to the measure of force applied against surrounding persons and property. Same word, two meanings: one for soldiers on a battlefield, one for police investigating a crime.

Neither body of law would gain anything in borrowing from the other here. It is sometimes unclear in a quickly shifting operational theater whether a situation of armed conflict exists, as indicated before. The soldier obeying "shoot-to-kill" rules of engagement seriously risks criminal liability if jury members later find that the condition of war had, perhaps only hours before, become a circumstance of peace. They may find that he should have sought to arrest his target rather than firing on him.[98] Down this road lies the point at which "a soldier on the battlefield can only fire in individual self-defense,"[99] narrowly interpreted, some protest. Since at least one scholar of international law seriously defends this result,[100] its invocation here in counterargument cannot be dismissed as a mere hypothetical *reductio ad absurdum*.

Administration defenders also observe that humanitarian law, though often ambiguous at the margins, is hardly novel or untried; it directly derives from just war theory, which is "one of the few basic fixtures of medieval philosophy to remain substantially unchallenged in the modern world," as one author notes.[101] This is not to say that, just because such law has been around for centuries, it should remain insulated from influence by more modern human rights ideas. It is only to register the fact that humanitarian law has a long and rich history of thinking through certain enduring problems presented by warfare in all its known forms, essential to the enterprise as such.

In any event, finding a similarity of purpose between humanitarian and human rights law at so high a level of abstraction as the defense of human dignity tells us little about how to resolve concrete problems, where the devil inevitably lies in the proverbial details. Much of modern law, after all, could be said to be concerned with protecting human dignity, in one way or another. The rules on releasing a person who has been incarcerated for coercive civil contempt, for instance, reflect an avowedly humanitarian concern with avoiding needless suffering by anyone demonstrating that he or she cannot be pressured into obeying the court's injunction.[102]

It is true, as one leading Swiss ICRC lawyer contends, that "both branches of law" – humanitarian and human rights – "try to protect people from unnecessary violence to the degree possible whilst respecting the perceived needs of society."[103] But the same could be said of many other legal rules, even the tort law of auto accidents, inasmuch as it seeks to reconcile society's desire for motor vehicles with its desire to minimize the unnecessary suffering of easily preventable accidents. The notions of human dignity and preventing unnecessary suffering thus provide no strong basis for yoking our two particular bodies of law together, for interpretive purposes, more than many other potential pairs.

The differences between humanitarian and human rights law are surely as salient as the similarities, moreover. The international law of human rights does not directly create any individual criminal liability. Human rights obligations are directly binding on states alone, whereas humanitarian law binds (and protects) both states and their nonstate antagonists. The ambit and approach of the two fields are therefore decidedly different.

There does exist an Optional Protocol to the Civil and Political Rights Convention enabling any state to charge another with human rights abuse occurring within the latter's home territory.[104] Yet most states have not ratified this Protocol, and no ratifier has ever invoked it.[105] The patent reason for both facts is that any state initiating such a formal proceeding against another may expect to have a similar charge promptly filed against it by the accused.[106] The Human Rights Committee charged with enforcing these treaties understands its mandate broadly and hence interprets the applicable law expansively. Thus, it is entirely plausible that the counterclaim would display sufficient legal merit to prove greatly embarrassing to the initial accuser, who would then also be an accused. The logic of reciprocity, in the sense of a propensity to meet like with like, thus explains the complete uselessness, in practical terms, of this entire Protocol.

In applying human rights law to situations of armed conflict, human rights courts also tend to push and arguably exceed the limits of their legal authority, their jurisdictional competence,[107] strictly speaking. This practice illustrates the larger problem that, when specialized courts stray beyond their immediate jurisdictional tether, they tend to privilege their own field's concerns over the other implicated bodies of law. The clearest case of this in the international arena is the treatment of environmental and human rights issues by the WTO.[108] Even defenders of the practice acknowledge that human rights courts have indeed "cloaked" the "implicit application" of humanitarian law doctrines "in the [Human Rights] Convention-specific categories" over which their authority uncontroversially extends.[109]

In recent years, international courts charged with applying humanitarian law have admittedly been almost equally expansive in interpreting their mandates, much enlarging the protections afforded by the law of war.[110] Yet such expansion has taken place by way of incorporating human rights, rather than overriding them. Even human rights law expressly authorizes derogation from most of its protections during declared emergencies, many of which are created by war.[111] President Bush did issue a November 2001 decree that sought to "proclaim a national emergency."[112] But derogation from human rights law requires officially reporting this to the UN and cannot in any event abrogate peremptory norms, as against torture, to which a state may be subject.[113]

Insofar as certain humanitarian norms *are* peremptory norms,[114] this fact becomes the basis for efforts by human rights advocates to subsume humanitarian law within their own domain, subordinating the rules of war – or elevating them, if you prefer – to higher moral standards. Even a revised Geneva Convention for fighting terrorists, if it sought to impose more stringent reciprocity conditions for favorable detainee treatment, could not today override the more onerous demands imposed by *jus cogens* norms derived from human rights law, including the Convention Against Torture.

Still, the United States interposed "reservations" to such treaties when ratifying them. These reservations have appeared to set limits, for instance, on the rights of aliens held overseas – perhaps especially those entrusted to other state parties to the Convention Against Torture. Whether U.S. constitutional rights applied to such persons at all, or with what restrictions, remained unsettled questions.[115] Many contend that this is why coercive interrogation has been taken offshore. In this way, the "boundaries of the firm" are altered without affecting the substance of production or, in this case, destruction. A legal critique of U.S. detention policy would therefore have to turn from treaty to customary international law. The United States had accepted parts of Geneva Additional Protocol I as reflective of binding custom,[116] but the most recent U.S. Operational Law Handbook abandons this position,[117] which never encompassed the provisions placing unprivileged belligerents in protective parity with combatants.[118]

If either body of law has fair claim today to gobble up the other, it is surely humanitarian law, not human rights. For the likelihood of further jihadist attacks on Western interests throughout the world and the legitimate concern with preventing them make it no longer possible to speak unequivocally of the periods between attacks as peaceful. The conceptual breakpoint between traditional war and other forms of violent conflict has been eroding for some time, and its effacement is certainly not unique to the conflict with Al Qaeda. The Cold War ignored that line as well. The period following World War II witnessed many guerrilla insurgencies, with their quintessential strategy of blending into a peaceful, civilian population.[119] Even the fiercest critics of the Bush administration have come to acknowledge that such "traditional legal categories" as war and peace had come to display "increasing incoherence and irrelevance."[120]

A conscientious military officer concerned with minimizing civilian casualties as much as with protecting his troops would very likely blanch at the insouciant statements of leading humanitarian lawyers on these matters. Such lawyers lecture one another that "human rights law . . . does not concern itself as to whether there is an armed conflict or not,"[121] or "in no circumstances can any of the two bodies of law [human rights and humanitarian] be invoked as curtailing the level of protection afforded to the individual under the other body of law,"[122] pronounces one Oxford don. The higher of the two standards must always prevail, in other words, which will generally be the human rights standard.

No legal authority is offered for this conclusion, nor other argument from practical reason of any sort. We soon see that the very opposite of this view will prove closer to the truth: that conflicts between humanitarian and human rights law are many and increasing (due to the latter's ever more capacious claims); that, during war, humanitarian law trumps human rights in the event of conflict; and that, even when human rights law is not displaced in this way, the human right to personal security prevails over other human rights that democratically accountable leadership finds inconsistent with it. For such writers as those just quoted, by contrast, the empire of human rights knows no limits; it knows exceptions "in no circumstances." A state of armed conflict is apparently irrelevant to whether or how human rights law should be applied, according to the first of these two authorities. There is no need for compromise or accommodation, in other words, between the differing purposes and provisions of each legal universe.

Faced with such preening aggrandizement, professional soldiers would rightly be tempted to go instead with their own situational judgment, to trust their ingrained sense of martial honor, and disregard altogether the clacking and strutting of the earnest jurists. Who needs them? And so, who needs the law for which they claim to speak? Such would be the natural and perfectly intelligible response to the hauteur veritably dripping from such statements. A very tempting response, surely, if ultimately misguided.

In vain, one searches the considerable scholarship on humanitarian law for any serious engagement with work on military history, military technology, military sociology, or security studies – in fact, for any awareness of the likely implications of particular legal rules (and their alternative interpretation) for the practice of war at the operational and tactical levels.[123] Any honest effort to apply such key legal concepts of proportionality and necessity to a given use of force, for instance, generally requires close attention to the relative capabilities of alternative weapons systems, knowledge in which few civilian humanitarian (much less human rights) lawyers show any interest. A knowledge of reconnaissance and intelligence-gathering methods would be equally essential to any attempt to apply the legal requirement that anyone who decides on an attack must do everything "feasible" to verify that objectives targeted are not actually civilian.[124] Instead, a few days of tourism on an aircraft carrier while at peace is apparently considered sufficient experience with the U.S. military to expatiate for Princeton University Press on how law should govern it.[125]

Distinguished human rights lawyers routinely exhort military officers and their JAG advisers to learn about how armed service activities are increasingly affected by developments in human rights law. But as just indicated, one sees virtually no corresponding effort on the part of human rights lawyers and even their judicial sympathizers to learn anything in depth about the military arts and how their technical nuances might affect the intelligent application of human rights law to armed conflict. For instance, one might naively suppose that a legal conclusion, such as Judge Christopher Weeramantry's in the World Court's Nuclear Weapons Advisory Opinion, that "there is no possibility whatsoever of a use or threat of use that does not offend the principles," i.e., of discrimination and proportionality,[126] – presumably even a threat to employ small-scale tactical weapons against warships on the high seas – would require at least a modicum of empirical support. It receives none, however. This is as if one were to write confidently about all of antitrust law while knowing no economics or to expound on patent law without any familiarity with engineering. One is tempted to say here, as Trotsky insisted of the dialectic, that international law and its practitioners are uninterested in the tactical and operational details of warfare does not mean that war is uninterested in them.[127]

Despite its alliterative appeal, to speak of a "coming clash" between humanitarian and human rights law (given the major differences between how the United States and most other states understand these bodies of law), understates the longstanding nature of the tension. But the increasing frequency of joint operations between America and its allies has accentuated it, to say nothing of the increasingly stringent demands of international human rights jurisprudence itself. In this clash, American JAGs will be called on to serve as implicit mediators between the opposing forces of United States military command and human rights advocates. The recent JAG Handbook and Counterinsurgency Field Manual both acknowledge that American troops will have to coordinate procedures with allied forces in most future operations and that Western European and Australian forces often seek to accord considerably more ample berth to human rights law within their rules of engagement than does the U.S. military.[128] The workaday imperatives of organizational "interoperability," further discussed in Chapter 12, therefore ensure that the "philosophical" differences will soon have very practical ramifications for joint military operations. Whether the JAGs can find creative and defensible ways to harmonize the conflicting approaches of American and allied armed forces toward the relation of humanitarian to human rights law remains an open question.

At very least, this and the previous chapter show that pertinent law – as properly understood in light of both international custom and America's very guarded incorporation of relevant treaties – does not unequivocally adopt a deontological view rejecting coercive interrogation and the other disputed practices here examined. The partisan scholarly effort to read such a view into the applicable legal sources, as Roth observes, "transmogrifies the [deontological moral] view from a shield" – against unjust state power – "into a sword, to slash through any positivistic obstacles that might impede the path to material justice *qua* authoritative vilification of those who have transgressed deontological norms,"[129] i.e., leading Bush administration lawyers like John Yoo.

HUMAN RIGHT VS. HUMAN RIGHT

Champions of international human rights law tell us that its failings are attributable to *anomie*: the weakness of its norms, their frail grip over our conscience and conduct. The greater problem, as the idea of human rights comes to be taken ever more seriously, may turn out to be their multiplicity. The effort in recent decades to pack virtually every potential source of human flourishing, including the right to annual paid holidays,[130] into one or another human rights treaty has ensured that almost no significant claim of right may be invoked without eliciting, in response, the reasonable invocation of a competing right, which is often incompatible. This has been observed by those on the left[131] no less than on the right, as well as by traditional liberals.

The human right to economic development, for instance, quickly runs afoul of the human right to environmental protection, the right to freedom of religion sits quite uneasily with the right to cultural preservation, and so forth, *ad infinitum*. Basic autonomy rights are often difficult to square fully with distributive rights (e.g., to social goods). And even within these two broad categories of right, conflicts are common, as between distributive claims by some people to this primary good versus demands by others to that one, given the likelihood of resource limitations. Similar conflicts arise within the traditional domain of autonomy rights. Rights of free association, for instance, regularly run up against rights against discrimination. Both are "fundamental."

In other areas of law a rule often cannot be applied without interpreting it in light of other rules abutting it, covering closely related issues, and thereby determining its ultimate scope and meaning. But that common task is more problematic still with human rights law. This difficulty is caused by the breadth and imprecision of many of its key concepts, as well as the range of human activities now encompassed under this field's broad canopy. The upshot is that not only is international human rights law frequently dissonant with several other fields of domestic and international law (environmental, trade,[132] health and safety, etc.) but the field is also conflicted internally, often virtually at war with itself.

Because they seek to embody the highest ideals of our species, human rights treaties tend to be drafted in more loosely capacious language than

ordinary legislation or other treaties. Well-crafted legal documents anticipate the possibility of normative conflict among their respective provisions,
as well as between their terms and those of other applicable legal authorities. A careful attorney prepares documents so that they establish priorities
that will help resolve such conflicts, as by specifying that "in no event shall
provision X be understood to interfere with the operation of provision Y,"
thereby subordinating X to Y if conflict between them arises. In such ordinary, competent legal drafting, the door to a simple balancing of conflicting
rights-claims is often closed off by "limitation clauses," specifying where
and when particular claims do not apply or must be overridden by other
rights.

With few exceptions,[133] human rights treaties aim too high to allow their
drafters to stoop to such pedestrian lawyerly stuff – to these mundane
but indispensable professional tasks of qualifying and cabining. But for
this reason they also fall well short of any normal measure of lawyerly
proficiency. This leaves only the question of whether, as with such domestic
constitutional provisions as "due process," it is defensible to turn over
the resolution of the resulting normative conflict – even conflicts eminently
foreseeable when drafting – to the courts, domestic or international. Judges –
who in many countries are unelected and life-tenured – inevitably acquire
a great deal of power when virtually every provision of a human rights
treaty displays the same level of lucidity and exactitude as that of "equal
protection."[134]

More to the point, the human right not to be tortured or subjected
to detention without charges begins to run up against the human right
to "security of the person" – as from terrorism – guaranteed in the Universal Declaration of Human Rights, the International Covenant on Civil
and Political Rights, and the European Convention of Human Rights.[135] As
Waldron admits, "Rights versus rights is a different ballgame from rights
versus social utility. If security is also a matter of rights, then rights are at
stake on both sides of the equation, and it might seem that there is no violation of the trumping principle" – that basic rights trump social utility –
"or of the idea of lexical priority when some adjustment is made to the
balance."[136] According to the expressive theory of law on which Waldron
relies,[137] the policies at issue would be objectionable only if motivated and
publicly defended by straightforward reference to the desire to advance the
general welfare by avoiding future attack. But the same policies would be
constitutionally acceptable, on this view, if adopted for the reason of protecting the right to personal security, for then their expressive meaning would
be quite different. There is no principled objection, then, if democratic
leaders defend such policies in these rights-respecting terms.

Competing claims of human right are sometimes susceptible to possible resolution on the grounds that one such right is a *jus cogens*/peremptory norm, whereas the other is not; the former type of legal rule exercises supremacy over the latter, according to the Vienna Convention on the Law of Treaties.[138] It is possible, however, for two *jus cogens* norms (i.e., rules of equal standing at the top of the hierarchy of international legal sources) to run afoul of each other. The duty "to undertake to prevent" genocide, under the Genocide Convention, will often conflict with the UN Charter duty not to employ force or threat of force against a fellow member without approval of the Security Council. The Charter, in fact, asserts supremacy over other treaties when they conflict.[139] More pertinent to present concerns: The duty to investigate and prosecute crimes against humanity and grave breaches of the Geneva Conventions, enshrined in the International Criminal Court Statute,[140] will sometimes sit uneasily with the duty not to employ coercive methods of interrogation prohibited by the Convention Against Torture. Both norms are peremptory.[141]

In liberal theory, political society emerges from the state of nature through an exchange of unfettered freedom for enhanced security. As Hobbes famously held,[142] expressing a view endorsed by many since,[143] the right to personal security is a necessary condition of enjoying most other rights. This right is not similarly contingent on any other right.[144] The executive director of Amnesty International concedes that the right to be "free from the threat of terrorism is . . . our right as human beings," one that "terrorists surely vitiate when they injure or kill civilians."[145] One may wish to respond sardonically, that apparently "in this new era" of counterterrorism "fundamental human rights related to liberty and security can acquire radically new meanings,"[146] never intended.

Some might assert that such complaints ring hollow when proclaimed from political quarters sympathetic to notions of "dynamic" interpretation.[147] A dynamic approach allows longstanding legal provisions to be legitimately reinterpreted to promote greater horizontal coherence with the wider *corpus juris*, as the latter evolves in light of changing public perceptions of social need. The enhanced concern with terrorism, reflected in a post-9/11 UN Security Council Resolution and domestic legislation implementing it,[148] would presumably constitute one notable such change. If there is nothing amiss as such in the dynamic interpretation of statutes and treaties, then the method may presumably be employed for a wide variety of policy ends.

One might reply that the human right not to have one's personal security destroyed by terror is simply not justiciable in the way the right to be free from torture may readily be brought before the courts of the state responsible.[149] However, the international human right to security of person from violence, public or private, is now justiciable in certain countries, notably South Africa.[150] And many human rights, notably those in the Covenant on Economic, Social, and Cultural Rights, are no more easily (nor intended to be directly) justiciable than the right to personal security, though Canada and parts of Western Europe have successfully made them so in recent years.[151]

The binding legal status of such rights is insisted on by most who reject the human right to personal security as a legitimate basis for counterterrorism law and policy. But if the former can be made justiciable, so can the latter.[152] Closely related, some claim to distinguish the "negative" (and uncontroversial) elements of the right to security, requiring merely that the state not interfere with the individual's interest in physical integrity, from the right's "positive" aspects.[153] In the latter and more controversial sense, the right to personal security would entail proactive public measures designed to reduce the likelihood of terrorist attacks. These would likely encompass many of the policies adopted by the Bush administration.

But again, some might charge that such a distinction by human rights advocates rings false. After all, several existing human rights treaties require "positive" state provision of extensive social services. Either treaties may impose positive public duties on ratifying states or they may not. The legal duties invoked, moreover, involve not only those proclaiming rights in the domain of the economic, social, and cultural. Duties of public provision are said to derive from the right to security itself, now understood to demand distribution of material resources necessary to the full development and exercise of basic human capabilities.[154] From this perspective, the right to security might "thus entail not merely duties to avoid violating human dignity by discrete and direct acts of violence." It might also entail "duties affirmatively to protect the right-bearer from violence and from analogous inflictions with similarly dehumanizing effects."[155] If the world now has a proactive "responsibility to protect" victims of human rights abuse from criminal states, as influential cosmopolitans now widely maintain,[156] states themselves surely have a responsibility to protect their nationals from the existential threat to personal security represented by transnational jihadist terror.[157]

One may also question the wisdom of broadening the definition of the human right to security of person – as social democrats and others to their left seek to do – so far beyond its original treaty meaning: freedom from threat of violent harm to person. For it then becomes too expansive to offer much guidance on how to distribute scarce resources among competing public priorities in the security domain, now much enlarged. In theory, this human right justifies almost everything; in practice, it justifies virtually nothing whenever tradeoffs must be made. The law is then cast back toward upon a dreaded "balancing." This will often entail balancing not only the relative moral weight of conflicting abstract rights-claims but also the practical consequences of prioritizing one or the other in implementation.

There is "something almost always overlooked," Richard Tuck wisely reminds, in the current enthusiasm for human rights as an antidote to war's violence and to wartime restrictions on civil liberties. We tend to neglect that "unless certain special and unusual conditions are in place, a theory of natural or human rights is more likely to lead to a *weakening* of the civil liberties embedded in the legal system of a society. Utilitarian modes of thinking, surprisingly enough, can often *strengthen* them."[158] It is no accident, then, that "utilitarian philosophers were . . . notable fighters for a range of civil rights in their societies," whereas "the first generation of natural rights theorists . . . explicitly defended slavery and absolutism."[159] For the latter thinkers, "the first duty of any government, understood as the agents of its citizens, was to safeguard their natural rights."[160] The right to self-preservation was always the most fundamental of these natural rights, according to seventeenth-century rights theorists[161] – not only Hobbes, but also Grotius and Pufendorf, fathers of modern international law. More recently, the English social democrat Bernard Williams could still write that the first question of politics is always "the securing of order, protection, safety, trust, and the conditions of cooperation. It is 'first' because solving it is the condition of solving, indeed posing, any others."[162] An interpretation of human rights that privileges physical security of the person from terrorist attack hence does not require some novel extension of the doctrine beyond its original intentions, but simply a return to its first principles.[163]

The left's recent embrace of human rights rhetoric abandons Marxism's foundational dismissal of such rights as irremediably bourgeois, but preserves its view of the social order as a fiercely implacable force always – especially during concocted "emergencies" – bearing down upon the isolated individual, the exercise of whose rights are hence ever in danger of succumbing to repression. What endures in the social theory of the left after Marxism, in other words, is the view that the public order of Western liberal capitalism is solid enough that it can essentially take care of itself, that it is strong enough to fend off any current challengers, once from class-conscious mobilization, now from militant jihadist networks – and certainly from human rights movements. Those of other ideological orientations, especially but not exclusively traditional conservatives, have tended to view the social order as an acutely precarious achievement, ever in need of authoritative bolstering, in perennial danger of being sapped, even deliberately sabotaged, by exaggerated claims of individual right, whether couched as "human" or more routinely legislative. In this context, an insistence on reciprocity in social relations does take a necessarily "conservative" turn, insofar as human rights are understood (by many) as endorsing the claims of precisely those who refuse to reciprocate the benefits that state and society confer upon them. The ideal-typical terrorist embodies this refusal to accept a correlative and commensurate personal burden.

According to much modern political theory, if a state fails to provide its citizens with the most basic physical security from violence, it breaks the social contract on which its existence is justified. The law of military occupation partly adopts this reasoning, as shown in this book's Introduction. Throughout history, belligerents have sought, by attacks on civilian interests, to demonstrate to the enemy's population that its rulers are unable to perform this first duty of any sovereign, with a view to encouraging public repudiation of such rulers' authority.[164] "Your regime cannot protect you, so accept our rule."[165] This is both a threat and an offer.[166]

Today's terrorists do not make quite this claim, of course. But theirs is not far different: "Your regime cannot protect you, so pressure it to accept our terms"[167] regarding its policies toward the Muslim world. Terror aims to interfere with the state's performance of its first duty, preventing it from honoring the promise of physical security in exchange for which individuals abandon the liberties of a hypothetical state of nature. In this attack on the moral foundations of the liberal polity, terrorism presents a threat far more profound than any risk of death to the individual citizen. Yet the liberal state also breaks this contract if it violates the citizen's most valued civil and political liberties in hopes of providing such security. And no global social contract can compensate for this violation at the domestic level, even if it ensures other important public goods.

One definition of tragedy is an encounter of right against right. Befitting Europe's sanguinary history, its liberal and other methodological-individualist thinkers – from Hobbes through J. S. Mill, and beyond – readily acknowledged that claims to various liberties might well turn out to conflict.[168] Europe's recent history of genocide, in particular, ensures that the individual's right to dignified treatment leads to the criminalization of hateful speech of a variety that America's First Amendment protects and that an American can readily find online at any time.[169] In contrast to Europe, liberal political and legal thought in America, epitomized by Rawls and Dworkin, has been more cheerful and ambitious, avowedly "Herculean,"[170] preferring to see our liberties as unified into a single coherent system, so that – properly understood – they need never directly collide.[171] Dworkin concludes that freedom of speech, for instance, does not clash with hate speech, since the latter is neither a genuine freedom nor truly speech.[172] And freedom of association that runs afoul of anti-discrimination law isn't really free. One could presumably perform this magic trick *ad infinitum*, dispatching inconvenient rights at will.

The contemporary international celebration of human rights, inspired in no small part by the seeming success of America's postwar civil rights revolution, often uncritically partakes of this same heroic hope. Another strand of (European) liberalism has never succumbed to this illusion, however. It has consistently held, with Isaiah Berlin, that "reason underdetermines, if not basic values themselves, at least their relative weight and priority when they come into conflict. And they will," Galston adds, because "value pluralism defines an inharmonious moral universe."[173] When values "compete," the legal norm that each embodies simply defines the other's interpretive outer limits, permitting their coherence.

International law would do better to follow the European tack than the American here, for the plurality of values – and disagreement over their rank ordering – is still greater in the global order today than in the domestic. The sobering experience of international relations counsels caution about whether normative theory might someday resolve such intractable questions to widespread satisfaction. The tumultuous history of such relations lends the law an elective affinity for the more modest European approach to managing deep conflicts of value, rather than the more "Herculean" American attempt to resolve such conflict through some master moral theory.

Political and social freedom is not the natural or normal human condition, that which remains after the retreat of tyranny and repression. Rather, it is an artifact of a state that can ensure citizens' basic security. Some of the risks most threatening to human rights today no longer emanate from tyrannical states, but from weak or collapsed ones.[174] The right to physical integrity of person, then, has always implicitly required a state strong enough to provide such security. The most cursory historical inquiry suggests that the provision of security has invariably entailed certain costs to other liberties. Opinion surveys reveal Americans to be quick in their willingness to accept limits on their liberties in exchange for greater security from terrorism.[175] There is no reason to believe Americans are unique in this regard.[176]

The upshot of the preceding analysis is that any attempt to infuse the law of human rights into the law of war need not lead to repudiating reciprocity in terrorist war. Only a highly selective reading of the relevant treaties and an unconcern with actual state practice could proclaim this

result. Preserving its proper measure of independence from human rights
law allows humanitarian law to accord greater weight to reciprocity than if it
had to reinterpret its every doctrine in light of newer rules originally devised
for times of peace. To argue for retaining such conceptual autonomy is not
to imply that humanitarian law should not be made more demanding on
those its governs, as by more stringent understandings of humanitarian law
principles themselves. Further resources to this end are to be found within
the sphere of martial honor itself, in ways that Chapter 12 indicates.

It is true that *jus cogens* prohibitions, such as that against torture, occupy
higher rank in the hierarchy of legal sources than other human rights,[177]
presumably trumping the latter in the event of conflict. Yet crimes against
humanity (and grave breaches of Geneva law) surely rank very highly in any
such ordering, and the 9/11 attacks are widely characterized in these legal
terms.[178] When the right to security of person is thus violated by a crime
against humanity, it would be difficult to dismiss that right as subordinate
to any other. If this is the most fundamental human right, and if it can be
secured only through reciprocity, then the law of human rights must, by
implication, permit actions consistent with the reciprocity principle. At the
time of its formulation, the Universal Declaration was considered a success
precisely because its diverse drafters were able to agree on a set of practical
protections without need for consensus on their underlying rationale or
principles. Yet over time it became clear that "the absence of an official
theory of international human rights" became "an embarrassment," as Beitz
observes, for it meant that "there is no public basis for settling the problems
of interpretation and implementation that the framers bequeathed to their
successors."[179]

Nothing thus said seeks to deny that a philosophically defensible account
of human rights may be possible, providing a principled basis for inclusion
and exclusion of the myriad current claims to such lofty stature.[180] It is only
to observe that, even when unworthy aspirants to this status are pruned
away, there will remain conflicts of right vs. right, conflicts resoluble only
by appeal beyond the terms of human rights discourse itself. Human rights
treaties do not rank order the innumerable *desiderata* they enshrine,[181]
apart from the supremacy of certain *jus cogens* norms. Conflicting claims of
human right can hence only be resolved by reference to normative standards
external to the treaties themselves. The upshot is that conflicts of right vs.
right set severe limits to the ultimate value of human rights discourse in
deciding the direction of counterterrorism law and policy.[182]

This "deficiency," if it is one, should scarcely be surprising. After all,
the positive law of human rights today does not aspire to be a full-fledged

moral and political theory like utilitarianism or Rawlsianism.[183] It does not claim, in other words, to provide a complete blueprint for the design of all public institutions and the solution of tension among all competing public concerns. Liberal thinkers like Rawls, Bernard Williams, and Charles Taylor have been right to insist that any set of genuinely human rights – if it is to be convincing to most of the world's peoples – must not be tied to a single conception of the good, for any view of the good life will necessarily be controversial.[184] The rights designated as human must therefore be neither distinctively liberal in inspiration nor inconsistent with liberalism. Such a list would be short,[185] for the shorter the list, the less likelihood of conflict among its elements or of conflict between any such element and some contestable conception of the good. The reciprocity principle, for instance, occupies a central place within some such conceptions, scarcely any place within others. Many forms of communitarianism, in particular, would reject tit-for-tat as a central or even tolerable principle of social relations,[186] just as highly inegalitarian societies would reject reciprocity when understood as the like treatment of like cases – i.e., they would insist on differentiating 'like' cases on the basis of litigants' differing social status.

The language of human rights may even discourage the deliberation and negotiation – with their ethic of reciprocity – necessary to resolving such disagreements within constitutional democracies. For it invites "an imperialistic tendency toward non-negotiable confrontation," as one leading human rights advocate acknowledges.[187] This tendency ensures that human rights doctrine, in isolation from broader normative discourse, is often nearly useless in resolving pressing disputes. As Eric Posner correctly observes,

> People who use the language of human rights find that they cannot agree on such diverse topics as the death penalty, the role of religion in public life, female genital cutting, the treatment of women and criminal defendants under Sharia, regulation of hate speech and subversive political parties, and human rights limitations on military action – leading to religious-war style impasses that excite emotions and interfere with essential forms of international cooperation.[188]

Utilitarians like Posner are not alone in their doubts about human rights. American geopolitical "realists" largely unconcerned with morality, utilitarian or otherwise, have long been skeptical of any effort to juridify international relations along moral lines like those with which human rights advocates are especially concerned. Robert Kagan even suggests, with regard to foreign relations, that "Americans are from Mars, Western Europeans from Venus."[189] His allusion is not so much to the planets but to the ancient gods, for Mars was the god of war, Venus of love. If we may momentarily equate the love of humanity with a respect for its human rights, then the recent exhortations to infuse human rights ideas into the law of war may be seen as the attempt of Venus to seduce Mars into laying down his arms and at least briefly defer to love's knowledge. Whether he would be wise to do so today remains to be seen.

Some theory is surely needed to identify the subset of legal claims worthy of treatment specifically as human rights and of a corresponding rank within the normative hierarchy of a legal system. Current thinking about human rights wisely counsels that this worthy ideal, as a broad normative commitment, should not be confused with the ever-changing doctrinal details of the human rights law.[190] Formal codification and judicial enforcement of human rights inevitably align such ideals with the interests of those doing the codifying and enforcing. Even if 'distortion' of this sort could be avoided, human rights ideals enshrine ethical aspirations that go beyond a well-functioning body of administrative law bearing that name, that is, if the ideals are to continue to influence the assessment of positive law. "The translation of a moral right into a legal right comes at a price,"[191] these authors stress.

This is because public international law must serve purposes other than human rights, notably the autonomy of national communities to define their own conception of the good life and of the general welfare. A country's ability to defend itself in war is another such purpose, central to the current discussion. These legitimate goals constrain the scope of international human rights law in ways at odds with the normative theory often thought to fit and justify this legal domain. In fact, the judicial application of human rights law, even in peacetime, rarely refers directly to abstract moral concepts, much less their philosophical foundations, even if theorists like Dworkin believe it should.[192] Thus, the limitations of human rights law as a guide to the conduct of war may arise no less from the ambitious overbreadth of this burgeoning legal domain – emphasized in the preceding analysis – than from its underinclusiveness vis-à-vis the most general moral principles, undeniably relevant to fighting justly.

HUMANITARIAN LAW AS AN INVITATION TO WAR?
THE LAW OF WAR THROUGH A DARK, POSTMODERNIST LENS

This analysis carries the legal debate only a bit beyond where it currently rests. To shed new light on the key questions at this point requires an intellectual broadening of the discussion beyond current legal doctrine, however important that doctrine is to pending litigation. The preceding observations have sought to respond to urgent claims that novel notions of human rights should do more, assert themselves more vigorously, in relation to the older domain of humanitarian law. Yet equally worthy of consideration – and ultimately of refutation as well – is the concern that human rights law has done too much, albeit in ways unintended by its champions.

From this perspective, we should perhaps approach the entire "human-ization of humanitarian law," as ICTY President Meron heralds it and that tribunal sometimes elaborates it,[193] in much the same spirit as Foucault urged us to view the humanization of Western penal practices since the eighteenth century. Just as public torture was replaced – under an expressly humanitarian banner – by other, seemingly less brutal but equally effective methods of sanction and surveillance, so humanitarian law has been infused by human rights ideas, with no diminution in war's destructiveness.

Quite the contrary. However heartening, the history of doctrinal change – over which much scholarly ink is lovingly lavished – would tell us literally nothing about the measure of respect for humanitarian norms actually evidenced in armed conflict during this same period. For clearly, the most prominent and consistent trend throughout twentieth-century warfare was the increasing percentage of casualties suffered by civilians (and not just sexual violence to women) as a proportion of total wartime casualties. At the outset of the century, the combatant/civilian fatality rate was eight to one, whereas by 2000, it was one to eight.[194] Indeed, genocidal wars and "ethnic cleansing" campaigns like those of Rwanda and the former Yugoslavia target civilians intentionally.[195] In such conflicts, harm to noncombatants cannot be classed as incidental or collateral.

Foucault himself would surely have stressed how humanitarian law, while purporting to tame and limit war (and perhaps achieving this goal in modest respects), at once tacitly authorizes its practice, empowering its proponents in many ways.[196] Humanitarian law might even be said to resemble the many professional discourses that, Foucault claimed, enabled modern states to turn recalcitrant young ruffians into disciplined soldiers and industrial workers (as well as to regiment our polymorphous sensuality into a more domesticated heterosexuality).[197] It was this transformation of crude, coarse human material into self-disciplined modern citizens that made warfare more brutal than ever before, he argued.[198]

There is perhaps no better illustration of Foucault's contention about the link between the freedom of the modern subject and the enhanced violence of modern warfare than the fact that President Abraham Lincoln declared his Emancipation Proclamation at virtually the very moment that he authorized General Sherman's "hard war" against the Confederacy's civil infrastructure and economic base.[199] In fact, freeing the slaves *was* an attack on a cornerstone of that economic base. Enforcing their emancipation authorized greater violence to destroy both the Confederacy itself and the premodern social formation on which it rested. This same social structure, no less than southern armies, obstructed the creation of "free" labor markets in the South, with their own forms of discipline and unfreedom, in Foucault's view. In a similar spirit one might observe that in 1955, just as the United States ratified the 1949 Geneva Conventions, it also introduced the hydrogen bomb into its effective arsenal (i.e., the hitherto greatest threat to civilian immunity in the history of warfare).

The invocation of Foucault is somewhat facile here, however. The making of the modern subject had at least the alleged consequence of maintaining control over restive social forces and disruptive populations. Such control purportedly made possible modern liberal society as we know it, even if Foucault himself hardly heralded this result. To similar effect, modern Western militaries and the American in particular enlist the law at every point to render themselves more effective as killing machines. This is mostly the law of military discipline, of private contracting (for logistical supply), and administrative process, rather than the law of war as such. Yet America's armed forces increasingly invoke humanitarian law as well to justify the battlefield deaths – intended and unintended – that such law authorizes, even while these same international rules continue to impose greater limits on such violence. Humanitarian law's "bold new vocabulary," David Kennedy thus extravagantly writes, "beats plowshares into swords as often as the reverse."[200] This leads him to ponder charily, "What does it mean . . . to find the humanist vocabulary of international law mobilized by the military as a strategic asset?"[201] Or as Dawes puts it, "The unpredictably multiple functioning of all artifacts, including these [Geneva] treaties, forces the question: are the conventions tools to minimize violence or weapons to justify it? Is there, finally, any way to tell the difference?"[202]

Postmodernists emphasize the coercive power of language, the violence to which it surely contributes and sometimes even directly effects.[203] In contrast, deliberative democrats stress its emancipatory potential. Like other modes of discourse, international law can and does employ language to both ends, often in the same breath. If that conclusion appears banal, this is because the intriguing and morally trenchant issues about international law are not really about the nature of language as such. To be sure, international law must implicitly take sides on the question: "Is language violent because it names, or is violence released precisely when language fails to name effectively?"[204] Law adopts the second stance unequivocally and, for better or worse, never stops to look back. The acknowledged problems with well-intentioned law then always become ones of too little efficacy, never of too much. And "international law . . . is the limit case of the relationship between words and actions," as Dawes observes. "The power of the laws of war," in particular, "is the power, small and defiant, of speech in the face of overwhelming physical force."[205]

True, humanitarian law implicitly normalizes war's violence (i.e., the massive violence such law permits), even as it explicitly banishes war's excesses. The normalizing takes place precisely by means of the banishing and could not be effective without it. In this way, humanitarian law threatens to morph subtly from noble ideal into dubious ideology. Like other features of the liberal legality from which it derives, it "normalizes the indignities associated with the operation and maintenance of the prevailing order, while identifying as exceptional the harsh responses occasioned by that very order's contradictions."[206] The capitalist society that promises peace through the softening effects of sweet commerce does not deliver it, such critics avow. And without the resulting war, there could be no war crimes.

All this is surely true in at least a trivial sense. Even army physicians facilitate war, one could similarly say, by repairing wounded soldiers so that they may return to battle. This already begins to suggest, however, that there is nothing unique about humanitarian law . Many bodies of law both prohibit and permit, constrain and facilitate, even constitute – as in constitutional law and that of corporations – the entities or "subjects" they then also discipline and restrain. The law of war does the same. The distinguishing feature of humanitarian law may be that it so often fails in these respects. For many people, it no longer legitimates the suffering it generously authorizes. Yet neither does it effectively banish the harm it claims to prohibit. Even as it has become infused with and emboldened by human rights law, the law of war has failed effectively to control the practice of war. Whether the doctrinal progress has had any discernible impact on actual war in most parts of the world is highly questionable.

Still, war has grown decidedly more deadly to noncombatants despite, not because of, humanitarian law. Much of this harm ensues from the law's sheer violation and lack of effective enforcement.[207] If the law of war were really the supple tool of Western imperialism that some assert, it would not so often prove necessary for Western powers to violate it in order to do their will, as in Nicaragua during the early 1980s, in the 1999 Kosovo intervention, or the 2003 U.S. occupation of Iraq. The normative condition of much warfare today, especially in Africa but also in parts of Asia and Latin America, approximates the very antithesis of Foucault's vision: not one of subtle but omnipotent disciplinary mechanisms on all sides quietly eliminating human freedom, but instead a Durkheimian anomie, a noisy state of moral disorder in which fighters believe they can do whatever they wish. They are often correct in this belief and conduct themselves accordingly.[208]

If the most reprehensible wartime violence already contravenes humanitarian law, then there is no need to import into it notions of human rights in order to prohibit such harm. Where it is not already clearly illegal, this conduct may be restricted through more demanding interpretations of longstanding doctrines of humanitarian law itself, especially those of proportionality, military necessity,[209] and feasibility.[210] The combination of established jurisprudence with pertinent expert knowledge (of the sort employed in the U.S. military's "After-Action Reviews")[211] ensures that these concepts, properly understood, are not infinitely elastic, as some casually claim. One Scottish legal scholar, for instance, quotes with approval Talal Asad's contention: "Given the ultimate aim of victory, the notion of 'military necessity' can be extended indefinitely. Any measure that is intended as a contribution to that aim, no matter how much suffering it creates, may be justified in terms of military necessity."[212]

But in fact humanitarian law does not adopt so subjective a standard.[213] What was and was not necessary under the defendant's circumstances may be carefully ascertained in light of "objective" professional standards, established by way of expert testimony. This is not to deny that reasonable professionals may disagree in close cases. But that is true in all varieties of litigation. What is important is that crazed imaginings and paranoic delusion do not suffice to demonstrate the necessity of particular decisions.

Simply put, war remains different enough from other activities to warrant treatment mostly by its own rules, the stringency of which would be best enhanced not with reference to other bodies of law but simply by closer attention to war itself. Human rights advocates would do better to turn their attention to this task of internal criticism and rule revision of existing rules within humanitarian law,[214] long embraced by the professional culture of the officer class, than to incursions from without, which will necessarily appear imperialistic, self-aggrandizing, and opportunistic. Pursuing this alternative path, however, will require a willingness on the part of human rights advocates to familiarize themselves with knowledge they now disdain. Thus, to call for greater recognition of humanitarian law's continuing autonomy from human rights, and hence the continuing place of reciprocity within it, is not to seek greater protection of military prerogative against civilian "interference" with its workings.

In short, the law of war itself is not the primary problem here. When postmodernists like David Kennedy of Harvard Law School today blame humanitarian law for facilitating war and therefore also war crimes, they commit much the same error they now mock but earlier embraced. As earnest young progressives, they credited this body of law with the heroic power "to regulate swords into plowshares."[215] One prominent means to this end was always the attempt to infuse human rights concerns into the law of war. Such critics' understanding of law's role has shifted over time from perfectionist to predatory without losing any of its potency. Yet in neither respect – in its capacity to do good or ill – has this body of law ever demonstrated itself so all powerful.[216] It may be true that in international affairs "no century has seen better norms and worse realities" than the twentieth, as observes David Rieff.[217] But this does not mean, of course, that the better norms have caused or significantly contributed to the worse realities. Perhaps, the hardest thing for us law professors to understand and accept is that the world's workings are often indifferent to our professional preoccupations – that its course and contours are not always about us. If we are not to be altogether irrelevant, and if we cannot solve the world's problems, then we can at least lay claim to being part of them, still important as a source of them.

Where there has been genuine progress toward humanitarian aims, the law cannot receive much credit, however. The military arts of the richest Western democracies have become more discriminating in their ability to distinguish enemy fighter from innocent civilian. But it is their science that has permitted this and their political morality that has demanded it. Their law as such has made little independent contribution. The West's adversaries have found ever more ingenious ways of blurring that line.[218] This has much limited the discriminating capacity of even our most sophisticated weapons.[219]

The upshot of this chapter and the one preceding is that humanitarian law remains and should remain far more important than human rights in governing war and that humanitarian law gives a central place to the reciprocity principle, by way of its rules on retorsion and reprisal, particularly when one focuses on the state practice component of customary international law. If we combine these two conclusions, the effect is to undermine the widespread view that the Bush administration's counterterrorism policy was contrary to international law, that is, contrary to such international law as the United States has constitutionally adopted and incorporated into its own.

We have at this point exhausted what the law, in isolation from other considerations, can offer to guide our understanding in confronting the policy predicaments posed by the conflict with Al Qaeda. If there are good reasons for American restraint, they lie elsewhere. It is therefore necessary to turn to other fields of inquiry and to see how they may better inform and guide the law's response. The first of these fields is moral thought, to which this book's next part is devoted.

PART TWO

THE ETHICS OF TORTURE AS RECIPROCITY

4

Is Torture Uniquely Degrading?
The Unpersuasive Answer of Liberal Jurisprudence

Among the many critiques of the Bush administration's counterterrorism policies, the most penetrating and philosophically sophisticated is that of political and legal theorist, Jeremy Waldron. He focuses on torture and concludes that the practice should never be rendered lawful even if it is, he admits, morally defensible in the most extreme circumstances. This stance is wholly uncontroversial as a description of existing law, international and domestic. Yet Waldron oddly insists on resting the theoretical foundation for this anodyne conclusion uniquely on the shoulders of Ronald Dworkin. Dworkin's theory of judging and the conclusions about specific cases that Dworkin has drawn from it over the years are, by contrast, enormously controversial.[1]

Dworkin's views have rightly excited great interest among American legal thinkers for more than thirty years.[2] Their appeal lies in their promise to link practical judgment in real cases to our deepest moral commitments and to do so in a way that explains and justifies key judicial decisions that almost everyone believes were correct but that remain otherwise anomalous – that is, from the viewpoint of more standard theories of what judges, in applying the law, may rightly do. The influence of Dworkin's ideas on practicing bench and bar, to judge from judicial citations, has been almost literally nil, however.[3] These ideas require a belief in some rather contentious propositions: that the law consists not only of explicit rules but also more diffuse principles, often never fully articulated, with a "gravitational force" of uncertain reach beyond the more routine rule formulations within which they are likely to be conventionally codified.[4] Entire fields of law, though emerging over long periods from tangled histories of political conflict, are nonetheless said to display a latent "integrity"[5] in the sense of philosophical coherence, a unifying "spirit."[6]

These claims would be demonstrably inaccurate if treated as empirical propositions about the legislative process, about how statutes are enacted and applied. To this objection, Dworkin responds that his conclusions about how judges decide cases and legislators enact statutes are not really empirical at all, even if they are generally consistent with central features of observable practice in both areas. Neither do his contentions amount merely to normative exhortations about what good legislators and judges should do in their professional labors, he claims. For then, his arguments would have little claim to account for the actual activity of judges in deciding cases, a claim Dworkin wishes to make. Rather, law's integrity – neither empirical nor normative exactly – is said to be "interpretive." In practice, this assertion invariably turns out to mean that, seen in their "best light," our existing political and legal practices should properly be read to underwrite the standard, left liberal political program to which Dworkin subscribes. To be sure, Chapter 2 has already shown, by demonstrating the broad gravitational force of the reciprocity principle within humanitarian law, that this easy association between Dworkin's unorthodox procedures and his predictable results is not one of necessity and that his methods may readily be made to serve a politics he would never endorse.

Still, it is easy to see why the indistinct characterization of judicial decision making as interpretive is not entirely convincing, meaningful, or even intelligible to many of Dworkin's readers. They are told to rest assured that the requirements of legal integrity will be legible at least to the "Herculean" jurist, if not to mere mortals such as themselves. In Hercules' mind the "integrated whole"[7] of a legal field will somehow crystallize, notwithstanding its many loose threads and path dependencies. Opposing principles and policies, though equally embedded in the legal authorities applicable to a case, will necessarily differ in "weight."[8] They do not actually "conflict," though often they admittedly "compete."[9] A single right answer to every legal question is therefore always possible in even the hardest cases. Dworkin's views are invariably delivered in the most elegant and mellifluous prose. It is always tempting to let slip from mind, while luxuriating in his verbal artistry, that one must actually accept all of these remarkable contentions to find his view of judging and legislating passably persuasive.

WALDRON ON DWORKIN AND TORTURE

It is therefore odd that an essay avowedly designed as a political intervention – "Jurisprudence for the White House" is Waldron's subtitle – would wish to ground its support for what is already the settled, longstanding consensus on the key question – torture is and should remain illegal – on a theory of judging held by so small a minority of judges who, after all, apply such theories in practical contexts.[10] In short, if we need to enlist Dworkin for a "deeper" rationale for torture's banishment from our legal system (i.e., deeper than its positivist status as a well-established legal rule), then we are in deep trouble – and have new reason to worry, more than before Waldron's intercession. If one demurs from a Dworkinian understanding of our legal system, its continued repudiation of torture is rendered less likely, not more.

If this unfortunate implication is not immediately apparent, it is because Waldron almost seems less interested in criticizing torture by way of Dworkinian theory than in defending such theory by way of our already strong, considered judgments against torture.[11] Because we so deeply abhor its brutality, he suggests, we must adopt a legal theory guaranteeing its prohibition by any court asked to rule on the practice. Because Dworkin's methods furnish this result, but positivism – his perennial sparring partner – cannot, the former approach is superior. Here, the primary audience is revealed to be not the White House at all, nor even the federal courts, but Waldron's fellow jurisprudents.[12]

Waldron's central contention is that the torture prohibition is no ordinary legal rule. Ordinarily, legal rules are readily subject to revision in light of changing circumstances, positivism contends.[13] (Here, Waldron drops a footnote admitting that this statement is really "something of a caricature" of actual positivists, thereby all but conceding that he will proceed to fight a jurisprudential straw man.[14]) Rather, the torture prohibition reflects a deeper principle at the heart of our legal system: It repudiates degrading brutality as a means of achieving social order, because brutality in any form abases human dignity, which a liberal society must protect. The ban on torture is "archetypal" of this more general principle, which has far-reaching gravitational force. Its relaxation would therefore have dire and pervasive consequences for the many other legal rules that also reflect this principle.[15]

Hannah Arendt famously stressed the everyday banality beneath the Nazi state's extraordinary brutality. Reversing Arendt, Waldron wants to restore brutality's incommensurability with law's quotidian depredations. Arendt sought to show how the ignoble had come to seem commonplace, whereas Waldron wishes to render the arguably commonplace – degrading brutality – as ignobly unique. Just as Arendt's move sought to discourage the simple demonization of brutality's agents (or at least some of them, like Heidegger),[16] so too does Waldron's countermove seek to denounce those responsible for America's detainee policy. Its officiants are no mere world-weary civil servants, the once hopeful, now disillusioned cops in tough precincts or beleaguered bureaucrats like Eichmann. For Waldron, Bush's evil is not banal. It is not a mere failure to stop and think through the implications of what he and his advisers were doing.

Yet as two Bush administration defenders promptly replied to Waldron,

> The commitment to minimize law's brutality is on both sides of this argument. Where coercive interrogation can save lives, not engaging in it might seem the more brutal choice, especially to those whose lives are at stake. Those people might reasonably hold that there is a sort of brutal callousness, a self-absorbed moral precocity, in the decision to preserve that law's archetypal integrity by permitting third-party deaths to go unprevented.[17]

Their main point may be restated less provocatively in Dworkin's own idiom, in fact, in terms more congenial to Waldron. Several international treaties codify the human right to "security of the person," a right imperiled by terror. When a state ratifies such treaties, it commits itself to ensuring this right's protection.[18] The principle of nonbrutality embodied in the torture prohibition must therefore be "weighed" against the "competing" principle of personal security. Since there are now claims of principle – not merely policy or well-being – on both sides of the argument, neither assertion of right may simply "trump" the other. One could be forgiven for supposing that we here find ourselves cast back into a situation where we must merely "balance" claims that genuinely "conflict," the method so dreaded by civil libertarians and from which Dworkin claims he rescues us.

WAR IS BRUTAL, LAW PERMITS WAR, LAW IS BRUTAL

A more obvious difficulty with Waldron's position should be noted at this point. To avow that law *per se* stands for the principle of nonbrutality sits rather uneasily with the overwhelming brutality of war itself, which the law of war permits. Humanitarian law does not seek to bar such brutality, only to minimize suffering that is "superfluous" or "unnecessary" to war's ends, regardless of the nature of those ends. Most of war's suffering is inherent in the enterprise itself, however. Its standard, historic forms – which could only be called brutal – are laid out in innumerable treaties and treatises, where they meet full acceptance. In a war of self-defense, this brutality is even essential to securing justice. Law not merely allows brutality, then, but confessedly harnesses it to rightful ends. At such times, one might almost say that the law requires brutality to advance its primary moral purpose.

Even the training of soldiers, beginning in boot camp, has always been a brutalizing process:

> Individuals had to be broken down to be rebuilt as efficient fighting men. The basic tenets included depersonalization, uniforms, lack of privacy, forced social relationships, tight schedules, lack of sleep, disorientation followed by rites of reorganization according to military codes, arbitrary rules, and strict punishment. These methods of brutalization were similar to those carried out in regimes where men were taught to torture prisoners: the difference resided in the degree of violence involved, not its nature.[19]

All this is merely the brutality inflicted on the fighters themselves by war's preliminary preparations, before they see any combat. It says nothing yet concerning the brutality about to be suffered by their victims, military and civilian, once the fighting begins.

WAR AS TORTURE

A related problem with Waldron's argument is that in legal terms the line between ordinary acts of combatancy – what soldiers regularly do in war – and torture itself, which no one may ever do, is vanishingly thin. The act and its intention often are identical for both. It is only the surrounding circumstance of "armed conflict" that distinguishes the first from the second. Yet "armed conflict" itself is scarcely defined in international law.[20] The meaning of torture is somewhat clearer, consisting of "any act by which severe pain or suffering, whether physical or mental, is intentionally inflicted on a person . . . at the instigation of or with the consent or acquiescence of a public official or other person acting in an official capacity."[21] But combatants routinely do just this in war on a daily basis.

To amount to torture, the officially authorized, intentional infliction on a person of severe pain must also aim to advance at least one of several enumerated purposes. Some are very broad, however, and include "intimidating or coercing him or a third person" and "punishing him for an act he or a third person has committed or is suspected of having committed."[22] War's central purpose for belligerent states is often to "intimidate" their enemy into doing what it would prefer not to do.

States often also seek to "punish" their adversary for wrongs it has allegedly committed, before or during the armed conflict, even if punishment is no longer a lawful ground for initiating war, as it once was. To punish or intimidate a state, one must punish or intimidate its agents; that is, its combatants. Acts and intentions that would otherwise constitute torture are a principal means to this end. Therefore, lawful acts of warfare in their ample brutality do not merely resemble torture, as Elaine Scarry observed[23]: In a very real sense, they *are* torture.[24]

This conclusion must then take its place as a premise within a syllogism: There is a right not to be tortured; torture differs from lawful combatancy only insofar as it is unconnected to an ongoing armed conflict; the latter concept lacks legal definition and may well not encompass the tangle of loosely conjoined circumstances that the Bush administration describes as a "global war on terrorism."[25] Hence, many acts conducted pursuant to this enterprise entail torture. To observe as much is not even necessarily to condemn such acts. It may only be to disclose the inadequacy of the conceptual grid by which the law currently classifies them. The problem, in other words, may lie with the law, not with these purposes and activities.

Waldron must in any event distinguish brutality, which our system claims to reject, from "coercion,"[26] even the most "grueling" variety,[27] which he acknowledges as pervasive and perhaps even indispensable to that system, yet somehow "not on a continuum of brutality with torture."[28] It may well be possible to defend such a distinction, but Waldron scarcely tries, at least not in any sustained way. At the key point in this portion of the argument, his conclusions are stunningly conclusory; he simply proclaims, "Law is not brutal in its operation. Law is not savage. Law does not rule through . . . breaking the will."[29]

Noble sentiments, to be sure.

One wonders, however, what Waldron's response would be to the view that all serious punishment and certainly all incarceration are intentionally and necessarily degrading of human dignity and that both of punishment's principal purposes – retribution and deterrence – are advanced by precisely such degradation. This stance is admittedly disconcerting, but it is widely held and hence worthy of refutation. Proponents of retributive punishment from Kant onward often ignore even the possibility that degradation might be integral to it.[30] They apparently believe that any punishment required by justice cannot, by definition, be brutal.[31] (They here resemble neoclassical economists, who believe that exploitation is impossible in a competitive market, one in which the pricing mechanism ensures *ipso facto* that no one is paid more than what his services are truly worth to others. Here, Kantians and such economists may simply share an irrational measure of faith in human reason.[32])

This Kantian view reformulates the question in terms of what justice – rather than nonbrutality – warrants in a given case. That retort seems to deny by definitional fiat the possibility of a conflict between the two. Yet to say that incarceration as currently practiced in America is brutal and degrading is not to say that retributive punishment is necessarily so. A Kantian would surely respond that what makes such incarceration brutal and unjust may be precisely its disproportionality vis-à-vis most of the offenses (e.g., drug possession) engendering it.

Still, this response is insufficient in that it denies the very possibility that "part of what makes punishments effective is their power to degrade – their power to make the person feel diminished, lessened, lowered,"[33] as Whitman writes. On this view, "punishment only works when it succeeds in making the punished person feel like an inferior."[34] Like the act of military surrender at war's end,[35] punishment is an archetypal "degradation ceremony," a public ritual designed to demean offenders, diminishing both their self-esteem and social standing.[36] This degradation derives from the social meaning attached to the ritual dishonoring more than from the mechanics of its implementation on the body, which takes different form in various places and periods.[37] The astonishing revival of public "shaming" as a penal sanction[38] – long buried with the Puritans and their pillories – powerfully attests to a renewed appreciation that social order may at least partly be secured through public humiliation as the avowed goal.[39] Such sanctions also help the state preserve order without resort to incarceration or monetary penalties (which harm the convict's innocent dependents), much less to overt violence; hence, without any of the ambivalence these practices rightly evoke in us.[40]

HUMANITARIAN SENSIBILITY AND THE CONCEALMENT OF BRUTALITY: FORM VS. SUBSTANCE

We may accept that modern penality differs from torture in its characteristic form without accepting that it greatly differs in its substantive measure of brutality.[41] It is true that the enlargement of humanitarian sensibility in modern times has created a form of punishment that is more seemly, decorous, tasteful, and refined, even when arguably no less degrading to its recipients. The reader may react incredulously to this suggestion at first. Yet as David Garland, one of America's most distinguished criminologists and law professors, observes,

> The social degradation of having to share a tiny cell with strangers – which . . . involves not only a lack of privacy and personal security but often the necessity of having to perform one's bodily functions in front of others – is, in modern civilized society, a brutalizing and dehumanizing punishment in itself. But because these pains are mental and emotional

rather than physical, because they are corrosive over an extended period
rather than immediate, because they are removed from public view, and
because they are legally disguised as a simple "loss of liberty," they do
not greatly offend our sensibilities and they are permitted to form part of
public policy.[42]

The field of cognitive psychology further identifies the mental "heuristics"
by which this sanitizing process occurs in individual minds. "Unavailability
bias," in particular, leads us to underpredict the frequency of an event if an
example cannot readily be brought to mind.[43] By rendering penal brutality
invisible in this way, the modern prison renders it mentally unavailable
to us.[44] The official language of penal sanction contributes further to this
process, Garland continues:

> Dispassionate professionals ... see themselves as "running institutions"
> rather than delivering pain and suffering. Similarly the language of pun-
> ishment has been ... reformulated in euphemistic terms, so that prisons
> become "correctional facilities," guards become "officers," and prisoners
> become "inmates" or even "residents," all of which tends to sublimate a
> rather distasteful activity.[45]

Torture is very different in this regard:

> In the delivery of pain to a human being ... one always sees the immediate
> evidence of suffering, and the brutality involved is inescapable. The wince
> of pain and the scream of agony announce the fact of violence and render
> it visible, whereas the mental anguish and gradual deterioration of an
> incarcerated inmate is much more difficult to observe and much easier to
> overlook. The crucial difference between corporal punishments which are
> banned, and other punishments ... is not a matter of the intrinsic levels of
> pain and brutality involved. It is a matter of the form which that violence
> takes, and the extent to which it impinges upon public sensibilities.[46]

With beguiling nonchalance, Garland further notes that "corporal punishments" – of which torture is one – "can be inexpensive ... precisely
calibrated, their side-effects ... minimized," as by avoiding the collateral
damage to family members who are financially dependent on the incarcerated. Also, "they can be delivered reasonably efficiently and uniformly."[47]
Bentham said much the same.[48] We may take Garland's suggestion more
seriously here than he himself chooses to: Corporal punishment may sometimes be more ethically defensible than incarceration. Thus, in rejecting
corporal punishment in preference for incarceration – and of lengthier periods for even nonviolent offenses like drug use – only "the conflict between

our civilized sensibilities and the often brutal routines of punishment is minimized and made more tolerable."[49] Just as "efficient means of killing are perceived as less violent than messy ones," William Ian Miller adds, so too "imperceptible and sanitized means of brutality are perceived as less brutal than more conspicuously violent ones."[50]

One might observe in passing that Garland's rendering of the conflict between reality and our self-awareness is itself slightly sanitized, for though he chooses to couch it in neutral academic language, his is clearly a barely veiled accusation of hypocrisy. How else could one characterize three centuries of the most earnest humanitarian reform in penal practices as concerned chiefly with "aesthetics,"[51] with ensuring that the law's brutality does not "disturb the equanimity"[52] of the middle classes? This has been the "expressive" meaning of the legal reforms that he describes. The legal authorization of coercive interrogation expresses exactly the opposite, in Waldron's view: not civility, but brutality. Yet the logic and psychological dynamic of his response are the same as with Garland: State violence and attendant human suffering are rendered publicly illegitimate when publicly "expressed." Through the availability heuristic, the indignities of torture are mentally available to us in a way that those of incarceration are not.

THE MEANING OF BRUTALITY AND DEGRADATION

If one accepts any of Garland's analysis, one then confronts the problem that the Convention Against Torture flatly prohibits "degrading... punishment."[53] The avowed purpose of shaming is to degrade one's social status. The same could arguably be said of punishment generally, we have just seen. The Convention offers no definition here, but the first meaning of "degrading" offered by the Oxford English Dictionary (OED) – always a good point of departure, at least – is "to reduce from a higher to a lower rank, to depose from a position of honour or estimation . . . as an act of punishment."[54] The OED's definition of "brutality" is quite broad and requires no violence, moreover. It begins with the words "in want of intelligence" and encompasses any conduct that may be described as "coarse."[55] Brutality is not identical with degradation, to be sure. A brutal act is always intentionally so, whereas a regime of degrading treatment is not necessarily intended to have this effect. But to make our law turn on this distinction – permitting degradation but not brutality – is surely to accord undue weight to our intentionality and not enough to the actual human experience, objective and subjective, of the incarcerated. A similar point later arises regarding the excuse of incidental or collateral damage to civilians in warfare, where intentionality again must carry a moral weight it may no longer convincingly bear.

It is not difficult to imagine a system of punishment, including incarceration, that fully respects human dignity, even rights of privacy. Germany has apparently established one.[56] Yet it is an open question whether such nondegrading punishment can offer an effective deterrent within more violent societies, some of which have even restored the death penalty after experimenting with its abolition.[57] Still less clear is whether such dignified punishment can offer a sanction commensurate with the wrongfulness of the most heinous offenses.[58] To reject this concern is to abandon the goal of retribution altogether, one that Waldron does not disavow. It is therefore at least incumbent upon him to tell his readers what his conception of proportionate but nondegrading measures against terrorist violence might concretely entail.[59]

Perhaps the only answer can be that torture for purposes of interrogation is not punishment at all; the suffering it inflicts therefore should not be assessed by any notion of retributive "fit." But, then, we surely need some other, more pertinent standard for moral assessment of the practice, perhaps partly derived from our legal system's considerable experience with the practice of coercive civil contempt, by which people may be incarcerated for long periods until they agree to honor a court's prior injunction.[60]

THE LAW DOES NOT BRUTALIZE, AS AMERICA DOES NOT TORTURE

Waldron himself simply insists that any official degradation of human dignity is rejected "in principle" by "the law." This stance bears an awkward resemblance to that of President Bush himself who, in claiming that "the U.S. does not engage in torture," long relied on a Justice Department definition of that practice excluding coercive methods producing pain short of "organ failure." Similarly, Waldron appears to mandate an unduly narrow and *ex cathedra* definition of "the law." By excluding all forms of state-sanctioned brutality, however pervasive, he is content to conclude almost tautologically that "law is not brutal."

Waldron must also offer a credible account of the relation between the "*de facto* terrorizing," which he admits to be common within America's actual criminal justice system,[61] and that system's facial rejection of such brutality in any form, through its legal texts and public discourse. Again, it may well be possible to offer a reasoned basis for treating the unpalatable first of these as immaterial to the sublime second. But Waldron himself scarcely attempts this task. He displays little curiosity, in this regard, concerning the ample social science scholarship on police and prison brutality in the United States.[62]

Nowhere does he ask, for instance, how often do ordinary police interrogations for violent offenses employ deceptive and moderately violent – surely degrading – methods of the sort that such scholarship depicts as relatively routine.[63] How common would such practices have to be, one wonders, before Waldron would be prepared to acknowledge them as "systemic," in the sense of endemic to the workings of "the law"? Could they amount to the quotidian, as in many "Third World" countries,[64] without yet being regarded as truly part of the legal system? If so, then the meaning of these terms surely threatens to become mysterious, at least to any but Dworkin's most ardent epigones.

Particularly disappointing is the peremptory manner in which Waldron dispatches as "dogmatic" those like Garland who are inclined to focus on just such questions.[65] These people he dismisses as holding the view that "law's complicity with torture . . . is just business as usual."[66] (In generosity, let us set aside this hyperbolic characterization of their views.) Waldron "concedes" that prisoners are today sometimes disciplined with electric shocks, and criminal defendants regularly threatened – by prosecutors, in plea bargaining – with the likelihood of prison rape.[67] Yet he stresses that these practices nonetheless elicit both the "standard moral outrage" and the more pertinent charge that they constitute "an affront to the deeper traditions of Anglo-American law"[68] (i.e., to its archetypal principle of nonbrutality).

Perhaps.

But in any honest effort to understand our law, on what basis are we to privilege its rhetorical ideals over its more troubling empirical regularities? Any institution – like any person – is sure to appear in its "best light,"[69] after all, if we so charitably take it at its word, as it wishes to present itself to the world. What if the disparity between the law in action and on the books (or simply in our hearts, as with much of Dworkin's and Waldron's law *contra* brutality) is actually no mere fortuitous slippage or gratuitous "gap"? What if it is rather a central feature of that system itself, properly and more broadly understood?[70] And what if the noble ideal these liberal jurisprudents uphold, however appealing on its face, is in fact largely a legitimating mystification? What if it is, in other words, a public myth useful primarily in suppressing our full appreciation of that system's less attractive but integral features?

Waldron's approach to the difference between rhetoric and reality, such as it is, does not even admit this possibility, still less forthrightly confront it.[71] He condemns the "rigidly textualist" formalism of the administration's Geneva Convention interpretations.[72] He then promptly adopts a highly formalistic conception of brutality: If it lacks a formal, textual basis within our penal system, then – however pervasive in fact – it does not sully our law's deeper "integrity."[73] Interpreted in its best light, that legal system has not truly been dirtied.

One wonders here how Waldron would distinguish his view of American law from that of George W. Bush, who, when visiting Jordan just after public revelation of the Abu Ghraib mistreatment photographs, expressed his "sorrow that people who have been seeing those pictures didn't understand the true nature and heart of America."[74] Susan Sontag's reaction to this statement is telling, if predictably provocative. She suggests that the conduct depicted in "those pictures," however aberrational vis-à-vis most U.S. military personnel in Iraq, reflects essential features of our society and its norms. "It is hard to measure the increasing acceptance of brutality in American life," she admits, "but its evidence is everywhere, starting with the video games of killing that are a principal entertainment of boys – can the video game *Interrogating the Terrorists* really be far behind?"[75]

Actually, as she wrote those words, several such games were already entering the market.[76] "America has become a society," she concludes, "in which the fantasies and the practice of violence are seen as good entertainment, fun."[77] If Waldron wished to put all this in its best light, he might admittedly observe that we are at least consistent here. We display a species of Dworkinian integrity: If we are brutal in our torture of terror suspects, we are scarcely less brutal in how we treat one another – for our brutal fantasies, indulged by a huge entertainment industry, are very much part of our social reality.

All this would surprise no one less than Foucault, who viewed boot camp brutality in the disciplining of early modern soldiers as the historic archetype for the later constitution of the modern Western subject. Disciplined training to the requirements of obedient soldiering made possible modern war as we know it, in all its heightened brutality. So too, training to the constraints of modern liberal subjectivity, beginning in childhood, at once unleashes or engenders some very dark phantasms and fantasies,[78] however "playful." One need not go so far as Sontag or especially Foucault, who considered liberal society brutal to the bone, to find some value in this general line of analysis.

Taken seriously, then, a more skeptical view of the rhetoric–reality relationship within our legal systems could easily undermine Waldron's entire argument against torture. For that project seeks to show how torture and other coercive interrogation – he treats them as essentially one – may readily be distinguished from the ordinary coercion and violence at least tacitly authorized by our criminal justice system, in practices used to elicit obedience from the recalcitrant and speech from the reticent. If the highly coercive interrogation of terror suspects is indeed on the same "continuum of discomfort" as the larger legal system, then no "sacred" and categorical line is crossed by it,[79] no singular taboo violated. Torture may not be condemned on that particular basis, at least, for it simply falls at a different point along the spectrum with other forms of state brutality aimed at preserving public order. The practices at issue, one should perhaps recall here, entail sleep deprivation, forced standing, slapping, stress positions, isolation, loud noise, and waterboarding, not the "Hollywood" torture of fingernail extraction,[80] garrotting,[81] and such grotesqueries. As Senator Joseph Lieberman has said of the methods actually employed, "The person is in no real danger. The impact is psychological. It's not like putting burning coals on people's bodies."[82]

The skepticism raised here about Dworkinian jurisprudence normally sounds from the left – clearly Garland's stance. Yet the extent to which such doubts converge in certain ways with those of Vermeule and Posner, who defend coercive interrogation, is noteworthy. All three are legal realists, and realism has always cut both ways, ideologically.[83] Partisan preferences notwithstanding, both critiques pride themselves on their freedom from sentimental illusions about the coherent "integrity" of judicial decision making and the competence of judges in unfamiliar and demanding policy areas. Both correspondingly place more confidence in the avowedly political branches.

For the left, this has meant, since 1789 at least, placing more confidence in the democratic legislature, deliberating robustly and responsive to popular will, a position Waldron himself has elsewhere eloquently and incisively endorsed.[84] For Posner and Vermeule, it means according greater deference both to legislation and to the specialized knowledge of relevant professionals within the executive branch – here, those whose expertise lies in the compilation and assessment of complex foreign and domestic intelligence bearing on the threat of terror.[85]

THE EXPRESSIVE MEANING OF LAW'S BRUTALITY

For reasons never articulated, Waldron thinks it is especially important that our law not "express" brutality. A central concern with what law symbolically expresses, apart from what it otherwise does, may strike some as simply effete, a too-delicate preoccupation of the pampered. But for Waldron, law's expression of brutality amounts to a wrong independent of, and apparently on a par in odiousness with, its practice of brutality. This conclusion presumably holds true even if such brutality is necessary given our socioeconomic system, even if law's "terrorizing" effect has been essential to its relative efficacy (e.g., producing much lower crime rates since the 1990s).

Yet as Posner and Vermeule observe, "a brutal law" – authorizing coercive interrogation – "that does good," by preventing terrorist attack, "no longer expresses brutality in unambiguous form. Indeed, such laws do no more than symbolize the government's willingness to produce the greatest possible good overall. . . . If we . . . tolerate them because they produce some good, their symbolic meaning" (i.e., the public ratification of brutality) "falls by the wayside,"[86] on this view. This observation should strike a resonant chord with anyone who regards her moral standpoint as at all consequentialist. One might also ask: What social meaning does the law of a highly developed society express when it fails to provide the elemental measure of security necessary to prevent attacks on the scale of 9/11 or those in London and Madrid?

Thus, even if the law's expressive function warranted as much weight as its instrumental – a questionable claim – the message expressed in authorizing an effective regime of coercive interrogation would be, at worst, somewhat mixed, rather than unequivocally indefensible, much less evil. In any event, only an undue preoccupation with expressive meaning over the harder reality of more palpable social practices, would allow one to concur with Waldron that torture and accepted American modes of punishment do not at least lie "on the same continuum." Because torture is not unique in its brutality, such brutality cannot then be the basis for its absolute prohibition. If it is to be barred, the reasons must be sought not in Dworkin but elsewhere, as Part Four of this book seeks to do.

THE ATTRACTIONS OF LEGAL AMBIGUITY

Finally, Waldron doubts even the desirability of a clear legal boundary between prohibited and permissible conduct in interrogation. He suggests that such a bright-line rule would encourage bad faith efforts by interrogators to "push the envelope,"[87] since they would then know just how far they could go in coercing a suspect without risking criminal liability. The law should not adopt such an approach for *mala in se* crimes, he argues, where law's gravitational force rightly extends beyond its formal letter. For some time, importuning by interrogators was indeed chilled by ambiguity about the scope of their potential liability,[88] a source of serious concern at the time to David Addington, counsel to the vice president.[89] So much the better, Waldron implies. The insistent questions that military interrogators posed to their JAG advisers, transmitted up the chain of command, even played some role in the later decision of JAG generals and admirals to challenge the Justice Department's indulgent legal view of coercive methods.[90]

Yet Waldron's defense of legal ambiguity here does not accord due importance to several attractions of such vagueness from the administration's perspective. First, civil suits against public servants must be dismissed where the illegality of their conduct was not yet "clearly established" at the time it occurred.[91] This rule has led to dismissal of several suits against executive officials alleging unconstitutional detention and treatment of foreign citizens held abroad or at Guantánamo.[92] The illegality of this practice remains "unsettled," as it is, at present writing, the subject of pending litigation before the Supreme Court.[93] Vagueness here is exculpatory.

Second and closely related, legal ambiguity appeals to the potential torturer and his superiors because it precludes their prosecutor from establishing the disputed conduct as "manifestly" illegal. The state must show this to overcome the defense of obedience to one's superior's orders.[94] Finally, the law must clearly identify the practices it prohibits. This requirement makes many gruesome practices hard to justify, because the law must describe them with grisly precision.[95] Atrocious practices more readily survive when loosely described, for instance, as "the third degree" than as waterboarding, and then accompanied by a careful definition. A well-drafted regulatory authorization of waterboarding would require its explicit verbal delineation, which would not be pretty and is to be avoided.

It was no small political achievement in itself that the administration was successful in preserving a significant measure of legal unclarity for as long as it did. Several investigations into detainee abuse at Abu Ghraib concluded that, for several years after 9/11, the Pentagon declined to establish uniform standards for even military interrogations worldwide.[96] As late as November 2007, the Legal Advisor to the State Department was publicly complaining in this regard that "there is a growing recognition . . . about the need for greater clarity about what is permitted and what is prohibited."[97] Waldron is hence also mistaken about the consequences of vagueness in the legal definition of the practices he abhors. Still, it is he who has thus far offered the most searching and trenchant insight into the jurisprudential problems at hand.

5

Fairness in Terrorist War (1):
Rawlsian Reciprocity

Does the law of war provide rules that are fair for fighting terrorists? How would we go about devising such rules if we were to start from scratch, rather than merely tinkering with the intellectual legacy we have inherited from centuries of reflection on rather different kinds of armed conflict?

These large questions should be divided into parts. First, there is disagreement about whether humanitarian law is even much concerned with ensuring a fair fight. One prominent view holds that law's aspiration is more modest: merely to minimize superfluous suffering, in the language of the Geneva Conventions. Leading scholar/practitioner Michael Schmitt thus writes that "'humanitarian law . . . is neither intended nor designed to ensure a 'fair fight.'" Belligerent reprisals, in particular, "have never been justified on the basis that it is unfair for one side to be limited by humanitarian law when the other ignores it,"[1] he contends.

Still, causing suffering that is unnecessary to a state's military triumph could surely be described as unfair to those – both civilian and soldier – personally experiencing it. The law of war is very much concerned with fairness in this sense.[2] But more in question, perhaps, is whether humanitarian law is much dedicated to achieving fairness between antagonists. The notion of avoiding unfair advantage between such entities finds no textual expression in the Conventions themselves or their drafting history. Yet it is hard to imagine any other basis for it, and Schmitt cites no evidence or authority, historical or contemporary, for his conclusion. Perhaps he has in mind the legal requirement that reprisals be employed "for the sole purpose of compelling the adverse party to cease committing violations" of humanitarian law.[3] The right of reprisal is therefore reserved, as by Britain with this quoted language, as permissible only to the extent necessary and proportionate to protection of the retaliating state's own troops and civilians.

Since its very inception, humanitarian law has regularly spoken of seeking a "fair contest," as Gentili put it,[4] as when abjuring poison as "treacherous,"[5] on the grounds that a combatant must not be denied the "chance to defend himself," in Grotius's words.[6] The law of war has always prohibited perfidy, defined as "acts inviting the confidence of an adversary to lead him to believe that he is entitled to, or is obliged to accord, protection . . . with intent to betray that confidence."[7] Perfidy is presumably prohibited because it is considered unfair. Similarly, the law of war has long condemned the assassination of political leaders as "infamous and execrable,"[8] language surely suggesting unfairness. The early modern *jus in bello* from which today's humanitarian law derives was also designed to apply identically to aggressor and aggrieved – regardless of the justice of the larger cause for which each fought. This suggests that concerns with fairness of process were not far from the minds of the law's creators, who were steeped in doctrines of natural right.

The alternative aim – preventing needless suffering – might at first seem humbler and more readily attainable; hence, a more realistic goal for the law of war. One could easily interpret that aim in quite demanding terms, however. It would not be easy for a belligerent's leaders to provide clear and convincing evidence, if required by a court of law, that all the vast suffering to which they contributed through their operational decisions was, in fact, absolutely necessary to achieving their principal objectives. It is almost never entirely clear *ex post*, much less *ex ante*, precisely how much force will be required for "victory," the proper meaning of which is itself often subject to dispute.[9] Such uncertainties exist in equal measure at any level of combat – tactical, operational, or strategic – and may be especially true of "irregular warfare," to which standard measures of military success do not readily apply, experts acknowledge.[10]

These matters were once simpler. "Who now worries about whether Nelson or any other great military leader might have secured his victories with fifty less lives, or thousands? At this remove, it does not seem to matter,"[11] observes one contemporary strategist. Today, by contrast, such a question matters intensely to many people, on both sides of the battle lines and beyond. The answer is increasingly sought through litigation.[12] Prosecutors of military and civilian leadership may not need to show exactly how much suffering was really necessary for victory to establish that a *particular* exercise of violence was excessive (in relation to such quantum), especially if the excess was obvious. In fact, most litigated cases have been "easy" in this sense – involving transparent excess. Courts have therefore been able to apply the "unnecessary suffering" standard with relative ease and have condemned the monumental abuses brought before them.

However, the duty to avoid unnecessary suffering need not be understood so indulgently.[13] The ICRC – joined more recently by several prominent human rights NGOs – has long advocated more stringent interpretation. Properly understood, unnecessary suffering may then ultimately prove no less demanding a goal for humanitarian law than securing a fair fight, which is superficially the more ambitious goal.

The global spread of a humanitarian sensibility ensures that humanitarian law is today asked to shoulder a heavier moral burden than it has in the past. Why might it not therefore strive to make the fight as fair as practically possible, interpreting extant rules (and sometimes revising them) accordingly? We might then ask what conception of fairness should inform such law.

In particular, what rules would parties choose from behind a veil of ignorance in the "original position,"[14] unaware of their relative future strengths and weaknesses? And would the parties engaged in choosing such a theory include only the combatants themselves or also the (far more numerous) prospective victims among noncombatants?[15] Such questions may at first strike the worldly reader as posed from too far beyond the Beltway for serious consideration in the contemporary torture debate. This vantage point might better be described, however, as simply "above the battle," though by no means Olympian.

RAWLS ON RECIPROCITY

John Rawls himself stresses that any theory of justice and the rules derived from it must acknowledge the "deep psychological fact" of "reciprocity, a tendency to answer in kind."[16] One displays this tendency in conduct toward one's benefactors and perhaps also toward one's detractors. But for reciprocity, "our nature would be very different and fruitful social cooperation fragile if not impossible. . . . If we answered love with hate, or came to dislike those who acted fairly toward us . . . a community would soon dissolve," Rawls writes. "Responses in kind," he continues, tend to build up "a capacity for a sense of justice" that, in turn, provides "a condition of human sociability." The "most stable conceptions of justice" are "firmly based on these tendencies." In fact, "the idea of reciprocity is implicit in the notion of a well-ordered society."

As a follower of Rawls, Ronald Dworkin says much the same, acknowledging that "reciprocity is prominent among the . . . conditions" necessary to create what he calls "associative obligations" among people (i.e., where they have significant ties but lack explicit agreement over the exact nature and scope of their legitimate claims on one another). "I have special responsibilities to my brother," Dworkin writes, "in virtue of our brotherhood, but these are sensitive to the degree to which he accepts such responsibilities toward me; my responsibilities toward those who claim that we are friends or lovers or neighbors or colleagues or countrymen are equally contingent on reciprocity."[17]

Rawls constructs his own conception of justice on such foundations. The people who must agree about the nature of justice and its institutions are neither highly altruistic nor completely egotistical,[18] but simply reasonable. People are reasonable insofar as "they are ready to propose principles and standards as fair terms of cooperation and to abide by them willingly, given the assurance that others will likewise do so."[19] In this way, the notion of "the reasonable leads to the idea of reciprocity," in that reasonable parties "are willing to follow faithfully" fair rules of cooperation "provided the others did so as well."[20] Reasonable parties "insist that reciprocity should hold within [their] world so that each benefits along with the others."[21] This is not the mere "mutual advantage" sought by egoistic rationalists. For as one prominent Rawls scholar writes,

> A person who is rational but not reasonable may be willing to comply with terms of cooperation that are mutually advantageous. But unlike the reasonable person he has no idea of fair terms of cooperation independent of the bargains and compromises that can be negotiated with others on the basis of competing interests.[22]

Like virtually all other thinkers who seriously consider the concept, Rawls too examines both reciprocity's short-term, bilateral form and its long-term, multilateral manifestations. He focuses on the first in *A Theory of Justice*, the second in *Political Liberalism*.[23] Even the latter discussion, however, sticks to the view that the benefits and burdens of any just scheme of social cooperation must be to the overall advantage of the particular people acquiring them. This view is consistent with Rawls's methodological individualism.[24] Multilateral reciprocity grows out of bilateral reciprocity, in fact. Where justice reigns – whether in society at large or in interpersonal relations – individuals are prepared to accept the going terms of cooperation because they know others will do the same.[25] Pithily parsing Rawls here, Martin Hollis describes the attendant transition from micro to macro with this example:

> Among mutual back-scratchers, reciprocity is at heart bilateral: you scratch my back and I scratch yours; if you scratched mine yesterday, I owe you one today. But the circle can be expanded, so that I can pay my debt by scratching the back of someone who scratches yours, or someone who

scratches someone's who scratches yours. As this ramifies, we can form a backscratchers' association, where scratching any back gains a credit, cashed in by having one's back scratched by anyone wanting a credit in their (sic) turn. Baby-sitting rings often work in this way, with a system of vouchers so that all parents sit and are sat for without its needing to be true that, if A has sat for B, then B will have sat for A. (Interestingly, such rings often insist on payment in kind, not cash, so that all parents shall do their bit in person.) Reciprocity, which starts as bilateral, can thus be generalized.[26]

The same process can work in reverse, Hollis adds, as in the revenge cycle of interfamilial vendetta between the Capulets and Montagues in *Romeo and Juliet.* Such downward devolution may at first seem the very opposite of the upward evolution he initially describes in the quoted passage. Yet it too manifests the process of "generalized reciprocity," albeit now "involving . . . reasons for doing what, here, is not to mutual advantage."[27]

Rawls offers several examples of reciprocity in social life, all reflecting cooperative or loving behavior being met with comparably positive conduct in response. Yet one might as easily illustrate Rawls's general point, as does Hollis, with examples of uncooperative behavior eliciting comparably negative conduct or at least the withdrawal of cooperation.[28] Two leading theorists thus recently write, "A strongly reciprocal individual responds kindly toward actions that are perceived to be kind and hostilely toward actions that are perceived to be hostile. Whether an action is perceived to be kind or hostile depends on the fairness or unfairness of the intention underlying the action."[29]

Might not this "fact" or "law" of human psychology, as Rawls alternately calls it, legitimately influence the U.S. response to Al Qaeda and other jihadist terrorists? Must the law not find some suitable place for it?

The Rawlsian question is, What principles and rules would reasonable people choose behind a veil of ignorance, where they do not know what position they will later occupy in society – in this case, as belligerents in war? The answer turns out to differ depending on what features of the self are included within the original position. Some answers suggest that the notion of a fair fight requires the right to retaliate for an enemy's consistent legal breaches. Others do not. In developing an ideal theory, one may assume good faith compliance by all concerned. One would surely then choose rules, from behind such a veil, prohibiting terrorism and torture, in order to avoid being subject to such wretched practices. But what happens once we shift to the world of nonideal theory, where rule adherence cannot be taken for granted?

In particular, what rules would one choose to fight by if one knew that one of the belligerents would fight dirty but did not know which one – possibly one's foe, possibly oneself? When we revise the original position in *these* terms, we remain impartial vis-à-vis the two belligerents. But now it is surely clear that, anticipating itself as the worse off of the two, any risk-averse belligerent would select rules ensuring that it did not suffer an adversary's illicit methods. It would therefore choose norms permitting self-protective retaliation in some form against uncooperative conduct whenever such conduct threatened to subject it to disadvantage. It might decide not to exercise its retaliatory right in a given situation, but it would certainly choose to preserve the option, assuming (as always) that there exists no central state to defend it on behalf of society at large.

Behind a veil of ignorance, then, states in the original position would not foreclose a right of reprisal if no effective multilateral means of collective security were to be put in its place. This proposition should be understood, at the very least, as a requirement of Rawlsian justice. Yet it is equally compelling as a description of the likely intent of state parties when ratifying the UN Charter and 1949 Geneva Conventions, with their restrictions on resort to force and to forceful reprisals in particular. Had the state parties known behind the veil that the Security Council would prove so pitiably weak a provider of collective security against breaches of humanitarian law,[30] they would never have agreed to forswear their longstanding rights of reprisal.[31]

Thus, the aim of ensuring a fair fight, if taken seriously, would justify granting a place to this expression of the reciprocity norm within humanitarian law. This should be true even when reprisal by one side would have little chance of establishing a cooperative equilibrium with its enemy. That is almost certainly the case, for instance, in the U.S. conflict with Al Qaeda and kindred groups, where no amount of U.S. reprisals against Al Qaeda detainees would likely dampen their leaders' predilection for unlawful methods of warfare. In other words, the ideal of fairness – as Rawls elucidates it – lends normative support to some legal recognition of reciprocity, entirely apart from tit-for-tat's occasional efficacy as an enforcement mechanism. The next question is whether a party fighting jihadist militants will suffer a significant disadvantage by adhering to humanitarian norms.

The Rawlsian query might be formulated in slightly different terms, however. We might ask: Would one agree to rules that would allow the other side to breach humanitarian norms in the treatment of detained enemy fighters if one knew that one would enjoy other advantages; for instance, greater financial and material resources? The answer to this question would presumably depend on the extent to which the enemy's use of dirty tactics would overcome one's own advantages in other areas.

If one were to contemplate oneself as the worst off – that is, the belligerent with fewer resources than the adversary – one might well agree to such a rule to ensure some means of overcoming that material disadvantage. If the Rawlsian question is posed in this way, the answer would be quite different from that suggested just above, again assuming risk aversion on all sides. Reciprocity, on this view, merely means that one party's breach of its treaty duties should excuse the other from those same duties, so that both may effectively fight by the same rules. Reciprocity does not require that all parties must choose to fight – within such rules – by identical means (e.g., the same weapons systems or tactical methods). One might employ terror, for example; the other might use targeted killings, sustained detention, and coercive interrogation.

WHEN JUSTICE REQUIRES DIFFERENT RULES FOR DIFFERENT PARTIES: GENEVA ADDITIONAL PROTOCOL I

When rules are written in a way that heavily favors one side over the other, fairness surely need not require that both play equally by them. For instance, democratic insurgents fighting repressive regimes rightly see the traditional international law of armed conflict as stacked against them. In fact, such insurgents view themselves as the ultimate protector of those for whom the rules are not providing adequate safeguards.[32] Jihadist militants often view themselves similarly.

Geneva Additional Protocol I was partly inspired by the idea that insurgents for national liberation movements against colonizing states should not be required to meet the same legal standards as those of their state antagonists. The drafters of this Protocol believed that fairness of result here required precisely that the parties be governed by *different* rules.[33] The departures thereby authorized from traditional standards were quite modest. These concerned only the question of how far, in advance of actual confrontation, belligerents must openly display distinguishing emblems and arms.

Like the advantages that law gives to national liberation movements, fair rules for fighting terrorists might permit those victimized by illicit methods to respond with means of warfare otherwise foreclosed to them. This might be described as playing by different rules: The initial terrorist recourse to illicit methods was unauthorized, whereas the victim's response to it was legally permissible. Alternatively and more accurately, this situation could be described as playing by the *same* rules, insofar as terrorism's victim might use methods otherwise prohibited *prima facie*, in response to terrorist violations of similar prohibitions.

Consider a third possible iteration of the Rawlsian question. Applying his "maximin" principle, it might seem that belligerents behind a veil of ignorance would choose to maximize the minimum threshold, or "floor" of acceptable conduct.[34] They might insist on highly demanding rules of humane treatment for all detainees. Being risk averse,[35] they must anticipate becoming such detainees themselves, not only possible captors.

Yet suicide bombers are neither risk averse nor much given to self-interest (as generally understood to include the instinct for self-preservation),[36] as one would expect them to be behind the Rawlsian veil. So, to participate in such an exercise, they would have to be stripped of features defining their essential character, embodying their constitutive attachments.[37] This impersonalization may seem unfair to them no less than to their adversaries, who must defend themselves against the actual methods of warfare (chosen by other deliberative methods). Yet such a stripping away of morally arbitrary features is precisely the point of the veil of ignorance in the first place, Rawls replies.

The fact that slightly different formulations of the Rawlsian question yield such disparate answers points to a deeper problem, one that ultimately renders *A Theory of Justice* singularly unhelpful in devising rules for fighting jihadist terror. Rawls assumes that persons in the original position are motivated fundamentally by a desire to live in the same society on terms that everyone, regardless of his or her conception of the good life, can regard as fair. If jihadist suicide bombers and their leaders are unwilling to make this assumption,[38] then they cannot be thought of as persons in the original position. A legal regime for war derived from within that position then could not fairly be expected to govern others' relations with them.

If this is the case, an altogether different conceptual frame is necessary for thinking about the relation between "us" and "them." Whether it can be a frame much concerned with justice – or at least with justice as fairness – remains an open question. Rawls offers little help in answering it. It may be no accident, then, that he applies his theory only to devising rules of warfare between "decent" peoples. In other words, his theory does not apply to wars in which one side is unwilling to live within the same international society, governed by shared rules, as the other. To acknowledge that reciprocity is a psychological fact with which any theory of justice must be consistent, then, does not carry us very far toward satisfactory answers to our practical questions. It does not much help us write a set of rules for fighting fairly against antagonists who wish to place themselves altogether outside of international society as it exists or might peaceably be reformed.

RAWLS'S "LAW OF PEOPLES" AND TERRORIST WAR

In *The Law of Peoples*, Rawls does seek to develop moral principles to govern the foreign policy of a liberal state toward illiberal ones, with a view to thereby ensuring "perpetual peace." To what extent, he asks, do the practices of illiberal peoples warrant our respect, even though they live by principles that would not be acceptable to us, as citizens of Western constitutional democracies, nor consistent with the principles we would choose for ourselves from within the original position?

He concludes that a just international order would fully respect peoples who, though illiberal and more rigidly hierarchical, are nonetheless "decent," in that they are peaceful and nonaggressive toward other peoples. (He may have had principally in mind such stable, "traditionalist" or "neo-traditionalist" Muslim countries as Kuwait and Saudi Arabia.[39]) He aspires here to what he calls a "realistic utopia,"[40] in that it would be "an ideal design that withal arises out of and reflects the way of the world."[41] He shares with Habermas, who follows him here, the search for "traces of a reason that unites without effacing separation, that binds without unnaming difference, that points out the common and the shared among strangers, without depriving the other of otherness."[42] Decent but illiberal peoples, Rawls infers, would agree to a narrower range of rights in their mutual relations than would liberal democracies or their citizens. An "overlapping consensus" on certain rights would nonetheless emerge from their choices behind the veil. There, in the original position, they would not know what sort of decent society they would be or become: liberal or illiberal.

Yet jihadist suicide bombers fail even this undemanding test, one avowedly designed to be tolerant and anti-imperialist[43] and consequently rejected by those championing a broader and more demanding conception of international human rights.[44] Just principles of social order can emerge only from and apply to "circumstances of justice,"[45] in which cooperation is both necessary and possible, writes Rawls (following Hume). Cooperation is necessary because social interdependence is inescapable under the circumstances.[46] Cooperation is possible because differing interests, though real, are not so great as to preclude consensus on basic rules of public order. That these two conditions for justice are also necessary for reciprocity, as the term is here used, is no accident.[47]

The circumstances of justice, so characterized, do not describe America's "relationship" with jihadist terrorists, however. It does not need them, and they do not need it. Or more precisely, terrorists need certain modern creations – the Internet,[48] mass media spectacle, aeronautics, and financial institutions – only to the extent necessary to destroy America.[49] This need cannot be the basis for any sustained sociality. "We are not fighting so that you will offer us something," calmly explains Hezbollah leader Hussein Massawi. "We are fighting to eliminate you."[50] Obviously, there is no basis for overlapping consensus regarding possible rules of international society if our enemies could never agree to occupy any such society with us.

Their apparent unwillingness to do so is an empirical question, subject to some spirited debate. Some contend, in particular, that they "hate us not for what we are, but rather for what we do" (i.e., for U.S. foreign policy in the Middle East).[51] Modifying foreign policy in relevant respects might enable our adversaries to imagine occupying the same international society with us. If so, there remains the possibility of satisfying at least one of the two necessary conditions to establish circumstances of justice. Shared membership in a single international society might someday be possible, presumably on the basis of some account of tolerance requiring a particular interpretation of the Koran,[52] one that has occasionally surfaced, if only due to Western influence.[53] Or there might simply arise, after exhaustion from an extended period of armed conflict, a tacit *modus vivendi*, an "untheorized agreement" to refrain from direct confrontation.[54] But unless and until both of Rawls's conditions for justice are satisfied, the principles of just conduct derived from such circumstances will not be helpful in governing America's conflict with militant jihadists. And where the circumstances of justice do not exist, justice is no longer the "first virtue" of institutions, as it would otherwise be, in Rawls's view.[55]

To be sure, behaving justly is often "contagious," Rawls rightly observes. For as Sandel points out (parsing Rawls), "acting out of a sense of justice . . . reinforces the assumptions it presupposes and enhances its own stability by encouraging and affirming like motivations in others."[56] Yet it is "inappropriate" to act on principles of justice where there exist no "circumstances of justice," Rawls acknowledges. In their absence, actions prompted by a sense of justice often will not "have the self-fulfilling effect of bringing about the conditions under which they would have been appropriate."[57] Indeed, "in this case justice will not have been a virtue but a vice,"[58] Sandel rightly counsels. In circumstances of benevolence or fraternity, for instance, to conduct oneself justly would be seen as falling well short of the situation's

moral requirements. Conversely, exceeding such requirements, as by acting on a sense of justice when others are unreasonable, incapable even of
limited altruism, unconcerned with securing primary goods, and unwilling
to engage in cooperative endeavor, can prove equally misguided – certainly
perilous and sometimes self-destructive.

Circumstances of justice do not exist in relations with peoples who lack
"decency." For this reason, "liberal and decent peoples have the right, under
the Law of Peoples, not to tolerate outlaw states" and so presumably also to
eschew toleration of outlaw nonstates. "These are aggressive and dangerous;
all peoples are safer and more secure if [they] change, or are forced to
change."[59] Kant said much the same, in "Perpetual Peace."[60] Unlike Rawls,
he saw no need even to make any special accommodation for peoples who,
though illiberal, could still be considered morally decent. The point of liberal
political theory is not to find a mode of civil accommodation with such
antagonists, but simply to eliminate the threat they pose. No international
society of decent peoples need tolerate groups whose peculiar conception
of the good life leads them actively to seek elimination of any other. Rawls's
liberalism here turns quite unforgiving, lacking in magnanimity.

In fact, the closer a society approximates the ideal of justice, the more
punitive it is likely to become toward those who persist in flouting its
criminal law.[61] Their resistance to its demands reflects resistance to justice
itself. This resistance can hence have no source other than their own eccentric
choice of nonconformity or simply a willful moral perversity. "Criminality
does not surface in a well-ordered regime," writes one of Rawls's leading
interpreters, and so "the institutionalization of justice makes magnanimity
unnecessary."[62]

This is as true of individuals within domestic society as of groups within
international society. As countries ratify and courts apply humanitarian law
with increasing frequency, its violators can expect decreasing sympathy –
for their deviations will no longer reflect the law's own defects. To disregard
an increasingly just and clarified humanitarian law is to display a willful
moral perversity, now at the collective level of standards for armed conflict.
Those who will not sign this social contract remain in the state of nature,
where nothing done to or by them can hence be considered unjust.[63] On
Rawls's view, if we do not share circumstances of justice with an indecent
opponent, tolerating even his continued existence can be dangerous. There
is certainly no ethical duty to do so.

Yet in the conflict with Al Qaeda, we must continue to make clear our willingness to coexist nonetheless, if only that entity's members will alter certain
relevant features of their conduct toward us. Tolerance in this sense remains

conceivable, desirable, even noble.[64] We should not deny the possibility of coexistence with those who support the suicide bomber, for instance, even if they currently deny it with us. By doing so, we would then likely overlook future prospects for cooperation with them, where they may arise. Hopes for later reciprocation thus rely on our continued capacity for tolerance – both real and perceived.

Tolerance is not the only virtue on which the social process of reciprocity depends. A second such virtue – more intellectual than moral – demands that we engage rationally with our adversaries. To reciprocate my opponent's good and bad deeds with my own, I must be attentive to its behavior and understand the real reasons for it. To respond aptly, I must know what it is doing; otherwise, I would be misled by apparently friendly behavior that is treacherous and by seemingly hostile behavior that is indifferent or beneficial to me. That suicide bombers will not rationally engage with us and do not care what we think about them does not mean that we should cease to engage with them, to make every effort to understand them.

Though reciprocity is not itself a virtue, its operation hence relies on two important virtues. We must retain a commitment to these virtues, even as our opponent entirely refuses to reciprocate. They remain rightly appealing to us on their own terms, ethically and strategically. We should therefore continue to cultivate and display reciprocity's constituent virtues, even as reciprocity itself remains impossible for the foreseeable future.

But if the notion of a fair fight makes any sense at all in the conflict with militant jihadists, it is thus not to be found by way of Rawls's theory of justice as fairness. That theory's endorsement of reciprocity, and the practical worldliness this seems to augur, ultimately proves a false lead. Rawls himself would here surely stress the limited scope of his concerns and hence acknowledge the limitations of his theory's relevance beyond them. Still, this is to admit that the best intellectual resources of contemporary liberalism leave us grasping at conceptual straws in confronting the present predicament, consistent with the best in our moral traditions. This is not to say that justice *tout court*, or morality more broadly, is rendered irrelevant to the current conflict, for Western thinking about humanitarianism in war has a much longer history. The next two chapters draw on other elements of that history, which prove more helpful in discerning what it might mean to fight fairly in a war against terrorists.

6

Fairness in Terrorist War (2):
Kantian Reciprocity

One widely held view of law's primary purpose is "to create and maintain the objective conditions of trust . . . that make it reasonable for citizens to trust one another even when they are strangers who lack the kind of personal relationship that can ground trust outside the law."[1] The general belief that no one will benefit through illegal conduct greatly contributes to such trust.[2] For the criminal code, this means, in particular, that all law must

> bring benefits (security, freedom) to all its citizens by imposing on them all the burdens of self-restraint involved in obeying the law. We can then say that a criminal, in breaking the law, takes an unfair advantage for herself over all those who obey the law. She accepts the benefits that flow from the law-abiding self-restraint of others but refuses to accept the burden of obeying the law herself. . . . She now deserves, as a matter of justice, to lose that unfair advantage, and punishment serves precisely to deprive her of it. By imposing an extra burden on her, it restores that fair balance of benefits and burdens that her crime disturbed.[3]

A principal goal of the criminal law has hence always been to discourage private retaliation as a means of restoring the balance, argues John Gardner[4] (following James Fitzjames Stephen).[5] Providing personal security against disruption of this balance is a central objective of the social contract.

Those who fight by means of terror benefit from the restraints that their state opponents may continue to honor, in conformity with humanitarian law. Yet such terrorists do not themselves endure the corresponding burdens of like compliance.[6] If they are responsible for great violence against innocents, they themselves are not innocent. The violence they suffer through coercive interrogation is hence very different in character from that suffered by the victims of 9/11, entirely apart from the disparity in magnitude. Unlike the World Trade Center victims, they have freely put themselves in a position where they can expect to meet with violence. This poses the unnerving question of what it might mean, if we will allow ourselves to entertain the idea, to respond to 9/11 "in kind." What are reciprocity's "terms of trade," in other words? We later return to this question in some detail.

We must now examine what inferences should be drawn, for America's response to terror, from a commitment to reciprocity. The injustice of terrorism consists partly in its rejection of rules universally endorsed by the international community, rules to which all reasonable, self-interested parties in circumstances of justice would agree behind a veil of ignorance.

The unfairness of terrorism partly consists in the choice to which terrorists put their adversaries. One reason for rejecting torture, after all, is that it violates the detainee's moral and psychological integrity by requiring him to betray, in interrogation, a cause to which he is committed.[7] This is presumably what Elaine Scarry has in mind when she writes, without any qualifying language, that "those who withstand torture without confessing should be honoured."[8] Yet the reasons that normally make us so solicitous of a prisoner's sense of integrity do not so clearly pertain to the ideal-typical terrorist. For as Sussman acknowledges (in passing, while concentrating on the wrongfulness of torture), the terrorist is someone who

> disregards the principles of just combat, striking at his enemies' loved ones simply because they are dear to him. The terrorist makes no effort to distinguish himself from civilians . . . , forcing his foe into the terrible choice of either waging war against innocents or failing to protect himself and those near to him. Given that the terrorist attacks his enemy's own integrity in this way, it is hard to see how he is entitled to terms of surrender that do not in any way require him to compromise his cause. Plausibly, such terms should be reserved for combatants who accept certain risks (by wearing uniforms, living apart from the civilian population, and so on) and do so in order to allow fighting to proceed without forcing combatants to make such self-disfiguring choices.[9]

One might even say that, just as the torturer puts the suspected terrorist to an unfair choice, one that disfigures his integrity (moral, no less than physical), so too does the terrorist put his victims to such a choice: They may have reason to believe they must violate their own scruples – their aversion to coercion, in particular – most effectively to defend themselves. Golda Meir once told an Egyptian interlocutor in a similar spirit, "We can perhaps someday forgive you for killing our children, but we cannot forgive you for making us kill *your* children."[10]

In the passage quoted earlier, Sussman fails only to complete his syllogism, making explicit its final inference. Fairness requires symmetry of risk; terrorism disrupts such symmetry by imposing choices that violate integrity and are therefore unfair; law must restore this symmetry, either by punishing legal breach or excusing its victim from comparable conduct, whether as punishment, self-defense, corrective justice, or all three. In the interests of fairness, the rules of warfare must strive for symmetry of risk in the methods of fighting that they permit. This remains true regardless of whether the disruption of such symmetry actually affects the war's outcome. The latter question regarding impact will often be impossible to answer *ex ante.* The wrong lies as much in the failure of self-restraint and the resulting imbalance of benefit and burden between belligerents, as in its effect on the conflict's result. This lack of restraint is simply unfair as a matter of process, which has been the law's chief concern here. The next chapter, on corrective justice, further develops this line of analysis.

At first, it seems utterly innocuous to observe that the law affords certain benefits to citizens in return for imposing correlative burdens, as Kant and other liberals contend. This proposition nonetheless turns out to provide the basis for a subtle and quite controversial argument for reciprocity in the law of war, as a requirement of fairness. On this view of fairness, each participant in a social interaction may impose certain risks on the other only so long as the other may in turn impose such risks on him or her. The categorical imperative, like the Golden Rule it arises from, so requires. The resulting rules are often described as reciprocal.[11]

Risks are reciprocal where they offset one another. They do so when their expected value or disvalue is equivalent. The risks one must assume within organized society should be equivalent to the risks one is permitted to impose on others. So too in international society. The Geneva Conventions expressly enshrine risk symmetry in many places, as in the requirement that POWs be criminally "sentenced only if the sentence has been pronounced by the same courts according to the same procedure as in the case of members of the armed forces of the Detaining Power."[12] When prosecuting war crime, in short, the rule is, do unto others as you do unto yourselves.

Risks may be symmetrical though they differ in form, in the nature and sources of the danger they present, Jules Coleman adds.[13] But the central idea is that "reciprocity of risk draws its normative power from the fact that it defines a regime of equal freedom," notes one Kantian lawyer[14] – and also, by implication, a regime of equal constraint. Kant's "moral agent" is willing to live under such a regime because she is "capable of acknowledging that what one claims for oneself as a right one can claim only as an equal to everyone else,"[15] Kateb writes.

Legal justice entails the enactment and enforcement of rules establishing an acceptable balance of benefits and burdens. Rule violations are unfair because they upset this balance. Their redress requires its restoration. To permit violations to go unanswered is to allow the violator to reap the benefits of a cooperative scheme without incurring the correlative burdens. The victims, conversely, have been asked to bear the legal burdens of social cooperation without receiving the benefits they were promised. On both sides the result is unjust, Kant would say.

The chief task of legal justice is hence to restore the symmetry of risk that rules had sought to establish, as an expression of the social contract. The state and its courts should correct the imbalance.[16] Where these institutions do not exist, however, fair balance might be reestablished in other ways – perhaps bilaterally, between the parties themselves. When the parties to a conflict are willing to play tit-for-tat, in particular, the renewal of cooperative equilibrium becomes possible even under conditions of anarchy, of statelessness.

Symmetry of legal risk is possible without satisfying the "circumstances of justice" necessary to fairness for Rawls and Hume. Such circumstances are lacking in war against belligerents that are not "decent," we have seen. Rawls therefore does not seek to apply his conclusions about humanitarian law to such warfare. Kant's essay, "Perpetual Peace," however, admits no such qualifications to his conception of the *jus in bello*. Symmetry is achieved whenever a given maxim for conduct can, in principle, be extended to all concerned, governing them equally. Variations in historical circumstance are largely immaterial, even when they greatly affect the likely consequences of acting on principle.[17]

The parties might be, let us say, belligerents in an armed conflict. Al Qaeda and the United States could agree, explicitly or tacitly, to fight by certain rules, whether those of current humanitarian law or others. One belligerent might, through its initial conduct, communicate to the other the nature of the rules by which it intended to fight. The other would implicitly agree to these rules simply by conducting itself in accordance with them, whatever its initial preferences to the contrary. Or it might respond by conduct that effectively proffers a different set of rules. Oversimplifying only a bit, this is in fact precisely what occurs during most actual warfare, as we see from the historical record discussed in Chapter 10. Through reciprocal interaction, the parties find an equilibrium – however distasteful in many cases – that they are "prepared to live with," though it may shift over time, altering upward or downward the measure of moral restraint they choose to impose upon themselves.

The rules implicit in Al Qaeda's chosen methods of warfare, when imaginatively universalized, are abominable in the extreme. If they were generalized to allow like conduct by Al Qaeda's victims, the ensuing world would be very unpleasant indeed. No rational agent would choose to live in it. The rules of the game could nonetheless be described as fair in procedural terms insofar as both sides were permitted and willing to play equally by them. Bin Laden might even say that, if America refuses to agree to his rules, that is its problem, not his. He has made clear the measure of moral restraint he is prepared to exercise. Because he is human and therefore capable of rationality, he should be treated accordingly, as if he were willing to generalize the principles reflected in his freely chosen conduct. He and his followers are, in fact, unwilling to endorse the consequences of generalizing their proffered rules of conduct. But this may simply be because they are more concerned with life in the next world than with the likely consequences of such rules in this one.

It is surely possible, in one sense, to imagine accepting the rules that bin Laden "proposes," even if it is painful to envisage our life within that universe. Still, a social world in which one were permitted to defend oneself against wrongful conduct through like conduct would surely be preferable to a world in which one enjoyed no such right. A reasonable nation-state would likely choose to exercise that right where international law failed effectively to enforce its writ. This has been the principal reason that the law of war saw fit to authorize belligerent reprisal throughout most of military history. One would reluctantly agree, on grounds of both fairness and self-interest, to play by substantively abhorrent rules if the alternative were the serious possibility of destruction at the hands of an enemy who persisted in acting on them.

There would still remain the question of whether it is logically possible to picture the resulting state of affairs (i.e., whether it would be sustainable or humanly inhabitable). To conclude that a maxim of conduct is susceptible to universalization, Kant requires that such sustainability be established. Assume that bin Laden's imagined world (and the maxims of conduct his followers adopt to instantiate it) is one that requires eliminating all people unlike themselves. Assume further that those to be eliminated will in turn imagine a world that must be culled of people like bin Laden's followers. Then the logical result – if uninhibited by other factors or third parties – would seem to be mutual annihilation. The two categories of people just described exhaust the universe of possible human types, in fact, so there exist no such third parties. A war fought reciprocally by such rules could have only one result: the species' extinction. The rules by which Al Qaeda proposes to fight would thus, if universalized, lead straight to the end of human habitation of the planet. The fact that such rules would also fail Kant's definition of justice would then presumably be among the least of our concerns.[18]

Yet even if bin Laden desires, in his dreams, to cleanse the earth of all infidels, it is safe to say that he will never acquire the capacity to do so. This may be irrelevant for Kant, as he is chiefly concerned with pure motivation and where it leads when extrapolated (i.e., hypothetically and subjunctively). But material capabilities are highly pertinent to any practical reasoning that remains attentive to consequences in the "phenomenal" world. Concerns about scarce capacities have begun to assert themselves even on the American side of the conflict. Some now contend, in criticism of the Bush administration's martial tropes, that jihadist militants should be viewed more as an ineliminable risk to be managed than as an enemy in a war to be won.[19] After all, a military victory – no matter how decisive – might prove to be beside the point, even counterproductive, if the enemy that is violently destroyed remains part of a much larger Muslim population sympathetic to some of its central aspirations and hence unwilling to condemn it unequivocally.

We should also here recall that bin Laden himself sometimes speaks, as in his epigraphs to this book, as if he fully respects the reciprocity principle, normatively embraces it, and consistently acts on it in practice. He would be perfectly prepared to exchange good conduct for like behavior from the United States, he tells us. He simply hasn't seen much goodness from America and so doesn't expect to, in the foreseeable future. Until he does, he will continue to reciprocate bad for bad, "blood for blood, destruction for destruction," in his words. Clear here is the importance of differences in perceptions – to which game theory does not attend: Osama bin Laden apparently understands himself to be behaving consistently with reciprocity's requirements (i.e., returning bad for bad), even as his Western opponents see him very differently. In fact, they view his strategy as virtually defined by its rejection of reciprocity; that is, by his refusal to return good for good.

TERROR, TORTURE, AND THE SYMMETRY OF RISK

A concern with preserving fairness in the sense of risk symmetry often finds its way into discussions of torture, albeit sometimes *sub rosa*. Consider, for instance, philosophy's recurrent effort to contrast the wrongfulness of torture with the moral acceptability of killing in war. The detainee who is subject to torture is considered utterly defenseless, whereas the enemy soldier is armed and trained to defend himself against attack, we are told.[20] The torturer's invulnerability is as absolute as the powerlessness of his victim, who is entirely at his mercy. Torture's wrongfulness lies in precisely this asymmetry, by some accounts.[21]

Yet if the candidate for torture is *ex hypothesi* a terrorist in possession of life-saving (which is also to say life-threatening) information, then he can hardly be described as powerless, and the potential torturer – the society he seeks to protect, that is – faces genuine risk. In the ticking time bomb scenario[22] in particular, the terrorist's "placing of the bomb was the beginning of an attack on us; his silence is . . . voluntary behavior undertaken for the sake of bringing that act to completion,"[23] Sussman argues. The detained terrorist thus remains in a position – through speech or silence – to impose risk; he is hence as legitimately subject to force as he was when unencumbered by captivity. For as Paul Kahn writes, "The fundamental principle of the morality of warfare is a right to exercise self-defense within the conditions of mutual imposition of risk. . . . Combatants are allowed to injure each other as long as they stand in relationship of mutual risk."[24] Such a captive terrorist retains the power not only to inflict harm but also to improve his treatment by disclosing information about his organization and its plans. The risk of being unjustly harmed, then, exists on both sides of such an interaction, no less than the possibility of unjustly harming. Any moral argument against torture that assumes a complete asymmetry of risk between interrogator and interrogated therefore fails.

The problem with this argument, the reader may retort, is that it does not distinguish the terrorist from the ordinary POW who has committed no war crime or crime against humanity and who may possess equally valuable information about the enemy's location, organization, and plans. If we believe that coercively interrogating ordinary POWs – including high-level officers sure to have such information – is wrong, then the preceding argument proves too much, for it justifies that practice beyond the population of terrorists. The argument could readily be revised, however, to incorporate the moral distinction between intentional civilian targeting and lawful means of combat. Those who employ lawful means of war can fairly anticipate better treatment than those who do not. The remaining question is whether this distinction can bear that much weight, in light of the ensuing disparity in likely treatment.

H. L. A. HART ON "FAIR PLAY"

Like Kant, Rawls, and Dworkin, H. L. A. Hart defends a similar notion of "fair play," understood in terms of a "mutuality of restrictions." A concern with reciprocity lies very close to the surface here, though Hart does not employ the word. Fair play, he writes, requires "maintaining an equal distribution of restrictions and so of freedom"[25] among pertinent parties. "When a number of persons conduct any joint enterprise according to rules and thus restrict their liberty, those who have submitted to these restrictions when required have a right to a similar submission from those who have benefited by their submission."[26]

With that last clause, Hart introduces qualifications that limit the relevance of his position to the conflict with Al Qaeda and kindred groups. At first glance, it would appear that because the United States has formally submitted to the Geneva Conventions and largely honored them in many conflicts, fair play requires reciprocal compliance by the beneficiaries of such law abidingness throughout the world. And because *erga omnes* duties are by nature owed to international society at large, all within it have been served by American adherence to them.

Al Qaeda's defenders would retort that Hart's argument, however compelling perhaps as moral theory, simply does not have any real bearing on the facts of their situation, properly understood. First, their organization has never "submitted" itself to the rules of humanitarian law. They would reject Jinks's claim that Al Qaeda members are bound as nationals of states that have ratified the Geneva Conventions, even when not fighting for such states, arguing along much the same lines as in Chapter 2. Insofar as Al Qaeda's warriors are not bound by these treaties, there exists no "joint enterprise," in Hart's terms, linking the United States to Al Qaeda in any relevant respect.

Al Qaeda supporters would further respond that they, and those they claim to defend, have not actually benefited from humanitarian law, inasmuch as it has not effectively protected fellow Muslims during myriad wars with the West – in Chechnya, Bosnia, Somalia, Iraq, Palestine, the Philippines, and elsewhere. This view rejects the moral distinction, long embodied in the law of war, between intentional harm and side effects. It also fails to distinguish situations in which much greater forbearance was shown (e.g., NATO action in Bosnia) from others (Russian action in Chechnya).[27] Still, because jihadist terrorists have neither endorsed humanitarian law nor believe they have profited from it, they consider themselves bound by no duty of fair play, in Hart's sense, that would compel them to respect such law when attacking Westerners. It would also follow from all this, however, that the United States enjoys "equal freedom" to defend itself against such antagonists. It will be free of the "mutuality of restrictions" to which it would be subject when fighting enemies who have accepted and profited from the protections of humanitarian law.

Does the terrorist's unfairness justify or excuse the torturer's conduct, in the interests of restoring a level field of play? Specifically, in armed conflict with the organization responsible for 9/11, do long-term detention and coercive interrogation of its members, as well as targeted killings of its leaders, restore in any way the fair play and symmetry of risk that humanitarian law seeks to establish? These key questions are not encountered in any of the considerable writing on counterterrorist law and policy. They are nevertheless the key questions Americans should be asking themselves.

The terrorist's victim has a right to security of person that the state must therefore ensure. So too, the terrorist has a human right to respect for his integrity. But the latter right may be presumptive only; that is, a presumption that might be rebutted and overridden by his own disrespect for the integrity of his intended victims, especially to the extent that they thereby suffer unfair disadvantage in resisting his efforts to destroy them. By their inhumane deeds, certain men may make themselves unworthy of their humanity, as Kant put it.[28] They do this by ceasing to act in ways consonant with the humanity within them or with respect for the humanity of others.

The upshot of this analysis, in the present and preceding chapters, is that the notion of reciprocity, as requiring rules to ensure a fair fight, cannot convincingly justify a policy of forbearance in the U.S. treatment of jihadist leaders and detainees. In fact, liberal moral theories of reciprocity could readily be employed to justify coercive measures – though forbidden presumptively – as a means of restoring the fair play and symmetry of risk disrupted by 9/11's massive crimes against humanity.

THE LAW FOR TERRORISTS IS NOT THE LAW FOR NATIONAL LIBERATION MOVEMENTS

As indicated before, in agreeing to Geneva Additional Protocol I, most states rejected the notion that all belligerents must play by the same rules. Specifically, they did not demand that all nonstate belligerents play by the same rules as states in noninternational armed conflict. These states did not believe that justice in war invariably requires the same rules for all antagonists. In fact, they appeared to conclude that securing just results – that is, the success of anticolonial and antiapartheid resistance movements – required quite the reverse.

A prohibition on attacking insurgents or terrorists who could instead readily be arrested, as several authorities now demand,[29] would move the law still further in this direction. The rebels themselves would not generally be in any position to "arrest" and prosecute members of the state's armed forces, unless the insurgents effectively controlled enough territory to have established state-like institutions therein. Still, domestic insurgents remain criminals under municipal law, which puts them at a considerable disadvantage in fighting a state on its territory. International humanitarian law entirely respects their domestic legal treatment in this manner.[30] No self-interested state would *want* to give domestic insurgents against it the same measure of rights the state's army enjoys in seeking to suppress them. This situation further illustrates the fact that states do not actually demand a humanitarian law equally applicable to all belligerents. They do not believe that justice requires or permits such perfect reciprocity in all situations. Just as anticolonial movements receive more legal protection than the colonial states they fight, so domestic insurgents are accorded less.

The bearing of this point on present concerns is slight, however: The law does not permit jihadists to attack civilians and civilian objects, any more than it is now understood to permit the United States to retaliate with torture, targeted killings, and sustained detention. Here, then, law *does* insist on the same rules for all parties. And no one proposes legally authorizing jihadist terror tactics, much less without permitting some form of reciprocity; that is, other than jihadists themselves, presumably. Whatever its many disagreements in such matters, the world accepts the distinction between jihadist terrorists and legitimate national liberation movements against colonial powers, movements of the sort that Additional Protocol I set out to protect.

The moral basis of this distinction deserves emphasis. Like national liberation movements, Al Qaeda views itself as ridding its corner of the world from American colonialist domination, and therefore presumably deserving of the same protections afforded such movements. By its terms, the Protocol does not provide any real guidance for distinguishing legitimate anticolonial resistance from its simulacrum and rhetorical invocation. Still, anticolonial guerrillas receive the rights of combatants under the Protocol on terms that are at least partly reciprocal. Such rights were, one leading international lawyer writes,

> part of a bargain whereby guerrilla groups received the protections of international humanitarian law in exchange for obligations on their own

to respect that law. . . . With terrorists, though, the calculus is totally differ-ent. If nonstate actors have simply created terrorist groups to kill innocent people and terrorize a population, why should governments assume that such conflicts deserve regulation by detailed rules of international human-itarian law? When the goal of a group is so beyond acceptable conduct that it finds no defenders among governments [unlike most national liberation movements], extending the protections of international humanitarian law to such conflicts and to such combatants, I think, only serves to legitimize them and is thus not acceptable.[31]

He concludes, "I do not think that this idea of non-reciprocity is or should be so all-encompassing." According rights of combatancy to terrorists, in fact, "has the risk of turning every act of violence into an act of war and all those who commit it into lawful combatants who enjoy the combatant's privilege"[32] (i.e., to kill other combatants). Geneva Additional Protocol II, though it does not confer POW status on domestic insurgents, encourages granting them amnesty from prosecution, in recognition of the fact that they, though lacking combatant immunity under international law, are not necessarily thugs or terrorists. They should thus be treated as criminals only where they commit what would be war crimes even by an official state combatant.

EXAMPLES OF FAIRNESS AS COMMON RULES

It would be helpful as this point to put some factual flesh on our skeletal theorizing. Let us pause briefly then to consider two practical situations in which it has proven important to respect the principle of reciprocity as fairness through common rules that balance benefits and burdens.

1. *The International Criminal Court and Universal Jurisdiction: Doubts Based on Reciprocity*

A major objection to the new International Criminal Court (ICC) con-cerns the failure of its statute to honor the principle of reciprocity as rules equally binding on all. American critics of the court, in particular, stress this conspicuous defect.[33] In humanitarian interventions throughout the world, including those authorized by the United Nations, U.S. armed forces are often at the forefront, incurring significant costs and risks. The ICC may someday choose to prosecute American military leaders for their conduct during such operations, just as the International Criminal Tribunal for the former Yugoslavia seriously considered prosecuting U.S. leaders for NATO peace operations against Slobodan Milošević in 1999.[34]

Under the terms of the treaty creating it, the ICC may even prosecute when the country on whose territory the wrongs occur is not party to the court's statute. The nonratifying state need only invoke Article 12(3) to grant *ad hoc* authority to the court. The United States, however, could not do the same concerning comparable misconduct by its antagonist – that is, unless the violations occur on U.S. soil. The situation, in a word, is nonreciprocal. The head of state responsible for ordering war crimes against U.S. troops could even vacation in The Hague itself – the court's home – without being subject to ICC jurisdiction.[35] As a result, JAG Col. Lietzau points out,

> Any peacekeeper or peace enforcer sent to quash an ongoing humanitarian disaster, and perhaps to bring its perpetrators to justice, would not enjoy the same ICC immunity as the rogue state actors themselves. For instance, absent a Security Council referral, Milošević would be immune from jurisdiction for any offense committed against his people, but NATO aircrews attempting to stop his forces from committing atrocities would not be.[36]

The upshot is that the ICC may "do actual harm by discouraging the United States from engaging in various human rights-protecting activities. And this, in turn, may increase rather than decrease the impunity of those who violate human rights."[37]

Concerns about reciprocity also come to the fore in discussions of "universal jurisdiction," the doctrine allowing any country to prosecute those responsible for certain grave offenses, regardless of where the crimes occur and the victim's or perpetrator's nationality. When the charge is genocide (or also torture, as in the case against General Augusto Pinochet before the British Law Lords[38]), it has been tempting to allow such extraterritorial assertions by national courts, as terms of the Geneva Conventions and Convention Against Torture all but require.[39] Yet a moment's reflection presents the serious prospect of total anarchy,[40] as states begin accusing one another's leaders of crimes against humanity, a capacious category arguably encompassing the policies of many states toward portions of their populations or their immediate neighbors.

Accusations of war crime, too, could easily become the basis for widespread extraterritorial trials, due in part to the imprecision of key rules. Like the Convention Against Torture, the Geneva Conventions not only authorize universal jurisdiction but indeed also require all ratifying states to prosecute (or extradite for prosecution elsewhere) those responsible for grave breaches, regardless of a malefactor's nationality. If this virtually never happens in fact, it is because states contemplating doing so rightly anticipate retaliation against them and their nationals.[41] It is then scarcely surprising that the doctrine has proven so unappealing to states or that it has not prospered in national courts virtually anywhere, despite its clear textual grounding in several treaties and its facial normative appeal. Where the symmetrical invocation of the right by all concerned is practically impossible, it has proven preferable to ignore the right entirely. Here, the effect of the reciprocity principle, when set against the constraints of *realpolitik*, is to stifle entirely the development of a legal practice with a long history (beginning with piracy and slave trade prosecutions) and with heartening possibilities, but also with perilous prospects.

2. *Reciprocity in International Regulatory Regimes*

Public international law relies on reciprocity not only when regulating weapons and other aspects of war, but in many other areas as well. One key issue over which there is some lively disagreement concerns the inclusiveness versus exclusiveness of international regulatory regimes[42] in addressing global problems through legal cooperation. Must the ideal distribution of burdens and benefits be fixed at the outset or evolve over time as nations conform to regulatory goals, with the benefit-burden distribution shifting as circumstances permit? Some contend that such regimes work best by conferring benefits only as states accept corresponding burdens. Imposing such burdens on members is generally necessary to make any regime effective in soon achieving its policy aims.

But this approach often leads to a much smaller initial membership in the regime than is required to attain its objectives. Incentives for a state to ratify the treaty and incur the costs of compliance arise from its benefits: They are contingent on each other. There is a stable balance of benefits for burdens from the beginning. An example would be an arms control treaty between two military rivals. As early members begin to reap the benefits, the regime's appeal will become apparent to interested nonmembers, it is thought. As they come to see that pros outweigh cons, they will eventually join the regime. Economists and international-relations rationalists favor this approach to institutional design, for it is congenial with their view of mutually advantageous exchange as the principal basis of social cooperation.

The opposing view favors fewer upfront membership costs in the new regulatory regime. As much as possible, it rejects jot-for-jot, burden-benefit reciprocity as essential from the outset. Such a regime makes benefits available nonetheless, if only by deferring correlative costs to a later time. The value of early benefits will, however, be less than under the first approach. In fact, such treaties often serve only as "frameworks" for further negotiation on matters of deeper import and continuing disagreement.

This method has worked well in some areas of environmental law, such as ozone depletion. Framework agreements may not even be treaties at all, but simply nonbinding pledges or informal memoranda of understanding. In some issue-areas, at least, this approach has proven quite effective in harmonizing conduct among states.[43] A more inclusive regime with fewer demands (and concomitantly smaller payouts) is preferable at first, in this view, to an exclusive arrangement with greater requirements and payoffs. Those favoring this approach tend to include human rights advocates, sociologists, and some international lawyers. These people harbor greater hope that the foundations of social order, even at the international level, might lie not only in reciprocal exchange – immediate, bilateral, and substantial – but also in shared ethical norms governing human interaction.

Through such interaction, reciprocity is not so much transcended as subtly transformed along the lines Piaget described as taking place over a few years in the child's moral development.[44] In this way, as Wendt writes,

> Even if states initially comply . . . for reasons of . . . self-interest, continuing adherence over time will tend to produce conceptions of identity and interest which presuppose its legitimacy, making compliance habitual or second nature. External constraints become internal constraints, so that social control is achieved primarily through self-control. Reciprocity is important in this context, since it is through this mechanism that states teach each other that following rules is worthwhile. . . . By observing each other's habitual compliance . . . states gradually learn that others have no desire to break the rules nor are they likely to seize opportunities for doing so, and as such can be trusted.[45]

Those who view humanitarian law in these terms – as capable of altering a state's self-understanding – do not interpret the Geneva Conventions primarily as a calculated exchange of rights for duties, benefits for costs, among potential belligerents. They understand these treaties, rather, as a prayer or gamble that the most fundamental and widely endorsed norms can be sustained on a nonreciprocal basis, simply through the shared belief in their desirability, which our successful social interaction confirms. Such norms may then become integral to the very identity of national leaders, to their view of themselves as rulers of law-abiding nations, which are members in good standing of the international community. Compliance will at least partly ensue for this reason alone, irrespective of instantaneous reciprocation by others.

The Geneva and Hague Conventions are highly inclusive in that virtually all states have found it possible to ratify them quickly.[46] They also impose rather exacting duties at war. Whereas compliance is relatively easy with regard to POW treatment, it has proven much more difficult in other areas, including the central principles of distinction (between the enemy's combatants and its noncombatants) and proportionality in the use of force, many conclude. We might thus describe the Conventions, by their formal terms at least, as relatively heavy on both benefits and burdens. Their near-universal ratification flows from the fact that, at the time, states assumed no true enforcement agency would soon arise. As with human rights treaties, ratification of humanitarian law conventions was perceived as "costless,"[47] an easy way to signal to the world community that one's state was a "good type." Most rules within these Conventions were also seen as consistent with state interests and as self-enforcing through the dynamics of reciprocity.

However, as international criminal law has burgeoned since 1990, with the addition of several new judicial institutions, future humanitarian treaties will not likely be ratified as unreflectively as the Geneva and Hague Conventions. The point for present purposes is simply that reasonable differences of opinion exist over the extent to which humanitarian law treaties, like other international regulatory regimes, should make the provision of generous benefits contingent upon fulfilling major burdens.

BEYOND RECIPROCITY, BEYOND JUSTICE

For all the liberal thinkers here discussed, reciprocity occupies an integral place in their accounts of justice. For none, however, does it constitute the whole of justice. Still, "it is not reciprocity's job, within a pluralistic theory, to justify everything worth justifying," as Schmidtz replies.[48] This is as true of reciprocity between national societies as within them. Whether we are dealing with single persons or large collectivities, those who cannot contribute in some way are still entitled to satisfaction of their most basic needs, however narrowly construed. These rights will not be grounded in reciprocity, but in respect for their human dignity[49] or simply on the basis of their capacity for suffering and the ready ability of others to prevent it. If their moral status demands our concern, this status and that concern must rest on something other than their current contributions to society, a burden they assume in exchange for societal benefits.

No one would claim that an incarcerated criminal, having failed to honor society's most basic rules and no longer contributing to it in the normal sense, forfeits all rights to humane treatment of any sort thereafter. None would even claim that those, like neo-Nazis, who would deny civil rights to groups they despise should in turn be denied all such rights themselves. But alas, liberal theory has had remarkably little to say about where the limits of reciprocity lie, at least not with any precision. As Allan Gibbard acknowledges, "Respecting a person will motivate one to certain restraints, to according him certain protections. [But] the content of those protections will normally have much to do with whatever social arrangements have been familiar. . . . Respect comes to be felt as entailing certain things, but the socio-psychic dynamics of what those things are must be complex" and will be resolved by whatever "arrangements will seem natural . . . familiar."[50]

The problem today is that central dimensions of the conflict with jihadist militants are entirely unfamiliar, so that many of the questions America faces do not readily offer any answers that "seem natural" to many of us. Our moral intuitions are trustworthy as far as they go, Gibbard counsels. But they may not take us far enough, with sufficient specificity.[51] Searching his mind for some natural and familiar terms of trade, conservative columnist Jonah Goldberg finds himself venturing, "I do not weep that Khalid Sheik Mohammed spent somewhere between .03 and .06 seconds feeling like he was drowning for every person he allegedly helped murder on 9/11." Yet Goldberg recoils immediately from his own suggestion: "Then again I think it would be horrific if we used that logic to justify waterboarding. It is not a technique that should be used for punishment"[52] (i.e., for retribution), with which Goldberg had momentarily confused it.

Respect for another's humanity may require many things and may vary with each conception of the principle, from the most modest and disengaged right up to ensuring all others equal capabilities through a generous welfare state.[53] The present problem in regard to jihadist terror suspects arises because our inclinations to behave respectfully begin to run afoul of our concurrent disposition to expect some reciprocation for our consistent contributions to a cooperative scheme – such as humanitarian law – from which the other benefits. These latter sentiments and moral intuitions are no less integral to the human experience than the former.

Though the idea of human rights aims to limit our expectations of reciprocity from others, one leading philosophical critic of reciprocity, Allen Buchanan, concedes that reciprocity remains relevant when the stakes involve risk of violent death. "Being obligated to bear the 'cost' of a risk of violent death," he writes, "seems to be a different matter"; that is, different from other nonreciprocal risks. "Here the lack of reciprocity seems to count . . . (i.e., reciprocity of risk of violent death)."[54] A nonreciprocal risk of violent death well describes the relation between belligerents who employ terror by directly targeting civilians and those refraining from that method of warfare. One might hence ask: Why should American citizens accept the risk of death – by fully honoring humanitarian law treaties – to release detained Al Qaeda suspects who will not accept the risk of death to save the lives of Western civilians (i.e., since Al Qaeda is an organization whose members risk death precisely to kill such civilians).

Buchanan even acknowledges that a lack of reciprocity largely explains the failure of developed democracies to intervene militarily to stop ongoing genocides.[55] "The citizens of the countries that are able to undertake effective intervention are generally the least vulnerable to violations of their basic human rights and those whose basic human rights they would protect through intervention are in no position to help protect the rights of the interveners. The reciprocity condition that makes the obligation to risk violent death plausible does not obtain."[56] In short, we have a duty to risk our lives for another only if the other is willing and able to do the same for us. Buchanan concludes that humanitarian intervention – though morally permissible and often laudable – is not obligatory. For it to be mandatory, its beneficiaries would have to be able to reciprocate the favor in some comparable way, at some point in the foreseeable future. That capacity would make them parties to either an implicit social contract. Even the basic human right not to suffer genocide is thus insufficient, in moral-theoretical terms, to create a duty in the rest of us to risk our lives to halt such grievous wrongdoing. And this in a philosophical account chiefly and avowedly aimed at confining reciprocity to a more limited place than that it occupies in other understandings of morality.

The next and final chapter on reciprocity as a moral principle assesses, and applies to the current conundrum, the novel view that humanitarian law's central purpose is often "corrective," in the sense of correcting for an ethical balance disrupted by behavior that rejects the legitimate claims of reciprocity. This view of law, more generally, has been salient in Western thought since the Greeks, so we will advance our argument by briefly moving still further backward in time, as we first did from Rawls to Kant and now onward to Aristotle.

7

Humanitarian Law as Corrective Justice:
Do Targeted Killing and Torture "Correct" for Terror?

A FAIR FIGHT IS A MEANINGFUL AIM,
DESPITE RESOURCE DISPARITY

Some would say that, if the Geneva and Hague Conventions harbor any implicit conception of a fair fight, it must surely be quite thin, for they have never required equality of arms. These treaties and related customary law have always permitted vast disparities in resources between military antagonists – and the consequent disparities in human suffering. That a superpower's superior matériel lets it impose certain asymmetrical risks on its foes – for example, much weaker roguish states and terrorist networks – is normatively irrelevant, according to the law of war.[1]

The type of reciprocity enshrined in humanitarian law is also compatible with the violent subordination of one belligerent by the other, which often results at least partly from resource disparities. To be lawful, such domination need only be effected without recourse to genocide, crimes against humanity, war crimes, and violations of the law of military occupation. The law aims to accommodate "realism" to this extent,[2] in that it does not actively interfere with more obvious forms of military domination. If it chose to, a more demanding understanding of reciprocity would be a good way to do so. Of course, other moral systems throughout history, including even the sexual ethics of the ancient Greeks,[3] set similar limitations on their ambitions, and so too on the scope of reciprocity, as a means of reconciling with the most entrenched features of existing power relations.

Some find humanitarian law's disregard for resource disparity to be very troubling. Yale law professor Paul Kahn,[4] for instance, writes that Iraq was foolish to obey international law and release its Western hostages in 1991, the only bargaining chip it had against its more powerful military opponents.[5] A law that denies a belligerent its only credible source of influence over events cannot "realistically expect . . . to gain the respect of countries that are more likely to be the victims than the allies of great powers," he adds.[6] On Kahn's account, jihadist terror does not turn contemporary warfare asymmetrical. In fact, it does the very opposite, restoring a measure of symmetry earlier disrupted by the suddenly overwhelming might of American armed forces after 1990.

Yet much of the material advantage (in long-range missiles, nuclear warheads, aircraft carriers, etc.) enjoyed by the United States proves almost entirely irrelevant in practical terms to winning conflicts with terrorist networks. Timely human intelligence from informants in the field,[7] followed by the rapid response of lightly armed forces,[8] is more often decisive. Asymmetrical warfare of the sort that jihadist terror represents is virtually defined by its effective circumvention of its adversary's material supremacy. This supposed supremacy proves evanescent, offering little protection against the terrorist's shrewd pinpointing of latent susceptibilities. The greater its material power, the greater its corresponding vulnerabilities and concomitant martial weaknesses.

These areas of exposure include more than the West's far-reaching dependence on computers, and thus its acute vulnerability to "information warfare" aimed at disabling them.[9] Such areas also encompass more mundane targets like transport hubs (e.g., airports and container port facilities) that are peculiarly susceptible to disruption by very small numbers of dedicated people.[10] As two military strategists remind us, "Despite owning the most powerful army, navy, air force, marines and space force in the history of human existence, the U.S. was unable either to deter or prevent some twenty individuals from making unopposed attacks on its national capital and its most iconic city in broad daylight."[11] The undoubted strengths of such a supposed "hyperpower" – indeed, the source of its prosperity, freedom, and power – are also its very weaknesses or at least inseparable from them.[12] Its vulnerability derives from its specifically modern form of social solidarity – organic, as Durkheim called it – reflecting the intricacy of its interdependencies.

A country's possession of greater material resources than those of its enemy will sometimes also render its legal duties more stringent.[13] Whether the incidental civilian damage done by each side has been "excessive" depends on each one's resources and resulting capabilities to distinguish between combatant and noncombatant. A belligerent with precision-guided missiles, for instance, will be held to a higher legal standard than one whose weaponry is much less sophisticated. On its face, the rule is the same for both: Civilian damage must be "proportionate" to military advantage anticipated from the particular use of force. Yet the rule means something quite different, depending on the respective material circumstances of each belligerent. This difference is considered fair because, as in all corrective justice, the baseline for legal judgment is the parties' position on entering the pertinent interaction – here, the particular armed conflict. That the "haves" previously chose to expend more of their national savings than the "have-nots" (even where the latter enjoy great wealth) to acquire more discriminating weapons systems becomes immaterial to their legal duties once war begins. It is the possession or nonpossession of those weapons that governs the scope and meaning of their legal duty to minimize unnecessary suffering.

How far should the preceding argument carry, however? Consider, in particular, its natural corollary. Interpreting humanitarian law to impose more stringent duties on belligerents with greater resources, more advanced technologies, and more developed organizational capacities entails less stringent duties for belligerents that lack substantial resources. Unless there was some defensible way of limiting its scope, the rule would subject belligerents with fewer and fewer resources to less and less stringent legal demands – until, with terrorists perhaps, it reached law's vanishing point.

Partisans and guerrillas throughout history, much like most terrorist groups today, are often incapable of taking prisoners because they hold no territory (other than perhaps a "safe house" here or there). They certainly hold no territory so large that it would be possible for them to establish fixed locales for POW detention consistent with standard requirements of humanitarian law. Yet the inability of these belligerents to conform their conduct to such universally accepted international norms surely does not legally excuse their noncompliance. Such a rule would exculpate, for instance, Confederate guerrilla fighter Nathan Bedford Forrest who, on capturing Fort Pillow during the American Civil War, refused the proffered surrender of more than a hundred soldiers, most of them black, "even as they fell to their knees with uplifted hands and screamed for mercy."[14] The southern partisans controlled no territory for holding POWs. Still, the law's logic surely should not extend so far as to excuse and incentivize such egregious misconduct.

When modern Western armies have defeated a more "primitive" enemy, moreover, this victory has often not been achieved through resource superiority but rather by wisely emulating the enemy's ways. As one scholar writes, in such circumstances "primitive tactics are superior, since civilized forces must adopt most of them – despite already possessing an often stupendous superiority in weapons, manpower, and supplies – in order to triumph over guerrilla adversaries."[15] Lt. Col. Ralph Peters puts the point more pungently:

After spending trillions of dollars on high-tech armaments, the U.S. finds itself confounded by a dirt-cheap weapon of genius: the suicide bomber.

The ultimate precision weapon and genuine "smart bomb," the suicide bomber is hard to deter and exasperatingly difficult to defeat. This is the "poor man's nuke." For a few hundred dollars (or less) and a human life, a suicide bomber can achieve strategic effects the U.S. Air Force can only envy. For all the claims that technology would dominate the twenty-first century, . . . we find that impassioned faith still trumps microchips.[16]

This fact was often lost upon the Bush administration's critics.[17] The West's military susceptibility to asymmetrical challenge did not begin with jihadist terror, of course. Throughout the modern history of response to insurgency movements, states have repeatedly discovered that "no matter how many soldiers and civilians were killed, how much money was spent, how powerful and sophisticated were the arms employed, foreigners cannot militarily defeat a determined insurgency except by virtual genocide,"[18] as one scholar of the subject concludes, with some hyperbole. A more sober assessment similarly concludes that powerful democracies, in particular, often "fail in small wars because they cannot find a winning balance between the costs of the war in human lives [to their own forces] and the political cost incurred by controlling these costs with force, between acceptable levels of casualties and acceptable levels of brutality."[19]

For the larger belligerent in such conflicts to invoke the language of fairness is therefore by no means preposterous, however risible many may initially find it. Some will of course find unconvincing any account of reciprocity as fairness in the allocation of risk that ignores resource disparities. For it must call to mind the notorious aphorism that the law, in its majestic fairness, equally prohibits the rich and the poor of Paris from sleeping beneath their good city's bridges, begging in its streets, and stealing bread.[20] However, the fact that humanitarian law ignores resource disparities between belligerents does not mean that it lacks an intelligible and coherent notion of a fair fight. The fairness of the fight is enforced and remedied through mechanisms of corrective justice.

FROM CIVIL TO CRIMINAL PROCESS:
HUMANITARIAN LAW'S CHANGING FOCUS

Humanitarian law can still hold states like Serbia civilly liable for failing to prevent or punish genocide.[21] Yet in its current concern with the prosecution of natural persons, humanitarian law has become increasingly penal in focus and so aims to deter individuals from crime and to exact retribution from those who cannot be deterred. It is only in recent decades, however, that humanitarian law has come to be understood in this way. For all of its modern history until the Nuremberg proceedings, it threatened only civil liability between states, as if merely redressing a private dispute rather than sewing up ruptures in a wider social contract.[22] Since the Middle Ages,[23] the remedy for unjust war making and unjust methods of fighting was restitution – the return of property wrongfully taken – or compensation of the aggrieved state's losses.[24] The right of reprisal was considered a means to that end, hence not initially understood as punishment.[25] The prevailing party was the state itself, however, the leaders of which might do whatever they wished with their legal recovery. The nationals of the victim state were not themselves entitled to anything at international law: not to damages suffered, much less a criminal prosecution of their individual victimizers.[26]

It might be said that, as humanitarian law becomes less active in civil litigation and more criminal in focus, its purposes must correspondingly evolve from corrective and compensatory to retributive and deterrent. There is still a debt to be repaid, to be sure, and it is still repaid to the victim. But the victim is now understood, more broadly, as the world at large, not simply the immediate sufferers. The fitting measure of sanction also increasingly turns not only on how greatly the victims – broad and narrow – have suffered or lost but also on the reprehensibility of the malefactor's mental state.

Even so, the law of war remains in key respects an exercise in corrective justice, aimed at restoring a wrongfully disrupted *status quo ante* between "private" parties. That is the point in time before a wrongful resort to force (*jus ad bellum*) occurred and/or before belligerents resorted to wrongful fighting methods (*jus in bello*). Thus, compensation for war crimes, aggression, torture, and crimes against humanity has been available through civil suit before the International Court of Justice.[27] Correction of the harms brought about by unjust warfare has been its aim.

Other aspects of humanitarian law display a similar concern with correcting wrongs between particular parties, no less than vindicating larger societal norms through punishment. Just as an award of money damages should not overcompensate, so too a belligerent reprisal, to be lawful, must be proportionate to the prior wrong it professes to redress. It would otherwise cause more harm than necessary to correct that wrong and grant the repriser more than necessary to secure its rightful position. Another example: Today the *jus ad bellum* has narrowed almost entirely to the right of self-defense, on how the victim of an armed attack may seek redress, restore itself to a previous condition, taken as the relevant baseline. When country A attacks country B, the latter's lawful acts of self-defense permit it to "correct" the consequences of A's misconduct, driving it from B's territory.

A final illustration: Geneva's Additional Protocol I's dispensation for national liberation movements, demanding less of them than their state opponents in distinctive dress and open display of weaponry, is sometimes rejected for breaching the traditional wall between *jus ad bellum* and *jus in bello* rules. Even this rule, however, is avowedly a means for remedying the injustices of colonialism and is hence defended as an instrument of corrective justice.

If some of humanitarian law is *not* about correcting past injustice, this is partly because certain wrongs have been regarded as entirely beyond the scope of justice at all – corrective, distributive, retributive, or otherwise. From Kant in the eighteenth century through the Lieber Code in the nineteenth up to the current Geneva Conventions, a recurrent concern in formulating norms of warfare has been to prevent either side from engaging in the kind of actions – atrocities, in a word, as distinguished from killing combatants in battle – that would greatly prejudice the possibility of harmonious relations between them at war's end.[28] The wrong of mass atrocity consisted in the wrongdoer's adoption of maxims of conduct that, if universalized, would make lasting peace impossible, because of the inconsolable sorrow and depth of indignation thereby aroused, according to Kant.[29]

This formulation may seem to us today rather quirky. But it is no coincidence that atrocities in international war were always the sort of injustices that could not readily be redressed, if at all, by civil or private law. They seemed, at least until the advent of international criminal courts in the mid-twentieth century,[30] to lie entirely beyond the reach of legal justice *tout court*, and hence were particularly important to prevent *ex ante*. Of course, corrective justice can only effectively address injustices of a sort susceptible to correction through restoring a *status quo ante*. This is impossible where people have died. Yet even here, the partial and more modest achievements of corrective justice in its material modality should not be dismissed as unworthy, though it addresses the symptoms rather than sources of warfare. Law rarely goes to the root causes of anything, after all.

Resource disparity, by contrast, is a matter of distributive justice. Correcting such disparity is a more heroic ambition that necessarily raises larger and more controversial questions,[31] ones that the law of war – in its realistic humility – has never addressed, much less answered. Law is modest here for the same reason that states do not form a true world government,[32] even a federal one, capable of solving problems the UN now apparently cannot. The depth of moral disagreement, no less than of conflicting interests, is too great.

Corrective justice aims its sights somewhat lower than distributive justice. Yet at least since Aristotle it has been regarded as a distinct and genuine form of justice.[33] In any event, the "best" should never become the enemy of the "good." And if distributive justice is simply inapt to a given situation, then it is not really "the best" at all.[34] In this vein, Weinrib contends,

> Corrective and distributive justice embody categorically different structures of justification. Corrective justice links the doer and sufferer of an injustice in terms of their correlative positions. Distributive justice, on the other hand, deals with the sharing of a benefit or burden; it involves comparing the potential parties to the distribution in terms of a distribution criterion.... The categorical distinction between correlativity and comparison is made clear in the difference between the numbers of parties that each admits.... Distributive justice admits any number of parties because, in principle, no limit exists for the number of persons who can be compared and among whom something can be divided.[35]

It follows that, "for purposes of justifying a determination of liability, corrective justice is independent of distributive justice. No distributive criterion can serve as a justification for holding one person liable to another."[36] Moreover, "within the corrective justice framework, rights cannot be understood . . . simply as bundles of welfare, for then liability would ultimately be only a mechanism for adjusting the relative welfare of the parties."[37] With corrective justice, "the reasons that justify the protection of the plaintiff's right are the same as the reasons that justify the existence of the defendant's duty."[38] Thus, "the doing and the suffering of injustice form a single juridical sequence in which each party participates only through the presence of the other."[39]

Everything Weinrib says here about corrective justice, and nothing that he says about distributive justice, squarely applies to the concerns and content of humanitarian law.[40] Humanitarian law is concerned with establishing the criminal liability of torturers, those who commit grave breaches of the Geneva Conventions, and with the civil liability of the states they serve. It does not establish grounds for distributing primary social goods, like education, but rather for defining and preventing a social evil: unnecessary suffering. Criminal law also seeks to redress a loss to the victim (i.e., society at large) by imposing a corresponding loss on the wrongdoer. Punishment under humanitarian law, in particular, aims to offset a loss to international peace and security by means of a corresponding gain in deterrence,[41] both general and specific, as well as in the expressive reaffirmation of moral principles central to the global social contract.

Criminal law, whether domestic or international, is always corrective insofar as the beneficiary of these several gains is the public at large, rather than the perpetrator's more immediate, individual victim, who may be compensated by civil lawsuit – in the International Court of Justice, when the victim is a state. The fact that criminal and humanitarian law require *courts* to effectuate the shift of loss, to restore the risk symmetry, is hardly a distinguishing feature of these bodies of "public" law. The "private" law of tort, after all, also requires third-party intermediaries to achieve that end and so is never entirely bilateral in structure.

SYMMETRY OF RISK WITHIN HUMANITARIAN LAW

Humanitarian law is committed to symmetry of risk only in relevant respect, and some disparities are morally immaterial. "The standard of justice that the principle of reciprocity of risk exemplifies," Jules Coleman notes, "should reflect the standing of individuals relative to one another in some appropriate dimension."[42] What makes a dimension "appropriate" for such purposes? One may initially be tempted to regard all risk as morally relevant, so that all nontrivial risk asymmetry renders illegitimate any legal rules permitting it. This is no mere *reductio ad absurdum* on my part, for others have seriously defended this position. Rules allowing asymmetrical risk arising from resource disparity "are unstable," Paul Kahn writes, "because they compel innovation by the disadvantaged side," particularly via "the infliction of reciprocal injury on a morally innocent civilian population."[43]

In other words, by an almost implacable logic, an inexorable rhythm, the impulse to impose "reciprocal injury" – or reciprocal risk, in present terms – will find a way to assert itself willy-nilly. If one rejects such anthropomorphic metaphors, one might say that the impulse to reciprocate risk is a force of nature; it behaves like water, especially a powerful river, ultimately finding its natural course regardless of the flimsy human obstacles erected in its path. Hence, for instance, "if the Palestinians cannot hope realistically to create a reciprocal risk for the Israeli military, they will direct the risk of injury at civilians," Kahn contends. "For the asymmetrically powerful to insist on the maintenance of the combatant-noncombatant distinction has the appearance of self-serving moralizing."[44] Kahn stops just short of saying that this "appearance" is also the relevant reality. The repudiation of the moral distinction between civilian and combatant is not likely to prove the end of the story, he concedes. "Just as it is practically intolerable to suffer an asymmetrical use of force, it is intolerable to suffer an asymmetrical risk to a civilian population. There is likely to be a cycle of escalation, as each side responds to the other's infliction of risk upon noncombatants. The bombing of London was followed by the bombing of Berlin."[45]

"If it became clear that Iraq was responsible for the release of anthrax in this country," which caused the deaths of several civilians, "would the American response respect the line separating combatants from noncombatants?" Kahn pondered in 2002. "The Israelis allegedly threatened Iraq with just such a retaliation when they perceived a threat of attack by chemical weapons during the [1991] Gulf War. It is hard to believe that any country would act differently."[46] Kahn credits the Israeli threat for Iraq's decision not to go chemical, inferring a broader point: "The lesson may be that reciprocity is still the most effective enforcement mechanism for the rules of warfare."[47]

In sum, law's efforts to tame such powerful impulses will prove as futile as those of the Army Corps of Engineers to tame the Mississippi, in Kahn's view. It is only the lawyers and the engineers who will emerge the worse for wear, if not entirely swept away by ensuing floods. Weaker parties will simply find a way to improve their strategic posture vis-à-vis more powerful adversaries, on this reasoning. If that means violating rules written by the latter, so be it. So much the better, in fact. Only lawyers who know nothing of war – or the world, for that matter – could ever have thought otherwise, Kahn implies. Law ignores such unsavory realities of warfare at its peril. War itself will follow its own course, blithely thumbing its nose at any law purporting to override such harsh but inexorable realities. Kahn here essentially embraces General William T. Sherman's argument, announced on ordering the expulsion of all civilians from Atlanta, before torching the city: "You might as well appeal against the thunderstorm as against these terrible hardships of war. If we must be enemies, let us be men and fight it out . . . and not deal in such hypocritical appeals to God and humanity."[48]

Whenever highbrow academicians defend their views with such hardheadedness, assuming the anti-intellectual mantle, there is usually reason to delve deeper, however. Despite Kahn's urgings here, most inequality of arms may properly remain extraneous to the concerns of humanitarian law. It is no accident that those generally most concerned with inequality between North and South in the world today rarely extend this concern to the domain of military hardware, urging poor countries to acquire more arms.[49] Nor does our sympathy for the truly wretched of the earth really require us to root, in every armed conflict, for the military "underdog" – and interpret the laws of war accordingly – no matter how aggressive its aims and egregious its martial misconduct. No one but a Yale law professor would seriously entertain the thought that the solution to the "problem" of Saddam Hussein's or Al Qaeda's inferior weaponry vis-à-vis the United States would be urging Saddam to keep his civilian hostages or releasing jihadists from other humanitarian law norms, so as to permit them, like Saddam, to harm civilians intentionally.[50]

Yet just after the 1991 Gulf War, Kahn wrote, "To assert that massive aerial bombardment – with its inevitable civilian casualties – complies with the international law of warfare, but that *reciprocal* efforts by a third-world country to put civilian populations at risk violate international law only reveals one's own political interests."[51] And if, by Kahn's logic, Iraq in 1990 – with its huge army and nonconventional weapons programs – may employ such means when fighting a superpower, then surely a much weaker, nonstate belligerent may do the same, *a fortiori*.

On a more generous reading, Kahn may simply be suggesting that current humanitarian law, by authorizing certain methods of warfare but not others, favors more powerful states over less powerful ones. Yet this assertion all but ignores the moral difference between intentionally targeting civilians and the many lawful methods of force that humanitarian law permits. Kahn does not apparently question the defensibility of that distinction, one long enshrined in the law of war.[52] If this distinction reflects a duty properly binding on all, then the fact that it may sometimes favor one belligerent over its adversary is immaterial from a moral point of view, which is presumably the point of view that humanitarian law should adopt. Virtually all legal rules turn out to burden some more than others, after all.

HUMANITARIAN LAW AS SIDE-CONSTRAINT

Noncombatant immunity is simply a side-constraint on what belligerents may do to one another in war, whatever their larger purposes. In this light, Kahn should be seen as making merely a prudential point about the need to write rules with which all parties will be sufficiently disposed to comply, given whatever enforcement mechanisms exist. The considerable regulatory constraints on tax accountants do not burden me at all, for instance, as long as I do not enter that profession. The analogous claim would be that those who intentionally attack civilians are not playing the same 'game' as those who refrain from doing so (i.e., those who attack only in ways consistent with humanitarian law). The activity in which they engage, in other words, is not warfare. It is merely murder, which is a war crime; that is, a crime even within the lethal context of war.

The proclivity to evade the law's constraints through innovation, by developing new methods of accomplishing the same ends, is by no means unique to the powerless. It is, in fact, more common among the powerful. Kahn does not suggest that the propensity of tax attorneys to devise creative tax avoidance schemes through corporate restructurings for their wealthy business clients is a force of nature too powerful to warrant law's efforts at redress. Why should the first variety of creative evasion deserve our sympathetic understanding, even quasi-endorsement, whereas this second receives only our moral reprobation – that is, unless all disparity in wealth and power is *ipso facto* illegitimate? The latter is a position Kahn presumably would not defend. Why should a world-weary prudence override moral principle in law's efforts to punish mass atrocity but not securities and tax fraud?

Jean Baudrillard, an influential postmodernist thinker, carries Kahn's line of analysis a step further. Jihadists cannot be blamed for the fact that the global system, including its humanitarian law, does not allow them to pursue their goals effectively. Like others who also oppose the spread of Western capitalism, jihadists are entitled to revise the rules of the 'game' in any way that will permit this legitimate objective to become the realistic aspiration it otherwise could never be. "It was the system itself which created the objective conditions for this brutal retaliation," Baudrillard thus argues. "By seizing all the cards for itself, it forced the Other to change the rules. And the new rules are fierce ones, because the stakes are fierce."[53]

One such rule change has been to permit methods of contestation to which response in kind is practically impossible, almost unimaginable. "To a system whose very excess of power poses an insoluble challenge, the terrorists respond with a definitive act which is also not susceptible of exchange. Terrorism is the act that restores an irreducible singularity to the heart of a system of generalized exchange."[54] The "singularity" lies in the novel method: the suicidal attack designed to cause maximum civilian deaths. This method is "not susceptible of exchange" because the United States is unable to respond in the same currency. Or, as a more conventional foreign policy analyst puts it, "How do you stop a foe whose tolerance for pain exceeds your willingness to inflict it?"[55] Just as a gift too generous to be reciprocated establishes a certain power over its humbled recipient, so can a wrong too odious to reciprocate disable its victim from retaliation. In the first case, it is the recipient's poverty that creates the disparity; in the second, it is the victim's wealth or "civilization" and the higher ethical standard attending it.

The "system of generalized exchange" in international relations (and in interstate warfare particularly) has hitherto operated by the principle of reciprocity, which the West – and most of the rest – find inconceivable here. This is why the 9/11 attacks go to "the heart" of that system, as Baudrillard writes. He thus exhorts jihadists: "Defy the system by a gift to which it cannot respond except by its own death and its own collapse"[56] (i.e., by violating everything it claims to stand for). "The terrorist hypothesis is that the system itself will commit suicide" – destroy everything that morally distinguishes it from its adversary, thereby losing its very springs of support – "in response to the multiple challenges posed by deaths and suicides. . . . This is the spirit of terrorism."[57] It is a spirit Baudrillard incisively interprets,[58] it must be said, even if he all but celebrates it.

The antagonists in this struggle are well paired, he continues, despite the differing methods they are prepared to employ against each other. For in the conflict between the suicide bomber and global capitalism with its myriad methods of coopting all challengers (to say nothing of its law, wealth, and state power), "this is terror against terror."[59] The jihadists employ "asymmetric terror,"[60] Baudrillard acknowledges, but it is well chosen for precisely this reason. America's unwillingness to respond with proportionate reprisal, jot for jot, reveals that this "is [an] asymmetry which leaves global omnipotence entirely disarmed." For "the system survives only by constantly drawing those attacking it into fighting on the ground of reality, which is always its own. . . . If they were content just to fight the system with its own weapons," respecting its own law, in particular, "they would immediately be eliminated."[61]

The 9/11 attackers were therefore wise instead "to shift the struggle into the symbolic sphere,"[62] where they have gloriously triumphed, he concludes. Their act symbolically exposed the dependence of America's very potency on its most acute vulnerabilities, technical and moral. Some will say, he admits, that "these terrorists exchanged their deaths for a place in paradise. There again, then, they are not fighting fair, since they get salvation, which we [secular moderns] cannot even continue to hope for. So we mourn our deaths" – those of our civilian victims and soldiers – "while they can turn theirs into very high-definition stakes."[63]

RESPONSE "IN KIND"? FINDING RECIPROCITY'S TERMS OF TRADE

Although the law of war has always been centrally concerned with matters of corrective justice, it has treated those of distributive justice as beyond its ken. The injustices requiring correction are those violating a principle of fairness, understood as the idea that each side be permitted to subject the other to the same general category of risk. As George Fletcher writes, "Implicit in the concept of reciprocity" is the notion 'that risks are fungible with others of the same 'kind.'"[64] The remedy for asymmetrical risk imposition may be either liability as found by a court of law, where that is practical, or release from a corresponding prohibition, where it is not.

Even granting this point leaves open the question, "How does one determine when risks are counterpoised as species of the same genus?"[65] Or as Gibbard more colloquially puts it, if the concept is to be rendered operational, "reciprocity needs terms of trade."[66] Such terms must be found if law's remedy for its breach is to redistribute risk more symmetrically. Sometimes these terms are well established, either by express rule or custom, when etiquette forbids explicit expression. Yet often disagreements arise over whether the *quo* was worth all the *quid*, especially in the context of foreign aid programs.[67]

The same issue arises in the area of armed conflict, particularly in connection with belligerent reprisals. Cassese hence notes that "lawful belligerent reprisals... may include the use of prohibited weapons as a response to serious violations of international humanitarian law... like the killing of prisoners of war or the intentional shelling of civilians."[68] The question of fungibility here tends to be couched in terms of proportionality, a doctrine in the law of war that – though ancient – has never attained much clarity, jurists concur. Talk about proportionality or "terms of trade" suggests a numerical precision that is inapt in the context of armed conflict, for even the most economically minded of military strategists are quick to concede that wartime bargaining between belligerents, especially by way of reprisals, involves an "idiom" that is highly "symbolic."[69] Even when money is used to measure the parties' respective contributions to a cooperative scheme, disagreements often arise over how much each side's concessions to the other are really worth.[70]

Reciprocity's "terms of trade" are often wildly unequal, moreover, as among patrons and clients in traditional and feudal societies, master craftsmen and junior apprentices, or lords and vassals.[71] And where women produce the actual goods offered up to the community at certain tribal potlatches, often only their husbands derive social status from the ensuing cycle of exchange.[72] Yet social scientists and historians often employ the term "reciprocity" to describe such exchange relationships, for there exist well-settled expectations, sometimes enforceable through law or politics, on all sides about who owes what to whom in response to which sort of offering.[73] Though infected by power disparities, the expectations of subordinates – when dishonored by superiors – generate resentment, some-times even organized revolt. As Taussig thus writes of Peruvian tribes in the early years of Spanish conquest,

> The Indians continued to evaluate their relationships to their new masters . . . by the criteria of reciprocity, despite its being constantly abused or denied. So long as this principle of reciprocity was a living force in the minds of the Indians, it meant trouble. To . . . deny reciprocity is to invoke war and the wrath of the gods.[74]

Whenever such reciprocity does not take the form of exchanging one thing for an identical counterpart, judgments of fungibility are necessary. In social life generally, no less than in the conflict with Al Qaeda, these judgments require assessments of equivalence, which are more evaluative than empirical. And "there can be heated disputes about which symmetries are germane,"[75] Gibbard adds.[76] One might ask, for instance: What relation exists between the risk of having one's skyscrapers destroyed by hijacked civilian aircraft and the risk of having one's partisans coercively interrogated for information about those responsible for such attacks, with a view to preventing future ones?

In other words, even if one were to agree to play the game of terrorist war according to the rules of *lex talionis* – an eye for an eye, a tooth for a tooth – one then faces the question: If terror is an "eye," isn't sustained detention perhaps merely a "tooth," i.e., a body part – dentally replaceable at that – of much lesser value to its possessor than his vision? Even torture for terror is surely rather more like a tooth for an eye, if one will endure the distasteful metaphor for a moment longer.

Would not true reciprocity in the full *lex talionis* sense therefore authorize the United States to hijack a Saudi Airlines jumbo jet and fly it into the great mosque at Mecca during the annual Haj? Virtually none of the Muslim religious observers thereby killed would have borne any responsibility for the 9/11 attacks, of course, just as virtually none of those killed in the U.S. on that day bore any measure of responsibility for the wrongs bin Laden ascribes to America. At least in this sense, one of the senses intended by this book's title, the age of reciprocity has indeed definitively ended. We immediately repudiate this distasteful hypothetical analogy.

This is also one plausible reading of Baudrillard's Delphic observation: "What terrorism revives is something that cannot be traded in a system of . . . generalized exchange. . . . For the system can function only if it can exchange itself for its own image, reflect itself like the towers in their twinness."[77] This interpretation sits uneasily, however, with his repeated assertions that jihadist terror simply mirrors back at America the oppressive terror of the global capitalism that the country has foisted on the world. Yet Baudrillard may nonetheless be implicitly conceding that even America, though its mischief may be fungible with that of Al Qaeda in other respects, is unwilling to retaliate in kind for 9/11, in any literal sense. That bin Laden thereby may gain the martial upper hand over his nemesis does not apparently trouble Baudrillard in the least.

What then happens when the reciprocity principle would, in isolation from other weightier considerations, permit retaliation proportionate to the initial wrong – whatever that might entail in regard to 9/11 – but where that measure of retaliation is barred by the victim's own ethical identity (and self-interest)? Does it mean that any lesser measure of reciprocation is therefore permissible *a fortiori*? Even the United States' fiercest critics would surely acknowledge that it would never descend to reciprocity of the kind illustrated in the Haj hypothetical. But more moderate variants of reciprocation are readily conceivable, and morally defensible under both Kantian and corrective justice theories – again, in isolation from other considerations.

Consider, for instance, that Al Qaeda rejects the distinction between combatants and noncombatants by directly targeting the latter, as in the 9/11 attacks. Acting on the principle of reciprocity, the United States might decline to respect that same distinction, not by committing random attacks on noncombatants, but in other, more discriminating ways. Might it not, for instance, detain Al Qaeda members until they would no longer pose serious danger, even though they do not qualify as "combatants"?[78]

This is precisely what the United States has done, of course. Yet the Bush administration has defended this course of action with very shaky legal arguments. The foregoing discussion, however, outlines a strong moral argument – from reciprocity as common rules – in support of this course of action. No one could argue, moreover, that the U.S. response, insofar at it disregarded the traditional legal line between combatant and noncombatant, was disproportionate to the violation of that line eliciting such response. And because the reciprocity principle so thoroughly infuses international law, including the customary law of war, the moral rationale becomes the basis for a legal argument as well.

Still, the law of reprisal retains specific doctrinal requirements of its own that do not perfectly match this more general argument from principle. The conduct that reprisal permits must be prospective in focus – that is, motivated and calculated to return the violator to compliance, to restoring a fair baseline as the law of war understands this goal. The Bush administration sought to defend its policies on targeted killing, detention, and interrogation neither in terms of retributive punishment nor prospective inducement of Al Qaeda's future compliance. So the logic of reciprocity, to the extent it tacitly informs administration policy in these areas, conforms neither to the black letter law of reprisal nor the purposes of punishment. These policies were instead defended simply as a means of dismantling and defeating Al Qaeda.

Some will contend that the risks presented by terror and by torture are reasonably symmetrical. Not only are both grave breaches of the Geneva Conventions,[79] but more to the point: "torture terrorizes," as Luban observes. Its *in terrorem* effect "is rooted in pain's biological function of impelling us in the most urgent way possible to escape from the source of pain – for that impulse is indistinguishable from panic."[80] Torture has hence often been a major tool for terrorizing the subject populations of colonial empires,[81] personalist dictatorships,[82] and modern military regimes.[83] Since Voltaire, its earliest modern associations are with tyranny, not warfare.

Yet even conventional warfare, in which one's antagonists do not attack civilian populations, is very much about terror. For success in war always requires forcing another to submit to one's will and to act against his own, as Clausewitz stressed. One's enemy will do so only from fear of great pain and violent death, a state of mind that virtually defines the psychological experience of terror. Terror and torture both instill a helplessness in their victim by destroying the sense of ordinariness in which emotional equanimity and stable identity reside.[84] It is tempting to dismiss the ordinary and its preservation as too humble and bland an ideal. Yet as philosopher Charles Taylor notes,

> The sense of the importance of the everyday in human life, along with its corollary about the importance of suffering, colours our whole understanding of what it is truly to respect human life and integrity. Along with the central place given to autonomy, it defines a version of this demand which is peculiar to our civilization, the modern West.[85]

The two are connected, in fact: "An affirmation of the value of ordinary life . . . is also seen as establishing the individual's freedom to determine the goals of his or her own life and own definition of happiness."[86] Another political theorist similarly observes,

> The ordinary gives us a sense of comfort; it allows us to make certain predictions about what will happen. . . . It allows a certain constancy of life.

It is reliable. The sun sets, the sun rises, another day of life begins. . . . And so we celebrate the ordinary as the practical form that peaceable living takes when life is good, and we cling to any vestiges of the ordinary that survive when catastrophe takes hold of us.[87]

Even these simple comforts threaten to dissolve, however, once terror becomes commonplace, the now ordinary, "the new normal." In this sense, both terror and torture are "catastrophes" that leave us clinging to what remains of the ordinary in one's life. This effect upon the individual ramifies in turn throughout society. Scheffler captures this in suggesting that "terrorism is morally distinctive insofar as it seeks to exploit the nexus of violence and fear in such a way as to degrade or destabilize an existing social order."[88]

Whether these risks of terror and torture are readily fungible, in Fletcher's terms, is a possibility that must be seriously considered. Are torture, sustained detention, and targeted killing ever a commensurate response to terror?[89] Do they contribute to restoring the symmetry of risk that humanitarian law seeks to maintain? In the extensive public debate over torture, dominated as it is by lawyers, this question has not even been posed. No one has asked whether these two types of risk – though perhaps not exactly "the same kind," in Fletcher's terms – might be at least commensurable. Can the threat of coercive interrogation and long but sanitary detention constitute a fair response to the mass murder of thousands, insofar as the former imposes risks of lesser moral magnitude?

Recall that Kahn's view is that it is too much to expect adherence to common rules from those possessing radically unequal arms. However, we should not confuse the search for fair rules for the search for rules that Al Qaeda will accept. A set of rules might be perfectly fair in the sense that they would be chosen by all reasonable, self-interested parties behind a veil of ignorance, without necessarily eliciting the consent of those actually concerned once they no longer occupy the original position. More to the point, rules of humanitarian law are not unfair simply because the possibility of victory under them is not entirely equal. Respect for the rules need promise only a nontrivial hope of victory[90] to satisfy Rawls's "strains of commitment." A reasonable belligerent in the original position might well accept rules permitting it somewhat less than a 50 percent chance of prevailing, in particular, if those rules also precluded its complete annihilation and enslavement on defeat, as modern humanitarian law has always done. Such rules would surely be chosen in the Rawlsian original position as well.

Humanitarian law here understands fairness as a matter of process, not result, and in this respect departs from Rawls, who is concerned with both. But a concern with both process and results characterizes all other rules of fair competition, from the law of antitrust and electoral campaigns to that of legal ethics. And war is necessarily competitive, of course, though it is also cooperative in certain respects. In antitrust and legal ethics, the law considers just results more likely to result from fair process than from unfair. Humanitarian law focuses similarly on the process of armed conflict, not on ensuring that the initial aggressor does not prevail over its victim.

Such law regulates an issue-area, however, about which more substantive agreement about justice's requirements is unlikely. For antitrust law, it is enough that economic competition in the marketplace advances efficiency and material welfare. For the law of lawyering, it is sufficient that adversarial competition in the courtroom often helps advance the discovery of truth and thereby substantive justice as well. But here the analogy with humanitarian law breaks down. Military competition in warfare cannot be said to advance any such social objective. Humanitarian law seeks to minimize superfluous suffering, a modest but worthy goal. It does not, however, generally seek to ensure that the aggrieved victim in war prevails against the aggressor, a more ambitious aim. It does not, in other words, aim to secure a just result to the underlying dispute between the belligerents.

One is tempted to say that the very level of controversy surrounding the question of just results is reason enough, in the interests of reaching interstate agreement on common rules, to remove it from the table entirely. Better to insulate humanitarian law altogether from questions of distributive justice as well. For those concerned with separating adjudication from "politics," it is often sufficient that "even if corrective justice works against a distributive background," one that it does not question, "it does not incorporate the justification of the distribution into its own structure"[91] and so retains an autonomy from more contentious distributive debate. This answer will satisfy only the formalist, however. It will not satisfy anyone viewing law primarily as an instrument for achieving social purposes.

Hiving off the distributive question from adjudication's concern hardly removes it, however. In fact, excluding distributive issues simply lets the burdens of inequity lie where they fall and so implicitly takes sides on the issue, rather than remaining truly agnostic toward it. As Kress observes, "Politics enters into the decision of whether a particular human activity is to be ordered by corrective justice or by distributive. . . . For example, a political decision, or lack of one, determines whether auto accidents are to be regulated by tort law (corrective justice) or . . . by a compensation scheme (distributive justice)."[92] Nor is it possible to say that corrective justice is the exclusive concern of private law, and distributive justice that of public. For both bodies of law, on closer inspection, turn out to be regularly enlisted in service of the other.[93]

NATIONAL WEALTH, WARTIME RESOURCE DISPARITY, AND HUMANITARIAN LAW

Rapid economic growth often disrupts domestic social and political hierarchies, and the legal changes necessary to accommodate such growth are therefore frequently resisted.[94] Yet wealth is not inherently zero-sum, and international humanitarian law cannot correct the wealth disparities that international economic law may produce, short of authorizing the Global South to sack the North as the Visigoths sacked Rome. This is one reason why the question of equalizing military resources is one of distributive justice, not corrective. As such, the entire question properly lies beyond the ken of humanitarian law, even if its answer were necessarily damning of existing disparities, which it need not be.

Still, the prudential fact Kahn highlights earlier – that the underdog will never follow rules of warfare guaranteeing its destruction – is undoubtedly pertinent to any nonideal theory of humanitarian law.[95] Such law must be designed to elicit both *de jure* acceptance and *de facto* compliance in a decidedly nonideal world. If violating humanitarian law is the only way in which militant jihadists can win what they seek, then this is what they will almost certainly do. It is best for their adversaries to operate on this assumption, at least. Kahn is correct that it may have been only Saddam's insufficient strategic savvy that led him to release his Western hostages in 1990, the most important source of power he had against the West in its imminent war against him.

"STRAINS OF COMMITMENT" TO HUMANITARIAN LAW

"When we enter an agreement," Rawls writes, "we must be able to honor it even should the worst possibilities prove to be the case. Otherwise, we have not acted in good faith."[96] The whole point of the original position is to be able to derive rules that can be justified to those who will turn out to fare least well under their application. An agreement that imposed duties too onerous to accept in practice would create intolerable "strains of commitment,"[97] he admits.

In a "well-ordered society," rules will be relatively stable, including rules of warfare within international society. To attain stability, they must be freely acceptable to all members of that society "who desire to act as the principles of justice require,"[98] whatever these may prove to be. Militant jihadists will simply reject any rules of humanitarian law greatly prejudicing the possibility of obtaining their political goals, Kahn suggests. In other words, current rules of humanitarian law – however otherwise defensible – might therefore fail the strains of commitment test.

Rawls himself acknowledges that parties behind the veil of ignorance would agree to just "penalties that stabilize a scheme of cooperation." He adds that "those who find that being disposed to act justly is not a good for them cannot deny" that "it is rational to authorize the measures needed to maintain just institutions."[99] It may therefore be, as Brian Barry suggests, that "it is simply a brute fact that some people will be reluctant to do what there are good independent reasons for saying justice demands." If so, he continues, then "people in the original position should be content if the principles they arrived at could be . . . stable . . . by coercing those who do not accept them freely."[100]

The current rules of humanitarian law offer much better treatment to the "worst off" (i.e. war's losers and the victims of its horrors on both sides) than rules that might permit their enslavement, torture, or extermination – common practices throughout human history.[101] Many other doctrines of just war, religious and secular, have been far less generous. It was precisely to foreclose more ruthlessly utilitarian rules, allowing sacrifice of the worst-off for the welfare of everyone else, that Rawls introduced the "strains of commitment" idea.[102] The idea recognizes that there is surely some level of well-being below which no one can be expected voluntarily to fall.[103]

Any defensible rules of humanitarian law must be so compelling that even war's losers should not be able reasonably to withhold their consent from them. It is easy to imagine, in fact, that prospective belligerents in the original position, ignorant of what sort of belligerent (state or nonstate) they might later turn out to be, would choose more or less the rules that humanitarian law currently enshrines, for these entirely foreclose the truly worst-case scenarios in defeat (extermination, enslavement, etc.). No one who is risk averse and has limited altruism – that is, no one in Rawls's original position or something approximating it – would settle for less in contemplating his own military defeat.

That belligerent would also insist on no more. The far more ambitious goal of guaranteeing an equal probability of victory to both sides would be impossible to define, much less to implement. Victory most often turns less on raw numbers – of guns and troops – than on social cohesion in combat and the tactical intelligence with which such resources and personnel are commanded.[104] To meet the demands of distributive justice as some understand it, humanitarian law would then presumably need to ensure that such intelligence was equally distributed between the belligerents' leaderships. If the law must satisfy this requirement to be passably just, then humanitarian law will never remotely approximate justice. If it must do so to warrant its very endeavor, then it should give up and acknowledge that its very discourse has always been a mystification.

Recall that Jinks contends the jihadists are bound to and therefore (more important to him) protected by Geneva law as nationals of states that have ratified it. The earlier discussion suggested that this conclusion was too generous to Al Qaeda members. It is not generous enough from Kahn's standpoint, however, for it emphasizes that they are not merely protected but also genuinely bound by rules doubtlessly stacked against them. Why would any belligerent, Kahn taunts, ever rationally accept a set of rules ensuring that its compliance will doom it to defeat and often complete destruction? As if making Kahn's point for him, an American soldier recently wounded in an Iraqi ambush, when interviewed on television, "shrugged and, with striking dispassion, conceded that, given the great imbalance of firepower between the Coalition and Saddam Hussein's Iraq, he could hardly blame his attackers for their murderous ruse."[105] Actually, ruses are permitted by the law of war, so long as they do not involve perfidy (e.g., waving a white flag of surrender to encourage the enemy to let down its guard before attacking). This point simply underlines the fact that it was not necessary for the Iraqi insurgents to violate humanitarian law here to secure the advantage they sought and achieved.

Baudrillard writes of the 9/11 attackers, "Admittedly, in terms of our system of values, they are cheating. But this does not trouble them, and the new rules are not ours to determine."[106] It is not the United States but Al Qaeda and its kindred spirits, one military thinker agrees, who "will redefine the terms under which the West will fight the wars of the future."[107] If one grants this point, then an unsettling possibility begins inexorably to emerge and demand our reluctant consideration: Stated bluntly, if fairness as symmetry of relevant risk requires that both sides be permitted to play by the same rules, and if it is unrealistic – perhaps even unfair – to expect the present opponent to play by ours, then perhaps it would be fairest to let us play by its. Pertinent to whether torture might then ever constitute a fair,

corrective response to terror is this recent contention of the distinguished
moral philosopher, Virginia Held:

> On grounds of justice, it is better to equalize rights violations in a transition
> to bring an end to rights violations than it is to subject a given group
> that has already suffered extensive rights violations to continued such
> violations, if the degree of severity of the two violations is similar. . . . If
> we must have rights violations, a more equitable distribution of such
> violations is better than a less equitable distribution.[108]

Put aside the logical merits of this argument for a moment and simply
apply it to present circumstances. Held here invokes both the rationale of
balancing benefits and burden – "a more equitable distribution of such violations" – and the enforcement rationale: "to bring an end to rights violations." She might well be contending that "to bring an end to rights
violations," of the crimes against humanity epitomized in the 9/11 attacks,
their victim, the United States would be entitled to respond in kind, "to
equalize rights violations," at least in the short term (i.e., "a transition"). To
prevent further acts of terror, in other words, terrorists might therefore be
indefinitely detained and coercively interrogated and their leaders subject
to targeted killing when it is difficult to prosecute them. Or so one could
reasonably infer from Held's words.

In fact, however, their context makes unequivocal that she intends her
argument as the very opposite: not as a defense of state torture in response
to nonstate terrorism, but a defense of nonstate terrorism in response to
state-sponsored rights abuse, such as the pervasive torture of dissidents in
repressive regimes.[109] Read it again, and you will see that her argument
runs in both directions, as would any case for reciprocity, consistently
applied. The argument offered by Held – better known for her tender-
hearted, feminist "ethics of care"[110] – is readily reversible, permitting its easy
invocation on behalf of myriad savageries, by both states and nonstates, of
every imaginable ideological coloration. This should give us pause about
upholding reciprocity as a workable, defensible norm governing the range
of lawful responses to mass atrocity.

REPRISAL AS RECIPROCITY IN SAVAGERY?

Perhaps the century-long effort of the earnest international lawyers to outlaw
belligerent reprisals[111] was better conceived than the latest "cutting-edge"
social science (discussed in Chapter 10) acknowledges. "Every terrorist in the
world claims to be responding in self-defense to a prior terrorism on the part

of the state," Derrida rightly observes, "one that simply went by other names and covered itself with all sorts of more or less credible justifications."[112] And as a careful scholar of premodern wartime atrocities adds, "Apologists for such massacres always claim that their perpetrators were 'provoked.' But war always seems full to overflowing with provocation."[113]

Osama bin Laden and other militant jihadists find entirely congenial the notion that their adversary's prior violations should release them from all prohibitions of humanitarian law. "We treat others like they treat us," bin Laden has said.[114] The Koran itself exhorts, "Whoever transgresses against you, respond in kind."[115] An Al Qaeda spokesman thus expatiates,

> Those killed in the World Trade Center and the Pentagon were no more than a fair exchange for the ones killed in the al-Amiriy shelter in Iraq [in 1991], and are but a tiny part of the exchange for those killed in Palestine, Somalia, Sudan, the Philippines, Bosnia, Kashmir, Chechnya, and Afghanistan. . . . We have not reached parity with them. We have the right to kill four million Americans, two million of them children, and to exile twice as many and wound and cripple hundreds of thousands. Furthermore, it is our right to fight them with chemical and biological weapons.[116]

The spokesman does not exactly offer, as a rationale for such response to Western misconduct, Kant's argument for restoring a fair balance of benefits and burdens, though bin Laden himself has written that "reciprocal treatment is a part of justice."[117] Yet it is the perception of such imbalance that gives rise to indignation of the sort acknowledged, even exalted, in the quoted words. The intuition there expressed is much closer, at least, to our second variety of reciprocity – restoring equitable balance established by common standards of conduct – than to the first, fostering cooperation via tit-for-tat. There is no hint in these words of a desire to establish any form of stable and enduring equilibrium or cooperative interaction. Moreover, sanctions against the West need not be mild because, unlike the logic of rational choice, the wrath of Allah need not, apparently, be "nice."

Yet in at least one interview, even bin Laden has said that an *additional* reason for punishing America and other Westerners in such uncivil ways is to deter them from continuing to kill Muslim civilians in the future. His fatwas quoted in this book's epigraphs might be read as intended in a similar spirit. In such interjections, one may hope for a basis of future restraint, if only through a coldly rationalistic tit-for-tat. In assessing their relative significance, however, it is important to recall that most of bin Laden's proffered justifications for attacking Western civilians are retributive in rationale, rather than deterrent. And his occasional invocations of reciprocity as a principle that will govern his war on America have suggested that he is more interested, for the foreseeable future, in reciprocating bad for bad than good for good. Measuring terms of trade is for him a matter of retributive "fit," not of correcting through compensation, much less seeking sustainable future cooperation. "You love life and we love death"[118] is not the language of someone interested in playing tit-for-tat.

Some may say that it is too much to expect greater consistency here; political actors rarely adhere strictly to any general theory of social action, after all. The Bush administration itself was not entirely consistent in its views on such matters. On the one hand, it generally defended its policies on the basis of Al Qaeda's insusceptibility to deterrence through tit-for-tat. Yet some in the administration also apparently thought "that if it is known in the terrorist community that detainees will not get the benefit of ordinary rules that prohibit torture, arbitrary detention and disappearance, then that will serve as a brutal deterrent."[119] If Al Qaeda members are capable of being deterred through such threats of violence, however, then they are likely capable of playing tit-for-tat. Too much is at stake here to dismiss a concern with consistency as the proverbial "hobgoblin of small minds."

The upshot of this book's Part Two is that morality, properly understood, does not preclude the targeted killing of Al Qaeda leaders or coercive interrogation and sustained detention of their followers, just as Part One established legal grounds for permitting these practices at times. But insofar as humanitarian law remains an exercise in corrective justice among organized belligerents (i.e., not only in retributive justice, imposed by the international community on criminal individuals), a victim state may decline to correct the imbalance created by its enemy's legal infractions. That law and morality permit response in kind is not to say that they require it. Parts Three and Four offer good reasons why America should choose not to exercise all its moral and legal options to this end. Part Two explores how social thought, encompassing but extending beyond the positivist social sciences, points toward this conclusion.

PART THREE

RECIPROCITY IN THE SOCIAL SCIENCE OF WAR

8

Reciprocity as Civilization:
The Terrorist as Savage

Victorian jurisprudents deemed a country's "civilized" and eligible for membership in international society if it demonstrated a capacity for reciprocity in its international relations. Civilizations incapable of reciprocity with others were "barbaric." Islamic peoples were more suspect than Buddhists or Confucians in this respect, one major legal thinker contended, because 'the moral code of the Koran is at the same time a code of international law . . . one that prohibits relations of equality and reciprocity between the house of Islam and infidel countries."'[1] Conversely, critics of colonialism invoked the rhetoric of reciprocity against the West itself, observing for instance that since Britain required Turkish citizens to submit to British law when in the West, Turkey could legitimately apply its own law to visiting Westerners, a practice that certain Western states then resisted. Britain's failure to reciprocate revealed its flagrant hypocrisy and disrespect for Islam, argued Italian Antonio Gallenga in 1868.[2]

The terms of that antique debate resonate today and may seem, in fact, little changed. "Postcolonialism" is a particularly influential current in contemporary analysis of relations between the Western and non-Western worlds. Critics of the Enlightenment have long viewed its alluring dream of human liberation as leading to new forms of enslavement, substituting one mythology or superstition for another.[3] In this spirit, postcolonial critics now rightly caution the West about the danger of conceiving "the Muslim terrorist" in much the same way it earlier conceived the Indian "savage" and, more generally, the Oriental Other.[4] We are remonstrated that similar misperceptions will likely lead to similar misjudgments of policy and law. In our assessment of other peoples' modes of contention, we must be wary of how their apparent "wildness has been continually invoked in the name of order, and how savage instincts have been manufactured from the fears of the colonizer's imagination."[5] According to a leading anthropologist, in fact, "the colonizer reifies his myths about the savage, becomes subject to their power, and in so doing seeks salvation from the civilization that torments him as much as from the savage on whom he has projected his anti-self."[6] In its condemnation of non-Western warfare as uncivilized, the modern West thereby became enslaved to a superstition of its own making.

The same misassessment takes place today, the argument continues, with regard to the terrorist. As early as the mid-1970s, Edmund Leach argued, for instance, that "if the lack of shared moral values is so complete that the 'other' comes to be categorized as a wild animal, then every imaginable form of terroristic atrocity is not only attributed to the other side but becomes permissible for oneself."[7] For one is then fighting off a wild animal, which will stop at nothing to devour its enemy – the sort of being, in other words, with whom no restraint through reciprocity is possible. If that being cannot be encaged or otherwise contained, it must be destroyed. So implies this way of thinking, first offered by John Locke.[8]

Some critics now urge, in fact, that the discredited basis for an "earlier exclusion of non-Western peoples" from the law's protection has risen again. The Bush administration's arguments that Al Qaeda members escape humanitarian law's coverage "mimic[s] in every shade . . . the structure and tone"[9] of these earlier grounds for exclusion.[10] In his argument to this effect, Fréderic Mégret develops central themes and arguments of postcolonial theory and so may here be taken as representative of its concerns and viewpoints. Some of the most important postmodernists, from whom postcolonial critics draw their primary inspiration,[11] have given pride of place to the discourse of military discipline in their understanding of the origins of modernity itself.[12]

Mégret claims to find, in U.S. disrespect for the asserted rights of the unprivileged belligerent, a "resurgence of the 'savage,'"[13] a "recycling" of the most reprehensible stereotypes about non-Western warfare. These older views deserve some elaboration before we can assess how much current positions resemble them.

European military thought, well before Western colonization, has long disdained features of the martial conduct of indigenous peoples. The ancient Greeks already regarded any methods other than direct, daylight confrontation between opposing phalanxes of heavily armored, socially respectable men on an open battlefield as an "unfair fight."[14] Medieval Crusaders thought much the same.[15] Delivering knockout blows in decisive battles employing overwhelming force also avoided more protracted wars, it was thought,[16] thereby diminishing overall suffering, to the extent that this mattered to anyone. Hence, there was nothing peculiarly colonialist or racist in the later animosity of European militaries toward evasive and surreptitious tactics.

The Persians' use of archers and javelin throwers elicited the Greeks' moral opprobrium because they fought furtively, often from afar, and were staffed by lightly equipped irregulars of lower social rank.[17] Though highly effective, archers were particularly repugnant because arrows, as Thucydides wrote, cannot pick out the cowards from the brave and so do not permit the brave to display their martial honor in the face of their foe.[18] This insistence on one's chance for glory was also profoundly irrational, of course, then as now, when considered from a less sentimental standpoint concerned only with defeating one's adversary rather than enhancing one's own fame.[19] If not for this anachronistic attitude toward innovation and the static conception of honor underlying it, "how else can we explain the carnage caused by those who adopted this absurd manner of battle at the Somme, or Verdun or Omaha Beach?" asks a leading military historian.[20]

This historian stresses the Attic warriors' "primitive animality," the "savagery in the fighting between armored men . . . an experience unrivaled in its brutality by the modern firefight in the jungle, or the weeks of shelling in the trenches."[21] International law in antiquity, such as it was, allowed noncombatants to be enslaved and surrendering enemy soldiers to be killed outright.[22] Massacres were therefore common. Their victims and perpetrators were both "Western." Yet as face-to-face confrontation, such savagery – as we now see it – was uniformly considered honorable.

RECIPROCITY IN EARLY COLONIAL WARFARE

Law, and international law particularly, provided a lens through which early British colonizers viewed native methods of warfare. Such settlers often expressly invoked the "law of nature and nations" in decrying the "barbarous . . . inhuman, felonious and piratical" methods employed by Native Americans,[23] historian Peter Silver recently observes.

Particularly offensive to colonialist sensibilities, as these were shaped by leading international law texts of the day,[24] were the killing of women, children, old men, and the scalping and burning (rather than burial) of victims' bodies. Also deeply disturbing was "simply the helplessness of the people killed . . . [their] incapacity or unreadiness for resistance,"[25] as in the case of farmers attacked while tilling their fields. The Swiss jurist Emmerich de Vattel, whose works were found in most colonial libraries, taught eighteenth-century settlers that they owed few duties to those who chose to disregard the laws of nations in such ways. Colonists considered indigenous warriors bound by the law of nations because it was thought to reflect the law of nature and was therefore intuitively accessible to all.[26] Natural law, in turn, embodied the principle of reciprocity, Vattel contended.[27] An increase in native attacks on settler noncombatants thus meant that "the gloves came off," to adopt a more recent idiom, in the methods of warfare that British colonizers thereafter used.

The very concept of noncombatant immunity was not, however, endorsed by – or even familiar to – Native American tribes, a fact consistently reflected in the nature of intertribal warfare. Abduction of enemy women and children, for instance, was especially common, much as in the ancient Israel described by the Old Testament.[28] In other words, tribal warriors treated colonizers little differently from fellow natives, whose captives they often tortured,[29] as best one may discern from available scholarship.[30] Native American warriors traveled alongside other tribal members and resided cheek by jowl with extended family in nomadic encampments. Native tribes did not have professionalized armies whose troops did nothing else but fight and who lived together isolated from civilians.[31] To attack an enemy tribe's warriors without attacking its "civilians" would thus have been difficult as a practical matter, even if there had existed some moral reprobation against so doing. Those defending the settler communities were themselves mostly farmers or engaged primarily in other nonmilitary vocations.[32] The challenge of "discriminating," as the law of war now describes it, between combatant and noncombatant among adult white male settlers, at least, would have scarcely been much easier for tribal warriors than when they fought one another.

Much later, in the nineteenth century, U.S. military forces were to employ equally indiscriminate methods against native villages, justifying such attacks on grounds that resonate with contemporary counterterrorism: "Indians normally avoided battle . . . and their small numbers and high mobility made them hard to locate amid the vastness of the Far West," writes a leading historian. When they could be found at all, they were enveloped in what today would be called a civilian shield. "Accordingly," he continues, "one of the army's favorite tactics was to swoop down upon a hostile party while it was ensconced in a village, ideally at dawn. This tactic practically guaranteed casualties among Native American women, children, and the elderly."[33] The intermingling of "combatants" with "noncombatants" – to use admittedly anachronistic terms – was not the U.S. government's doing, of course, but it was knowingly exploited through such modes of raiding. "The greatest opportunity for white victory would occur when the presence of women and children *immobilized* the warriors and forced them to defend their ground."[34]

The international law of the time, purporting to reflect the law of nature, endowed colonists with their acute and righteous sense that "Indian violence . . . swerved away from what seemed normal to them, even for a world at war," Silver concludes.[35] Writing in 2008, he adds what appears a furtive allusion to the present: "The sense of indignant vulnerability that many Americans felt – what could literally be called their violent self-pity – would be one of the new nation's most characteristic and long-lasting cultural products."[36]

Mégret seeks to make much of the seeming similarities here. "Although international law is supposed to have shed its racist past, the laws of war," as the United States applies them to Al Qaeda members, "nonetheless clearly end up excluding a category of individuals on exactly the same grounds that they previously excluded 'savages.'"[37] The "grounds" in question turn out to be, in particular, the inability or refusal to reciprocate restraint.[38] This is a common thread, he suggests, connecting the contemporary American refusal to grant humanitarian law's full protections to Al Qaeda members with the nineteenth-century refusal of Western colonizers to extend *jus in bello* restraints to indigenous peoples, from Andrew Jackson's Indian campaigns through de Gaulle's Algerian War.[39]

One of Mégret's rhetorical moves, like that of many postcolonial critics,[40] is to tar recent Western humanitarian initiatives in poor non-Western countries by association with older, now-discredited efforts in these same places carried out under the banner of a "civilizing mission."[41] It is true that from 1830 through 1930 a subtle shift occurred in the articulate defense of such initiatives, including the elimination of slavery, from a "civilizing" to a "humanizing" mission, later assuming the moniker of "humanitarian intervention." This discursive reorientation finds reflection in the law of armed conflict itself. By at least the late nineteenth century, as Mégret notes, "from an attribute of civilization, restrained warfare was fast on its way to being recognized as an attribute of humanity."[42]

Because no idea is ever entirely new, one can almost always find an intellectual antecedent, long discredited, for the views of one's opponent, who may then be found guilty by association, albeit artificially imposed. A distinguished Marxist sociologist of literature once observed, for instance, the close resemblance between the pervasive disdain of leftist intellectuals for how the "masses" spend their leisure time, in watching television or following celebrities' peccadillos, and the centuries of contempt by Protestant clergy for members of their flock who did not spend more time reading the Bible.[43] Tarnished with that unflattering but telling association, the erudite critique of mass culture seems rather less compelling.[44] In fact, the sociologist's observation proves quite apt here, for a "fear of the savage" would better describe the predominant attitude of intellectual cognoscenti toward the vulgarity or "detritus" – as they like to call it – of mass culture and its purveyors than that of Western counterterrorism analysts toward militant jihadists.

But guilt by imposed association is a standard rhetorical trick that may always be played by both sides. We should resist "the overwhelming tendency to read the strange back into the familiar,"[45] as Villa writes, for instance, in his insistence on the novelties of totalitarian terror as against older forms of tyranny.

THEN AND NOW: DIFFERENCES

Two responses to the postcolonial critique of counterterrorism law as a covert form of colonialism are available. The first rightly shows the major differences between older and newer humanitarian reforms and, in particular, their very different view of the Other's social practices; the second is described in the next section.

Colonialist political and legal discourse often attributed cultural differences to racial inferiority. As recently as World War II, for that matter, Americans at home often portrayed their military adversaries in racial terms. In contrast, the Bush administration took every opportunity to emphasize that its adversary was not Islam or the Arab peoples,[46] even if many Muslims view the conflict in precisely these terms. Colonialist discourse also denied any rights to conquered peoples on the grounds that they lacked "civilized states" (i.e., Christian polities of the European variety, the only entities then acknowledged as bearing rights in international law).[47] The Bush administration's disinclination to extend Geneva rights to Al Qaeda members makes none of these claims.

Many nineteenth-century reformers also viewed non-Westerners, including their warriors, as imbecilic and irrationally crazed for failing to honor Western chivalric codes. By contrast, more recent thinking about non-Western warfare (beginning even before T. E. Lawrence)[48] stresses its efficacy for fighting more conventional, bureaucratic armies, even seeking to emulate its ways[49] – as Lawrence himself did so effectively in fighting the Ottoman empire.[50] For instance, the Apaches, writes a leading scholar, "survived civilized military pressure for over 300 years and were defeated only by primitive methods – literally by other Apaches wearing U.S. Army uniforms."[51]

This offers an early illustration of the counsel, since offered by leading twentieth-century American strategists like Bernard Brodie, that "good strategy presumes good anthropology and sociology."[52] The rationality of mimicking an enemy's more "primitive" methods of warfare, in particular, today explains the renewed prominence of "Special Operations"[53] forces, as in Afghanistan and Iraq, in an era that – it was supposed until recently – would be dominated instead by the much more sophisticated methods of cyberwar, space-based weaponry, and nanotechnology.[54] Even such left-leaning critics of the United States as Antonio Negri and Michael Hardt announce that it will not prevail in the fight against Al Qaeda unless it finds a way to adopt the latter's network form of organization.[55]

Neither is there any trace of a patronizing or paternalistic tone in most contemporary military discourse on insurgency warfare in places like Somalia, Afghanistan, and Iraq. "Your worst opponent is not the psychopathic terrorist of Hollywood," writes a leading, contemporary counterinsurgency thinker. "It is the charismatic follow-me warrior who would make your best platoon leader."[56] Such professional discourse is thus today highly respectful of the accomplishments of non-Western methods and closely attentive to the factors rendering them effective in particular situations.[57] If current analyses conclude, like their putative predecessor, that it is impractical to fight such an adversary while adhering to traditional Western law, this is not because the enemy continues to be seen as "unlike us" in its irrationality. Only the practice of self-protection by hiding among civilians is condemned for its "amoral" character,[58] because of its dangers to noncombatants. Earlier colonialist writings on fighting natives expressed no such concern for indigenous non-fighters.

Current Western military thinking recognizes, moreover, that unconventional adversaries fight differently simply because they realize that there is no other way to win against modern armies, that they cannot hope to prevail if they adhere to Western rules of warfare. In this respect, their strategic thinking is rational indeed, as current U.S. military thinking readily acknowledges of militant jihadists.[59] In sum, the reasons the Bush administration offered for why unconventional antagonists refuse to reciprocate the West's attempted adherence to humanitarian norms are meaningfully different from the earlier "Orientalist" discourse to which postcolonial criticism compares it.

According to Said, the Orientalist views the non-Westerner as docile, fatalistic, silent, unchanging, passive, and having nothing from which the West may learn.[60] Orientalism also apprehended the Other only through antiquated Western texts, rather than opening itself to direct interpersonal encounter with those it sought to understand and govern. Few if any of these traits are prominent in early American military discourse on fighting Native

Americans – and none at all in the contemporary discourse of counterinsurgency, counterterrorism, and their legal governance. Elite journalistic
discourse about the Arab world today would be better faulted for its accen-
tuation of the faint, frail, and often evanescent sproutings of liberalism, of
"a budding culture of change,"[61] as writes one prominent American reporter
specializing in the region, than for any preoccupation with institutional
sclerosis, as Islamic historian Juan Cole observes.[62]

At first glance, another similarity appears between the discourses of colonialism and of antiterrorism law: the state of dread, a raw Hobbesian fear –
almost paranoiac – of violent death as an omnipresent possibility. Taussig
eloquently captures this phantasmagoric mental universe in his account
of Peru's early Spanish conquistadors, who were suddenly immersed in
a strange world of poisonous insects, predatory animals, and sometimes
hostile natives:

> They saw danger everywhere and thought solely of the fact that they
> were surrounded by vipers, tigers, and cannibals. It is these ideas of
> death . . . which constantly struck their imagination, making them terrified
> and capable of any act. Like children who read the *Arabian Nights*, . . . they
> had nightmares of witches, evil spirits, death, treason and blood. The
> only way they could live in such a terrifying world . . . was by themselves
> inspiring terror.[63]

The analogy to more contemporary circumstances would presumably
run as follows: In half-delusional dread of another 9/11, the Bush administration felt itself suddenly thrown into "a terrifying world" of savagery.
Within that novel and unsettling universe, national self-defense seemed to
require "inspiring terror" through preventive war, torture, detention without charges, and targeted killing of terrorist leaders. There may even be
a germ of truth to this perhaps facile comparison, at the semi-conscious
level of moral genealogy, recoverable by historians perhaps only many years
hence from personal diaries of the key policymakers and ordinary citizens.

Yet the differences are surely more prominent than the similarities to the
mental universe of the early conquistadors. The closest we yet have to a
personal diary of how decisions on legal policy were made following 9/11 is
Jack Goldsmith's reflection on the climate of acute fear he encountered on
assuming leadership of the Office of Legal Counsel in early 2003.[64] There
is undoubtedly a Hobbesian element in this fear, but what is more striking
and telling about his account are three additional elements, utterly absent
from the minds of Taussig's conquistadors.

No one in the upper reaches of the Bush administration was especially preoccupied with the prospect of his or her own death. Rather, it was the future deaths – perhaps imminent – of many thousands of unknown fellow Americans that brought angst and nightmares. Second and closely related, it was the recognition that they, current legal policymakers, would soon be held politically accountable for their decisions if these proved too cautious and allowed another attack. Their fear, in other words, displayed an egalitarian and democratic character distinguishing it from Pizarro's in morally trenchant ways. Whereas "the savage instincts [of Peruvian natives] were manufactured largely in the imaginations of the whites," according to Taussig, the same cannot be said of the savage instincts inspiring 9/11 and related mass atrocities by militant jihadists in London, Madrid, Bali, Kenya, Tanzania, Casablanca, Istanbul, Riyadh, Baghdad, Jerusalem, Mombassa, and several other places.

Finally, for the conquistadors, like the Nazis to whom he compares them, the "very animality projected onto the racial Other," Taussig tells us, was in turn "mimicked as sadistic ritual, degradation, and ultimately in genocide against the Other."[65] There was sadism aplenty at Abu Ghraib, and likely considerable degradation at Guantánamo. American excesses in the conflict with Al Qaeda do not, however, remotely approximate genocide.

THEN AND NOW: SIMILARITIES

Long before the U.S. military learned to adopt indigenous methods of warfare, the earliest Pilgrims maintained an image of native warfare that was not altogether negative. Just as they saw initial native hospitality as evidence of "the Lord's mercy to His chosen people," they viewed savage warfare as evidence that "God must from time to time send a message to chastise His chosen people in their pride and their departure from His word."[66] Strikingly similar was the Rev. Jerry Falwell's initial response to 9/11: a jeremiad proclaiming that the very savagery of this attack represented God's punishment of America for straying from His ways.[67]

The second and more controversial response to the postcolonial point might thus admit that such critics have indeed discovered some nontrivial similarities between past and present discourse. There are indeed certain resemblances between the older and newer humanitarianism in Western views and policies toward poor countries and their fighters. Neither indigenous peoples nor today's jihadist militants, for instance, are parties to humanitarian law treaties nor are they agreeable to many of their terms.

Both U.S. Army Indian fighters in the nineteenth century and today's counterinsurgency thinkers,[68] moreover, stress the unwillingness and frequent inability of their adversaries to accept the surrender of prisoners or respect the distinction between fighters and civilians.

However, this is only because such similarities are genuine, demonstrably so,[69] not because both discourses are equally racist, as Mégret and other postcolonialists suggest.[70] This response to such a postcolonial critique would then proceed, on the basis of these acknowledged affinities, to reconsider the original articulations of Western moral concern. It would do so in a more sympathetic light than the current intellectual climate allows. Such an avowedly revisionist approach would begin, of course, by openly acknowledging that early reflections on non-Western warfare, in employing the prevailing language of the time, reflected the West's cultural prejudices. (It would be too much to describe such reflections as "investigations," much less as social science, as social observation had not yet become professionalized.)

The analysis would then, however, credibly disentangle these prejudices from the empirical observations, often accurate and even quite perceptive, of what is now widely described as "asymmetrical" warfare. In this type of armed conflict, the weaker party exploits the stronger's vulnerabilities through surprise (e.g., ambush), stealth, avoidance of direct battlefield confrontation (e.g., sniping, booby traps, and sabotage),[71] and hiding among civilians.[72] By breaching extant rules, the irregular attacker can derive great tactical benefits at small cost while inflicting enormous costs on the enemy. The 9/11 attacks, for instance, cost Al Qaeda about $200,000, yet inflicted many billions of dollars in direct and indirect damage on the United States.[73]

From this angle, the early reflections of Western colonizers and Native American fighters would then be acknowledged, even praised perhaps, for offering prescient glimmers of recognition that something genuinely new was afoot, outside the strategic imagination of classical, Clausewitzian thought with its statist assumptions.[74] It is therefore not unusual to encounter today, in military discussions of counterinsurgency operations, such observations as this: "Veterans of the Indian Wars appreciated the value of indigenous soldiers, who possessed a threefold advantage in their knowledge of the people, the terrain, and the language."[75] Those lacking the latest technology and bureaucratic organization that their enemies possess were simply doing what any economist or rational choice theorist would have recommended: play to your comparative advantage. The weapons of the weak in asymmetrical warfare are simply an application of this economic principle, albeit for purposes of destruction rather than production.

Such a rehabilitation of the nineteenth-century discourse would not allow the use of offensive language to characterize non-Western warfare – as "flighty," "rascally," "fiendish," and "frivolous," for instance[76] – to gainsay the elements of truth in such writings. The law of war has been struggling with the problems presented by asymmetrical warfare, under one label or another, ever since. Tribal warfare resembles more recent guerrilla warfare, in particular, in its devotion to the offensive; its use of stealth, surprise, and scouting reconnaissance; its tactical mobility; and its superior knowledge of terrain. Contemporary military thinkers should not then be embarrassed by such similarities nor the intellectual legacy through which they were first identified. "Every successful guerrilla campaign, however rare, is a demonstration that there is nothing contemptible about primitive military techniques,"[77] notes one contemporary scholar.

The same could be said of most successful *anti*-guerrilla campaigns.[78] "Anti-guerrilla warfare requires exactly the same tactical adjustments by conventional armies as were adopted to counter tribal warriors,"[79] remarks an anthropologist of warfare. One should hasten to add that "this does not mean," in the words of counterinsurgency scholar/adviser David Kilcullen, "that [counterinsurgents] should be 'irregular' in the sense of being brutal, or outside proper control. Rather, they should move, equip, and organize like the insurgents."[80]

It would be puerile if the tacit appeal in such a rehabilitation of discredited "ancestors" lay in the surreptitious *frisson* of the forbidden. At the risk of seeming to succumb to such guilty pleasures, it is worth seriously entertaining, in a spirit of candor that statesmen themselves cannot indulge, whether the notion of a civilizing mission, so central to the rhetoric of Western imperialism, was actually onto something, albeit not from its very beginnings in the brutal Spanish conquest of the Americas or the later trade with African slave dealers, of course. Terry Eagleton cannot be faulted for delicately observing that the West has been "a civilization that for centuries has wreaked untold carnage throughout the world."[81]

Among other things.

And among the other things it has wrought, at the bottom of Pandora's box may be found what we now call universal human rights, enshrined as such within international law. These would always prove to be the essential normative commitment and world-historical contribution of Western civilization, understood in its best light, at least since the Enlightenment.[82] "To the imperial eye," Peter Fitzpatrick mockingly writes, "law was preeminent among the 'gifts' of an expansive civilization, one which would extend in its abounding generosity to the entire globe."[83] Yet gifts are never entirely disinterested, even in the most intimate venues. So a measure of self-interest in the offering does not deprive it of that designation, as we later see.

In any event, the West's rule of law and human rights ideals were rightly thrown back in its face by many nationalist, anticolonial movements (often led by lawyers like Gandhi, Nehru, and Jinnah), confirming its utility to the oppressed as a universal standard for identifying and chastising political injustice. And contemporary rules of international human rights, particularly civil and political rights, were later to emerge largely as ramifications and permutations of this same liberal legal ideal as it worked itself pure (i.e., pure of its early contamination by colonial self-interest).[84] Or are we to believe that the Chinese students who marched behind a model of the Statute of Liberty were simply misguided agents of Western cultural imperialism? So too Ho Chi Minh, presumably, when he quoted America's Declaration of Independence in demanding Vietnam's right to national self-determination?

Much as the West has often opened itself to external influence – adopting Native American military tactics was the least of this[85] – so the non-West has stood something to gain from attending to Western innovations, again beginning with military methods[86] but soon extending far beyond. Such borrowing may not be entirely necessary insofar as strong traces of analogous ideas prove readily recoverable from within indigenous traditions of thought,[87] ideas that Western influence may help reinvigorate, inspire to confidence, and perhaps coax into greater political prominence. There is a considerable effort to this effect, after all, in the attempt to discover an intellectual foundation for international human rights within authoritative Islamic texts of much older provenance.

One may fairly describe as "missionary," without straining the metaphor, any such effort – deliberate, continuous, and unapologetic – to encourage members of another culture to reconsider some of its presuppositions in light of foreign experience with differing ones.[88] Such an effort might even be called "civilizing" insofar as it involves the willful dissemination of ideas originating within one civilization to others, ideas that the missionary believes will enhance human capabilities and well-being everywhere.[89] This is not to say anything as general or absurd as that the recipients are lacking in civilization *tout court*, of course. The present suggestion is entirely consistent, in fact, with a view of civilizational change as a process of hybridization,[90] in the sense that each such entity at times adopts this or that practice, product, or idea from another, allowing its repercussions to ripple through, without fear of losing any putative purity, integrity, or authenticity.[91] In this sense, various peoples may simultaneously "civilize" one another.[92]

One requirement of rationality is moral in nature: the modesty to admit the possible existence of better options wherever they may be found. As Georgia Warnke observes, "The awareness that one's knowledge is always open to refutation or modification from the vantage point of another perspective is not a basis for suspending confidence in the idea of reason, but rather represents the very possibility of rational progress."[93] What she luminously describes here is an expression of the fourth variety of reciprocity that this study identifies, that implicit in any mutually respectful conversation.[94] Islamic historian Juan Cole makes passing reference, in this connection, to small circles of Afghani and Iranian clerics who read Western political theory and have shown themselves open to genuine dialogue with non-Islamists. "Habermasian mullahs," Cole calls them. He quickly counsels, however, that they constitute an extremely small minority, scarcely a handful, and that they exercise no political influence.[95]

INVENTING A PLAYMATE: FROM OTHER INTO OPPONENT

A still more radical critique of reciprocity as an enforcement strategy, also inspired by postmodernism, emerges from the cheeky little subfield of "critical security studies."[96] From its standpoint, all talk of national security becomes a mysterious and distorted lens through which particular interests come to be seen as national interests and individual persons come to view their own interests as identical with those of the nation, so understood. In this way, national security discourse does not so much respond to personal security threats as imaginatively re-apprehend them – "create: them, one might almost say. The law of national security is an integral component of such discourse. Through its rules and the rights they create, "states are . . . reproduced as actors with particular kinds of interests in representations of their insecurity."[97]

This view objects even to our thinking about America's vexed encounter with jihadist terror in terms of its amenability to restraint through tit-for-tat. It contends that this very approach is part of the problem. Reciprocity-speak – much like "rights talk" in this regard[98] – is but another source of binary oppositions and conflictive self-identification. Reprisal and other retaliation for legal breach, seen in this light, are not really tools for implementing humanitarian law within armed conflict. For that assumes the existence of at least two well-demarcated belligerents, capable of having rights and responsibilities vis-à-vis each other.

The roots of the Rwandan genocide have sometimes been partly traced to just such a misclassification. Colonial rulers had sought, for administrative convenience, to draw a bright line between Tutsis and Hutus, lending the demarcation a legal rigidity that it lacked at the level of social relations. This step effectively transformed into a binary opposition what had been a more richly variegated social tableau within which multiple patterns of mixing – interpersonal, marital, cultural – had been pervasive. Once distinct groups were said to exist, there then arose the need to establish mutually satisfactory terms of relations between them, including power sharing (i.e., terms acceptable to rivalrous leaders on both sides of the newly entrenched line). The consistent failure to discover such terms led to a series of violent conflicts, culminating in the 1993 genocide. The aims of German and Belgian rulers may have been well served by this "divide and conquer" approach to colonial administration. Yet it was their insistence upon so watertight a binary division between the two "peoples" that created the necessary (though insufficient) conditions for later genocide. Later on, state failure ensured that Rwandans themselves could not establish reciprocity through any social contract. Concepts thus have consequences, sometimes lethal.

Reciprocity may at first appear a merely theoretical concept or approach, salutary – at worst innocuous – in its promise to help enforce humanitarian law. Yet in fact, it contributes at least subliminally to constituting the very opponents who, so conceived, find themselves then notionally pitted against each other. The dichotomy on which such confrontations are constructed may be false or true only through its susceptibility to self-fulfillment. For if tit-for-tat has often shown itself a good way to resolve conflict, then it is tempting to fit the facts of any particular disaccord into terms amenable to this analysis. Once the Other comes to be seen as an adversary in a game, it is expected to "play" by the game's rules. If it refuses to do so, if only because it does not entirely understand those rules, it may then quickly come to be viewed as an outright enemy, which in turn authorizes violence against it, and perhaps even its destruction. This is true even if the game itself is one allowing for mutually beneficial cooperation among players if they adhere to its strictures.

In a Foucaultian spirit, one could say that the aim of inducing reciprocal restraint in terrorists through tit-for-tat involves an effort to "bring terror within the political rationalities and calculative control of western security technologies."[99] The most important of these technologies are always intellectual rather than industrial fabrications. Yet terrorists and their fellow travelers resist any such attempt to form them into a variety of "subject" different from what they are or wish to become. For this reason, the West-ern strategy of what one might call "governing terror through reciprocity," through tit-for-tat, is doomed to failure. More colloquially, one might say that, once such reciprocity becomes the principal tool for pounding out international disagreement, then too much of the world will start to look like a nail – and be hammered accordingly. To extend the tool shop metaphor, all that might actually be needed may be some fine-grained sandpaper to smooth out a few rough spots. A particular danger here arises from the fact that, as a conceptual "security technology," tit-for-tat assumes a low level of trust between actors, an assumption that – when consistently acted on – generally confirms itself.[100] Opportunities between potential antagonists for establishing and enhancing trust – rather than mere respect for each other's rationality – will tend to go unrecognized and so fail to be exploited.

This is not to say that there is any basis today for trust in Osama bin Laden that he will honor promises he might make to the West, of course, other than perhaps to destroy everything he believes it stands for. But this is just the point at which it is most crucial to call to mind the distinctions between bin Laden and others with whom he shares salient properties. For the political dynamics of retaliation reverberate with third parties in ways that quickly escape tit-for-tat's bilateral logic. When the Bush administration privately cajoled Pakistani President Pervez Musharraf to pursue militant jihadists more aggressively, for instance, he insistently replied that it was important to distinguish "anti-U.S. terrorists affiliated with Al Qaeda, who need to be fought or eliminated, from local Islamist insurgents (whether Afghan, Pakistani, or Kashmiri) who can be engaged in dialogue."[101] There is some reason to think his particular judgments in this regard were seriously mistaken.[102] But his commitment to respecting such a distinction – in principle, wherever the facts permit it – is clearly a good one. To resist binary thinking requires that one keep several distinctions at once in mind: that not all Muslims are Islamists (i.e., *shari'a* theocrats),[103] that there are both literalist and liberal-purposive interpretations of *shari'a*, that not all Islamists are jihadists, that not all jihadists employ violence, and that not all violent jihadists endorse attacks on civilians,[104] and so forth.

Forbearing from punitive tit-for-tat, with its easy susceptibility to excess and counter-reprisal, is likely to dissuade people in each of these categories from making the next move in this downward spiral of hate. This is not to suggest, however, that American mistreatment of terror suspects has caused many sympathizers to take the further step of becoming suicide bombers, as some leading Bush administration critics suggest.[105] Even so, with this possible result in mind, Khaled Abou El Fadl observes a dynamic of dichotomization from within one Islamic community:

> In response to the often searing criticisms of Orientalists, Muslims have been motivated to close ranks and to engage in a type of unthinking cheer-leading on behalf of the Islamic tradition. The most common comment that a Muslim critic hears from fellow Muslims is "Yes, you're making good points, but you are also playing into the hands of the enemies of Islam."[106]

El Fadl persists in his criticism, on the grounds that "the Qur'an instructs a Muslim to bear witness to the truth even if it is against oneself or against loved ones."[107] His brethren are well disposed to make the relevant distinctions: Opinion surveys in the Middle East clearly reveal that positive views of Osama bin Laden, though pervasive, stem largely from his perceived ability to stand up to U.S. meddling in the region, as so many corrupt and incompetent states there do not, rather than from his methods of warfare or goal of restoring a pan-Muslim caliphate.[108]

Shortly after 9/11, President Bush vowed to the world, "Either you are with us or you are with the terrorists."[109] There could be no better articulation of the binary logic on which reciprocity thinking depends. Then, what is to happen to those who continue to insist that they are neither against us, in the sense of hating America, nor with us, in the sense of endorsing President Bush's conception of the conflict with its disparate opponents in the Muslim world in terms of a "global war on terror"? The law of war itself, one must add, insists on the rights of nonbelligerents in an armed conflict to remain neutral and hence to continue interaction with both sides.[110]

The binary oppositions of reciprocity-speak do not, at the very least, discourage the polarizing descent that El Fadl describes and laments among his fellow Muslims, a process set loose by the West's own initial oversimplifications, he believes. The process might as easily have begun from the other direction, of course, through bin Laden's announced strategy to "provoke and bait" the United States into "bleeding wars on Muslim ground." Wherever it started, the very polarities implicit in reciprocity as a way of apprehending international relations, especially at the intercultural level, already privilege and accentuate differences over commonalities across existing lines of undoubted disagreement. This is pernicious in the same way as is the notion of a "clash of civilizations." Both encourage each side to think primarily in terms of the polarities of "us/them, here/there, friends/enemies, inside/outside."[111] There must be at least two distinct entities capable of facing off and resolving the face-off through reciprocal exchange, nonviolent or otherwise, for the notion of reciprocity between parties to make any sense, after all.[112]

What was at first merely a heuristic device for understanding an ever-shifting and elusive boundary somehow becomes hypostasized into a chasm that cannot be crossed. Tit-for-tat may be fine for reaching equilibrium with an opponent. Yet what if most people across the relevant divide are not true opponents? Lines will tend to harden, as shades of gray dissolve into black and white. Relations between neighboring and perhaps wary acquaintances threaten to become a Schmittian confrontation of friend and foe.[113] Muslims who are Islamists but not violent, even Muslims who are not Islamists, are then in peril of being herded into the same conceptual corral as the most violent jihadists – and treated accordingly. So too the jihadists' seeming equation of all Americans with either the most extreme Christian evangelicals or *Sex and the City* sybarites.

The immediate question of how America should apprehend its relation to Al Qaeda unfortunately implicates the larger question of how Americans are to understand their relations with the Islamic world as a whole. On all accounts, there is widespread sympathy within that world for some of Al Qaeda's principal policy aims, a sympathy not entirely overridden by opposition to its methods. The United States hence risks antagonizing many Muslims by conceiving Al Qaeda and all kindred spirits as unqualifiedly evil, as nothing more than a military adversary to be destroyed – or even managed, through tit-for-tat, if that someday proves possible.

To understand the conflicts in Lebanon alone, for example, one must strive to master the sometimes subtle differences among at least eleven ethnoreligious communities and armed groups. To render manageable any such complex reality, the beleaguered mind demands some simplification, and binary classification is always the easiest. It seems to offer us some security, even as acting on its oversimplifications may create insecurity for others.[114] Preoccupation with talking about one's own security "must continue to produce images of insecurity in order to retain its meaning,"[115] argue scholars of critical security studies.

CELEBRATING LEGAL HYBRIDITY AS CULTURAL MONGRELISM

The West and the Muslim world have profoundly influenced each other in many ways and have contributed to each other's core commitments and most prized achievements. They do not occupy separate cultural cocoons. Western science, in particular, was preserved and cultivated for several centuries in medieval Muslim Spain, a period in which Europe itself no longer did so.[116] There, in Andalucia, even arguments for military forbearance, derived from the Islamic law of war, found crucial support in interpretive methods borrowed from such Western authors as Aristotle.[117] Even the interpretations of Islam most hostile to the West, such as those of Qutb, draw heavily on Western ideas, as Leonard Binder showed a generation ago.[118] This variety of sharing sits uneasily with the very idea of reciprocity. For as Sandel writes, "While 'reciprocity' implies a principle of exchange and hence a plurality of agents, the notion of 'sharing' may suggest a solidarity such that no exchange need be involved, as in sharing a joke, or an aspiration, or an understanding."[119]

Once one acknowledges the long legacy of such overlapping concerns and concepts, a return to reciprocity thinking can then only push one back into an undue reliance on insupportable distinctions. These threaten to reestablish a hierarchy of civilizations (i.e., a dichotomy between those capable of reciprocity in war and those incapable of it). This way of thinking creates what Antony Anghie calls a self-perpetuating dynamic of difference.[120] Once this rhythm is set in motion, gradually all the genuine doubts that we harbor (even pride ourselves in holding) about our own way of life – about the widely acknowledged downsides of modern, liberal, industrial, secular rationality,[121] if you will – are forgotten at the moment we turn our attention from assessing ourselves to understanding the non-Western Other. Earlier in these very pages, for that matter, the policy of enforcing humanitarian law through reprisal (i.e., private tit-for-tat) was described as quite primitive, compared to the possibility of collective security through effective international bodies of the sort widely contemplated in 1945. As early as 1923, one leading international lawyer could write that, insofar as "reprisal suggests a crude legal notion of joint responsibility of a community for actions of its members," it is "symptomatic of lawlessness and barbarism."[122] At the present turn in the argument, then, how did such reciprocity itself – only guardedly defended as a lesser evil to total nonenforcement – suddenly become the very mark of civilization, the moral touchstone by which we now set ourselves above our more primitive adversary?[123]

Notions of reciprocity also inspired the Cold War's strategy of "mutually assured destruction," as Chapter 1 suggests. That dangerous doctrine was broadly decried at the time as immoral by even the archest of cold warriors, notably Ronald Reagan, who defended his program for a missile shield on this basis. In that Cold War form, the practice of reciprocity seemed to augur the end of all human civilization on the planet, many believed. Yet barely a decade later, the conflicts with Iraq, Iran, North Korea, and

Al Qaeda have ensured, as one strategist notes, that "suddenly the absurdity of it all [M.A.D.] faded away" for critics of the Bush administration. "All the [dubious] assumptions of human nature, the ability to tightly manage crisis, the idea that not only would the 'Russians love their children too,' they would also act in ways that fitted into game theoretical matrixes, as indeed would the U.S. chain of command.... All these highly contested notions suddenly became the holy grail of strategy – often for the very people who had criticized them during the Cold War – because deterrence [now] seemed a moderate and sensible alternative to the new doctrine . . . of pre-emption,"[124] conducted through targeted killing, sustained detention, and torture.

Earlier too, the present analysis judged the concept of human rights as largely useless in resolving hard questions of counterterrorism law and policy.[125] Yet here the idea of human rights has somehow morphed into the West's crowning achievement. We now invoke human rights to define ourselves in opposition to radical Islam, whereas just a moment ago we found the international jurisprudence of human rights hopelessly indeterminate and hence lacking in practical value. Can it really be so categorical an improvement on other modes of deliberation and conflict resolution that we Westerners today talk through our disagreements in terms of the relative weight of competing claims of human right? It is not difficult to discover social practices in the non-West that are rights supportive, even if not defended in such terms, just as it is easy to find social practices in the West that are not conducive to the exercise of human rights. Here too, then, one finds oneself, as Taussig writes, unwittingly minimizing the "mosaic of . . . hybridities seething with instability," because it "threatens [one's] First World quest for a decent fix of straightforward Othering."[126]

The West only civilized itself gradually, after all, finally abolishing slavery only after the mid-nineteenth century. More intimate expressions of civility are also quite modern, as in the restraint of violence within personal relations and the suppression of aggressive emotions, Norbert Elias shows.[127] Sociologists have discovered that such habits of civility are still quite unevenly distributed across the general population.[128] Even the West's own recent human rights agenda, particularly the right of peoples to self-determination, has been the product of its recent "dialogue" with the non-West. It is in significant measure a result of what the West learned from the anticolonial, antiapartheid, and other struggles marking its retreat from empire.[129]

This is a fitting conclusion to a tradition of thought that began, in early modern doctrines of natural right, precisely with the question of how

Western conquerors should behave toward newly encountered peoples in an anarchic international arena.[130] Natural rights doctrine was developed by a group of thinkers directly sponsored by ambitious state rulers seeking intellectual rationales for colonial expansion. Yet it evolved over time into a doctrine chiefly concerned with repudiating the imperial venture in all its forms.

FROM MARTIAL MORALITY TO METAPHYSICS

It is tempting to elevate the difference between "them and us" from one of martial methods and the morality underlying them to one of metaphysics, as some philosophers and military strategists have sought to do.[131] Even the cautious, sober 9/11 Commission Report concluded in this respect that bin Laden's program "is not a position with which America can bargain or negotiate. With it there is no common ground – not even respect for life – on which to begin a dialogue. It can only be destroyed or utterly isolated."[132]

From this "elevated" view of the struggle, acts of terror and death that Westerners find senseless and life-denying the 9/11 attackers and kindred spirits find life–affirming, because they are rich with meaning of personal salvation through righteous struggle. Another difference approximating the metaphysical: Western military officers today reject the notion that inhumanity (i.e., behaving inhumanely in war) is a necessary condition for the successful practice of their vocation.[133] Their current adversaries, scornful of secular civilian values, seemingly embrace this notion. For us, war is instrumental, a prudent matching of means to ends; for them, it is essentially symbolic, even existential.

There may be an element of truth to such dichotomies. Yet one can as easily point to many congruities, even to polarities running in the opposite direction. Osama bin Laden professes no qualms, for instance, about employing nuclear and other unconventional weapons against his enemy,[134] a thoroughly instrumental view of such methods. The West often speaks expressly and unapologetically in the language of superstition: of a "taboo" on the use of such weapons against anyone, ever.[135] Tens of thousands of Americans volunteered to serve in Iraq, presumably finding such national service, even the prospect of death in that conflict, deeply meaningful at the level of personal identity (i.e., in "existential" terms).[136] Jihadist suicide bombers, by contrast, have often volunteered themselves for the most secular, pedestrian – all too human – of motivations, according to the closest study of them to date.[137]

The phantasmagoric spectacle of bringing down the World Trade Center may have been a richly symbolic way of suggesting global capitalism's vulnerabilities without actually making more than the smallest dent in its ongoing operation. But it also had considerable instrumental success in causing billions of dollars in material damage (and untold suffering). Conversely, the visual "shock and awe" of America's 2003 Iraq bombing campaign were not exactly unconcerned with the spectacular dimension of power. Shrewd use of symbols often helps advance a political agenda in "modern," no less than "traditional," society. Such congruences and others further efface the "us vs. them" polarity on which reciprocity-think relies.

Still, the dynamic of differentiation need not prove uniformly negative in its consequences. According to a different and more intriguing account of that process, a belligerent's effort to distinguish itself ethically from its military foe may induce it to take its own professed ideals more seriously as a way of accentuating its adversary's corresponding moral failings. This may be crucial to a larger contest for the opinion of third parties, perhaps the world at large, as during the Cold War. What begins as only a proclaimed virtue, much exaggerated – racial equality, for instance – actually becomes more genuinely realized. This is the beguiling suggestion, at least, of a rather different strain of postmodernism.[138] It compels us to acknowledge that, although war often leads antagonists to mimic each other in the most loathsome ways, it sometimes also induces them to distinguish themselves morally from each other, to appeal for the support of third parties. Senator John McCain has said that he could not have survived his five and a half years as a prisoner of war unless he believed that his country would not mistreat Viet Cong and North Vietnamese soldiers as he was abused.[139] In a similar spirit, the most noteworthy invocations of "what we stand for" as a rationale for national policy during the twentieth century arose during regime transitions from dictatorial, military, and/or communist rule to constitutional democracy. The consistent claim of new rulers was that we must mark our moral difference from the discredited autocrats whom we displace. To this end, when prosecuting former rulers for their crimes, we must afford punctilious due process of exactly the sort they denied their victims, thereby symbolically distancing ourselves from their lawless practices.[140] Political rivalry between competing elites thus sets in motion a moral "race to the top."

The more perennial argument is, rather, that the dynamic of differentiation between West and "rest" is unambiguously pernicious. It leads straight to imperialism, and then – when that is no longer permitted – to neoliberal neoimperialism.[141] If this is where reciprocity-think leads, then we must be more wary, at the very least, of "the slipperiness of our significations,"[142] especially those by which we define the Other as an adversary, even if only in an initially nonviolent game. The problem then is not so much the Other's inability or unwillingness to see its interactions with us through the lens of reciprocity, but the very opposite: our own excessive inclination to that end. This point should be deeply sobering for anyone with the faintest sympathies for game-theoretic approaches to international conflict resolution.

Governing war through reciprocity was an intellectual artifact of a world of jealously independent sovereign states that could imaginatively be pitted against each other with great plausibility. Today, most cross-border interaction no longer involves formal, interstate exchange, but rather unceremonious and often unlawful streams of people and things – finance, weapons, food, drugs, disease, energy, information, images, grievances, and ideas of the good life.[143] This is a relatively informal process not amenable to satisfactory analysis through longstanding conceptions of international relations.[144] We have entered, Taussig proclaims, "an era of the borderland where 'us' and 'them' lose their polarity and swim in and out of focus."[145]

This is what others have in mind when they speak of the emergence of a world society, not merely international society; that is, the society of autonomous states.[146] If true world societies of any social depth are ever to emerge, they will surely arise more through the largely spontaneous ordering of such flows – from the bottom up,[147] as it were – than from diplomatic machinations over the proper wording of interstate treaties. The Wikipedia and other participatory, open-source software become the new template for global social organization, from this perspective.

This is a pretty picture indeed. Yet one small quibble with this otherwise elegant, evocative, and altogether alluring stance is that it ignores the demonstrable fact that there are plenty of angry people who – not to put too fine a point on it – want us dead and seek to kill us, at the very least to terrorize us, itself a war crime.[148] As many of us as possible. They have either acquired or are energetically striving to acquire the capabilities to do so. They have had notable successes. No clever deconstruction of the terms by which they are to be designated can make them go away. "The criticism of language may be required for the criticism of politics, but politics is not mainly language," as Leon Wieseltier wisely warns.[149] If we stop seeing Al Qaeda members through the lens of their distaste for reciprocity with us, they will not cease to present a threat, even if we no longer exaggerate and perhaps aggravate that threat through our own classificatory grid. If defenders of a war on terrorism, through their carelessly overinclusive idiom, sometimes exaggerate the scope of the West's true adversary, postcolonial critics – through a corresponding linguistic underinclusiveness – seek to make the very possibility of such an enemy disappear entirely, by talismanic verbal trick.

More precisely, in their barely concealed sympathy for many goals of the 9/11 attackers, such critics do not actually wish them literally to disappear, but only to disappear *qua* enemies from the gaze of a neocolonial Western *mentalité*.

To be sure, all collective entities, including all nations and the Muslim *ummah* itself,[150] are historically contingent and culturally constructed, if the reader will forgive such clichés. But that fact does not make them any less real for practical purposes – moral, political, legal, or military. Deconstructing the key terms of public debate can be helpful here to the extent that this exercise counsels caution about the language through which we identify and understand other human beings, especially those who may be conceived as enemies. This is valuable even if deconstruction itself is rarely a model of such clarity and certainly may claim no monopoly to it.

But deconstruction's view of the predicament is vastly overbroad if it can be redressed simply with greater verbal and empirical precision. There is no such solution if the problem inheres in the nature of language and if language is all we have for apprehending reality. This is the deconstructionist's distinctive claim: "There is nothing beyond the text." That mantra is understandably appealing to anyone wishing to argue, like one postmodernist reviewer of this book in manuscript, that not only a "war on terrorism," but even one on "jihadist terrorists," still yet on "something called Al Qaeda"[151] is an impossibility, simply a naïve linguistic mistake. Any such terms, because there is some gray around their edges, are thus repudiated as oversimplifications and so barred from acceptable discourse, on this view.

As flesh-and-blood beings, however, the 9/11 attackers and their many active supporters, widely reported to be increasing in number, do indeed lie "beyond the text," alas. Such persons are no figment of the Orientalist imagination, and it shows them no respect – multicultural or otherwise – to speak of them as if they were.[152]

Other varieties of social thought provide better leads in guiding U.S. policy. The next two of these, employed in the next chapter, are those of cultural sociology and Nietzschean genealogy.

9

The Inflationary Rhetoric of Terrorist Threat: Humanitarian Law as Deflationary Check

However intense the passions leading to war may often be, each belligerent must view its enemy as resembling it in key respects if there is to be any possibility of restraint through reciprocity. This paradox explains why the argument against forbearance in war is always some version of the claim that the enemy is entirely different from us in ways that make it incapable of rationally playing tit-for-tat. We must therefore consider the rhetorical tool kit with which proponents of the argument against restraint come to formulate it and the recurrent role of humanitarian law in refuting it.

The public argument for going to war has almost never been couched in simple terms of efficiency or social utility. To justify war's predictable horrors – especially to democratic voters – demands a rhetorical mode altogether distinct from the utilitarian, with its sober and uninflected tone. The public is never simply told that the lesser pain of war, correctly calculated, is preferable to the greater prospective pain of not fighting, that this calculus provides sufficient grounds for entering the fight, even in self-defense.

Rather, "wars are born and sustained in rivers of language about what it means to serve the cause, to kill the enemy, and to die with dignity; and they are reintegrated into a collective historical self-understanding through a ritualistic overplus of the language of commemoration,"[1] observes literary critic James Dawes. If such language amply allows for the expression of many emotions, it also constrains the range of available reasons for war. Dawes continues,

> Moral talk constrains what we can say, even in the face of what might be our overwhelming . . . power. It forces us to tell a very special story to justify our actions, a story that is vulnerable to all the rules of evidence and credibility. An invasion that is called just is not . . . an invasion that

simply enjoys approbation; it is an invasion that enjoys approbation for particular reasons, and anyone asserting its "justice" is required to provide particular sorts of evidence.... One reinforces the legitimacy of particular moral obligations even if one enters into rational discourse only to assert, disingenuously, that one has not violated them.[2]

Legal talk – and talk about the law of war in particular – does the same by "establishing an overlapping vocabulary between belligerents,"[3] Dawes adds. And what is true of arguments for war in this respect is also true of efforts to justify resort to warfare's most inhumane methods, such as torture and the targeted killing of enemy leaders. Even General Sherman invoked the law of war when justifying his shelling of Atlanta, pointing out that it was "a fortified town, with magazines, arsenals, founderies,"[4] and therefore a legitimate military objective. Contrary to his more famous pronouncement on the subject, it turns out that war's "cruelty" could in this way, after all, be "refined"[5] in light of the call of "God and humanity."

Surely, this is not the stuff of economics, one would suppose. Still, Posner the Younger does go so far as to defend – with seemingly bellicose bluster – the Bush administration's strategic doctrine of preventive self-defense on an economic theory of "optimal war."[6] Posner the Elder wisely chides, however, that a decision to go to war should not be taken simply on the basis of an assessment that national benefits will exceed the costs. Otherwise, he warns, the United States might blithely decide to invade Canada.[7] Any sober prognosis of the far-ranging costs of war, grounded in careful attention to historical experience, would in any event often prove highly cautionary. War is usually quite inefficient in a Paretian sense, whatever other, more obvious criticisms are often made of it.[8] But this is not the language in which war has ever been publicly debated.

One instead tends to hear a discourse of high drama – melodrama, in fact. Resort to criminal methods of warfare, like recourse to war itself, requires the framing of events according to a legitimating narrative of apocalypse, of good and evil, not cost and benefit. Leaders must persuade publics, often initially skeptical, that the very survival of the country and its institutions is at stake, so the choice they collectively face is do-or-die. Hence, for instance, in their defense of Bush administration counterterrorism policy, David Frum and Richard Perle write, "There is no middle way for Americans: it is either victory or holocaust."[9] In response to this claim, James Traub mockingly continues, "In the face of extinction, only a Democrat or a diplomat or a member of the liberal media would trifle over civil liberties or the use of torture."[10]

THE DISCOURSE OF WAR: A CULTURAL SOCIOLOGY

To cast a conflict in such do-or-die terms demands an "inflationary" assessment of threat, as sociologists Jeffrey Alexander and Philip Smith contend.[11] It entails characterizing the potential enemy as "not like us"; that is, immune to sensible argument, incapable of rational negotiation, insusceptible even to deterrence through prudent assessment of its self-interest in avoiding destruction.[12] To speak of an "axis of evil" is thus not a thoughtless, careless slip of the tongue, as some have suggested,[13] but rather the only culturally acceptable narrative for framing a decision to abandon rule adherence and mundane diplomatic negotiation, where one may split the difference. "When radical evil is afoot in the world," writes sociologist Philip Smith, "there can be no compromise . . . no prudent efforts to effect sanctions or maintain a balance of power. The evil is so absolute that there is no possibility for trust. . . . Events are seen as unequivocally world-historical . . . in need of heroic interventions, for the object of struggle is the future . . . of civilization."[14]

British Prime Minister Tony Blair expressed just such a view of the conflict with Al Qaeda:

> They have no moral inhibition on the slaughter of the innocent. If they could have murdered not 7,000 but 70,000, does anyone doubt that they would have done so and rejoiced in it? There is no compromise possible with such people, no meeting of minds, no point of understanding with such terror. Just a choice: defeat it or be defeated by it. And defeat it we must.[15]

In such a struggle, the outcome, Smith continues, is entirely "dependent on faith, decisiveness, and resolve," and for this reason "internalized motivational fidelity to higher ideals" is "a more important criterion for evaluating action than budgets and established procedure." As a theist with evangelical leanings, President Bush presumably has some affinity for thinking in apocalyptic rather than utilitarian terms. But so too do his critics employ near-apocalyptic allusions in decrying the threat he purportedly posed to civil liberties.[16]

The state of inflationary excitation just described is quite precarious, however. As Smith writes, because political leaders favoring war

> have raised the stakes so high, they are exposed to risks of deflation. Those encoded as pure and those encoded as polluted must act in ways that sustain this imagined scripting. If the gap starts to close between the good and the evil or events start to look less apocalyptic, we can negotiate. If the

object of struggle turns out to be simply some local issue, then the future
of the world is no longer at stake and we need not send troops to die for
it. Efforts to de-legitimate war typically involve these kinds of attempts
to prick the balloon of apocalypticism through redescription of objects,
actors, and motivations and thereby move our cultural frame of reference
back down the . . . hierarchy.

He refers here to the hierarchy from melodrama to tragedy, the latter
a genre that accentuates "the suffering of innocents" in a world of "documented futility and chaos." In tragedy, one's adversaries are "complex in
their motivations and . . . essentially 'just like us' in their ambitions and
powers of action."[17] Smith sees this "low mimetic mode" of description,
as he calls it, to be "the predominant narrative for our understanding
of everyday politics," where we face "business as usual." At such times,
extraordinary, "existential threats to national survival" are not in play, and
the "binary modes of sacred and profane" cannot credibly be brought to
bear in characterizing the protagonists. The latter are instead "drab and
routinized." We can see "the shades of gray that mark personalities in realist
fiction," rather than the histrionically operatic, "iconic, stylized character
qualities . . . emblematic of overarching moral positions." Such qualities and
positions make sense only in a world already intensely polarized, lacking
psychological ambiguity and emotional range.

Such a perspective on a country's internal disagreements over war and
war's acceptable methods encourages us to "think of this agonistic struggle
as a genre war" – melodrama vs. tragedy – "in which interested parties try
to impose their version of reality by . . . attempting to institutionalize and
disseminate a broader, more diffuse and therefore more powerful genre of
interpretation through the public sphere. . . . Narrative inflation and defla-
tion through the genre gamut is pivotal to this ramping up or talking down
of threats," Smith concludes. In sum, as Elaine Scarry once observed, war is
always a "reality duel . . . a contest to out-describe."[18]

LAW'S EFFECT ON PUBLIC RHETORIC

How does the introduction of international law into public debate affect
this rhythm of rhetorical escalation and deescalation? Clearly, its consistent
effect, when taken even half-seriously, is to deflate the claims of the war
party.[19] The *jus ad bellum* historically imposed a list of stringent conditions, such as "last resort" and pure intention, requiring clear satisfaction
before a state could lawfully resort to force. The UN Charter ratcheted
the threshold still higher, repudiating arguments for war that had been

accepted throughout much of history until very recently, essentially leaving only self-defense.[20]

Similarly deflationary is the *jus in bello* on acceptable methods of fighting, in rendering irrelevant the enemy's moral character and motivations for entering combat. That one's enemy is the aggressor, in particular, permits the aggrieved nation no special dispensation to employ methods impermissible to its antagonist. Once war begins, aggression's victim stands on a par and must thereafter play by the same rules as its perpetrator. In this way, the key to apocalyptic narration – the enemy as monstrously irremediable villain – becomes immaterial to the question of how it may be resisted. The antagonist who is truly seeking world domination within its grasp must be fought by the same rules as an enemy seeking only to defend itself or to reannex a small piece of adjoining land historically part of its territory and wrongfully taken from it.

This entire approach will initially strike the neophyte as counterintuitive, even indefensible, as it continues to appear to leading philosophers.[21] Among its longstanding rationales, however, has been the view that belligerents, whether aggressor or aggrieved, resemble one another – our enemies are "like us" – in their susceptibility to deterrence through retaliation.[22] The doctrine of belligerent reprisals helped codify this assumption into the law, first customary then treaty law. Humanitarian law has thereby always sought to resist the apocalyptic cultural script according to which the enemy must be destroyed or must submit to truly "unconditional" surrender. It thus deflates the operative genre through which a conflict may be described. It does so by presuming the possibility of reciprocity with one's enemy, whether through reprisal – now disfavored – or, more broadly, through lawful retaliation (i.e., retorsion).

This presumption made sense as long as retaliation by reprisal – a lofty term for a decidedly unlovely reality – was accepted practice and passable as legal doctrine. Today, such reprisal is no longer widely acceptable, however, in many respects. We are left with the law still engaged in telling a deflationary story about the enemy that is no longer so obviously sensible, insofar as the enemy – no longer mirroring us – is apparently insusceptible to deterrence through lawful reprisal or other retaliation.

The Bush administration's desire to tell an inflationary story about the incorrigible character of its adversary has therefore required resort to extralegal argument – that is, to the contention that the law, however technically applicable by its terms perhaps, was simply not drafted with anything like America's present predicament in mind. The only way to circumvent law's deflationary drag on the story of how to fight terrorists is thus to describe this predicament in highly inflationary terms and urge that the law is defective in failing to permit our appreciation of this true and more threatening reality.

Any deflationary response to this narrative must seek, in turn, to shove the facts back into the genre conventions of tragedy, away from those of melodrama. It must argue that Al Qaeda seeks only to modify U.S. foreign policy in the region, a truly mundane political objective. Osama bin Laden strives primarily to reduce American influence in the Middle East, a strategic, geopolitical goal of the most traditional sort, in this view. And in fact, the most careful aggregate data analysis of suicide bombings since 1980 concludes that "what nearly all suicide terrorist campaigns have in common is a specific secular and strategic goal to compel liberal democracies to withdraw military forces from territory that the terrorists consider to be their homeland."[23]

Thus, despite the occasional attack on mere symbols of cultural decadence – the unchaste, debauched women of London's discotheques – jihadists do not really hate us "for who we are,"[24] and the conflict with them therefore is not apocalyptic. Through this lens, jihadist militants depart from a certain Asian and Middle Eastern "occidentalism" for which "whatever the U.S. government does or does not do is often besides the point,"[25] because of "the Crusader spirit that all Westerners carry in their blood,"[26] as argued the highly influential Sayyid Qutb. Such militants are opposed, argue Buruma and Margalit, "not so much to American policies, but to the idea of America itself, as a rootless, cosmopolitan, superficial, trivial, materialistic, racially mixed, fashion-addicted civilization."[27]

Occidentalism of this sort is a useful concept, if taken only as an ideal-type, i.e., regardless of whether it provides a fully accurate characterization of anyone's actual views on America, views that are likely to be more complex.[28] It is especially striking that so much of Occidentalist criticism of the West has largely accepted the empirical substance of the Orientalist discourse about the East, simply inverting the value signs, transvaluing negatives into positives and vice versa.[29]

The question of who we *are* may be inseparable, of course, from that of what we *do* in our foreign policy. In particular, our insatiable search for oil as a means to material wealth might flow inexorably from our godless, spiritual bankruptcy. Yet if who we are and what we do can be separated, a deflationary story may be told, perhaps convincingly. This story of separation cannot be told specifically *through* law, however, in that law itself does not really facilitate the telling. By contrast, the law of reprisal advanced the telling of a deflationary story about deterrence, on the basis of a shared human capacity for calculative reason. Yet even the Bush administration's critics admit that jihadist suicide bombers cannot be deterred from war crimes and crimes against humanity in the way the law has always presumed.[30] This is not to gainsay that even certain factions within Al Qaeda sometimes favor forbearance (on televised beheadings, for instance, and causing too many civilian deaths) for other reasons.[31]

The law must pursue a different path if it is to contribute to a deflationary narrative. This path today resides in the law of human rights. Even suicidal jihadists resemble us in being members of the same species, endowed with corresponding rights, according to this recent body of international law. Violent jihadists may be unwilling to reciprocate our restraint, the argument goes, but they are still human beings. One seeks to deescalate demands for war with another country by stressing the demonstrably prosaic and negotiable quality of its ambitions. So too, one deflates calls for coercive interrogation of detainees and targeted killings of their leaders by emphasizing their essential humanity. One tries to "talk down," in Smith's terms, their apparent membership in a sectarian ideological group seeking mass destruction, as not germane to the question of their treatment after capture.

Hence the considerable intellectual effort, examined in Chapter 3, to read the law of human rights into humanitarian law, a sort of "incorporation by reference" to the common purpose of safeguarding human dignity from threat by political strife.[32] Now, the deflationary story can be told by accentuating commonalities across the battle lines, albeit ones of philosophical anthropology, rather than self-interested rationality. The source of restraint in war then resides not in our shared capacity for reciprocity but in our shared humanity and our subjective appreciation of its moral importance.

This is a species of the social solidarity that Durkheim called "mechanical," in contrast to the "organic" solidarity among people occupying complementary roles within a division of labor.[33] He observed that breaches of mechanical solidarity are always enforced by criminal law,[34] of which much of international humanitarian law is now a part. Mechanical solidarity is precarious enough in small societies, Durkheim added. There, cultural sameness and a lack of interdependence – where all engage in the same economic activity – facilitate secession whenever disagreements arise. When sameness of worldview dissolves, so does society itself, for it is brittle and vulnerable to breakup through mere difference of opinion.

At the international level, sameness of worldview is rare, of course, leaving only our common humanity, and its recognition in "the cult of the individual"[35] – Durkheim's term – as a basis for this sort of solidarity. Yet the disagreements dividing Western liberal society[36] from violent jihadists, combined with the lack of economic or other ties, make it difficult for many Americans to give pride of place, in treatment of detainees and their fugitive leaders, to this common humanity. The collective conscience on which such sentiments must rest is weak.[37]

Arendt invoked the true political refugee – someone who should readily elicit our sympathies – to illustrate this point. She observed the disconcerting irony that when this refugee is seen as simply a human being, stripped by statelessness of all social and cultural attachments, he is then generally classified and so treated as no one at all.[38] This is the human person reduced to the bare essentials (i.e., precisely the figure whose entitlements and claims on us can derive only from the law of human rights). The refugee therefore tests our commitment to that legal ideal. Yet in the darkest days of mid-century Europe (as Jews sought shelter from the Nazis and their many collaborators throughout Europe), to warrant treatment as a fellow human being, Arendt reminds us, turned out to require stronger, more specific affiliations than with the species at large, membership in which counted for nothing at all in practical terms.[39] It was only much thicker attachments and the social bonds of reciprocity they entailed – the Danish churches, the Dutch physicians, for instance – that engendered meaningful support for those most vulnerable and the attendant resistance to their oppressors that this support required.

Even such deeper, organic solidarity of the Durkheimian sort is neither cure for social conflict nor guarantee of fellow-feeling. Some of the Muslims who have benefited materially from economic integration with the West are prominent among the jihadists. The beneficiaries of petroleum markets, in particular, on both sides of the exchange certainly do share an organic interdependence that generally keeps their mutual resentments politically in check. Yet even here the exceptions, beginning with Osama bin Laden himself,[40] certainly test the rule and undermine its claims, in ways Durkheim did not anticipate. Many of the 9/11 hijackers themselves had received higher education in the West, training for careers that would have involved enduring interaction with Westerners in the technical professions. Bin Laden, for example, was schooled to be a modern engineer. Even Durkheim, for all his faith in organic, economic forms of solidarity, ultimately came around to the view that social order continued to require a collective conscience, one now based on the "cult of the individual" or what today we would call human rights.

It is questionable whether, in the face of counterpressures, this merely mechanical sort of solidarity that is shared with jihadist detainees will ever prove as salient a source of forbearance as organic solidarity often has.[41] The humanitarian sensibility, in its affective attention to other peoples' suffering, requires a cosmopolitan self-understanding according to which we are all, first and foremost, "citizens of the world" more than citizens of our particular nation-states[42] – even at moments of intensely felt threat to our security as nationals of such states. This is a tall order. One scholar of military affairs concisely articulates the limits of humanitarianism today, both American and European: "U.S. soldiers are humanitarian enough to kill on behalf of an oppressed group, but they are not prepared to die for its members."[43]

Yet it is just such arguments about shared humanity that provide the discursive structure or cultural logic on which the Bush administration's critics tacitly relied. Seen from an historical perspective covering the last 150 years (i.e., starting with the abolition of slavery), the diffusion of humanitarian sensibility throughout the world is doubtless impressive, even remarkable.[44] At any point in time, however, the progress from one step to the next has inevitably seemed almost glacial, with major periodic steps backward.[45]

Even in the eighteenth century, Kant could already precociously proclaim that "the people of the earth have . . . entered . . . into a universal community, and it has developed to the point where a violation of rights in one part of the world is felt everywhere."[46] Perhaps. But humanitarian sentiment – when it demands any serious sacrifice – is difficult enough to sustain toward those of incompatible views from disparate cultures on the other side of the world, with whom one's ties – through commerce and other communication – are extremely weak.[47] Still harder is it to sustain such sympathy toward those who appear to labor diligently, through free will and with passionate commitment, toward one's destruction.

Whether Americans should now be telling themselves an inflationary or deflationary story – in the face of conflicting evidence, supporting and undermining both sorts of narrative – is not a question that the cultural sociology of war's discourse seeks to address. It teaches us only to be attuned to the rhetorical stratagems in which claim and counterclaim are couched, through which certain evidence is highlighted and the rest deemphasized. It does not grant us wisdom, and as William James wrote, "The art of being wise is the art of knowing what to overlook."[48] No theory has ever been devised that can confer judgment about which features of a complex and inconsistent reality to ignore and which to dwell upon.

Two types of error are possible here. Just as one may overlook subtle evidence of possibilities for a conflict's peaceful resolution, one may also sometimes overlook the need to prepare for (or acknowledge a *de facto* state of) war, prematurely declaring "peace in our time,"[49] for instance. Similarly, one may overlook the need or moral/legal permissibility to relax certain restrictions on war's traditional methods of prosecution. The wisdom required in such circumstances is an attribute of "statesmanship," Rawls acknowledges,[50] and the great theorist remains aptly cryptic about what, if anything, a statesman may gain here from theory.

Very little, presumably.[51]

TERROR–TORTURE AS MIRROR IMAGE?

Until recently, the United States had represented the rule of law – no less than the freedom and prosperity such law permits – to the rest of the world. What better way for jihadist militants to erode this potent appeal than to "lure the U.S. into a matching descent into lawlessness," as one British scholar decries.[52] The similarities are indeed troubling. Each side has adopted an increasingly expansive doctrine of self-defense. The Bush administration's version rejects secular international law,[53] much as bin Laden's version departs from most Koranic understandings.[54] Both reinterpretations seek to characterize what is essentially a first-strike policy as actually defensive, on the basis of the ubiquity of the enemy's lurking threat.[55] Both also extend responsibility/liability "vicariously" to those not immediately involved, whether by way of their assistance to direct participants (the United States to Israel) or simply their seeming neutrality (i.e., insufficient enthusiasm in cooperating with U.S. counterterrorism policy).[56]

The breadth with which both sides define self-defense is matched by a narrowness in their understanding of other key terms. Many Muslim legal scholars, for instance, avow that even the martial variety of jihad does not permit terrorism. Yet their definitions of that term often prove quite restrictive, excluding conduct that most nonmilitants would surely include, such as attacks on Israeli civilians or Jewish civilian organizations presumed to be sympathetic to Israel (as in the Buenos Aires bombings),[57] and certainly on Americans, because their country acts "in concert" with Israel.[58] Thus, any violence identified with the Palestinian cause would not necessarily count as terrorism. In this way, such writers – who invariably surround the term with quotation marks – all but define terrorism out of existence.[59] This makes it easy for them, in turn, to claim publicly that they "oppose all terrorism." In its dubious narrowness, this approach to defining terrorism uncomfortably approximates President Bush's approach to defining torture. The metaphor of the mirror again becomes tempting, if not irresistible.

Each side views its adversary as harboring the grandest of imperial ambitions, whether spreading Islamic theocracy or "the freedom agenda," as proclaimed in the 2006 U.S. National Security Strategy.[60] In a November 11, 2005, speech, President Bush warned, "We're facing a radical ideology with inalterable objectives, to enslave whole nations and intimidate the world. . . . They have endless ambitions of imperial domination and they wish to make everyone powerless except themselves." Yet even those who are willing to acknowledge that, "doubtless, the President was correct" in this regard, then proceed to criticize what they view as his "projecting on to one's fundamentalist opponent one's own exaggerated ambitions . . . for a 'benevolent hegemony,'" which entails "a project no less grand."[61] Some have indeed described American liberalism today as fundamentalist.

As mirror images, these fundamentalisms, Tariq Ramadan contends, may even "feed into one another and, each reinforces the other with its alter ego."[62] The core message of the conflict reads much the same from either end, like some perverse political palindrome. Even avowedly "adversarial" institutions often end up resembling the mainstream ones they attack, more than they would like to think. The "critical alternatives" they devise are always formed and deformed by those with which they joust; certain strands of the New Left ended up no less authoritarian, to put it mildly, than the liberal educational authority they denounced for its authoritarianism.

The metaphor of the mirror may not always be quite correct, however, unless one has in mind a fun-house mirror or a game with mirrors, as Taussig observes.[63] For what is mimicked is often each side's image of the other more than any demonstrable facts about the opponent. Children throughout the Arab world now carry images of Abu Ghraib on their cell phones, and Al Qaeda recruitment videos invoke Guantánamo to persuade viewers that America has no respect for Muslims, as if these were proof to that effect. "No wonder the Islamist equation" of such mistreatment to the 9/11 attacks "was credible to many ordinary Muslims," writes Shaw.[64] In such mental mirroring, each side begins to enter not only the other's calculations but also its cosmology. By late 2007, the Bush administration's proclaimed war on terrorism had become as central as abortion and same-sex marriage to the evolving worldview of Christian evangelicals, by some accounts.[65]

A game theorist might too quickly characterize this process in terms of a "grim trigger," a self-reinforcing cycle of defections from cooperation, but even that does not capture its full measure of perversity. For the problem is not merely that each side seeks to punish the other's defections *ad infinitum*, escalating its sanction from every round to the next. The problem is that each side comes increasingly to resemble the other by refining itself in light of the other's latest moves, where each move alters the nature of the mover. If each acts increasingly like the other, this is because each increasingly becomes obsessed with the other, almost to the point of becoming the other.

The mutual mimesis begins at the level of tactics. That Al Qaeda has reportedly added waterboarding to its training programs should then come as no surprise, much as the early British settlers in North America soon adopted the practice of "scalping" from the indigenous peoples they fought.[66] The gruesome history of counterinsurgency warfare has similarly led some to conclude that "the easy and reliable way of defeating all insurgencies everywhere," as strategist Edward Luttwak mockingly writes, is to "out-terrorize the insurgents, so that fear of reprisals outweighs the desire to help the insurgents."[67]

What is first defended simply as smart strategy threatens to become true as a deeper ontology – a stance on what is real and unreal – much as early game theory, designed only to model and explain existing behavior, quickly began to influence first the nuclear strategy of Cold War superpowers and then the foreign policy of the strategizers more broadly. Taussig describes a variation on this theme quite evocatively, if elusively, in the context of colonial slavery in Peru and the Congo:

> The system of torture they [the colonizers] devised . . . mirrored the horror of the savagery they so feared, condemned – and fictionalized. . . . [Hence] the mimesis between the savagery attributed to the Indians by the colonists and the savagery perpetuated by the colonists in the name of . . . civilization. This reciprocating yet distorted mimesis has been . . . the colonial mirror that reflects back onto the colonists the barbarity of their own social relations, but as imputed to the savage. . . . And what is put into discourse through the artful story telling . . . is the same as what they practiced on the bodies of Indians.[68]

Taussig's discussion of this perverse species of mimetic reciprocity leaves no doubt about its contemporary repercussions, as he sees them. Writing in the early 1980s, under the shadow of U.S. support for anti-communist forces in Central America, he continues, "The military and the New Right, like the conquerors of old, discover the evil they have imputed to these aliens, and mimic the savagery they have imputed. . . . For it is not the victim as animal that gratifies the torturer, but the fact that the victim is human, thus enabling the torturer to become the savage."[69]

Perhaps even more than the colonial encounter with its racial tensions, conflicts between antagonists sharing a line of descent, as with brothers in Greek mythology or modern civil wars, have often been particularly uninhibited.[70] International law has indulged this unrestraint. Civil wars begin, at least, as domestic rebellions against lawful authority, which states everywhere in their domestic law have always treated as simply criminal. This is a treatment that international law, created by such states, has only recently and modestly ventured to regulate.[71] It would be difficult, however, to construct an explanation of restraint in war that could account for the possibility that the "gloves come off" more readily in fights both between belligerents who are most different (colonial conquest) and also between those who are most alike (civil wars within ethnically homogeneous societies; that is, between northern and southern whites in 1860s America). The evidence for the first of these two propositions, by the way, is much stronger than for the second.[72] Without more comparative research on the question, however, it is better to be wary of all such hasty generalizations.[73]

Internecine confrontations surely harbor violently intermingled imaginings of the sort Taussig describes in the colonial context. Through the peculiar dynamic of fratricidal conflict, René Girard suggests,

> Each party progresses rapidly in uncovering the truth about the other, without ever recognizing the truth about himself. Each sees in the other the usurper of a legitimacy that he thinks he is defending but that he is in fact undermining.... Reciprocity is busy aiding each party in his own destruction.... Violent reciprocity is left in sole command of the battlefield.... There is never anything on one side of the system that cannot be found on the other side, provided we wait long enough. The quicker the rhythm of reprisals, the shorter the wait.... On both sides everything is equal: not only the desire, the violence, the strategy, but also the alternation of victory and defeat, of exaltation and despair.... There is no monster that does not tend to duplicate himself or to "marry" another monster.... Under the heading of *monstrous double* we shall call all the hallucinatory phenomena provoked at the height of unrecognized reciprocity.[74]

Each party engages in increasingly desperate efforts to differentiate itself from its adversary, but in surpassing its novel methods and beating it at its own game, the one becomes the other in this very respect. Each seeks to become only a subversive simulacrum, not a perfect photocopy,[75] but becomes instead a copy of a copy of itself. Each initially may employ mimicry almost in parody, but ends up locked into its inherent logic.

Outsiders readily perceive the resulting convergence, whereas the parties themselves see only the differences between them, even as these grow ever smaller. They become mutually self-consumed in a narcissism of small differences. In his novel *The Red and the Black*, Stendhal first observed the dynamic in the most intimate of settings: When two men compete vigorously for the romantic attention of a single woman, they both often find it necessary to employ stratagems that only alienate her affections entirely, so that she prefers solitude or someone less obsessively interested in her.[76]

Girard's observations, notwithstanding some portentous hyperbole, shed light on certain aspects of armed conflict, and not only in civil war. In the early modern era, competition for New World colonies led Western imperial powers to mimic one another's methods and stratagems.[77] Such mirroring sometimes has its gravest consequences for third parties drawn into the vortex of what was initially only a bilateral contest. During the Cold War, for instance, the dueling superpowers each denied the possibility of a genuine "third way."[78] Each often seized on the smallest deviation by other states from its own, favored social model as evidence of slippage toward the rival model. Yet like the female object of affection for Stendhal's romantic rivals, many such states – heralding their "nonaligned" status – ultimately sought to avoid the overbearing attention of both superpowers. In the face of this persistent independent-mindedness, however, each superpower could perceive only a surreptitious coddling up to its adversary.

Girard's insights counsel similar caution in American counterterrorism policy, for most of the Muslim world wishes wholly to embrace neither Al Qaeda's agenda nor America's way of life, it is safe to say. Talk of dueling fundamentalisms in the conflict with Al Qaeda is appealing to critics of President Bush, as well as his Christian constituencies. Liberalism may today be very expansive in the geographical scope of its aspirations to human liberation from oppression. Yet it nonetheless differs crucially from radical Islam in its tolerance, even encouragement, of myriad conceptions of the good life – all but the theocratic and violently xenophobic, in fact.[79] The equation of the two, in its implication of moral equivalence, is hence dangerously misconceived. It is also a rhetorical device unnecessary to making a convincing argument for American inhibition.

Abundant evidence from military history does suggest that, when each side to a brewing conflict perceives the other's intentions as more aggressive than they actually were, their mutual misperceptions become self-fulfilling.[80] There are even demonstrable micro-foundations, at the level of individual psychology, to this macro-pattern in international politics. Experimental researchers have found that people generally attribute their own misconduct to the constraints of circumstance, whereas they ascribe the failure of others to stable dispositions of character.[81] These studies find many such self-serving biases to be pervasive, as when people are asked to compare their own support to a cooperative scheme relative to others' contributions.[82] Such tendencies are surely exacerbated by a climate of distrust between the parties. The relation between belligerents in war is surely the *ne plus ultra* of distrust. It is not surprising, then, that opportunities for international cooperation between geopolitical adversaries have regularly been missed, demonstrably so, as in the superpower rivalry of the Cold War, according to some careful recent historiography.[83]

In game-theoretic terms, a player who believes that the world is always "dog eat dog" cannot be proven wrong, because it will exploit a "good will" gesture from competitors, treating it as a ruse, thereby forcing others to defect from cooperation, just as anticipated from the beginning that they always would.[84] At the outset of most major episodes of mass atrocity, in fact, scholarship now suggests that many perpetrators sincerely believe – albeit often delusionally – that the group they target is itself about to perpetrate atrocities of its own (i.e., against the first group), whose members must therefore act preemptively against the imminent danger.[85]

This "matching descent" suggests a darker dynamic, altogether different from the processes examined thus far, though an extension of those assayed at the end of the preceding chapter.[86] Such a rhythm might even be described as a mutant form of reciprocity; it is clearly consistent with one definition of that phenomenon employed by leading sociologists: "the mutual enforcement by two parties of each other's actions."[87] Through this process, righteous indignation can devolve into wild, barely controllable rage. This is the devolution that many claimed to discern in relations between the Bush administration and major portions of the Muslim world.[88] This mutual reinforcement involves neither of the more salubrious types discussed thus far: that of the game theorists (restoring cooperation through tit-for-tat) nor of liberal moral theorists (invoking fairness).

Mirror imaging may take still other forms. A widely endorsed view of the conflict with Al Qaeda, not only among postmodernists, is that "the specter of terrorism is forcing the West to terrorize itself. . . . All the security strategies are merely extensions of terror. . . . And it is the real victory of terrorism that it has plunged the whole of the West into the obsession with security – that is to say, into a veiled form of perpetual terror."[89] The most extravagant version of this mirror-imaging thesis (from Baudrillard, again) contends that the 9/11 attackers merely helped kill off our already dying, self-destructive society. In their suicides, they mirror our own desire to die, just as in their homicides, they help put us out of our misery. In our *ennui* and alienation, we secretly want to be done with our petty, paltry lives. Those who attack us thus are "unconsciously on our side." The terrorists are really playing the same 'game,' advancing the same end. We might merely tell such people, "You cannot kill us, because we are already dead. . . . We have already devastated our world; what more do you want?"[90]

The answer to this question, Baudrillard continues, is that "we have merely devastated this world; it still has to be destroyed. Destroyed symbolically." And what better symbol of Western decadence than the Twin Towers – those hubristic heights of phallocentric fantasy – along with all the boring capitalist drones tediously toiling within? "Our despair is terminal, because it arises out of the fulfillment of all desires"[91] (i.e., our limitless wealth, power, and leisure), Baudrillard concludes.

Needless to say, this discussion takes place almost entirely among French postmodernist intellectuals, if one will forgive the cheap shot. More to the point, it doesn't much speak to either the normative or practical concerns of humanitarian law and to those of us concerned with making that law more principled and effective.

THE WILL TO TORTURE?
RECIPROCITY AS MASS PSYCHOPATHOLOGY

The Bush administration clearly believed it owed a lower measure of legal process to foreign terror detainees held at Guantánamo than indicated by the Geneva Conventions or the International Covenant on Civil and Political Rights. Yet the administration has never expressly defended this diminished process as reciprocation for Al Qaeda's own disrespect of legal process in its mistreatment – often beheadings, in fact – of Western or Asian captives and other civilian victims of its attacks. The United States has instead defended its detention irregularities as necessary in light of the threat posed by those detained.

This rationale has struck most of the world as specious and unconvincing, however, in no small part because of the failure for more than four years to initiate proceedings against most detainees, to assess that threat before a neutral fact-finder. This failure legitimately arouses the suspicion that the genealogy of such irregularities may more accurately be found elsewhere, perhaps in some notion of reciprocity, however inarticulate or semi-conscious.

In this vein, one leading American political thinker, Stephen Holmes, claims that the problem with current counterterrorism policy does not reside in any misapplication of cost-benefit analyses; hence, getting the numbers right will not solve it. The process of rational calculation has not gone astray in its details, for we are not really operating in the realm of rational assessment to begin with. Holmes instead detects what we might call a "Nietzschean" theme at the core of U.S. antiterrorism policy.[92] This is the notion that the world's sole super- or *über* power is "exceptional" in its immunity from ordinary prejudices about good and evil.[93] Such prejudices and resulting rules are based on the perennial resentment of the mediocre against their betters. The latter should simply indulge their expansive impulses, because a "will to power" and an attendant indifference to settled opinion (e.g., among other sovereign states) are essential to accomplishing anything original and important in life. Those capable of such *virtu* are hence "philosophers of the future," serving as "commanders and legislators who first determine the Whither and For What of man,"[94] Nietzsche writes.

One senses sentiments of this sort palpitating just beneath the surface of such statements by President Bush as "this country will define our times, not be defined by them."[95] His closest advisers privately proclaim, "We're an empire now, and when we act, we create our own reality. And while you're studying that reality – judiciously, as you will – we'll act again, creating other new realities. . . . We're history's actors . . . and you, all of you [journalists and scholars], will be left to just study what we do."[96]

Surely the superman, seeking to remake the world in his image, does not trifle over diplomatic etiquette and moral niceties, presumably including the prohibition against torturing his tormenters. Justice – in the sense of rules of right and wrong that are equally binding on all – is a petty and ignoble notion.[97] International law – with its first principle that all states deserve equal respect for their sovereignty – simply enshrines the slave morality of the mediocre. International humanitarian law may codify the world's most uniformly accepted judgments, to be sure. But such judgments are always the falsest, Nietzsche taught. Those who submit to such law hence succumb to "the herd instinct of obedience." If there is anything "healthy" and life-affirming about the enterprise, it is that customary international law, at least, permits its own transgression as a means of self-transformation,[98] a curious feature with no exact analogue in domestic law.

Holmes strikes another Nietzschean chord in suggesting that Bush administration counterterror policy is less concerned with national self-defense than with the sheer joy of lording the country's superior status over those on whom it vents its retributive wrath.[99] Self-defense is prospective, undertaken in light of current threats. Retribution is entirely retrospective. According to Nietzsche, indulging one's retributive emotions is also intensely pleasurable, for it enables one to demonstrate, even celebrate, one's elevated position over social/moral inferiors. Expecting no such self-indulgent sentiment in an arch "realist," many were surprised that former Secretary of State Henry Kissinger endorsed the 2003 Iraq war. Yet here is his explanation, offered in private conversation with a Bush administration speech writer: "Because Afghanistan wasn't enough, and we need to humiliate them . . . in order to make a point that we're not going to live in this world that they want for us."[100] Of course, even a realist may presumably indulge such sentiments if humiliating a rival or adversary is not an end in itself, but merely a means to more effective power over him.

The Bush administration's proffered rationale for coercive interrogation, targeted killing, and sustained detention of Al Qaeda suspects was the national defense, of course. The motive for self-defense is self-preservation, so its emotional tone is invariably temperate. Such *gravitas* was not always the moral register in which the Bush administration defended its "global war on terror," however. "Bring 'em on!" does not exactly display the modicum of sobriety befitting a matter necessarily involving the deaths of thousands, likely including many innocents. Though publicly propounded in terms of national defense, American policy thus differed from true self-defense, on this view, in both its temporal focus (retro- rather than prospective) and, more important, in its psychological roots. As sheer punitive rage, this form of "reciprocity," if it may be so called, does not figure in this book's initial typology. For unlike the other four types, it does not even profess to make a normative argument for the conduct encompassed. Its relation to the normative domain is more like Nietzsche's relation to moral philosophy – a field no one would confuse him of "practicing," though he remains impossible for moral theorists to ignore.

If one sees U.S. counterterrorism law as driven primarily by a punitive rage, then the theory of tit-for-tat (and Al Qaeda's refusal to play by its rules) must have been invoked merely to provide a rhetorically acceptable facade for far darker impulses. These impulses are unconcerned with utilitarian rationality and stand, in fact, much closer to mass psychopathology, on Holmes's reading.[101] Unwarranted detention and ineffective torture simply indulge a national lust for revenge in the face of impotence against an elusive and despised foe.[102] The public appeal of torture arises not despite its illegality, but precisely because of it, for violating a legal/moral "absolute" eloquently "sends a message about American determination, ruthlessness, and willingness to act without asking permission or making excuses."[103]

The public acceptance of unlawful detention is similarly enhanced by the very innocence of most detainees, on Holmes's view, for many Americans simply view the unjust detention of "their" (i.e., Muslim) innocents as a perfectly "appropriate response to 9/11," when "the hijackers killed perfectly

innocent people themselves."[104] Just as terror seeks to instill fear into everyday life, so the random prospect of torture sows fear into the population of
terrorists and potential terrorists. Poetic justice, one might more charitably
say: "For 'tis the sport to have the engineer," as Shakespeare rhapsodized,
"hoist with his own petard."[105] Such justice, if it may be so called, is almost
too perfect in its harmonious equilibrium to be entirely convincing as social
explanation. Society is rarely so symmetrical.

   Other clichés come equally to mind. Legal theorist George Fletcher, invoking Kant, writes that, with respect to the law of war, "what's good for the
goose is good for the gander."[106] "Fighting fire with fire," as Richard Posner
puts it, may be a better – and even more charitable – metaphor.[107] For it suggests the possibility, the occasional necessity even, of averting a particular
sort of threat by directing the same type of threat against it. This is precisely
the method that firefighters employ when starting one blaze in order to
combat another; doing so deprives the first of future fuel. Yet one ventures
to say that none of these platitudes fully capture our moral intuitions about
what is at stake here; that is, once we begin to speak of human beings rather
than geese and trees.

   Whatever the merits of Holmes's provocative account,[108] there is little
doubt that it effectively captures an important element of truth in how
others came to view us. The forceful U.S. government response to 9/11
is largely symbolic, on this view, providing reassurance to an emotional
public by focusing on areas (like reduced civil liberties) where there are few
quantifiable costs, rather than on those (e.g., port security) where major
risk reduction would be quite expensive. Studies also suggest that when
strong emotions of outrage lead people to focus on the wrongfulness of
given conduct, the probability of its recurrence is much exaggerated and
even ignored (i.e., in deciding how to respond).[109]

   Studies further show that "subjects exposed to stimuli designed to
heighten anger believed the risks of further terror attacks to be higher than
those exposed to fear stimuli." This finding suggests that "anger rather than
fear may better explain the substance of terrorism-inspired concerns."[110]
More Americans die every few years from bee stings than from jihadist
terror.[111] Administration critics invoking such numbers appear to imply that
Americans should regard the 9/11 attacks as the functional equivalent of a
national bee sting.[112] Yet the number of persons killed on that day obviously
does not exhaust the event's political, economic, or legal significance.

   Like Nietzsche's own genealogy of morals, Holmes's version is not readily susceptible to disconfirmation in the way that positivist social science

requires.[113] So much the worse for social science, both theorists would plausibly respond. Even the usually sober George Kateb contends that, today, "analysis should be guided by the thought that the motives of the Bush administration are not primarily the stated ones."[114] But the charge that an entire country is indulging a bout of outright sadism would seem to call for at least some sort of evidence. More important, Holmes's effort to psychologize and diagnose the nation's torturing temptation as ill-considered and unfocused rage, though perhaps insightful, declines to refute torture's claims on its own terms, which is also a more respectful posture toward one's opponents in democratic debate.

If the impulse to defend torture is simply an expression of unreason, then attempting to reason with those who succumb to it is senseless. Like madmen, those who would see U.S. law institutionalize the practice of coercive interrogation in the conflict with Al Qaeda should themselves presumably be institutionalized. It bears emphasis here that such proponents include not only such perennial headline seekers as Alan Dershowitz[115] but also much more sober, cautious, and respected intelligences in the legal academy.[116] Holmes's account also does not adequately explain why Americans would knowingly choose to resemble an adversary from whose illicit practices they would presumably wish to distinguish themselves.

For Aristotle and the ancient Greeks, at least, a victor's magnanimity toward vanquished foes was no minor virtue. It was a display of his nobility,[117] as well as a strategy for gaining support from the enemy's civilian population.[118] To retaliate in kind was to treat the adversary as a moral equal, whereas to desist from reprisal was to show one's indifference to the actions of an inferior and thereby display one's superiority over him. The forbearance that ensued arose in no way from any sympathy for its recipient, seen as a fellow member of the human species.[119] To the good warrior, such an opponent was not evil, requiring destruction, but merely bad, a force to be reckoned with, an obstacle with which one must contend.[120] If he must be struck, he should be struck only with the blunt side of one's sword.[121] This stance and its relevance to the current conflict are elaborated and defended in Chapters 11 and 12.

Yet first, we see in Chapter 10 how economics, particularly game theory and other rational choice thinking, might provide help in strategizing America's conflict with Al Qaeda and the place of law within that strategy.

10

Reciprocity as Tit-for-Tat:
Rational Retaliation in Modern War

MILITARY HISTORY THROUGH THE LENS OF SOCIAL SCIENCE

To answer convincingly this book's policy questions, we must first ask a more elemental empirical one: Do the Geneva Conventions really contribute much to restraint in war, to better treatment of enemy soldiers and civilians? Or, do the Conventions merely coordinate relations among states with preexisting cooperative interests, having no independent effect on their behavior?[1] Claims that relaxing legal restraints on combating terrorists will have dire consequences for human protection assume that these restraints have been effective. Yet how different would the last century's history of warfare have been if there had been no Hague or Geneva Conventions?[2] These questions presume that, when engaged in practical moral reasoning, we need to take consequences seriously, including consequences that are unintended but foreseeable.

Restraint in war has many sources in addition to those imposed by law. How important is the law, really, when compared to these other sources? There has always been intermittent evidence throughout military history for what might be called a sociology of martial restraint. In early modern Europe, historian Geoffrey Parker observes, especially at the local level,

> Where garrisons from opposing sides existed in close proximity, conventions emerged that anticipated the live and let live system on relatively quiet sectors of the trenches on the western front during World War I.... In order to remove the intolerable tensions of living on permanent alert, rival garrison commanders or neighboring (but opposed) communities would agree not to attack each other. There was even a ratchet effect, as cooperation on such basic matters led to deals in other areas, such as where each side might safely forage.[3]

Such recurrent historical experience of restraint through reciprocity may seem to suggest that its attendant sociology, however necessary to confronting the present predicament, does not require much attention to international law, even to the sociology of such law.

This is mistaken.

The view that the Geneva and Hague Conventions have had little real impact is surely worthy of serious consideration. In war, patterns that seem humane are not necessarily signs of humanity, much less of belief in a legal duty, argues international relations "realist" Eric Posner.[4] Often, "interest mimics altruism," as Elster puts it.[5] Consistent with this view, prisoners are not usually executed, but only because they are valuable as hostages and can be ransomed. Armies often spare the lives of noncombatants, but only because they pose no immediate threat, and killing them would simply antagonize enemy civilians who, if left alone, could also provide information and supplies.[6] Hence the historic rationale for the rule requiring belligerents to "grant quarter" was not the individual soldier's human rights; it was that surrender to the enemy renders him useless to the organization for which he has fought. Once he is useless in this sense, his death can yield no further military advantage. The suffering it entails is therefore superfluous, from a strictly martial standpoint. The contrary view of war mistakenly assumes that an army's aim is always to annihilate as many soldiers as possible, when it is more often to win territory and other resources.[7]

None of this should be surprising. It has been well known for more than forty years, after all, that contract law – to take just one empirically well-studied area – plays a relatively minor role in the actual workings of many markets, compared to one's reputation for trustworthiness and related, nonlegal sanctions.[8] Why shouldn't the same be true in the international arena, where law has enjoyed still weaker enforcement?

In recent years, even economists have come to recognize the importance of cooperative norms, relative to formal legal sanctions, in regulating social behavior; such norms often arise spontaneously over the course of repeated interaction among a limited set of otherwise self-interested actors.[9] Humanitarian law itself developed historically in just this way, as an informal, internal code of honor among aristocratic warrior elites in late medieval Europe, anticipating future martial encounters among themselves.[10] The process partly resembled that of "the law merchant," by which wool and wine traders in the same period developed rules of cross-border commerce and private courts to enforce them.[11] In fact, one might even describe recent social science findings as showing that, like the law merchant, the arcane formalities of humanitarian law do their job primarily by bolstering an informal reputational system.[12]

That system and its norms long antedate the Geneva Conventions. Only in the seventeenth century did humanitarian law become somewhat formalized into national treatises on natural and customary law. And only in the mid- to late nineteenth century did it begin to be codified into multilateral treaties. Thus, the view that armed conflict's excesses should be restrained primarily by widespread treaty ratification and, thereafter, by international judicial enforcement is relatively new to the history of efforts to tame the proverbial dogs of war. That informal mechanisms of diplomacy, often concerned with reputation, should remain more salient – their undoubted inadequacies notwithstanding – is hardly astonishing.

"Realists" contend that a state's treaty compliance does not mean that the country cares about the treaty as such, because states only sign agreements the terms of which they already intend to comply with from self-interest. Cases of compliance hence suffer from a huge selection bias.[13] If governments foresee enforcement problems with a provisional version of a treaty (i.e., noncompliance either by themselves or others), they may redraft it to facilitate ratification. Doing so may require watering down the treaty's demands to the point that its central concerns – say, fishery preservation – are not seriously addressed.[14] This strategy permits both *de jure* agreement and *de facto* compliance, but without solving the underlying problem that the treaty negotiations set out to tackle.

From such facts, realists infer that states settle on only such terms that will ensure the resulting treaties will readily be honored. Would that this were true! The norms embodied in humanitarian law treaties are widely violated in war,[15] often with complete impunity. States here show themselves entirely willing to ratify conventions the demands of which they are unwilling to honor, when push comes to shove. Signing such treaties is simply one of the many acts states know they must perform to be taken seriously in the world. To be treated as members of the international community, as players in that particular game, they must follow the cultural script of statehood, constructivists tell us.[16]

Another response to the realists is that the Geneva Conventions, through their formality and legal character, help states signal their intentions and stake their reputations. Through such treaties, states can lend some precision and credibility to their commitments. Treaties stabilize expectations about what conduct is unacceptable, a fact noted at least as early as the seventeenth century.[17] They also eliminate the transaction costs of bargaining over rules case by case, from one war to the next.[18] They screen out states as good or bad types, distinguishing those willing from those unwilling to make the relevant commitments.

For realists, though, all this is trivial, because – in an anarchic global system – states at war face each other in a series of bilateral prisoners' dilemmas, at best. When there are more than two belligerents, prospects for restraint through reciprocity drop still further, as laboratory experiments also find.[19] Formal commitments to the world at large, through multilateral treaties ratified many years before, count for little. A reputation for being law abiding will often be traded in for a reputation for protecting national interests vigorously, even ruthlessly.[20]

This move may not actually further a state's interests, some evidence suggests.[21] Yet states surely care more about winning the war – a 'game' that is ultimately zero-sum (because someone must win,[22] the other lose) – than continuing to play cooperatively whenever the two goals conflict, as they finally must, realists contend. No one can win at chess by playing with the primary goal of keeping as many pieces on the board as possible. And no one can ever truly win a war through strict adherence to tit-for-tat; and winning – not minimizing unnecessary suffering – is the ultimate objective of both sides. This fact gives rise to what two legal economists call "the familiar end-game problem"; that is, "the anticipation of the last transaction may cause the entire cooperative pattern to unravel as each party anticipates that the next interaction will be the last . . . and that the promissor might defect."[23] Treaties in humanitarian law differ here from those in other areas of international law, such as trade or the environment, where mutual gains from continued adherence often extend indefinitely, because the "shadow of the future" is perpetual, at least potentially.

The temptation to defect from cooperative "play" rises steeply as war draws to a close, realists stress. The likely winner can no longer be effectively deterred by the prospect of enemy punishment for war crimes. And the losing party is increasingly tempted to adopt dirty, "last ditch" methods of fighting, from which it may have previously refrained.[24] Facing what appears imminent destruction, its leaders conclude they have little to lose. Military "necessity" then seems to justify everything.[25] As the future's shadow shortens, any hope of a mutually beneficial equilibrium dissolves; cooperation succumbs to defection.[26] The targeting of civilian populations therefore increases in incidence as a war lasts longer and longer.[27] The mutual benefit in reducing avoidable costs of warfare – "unnecessary suffering" in the Geneva language – begins to dissolve over time. The thinking on one

side is, "I'm now so weak; how can I afford restraint?"[28] On the other, it
is, "I'm now so strong; why should I trouble to restrain myself before the
other side surrenders?" It is surely no coincidence that the United States
resorted to the direct targeting of Japanese civilian population centers only
at the very end of World War II,[29] when victory began to appear likely
(and prosecution for war crimes correspondingly unlikely), whereas Britain
adopted such methods much earlier in the war, when it was very much
on the defensive and its very survival seemed at stake.[30] Western bombing
strategy in that single conflict thus gives ample evidence of this hypothesis,
in both its avatars.

This realist/rationalist stance oversimplifies in several ways, however.
First, it assumes that it is possible to label a winner and loser, even when
both sides have been devastated and neither may feel that it has decisively
won or lost. Many wars end without either side completely achieving its
initial goals or only doing so at much greater cost than it would have been
prepared to assume *ex ante*. It is arguable whether either side really won the
Korean War, for instance, to say nothing of the many wars between England
and France from the thirteenth through the seventeenth centuries.

If the imminent winner adopts a generous policy for treating surrendering
enemy soldiers, moreover, then the loser's capacity to effect war crimes may
decline as defeat becomes more likely. Such a liberal policy ruptures the
unity of interest between commanders and lower echelons. Inferiors then
presumably become less likely to obey superiors' orders, realizing that their
interests no longer align with commander-principals whom the victor will
likely punish for such orders. On the other hand, when surrender becomes
difficult for any reason, soldiers do not distance themselves from superiors in
this way. Historians have recently adduced some good evidence supporting
these propositions.[31]

During the American Civil War, Union respect for civilian life and property in the Confederacy varied greatly from one part of it to another,
depending on the virulence with which a particular state had sought secession. Union forbearance was calculated to detach southern whites from
allegiance to the Confederacy. "White Southerners got off more easily the
more they seemed likely to resume their status as U.S. citizens," writes a
leading military historian, "because the goal was to restore the South to the
Union."[32] States like Georgia, having shown themselves least receptive to
this Union goal, bore the brunt of the worst northern violence. Much like
today's terrorists, they were considered beyond the reach of cooperation
through a policy of cooperative restraint. Martial restraint was employed

strategically, as an invitation to reconciliation where it seemed plausible, as in North Carolina. Abandoning forbearance is therefore not always in the self-interest of the imminent victor.

Yet another such qualification emerges when neutral parties are added to the picture. Game theory's much-touted strategy of tit-for-tat, derived from the study of bilateral interaction, is less useful in preserving a cooperative equilibrium as the relationships become trilateral or multilateral. Often, after all, actors are multiple and embedded in complex networks covering diverse issue-areas. Thus, the repercussions of state A's conduct toward B on matter X may run quite far afield, affecting states C, D, and E with respect to issues Y and Z.

Today, the management of international armed conflict, in particular, no longer chiefly concerns relations between two relatively equal parties, as between the Soviet Union and the United States. The Cold War, in fact, provided the historical template for most early game-theoretic thinking in international relations. When a regional power like Serbia, for instance, begins to oppress several of its immediate neighbors, other states beyond the region as well as multilateral organizations like NATO become crucial to the conflict's resolution. When the United States and European Union later pressure new Serbian leaders to prosecute war criminals domestically and extradite others to a UN-created tribunal in The Hague, still more countries and international organizations become directly involved. When Belgrade submits to such pressure regarding humanitarian law, it expects reciprocation in economic law (i.e., admission to the World Trade Organization and European Union).[33] Reciprocity must today be understood in light of such complex political ramifications among myriad states and nonstate organizations.

For all its avowed "sophistication," game theory has been remarkably slow to develop analytical tools for thinking about what happens to the interaction between A and B when both also have to deal with C.[34] Just as the addition of a third person to a conversational *tête-à-tête* entirely changes its course and contours, as Georg Simmel noted,[35] much the same is true when efforts to influence a military conflict between two countries requires attention to its ripple effects on third parties. At such times, the elegant, formal parsimony of bilateral models must give way to more messy empirical subtleties and the practical judgment that their wise management has throughout history invariably required. To be sure, because the addition of a third party always makes possible some coalition (A-B vs. C, A-C vs. B, or B-C vs. A), game theorists have been inclined quickly to reduce complex three-way interaction to variations on bilateral relations, which are more easily modeled.[36] But there are often tensions even within a coalition, rendering it precarious and vulnerable to recomposition.

Finally, during most of a period of belligerency, war is actually not a game of "winner take all," though of course it is never entirely cooperative. The game turns wholly zero-sum only at its endpoint, when someone must win and his opponent lose – to the extent these terms retain much meaning in contemporary warfare, for that matter. "For the duration," the experience of war is more often one of a "game" in which "conflict is mixed with mutual dependence,"[37] as Schelling observed of superpower confrontation during the Cold War. Humanitarian law seeks to build on the fact that interaction between belligerents can remain partly cooperative, for considerable periods at least.

WAR'S ENDGAME: THE DEATH OF COOPERATION AMONG BELLIGERENTS

Consider here how a war's imminent end affects each side's temptation to employ a legally prohibited weapon. According to the realist view of such restrictions,[38] reciprocal commitment to treaties regularly fails to restrain illegal usage. This is because a treaty requiring states to abandon a given weapon often turns out to mean much more to one side than the other. An arms control treaty that is neutral on its face can have distributional effects that are quite unbalanced.[39] Giving up the right to antipersonnel landmines means something rather different for South Korea than for Switzerland, for instance.[40] Similarly, before World War II, states could agree on banning poison gas, but not on banning unrestricted submarine warfare. This is because poison gas did not advantage any state over the rest for all had the capacity to make it. In contrast, the commercial shipping protected by the proposed treaty against submarine warfare was much more important to Britain than its continental rivals, who therefore blocked that treaty.

Let us now consider how this same distributional dynamic pertains to the issue of POW treatment. Requiring humane treatment of POWs may seem, at first, of equal benefit to both sides. Yet it may not be so in practice, because some states think treating POWs well is a good way to get enemy soldiers to surrender, whereas an adversary might think treating POWs inhumanely is an effective way to demoralize the enemy and persuade it to seek peace.[41] The leadership of such a country may not care that its opponent will retaliate for POW abuse with like treatment of its own soldiers.[42] In fact, it may want to threaten its soldiers with that very possibility to motivate them to fight harder. This was the avowed approach of Japan, for instance, in World War II and, to some extent, also of both sides on the Eastern front in the European theater.[43] Sometimes, the process displays a dynamic of its own. During the American Civil War, for instance, as black Union soldiers came to learn that the Confederates would not accept their surrender, and as their fellows experienced ever greater brutality from Confederate soldiers, they fought with increasing ferocity, writes Drew Faust.[44] This was not the intention, of course, of the Confederate officers who ordered the atrocities that induced such resolve.

Eric Posner here recognizes that social context – that is, differences in leadership, cultures, and history – rather than "stateness," affects a state's perceived interests, which in turn affect its decision to obey or disobey rules, including rules of POW treatment. In so recognizing, Posner departs from his realist and rationalist premises. But his factual point, as well as its corollary for law and policy, is surely correct, even as it undermines the value of his favored method for understanding such belligerent behavior.

RECENT LEGAL DEVELOPMENTS: THE MILITARY COMMISSIONS ACT

The U.S. legislation, the Military Commissions Act of 2006, itself relies heavily on the principle of reciprocity in denying Geneva rights to "unlawful enemy combatants," as the statute defines such persons. It could almost be said that rights that are made nonreciprocal by Geneva Common Article 3, such as certain procedural protections when prosecuted for war crimes, are in essence made reciprocal by the U.S. legislation, through prohibiting their direct invocation in commission proceedings.[45] In this way, belligerent forces obtain Geneva protections for their members only by lawful combat (i.e., honoring the Conventions' corresponding duties). Violate the duties, and one impliedly "waives" most of one's rights under these Conventions.

Bush administration lawyers privately report, in fact, that a central aim of the new legislation, in embracing the administration's concept of unlawful enemy combatant, was precisely to entitle U.S. forces to attack such persons,[46] against whom the only prior remedies, under the Fourth Geneva Convention, had been criminal prosecution and detention until the end of hostilities.[47] The norm of reciprocity offers the most credible rationale for the new approach: Because Al Qaeda attacks enemy civilians without qualm, its adversaries are justified in attacking – not merely detaining or prosecuting – civilians of any nationality who take up arms against it by joining Al Qaeda. America's adoption of a policy of extrajudicial execution is morally justified by the reciprocity principle.

Critics of the Military Commissions Act condemn the authority it gives the president to define the scope of protections under Common Article 3 of the Geneva Conventions, arguing that future antagonists may then do the same vis-à-vis America's own troops. Yet any future war with Iran or North Korea – America's most likely state antagonists – would be an "international armed conflict," to which Article 2, not Article 3, applies. Article 3 applies only to conflicts "not of an international character," including war with cross-border jihadist groups according to the Supreme Court's *Hamdan* decision.[48] This latter conflict is not between nation-states; hence, it is not international.

In resisting key features of the recent legislation, the JAGs' position was that disregarding the Geneva and antitorture treaties due to the supposed exigencies of the moment is short-sighted in view of likely future wars with more conventional enemies. But it is simply untrue that America's next enemy will torture U.S. POWs just because the United States violated humanitarian law by torturing jihadist detainees. As Eric Posner writes, "There is no reason to believe that North Korea will torture American POWs *because* U.S. forces tortured Iraqis. After all, if North Korea tortures American POWs, it can expect the United States to retaliate in some way. North Korea has no interest in vindicating the rights of Iraqis."[49] Still, future adversaries may understandably suspect America's propensity to such violations to surface in later conflicts, and this suspicion alone could lead them to mistreat U.S. POWs. From these inferences, others may initiate mistreatment of U.S. POWs, in the belief that America's recent track record suggests that it is disposed to do the same to theirs.

American, British, and other NATO soldiers undergo waterboarding as a routine part of training designed to prepare them to endure torture by a prospective enemy.[50] This is always the lesson of such training: Such is the treatment you should expect from an unscrupulous foe, even if we ourselves would never employ it. This teaching reveals that U.S. officers fully expect themselves and their troops to be treated far worse than they would ever treat enemy captives. One might first read this to suggest that such officers do not expect their enemy to reciprocate humanitarian treatment of captives. That conclusion may seem to sit uneasily with the officers' recent professions of concern about how best to protect Americans captured in future wars. But there is no contradiction in the officers' stance here. They regard adherence to Geneva norms as a necessary, albeit insufficient, condition for like treatment by prospective adversaries. One might alternatively say they are convinced that the probabilities of eliciting humane conduct for their own captured colleagues are at least nontrivially enhanced by humanitarian behavior toward enemy captives in one's own custody. However, there are no guarantees, they admit.

But if we were instead to play tit-for-tat (as strategists have taught us to do), returning bad for bad, we would then override our initial inclinations toward compliance with humanitarian law, thereby fulfilling the enemy's worst prophecies and teachings to their troops about us. Thus, the stage is set for a descending spiral of mutual abuse, with each round of putative reprisal misinterpreted as a new round of mistreatment, rather than as punishment for the preceding.

On its own, to be sure, the law seeks to tell a story in which the injustice of a war crime ends with a just act of reprisal. Like early Gothic tales, the legal narrative finishes with "a cruelty that will not escalate or be repaid," for "the villain is crushed."[51] Yet the story of reprisal as told by military history is often quite different, alas.[52] There may be no clear delineation of villains and heroes, much less a moral closure to anyone's satisfaction. The law's emplotment of the story, however accurate within its chosen temporal and spatial framing, both begins and ends in the wrong place. Military history itself succumbs to a similar problem, conventionally ending the narrative with one side's battlefield triumph over the other, without regard to the war's likely legacy of enduring suffering, sometimes for generations.[53]

Downward escalatory spirals have not been uncommon in modern international relations, not only in war but also in the area of foreign trade. Until the advent of the World Trade Organization, in particular, there had regularly occurred cycles of retaliation and counter-retaliation,[54] such as those following America's 1930 Smoot-Hawley Tariff Act,[55] by most accounts, one cause of World War II. This U.S. legislative effort to boost economic activity in the Depression sparked retaliatory tariffs by many countries, causing America's exports and imports to plummet quickly by more than half. Only with the postwar General Agreement on Tariffs and Trade (GATT) was retaliation for trade law violations limited and regularized, as by America's Section 301 proceedings (which gave target states a hearing for their views), to an extent that dissuaded counterretaliation in most cases.[56]

For tit-for-tat to reestablish a mutually beneficial equilibrium, not only must sanction be situation specific and short term (or "nice," in the game-theoretic lingo), it must also be perceived as such. The perennial "fog of war" often precludes such crystalline communication between foes, each already inclined to assume the worst about the other, to deny it the benefit of any doubt, and even to deny the existence of reasonable doubt where some genuinely remains.

In game-theoretic terms, the key obstacle to conducting an effective reprisal to level the playing field is the ease with which an opponent who is sincerely trying to play tit-for-tat can be confused, on account of war's considerable background "noise," with someone playing a less forgiving game. Such a person cares less about restoring long-term cooperation than simply punishing recent, past wrong – as he perceives it. In celebrating tit-for-tat as nearly a panacea for conflict resolution, Axelrod's influential account paid insufficient heed to this danger. The apparent implication was that the mathematical pyrotechnics of a computer programmers' tournament could eliminate the need for sober, practical judgment concerning the messy nuances of a factually complex and ambiguous situation involving strong emotions and limited information on both sides of the battlelines.

In the breathless wording quoted just below, for instance, Axelrod could barely contain his excitement over his elegantly simple model, an enthusiasm which proved quite infectious throughout social science for a generation:

> Once the word gets out that reciprocity works, it becomes the thing to do. If you expect others to reciprocate your defections as well as your cooperations, you will be wise to avoid starting trouble. Moreover, you will be wise to defect after someone else defects, showing that you will not be exploited. Thus you will be wise to use a strategy based on reciprocity. So will everyone else. In this manner the appreciation of the value of reciprocity becomes self-enforcing. Once it gets going, it gets stronger and stronger.[57]

But this observation may be as true of a cycle of defections as of a cycle of cooperation, especially wherever one's primary, proximate aim is simply to win the current contest, even if one also recognizes at some level that one must live with one's opponent (and/or his descendants) long thereafter, which will require preserving the conditions for cooperation. If Axelrod's rational actor is, at least, not traumatized by history's horrors – beyond the game's last steps – neither is he expected to envision the mid-range future, beyond his and his opponent's next move. This is simply not the human person as we know him. It is rather more like the brain-damaged, central character in the film *Memento*,[58] whose short-term memory is so impaired that he lives fecklessly in a perpetual present. His disability allows others to manipulate him into acts of great violence, the significance of which he cannot anticipate because of his foreshortened time horizon.

Still, Posner is almost certainly correct that America's future state adversaries will understand that how it treats terrorists is different from how it treats nation-states, which can be expected to play tit-for-tat with it because of their greater vulnerability to retaliation. They will prove able to make the relevant distinctions as easily as we Americans are doing among ourselves. There would then be no need to send a general and unqualified signal of willingness to comply in all future wars with all Geneva norms, in order to negotiate compliance with a particular adversary in a particular conflict, tailoring norms of forbearance to the singular enemy and its particular aims.

History suggests, realists observe, that effective restraints on war can only be specific to individual conflicts and to particular bilateral relationships, in fact, within a given war. Hence, the very different treatment that Nazi Germany afforded enemy POWs on the Eastern versus the Western fronts,[59] depending on whether its adversary had ratified the 1929 Geneva Conventions (France and Britain had, Russia had not).[60] The occasional Nazi mistreatment of Western POWs occurred in retaliation for the occasional Western mistreatment of German POWs.[61]

Memories in international relations may be short, especially during true emergencies. Some social science suggests that "when assessing credibility during crises, leaders focus on the 'here and now,' not on their adversaries' past behavior."[62] At such times, rivals appear to monitor each other closely from day to day, and often try to lure each other at least into a game of tit-for-tat (i.e., where far worse possibilities appear on the immediate horizon).[63] Longstanding reputation, especially for trustworthiness, seems to be a weightier factor in mundane interactions over a longer period. Even between highly competitive superpowers, relations can attain equilibrium on certain issues. They are based on patterns of expected behavior, often permitting considerable cooperation.[64] And even during crises, status quo powers, at least, often seek stability and to dampen conflict by rewarding a rival's good behavior more than punishing its bad.[65]

In the area of wartime conduct, the United States may not really want to encourage adversaries to have a very long memory, in any event, given its historical record, which is mixed at best – including not only Hiroshima and Nagasaki but also the firebombing of many Japanese cities, the Japanese-American internment, plus My Lai, No Gun Ri, now Fallujah, Haditha,[66] and so forth. In fact, playing tit-for-tat requires a decidedly short memory: Each party recalls only the other's prior move. A longer memory for still earlier defections from cooperation does not encourage the "forgiveness" on which tit-for-tat depends, on all accounts, for its success in restoring harmonious relations.

Just as armed conflicts in various places can follow different dynamics, moreover, so the "same" conflict may display different logics at various points in time. The U.S. struggle against terrorists might credibly be viewed less as a single conflict with multiple manifestations than as a series of largely separate engagements – from Malaysia and the Philippines to Israel and Saudi Arabia – with rather different kinds of antagonists, some more susceptible than others to reciprocity's rhythms. From this perspective, a new antagonist may choose to regard U.S. treatment of earlier detainees in other places and times as largely immaterial to how it will treat America's, here and now.

Yet one may also plausibly see the conflict against "global jihad" as a single, long-term enterprise, demanding greater consistency over time in America's treatment of its captives. On this view, it appears more likely that relaxing humanitarian standards in U.S. treatment of one set of detainees will prejudice enemy treatment of U.S. soldiers at a later point in the larger conflict. The likely costs of such relaxation become greater from this perspective. The key questions thus become: To what extent will militant jihadists throughout the world, past and present, identify with one another's struggles? What is the relative importance of local vs. translocal grievances within their political programs? To what extent does the United States face one adversary or many? If there are many, do the similarities predominate over the differences? Are the relevant differences only in how they themselves view one another? Or are they also partly in how we may legitimately choose to view them?

The evidence to date is inconclusive, but not encouraging (e.g., in that disparate jihadist groups often strongly identify with one another).[67] This means that mistreating jihadists in one operational theater may have costly consequences for the United States in others. In this case, the JAGs would be quite right to worry about future treatment of U.S. soldiers in later phases of the continuing armed conflict with a transnational jihadist "movement" of sorts. Jihadists' self-understandings here bear directly on the legal existence and scope of any armed conflict.[68] Strong mutual identification among the members of such groups, especially if combined with some exchange of information and resources, would begin to suggest a single armed conflict, persisting at least dormantly in periods between the separate terror attacks in various countries. The law of armed conflict would then govern U.S. response throughout, and especially when such law conflicted with that of human rights.[69]

Those who deny the existence of a single armed conflict, sometimes even of closely associated conflicts involving jihadist terror groups in distinct places throughout the world,[70] should closely consider what it would require to justify linking one or more such sites of sustained confrontation under this legal concept; that is, as a single armed conflict (or small number thereof).

Their answer must attend to definitional details, perhaps including how much direction one jihadist group exercises over a geographically distant cousin. Yet as a matter of practical politics – apart from these lawyerly intricacies – the answer is entirely different and readily apparent: "another 9/11." Bush's critics would be correct to retort that international law offers no warrant for a retroactive doctrinal move of this sort. This is because no *post facto* event or events, however colossally calamitous, could justify the *ex ante* legal treatment of jihadists across the globe as a single entity (i.e., for purposes of delineating the current conflict's true scope and identifying those who may rightly be considered belligerent parties to it). The most basic notion of due process should prevent the law from allowing only B's later conduct to render A's prior conduct part of an armed conflict, therefore governed by the law of war.

Still, an international law so aloof to geopolitical reality that it would regard further incidents of such magnitude as irrelevant is a law unworthy of great weight in the deliberations of democratic leaders, who are constitutionally duty bound to ensure their constituents' security. The Holmesian-pragmatist view of law adopted throughout these pages again compels the conclusion that, when the law thus ceases to respect such weighty principles and legitimate policy considerations (as well as inexorable institutional constraints), it is largely the law that will suffer, not these competing concerns, which are often no less compelling.[71] The very concept of customary international law, moreover, with its traditional attention to actual behavior beyond the realm of verbal formalities, displays an elective affinity for pragmatist and "realist" modes of legal reasoning.

STATISTICAL EVIDENCE OF RETALIATION IN WAR

What is the empirical record on whether humanitarian treaties actually make any difference to wartime conduct? And what place does retaliation for their violation occupy either in restoring order or aggravating the situation?

By far, the most important evidence comes from a recent study by James Morrow, using a data set of nearly all interstate wars for the last century.[72] The data show that treaties matter, but not in the way lawyers would expect – or desire. Treaties should be understood, not in contrast with retaliatory tit-for-tat, but as working best – perhaps only – when they strengthen the mechanisms through which reciprocity itself operates. Joint ratification of a humanitarian treaty – that is, by both parties to a conflict – strengthens not only adherence to its norms but also reciprocal response to their violation. Treaties increase compliance by facilitating retaliation commensurate with prior breaches. They do this by setting common standards through which potential violators are put on notice that certain sorts of naughtiness will have consequences.

Still, such reciprocity often works outside the treaty framework in that the treaties often do not themselves authorize most such retaliation for their breach. In other words, the treaty works because it helps state A know that state B will retaliate against particular kinds of conduct, at odds with treaty norms, even though the treaty itself or background law does not afford a reprisal remedy. Whereas lawyers here see simply noncompliance all around, breach by both sides, social science finds the practical potential for increased compliance through retaliatory tit-for-tat.

Inasmuch as most observers view such state practice as permissible, moreover, the customary international law thereby established would diverge from treaty law, as discussed in Chapter 2. In other words, Morrow's findings regarding the near ubiquity of retaliation, publicly defended as reprisal (or retorsion), for violations and perceived violations of humanitarian law suggest that state practice, a key element of customary international law, confirms a central place for the reciprocity principle beyond that granted by the Geneva Conventions. This is especially true if one adheres to longstanding understandings of custom, as employed by the U.S. Supreme Court in *The Paquete Habana*, which emphasize the nonverbal conduct of states – in that case, their failure to seize enemy merchant ships on the high seas.[73] Material conduct of this sort surely deserves greater weight in assessing state practice than the merely verbal protestations of officials (which they proceed to ignore) and the wishful pronouncements of scholar-activists.[74]

Yet international jurisprudence today pays little heed to the operational practice of armed forces.[75] This perceptible shift in judicial selectivity on sources receives no serious normative defense. Courts instead merely invoke – not the opinion of actual states – but rather a novel, so-called "*opinio necessitatis.*"[76] This is essentially a claim of moral necessity, less constrained than (and sometimes designed to trump) any defense of military necessity. This doctrinal trend further evidences the near-complete indifference to military considerations displayed by international jurists responsible for resolving law of war issues.[77]

In fact, customary law sometimes leads a life of its own, following a path quite distinct from that enshrined in treaty. Morrow's data suggest that throughout modern history the prevailing practice of states reflects widespread invocation and exercise of a right of reprisal in many situations where the postwar Geneva Conventions (both 1949 and 1977) would bar it. Accordingly, such treaties appear to repudiate existing custom, rather than merely codify it, their more modest and stated aim. But even treaties must be interpreted in light of subsequent state practice bearing on their norms, reflecting the parties' understandings of their duties.[78] The upshot is to reinject a broader role for the reciprocity principle back into humanitarian law by way of custom, even as treaties have increasingly sought to reject it.[79]

The best recent social science suggests, then, that the law reinforces rather than supplants reciprocity.[80] That is law's real contribution to humanitarianism, however paradoxical it may first seem, as Geoffrey Best mockingly writes in his epigraph to this book. One may analogize this contribution to that of most arms control agreements, which seek not to transcend the balance of power in international relations but rather, by setting numerical limits for particular weapons, to facilitate its more effective workings.

One could also say that law here contributes neither to a vicious cycle (bad creating worse) nor a virtuous cycle (good engendering better), but a kind of dialectic that is ultimately salubrious, through which things must get worse (by retaliation) before they can get better (in restored compliance). In fact, Morrow finds that virtually all cases of treaty noncompliance are met with retaliation by the victim state. Unilateral forbearance almost never occurs,[81] though it is sometimes entirely possible to defend in game-theoretic terms.[82] The only major counterexamples are Western nonretaliation for Japanese mistreatment of Allied POWs during World War II[83] and U.S. nonretaliation for similar violations by North Vietnam (including the Viet Cong) and Iraq (in 1991), during its military conflicts with those two states.

The United States treated captured Viet Cong as POWs, for instance, despite that adversary's failure to adhere consistently to several requirements for that status in the Third Geneva Convention. It is also noteworthy that, during World War II, the Allies held many Japanese and German POWs of high rank, including Rudolf Hess, a top Hitler deputy. Yet the Western powers did not coercively interrogate such prisoners for military intelligence, which some must surely have possessed.[84] Captors established a "give and take" relationship with captives, which sometimes yielded valuable information.[85] Seemingly unilateral restraint, as in both these cases, is sometimes partly inspired by hopes of eliciting reciprocal treatment for one's own POWs, in the long run if not necessarily the short.[86] For the United States, at least, other considerations were also operative, as we see later.

These episodes present important anomalies, difficult to square with any simplistically realist accounts of the relevant data, in that they represent the possibility of cooperative behavior, or humane treatment at least, in situations where realists would predict noncooperation. Anomalies within existing theories offer the key starting points for developing better ones.[87] In these "outlier" cases, U.S. aspirations to continued leadership of the "Free World" likely imposed a higher moral standard on it than on other belligerents, making it more willing to absorb greater costs. The anomaly can most easily be resolved, in other words, by reference to American aspirations to what is now called "soft power," the sort that springs from a country's attractiveness to others, the allure of its mores and way of life, enabling it to lead by example. This possibility is explored in some detail in Chapter 11. To lead by example, however, one must be prepared to set an example, to play by the same rules one desires others to adopt. This is one understanding of reciprocity, after all, the second conception in our initial typology.

Treaty compliance is greatest on issues where reciprocity has greatest sway, Morrow finds.[88] Thus, compliance is lowest with the rules protecting civilians, because civilians cannot retaliate against soldiers who abuse them. Threat of retaliation from enemy soldiers is much greater and more immediate, however, which in turn deters violations against such soldiers. The whole range of humanitarian law issues can be arrayed along this continuum; there is a strong correlation between the victim's power to retaliate against a norm's violation and a state's degree of compliance with that norm. A vivid illustration is the international law of occupation: Victors breach it regularly because the defeated adversary has no capacity to retaliate.[89]

The same may be observed of colonial occupation as of military occupation. Britain could so readily employ the most repressive methods against the increasingly restive Calcutta populace a century ago precisely because London's population had nothing to fear by way of retaliation. By contrast, the Cold War superpowers – in holding hostage each other's civilian populations – successfully deterred one another from direct aggression between themselves, fighting only in a more mediated manner through less fortunate proxies. From this perspective, Fanon's unapologetic call to arms – though defended in more psychological terms, as restoring self-respect and overcoming despair – would surely seem more convincing than Ghandi's to civil disobedience, with its riskier appeal to the colonizer's conscience, such as it was.

Such conclusions suggest that international law's century-long efforts to ban reprisals,[90] or at least severely limit them, may have been misconceived.[91] The rationale for such efforts had always been that even lawful reprisals are widely "misperceived" by their targets as new and independent violations and so tend to provoke still further violations, escalating conflict into retaliatory spirals rather than restoring cooperative equilibrium.[92] This peril appears to have been much exaggerated, if Morrow's statistical analysis is correct.

In fact, the current situation concerning treaty enforcement could accurately be described as "the worst of both worlds," as laments one leading scholar of international law, in that humanitarian law norms "lack an effective community-based enforcement mechanism (be it under general international law or specific treaty regimes) and on top of that, are deprived of the normal back-up of individual enforcement, whether reciprocal suspension or countermeasures."[93] It may be just as well that where humanitarian law rejects reciprocity, the law is largely ignored in practice. This does not speak well of law's understanding of the world it aspires to govern, however, a reality with which it appears wildly out of sync.

If retaliation works so well, then only one serious rationale remains for banning reprisals: the view that if we make it nearly impossible to fight war legally, then states will be less likely to fight at all[94] and will be more inclined to resolve their disputes peacefully. From this perspective, the very efficacy of reprisal in warfare (i.e., in accomplishing the belligerents' military goals) is precisely what makes its prohibition so essential. This view strikes Pentagon and Bush administration humanitarian law experts as utopian and hence misguided.[95]

Yet it finds much greater receptivity among lawyers in human rights NGOs and at the International Committee of the Red Cross,[96] an organization with some responsibility for interpreting the Geneva Conventions.[97] After all, in the last half-century entire industries have been put out of business or have lost most of their manufacturers, simply because of increased exposure to civil liability.[98] David Kennedy here candidly proclaims the humanitarian lawyer's dream, once his own: "The world of rules, of procedures, of wise management would, should, sneak up on war, infiltrate the military, overwhelm the evil statesman, and make war a matter of the past. We would regulate swords into plowshares."[99] If war was once the continuation of politics by other means, war would henceforth become the continuation of law by the same means.

There is a beguiling similarity here to the domestic law of judicial remedies, with which all civil litigators are familiar. If substantive rights establish the law's ends, then remedies are the means for achieving these. It is therefore common in domestic law for critics of a particular right, when they cannot greatly curtail or abolish it outright, to weaken the remedies by which courts may vindicate it. The analogous move in the law of war is that, if the resort to force cannot be effectively banished, then the means by which force is employed might at least be restricted in such a way, to such an extent, that it cannot take place without a high probability of liability – civil and/or criminal, individual, and/or state – for any prospective belligerent and its commanders.[100]

The key terms of art within humanitarian law – necessity, proportionality,[101] feasibility, even armed conflict itself[102] – remain defined in only the vaguest terms,[103] if at all. Those who invoke these terms to authorize force should construe them in the interests of humanity,[104] and those who violate them should incur liability. Interrogators have reason to worry here, even after receiving the green light from government lawyers. In February 2008, the Justice Department revealed that its internal ethics office was investigating the department's legal approval for waterboarding of Al Qaeda suspects by the CIA.[105] One might even contend, from an economic perspective, that a law of war that effectively precluded military victory would surely be the most socially efficient law imaginable. For it would prevent the consummate destructiveness of armed conflict itself, with all its ensuing disutilities.

The Bush administration's posture toward the question of law's vagueness was disingenuous. It argued at one moment that legal imprecision rendered international law useless in providing fair notice to U.S. forces of their concrete duties. At the next, the administration sought to preserve such opaqueness, instructing troops to provide "humane treatment, subject to military necessity."[106] Vagueness of this variety has the effect of distancing administration leaders from responsibility for such "freelance" sadism as at Abu Ghraib – an intentional effect, some would argue. Administration critics are sometimes equally disingenuous, however, insisting that, since humanitarian law is often vague, it is therefore open to their preferred interpretation, permitting broad charges of "torture," for instance.[107] They have sometimes claimed to find vagueness even in places where settled law is all too clearly against their position, for instance, regarding denial of POW status to detainees like Khalid Sheikh Mohammed.

HISTORY'S QUESTIONABLE RELEVANCE:
NEW ANTAGONISTS, NEW WARS

Morrow's data concern only interstate wars. Is there any reason to think his conclusions are pertinent to wars between states and terrorist organizations? Terrorist groups might not be susceptible to restraint through reciprocity, however, because they acquire military advantage, otherwise unattainable, through illicit methods.[108] Insurgents' preference for dirty tactics led states to limit legal protections to such forces in civil wars, agreeing only to the limited rights of Common Article 3 and Protocol II.[109] This explains why the combatant/noncombatant distinction received much greater respect in interstate wars than in civil wars.[110] Even where leaders of irregular forces might wish to honor legal restraints, their capacity to enforce humanitarian norms on their (often desultorily organized) forces was in doubt.[111]

Clearly, the willingness of militant jihadists to attack civilian institutions like the World Trade Center affords an operational advantage unavailable on a traditional, set-piece battlefield. Attacking civilians is also done on point of principle: It is a rejection of the traditional equation of civilian status with moral innocence. Lack of restraint here, however, does not necessarily entail nonrestraint on all issues and in all contexts. Holding POWs, instead of killing them, can increase the bargaining power of a nonstate belligerent in dealing with its adversary, just as it can for states. Militant groups employing terror often reach tacit understandings and respect certain rules with the states they fight. At the very least, they usually grant immunity to message bearers. They often try to force governments into negotiations and so refrain from the kind of humanitarian breaches that would imperil such negotiations. In many cases – South Africa, Spain, Northern Ireland, and Italy, for instance – terrorist organizations have evolved into political organizations capable of reaching formal agreement with states.[112]

Even Hamas and Hezbollah engage in prisoner exchanges and ceasefire agreements with Israel.[113] Some guerrilla groups in Colombia have trained their members in humanitarian law, according to Human Rights Watch.[114] The guerrilla movement in Guatemala made an agreement with the state to honor Geneva Additional Protocol II, despite its legal inapplicability, strictly speaking,[115] as did the African National Congress in its armed struggle against South Africa's apartheid regime.[116] And in El Salvador during the 1980s, both the rebels and the government independently decided to abide by Geneva Common Article 3 and Protocol II.[117] Such multilateral treaties thereby contribute to the *de facto* and customary restraints that evolved in prior wars between states and terrorist organizations, even if compliance was spotty at best.[118] These historical experiences should be examined carefully for the guidance they may offer today.[119] Where these undertakings were unilateral, there were no transaction costs, because no negotiations with the enemy were required.

Not every profession of willingness to reciprocate can be taken at face value, to be sure.[120] The captors of *Wall Street Journal* reporter Daniel Pearl publicly announced that his treatment would improve in response to any amelioration of conditions for Guantánamo detainees.[121] Yet given his kidnappers' intentions of decapitation and dismemberment, as well as their intense hatred of America – especially of American Jews like Pearl – his fate would probably not have been any different. It is difficult to imagine that any improvement in the U.S. treatment of Al Qaeda suspects would have much altered the worldview and resulting decision calculus of Pearl's apparent murderer, 9/11 mastermind Khalid Sheikh Mohammed.[122] Yet Osama bin Laden himself regularly and explicitly invokes reciprocity to justify his tactics: Because the United States and its allies are killing Muslim civilians around the world, he says, it is defensible for Al Qaeda to respond by targeting American civilians.[123]

THE RATIONALITY OF NONRECIPROCAL CONCESSION

Unilateral concessions are sometimes more effective than tit-for-tat retaliation in eliciting cooperation. In the negotiations that led to ending apartheid in South Africa, for instance, neither side (i.e., Nelson Mandela nor President F. W. de Klerk) insisted on concessions by the other as a condition of making its own. Prominent in their minds was the way that mutual conditioning of this sort had contributed to the recurrent failure of Palestinian-Israeli peace negotiations, since hardliners on both sides were then able to highlight unmet conditions, thereby justifying further violence.[124] Many South Koreans apparently think along similar lines with a view to improving their country's relations with the North.[125]

Insurrectionary groups like the Central American insurgencies of the 1980s sit somewhere in the middle of a spectrum between states, at one extreme, and most jihadist terrorists, on the other, in that they seek to acquire and hold territory, a traditional military aim, and have formal chains of command, minimizing freelance atrocity and the "noise" it creates about whether responsibility rests at the top.[126] The loose association of jihadist movements across the globe displays neither trait. Where there is no effective control over the small fry, no "responsible command" in Geneva law terms, there can be no command responsibility. Hence, leaders cannot on that basis be held legally responsible for their followers' criminal acts. If reciprocity through threat of retaliation – or of criminal prosecution, for that matter – is to induce policy change by the enemy, the enemy must be organized enough to enforce consistent policies.[127] As Geoffrey Best writes, "No armed force can be trusted to comply with the relevant international humanitarian law principles and rules and to enter into the implied relationship of reciprocity towards its opponents unless [that armed force] is cohesive and disciplined."[128]

Yet many jihadist groups in particular places, in both their narrower grievances and broader goals, avowedly seek to establish theocratic rule under *shari'a* in their homelands. To the extent that they seek the traditional goal of territorial control, as over Saudi Arabia's sacred cities, they may thus prove amenable to reciprocity as an enforcement strategy, under certain circumstances at least. It may even have been a mistake, from this perspective, to have ousted the Taliban from control over Afghanistan, insofar as confinement of violent jihadists from throughout the world to a single territory for their training and residence may have made the larger conflict more readily amenable at some point to realist/rationalist methods of restraint through reciprocity. A terrorist state is still a state, realists stress, and so remains subject to many of the standard methods of lawful pressure, such as "smart" sanctions, that more powerful states and the international community at large have sometimes brought to bear on those regarded as exceptionally roguish.[129] The moderation of Libya's foreign policy in recent years, apparently in response to Western sanctions,[130] offers a telling illustration of such possibilities.

A state's interest in forbearance by adversaries is often imperiled by its own soldiers' apparent interest in looting, pillaging, and seeking revenge for "buddies" recently killed in combat.[131] Conversely, soldiers sometimes seek to restrain superiors inclined to order highly risky operations against the enemy, even where such operations may serve state interests.[132] In both situations, gaps arise between the aims of states and of the individuals to whom humanitarian law now also applies.

International law seeks to link the fate of the two – superior and subordinate – through various doctrines of shared responsibility.[133] But these doctrines are flawed in various ways, ensuring recurrent disarticulation. Even where it would genuinely be in a state's interest to exercise forbearance in its detention and treatment of enemy fighters, its fighters and notional agents may regularly fail to do so. The problem is even more acute with militant jihadist networks, whose purported leaders surely exercise still less control over far-flung adherents and fellow travelers. These leaders may even wish to foster such "excess," because the law – acknowledging the limits of their control – cannot hold them accountable for it. Realist talk about "state interests" – in restraint or unrestraint – ignores these important complications.

Though Al Qaeda itself regained significant organizational coherence after its initial post-9/11 losses, on most accounts, it soon became simply one major piece of a larger puzzle of militant jihadist movements.[134] As such, it becomes even harder to imagine a deal on humanitarian law with America's adversaries, broadly understood. American leaders must almost long for the days when they could point to a single man, Osama bin Laden, with whom to negotiate, someone who could presumably order followers to treat Western prisoners and civilians humanely, for instance, in reciprocal exchange for some conceivable *quid pro quo*.

Within Al Qaeda itself, in contrast with the broader array of violent jihadist movements, there do exist chains of command – largely secret, but elaborate and relatively formal – linking its far-flung membership to Osama bin Laden, its head.[135] That organization has also waged war quite traditionally (and successfully) in battling the Pakistani army to a stalemate for control of territory – a classic military aim – on the Afghan-Pakistani border. Bin Laden's public statements, at least, have sometimes suggested conventional defensive purposes: "We want to defend our people and our land. That is why I say that if we don't get security, the Americans, too, would not get security. This is a simple formula . . . of live and let live."[136] Moreover, Al Qaeda's attacks on civilian population centers, as on 9/11, hardly distinguish its fighting methods from those of many states in World War II (on both sides) and often since.

On the basis of such similarities, one scholar thus asks, "Are suicide bombers that strike in cities so much worse than aerial bombers that also strike in cities" (i.e., different enough) "to make us think that one should be treated as outlaws and the other as full members of the international community?"[137] Privately, at least, some scholars even deride the "fetishizing" of Al Qaeda's civilian targeting on 9/11 as if it were some novel horror of jihadist terror,[138] rather than a recurrent feature of modern warfare – most distressing precisely in its near ubiquity.[139]

DO THE GENEVA CONVENTIONS REALLY MATTER?

Eric Posner argues that no reciprocity, and no restraint on that basis, is possible with Al Qaeda, much less the broader array of violent jihadist movements. The United States cannot expect to gain any benefits from Al Qaeda by treating its prisoners humanely, given Al Qaeda's deliberately inhumane treatment of enemy Western civilians on many occasions. American forbearance makes no sense from a rational choice perspective because the situation is asymmetrical: Al Qaeda gains much less by sparing Americans, if it had any,[140] than the United States gains by sparing Al Qaeda detainees.[141] What matters most is not that both sides might gain from restraint, but that one side will gain significantly more than the other, thereby nixing the possibility of cooperation. (This consideration is stressed by so-called neo-realists.[142])

That asymmetry would explain U.S. noncompliance with Geneva law. It also presumably justifies such noncompliance, in Posner's view, insofar as America wishes to act rationally in its national self-interest. This does not mean that the United States should not be attentive to signals of opportunities to create implicit norms of restraint that serve U.S. interests, he concedes. And the Geneva Conventions may serve as one helpful source of such restraining norms, among others.[143] Islamic law itself has long demanded forbearance of varying degrees in the treatment of certain enemy prisoners, one might add, including the torture and targeting of certain noncombatants,[144] though it has not historically sought to defend these restrictions through a concept of "human rights."[145] It is pertinent that the Islamic law of war endorses the reciprocity principle in key places, at least.[146]

Like the classic realists, Posner thinks that all states seek the same things from the international system, regardless of their internal composition. States are states, whether they be constitutional democracies, terrorist states, rogue states, or quasi-states.[147] They can all be deterred from humanitarian law violations by the threat of retaliation. Only such threats can hold restraints in place, in fact, and this threat has the same meaning to all rational actors, regardless of their regime type. Some data are consistent with this view.[148]

Morrow's data, however, suggest that this often is not so. The kind of regime makes a major difference, more than treaty ratification itself, he finds.[149] Ratification makes no difference at all, in fact, to compliance rates for nondemocracies, for its very costlessness makes it a poor predictor of subsequent state conduct. Morrow's finding here supports the so-called liberal theory of international relations, according to which democracies follow the law internationally because they are accustomed to following it domestically, whereas the converse is true of dictatorships. Democracies do not respect humanitarian norms merely because their diplomats have legally committed to them at Geneva many years ago.

Hence, Posner, for all his skepticism about the need for self-restraint versus jihadist terrorists, may actually be too optimistic. He assumes, after all, that reciprocity works even with nondemocratic states, even nonstate terrorist groups, to the extent they begin to approximate states, as had the Palestinian Authority under Yasser Arafat. The United States is not likely soon to be fighting any real democracies, unless one considers Iran partly in that category.[150] In fact, established democracies virtually never fight other democracies.[151] The American JAGs are thus likely wrong to expect forbearance from nondemocracies on the basis of their Geneva commitments. Specifically, they are wrong to think that America's future adversaries could be deterred from prisoner abuse by the logic of reciprocity.

It is noteworthy that terrorist networks and nondemocratic states, though different in many respects, have one notable common feature: Both lack internal *ex post* accountability mechanisms that would hold commanders responsible for subordinates' wrongful acts and elected leaders responsible to democratic voters for misguided and unsuccessful policies.[152] Bin Laden himself invokes the liberal democratic character of the U.S. political system to hold the American people collectively responsible, hence subject to civilian attacks, for Bush administration policies in the Middle East,[153] especially after President Bush's 2004 reelection. Some social science even suggests that a democratic regime may be more prone to target enemy civilians than other kinds of states, due to stronger popular pressure at home to minimize casualties among its own ranks and end the conflict quickly.[154] But the conclusions of empirical results here are mixed, with the better and more recent studies taking quite different views.[155]

So-called failed states resemble nondemocratic ones and terror networks in lacking such methods of internal accountability. To the extent that such a state ceases to display key attributes of statehood, its putative agents can no longer be deterred by threat of responsibility – legal or otherwise – for their actions ostensibly on its behalf. According to Bush administration lawyers, it follows that the Taliban's tenuous *de facto* hold over much of Afghanistan's territory during long years of civil war ensured that this adversary "was unlikely to respect the Geneva rights of any U.S. captive it took . . . and unlikely to reciprocate U.S. performance of Geneva standards."[156] In assuming a more "normal" fight, the JAGs are thus simply, according to influential military lawyer Hays Parks, "playing to the military's conventional mindset, i.e., you try to force the war to the war you trained for, rather than the threat you face."[157] Or, as strategist Edward Luttwak puts it, you hope against hope that the enemy will somehow be so foolish as to "assemble in conveniently targetable combat formations."[158]

The upshot would appear to be that relaxing U.S. adherence to Geneva norms in response to Al Qaeda's disrespect for them would not, through the logic of tit-for-tat, establish more cooperative relations with jihadists and deter them from future misconduct. If this is true, then the United States should adhere to such law in any event, as it has nothing to gain in anticipated reciprocation from the world's militant jihadists. This would be the conclusion, that is, unless it can be shown that the United States suffers an unfair disadvantage in nontrivial measure when so doing, a possibility examined at the end of Chapter 13.

Even those readily acknowledging that traditional tit-for-tat does not work against jihadist terror often find themselves drawn back, willy-nilly, to more nuanced versions of reciprocity analysis, in the hopes of finding some basis for forbearance in the treatment of Al Qaeda detainees. Notice the lingering allure of reciprocity logic, somewhat delicately submerged beneath the discourse of human rights, in the following passages by Larry May, for instance:

> To describe some humans [first pirates, now terrorists] as the enemies of humanity dehumanizes them and also causes them to think of themselves as different from, and enemies of, the rest of us, rather than as part of the same family. . . . To label an entire group of people, containing thousands of members, as enemies of humanity is also to risk the undermining of what has been the foundation of universal human rights protections, namely that we are all much more alike than different and that all are subject to the same law.[159]

Our aim should be to ensure that they are "not pushed outside the protection of that umbrella where they are far more likely to be true enemies of humanity.[160] . . . If Islamic terrorists see themselves primarily as fellow humans instead of enemies of those in the West, terrorist violence will likely be diminished, and all peoples will gain in security."[161]

One could criticize this passage for overestimating the effects of U.S. forbearance (and a resulting jihadist recognition of the common humanity shared with their enemies) and underestimating the effects of the militants' theological commitments, consistently articulated and repeatedly enacted, in governing their political aims and choice of targets. Yet most important for present purposes is the subtle reintroduction here of reciprocity calculus – without the usual assumption of rational self-interest, to be sure. We are told that jihadists must not, by our inhumane treatment of their detainees, be "pushed outside the protection" of human rights law, for then they will more likely behave like "true enemies of humanity."

This version of the reciprocity story takes a longer view of the relevant horizon than does tit-for-tat, and it foresees the socialization of jihadists to human rights norms – surely an optimistic scenario. Yet it is a reciprocity story nonetheless, for it tacitly tells us that, surely, they will ultimately acknowledge our humanity if only we clearly and persistently demonstrate our recognition of theirs. They will also presumably be less inclined to hate us "for who we are" if through our conscientious treatment of their detainees we show them what our character requires of us (i.e., that we remain humane even under the most exigent circumstances).

We could say that May here implicitly invokes a variation on Pascal's wager: It is rational to act as if we believe in Al Qaeda's future susceptibility to reciprocity, however little evidence there may be of it. If it turns out that none ever existed, the West – in treating jihadist detainees humanely – would only have lost some information about them. But if they someday proved open to reciprocity, it would then be too late to attain such an equilibrium, having damned ourselves in perpetuity by our mistreatment of them.

Such mistreatment would have foreclosed the genuine possibility of reciprocity that once lay at our doorstep, on this view. Such analysis assumes without evidence or argument, however, that the "some information" foregone would be inconsequential, which cannot clearly be known *ex ante* (i.e., before interrogation) or perhaps even *ex post.* But put that aside for a moment.

RECIPROCITY IN PRIVATE INTERNATIONAL LAW

The logic of May's argument, however unpersuasive it may prove in the present context, is not altogether alien to regular U.S. legal practice. Paradoxically perhaps, there are some circumstances in which the best way to elicit favorable treatment for oneself from another may be *not* to require such treatment from the other, even to flaunt one's failure to demand prior reciprocity, in fact. For instance, in hopes of obtaining greater recognition for U.S. civil judgments in foreign tribunals, American courts have generally adopted the practice of "comity." In other words, the United States does not demand that another country must have enforced American judgments before that country may expect the United States to enforce its own judgments.[162]

This effort to initiate more cooperation in judgment enforcement has produced positive results, according to some experts.[163] It was widely thought that the opposing approach, "examining the motives and policies of a foreign government and its judicial processes toward U.S. citizens," would generate needless controversy. As one scholar observes, "The intrusive inquiry into the judicial practices of other states would be particularly offensive to foreign sovereigns and a continuous embarrassment in the conduct of foreign relations."[164] Nevertheless, the American Law Institute has recently proposed legislation establishing a reciprocity requirement, in the view that the more indulgent approach toward foreign judgments had not elicited sufficient cooperation from other lands in enforcing American ones.[165]

Unilateral enforcement of foreign civil judgments seeks to induce future reciprocation by favorable treatment of the other state, irrespective of the other's prior mistreatment of the United States. As in a prisoners' dilemma, there are possible gains from cooperation here; but unlike that predicament, this is an "assurance game,"[166] in which the other's past defections are best ignored, or at least not immediately punished, if its cooperation is to be soon obtained. The 'game' of mutual enforcement of civil judgments is positive-sum and differs in this respect from war. "If comity is reciprocal," writes one scholar in the field, "both states are better off than they would have been if each simply applied its own law,"[167] rather than the law and judgments of the other.

We have seen that states differ in their understanding of rational self-interest (and their ability to act consistently on it), depending on regime type and regime strength. Nonstate actors in armed conflict also differ in their susceptibility to tit-for-tat. The threat of torture – and death under torture – invariably counts as a risk or "cost" from the standpoint of secular modernity.[168] Yet on a jihadist's mental map, martyrdom against the Western infidel might be tallied as a "benefit," an opportunity to pass the test of faith.[169] Thus, even bodily experience is not altogether physiologically determined, but is in part culturally interpreted. This presumably extends to the experience of pain.[170] Since many find sustained exposure to atonal music and contemporary art akin to torture, it is not surprising to learn that both have on occasion been used for precisely this purpose.[171] For the jihadist zealot, coercive interrogation would be subjectively experienced as a test of faith which he, as a true believer, looks forward to passing – admittedly, with trepidation. Martyrdom, in requiring self-sacrifice, reflects upon one's virtue, after all, and "virtue gains much by being put to the proof," Seneca remarked.[172]

Discomfort may even give one 'pleasure' insofar as one takes satisfaction in demonstrating – to oneself and to one's interrogator – one's ability to withstand it (i.e., without succumbing to the interrogator's wishes). We might therefore wonder whether the ensuing discomfort – since mixed with something distinctly positive[173] – might (beyond a reasonable doubt) be labeled "pain" or "suffering," much less "severe" forms of these, as required by the legal definition of torture. That definition, observes Talal Asad, presumes a utilitarian worldview according to which human subjectivity can always be measured along a single spectrum, with extreme pain and extreme pleasure at opposite ends, so that they may never coexist in one person at the same time. The more satisfaction one derives from the prospect of, and success in passing God's test, the less one's attendant suffering – if that is any longer quite the right word for this spiritual experience – may be unambiguously described as severe.[174] For such reasons, as Montaigne observed, "Tortures which are most ghastly to see are not always the harshest to suffer."[175]

To note the jihadist's "interest" in martyrdom – given his preferred metaphysics – is not to suggest that suicide bombers are "egoistic," in Durkheim's terms, a result of an individual's social isolation.[176] Such suicides are sometimes intensely "altruistic," springing from a strong sense of duty to one's community, perceived to be in need of such defense against oppressors and heretics, external and internal.[177] Yet such an understanding of self-sacrifice transforms the fulfillment of one's duty into the sort of virtue that is an end in itself, "its own reward." This is true regardless of the more material rewards that the terrorist organization will provide to a member's family[178] or the seventy-two virgins with whom he will cavort in heaven. The metaphysics of martyrdom thus transforms a secularist's cost into a spiritualist's benefit in ways that wreak havoc with any conventional application of utilitarianism to military strategy and specifically to counterterrorism policy. "I think the greatest mistake is assuming that people ... will be rational according to our definition of what is rational," said Paul Wolfowitz, when deputy secretary of defense.[179] To similar effect, two military strategists write, "If the concept of deterrence is to work, the protagonists must have a common definition of rationality."[180]

We should be wary of following where this path quickly leads, however, as most have acknowledged:

> If more and more enemies are believed to be outside the bounds of means-end rationality, then armed conflict can become much more ruthless. ... Enemies of a different rationality are subject to different rules from those codified in bureaucratic warfare. Thus, at the same time as the law and rules of war have become stricter than perhaps ever before, the enemies whom the West expects to fight in the future are increasingly seen as being outside these law and rules.[181]

There is nothing out of the ordinary in this last observation. Throughout much of modern history, belligerents have often contended that the laws of war, however stringent on their face, are technically inapplicable to the particular conduct in question. This has always been the most common demurrer by states to accusations of war crime.

It is also true, as constructivists contend, that conceptions of rationality and hence of rational self-interest are governed by ideologies, theologies, and cosmologies, not simply given *a priori*. Survivors of Nazi concentration camps, for instance, report that, at least for Communists and the most religiously devout, the experience – if not exactly life-affirming – was decidedly ideology-confirming in people whose ideologies were already life-defining.

For Communists, in particular, the very severity of their mistreatment confirmed their initial loathing of the Nazi regime, deepening their moral commitment to oppose it to their last breath. Mere social democrats and the religiously lapsed could find no such deeper meaning in their suffering and so endured it with greater difficulty, succumbing to it more quickly as a result, according to Bettelheim.[182]

The conception of rationality adopted by militant jihadists may be not only metaphysically different from ours but also emotionally sustaining and hence empowering, like that of German Communists. For Bettelheim's "informants," their political rationality made them fight harder to survive, whereas that of the jihadists leads them to fight harder to kill and die. But the similarity for present purposes is more important than this difference. As always, Baudrillard puts the point grandiloquently, but with unnerving insight:

> We, the powerful, sheltered now from death and overprotected on all sides, occupy exactly the position of the slave; whereas those whose deaths are at their own disposal, and who do not have survival as their exclusive aim, are the ones who today symbolically occupy the position of the master.[183]

COGNITIVE BIAS AND MISPERCEPTION: OBSTACLES TO RESTRAINT THROUGH RECIPROCITY

Tit-for-tat, whether in rewarding good behavior of an opponent or punishing bad, depends for its efficacy and equilibrium on both an accurate perception of the other's intentions and a rational assessment of one's strategic situation. Yet key features of that situation may long remain opaque. For instance, even in advanced democracies military elites often are not particularly rational about the fighting methods they choose. They repeatedly sacrifice military advantage to professional prejudices against new and more effective weapons systems, like the British antipathy in the 1930s toward submarines and their continuing affection for battleships. Intelligence agencies, as formal organizations, are subject to much the same species of distorted reasoning. It was such processes that led the FBI and CIA, in particular, to misconstrue abundant advance warning of the 9/11 attacks, long within their possession.[184] Such organizational culture affects how the strategic costs and benefits of alternative counterterrorism strategies and fighting methods are perceived and assessed.[185]

These assessments often prove mistaken.[186] The resulting restraints on warfare's methods derive not from moral commitments but cognitive impairments. A state's choices on how to fight can be only as rational as the organizations in which such decisions are made. This process proves a frail foundation on which to rest a rational choice approach to choosing means of warfare. Comparing expected costs with expected benefits leads one astray when one's expectations rest on major misconceptions about the relative efficacy of alternative strategies, tactics, and technologies.

To take one now-notorious example, losing the Vietnam War persuaded the U.S. officer corps to avoid future counterinsurgency warfare in favor of strategies of overwhelming force within more conventional armed confrontations. For a generation, the U.S. Army therefore ceased to study or train seriously for such conflicts, leaving it wholly unprepared for the invasions of Afghanistan and Iraq in 2002 and 2003. Its aversion to any such engagements continued thereafter for some time, facilitating the considerable successes of the Sunni insurgency in Iraq after 2004. In retrospect and perhaps *ex ante* as well, the officers' refusal to prepare for such inevitable confrontations could only be described as wishful thinking: preparing for the war you want, rather than the war you are likely to get, and likely to get precisely *because it is* the war you do not want. By 2005, this had come to seem the height of irrationality.

Perceptions of the efficacy of coercive interrogation may be similarly clouded. At the very least, they are perceived very differently in the FBI than in the CIA.[187] Both organizations may be right, but in ways that say as much about differences in organizational culture and concerns as about real ambiguity in the available data. Whereas coercive interrogation may well sometimes produce "actionable intelligence" about enemy plans and personnel – the CIA's chief objective – it is much less likely to yield evidence for criminal prosecution, the FBI's concern – for the very manner of its acquisition normally ensures its inadmissibility.[188] Each organization succumbs to its characteristic *déformation professionnelle*, seeing only its own small piece of the proverbial elephant.

In the immediate aftermath of 9/11, intelligence gathering about possible future attacks rightly took priority, but in ways that greatly prejudiced the later possibility of fair trials. The tension between the two policy objectives is a perennial one, an old chestnut of criminal law enforcement, long antedating the current conflict with Al Qaeda and certain to outlive it.

WHY NOT SUBJECT HUMAN RIGHTS TO COST-BENEFIT ANALYSIS?

The influence that cost-benefit analysis now exercises within circles of power, including those concerned with U.S. posture toward international law,[189] warrants serious attention if we are to ensure its proper application. Even Kenneth Roth, executive director of Human Rights Watch – presumably harboring no deep commitment to cost-benefit analysis – now chooses to speak of the "huge opportunity costs" that the United States incurs when it discourages potential informants from reporting suspicious activity, for fear of facilitating torture of those thereby detained.[190] He likewise condemns the "reverse incentives" for Muslim youth, alienated by U.S. mistreatment of detained religious brethren, to cross the line from vague sympathy into support for violent groups.[191] When Philip Zelikow, former counselor to Secretary of State Condoleezza Rice, publicly condemned U.S. interrogation policy as "immoral" – a statement widely reported in the world press – he actually devoted more space to showing how it was not "cost-beneficial."[192] And Cass Sunstein, a leading liberal Democratic legal thinker, unapologetically favors making national security policy under the aegis of an administrative law that gives pride of place to cost-benefit analysis.[193]

It is best to think of Posner's species of cost-benefit analysis in his defense of coercive interrogation of terror suspects as simply one language game, among others (including legal doctrine, moral philosophy, and social theory), with which any serious student of public policy must be passably conversant. Social science on the subject of "expert political judgment" suggests that the policy analyst should aspire to be a fox – who knows many small things – more than a hedgehog, knowing one big thing, the universal relevance of which he relentlessly avows.[194] That different social and moral theories, incompatible in their underlying premises, should reach an identical conclusion – an incompletely theorized agreement,[195] one might say – when applied to a concrete problem is perhaps the best evidence that one has reached the right result. It is therefore wrong to assume, as many do, that arriving at the right answer on public policy necessarily requires beginning with *the* correct theory. Felicitously, theories of virtue and of *realpolitik* turn out to coincide when one's interests and one's sense of honor independently counsel the same conduct. The remaining chapters show that they do.

The "Gift" of Humanitarianism:
Soft Power and Benevolent Signaling

One of America's greatest strengths is the soft power of our value system and how we treat prisoners of war.

  Tom Ridge, first Secretary of the Department of Homeland Security, Jan. 18, 2008[1]

Let us pause briefly to view the debate over detention, interrogation, and targeted killing in the wider context of debate within the Bush administration over geopolitical strategy. The 2003 invasion of Iraq was conducted in a way that reflected its origins in an uneasy alliance of hopeful "neoconservatives" and more wary realists. The neocons sought to create a model for democratic change throughout the region, whereas their more cautious counterparts feared that Saddam's removal would loose destabilizing ethnic and geopolitical forces beyond America's control.[2] This latter group, led by Brent Scowcroft, opposed any such intervention.[3] The military leadership sided with this group, but insisted that if the invasion were to proceed, it must be accompanied by a commitment of greater force from the start than key neocons thought necessary to ensure its success, as the Weinberger-Powell doctrine enjoined.[4]

The compromise struck by the two sides combined what proved to be the worst of both worlds: an invasion, but one perilously understaffed, especially when combined with the decision to disband the Iraqi army, police, and civil service.[5] The success of the 2008 "surge" in much reducing civil strife only left many inferring that sufficient resources at the outset in 2003 could well have prevented the problem from arising in the first place.[6] Neither party to this debate within the Bush administration initially anticipated the ensuing controversies surrounding the sustained detention and coercive interrogation of thousands of Muslims from throughout the region and beyond. Hence, neither group was much concerned with what that prospect might mean for the country's image in the region and world at large.

The neocons believed that the United States must serve as an inspirational model for regime change in the Middle East. But they anticipated that America's obvious prosperity and liberty, plus a little "public diplomacy," would suffice to this end; any short-term loss to the country's esteem, owing to the invasion itself and attendant dislocations, would soon be overcome by the establishment of popular democratic institutions on the Western model. As fellow peace-loving states, these states would quickly become America's natural allies, and Arab opinion of America would soon improve.[7]

The realists, by contrast, operated within an intellectual framework that enabled them to contemplate and confront the possibility of sustained detention and interrogation of many Muslims. This book therefore concentrates its criticism on the realist defense of such U.S. practices. Whatever their other possible failings, realists have always been more willing than idealists, among whom the neocons must here be counted, to anticipate unintended consequences and so to devise, when intentions go awry, a satisfactory "Plan B." Realist policies and the ideas underlying them are worth debating because they have, at least, confronted the essential questions – albeit largely *post facto* – rather than dreaming that these would never arise. By contrast, there was nothing in the neocons' world-historical imagination, their plan for an "end to history," that would have permitted them seriously to entertain the eventuality of the mass detentions that America soon confronted.

CAN MORAL RESTRAINT ENHANCE SOFT POWER?

Eric Posner is an unabashed "realist." What is most troubling about his argument, outlined in the previous chapter, is not its excessive optimism about restraining nondemocratic states (and similar state-like entities) from humanitarian law violations nor even its blithe indifference to humanitarian issues that are insusceptible to cost-benefit analysis. Still more perplexing is Posner's seeming disregard for how the United States most effectively exerts influence abroad. The JAG memoranda stress that forbearance in detainee treatment, even when – especially when – the adversary will not reciprocate, enhances American moral authority in the world.

Such moral authority is essential to the "soft power" to which the United States aspires today.[8] Soft power requires that others admire us, our way of living and acting; it is not enough that they fear us and respect our might.

America most effectively demonstrates the value of democratic freedoms through its own political practice of them. Its greatest influence across the globe derives, on this view, less from its military might than from the picture of personal liberty and prosperity it projects through its movie and television industries and the Internet, as well as the lure of its capital markets to foreign companies.[9] Yet the United States aspires to present more than just an alluring model, of course, something that Western Europe may offer as well or better. On the basis of its cultural allure and liberal legality, as much as its military and economic power, the United States also effectively claims the predominant role in global governance, in shaping the world's direction. In its response to 9/11, the Bush administration did not adequately appreciate this. As observes Paul Berman, a commentator often sympathetic to Bush's counterterrorism policies, "Laws, formal treaties, the customs of civilized nations, the legitimacy of international institutions – these were the dross of the past, and Bush was plunging into the future. And, as he plunged, he had no idea, nobody in his administration seemed to have any idea, that international law [and] . . . human rights had willy-nilly become the language of liberal democracy around the world."[10]

America's treatment of terror suspects and Iraqi civilians has greatly tarnished its image throughout the world, according to Pew surveys.[11] In early 2007, nearly 70 percent of world respondents disapproved of the U.S. handling of Guantánamo detainees, for instance.[12] Still more offensive has probably been the "willful failure to investigate" civilian deaths caused by U.S. armed forces, in the words of an internal U.S. military report.[13] The foreign criticisms may be exaggerated, and they are often simply inaccurate.[14] But they are very real in their effects on America's capacity to exert moral suasion on societies it may wish to influence, for "if men define situations as real, they are real in their consequences."[15]

American attorneys working in law reform programs throughout the world report that, from virtually every audience, they regularly receive a question – sometimes in a tone of barely concealed contempt – about Abu Ghraib and the attendant hypocrisy of U.S. efforts to present itself as a model to other countries for enhancing the "rule of law."[16] As Thomas Friedman observes, and any frequent traveler can attest, "Dive into a conversation about America in the Arab world today, or even in Europe and Africa, and it won't take 30 seconds before the words 'Abu Ghraib' and 'Guantánamo Bay' are thrown at you."[17] To be sure, there is hypocrisy all around on such matters: The same Western Europe that sharply criticizes U.S. treatment of terror suspects did little better, and in some cases far worse, in treatment of its own domestic terror suspects from the 1970s through the 1990s.[18]

And many of the non-Western statesmen who so vigorously denounced the events at Abu Ghraib would find more ample evidence of torture in their own countries' ordinary police practices and prisons, according to credible human rights groups.

Still, the global allure of the United States and the willingness to follow its lead spring in no small measure from its close historic association with the rule of law ideal, not simply its prosperity and political freedom. Much more is at stake for America's place in the world than whether its diplomats are snubbed at foreign embassies' cocktail parties. American military officers are well aware of this: In a Pentagon office, not long ago there prominently hung for a time – until superiors required its removal – photographs of the Abu Ghraib soldier/tormentors, with a caption reading: "the six morons who lost the war."[19]

Adherence to norms of restraint, even when not strictly applicable as a legal matter, can be advantageous in turning opinion against one's adversaries. Other countries have employed favorable detainee treatment in this way. During World War I, for instance, Japan honored its treaty duties toward POWs and used their good treatment to win sympathy among Western powers.[20] In fact, the competition between Russia and Japan for Western support in the Russo-Japanese War was couched precisely in terms of "which is the civilized power?," as George Kennan posed it, a question answered largely in terms of their relative measure of respect for the laws of war.[21]

America's humane disposition is especially helpful in relations with countries where opinion is divided or wavering, as was true in a number of moderate Muslim societies (Malaysia, Indonesia, Morocco, and Turkey, among others)[22] before the 2003 Iraq invasion. Relations with even close allies, on which the United States heavily depends for cooperation in the conflict with Al Qaeda, may have been somewhat prejudiced[23] by revelations that orders on detainee interrogation methods came directly from President Bush and Attorney General Gonzales.[24] As mentioned earlier, the 2006 Pew Survey revealed that 70 percent of world respondents had a less favorable view of the United States than they had five years earlier and that 85 percent had a less favorable view of U.S. foreign policy.[25] Learned conferences of diplomats and high-minded scholars have deliberated gravely on, in the title of one such gathering, "Guantánamo: Implications for U.S. Human Rights Leadership."[26] The *erga omnes* nature of U.S. duties under the Convention Against Torture and parts of the Geneva Conventions means that the rest of the world realizes that it has a legitimate stake in how America treats its detainees.

The negative impact on relations with close allies, at least, should not be exaggerated, however. Interagency cooperation in counterterrorist policy enforcement (over asset freezing and intelligence sharing, in particular) between high-ranking civil servants in both France and Germany and their U.S. counterparts did not greatly suffer during periods of even the most intense diplomatic tension over the Iraq war and U.S. detainee treatment.[27] This suggests that the strength of such administrative networks, often seen as transcending sovereignty, might actually reduce the cost of unilateral U.S. self-assertion. Such continuing cooperation also confirms realist and other rationalist views insofar as it reflects the weight of shared interests in preventing terrorism, regardless of opposing views on the importance of the law of war.

Even so, a concern about others' judgments of America's behavior is hardly alien to the history of its foreign policy. The country began, in its Declaration of Independence, professing its "decent Respect to the Opinions of Mankind."[28] During the Cold War, American presidents were acutely concerned with how countries in Asia, Latin America, and Africa perceived U.S. racial problems.[29] Today, as we see, there are good reasons to remain concerned with how others view us.

THE "AUDIENCE COSTS" OF HARD POWER

Opinion surveys in 2007 indicated that three-quarters of Americans were well aware that torture allegations against their country had damaged its image abroad.[30] "Audience costs," as the economists call them,[31] have been significant. Eric Posner rightly observes that "a common form of hubris is for increasingly successful people to violate increasingly important norms as a challenge; it is a way of saying, 'You need me more than I need you,'" a way of advertising that "others cannot afford to ostracize them."[32] But there are obvious limits on this stance, as the fate of many celebrities attests. Even the Supreme Court's current conservative majority cares enough about other countries' views to endorse the practice of judicial comity, even deferring to foreign courts' interpretations of treaties that the United States has also ratified.[33]

Earlier world powers, long before the age of CNN and Al Jazeera, have sometimes taken audience costs into account when contemplating war crimes. The desire to avoid antagonizing American opinion restrained Britain from directly targeting German population centers at the start of World War II, for instance.[34] That the law against such targeting "served as a focal point of the struggle to court neutral (and especially American) public opinion shows that norms often do not compete with strategic considerations," one scholar notes, "but rather alter the strategic calculus . . . that a state must consider."[35]

America may well be an empire, as critics charge.[36] But it is surely the only one in history that expects to be loved for it, loved for its very impact – often highly disruptive – on societies less powerful or economically dynamic. This expectation may be terribly naïve on its part. Yet it is also the only kind of empire Americans today will ever long endorse. Opinion surveys show they are not prepared to shoulder the costs of traditional, full-blown empire.[37] Soft power is now the only type of power with which Americans are truly comfortable, for very long, when projecting themselves abroad. Machiavelli famously taught that in seeking and exercising power it is more important to be feared than loved. But in so concluding, he thought it easy to instill fear without also inspiring hatred.[38] That may have been true in the early sixteenth century, a time as yet uninfluenced by modern ideals of equality.

Historic empires like the British or Byzantine empires at their apogee did not trouble themselves over how "lesser peoples" regarded their morals. However, a contemporary superpower whose greatest sway derives from the seductive allure of its form of life, its mode of being, must be concerned about such perceptions.[39] For such an "empire," if it may be so called, there is a much steeper discount rate on global influence from the demise of moral repute. The price of love lost is high for the United States as it never was for Rome.[40] In its foreign policy, the United States must strive to be, above all, a salesman for the American way of life, of which the rule of law is an integral feature. Any salesman, as Arthur Miller wrote of Willie Loman, is "a man out there in the blue, riding on a smile and a shoeshine. And when they stop smiling back – that's an earthquake. And then you get yourself a couple of spots on your hat, and you're finished."[41]

Newly attentive to such concerns with world opinion, the Bush administration briefly saw fit to hire a leading Madison Avenue advertising executive, Charlotte Beers, for the new position of under secretary of state for public diplomacy and public affairs. "I consider the marketing capacity of the United States to be our greatest unlisted asset," she breathlessly proclaimed. "This is the most sophisticated branding assignment I ever had," she adds. "It is almost as if we have to define what America is."[42]

Quite.

Others will reserve the right to make their own, independent judgments about what the United States represents to them. They will do so on the basis of how they observe America to be conducting itself. Judgments of this sort admittedly do not spring forth spontaneously and are sometimes subject to deliberate influence.[43] It is telling, however, that even privately owned media outlets in Arab countries largely rejected U.S. government advertising revenues from Ms. Beers' campaign.[44] Effective public diplomacy is indeed possible and can be quite valuable, as several Western European states have shown in their intraregional relations.[45] But it requires an openness to unscripted dialogue and "taking calculated risks,"[46] the immediate results of which will sometimes be embarrassing. It requires not merely eloquent speech but what we have here called deliberative reciprocity: evidence that one is willing to take the time to listen respectfully to painful criticism and reply with something more empathetic and compelling than a battery of pat, bullet-point retorts, however accurate.

THE REALISM OF SOFT POWER

"Realists," like other rationalists within international relations,[47] may be correct in denying any intrinsic interest in U.S. compliance with international law across the board. They must nonetheless acknowledge that other states, including most of America's major allies, take such law quite seriously. This fact itself becomes a feature of the global geopolitical reality that American realists must confront, however much they might wish others would think more "rationally." Cultivating global legitimacy now requires respecting the rule of law in one's dealings with other peoples. Even those concerned only with preserving and enhancing America's world primacy must now worry about the country's compliance with international law.

Tit-for-tat gamesmanship with adversaries, however effective on its own terms, does not always advance this larger objective. Attaining that goal sometimes requires a willingness to forgo temptation so as to preserve the integrity of an international legal system that regularly provides many other public goods.[48] One such temptation is to disregard norms of humanitarian law to which other states, including major allies, remain staunchly committed.

This stance is entirely consistent with the view, defended before, that public international law remains an *ad hoc* enterprise, the ideal scope of which can only be discovered through case-by-case experimentation. The concern with national reputation and its future payoffs within a larger system of international cooperation can be described as a concern with diffuse reciprocity, however attenuated the link between present cost and anticipated future benefits. There are plenty of precedents. During the Cold War, for instance, George Kennan argued for avoiding unnecessary confrontations with the Soviet Union and against antagonizing its leaders whenever possible. His reasoning was that Western economic and political institutions would eventually reveal their superiority. Time was on America's side. So there was no need to risk nuclear conflagration in a passing spat with the rival superpower.

Much the same logic pertains to the current conflict with militant jihadists. That they and their vision of the good life have little to offer of any appeal to almost anyone will become apparent enough to most sympathizers and apologists, many of whom resentfully root for any underdog without reflection. This requires, however, that "we act in a way that doesn't inflame our enemies' pride and anger and win them new recruits," one commentator adds. An "unambiguous renunciation of torture" would be one good step in this direction.[49]

A concern with soft power is perfectly consistent with "realism." Soft power is still power, albeit gained through nonmilitary means. Spreading America's best ideals and institutions is not an end in itself, on this view. In the "war on terror," it is the ambition for power – through power's own logic – that should lead to American restraint, more than any norms of law or morality. Most Americans care about preserving and enlarging the country's influence in the world.[50] Two-thirds believe it good that "American ideas and customs are spreading around the world."[51] Even liberal Democrats have come to view American power in the world as necessary and desirable,[52] a fact reflected in public debate among the party's presidential candidates.[53] And as Justice Stevens has recently said of our legal and political institutions, "Our system is the role model for the world."[54]

It is the "considered judgment"[55] across most of the American political spectrum that many other societies – especially poor and repressive ones – would stand to gain in freedom and prosperity from emulating many of our political and economic institutions. American counterterrorism policy must consistently accommodate this judgment. The two must work in "reflective equilibrium."[56] Counterterrorism policy must therefore project an image – and reflect an underlying reality – of a society that treats its most violent enemy captives with humanity as individuals, even as it most strenuously seeks to disable their operational capacity. An approach widely perceived as brutal, unnecessarily so, is incompatible with this aim. A foreign policy aimed at soft power hence requires a counterterrorism policy respectful of the world's nearly unequivocal embrace of the Geneva Conventions and Convention Against Torture.

DOUBTS ABOUT SOFT POWER

Not all Americans agree that the country's world influence is largely beneficial and its leadership mostly benevolent. They question whether such benefits to others, however genuine, are worth the costs to Americans themselves. Such Americans, to say nothing of America's foreign detractors, will be skeptical of basing counterterrorism policy on a desire to enhance U.S. influence. It is open to question whether any significant, actionable intelligence that could be gained through sustained detention and coercive interrogation should be forgone for the uncertain prospect of greater international allure. The first responsibility of national leadership is to protect the country's security. Preventing another 9/11 ought to take precedence over the wish to be emulated abroad, when these goals conflict. In any event, world opinion would likely indulge the rough treatment of a few top leaders of Al Qaeda,[57] albeit not the indiscriminate abuse of lowly minions.

Soft power today requires even more than U.S. compliance with humanitarian law. World opinion is no longer so easily satisfied. Such compliance, though necessary, is no longer sufficient. Many now see the law of war itself as part of the problem, as insufficiently attentive to the moral claims of weaker opponents and subject peoples. This is particularly true in the Muslim world, where large numbers of casualties suffered by noncombatant brethren are regarded as morally unacceptable, even when consistent with humanitarian law.[58] Variations on this theme are common in the writings of leading American intellectuals, such as John Updike:

> Can a nation war against a regime without warring against the people the regime rules? Is the very concept of "war crime" tautological, given the context of determined violence? As Kofi Annan, the UN Secretary General, said a few weeks ago, "War is always a catastrophe." Are discriminations possible between appropriate and excessive bombing, between legitimate and atrocious ship-sinkings, between proper combat of armed soldiers and such tactics as using civilians, including children, as human shields or disguising an ambush as a surrender?[59]

In posing these questions rhetorically, offering no analysis to follow, Updike wishes to imply that their answers are clearly negative. Whatever else might be said of this view, there is no doubt that it reflects a widespread sensibility. It would be too much to call it an argument, however, much less a good one.

It is true that casualties are often legally permissible as damage "incidental"[60] to the "military advantage" thereby obtained, if "proportionate"[61] and "necessary" to that end. Historically, the latter terms of art have often been indulgently construed, moreover, though they need not be so understood henceforth. The redirection of humanitarian law from state civil liability to personal criminal liability threatens to reinforce this indulgence, due to the longstanding interpretive maxim that penal statutes must be strictly construed, giving the defendant the benefit of ambiguity.[62] But outside military circles and official U.S. discourse, the term "collateral damage" is today employed largely in derision or at least with ample apologies for its confessedly "euphemistic" character.[63] Oxford's Chichele Professor of Social and Political Theory, G. A. Cohen, even writes that "holding everything else equal . . . killing two hundred innocents through foreseeable side-effect is actually worse than killing one innocent who is your target."[64] And Columbia Law professor Matthew Waxman is correct that today's political pressures to minimize civilian casualties "may reduce operational flexibility more severely than does adherence to international law."[65] In fact, that formulation rather understates the problem.

The argument that U.S. (and Israeli) "incidental damage" to Muslim civilians is not meaningfully different from Al Qaeda's (or Hezbollah's and Hamas's) intentional targeting of civilians quietly seeks to reestablish the "moral equality of soldiers"[66] on both sides of current battlelines. For it is this moral equality that always justified the law's like treatment of those who fought for the aggrieved and the aggressor (i.e., as long as the latter played no role, as do members of an army's general staff, in planning the aggression). Because they have simply done their duty, soldiers are moral equals, in the law's conventional account, even if the states and leaders for which they fight are not. That moral equality, and the rights to equal treatment it had long justified, surely struck most Westerners as lacking in the conflict with Al Qaeda, on account of its intentional killing of civilians.

Yet not everyone saw the moral inequality here as obvious.[67] At this point many remind us of state-sponsored terrorism, including that implicit in effective nuclear deterrence. They also insistently direct our attention to the extent of collateral damage caused by the organized armed forces of nation-states, perhaps especially but not only to Muslim peoples. The insinuation here of a deeper moral equivalence between antagonists does not wish to justify lowering the standards of treatment that jihadists may accord Western captives, but to urge improving the conditions of captured jihadists. These men have killed far fewer civilians, consequentialists would remind us, than have their adversaries. In distinguishing their greater culpability from that of our own troops, who kill civilians unintentionally, we display our legal "sophistication" perhaps.

But such distinctions, for an increasing number of people throughout the world, border on mere sophistry, and it is no coincidence that the two words share a single etymology. Nor is skepticism about the exculpatory upshot of "double effect"[68] a recent development, much less an exclusively non-Western insight. The distinguished liberal theorist H. L. A. Hart attacked the doctrine forty years ago.[69] In the Old Testament for that matter,

Abraham dares – on the grounds that innocent people will die – to question God's decision to destroy Sodom.[70] One could thus say that doubts about double effect are internal to Western moral thought from its inception.

Despite superficial disparities between today's rival belligerents, their conduct in the current conflict is more similar than different, the critics imply. The angry men who now appear to seek our destruction hence are not, despite initial appearances, our moral inferiors. And because they are our moral equals, they deserve treatment equal in its humanity to that which the Western soldier expects to receive. In suggesting that the rules they play by, though distinct from ours, are only trivially different in practical and moral terms (i.e., by the West's own metric of "body counts"), this argument implicitly reasserts the reciprocity principle – throwing back in its face the very norm the West accuses its adversary of violating.

Yet Islamic law itself sometimes accepts a version of double effect, punishing intended harm more seriously than foreseeable but unintended harm, especially if the latter harm bears a proportionate relation to lawful purposes.[71] In any event, the refusal to acknowledge any difference in moral significance between killing civilians intentionally and killing them as a proportionate, unintended consequence of warfare's lawful measures against armed combatants will strike anyone familiar with humanitarian law – and likely most other people – as obtuse, perhaps even obscene. But this initial reaction, though perfectly intelligible, should be chastened by the recognition that such a double effect rule proves readily susceptible, in the hands of an artful advocate, to the narrowing of liability beyond any defensible limits. No other illustration is necessary than the skillful sophistry performed by John Yoo and Jay Bybee on the mental state required for the crime of torture. The Convention Against Torture requires that the severe pain or suffering be "intentionally inflicted."[72] The U.S. "understanding" accompanying ratification and the implementing legislation specify that the painful effect must be "specifically intended."[73]

If interrogators employ coercion only for the specific purpose of eliciting actionable intelligence, they may not specifically intend the pain they necessarily produce to obtain that information. Such pain is an *un*intended byproduct, the secondary, ancillary, or "double" effect of their acts of coercion. The upshot: Only a true sadist (i.e., someone deriving personal pleasure from the pain of the interrogated) would be guilty of torture. Because the damage that U.S. interrogators inflict on detainees, however considerable, is "collateral" to their legitimate intention of eliciting life-saving information, their conduct does not constitute torture, on this interpretation. One can see why many recoil from the doctrine of double effect, if this is where it leads. In this case, however, it does not actually so lead, as other elements of torture's legal definition make clear that officials may not inflict severe pain for interrogative purposes.[74] The appeal to good intentions to deflect criticism for foreseeable civilian deaths has a longer and unpleasant place in twentieth-century American military history. One historian writes, in fact, "Americans have spent more time thinking about their good intentions than about how they could prevent more civilian deaths from their wars."[75]

In sum, entirely apart from what law may require, America's interest in maintaining the legitimacy of its leadership and the perception of its hegemony as generally benign demands forbearance in how it fights jihadist terror. "Specific" reciprocity plays no part here. Posner's preoccupation with it thus fails even as *realpolitik* – as a "realistic" concern with enhancing U.S. influence in the world. He admits that restraint is possible whenever antagonists within a bilateral conflict find moderation to be in their mutual interest. He says nothing, however, about the wider and longer-term interests of a superpower in fostering a favorable global view of itself and its way of life.

Thus, even if one were to accept cost-benefit analysis as the only relevant test, Posner's application of that method seriously underestimates a crucial benefit of restraint. Detainee abuse has already had diffuse but harmful consequences for American moral authority, as indicated. It has lent a harsher, meaner tone to U.S. relations with many other countries, in ways that are very real, albeit more subtle than rational choice or other social science methods readily capture.[76]

Strictly speaking, this defect may not be intrinsic to cost-benefit analysis, intelligently applied, and cost-benefit analysis is admittedly more philosophically sophisticated today than in the past.[77] And it is not an analytic truth that costs to moral authority, forfeited by the use of questionable fighting methods, must outweigh corresponding gains in military advantage against a foe, as Posner rightly responds.[78] Let us imagine, for instance, that the Third Reich had employed poison gas against Allied forces in the mid-1940s, killing many thousands and permitting the enduring occupation of innocent countries and the Holocaust's continuation. In fact, assume that the Nazi first use of chemical warfare was turning the war's tide in their favor. Under these circumstances, it is unlikely that the Allies would have continued to deny themselves the use of like weapons. Public sentiment would surely have clamored for such use, in fact. Initial concerns about costs to the country's moral authority from employing these methods would have been soon trumped by military considerations, underpinned by the moral repercussions of likely Nazi victory.

Still, reputational costs to a state from its war crimes and other treaty breaches may often be considerable. Japan continues to pay a price for such misconduct in its diplomatic and cultural relations with Asian trading partners. Such costs – though not illusory or ephemeral – are notoriously elusive, almost ethereal, and impossible to measure, especially compared to more palpable losses.[79] Uncertain future costs also tend to receive less attention in our minds than more certain, present costs; this is true even where the former will prove predictably heavier.[80] This cognitive distortion is pervasive in much managerial decision making.[81]

Long-term reputational costs from torturing detainees, after the nature of this treatment ultimately becomes known years later, may seem imponderable and speculative compared to the immediate cost of forgoing such methods in the face of their obdurate reticence during interrogation. Posner's own pre-9/11 writings, however, stress that people grasp the value of voluntarily contributing to collective goods to the extent that so doing wins them a reputation for moral virtues, which disposes others to enter interactions with them.[82] He applies this insight to a vast variety of social contexts, from family law to flag desecration. If it is pertinent to so much in relations among people, why not also among states?

By incurring slightly greater risk, the United States would incur corresponding benefits in enhanced good will – of smaller magnitude in any given action, but greater over a longer period. These benefits would take many forms, prominent among them a greater proclivity to respect international law (e.g., WTO judgments in favor of the United States). A loss to the United States of 5 units or utiles of intelligence value, say, from abjuring torture might yield a gain of 0.1 units in comity value from each of 100 other countries, for a total value of 10 and a net gain of 5. The number of states that might be drawn into the calculus, per unit of signaling effort, would likely be high because of the salience of "Abu Ghraib" and "Guantánamo" in world opinion. The prominence of these public concerns would contribute to broadcast efficiency, as economists call it, of any U.S. message aimed at redressing them.[83] America could soon recover its upfront costs in future payoffs.[84]

"STRONG" RECIPROCITY AND HEGEMONIC STABILITY

Forgoing the ephemeral benefits of violating Geneva law is one of the costs an international "hegemon" is expected to bear to preserve the stable legitimacy of a system it helps establish and oversee, one from which it greatly benefits.[85] That system pays its leading beneficiaries handsome long-term dividends in return for occasional, short-term expenditures. The

United States absorbed the lion's share of NATO's costs for a half-century, for instance, enduring innumerable indignities from less powerful members while displaying respectful appreciation for their often-paltry material contributions.[86] One might almost say that, within the theory of international relations, the place of the benevolent hegemon resembles that of the sun within ancient cosmologies: an original and powerful giver that cannot accept equivalent gifts in return, only sacrifices in its honor.

"Strong" reciprocators, unlike "conditional" ones, are prepared to incur costs to punish a rule violator, even when doing so brings them no immediate benefit. They accept these costs to preserve the larger order within which such rules are embedded, and they believe that justice requires punishment even when it is costly to those doing the punishing.[87] An economist like Posner could say nothing more about strong reciprocators than that they seem to have a "taste" or "appetite" for justice, as they understand its demands – while perhaps bemusedly wondering, "How strange!" Otherwise, their desire to punish, without expectation of corresponding gain to themselves, would have to be considered irrational.

A country is a strong reciprocator if, for instance, it imposes sanctions on another even when sanctions are unlikely to change the offender's trading policies; tariffs on imports always raise costs to domestic consumers of the products subject to them. Imposing trade sanctions hence punishes both sides. The United States has done precisely this on many occasions, both through and independently of multilateral trade organizations.[88] Benevolent hegemons are strong reciprocators for they are willing to absorb costs necessary to preserve a system. They do so because they believe this system generally to be just and they appreciate how it works in their long-term interests, even as they may seek to modify certain of its unwelcome rules.

As with trade, so with war. The United States has long strongly supported the development of international humanitarian law. It has heavily subsidized a number of international criminal tribunals, from Nuremberg through the Yugoslav and Rwandan experiences, as well as lower profile domestic prosecutions in Serbia and Croatia. The global order it oversees has at once also encouraged the participation of other states in the formation of many key institutions and policies. As Ikenberry observes,

> The American-centered Western order exhibits far more reciprocity and legitimacy than an order based solely on superordinate and subordinate relations. . . . The distinctive features of this system – particularly its transparency, the diffusion and power into many hands, and the multiple points of access to policymaking – have enabled Western Europeans and

Japanese allies to participate in policymaking for the overall system. As a result ... the arrows of influence ... run in both directions, producing a fundamentally reciprocal political order.[89]

When a legal regime consists of rules that serve a major state, that state's leaders should find adherence to "the rule of law" a good way of advancing national interests. Yet when the dominant power in such a regime starts to insist on taking the good without the bad, weaker states begin to question the larger social contract by which they agreed to respect a legal system not so obviously and consistently in their interests. The potential global costs to the United States from its legally questionable conduct in the conflict with Al Qaeda are hence momentous.

DISTINGUISHING ONESELF FROM ONE'S FOE
AS A SOURCE OF SOFT POWER

When a constitutional democracy wishes to distinguish its martial prac-tices from more dubious ones of nondemocratic foes, it emphasizes how its principles differ from those of its adversary. Hence, for instance, the stir-ring language of Justice Wiley Rutledge's *Yamashita* dissent. Opposing the prosecution of a Japanese general by military commission, he wrote that the "long held attachment" to our "great constitutional traditions ... marks the great divide between our enemies and ourselves. Theirs was a philosophy of universal force. Ours is one of universal law, albeit imperfectly made flesh of our systems."[90] Why does this same impulse to distinguish itself from its enemies not find comparable expression and force in American politics today?

History offers a partial answer here. Some historians now claim that it was U.S. interests in world domination that led it to take seriously, for the first time, the civil rights of African Americans, so as to distinguish the country's moral standards from those of its Cold War adversary, reflected in sundry Soviet barbarities.[91] The Soviet "Other" – its human rights abuses – came to define American political identity, in this view, more than any intrinsic commitment to realizing our own essential constitutional ideals.[92] The positive consequences ran quite far afield. Just after World War II, the American fear of possible creeping Soviet influence over an economically devastated Western Europe (of the sort soon attained through suzerainty over Finland) was a major inspiration for America's Marshall Plan.[93]

Along with the U.S. lend-lease program during the war itself, the Marshall Plan became the legal template for two generations of ensuing American foreign aid to much of the world. Foreign aid between rich and poor countries closely resembles gift exchange between tribal clans in the denial of any explicit *quid pro quo*. In both types of interaction, there is a shared public face of gracious disinterestedness. It is combined, however, with a mutual understanding that is exactly the opposite. That a two-way exchange has even taken place, much less its precise terms, is disavowed or at least ritually dissimulated. Openly acknowledging the expectation of reciprocity would "commodify" and thereby demean the relationship.

American foreign postwar assistance programs reflected a dynamic common to the history of intergroup relations under primitive conditions of cooperation, as we now see: the tendency for fear – of Communism in this case – to inspire gifts aimed at stabilizing relations while exercising influence.[94] The European Left immediately recognized the Marshall Plan for what it was, in this respect. Frenchman George Bataille, for instance, welcomed American aid only because of his confidence that "working class agitation" and the salubrious influence of Western Communist parties would "reduce the risk that the intervention might turn into a conquest."[95]

Let us assume *arguendo* that the Cold War heavily inspired America's court-enforced racial integration and its financial commitment to aiding poor countries. Let us also assume that both were unequivocally positive developments. Cold Warriors may then fairly respond that these then were just two more good consequences, albeit perhaps unintended, of the country's resolve to win that superpower conflict. One might even say that superpower rivalry strengthened incentives to improve America's proffered product – capitalist democracy – in a competitive market for influence over the "Third World." Monopolists, by contrast, tend to rest on their laurels, in international relations no less than in the business world.

From either viewpoint, however, the question arises: In the absence of a strong geopolitical rival, what political counterforce might hold America to its own professed ethical standards, in the face of powerful temptations to the contrary? One might think that Al Qaeda's conspicuous violations of humanitarian law should have proven sufficient for purposes of moral contrast. Unlike Communism during much of its early history, Al Qaeda does not present an appealing alternative model of the good life.

The Soviet counterweight to U.S. temptation was much stronger for this reason. America does not require a spotless record of humanitarian restraint to persuade most people throughout the world of its superiority – moral and otherwise – to its current foe. Yet the very measure of that superiority vis-à-vis Al Qaeda creates a wider margin for moral error and so an unfortunate carelessless about the risk of succumbing to it. Today, the United States has reason to fear not only the violent terror of militant jihadists but also, owing to the Bush administration's response, an increasing global skepticism about the wisdom of U.S. leadership over the international order as a whole. That skepticism would be most prejudicial to the country's interests and ideals if it were to lead many abroad to question the desirability of continued globalization under American stewardship and institutional inspiration.

SIGNALING THE LEGITIMACY OF AMERICA'S WORLD LEADERSHIP

More humane treatment of Al Qaeda suspects would improve America's image throughout the world. But how does enhanced imagery translate into power – soft or otherwise? What is the mechanism by which the country's willing assumption of greater burdens is likely to be repaid in increased benefits? This prospect becomes a major reason for restraint, after all, once morality and law, as preceding chapters show, no longer unequivocally demand it.

Many countries' leaders have found it expedient to invoke international law to justify action that would be domestically unpopular, shifting the blame from their own shoulders to the irresistible demands of the world community. At these times, a major function of international law is precisely the face-saving façade it permits such leaders,[96] even if domestic respect for such law in their countries is prejudiced in the process. America, however, is probably the only country where political leaders have never seriously tried this tactic, because they recognize that it will not work here. Invoking the constraints imposed by international law (insofar as the United States has endorsed it) would be neither factually credible nor politically viable. If the United States is to come into compliance with humanitarian law norms as generally understood, it must be persuaded by way of a rather different discourse.

It is useful to think of humane treatment for Al Qaeda suspects as a species of signal by which America indicates the benevolence of its global leadership and the value it attaches to relationships with other nation-states. Incurring the costs of such humanitarianism is also a way of buying insurance against system instability.[97] Helpful here is the theory of "costly signaling,"[98] developed contemporaneously by economists and biologists. Animals seeking a mate in the wild engage in activities, such as showy exhibitions of plumage, designed to convey information about their valuable traits. Potential prey, when warding off a predator, find ways to signal their prowess, exaggerating their capacity to resist attack. A defining feature of costly signaling is that it "does not entail conditional reciprocity."[99] Little or nothing is expected from the other in return, and certainly no comparably lavish expenditure. Costly signaling tends to arise, in fact, "where conditional reciprocity is unlikely to emerge and is vulnerable to free-riding."[100] Parties turn instead to unilateral signaling when they find that they cannot rely on tit-for-tat or other forms of immediate, bilateral *quid pro quo*.

In the wild, costly signaling permits evolutionary stability despite natural selection and the conflicts of interest it engenders. In the international arena, such signaling permits a measure of stability in interstate relations despite the conflicts of interest flowing from conditions of anarchy posed by the absence of a global sovereign. From this perspective, the problem with torture and indefinite detention is not their intrinsic immorality or illegality. Rather, the problem lies in the irrational brevity of the time horizon from which defenders of such practices derive so steep a discount rate on the value of America's reputation. Abstaining from torture and sustained detention without trial signals the benevolence of U.S. hegemony over international affairs. The appearance of costliness to America would even be desirable, on this account, because such very "extravagance" is necessary to the signal that its leaders would wish to send. Extravagance is necessary to that signal's clarity and broadcast efficacy.

The theory of costly signaling was designed to account for how markets handle asymmetry in the distribution of information; that is, in situations in which parties cannot or will not directly communicate all pertinent data about the quality of their goods or services. The model was first developed in the context of labor markets. There, employees signal their relative skills to prospective employers by obtaining a certain amount of education, a process that is costly to them. Employers pay higher wages to more educated employees because they recognize that the percentage of employees with high abilities is greater among the educated ones. This is because it is less costly for such employees to acquire education than for those with lesser talents. For the theory to work, it is unnecessary that education have any intrinsic value, as long as it communicates relevant information about the sender to the recipient because the signal is costly.

The theory's creator, Michael Spence, hence told us – of course, before becoming dean of Stanford Business School – that there is little in the actual content of an expensive MBA education that can only be learned in that fashion.[101] So too, there is little in a particular peacock's tail that makes it a better mate for the peahen, all things considered. And there is little in America's better treatment of terror suspects as such that proves that its global hegemony, broadly understood, will be consistent with the interests of everyone else.

The data contained in the signal, in other words, do not themselves signify a very deep, true benevolence on America's part toward the rest of the
world in other issue-areas. Still, few markets are really so inefficient, so completely dysfunctional, that the signs sellers employ as signals bear no relation
whatever to the information their senders are seeking to communicate. This
is true even of the market for international political influence, however
monopolized it may today be. What one learns at Stanford Business School
is not completely irrelevant, for that matter, to what one may later do as
a corporate manager. America's true measure of benevolence is difficult to
determine, especially because many of its foreign commitments manage to
benefit both itself and others at once, in differing measure at different times
and places. Signaling benevolence also helps resolve ambiguities in others'
minds about how to assess the uncertain mix of costs and benefits associated
with mimicking the American political and economic model, including its
understanding of the rule of law.

From a somewhat different view, abjuring torture would be not so much
a gesture to the world of disinterested goodness nor even of deference to the
opinion of coequal sovereign states as such. Rather, forbearance could reflect
something more like the savvy, power-confirming, status-enhancing "gift"
that has transfixed anthropologists for nearly a century.[102] Gifts, unlike
mere signals, anticipate reciprocation, however. The analogy may at first
seem counterintuitive, perhaps bizarre. It thus requires some elaborative
background.

In premodern societies, the link between gift exchange and the exercise of power is much clearer than in the modern West. Potlatches among
Indians of the Pacific Northwest,[103] for instance, accomplish two very different aims at once. They neutralize tensions between competitive tribes,
substituting the pacifications of trade for the prospect of war.[104] Taussig
thus writes of such societies, "As written into the morality and aesthetics
of gift exchange, reciprocity aims to buy peace."[105] A potlatch also provides
an outlet for nonviolent competition between such tribes through lavish
presentations by which the recipient – if it cannot afford fully to repay –
becomes permanently indebted, and thereby socially subordinate, to the
donor. (Thorsten Veblen much elaborated on this competitive element of
gift exchange in his theory of "conspicuous consumption."[106]) In tribal
societies, the extravagant gratuitousness of the ritual exhibition serves both
purposes. It helps overcome the recipient's recurrent fear of its rival while
advancing the donor's desire for supremacy, gained by nonviolent means.

Whether this link between the exercise of power and the conferral of
gifts has truly disappeared in modern society or merely become subtly

sublimated is a question that continues to fascinate contemporary social thought.[107] Even today, insists William Ian Miller,

> The norm of reciprocity still works to give gifts the power to honor and dishonor, to bind people to one another, and hence to impose on them. But we prefer to deny that; because we long ago delegitimized the homology of gift exchange and vengeance we have been able to construct for ourselves an ideology of the free gift, the gift that looks for no return.... There appears to be an intimate connection between our official view of the sweet disinterest of the pure gift and the official view of evil and senseless vengeance, condemned both as immoral by moralists and irrational by economists. Lowering the morality of vengeance raised the morality of the gift. So we criminalized vengeance and decriminalized debt: The law of the talon gave way to the law of bankruptcy.[108]

International law underwent much the same transition. Barely more than a century ago, the law of war fully authorized a state in resorting to force to secure repayment of a foreign debt.[109] Today, the practice is criminalized as aggression. States may effectively declare "bankruptcy" by defaulting on their foreign loans without fear of violent vengeance by creditors.

Just as gifts can be assertions of power, it has also been often true that "gifts and violence ran in the same grooves,"[110] as Miller observes of medieval Icelandic sagas. Or as Bourdieu remarks, violence "obeys the same logic as gift exchange."[111] Both forms of interaction play central roles within a larger process of "generalized exchange," as Lévi-Strauss calls it, by which premodern societies at once sustain themselves over time and allow some measure of change, including social mobility. Within this broader context, violence is almost never truly "senseless," any more than gifts are ever entirely disinterested or "free," and for the same reason.[112]

More humane treatment of Al Qaeda suspects would nonetheless be truly a "free gift" to them, because it need not be defended in terms of their legal rights, human or otherwise, against their captors.[113] It is also free because their organization could not soon be expected to return the favor, to reciprocate good for good. If there were any exchange involved, it would take place between America and the rest of the world, with the detainees as mere third-party beneficiaries to it. A countergift may be anticipated from allies and estranged allies (i.e., states that have chosen to distance themselves from the United States since President Bush declared the "war on terrorism"). America might expect such states to repay, in myriad small ways, such a gift of humanitarianism.[114] Reciprocation would come in the forms of enhanced counterterrorism cooperation and in other diplomatic currency.[115]

That such a palpable return is envisaged from the outset does not disqualify the initial offering as a gift, in the anthropological sense. To the contrary, this is exactly the sort of proffering that anthropologists have so widely found within stateless societies throughout the world. It would be designed to serve precisely the same ends as in those places and periods: asserting power through an act of beneficence that creates a debt that must be discharged in some way. This effect requires reciprocation and goes beyond mere benevolent signaling. The countergift cannot be legally guaranteed and hence always involves something of a gamble on the strength of less formal social ties.

Modern humanitarianism has clear roots in ancient notions of magnanimity (also translated as magnificence), which was itself understood as a species of generosity (or liberality, in some translations). For Aristotle, "magnificence is the variety of liberality which related to gifts to the community. ... The magnificent man ... gives without receiving presents in exchange. He devotes his fortune to higher values, civic or religious, and does not introduce his bounty into the system of exchange of favours that characterizes the more modest virtue of liberality."[116] It is precisely its supererogatory nature – how the magnificent bequest transcends any call of duty and the logic of social exchange – that endows it with its special aura, its ineffable allure. In short, the noble person (including the noble soldier) disdains reciprocity in human relations, no less than the suicide bomber for militant jihad, albeit for very different reasons.

Aquinas treated magnanimity by war's victors under the more general virtue of temperance.[117] Even Grotius, who sought to reestablish the law of war on the more impersonal basis of rights and rules, similarly heralded martial restraint – *temperantia belli,* as the Latin suggests – in terms of this same personal virtue.[118] And early nineteenth-century formulations of international humanitarian law norms referred expressly to magnanimity as the source of their ethical inspiration.

Such language is today admittedly very uncommon in public; it has been replaced by the modern idiom of rights. In the contemporary debate over Guantánamo, for instance, the only person to have explicitly invoked this historically Western and "Christian" virtue in defending the more temperate treatment of jihadist detainees, to judge from a quick Web search, is an isolated Muslim blogger in India.[119] In interpersonal interaction, a gesture of magnanimity cannot intend to elicit a reciprocal gesture of any sort without ceasing to be magnanimous. The possibility of a like gesture in response cannot be acknowledged without compromising the gift's necessary appearance as free or altruistic.

This ambiguous status of the gift – the tension between its avowed purpose and subterranean social function – has had far-reaching ramifications for modern law. In elections to political office, for instance, campaign contributions are not treated as gifts for tax purposes because they often seek to influence public policy in ways favorable to donor interests, even to facilitate the donor's appointment to office. Yet the exact terms of how much influence a donor expects from a candidate-donee in exchange for how large of a contribution cannot be made explicit without amounting to the criminal offense of bribery.[120] So too the candidate cannot tell potential donors that favorable treatment of their interests is contingent on a contribution (i.e., without committing the crime of extortion).

The general rule is nonetheless that the implicit "purchase of favorable official action with campaign contributions is not a corrupt practice, as long as the 'contributions' do not benefit candidates in their personal lives and as long as the 'purchases' are voluntary."[121] Public policy, reflected in campaign finance law, aims not to banish this market in political influence, but to render it more perfectly competitive. Contributions to electoral candidates straddle the line between the public-spirited free gift, to which no strings may be attached, and a confessedly self-interested *quid pro quo*. The law is unsatisfyingly imprecise concerning the line between lawful influence and criminal transaction, giving only the vaguest of warnings when it is being crossed.[122]

In international relations, unlike the domestic and especially the interpersonal, the ideology of the free gift barely exists. There is no expectation that any valued prestation between states will be altruistic. In even the most avowedly "humanitarian" of military interventions, for instance, it is often easy to identify the vindication of national interest in some nontrivial degree, such as that of Kenya – when overthrowing Idi Amin – in avoiding refugee flows from Uganda. It is enough that international policymakers are "likely to infer that a costly concession is sincerely motivated by the desire for an agreement or better relations,"[123] remarks one leading scholar of the subject. As in domestic electoral campaigns, the terms of trade are left willfully ambiguous. In addition to the reasons just mentioned, there is also the wish to avoid offending the recipient state's pride in its independence. The foreign donor's bestowal itself gives no evidence on its face of any transaction at all (i.e., that it expects anything in return). As with any important gift, the real transaction "takes place in the mind,"[124] Seneca long ago observed.[125] It is a genuine transaction, nonetheless.

Such uncertainty combines with other considerations to ensure that there is often little correspondence between the dollar amount of assistance a country receives and the degree of influence thereby secured. To take a particularly pertinent example, informed analyses of U.S.-Pakistani relations since 9/11 conclude that America's $10 billion in acknowledged assistance won it little in effective counterterrorism policy, still less in public regard – Pakistani or global.[126] In response to the promise of generous aid, President Pervez Musharraf did make a public shift in policy from endorsing to opposing the Taliban. But he was either unable or unwilling to implement it operationally in key respects. The vast bulk of U.S. foreign aid went to purchase U.S.-manufactured weaponry for the country's armed forces,[127] thereby further strengthening the military's domestic political power within society. Yet the Pakistani officer corps, like the country at large, remained deeply split over whether the country should subordinate its foreign policy to American geopolitical interests[128] – which favored rapprochement with India, among other aims objectionable to the officers on nationalist grounds.

Only a small proportion of U.S. aid found its way into the hands of anyone beyond the officers' public and private coffers,[129] much less the worst off[130] (i.e., those especially susceptible to the message of militant jihad). Repressing most internal dissent with now much-enhanced weaponry, Musharraf – though initially popular – soon became widely disliked as a dictator. Because America was by then his principal source of financial and international political support, the United States soon came to be widely resented by the Pakistani public. Derided as America's "Viceroy," Musharraf was decisively voted from office in February 2008. Whether its $10 billion had won the United States any enhancement in national security at all was, to say the least, open to question.

The Marshall Plan, this wasn't. In fact, Benazir Bhutto aptly called it instead "the Martial Plan."[131] In close personal relations, one learns a great deal about another from the other's gifts: whether they reveal an appreciation of what the recipient truly values and needs or rather what the giver thinks the recipient *should* value (i.e., what the giver him- or herself values). Much the same is true in foreign aid. Because the gift to Pakistan from its American friend took place bilaterally and noncontractually, there was no state or international legal apparatus through which to enforce its terms, whatever they may have been. Predictably, political science has discovered no method for discerning foreign aid's true terms of trade, in this case or any other, apart from through such trivia as voting patterns in the UN General Assembly.[132]

THE "GIFT" AS INTERGROUP RECIPROCITY

There is more use for humble processes of fence-mending in international relations than we may generally assume. Gifts between sovereigns – as well as complaints of their inadequacy in relation to the receiver's own prior gifts – have been an integral, ritualized component of diplomacy from its recorded beginnings in the ancient Near East.[133] Such exchanges became part of an elaborate language of diplomatic communication, character-ized by standardized signals and hermeneutics for decoding them.[134] For resolving interstate conflicts today, there have developed formal, stylized measures – derived from reflection on bargaining experience in many types of negotiations – for international "confidence-building."[135]

If they were not part of a negotiation, such measures often involve what might almost be called gifts[136]; that is, conspicuous gestures of "generosity" designed to soothe tensions between troubled parties at key points in a deliberative interaction. Unlike true gifts, they may be declined without breach of etiquette. Yet they are designed to stimulate cooperation with a rival and in this sense resemble gift exchange within preindustrial societies. An accepted maxim in international negotiation today is that "reciprocity requires that concessions be matched,"[137] if the concession is accepted. Under a different guise, then, the social mechanisms that have always lain beneath gift exchange between peoples persist in many ways. The dynamics of reciprocal gift giving in intergroup conflict resolution display significant similarities between times and places, whether the "tribes" in question are Haida and Tlingit[138] or statesmen-diplomats from the United States and Western Europe.

The principal change is that the gift concession is now part and parcel of the negotiation process, whereas a distinguishing feature of archaic gift exchange – certainly as an ideal-type, at least – was precisely the absence of negotiation, though the latter process is rich in interactive meaning. If a gift is aimed at preserving and consolidating an existing state of stable relations, then the terms of trade will have been largely settled by customary practice (i.e., tradition). If the gift is competitive in spirit, aimed at enhancing power, then the donor is perfectly content to proffer more than the recipient can reciprocate. Short of declining the gift outright, which is usually a major breach of social etiquette in any society, there is little the recipient can do. Here too, no negotiation is required or even possible. And if the gift is truly altruistic – "no strings attached" – then the donor intends that the donee should be the only party to profit from the interaction. The donor seeks nothing in return, so yet again, no negotiation occurs. In all three of these instantiations, the gift is the antithesis of what Sahlins once called "the oriental confrontation of buyer and seller in higgle-haggle . . . the morality of the bazaar."[139] Similarly, no negotiation between America and the world need be entailed in a gift of humanitarianism in the treatment of Al Qaeda suspects.[140]

In tribal societies, the gift conferred power over the recipient partly because it continued to be imbued with the spirit of the giver. The object transmitted through rituals of reciprocity retained the aura of the person who had owned it. In fact, the gift often *was* a person, hitherto a member of the donor clan (i.e., one of its women offered in marriage to the recipient clan). Links to her group of origin and early socialization inevitably endured as she became gradually integrated into the new group. Even gifts of material things were not yet conceived as entirely separate from the persons who had proffered them. Mauss thus naturally turned to Roman law for contrast here,[141] since that was where the distinction between persons and their things was first clearly introduced into Western juridical life.

From the American perspective, the hundreds of terror suspects released from Guantánamo constitute a kind of human gift to the international community, one could say, because the United States did not confer their freedom in recognition of any claim of legal right nor in exchange for benefits from anyone. So too, the more humane treatment accorded since 2003 to those who remained in custody, particularly their greater freedom from coercive interrogation, should be conceived in this way. Even modern gifts remain at least somewhat imbued with their giver's spirit. But it would not be easy to say exactly in what that spirit might here consist. The humanity retained, preserved, and honored in these gifts, we are sure to say, is that of persons themselves released from custody without charges or exempt from degrading methods of interrogation.

SOLIDARITY WITHOUT THE STATE: THE ROLE OF GIFTS

It may at first seem that, as a basis for restoring a ruptured solidarity, gift giving is uniquely suited to small and "primitive" societies. Yet more important than their size or economic development is their lack of a central state that codifies and enforces terms of a broad-ranging social (i.e., multilateral) contract. The state's nonexistence is the defining feature of international society no less than of premodern society.[142] The ideology of the free gift – as Derrida extols it, for instance[143] – has no place in either arena.[144] If gifts are the primitive analogue of the social contract, as Mauss and Sahlins argued, this is because they serve societal purposes assumed by the state in centralized polities.[145]

The very "primitiveness" of gift exchange is what makes it so suitable as a means of defusing conflict and mollifying rivals in international relations, no less than in intertribal ones. A gift is traditionally bilateral because there is no state or market through which exchange – and the solidarities it creates – could be rendered multilateral. The "circumstances of gifting" exist whenever there is a recurrent threat of coercion among those who, though morally averse to unrestrained reliance on market mechanisms in their interrelations, nonetheless remain economically interdependent, and a central polity to enforce a multilateral social contract among them all is impracticable. "There is no international government," notes Richard Posner, "yet extensive cooperative relationships are established and maintained across national boundaries. People travel and trade more or less securely in most areas at most times. Reciprocity and retaliation maintain a tolerably stable international order." As in intertribal relations, reciprocity is 'presented as an attainable ideal of social interactions outside the *oikos* [home] – a substitute for the "night-watchman" state,'[146] he concludes.

The international arena resembles archaic societies in this way. In relations among ancient Greek city-states, for instance, "the act of giving was . . . always the first half of a reciprocal action, the other half of which was a counter-gift,"[147] writes a leading classicist. In reflecting on such societies, legal theorist Lon Fuller further concludes, "The central principle of customary law is a reciprocity of benefits conferred . . . suggest[ing] that the sanction which insures compliance with the rules . . . lies in a tacit threat that if a man does not make his contribution, others may withhold theirs."[148]

Just as archaic gifting exercised certain functions now assumed by the state, it performed others that today are carried out by markets. In tribal exchange, writes Mary Douglas, Mauss had "discovered a mechanism by which individual interest combines to make a social system, without engaging in market exchange. . . . Like the market, it supplies each individual with personal incentives for collaborating in the pattern of exchanges." In this way, she concludes, "The gift cycle echoes Adam Smith's invisible hand,"[149] notwithstanding the conventional opposition of self-interest and free gift, which (following Mauss) she rejects. Nothing could be more modern, in this respect, as a means of easing tensions among interdependent but mutually fearful "tribes" – lacking a central state to establish and enforce a wider social contract among them – than the seemingly anachronistic theory of the premodern gift. And nothing could be more useful to America, in its vexed relations with allies over its "war on terrorism", than to profit from the ancient but timeless fence-mending practice of the peace offering.

Abstaining from gratuitous sadism of the Abu Ghraib variety may not qualify as a very generous gift, hence as a true display of magnanimity, given the transparent illegality and sheer pointlessness of such abuse. But according full POW rights and federal *habeas corpus* to all Guantánamo detainees would, for those actions would entail accepting a somewhat higher level of national risk. Any voluntary release of those organizational members whose previous detainees had already returned in significant numbers to the fight could nonetheless be described, in some circles, as an extravagant expenditure indeed. Yet a gift cannot be miserly if it is to elicit a non-trivial countergift. Like any conspicuous exercise of magnanimity, power-enhancing gifts generally involve "an exuberant display of abundance," Polanyi observes.[150] They resemble costly signaling in this regard. There is little danger of dissipatory excess in the relations of states within the contemporary international arena, of course. Even America's most ostentatious foreign gift, the Marshall Plan, cost the country's taxpayers less than their annual consumption of alcohol at the time.[151] No one would really have expected America to incur greater cost, and its foreign aid budget never again reached even that share (2 percent) of GDP.

Still, there are certain mental and social states, Elster observes, that "can only come about as the byproduct of actions undertaken for other ends. They can never, that is, be brought about intentionally, because the very attempt to do so precludes the state one is trying to bring about."[152] There is a fallacy in "searching for the things that recede before the hand that reaches out for them."[153] The class of "states that are essentially byproducts," includes phenomena "as diverse as sleep, class-consciousness, benevolence, magnificence, the contribution of jury participation to civic education, and self-respect." This is not to deny "the widespread tendency to erect into goals for political action effects that can only be byproducts."[154] It is only to say that such efforts are doomed to fail.

Is soft power such a beast? Must it not emanate spontaneously from features of American society cultivated entirely for other ends, features intrinsically appealing to others only so long as they are not designed to be or not intended as such? On Elster's own list of states that are "essentially byproducts" we find "benevolence" and "magnificence," after all themselves surely among the key ingredients of soft power in international relations. So too is magnanimity closely related to both. For purposes of soft power, the *appearance* of magnanimity would suffice and might be intentionally cultivated. But it is probably too difficult credibly to simulate. Seneca observed that it is crucial to securing the advantage gained by giving gifts that this advantage should appear to be entirely beside the point, beneath the giver's dignity to consider, beyond his or her consciousness. Gift giving as a social practice communicates information about one's trustworthy character.[155] If the true message is that one is self-interested, because one gives only to receive repayment of a sort, then the recipient recognizes that the donor is not very deeply committed to a relationship after all. The gift is then pointless, ineffective even as a signal of benevolence, much less of loyalty and relational commitment.

Still, in interstate relations there is no expectation of disinterestedness in the first place, as indicated. If such "gifts" as foreign aid are extrinsically motivated, and thus display no true magnanimity, this does not discount their value as currency in the exercise of influence, unlike in the realm of interpersonal relations. That America's forbearance toward terror suspects may not manifest much true virtue in others' eyes effects only a slight reputational discount. It is enough that such prestations signal a desire to reestablish more friendly relations, as well as the giver's generic benevolence.

The international community regards its demands for melioration of detainee treatment as based in law. Its members hence would not endorse any interpretation of such U.S. forbearance as reflecting true magnanimity. They would likely take offense at the very suggestion. Even if they privately acknowledged the desirability of such magnanimity from America, they would have little standing to demand it. In fact, if Western Europe were not itself the target of jihadist terror and allied in the fight against it, European statesmen would be presumptuous in insisting on this virtue from U.S. foreign policy. The expectation that another party show courtesy toward its adversary is inapt in someone not immediately party to the dispute, Montaigne observed. Whereas "you yourself can and must show [courtesy] to your enemy when you have reduced him to a sorry state and have him at great disadvantage" – the situation of the detained terror suspect, for instance – such a stance is unsuited to the "second" in a duel,[156] who should be neither "just nor courteous" in showing mercy to his opposite number "at the expense of the one to whom he had lent his support."[157]

The current conflict is not one exclusively between the United States and Al Qaeda, however. Western Europe is very much party to it, and not as America's "second." Still, each party-belligerent is entitled to make its own assessment of how it will conduct itself within the discretion afforded by law and moral principle. Both sets of norms allow greater discretion to America than generally believed, as argued in Chapters 2–7.

There is no right to gratitude or to magnanimity, in any event. They would likely take offense at the very suggestion. Personal experience offers ample opportunity to display gratitude toward someone whose gift one did not especially desire and that will not thereafter afford any particular enjoyment. But how should one respond on receiving something one has intensely sought, but not in the form of a gift?

Peace offerings have always been enveloped in ritual. As Lévi-Strauss observed of the Kwakiutl potlatch,

> The process of reciprocal gifts . . . brings about the transition from hostility to alliance, from anxiety to confidence, and from fear to friendship . . . the passing of war into peace or at least of hostility into cordiality operates through the intermediary of ritual gestures: the adversaries feel each other out, and with gestures that still retain something of the attitudes of combat, inspect the necklaces, earrings, bracelets, and feathered ornaments of one another with admiring comments.[158]

We may safely leave it to today's diplomats to work out the corresponding details, *mutatis mutandis*. But why should the world feel any duty to reciprocate in the present case? Why should the gift of humanitarianism, like that of the competitive Kwakiutl chieftain, establish any sense of indebtedness in their third-party beneficiaries – the only beneficiaries even potentially disposed here to positive reciprocity with America?

America should anticipate no expression of gratitude, of course, from Western Europe or the rest of the world for doing what they believed had been its legal duty from the beginning. A fitting response would be not gratitude, but rather enhanced comity in recognition that the world's concerns, though not shared, have been acknowledged and accommodated. Increased cordiality should ensue, in fact, precisely *because* the world recognizes that its concerns were not shared, but were accommodated nonetheless, at some perceived cost and enhanced risk. The cordiality of comity, then, is the apt disposition to display in response to such a diplomatic foray. Comity involves a weaker form of reciprocity than strict *quid pro quo* or tit-for-tat, much less the more demanding diffuse and multilateral variety. Yet neither is it entirely bilateral, for it has always been understood as a property or institutional feature of the international *system*, legal and political.[159] Still, it entails no more than a predisposition to look favorably on other parties and their actions, in some modest expectation that this posture and its underlying attitude will be reciprocated, albeit perhaps in congenial behavior on entirely different issues. Comity's reciprocity is "diffuse" in that respect, as the study of international relations, following Keohane, employs the term.

When at least 10 percent of those released from Guantánamo are soon recaptured after returning to violent militance,[160] there can be little doubt that granting them such freedom poses real risks – to the grantor/donor and its allies. That the law arguably requires America to incur these risks in no way gainsays their risky character. It is also costly for democratic leaders to incur such risks on their country's behalf, for they know that they will suffer the political consequences if these materialize. Allied statesmen will surely understand that U.S. leaders therefore perceive such melioration of treatment as costly.

Even without reciprocation from such allies, the gesture of humanitarianism sends a signal that America is a society still worthy of emulation – that with regard to the rule of law, it still practices what it preaches. And at the very least, a gift of humanitarianism signals that America still values the good will and sociability of other peoples with whom it nonetheless disagrees on key questions. In international relations, as in much else, there are decreasing levels of difficulty in moving from a prestation that can be expected to elicit a countergift, to one that signals benevolence, to one signaling only a desire for closer relations (i.e., to mend fences without protestations to disinterestedness). This is the best counsel that social thought can today provide regarding the ramifications of U.S. counterterrorism policy for the country's international relations.

The next chapter shifts the focus back to the domestic arena, examining the contribution of the American JAGs to the torture debate. That discussion draws on the sociology of professions and on recent political thinking about the perplexing place of honor within modern society.

PART FOUR

THE END OF RECIPROCITY

Martial Honor in Modern Democracy: The JAGs as a Source of National Restraint

RESTRAINT THROUGH PROFESSIONAL ETHICS

The chief influence of American military lawyers on the 2006 Military Commissions Act was to ensure that commission proceedings could not rely on evidence kept secret from defense counsel.[1] The JAGs also persuaded Secretary of Defense Donald Rumsfeld to withdraw approval for certain interrogation techniques.[2] In other respects, their views were largely rejected,[3] though they continued to resist the system of military commissions established by the Bush administration with congressional approval.[4] In particular, they had sought to show how the Geneva Conventions require Al Qaeda members to be prosecuted in the equivalent of regular courts-martial, rather than in a venue affording defendants weaker procedural protections.[5] The JAGs are empowered by statute to administer the country's courts-martial.

The controversy between the military lawyers and the White House had a longer history than reflected in the 2006 legislative debate. It began in the early 1990s when Dick Cheney, then secretary of defense in the Bush-Quayle administration, sought to curtail the JAGs' independence by subordinating the top military lawyer in each branch to a "general counsel," a civilian political appointee. When Congress rejected Cheney's proposal, he sought to implement it by way of administrative orders, but met with resistance. As vice president, Cheney renewed his efforts. At that point, retired JAGs asked the Senate Armed Services Committee to intercede. Congress responded with legislation in late 2004 preserving the civilian general counsels but forbidding them from interfering with the JAGs' duty to "give independent legal advice" directly to military leaders, both field commanders and the civilian service secretaries for each branch.

There followed a period of noncompliance by the White House, which led the Senate to pass a bill cutting off all funds for Air Force legal services, thereby forcing the administration to capitulate. Retired JAGs then sought to persuade Congress to raise the rank of the top-service JAG from a two- to three-star general, in hopes that doing so would bolster military lawyers' access to and influence within key deliberations. White House opposition to the measure prevailed, however. Assessing this troubled history, one knowledgeable observer has said, "The administration believes that the political appointees," i.e., the civilian general counsels, "will not contest what the president wants to do, whereas the uniformed lawyers . . . are going to push back."[6]

The intervention of the military lawyers in the torture debate after 9/11 was prompted not only by the peril they perceived to U.S. forces in future wars from the current mistreatment of detained Al Qaeda suspects. The JAGs also feared that the armed forces' apparent involvement in such practices would sully their image with the American public – a reputation that had been positive for nearly a generation.[7] After the My Lai massacre, regaining public trust on such matters took a very long time. This trust is essential to the popular support needed to sustain international commitments that are difficult and costly, especially where an immediate national interest is not obvious, as in humanitarian interventions.

Because of the Iraq imbroglio and especially the revelations of detainee abuse, there has been some concern among American military leaders, reflected in the JAGs' memoranda,[8] about a possible return to the "broken army" of the 1970s – seriously diminished in both the country's esteem and its own morale.[9] The danger to U.S. military esprit from revelations of involvement in detainee abuse finds prominent expression in the memos.[10] Current leaders of the officer corps all entered the profession when it was at its nadir in the public eye and are rightly proud of the role they played in its difficult but successful return to public respectability.[11]

For the JAGs, certain practices – like certain weapons systems – must be morally stigmatized and abjured, regardless of their possible utility, because their use is simply considered inconsistent with "who we are, what we've stood for,"[12] as Admiral John Hutson put it before the Senate Armed Services Committee. The frequency with which these very words are invoked by American officers[13] (and many ordinary citizens) in this context warrants reflection. In another frequent formulation, "It's not about them. It is about us," as writes Lt. Commander Charles Swift, Hamdan's JAG defender, in explaining why Al Qaeda's mistreatment of civilians should be irrelevant to how the United States treats Al Qaeda fighters.[14]

Hence, the JAGs' fervent vow that certain means of coercive interrogation, "while technically legal, are inconsistent with our most fundamental values."[15] A JAG memorandum similarly asks, rhetorically, of detainee abuse: "Is this the 'right thing' for U.S. military personnel?"[16] From what JAG insiders report, it is *this* way of thinking, more than rationalist reciprocity calculus, that really motivated their legislative intervention.[17] Officers find particularly repellent the "realist" insinuation that they restrain themselves in the use of force only from rationalist self-interest – where violence serves no instrumental purpose and secures no tangible benefit.[18] All pride themselves on distinguishing what they do from murder, and murder can sometimes be highly advantageous, after all. It is humanitarian law that draws the line between murder and legitimate killing in war, and for this reason professional soldiers have rarely been dismissive of it. Such norms help constitute their very identity as law abiding, even for officers otherwise skeptical of airy claims on them by "the international community." These are norms to which generations of professional soldiers have contributed, establishing a tradition that their successors willingly embrace, internalize – and occasionally revise. To be sure, for one's identity as law abiding to engender greater restraint in the conflict with Al Qaeda, one must believe that the relevant law requires such forbearance. The analysis in Chapters 2 and 3 suggested that this may not necessarily be the case. More relevant here, however, is the JAGs' own view of the legality of the disputed U.S. counterterrorism practices, not my opinion.

The concept of martial honor is crucial here. The present discussion refers to three features of honor that are distinct but compatible and, in fact, often mutually reinforcing. Honor is public in that it entails external recognition. Its requirements for conduct are reflected in codes of honor, enshrining a community's ideals of conduct for all members. Finally, honor is a quality of character. The last of these characteristics relates to the preceding two in that it entails "the ambitious desire to live up to one's code and to be publicly recognized for doing so."[19]

The honor of the professional soldier should be seen as a sort of "internal morality,"[20] carrying much the same meaning for professional soldiers that the rule of law carries for lawyers.[21] But humanitarian law does not, in this manner, create merely a private language in Wittgenstein's terms, intelligible only to initiates.[22] It must also serve as a conceptual boundary between the language of war and other activities, some of which it uncomfortably resembles, particularly murder. Moral theorists have the luxury of asking the larger question of whether there exists a coherent, morally defensible distinction between war and massacre, taking humanitarian law's answer to that question as merely a social convention, open to scrutiny. Humanitarian lawyers, in contrast, have the task of assuming an affirmative answer to such deeper questions and must concern themselves simply with fixing an acceptable line between the two activities, asking instead, "*At what point does war become murder, turn into atrocity?*"

Martial honor embodies the virtues that constitute good soldiering, intrinsic to the calling, rather than imposed from the environing society. Individual officers are therefore to think of their personal honor in terms of adherence to their profession's code of honor. They should respect themselves as professionals to the extent that they conform to that code's terms. In this way, self-respect is possible for any officer who understands honor's requirements in a particular situation.[23] For this reason, "self-respect cannot be an idiosyncracy; it is not a matter of will. In any substantive sense, it is a matter of membership," Walzer writes.[24]

This sense of honor has often required more of soldiers than has international law, and so they are accustomed to aspiring to standards "beyond the call of duty."[25] Sympathetic responses to the JAG memoranda by civilian lawyers deemed them "heroic."[26] Yet legal ethicist Bradley Wendel may also be right that "it says a good deal about the current operating environment for government lawyers that [their] traditional role should now be deemed supererogatory."[27] In any event, it is no coincidence that these "courageous" views issued from the pens of lawyers who were also career-long professional soldiers, voicing the views of most comrades-in-arms.[28]

From the perspective of many such officers, as reflected in their Senate testimony, Common Article 3 of the Geneva Conventions should be seen as setting a "floor" beneath which no honorable soldier would descend, but demanding less than the standard the soldier is actually trained to meet.[29] Conduct flows from character more than from conscious subscription to legal norms, on this view. And character consists of habituated dispositions, manifested not in rote rule following but in good judgment, needed especially when the rules provide inadequate answers or none at all.[30] One cultivates practical judgment in confrontation with concrete situations, real or simulated.[31] Military ethics has almost always been taught in this way,[32] rather than as the application of universal principles relevant to all, irrespective of vocation.[33]

By contrast, in intellectually "serious" moral argument (i.e., within elite universities), "one's station and its duties" has long been thoroughly disdained as butler's ethics, the moral vision of a clerk.[34] "Duty, Honor, Country" is dismissed as a meaningless mantra, incapable of offering real guidance in confronting difficult ethical choices. The notion that one may ever trust to such simple verities is, well, simplistic – even if the verity is *veritas* itself and emblazoned on one's escutcheon. "Conduct unbecoming an officer," a criminal offense in the Uniform Code of Military Justice, seems intolerably vague, hence inconsistent with established notions of due process.[35] The only nontrivial question about the notion that virtue might be "its own reward" is whether this absurdity is better characterized as a tautology or a *non sequitur*. And "habit" is disdained as a "nonstarter" in the justification of any social institution, its irrelevance a "no brainer."[36] Yet here is the recent defense offered by JAG Gen. Jack Rives for forbearance in detainee treatment:

> The use of the more extreme interrogation techniques simply is not how the U.S. armed forces have operated in recent history. We have taken the legal and moral "high road" in the conduct of our military operations regardless of how others may operate. . . . We need to consider the overall impact of . . . giving official approval and legal sanction to the application of interrogation techniques that U.S. forces have consistently been trained [to believe] are unlawful.[37]

JAGs like Gen. Rives play a major role in drafting the simulation exercises in which soldiers learn to apply humanitarian law; they view such habituated judgment as a better means of avoiding war crime than the threat of later court-martial or other prosecution.[38] In debate over the "torture memos" within the Bush administration, General Richard Myers, chairman of the Joint Chiefs of Staff, argued vehemently that the Geneva Conventions were "ingrained in U.S. military culture" and that "an American soldier's self-image is bound up with the Conventions."[39] Compliance with humanitarian law has increased as a result of the ensuing "internalization of noncombatant immunity within the U.S. military's organizational culture, especially since the Vietnam War," one independent empirical study recently concludes.[40]

For present purposes, the most apposite feature of martial honor is less its habitual than its nonconsequentialist cast: Virtue indeed becomes an end in itself. It impels conduct for the sake of its claims, rather than simply in accordance with them.[41] The satisfaction and even pride that follow from attaining high professional standards enable the virtuous practitioner to withstand temptation, where self-interest indicates a contrary course of action, as it might when interrogating a reticent Al Qaeda detainee.

It is tempting readily to "reconcile" an ethics of principle with one of virtue by viewing the latter as merely the former's internalization, the person's socialization to such principles at the level of individual psychology, so that he is motivated to act on them. On this account, virtue is simply the disposition to act on principles of morality, with the disposition or psychological trait itself doing no real, normative work. An ethics of virtue differs more profoundly from one of principle than this account suggests, however, in that – when seeking virtue – one strives not to live in conscious accordance with abstract principles applicable to all, but to model oneself on heroic archetypes of one's profession, its most stellar representatives throughout history, to the unabashed end of social esteem among valued brethren – here, comrades-in-arms.[42]

In this way, one seeks individual meaning and social distinction in one's life, as well as a place in the hearts and memory of one's peers, by honoring their distinctive and internal traditions of excellence.[43] Such standards will sometimes depart from the expectations of the market and the state, requiring a measure of autonomy from both.[44] Hence, as Simon Weil observed, "For the need of honor to be satisfied in professional life, every profession must have some association really capable of keeping alive the memory of all the . . . nobility, heroism, probity, generosity, and genius spent in the exercise of that profession."[45]

Codes of honor, including martial honor, are irreducible to any meaningful statement of general principle or rule. This remains true even while rules of international law increasingly permeate military self-understanding, as we see later in this chapter. If asked to state what general principles these codes and traditions embody, even the most virtuous practitioner is likely to be at a loss for words or to utter only the most unhelpful platitudes, the inadequacy of which she will be the first to concede. That glittering generalities of this sort occupy so small a place in the self-understanding of a field's most distinguished practitioners is telling evidence of their near irrelevance to any proper understanding of what is truly involved in the exercise of vocational virtuosity.

For military officers, in particular, it is apparently enough for them to observe that great soldiers do not practice torture, however simplistic this may sound as a philosophy of professionalism (i.e., to the more theoretically "sophisticated").[46] Torture is dishonorable. Period. This lesson is then conveyed to their subordinates in even more simple terms: "Marines don't do that!" In these very words, an officer urgently communicates that the group's code of honor does not permit an imminent atrocity.[47] Traditional concerns with collective identity also inform the aversion of many American officers to assassination, even of terrorist leaders after 9/11. "I've heard this – 'It's not American' – from the military leadership,"[48] reports a Pentagon adviser who worked for Defense Secretary Donald Rumsfeld. Adds a colonel and former member of high-level planning staffs at the Pentagon:

The civilians running the Pentagon are no longer trying to avoid the gray area.... It is not unlawful, but ethics is about what we ought to do in our position as the most powerful country in human history. Strategic deception plans, global assassinations done by the military – all will define who we are and what we want to become as a nation.[49]

On this view, their sense of honor is what keeps good soldiers out of "the gray area," from straying onto legally questionable terrain.

Aristotle emphasizes the historical specificity of the virtues, how their meaning is redefined by certain periods and social groups. MacIntyre hence observes that if there is any enduring appeal in their particular instantiations – even the virtue of martial courage, presumably – it may only be found "in retrospect," for "the heroic self does not aspire to universality." It is inspired and deeply informed by past achievements, but does not aim to articulate or advance universal standards of either excellence or ethics.

AN ECONOMICS OF VIRTUE?

The cost-benefit theory in which the Posners trade has a hard time getting its mind around any of these considerations. It can speak only vaguely, metaphorically, of how self-interest may be "thickened" by self-imposed restraints of this sort.[50] Such marginal amendments to the theory are inadequate inasmuch as the capacity to revise our understanding of self-interest in light of our moral commitments is surely essential to what makes us human.[51] The JAGs' legislative intervention should be understood in this light.

We are normally skeptical of guild-type norms and resulting policy prescriptions, a skepticism encouraged by economic analysis.[52] And the JAGs' desire to preserve the military's self-respect and public esteem reflects a professional self-interest that is not necessarily identical to the national interest. In conversations among themselves, JAGs sometimes speak in candidly guild-like terms. "Who owns the law of war?" rhetorically asks former My Lai prosecutor William Eckhardt at one such gathering. "We do: the profession of arms," he immediately answers. "It's time to take it back," he adds, alluding to the Office of Legal Counsel's temporary, recent hijacking of the field.[53]

It is true that the law of war long primarily served professional warriors themselves, subordinating the concerns and interests of others whenever they conflicted with those of the warrior class. It is also true that this subordination is today neither possible nor desirable. Why should there be any legitimate interest, for that matter, in dusting off the seemingly anachronistic notion of martial honor itself, with its musty overtones of besmirched escutcheons, tailored gauntlets, frivolous duels, damsels in distress, and such rot – today perhaps even "honor killings" of women throughout the Muslim world?[54] Military law's stakeholders and constituencies today encompass many others besides the officer corps itself. A set of rules written exclusively by soldiers, reflecting only warrior virtues, would be impossible to defend before a modern democratic public, perhaps especially one victimized by terrorist violence.

The relation of martial honor to military self-interest is complex, however. The "notion of honor," as Sharon Krause observes,

> challenges the familiar dichotomy between interest and obligation according to which interests are what we do for ourselves and obligations are what we owe to others. It recognizes that what we do for ourselves ought not be limited to our interests and that what we do for others does not exhaust our obligations.... Honor as a form of motivation cannot be reduced to self-interest, or civic virtue, or the sense of justice.... It is a motive ... grounded in a sense of personal obligation, but in an obligation to oneself.... Though there are dimensions of honor that may be construed in instrumental terms, such as the desire for the self-respect and public recognition that come from living up to one's code, these aspects of honor are inseparable from the noninstrumental, categorical sense that living up to one's code is something one *must* do.[55]

The autonomy that the top JAGs showed from their commander-in-chief was unprecedented in U.S. military history, much less by military lawyers in other nations. It was lawful, as they did not use "contemptuous words" in their criticism of the president and his policies, the test for court-martial under the Uniform Code of Military Justice.[56] And there was, in truth, little actual risk to their careers, as they were all on the verge of retirement from the military,[57] at the point of entering the private bar, where professional opinion was already skeptical of the president's views on the Geneva Conventions.[58]

JAG officers just beneath the very highest echelons did, by contrast, take some professional risks. They provided the collective stimulus prompting their superiors to act. James Walker, the intellectual leader of the Marine Corps' antitorture stance, was thereafter promoted to brigadier general and top-staff JAG for his branch of service. All the services joined forces after reaching provisional consensus on their own. The experience illustrates the pattern, confirmed by psychological studies, that people sharing an initial predisposition confirm and harden their views on meeting up and discussing the question with others already similarly disposed.[59] "It was one of those rare Pentagon events," one participant claims, "that had no hidden political agenda, no inter-service motive, no personal aggrandizement aspect."[60]

The JAGs were questioning not only the legality of U.S. interrogation practices but also their political viability, including in America's relations with Western Europe. Their intervention hence seemed to border on challenging civilian supremacy, a central constitutional principle, and thus invited some superficial comparison, at least, with Gen. Douglas MacArthur's infamous challenge to President Truman's decision-making authority in the Korean War.[61] John Yoo has even suggested, with respect to the JAGs' intercessions against torture and military commissions, that like MacArthur they "appear to share a similar attitude that civilian leaders are, at best, temporary office holders to be outmaneuvered or outlasted."[62] Inasmuch as the JAGs' views have been much influenced by conversation with military lawyers from allied countries, moreover, Yoo might view the JAGs as virtually a "fifth column," representing only a "new class" of rootless transnational elites, unaccountable to democratic publics in any country – least of all America.

CROSS-BORDER NETWORKS OF MILITARY LAWYERS

"Mil-to-mil" networks, as they are called in the trade, including links between military lawyers (from the rank of lieutenant colonel upward), are today crucial channels of communication between the U.S. armed forces and their allies. Western European military lawyers, in particular, made clear to their U.S. counterparts their reluctance to authorize the transfer of Al Qaeda suspects to the United States because of possible mistreatment here. The European lawyers also sought to block the transfer of suspects to U.S. allies, such as Egypt, where they believed still worse mistreatment was likely. Unlike the United States, its Continental allies had ratified Geneva Additional Protocol I, with standards somewhat more demanding than the 1949 versions. The Europeans and Australians also interpreted Common Article 3 more generously with respect to detainees than did the Bush administration.[63]

These critical communications were not among strangers or intermittent acquaintances with little trust in or influence over one another. The European and Australian military lawyers interact regularly with American JAGs both at annual meetings of the European Command Legal Conference and, more informally, in frequent conversations with visiting U.S. staff judge advocates. The same is true in other theater commands, especially the

Pacific. Expressions of concern about detainee abuse from military lawyers of global allies played a significant part in the decision of the leading JAGs to oppose such mistreatment in their private memoranda and later public testimony.[64] The irony here is, of course, that at the very moment in history when the U.S. government claimed to be engaged in spreading the rule of law ideal to other parts of the world, it was others who in fact held America to its longstanding, but recently neglected, legal commitments to the world community.

The broader context of such mil-to-mil lawyer conversations involved the question of whether the United States should join the new International Criminal Court. The JAGs' stated position had come to be that so doing was unnecessary, given the quality of the U.S. military justice system and its capacity to prosecute the offenses over which the ICC would also acquire jurisdiction. The European and other military lawyers rightly responded, however, that if this domestic system were so just and effective, then the United States should have nothing to fear from ratifying the Court's Rome Statute. Under the court's "complementarity" rule,[65] it has no jurisdiction where the relevant state shows itself able and willing to prosecute the offender in its national courts, including courts-martial. To refuse to ratify the new court's Rome Statute thus seemed to imply that the United States did not actually have such an impartial and effective military justice system after all; that is, one sufficiently independent of presidential and other command interference to ensure domestic prosecution of U.S. war criminals, especially politically influential ones. For the United States would fear the new court only if it knew that its domestic judicial system would prove unwilling to prosecute war-related offenses by such leaders.

The JAGs pride themselves not only as officers but also on their status as independent professionals like their peers at the bar. For a half-century, they have been cultivating and exercising that independence under the Uniform Code of Military Justice.[66] America's failure to employ its military justice system more aggressively against detainee abuse suggested that the president feared this very independence from his command influence. Military lawyers elsewhere thus inferred that, though the JAGs themselves were perfectly able to prosecute terrorists and ranking American war criminals, the president and his legal policy advisers were unwilling to let them do so.

The JAGs thus came to feel that, under either analysis, their reputation among international brethren as truly independent from executive superiors was on the line. It had become necessary, they felt, to display greater autonomy from the president by repudiating his Office of Legal Counsel's misreadings of the Geneva Conventions. The failure of several federal investigations into the Abu Ghraib abuses to produce indictments of ranking military or civilian leaders seemed to confirm the worst suspicions of the Western military lawyers whose professional respect American JAGs had come to value.

At the time, the United States seemed rather far from joining the ICC, to be sure. The officer corps itself retained deep doubts about so doing, for that matter, though they were by no means uniformly hostile to this possibility. Still, the gist of mil-to-mil conversations suggested that their professional integrity was at stake. If the American court-martial system was as independent and effective as American JAGs claimed it to be, they should demand its use, here and now, for both Al Qaeda suspects and any American military personnel responsible for war crimes in Iraq or Afghanistan. Collegial cajoling hence helped spur the JAGs to action. Also important were the persistent questions from U.S. military interrogators about the legality of coercive methods they were asked to employ. An intended audience for the JAGs' display of professional autonomy hence consisted not only of the president himself but also military legal colleagues from America's key allies.

John Yoo sees all this rather differently, of course, with causation running in the other direction. He believes that what occurred was not an effort by allied military lawyers to persuade their U.S. brethren, but rather a power play by the American JAGs, who sought out the opinion of others, such as foreign military brethren and the civilian New York City Bar Association, "because this would allow them more autonomy"[67] from the president, their executive superior.[68] The JAGs indeed sought out the Bar Association's counsel, essentially inviting a civilian legal opinion that would ethically preclude their participation in enforcing administration policy. And Yoo is correct in observing that the entire episode can be fully understood only in the political context of the JAGs' bitter opposition to their partial displacement by civilian general counsels of the various armed services, a change that Vice President Dick Cheney had introduced a decade earlier when serving as secretary of defense. As mentioned, the military lawyers had responded by pressing for legislation raising the rank of the top JAG officers, a reform that would have given them greater influence within top-level Pentagon decision making.

The failure of that effort, combined with Cheney's successful imposition of the tier of civilian superiors between top-service JAGs and the secretary of defense, created a reservoir of political resentment among the JAGs that was easily tapped when disagreement later arose over the unrelated matter of detainee torture. In Max Weber's terms,[69] the "ideal interest" of the armed service lawyers in martial honor was therefore not the only JAG interest in play. Still later, many top JAGs further resented having been outmaneuvered by Justice Department attorneys in the interagency competition for the president's ear on how to handle and prosecute detainees.[70] Yoo's contentions about the workings of political ambition within "palace wars"[71] therefore have some factual basis. Major law firms agreed to represent Guantánamo detainees *pro bono* in part through earlier contacts with JAGs.[72] The private bar approached the litigation not in terms of its implications for international humanitarian law, about which its lawyers previously knew virtually nothing. Still less did the civilian bar have any particular concern with preserving martial honor. Rather, it viewed these cases as an extension of the struggle for civil rights within American constitutional law, a struggle in which civil litigators like themselves had played a crucial role, empowering at once both racial minorities and the social stature of their profession. By framing the issues in terms of civil rights, the civilian bar helped banish the reciprocity principle from central consideration in the legal and political debate, because such rights – like international human rights – are owed by states toward their denizens, irrespective of any duties also running in the other direction.

The subtle mix of ideals and interests in the motivations of civilian counsel comes across vividly in Neal Katyal's candid and revealing account to a sympathetic readership in *The Nation*: "This is the new civil rights movement. Now it's international law, and especially international humanitarian law. This is a field of law which isn't very well developed and doesn't have a lot of senior people with expertise, so young lawyers and lawyers with little practical experience can learn the field and have a real impact."[73] The *National Law Journal* named Katyal himself as one of America's leading "40 lawyers under 40" for his representation of Salim Ahmed Hamdan before the federal courts.[74] In statements like his just quoted, it is easy to discern how moral aspiration and personal ambition are virtually coded onto the same strand of DNA, as anyone who attends an elite American law school can readily observe. One need not doubt, in other words, the sincerity of moral commitment here. There is little point in disentangling the mixed motives to measure their relative causal weight. The more interesting and important question is whether this distinctively American amalgam of ethical idealism and lawyerly self-aggrandizement will ultimately evoke the same powerful democratic backlash it did within American politics since 1980, in reaction to preceding years of federal judicial assertiveness over civil rights. After all, public opinion was much more indulgent of Bush administration counterterrorism policy than the elite bar. That divide is likely only to widen with the next terror attack on American soil. The axis of political division thus emerged with increasing clarity: On one side could be found what Garth and Dezalay describe as "a liberal fraction of the establishment," including a handful of journalists for the elite press, "and a portion of the left coming from the civil rights movement," people who had gone on to create and occupy international human rights NGOs.[75] On the other side were the Bush administration, its allies in Congress and the federal courts, and the considerable portion of the American public still favoring a "get tough" approach to treatment of terrorist suspects.

In sum, the lawyers' alliance against torture, as we may call it, emerged from two quite different quarters, each opposed – for distinct reasons – to reciprocity as the moral touchstone for fighting militant jihad. On the one hand, there are the JAGs, whose antireciprocity was rooted in martial honor; on the other, the elite private bar, whose antireciprocity rested on the legacy of civil rights, now transmuted into international human rights.

LEGAL "INTEROPERABILITY"

Joint operations with allies, in Afghanistan, Iraq, and elsewhere, require interoperability between the armed forces of different nations. Incentives to harmonize standards are therefore strong. This is the case even when such harmonization can sometimes be achieved only at a suboptimal standard (i.e., lower than that attainable by the wealthiest states in an alliance). The technological and logistical dimensions of this problem are familiar and relatively well studied by security specialists.

Legal interoperability has only recently come to the fore; it allows armies to play by the same rules – now for efficacy, rather than fairness. It has been especially important during joint "rule of law operations" aimed at establishing working courts, police forces, and prisons in "postconflict" societies.[76] In uncharacteristically pithy language, the new U.S. Counterinsurgency Field Manual thus proclaims that "coordination and synchronization is to the rule of law what fires and maneuver is to the high intensity conflict."[77] According to the new Rule of Law Handbook for JAGs, moreover, "the first in command naturally turns to the legal expert within the task force to plan . . . coordinate and evaluate rule of law efforts." For this reason, "the JAG Corps owes these lawyers at the tip of the spear" (i.e., on the front lines) "practical guidance."[78]

Legal memoranda of understanding (MOUs) are now common between the administrative agencies of Western nations, coordinating the implementation of national regulations on problems with international dimensions.[79] Their aim is "uniformity without centralization"[80] (i.e., centralization of the sort traditionally sought in multilateral treaties and international organizations for their enforcement). It would hence be natural to expect such

MOUs between national armed forces, in the interests of interoperability, regarding their understanding of ambiguous provisions within the Geneva Conventions. Disagreements between America and its allies over the scope of Geneva protections, however, have precluded such MOUs in this area.

When states differ in their interpretations of humanitarian law, these differences find their way into rules of engagement for their national forces, rules drafted by military lawyers for each country. When the armed forces of several countries must then collaborate, whether in battle or in operations other than war, legal obstacles arise. International military coordination requires some accommodation of these conflicts of law. Through NATO, this accommodation has been achieved to a great degree. One leading military law practitioner even writes that today "when the U.S. is engaged in coalition warfare with . . . allies, America is effectively bound by Additional Protocol I, despite not having ratified. . . . Prospects for U.S. ratification remain dim, but it hardly matters."[81] In fact, the most heated disagreements since 2002 have not been among Western military lawyers themselves, but between American JAGs and their civilian superiors in the Pentagon, as well as with other lawyers in the executive branch, notably the Justice Department and the Office of the Vice President.

Prevailing sentiment among American JAGs themselves is well captured in their recent Rule of Law Handbook.[82] Drafted by young U.S., British, and German military lawyers, it stresses that it is "essential for Judge Advocates to know about the philosophy, goals and structure of coalition forces," with which joint operations are now regularly conducted.[83] Prominent among such "philosophical" differences, it continues, is the fact that "while U.S. military operations are primarily motivated by national interests," America's allies sometimes also "focus on the prevention and ending of violence, the establishment of the rule of law in international relations, and support of underdeveloped countries, even independent from national interests."[84] American JAGs also "need to know that the coalition partners' understanding of rule of law activities might be very different from the U.S. understanding."[85] In particular, "European coalition partners" sometimes believe that their obligations under European human rights law apply extraterritorially, to military operations beyond the European Union itself.[86] The United States, in contrast, does not view its treaty commitments on international human rights as much applicable beyond its borders, the JAGs acknowledge.[87] Their Handbook now nonetheless emphasizes:

> Even if one were to ignore legal obligations, in post-conflict situations rule of law operations should be guided and informed by human rights law purely as a matter of efficacy. While U.S. operations are controlled, as a

matter of policy by the *lex specialis* of the law of war, the host nation may be bound by other human rights obligations. U.S. forces should model behavior for, and encourage actions by, the host nation government that will encourage the host nation to adopt and practice strong human rights norms. For example, while detention operations by U.S. forces may legally be conducted in accordance with law of war requirements, the detention procedures adopted by U.S. forces during the post-conflict phase may serve as a model for the administrative detention procedures that the host nation adopts for domestic use, and should consequently comply with international human rights norms.[88]

The Counterinsurgency Manual, which several JAGs joined in writing, similarly stresses that "in light of the need to establish legitimacy of the rule of law among the host nation's populace, conduct by U.S. forces that would be questionable under any mainstream interpretation of international human rights law is unlikely to have a place in rule of law operations."[89] That sentence is artfully worded to manifest a sensitivity to the opinions of military lawyers among Western allies, when they differ significantly from America's own. The authors add that detention and interrogation activities during counterinsurgency operations must honor the United States' international legal commitments, particularly Common Article 3 of the Geneva Conventions,[90] a position the Bush administration consistently opposed until chastened by the Supreme Court in the 2006 *Hamdan* decision. Commenting on the Manual, one legal scholar even reads it to

> acknowledge that counterinsurgency actions will be measured against applicable rules and standards found in international law, even when insurgents show no respect for any legal rules. In this sense, dismissing or marginalizing international law proves harmful to counterinsurgency efforts to compete for legitimacy and power and to convince the target population that the rule of law informs not only the ultimate objective but the way in which legitimate government will be created. . . . Counterinsurgency doctrine incorporates international law as a strategically and tactically important instrument.[91]

One could not imagine a more thorough rejection of the notion that, to counter an insurgency, one must "fight fire with fire," retaliate in kind to the enemy's legal transgressions (e.g., counter terror with torture).

To observe that the JAGs and, to a somewhat lesser extent, other American officers now identify themselves in this way as respectful of international law, even where others understand it differently, is to say that the duty to comply with such law has entered into their professional self-understanding as virtuous soldiers. At this point, the philosopher's tired contrast between an ethics of virtue and an ethics of rules and principles, though heuristically helpful, begins to break down in practice. Disputes about what international law requires in a contentious set of facts become integral to the effort to understand what martial honor demands of the profession of arms. Even questions about the proper relation of humanitarian law to human rights law must then begin to enter the penumbra, at least, of professional consciousness. This process, though well advanced within the JAGs' vocational domain, has not yet much penetrated public discourse on these issues, as we see later, for international law played only the smallest role in the senatorial deliberations – though spurred by current JAGs and former officers within that chamber – leading to passage of the Military Commissions Act of 2006.

MARTIAL HONOR AND PROFESSIONAL INDEPENDENCE

The JAGs' memoranda against torture and their 2006 Senate testimony to similar effect embody the kind of critical independence from both public opinion and executive superiors that modern social thought, since Durkheim and Tawney, has always hoped would come from the professions.[92] Such thinking long held that resistance by professionals to the corrupting influence of money and power would arise not by way of courageous, individual conscience of the sort stressed by moral philosophers. It would spring rather from the stronger, sounder "*professional* grounds that the basic value or purpose of a discipline is being perverted."[93]

In this spirit, Krause contends that professional "honor is more reliable than altruistic obligations to others and braver than self-interest. . . . The partial desire for self-respect reflects the undying self-concern at the heart of honor, which distinguishes honor from altruism, however general its codes may be."[94] It was long believed that, through their very monopoly of certain essential services, professionals could maintain a measure of disinterestedness in assessing the public good, despite contrary pressures from immediate clients and employers.[95] Tocqueville already observed this in the American lawyer-statesmen he met in the 1830s.[96] Warm professional collegiality was not at odds with intense competition and respectful criticism among peers, in light of shared standards of ethics and excellence. For such "mutual criticism is motivated by a tacit understanding of the long-term interests of the profession, not self-abnegation,"[97] Haskell observes.

In the 1960s and 70s, social critics widely feared, to the contrary, that the professions had come to exercise too much control over their respective domains – including influence by the officer corps over foreign policy. But by the 1990s the more common complaint was again that professionals possessed too little control, as in physicians' submission to intrusive over-sight from health maintenance organizations and insurance companies. Any public-interested display of professional self-assertion today is there-fore noteworthy, for the reasons that social theory historically looked to it. The JAGs' vociferousness may be contrasted here with the reticence, and perhaps pusillanimity, of the American Medical Association on the role of physicians during Guantánamo interrogations.[98]

Autonomy from the state, no less than from the marketplace, was consid-ered (by Durkheim, Tawney, and later sociologists) the crucial institutional predicate for any serious exercise of independent judgment by members of the professions. Yet surely no profession is more tightly integrated into the state and central to its core functions than the armed forces and its officer class. The robust resistance of that profession to Bush administration coun-terterrorism practices would thus appear, from a sociological perspective, all but inconceivable and unimaginable.

MARTIAL HONOR IN TERRORIST WAR: AN OXYMORON?

The charge might be levied that, in attempting to uphold traditional soldierly ideals, the JAGs seek a chance to display ancient military virtue where none exists. "For what room is there for courage or honor in the face of evasion [by terrorists of direct military combat] and the absence of any possibility of genuine reciprocity?" asks a British commentator.[99] After all, the heroes of 9/11 were not soldiers, but policemen and firefighters, often victims themselves. Their undoubted courage bore only an uncertain resemblance to traditional martial ideals.

The JAG officers' motives may not be entirely improper, however, in light of the armed forces' sincere and longstanding efforts to overcome the legacy of My Lai. As My Lai prosecutor Bill Eckhardt puts it, "We helped the military get back its profession."[100] The importance of the lawyers' contribution in this regard is a recurrent theme in the recent JAG memoranda on detainee abuse and in in-house conversation.[101] Like other professional norms and traditions, military ones can be reinterpreted in light of new circumstances and can reach beyond self-interest.

Consider in this regard the response of JAG Admiral Hutson, at Senate hearings preceding enactment of the Military Commissions Act, to Sena-tor Inhofe's question, referring to language in Geneva Conventions Com-mon Article 3: "Exactly what does 'humiliating treatment' mean? What does 'degrading treatment' mean?" Hutson's answer: "Part of the definition comes from the Army Field Manual. Part of the definition comes from

200 years of tradition."[102] And Lt. Cmdr. Swift, in publicly explaining his vigorous defense of Hamdan to the Supreme Court, similarly remarks, "I did what the tradition expected of me," referring to the JAGs who contested, before the Supreme Court, Gen. Yamashita's 1946 conviction by military commission.[103]

Martial ideals had already evolved in ways more consistent with contemporary challenges and ethical sensibilities. One may win medals in the U.S. military today, for instance, not only by risking one's life to kill enemy fighters but also by saving enemy noncombatants, as by holding fire until their protected status is finally determined.[104] Martial honor now clearly encompasses restraint in one's treatment of enemy suspects as well, the JAG memoranda suggest. By no means were these the first efforts to reimagine the concept of martial honor. If these efforts seem radical, we should recall that as early as the sixteenth century Montaigne, more ambitiously still, sought to redefine valor in combat, a principal expression of martial honor, to focus no longer on one's glory in victory but rather on bravery in enduring defeat and captivity.[105]

Though traditional notions of martial honor stood very much at odds with humanitarian and egalitarian sensibilities, American officers and their lawyers have clearly come to understand the concept quite differently today. Honor is not a virtue specific to liberal society. But it has felicitously mutated from one incompatible with this form of social order to one largely congenial to it. In this respect, its reinterpretation resembles the efforts of contemporary Western Muslims to reinterpret the Koran in light of international human rights norms that they find compelling.

New conceptions of good soldiering at least partly have replaced older ones. "Nobody now can be a Hector or a Gisli" (a medieval Icelandic warrior), Alasdair MacIntyre regretfully remarks.[106] His lamentation is shared here by some leading postmodernists who, following Foucault, see no allure in the more "docile" life of the obedient modern soldier.[107] The "heroic virtues" of the medieval warrior, to be sure, "required for their exercise the presence of a kind of social structure which is now irrevocably lost," MacIntyre adds.

Yet martial courage has come to mean something rather different to soldiers in contemporary society. It remains equally true, as it did in the Middle Ages, that "the ethic of honour sees the love and fame of immortality as the source of great deeds and exemplary courage."[108] It is simply that courageous deeds may today take novel form. A soldier might today display such courage and practical wisdom, for instance, in recognizing that a given jihadist detainee does *not* present the "ticking time bomb" scenario – and acting accordingly, despite some situational pressure to the contrary. In fact, such forbearance would be entirely consistent with his prior training. It would hence seem less heroic than habituated. Since the early 1980s, U.S. forces have been taught to treat all enemy detainees consistently with Geneva Common Article 3, regardless of enemy treatment of U.S. forces, as the JAG memoranda observe. The JAG memoranda further imply that this training built the rejection of reciprocity into American martial identity.[109]

It is a curious paradox of international relations – a perverse tribute to realism – that even when our private motives are sincerely ethical, we think it necessary to defend our public views in the colder, rationalist idiom of national self-interest. Self-proclaimed realists profess to find self-interest masquerading as disinterested humanitarianism.[110] In the JAGs' public interventions, however, we see something close to the very opposite: professional ethics and humanitarianism masquerading as a tougher, harder rationalism or "realism." For the realist's rhetoric, at least, still sets the terms. It is the dominant discourse of mainstream foreign policy debate in the United States, unlike in Western Europe.[111]

Yet one may rightly ask: What moral standing do professional soldiers have to make such assertions about what We, the American People, stand for? Our elected representatives would seem better placed to speak for us here, and such legislators – reflecting public opinion, as consistently registered by survey research – have been more deferential to President Bush's counterterrorism practices than has the country's officer corps. Given that law and morality afford such unanticipated latitude in U.S. treatment of terrorists (as Parts One and Two of this book showed), why should the public defer to officers' interest in preserving a caste virtue, albeit now dressed up in more modern idiom? The desire to project American soft power may add little real support for restraint here, moreover, insofar as few Americans are prepared to incur significant national sacrifice to advance the freedom and prosperity of other peoples, where U.S. interests are not clearly implicated. And some measure of self-sacrifice is entailed in any serious exercise of restraint toward terrorist suspects, especially their leaders.

FROM PROFESSIONAL IDEALS TO NATIONAL IDEALS

Might the prohibition on torture someday become as important to America's national identity as to the professional identity of its officers? That the national identity is indeed at stake has been noted by many. Prominent liberal journalist Peter Beinart, for instance, writes that "how the United States fights . . . the war on terror . . . will help shape the kind of country it becomes in this young century."[112] The *New York Times* editorializes, concerning Bush administration counterterrorism policy, "There are too many moments these days when we cannot recognize our country."[113] In such policy, it is now

> impossible to see the founding principles of the greatest democracy in the contempt these men and their bosses showed for the Constitution, the rule of law and human decency. . . . Out of panic and ideology, President Bush squandered America's position of moral and political leadership, swept aside international institutions and treaties, sullied America's global image, and trampled on the constitutional pillars that have supported our democracy through the most terrifying and challenging times. These policies have fed the world's anger and alienation and have not made any of us safer.[114]

If America defines its national identity in terms of certain ideas – such as ideals of humane treatment – then any measures purportedly taken in the national defense but departing from these constitutive commitments are logically foreclosed. It's as simple as that. In this spirit, Kutz contends, "By removing politics from the formal legal restraints that legitimate it," the Bush administration's detention and interrogation policies "transform necessity into a device for overriding all rights in the name of the security of a nation whose political identity has perforce been lost."[115] In grounding identity on adherence to universal principle, Kutz here invokes, one could say, a Kantian version of virtue ethics – focused on preserving the virtue of the American nation.

One need not be convinced by this casual privileging of our civic identity as liberal citizens over the more palpable material interest we share with our fellow Americans as potential victims of jihadist terror. An astringently civic conception of national identity like Kutz's is something of a legal fiction, appealing chiefly to liberal theorists and their lawyerly academic epigones. Yet a more full-bodied, "sociological" conception of national identity demands a level of communal attachment and fellow-feeling rare in our mobile society. Kutz is still helpful in implicitly identifying a telling ambiguity in the JAGs' question about "who we are." Who is the "we," exactly? Does the rest of the sentence implicitly read: Who we are "as soldiers," "as Americans," or simply "as human beings"?[116] There may be good reasons to leave the "we" studiously vague, for the notion that we stand for norms of humane treatment might mean rather different things to different people.

It might mean that we are, as Samuel Huntington puts it, "a universal nation based on values common to all humanity and in principle embracing all peoples."[117] In that case, what America stands for is in no way distinctively American, but rather embodies principles shared with many others. If this is identity politics, it is of a singularly Kantian sort. It would then be perfectly sensible that America, through its JAG leadership, should take welcome counsel from the military lawyers of our European and Australian allies, for instance, in understanding general principles of humanitarian law, regardless of the details of our particular national reservations to and non-ratifications of given treaties. For the interpretation of shared commitments is necessarily a common enterprise. There would be nothing amiss in "the growing commitment of elites," such as top American JAGs, "to cosmopolitan and transnational identities,"[118] a development that avowed nationalists like Huntington bemoan. Former Office of Legal Counsel lawyer John Yoo (and co-author) goes so far as to charge,

> Unregulated deference to the JAGs has limited some combat operations, and will continue to do so. Civilian leaders should remain aware that the growth in JAG influence can have detrimental impact on the nation's ability to win wars. Leaders have allowed a regime to arise in which the JAGs advise, within the confines of the law, the best means of achieving military objectives. American combat officers must now seek out JAGs for rulings on the incorporation of the law of armed conflict into their ongoing operations. . . . Their enthusiasm in providing advice on operational matters will be viewed by some as challenges to civilian control of the armed forces.[119]

Yoo also chastises the JAGs for going "in secret to private attorneys to urge them to bring suit on behalf of detainees held at Guantanamo Bay."[120] He recommends that they be "punished" for so doing.

Major General Charles Dunlap, an Air Force JAG, responds that military lawyers have a legal duty, under their statutory code of ethics – modeled on that in the private sector – to exercise independent professional judgment on questions within their relevant expertise.[121] Yoo's remarkable allegation that American JAGs have usurped the president's constitutional authority also expressly relies on an understanding of such authority grounded in the theory of the "unitary executive," which (in such extreme form) has been accepted by few constitutional lawyers and resisted by the Supreme Court. This theory holds that the president exercises hierarchical control over all interpretation and implementation of federal law, so that the relation between him and all other members of the executive branch is essentially one of principal to agent, as Yoo himself characterizes it.[122]

REASONS FOR HUMANE TREATMENT:
NATIONAL HONOR VS. HUMAN RIGHTS

When the armed services and their senatorial champions – John McCain, John Warner, and Lindsay Graham – demand more humane treatment standards, they are, as Roth observes, "notably uninterested in international human rights as such."[123] This is evidenced in the details of the Detainee Treatment Act they sponsored. That legislation provided only truncated processes of appeal that, unless creatively interpreted, fell well short of normal due process requirements. The Graham-Levin amendment further denied detainees the writ of *habeas corpus*, which would establish judicial supervision over conditions of detention as well as authorize injunctions and damages remedies against the government and its agents for violation of the Convention Against Torture's "cruel, inhuman and degrading treatment" prohibition. When the Supreme Court held in June 2008 that aliens detained at Guantánamo were constitutionally entitled to bring *habeas* actions in U.S. federal courts, McCain described the ruling as "one of the worst decisions in the history of the country."[124]

This seeming indifference to rights – human and constitutional – means that, far from submitting themselves to universal standards endorsed by many, when such leaders oppose torture they see themselves as instead reaffirming a national exceptionalism. "When the principle of reciprocity does not apply," McCain argued, "we must instead remember the principles by which our nation conducts its affairs. . . . Were we to abandon the principles of wartime conduct to which we have freely committed ourselves, we would lose the moral standing that has made America unique in the world."[125] In other words, such leaders argue that we are simply following our own particular traditions, irrespective of whether the world concurs, even as doing so leads us paradoxically to comply with international law – fortuitously, almost apologetically.

When Hamdan argued that it was unlawful to exclude him from his trial, his JAG counsel appealed not only to the UCMJ but also to "the American conception of fundamental fairness" embodied in the U.S. Constitution.[126] When John McCain spoke passionately in presidential debates against the U.S. use of waterboarding on terror suspects, and commanded such deference from competing candidates, no sensate, sentient listener could harbor any doubt that he sought to speak from his experience as an American combat veteran tortured by the North Vietnamese,[127] not as a servant of, or spokesperson for, international law. "We" – that is, we Americans – was equally the clear referent for Attorney General designate Michael Mukasey when testifying in confirmation hearings that torture "is not what this country is about. It is not what this country stands for. It's antithetical to everything this country stands for."[128]

Col. Morris Davis, the JAG who briefly served as chief prosecutor for the Guantánamo military commissions, ruled that evidence derived from waterboarding would be inadmissible, a decision on which he was later overruled. The reasoning for his decision is revealing in its simultaneous appeal to virtue and its repudiation of reciprocity, both by way of a single story:

> Twenty-seven years ago, in the final days of the Iran hostage crisis, the CIA's Tehran station chief, Tom Ahern, faced his principal interrogator for the last time. The interrogator said the abuse Mr. Ahern had suffered was inconsistent with his own personal values and with the values of Islam and, as if to wipe the slate clean, he offered Mr. Ahern a chance to abuse him just as he had abused the hostages. Mr. Ahern looked the interrogator in the eyes and said, "We don't do stuff like that." Today, Tom Ahern might have to say: "We don't do stuff like that very often." Or, "We generally don't do stuff like that." That is a shame. Virtues requiring caveats are not virtues.[129]

Not a word about rights, much less those of international human rights law. Much the same came from Senator and Republican presidential candidate John McCain. Consider this typical statement: "I hold no brief for the prisoners, but I do hold a brief for the reputation of the U.S. as to adhering to certain standards of treatment of people, no matter how evil or terrible they might be."[130]

All these men consistently emphasized the need for America to uphold standards of honorable conduct. They said as little as possible, however, about whether alien detainees should be regarded as rights-bearers at all. If they were to acknowlege humane treatment to be required as a matter of right, then confessing such treatment would not count as an exercise of honor and identity, national or martial. Merely respecting our legal obligations does not qualify as superogatory and so does not permit us to display our nobility. This explains the paradox that Senators McCain, Graham, and Warner continued to oppose legislation and criticize judicial decisions seeking to require martial restraint of the very sort they themselves advocated – in practice, albeit not by law. The problem here was that the high standards of detainee treatment that such officers wished to meet, but to view as beyond the call of duty, actually fell squarely within it, according to human rights advocates.[131] Here lay the crux of the disagreement, though never articulated as such.

A legislative move, as in the Detainee Treatment Act and Military Commissions Act, to restrict detainee rights (to *habeas*, in this case) is almost essential to creating the opportunity to engage in heroics, viewed as more virtuous than mere rule following. The clear implication was that we should treat others honorably because that is how we may display our virtue. For virtue is a property of our character, not of our relations with others, even if evidenced in such relations. In arguing for national self-restraint, they thus sought not to minimize the threat that America faces – as did many critics of Bush administration counterterrorism policies – but instead to suggest the need for courage in the face of it. And courage, like any "virtue presupposes difficulty and opposition, and cannot be exercised without a struggle,"[132] as Montaigne observed, parsing the Stoics. Courage is a virtue widely sought in political leadership.

The present discussion of virtue has focused on magnanimity, however, rather than courage. The circumstances suitable for the display of one are rarely apt for the other. Yet a curious feature of America's current conundrum regarding those it has detained as terror suspects is that such men, though incarcerated and therefore situated as conventional beneficiaries of magnanimity, are prospectively also often very dangerous. This means that their release from detention entails significant avoidable risk, the voluntary acceptance of which always demands some measure of courage. Here the requirements of courage and of magnanimity operate in tandem and reinforce each other. That these virtues lead to much the same conduct as if America set out to respect the human rights and dignity of such men is a mere coincidence from this perspective. It arises from the fortuitous fact that neither human rights nor virtue ethics relies on reciprocity.

In displaying magnanimity, America would not be simply extending a right to be treated honorably beyond its existing boundaries of national citizenship,[133] for what is at stake is not truly a matter of respecting anyone's rights at all. The notion of a right to be treated honorably is, in any event, itself an incongruous pairing of inconsistent moral idioms. In other words, because Al Qaeda suspects are not party to any discernible social contract with us, America's decision to treat them humanely cannot rest on any such claim of right against us. Our decision can only be a signal of beneficence or a gift of magnanimity, as shown in Chapter 11. Such gifts derive, as Nietzsche wrote, "from another economy that precedes 'legal subjects,' 'personal legal rights,' and even man,"[134] and therefore certainly any notion of human right.

Yet may Mukasey, McCain, and the other senators here speak for the rest of America? And just what sort of statement, exactly, is involved in asserting "what we are": empirical, definitional, normative, interpretive, performative, or something else? Is it merely a definitional dictate, a stipulative fiat? If so, then it carries little weight in political argument, which rightly focuses on facts concerning what the country has recently done, and may still be doing, to detained Al Qaeda suspects. The same is true if the statement is merely normative, an affirmation of the speaker's ideal for his country in ideal circumstances.

As an empirical claim, such statements as those of the JAGs or Mukasey about "who we are" are questionable for still other reasons. After 9/11, Americans were at first quite willing to endorse the use of torture against terror suspects, surveys found.[135] The U.S. practice of torture even survived its public revelation at Abu Ghraib and since – a fact particularly shocking to liberals here and abroad.[136] The moral plurality that inhabits and unsettles humanitarian law itself, as we saw in Chapter 2, equally inhabits public opinion. Hence, any factual assertion about the political morality to which "we" – the American nation – are committed is subject to similar instability and indeterminacy. There is abundant evidence in the opinion polls that many Americans, including many rank-and-file soldiers, view the country's political morality as perfectly consistent with forms of state conduct condemned by JAG champions of martial honor and corresponding notions of civic virtue. Torture did decline in frequency after 2002,[137] at least in the interrogation of ordinary Al Qaeda members, as the CIA – having no trained interrogators on staff before 9/11 – eventually "learned the art of interrogation," according to Robert Grenier, its counterterrorism chief.[138] Yet torture's public disclosure nonetheless did not prevent the reelection of a president responsible for it. For much of the world, looking at such facts, torture of terror suspects is precisely what we stand for. On what basis may one assert that these facts are irrelevant in determining "who we are"?[139]

One might alternatively take the affirmations of the JAGs, senators, and Mukasey simply as an interpretation of American character or culture. National character is a species of "social character," a concept that has not received serious elaboration since the 1950s, when it was thought (in the influential work of Erich Fromm particularly) "not to comprise the whole of an individual's personality, but only those traits he shared with others as a result of shared experiences."[140] But wooly talk of national character is no longer intellectually respectable.[141] We now recognize the complexities of intracultural plurality – of religion and national ancestry, in particular. Through periodic waves of mass immigration, the foreign-born population is today larger proportionately than at any point since the early twentieth century.[142] We now also debate the meaning of national histories and accept shifting majority views on key character-related issues.[143] Talk about national culture or character today quickly degenerates into caricature, which discourages such talk, even as careful empirical studies all but confirm some of these stereotypes.[144]

Americans may desire a national character or identity, for the greater sense of community that would presumably ensue. Yet there is considerable ambivalence about even this desire, statistically reflected in the fact that though two-thirds of native-born Americans describe their country as composed of many cultures, the same proportion say they believe that immigrants should adopt American values.[145] One may also wonder why, "in a country where it is so unclear what *is* American, do people worry so much about the threat of things 'un-American,'"[146] as historian Michael Kammen wryly remarks. One might infer that the very elusiveness of our collective identity is precisely what has sometimes led to such acute fear of seeming threats to it. But a society committed to liberalism as its public philosophy – with all this implies for self-fashioning – can possess only a "thin" conception of national identity, Kymlicka rightly contends.[147]

In statistical studies, several characteristics are often found to distinguish Americans from others. A number of these – self-reliance, autonomy, and independence[148] – are entirely consistent with a collective decision to ignore what others, including friendly nations, think of our conduct. Surveys also find that quintessentially American traits include cooperation with neighbors, communal action, trust in others, and equality.[149] All these traits should presumably induce an acute sensitivity to others' views.

Some contend that foreign policy does not so much reflect a preexisting national identity as continually construct one, performatively redefining the national self through speech and deed. We are, or can become, whatever we want to be. Large communities of any sort are necessarily "imagined." At times, especially in war, national communities define themselves in terms of their putative differences from their adversaries.[150] The most divergent of these others locate a "geography of evil,"[151] enabling an "evangelism of fear."[152] Or as another author writes, "Don't ask what a people is . . . ask how an order of fear forms a people."[153] For all nations, then, "their enemies define them. In choosing what they will reject nations determine what they signify."[154]

This line of thinking would suggest that our failure to reject torture determines how we signify ourselves to the world. Yet whatever it is that a nation rejects in one respect does not necessarily fix what it will accept in another. The relevant conceptual schema – for defining national identities, in this case – is not binary. We need not understand and conduct ourselves primarily as either torturers or terror's victims. And there is more than one pertinent issue-area to consider. If we have accepted torture, we have nonetheless – through our law and politics – rejected not only theocratically inspired terror but also myriad lesser forms of illiberal intolerance. We react to many practices this way, and we are not always perfectly consistent. Postmodern mantras about defining ourselves in terms of what we disdain or disclaim on a single, particular issue therefore ultimately tell us little about ourselves.

A preoccupation with performances of the moment, however grand the world stage, also fails to do justice to key fixed points of historical reference, in relation to which all thoughtful Americans define their country. These points begin with the Declaration of Independence and the Constitution, surely encompassing as well the Gettysburg Address and the Rev. Martin Luther King's "I Have a Dream" peroration. Though we may differ over their proper meaning, the tradition that these documents establish is not "invented,"[155] in the sense of deliberately manufactured *as* a tradition out of whole cloth, much less as one making false factual claims about the past.[156]

THE ROLE OF LAW IN DEFINING "WHAT WE STAND FOR"

There is another, closely related understanding of the "what we stand for" or "who we are" question. It is that, regardless of its frequently violent and oppressive past (with which American history is replete), a country is always free – and thus responsible for – what it chooses to make of itself in the present and future. Societies, like persons, have no predefined essence or fixed meaning. They continually redefine themselves in terms of what they seek to become, as their lives arc played out in response to the world's challenges. A society that tortures chooses to make itself cruel, by this reasoning, regardless of the ideals enshrined in its foundational legal texts penned centuries ago. This is the basis today for the widespread concern, less with the effects of torture on the tortured, than on the torturer – both individual and collective/national. Though this analytical tack has the ring of existentialism, it also sounds in virtue ethics, in its attention to how character may be chosen and confirmed through consistent conduct.[157]

A secondary but still important motif in the "who we are" debate – apart from the query of whether we are torturers – is the question of whether we are also hypocrites. The Bush administration, after all, displayed a conspicuous lack of public transparency in its handling of detention and interrogation policy for some time. For nearly three years following 9/11, it sought to keep its practices almost entirely secret.[158] Then, it was forced to admit, in the most general terms and only after some investigative reporting by the elite press, that it employed "an alternative set of procedures"[159] for interrogation of suspected Al Qaeda leaders, that it had been necessary to "take the gloves off," in Cofer Black's notorious euphemism. Information about the exact nature of these methods then began to leak out, often from lawyers representing detainees and from human rights organizations like the ICRC.

It was in this way that the public ultimately learned that harsh treatment regularly extended beyond the top ranks of known Al Qaeda leaders. Only then did a full, public, legal defense of the administration's interrogation methods become unavoidable. But presidential spokesmen employed agonizingly narrow definitions of torture, as of other key concepts in international conventions. If the methods employed had been legally defensible in the first place, many asked, why did the administration need to keep them secret for so long?[160] Any such *ex post* justification of practices long denied was certain to meet with skepticism from many quarters.

The true definition of hypocrisy is not really "the tribute vice pays to virtue."[161] It is rather "a feigning to be what one is not ... especially: the false assumption of an appearance of virtue."[162] A nation whose members do this in their common affairs lives a life of deception. That this may be accompanied by some measure of self-deception only aggravates the situation. And a nation that long feigns to employ only lawful methods of warfare, when in fact it does not, and that "renders" terror suspects to authoritarian allies for likely torture so that it may assert that it "does not engage in torture," might fairly be called a nation of hypocrites. This is not to say that doing all of this openly would necessarily have been any better, for as Žižek quips, "Well, if this is 'honesty,' I think I'll stick with hypocrisy."[163]

However, such palpable hypocrisy is not a good recipe for soft power. Whenever President Bush criticized Russia's practices in Chechnya and elsewhere, Russian President Vladimir Putin deftly invoked America's practices in its "war on terrorism." Such Russian criticism might have been readily dismissed as a pretext for what Putin would likely have done there anyway, but for the fact that the United States had sought to found its claim to global stewardship – within Russia's traditional sphere of influence, specifically – precisely on the basis of its adherence to the rule of law and respect for human rights. Putin's analogies hence found great resonance in Russian public opinion. The Bush administration's preoccupation with the impossibility of bilateral reciprocity in relation to Al Qaeda again led it to underestimate the costs of its policies vis-à-vis third parties over which it sought influence and with which a more diffuse reciprocity was necessary.

In light of all the recent American talk about national identity and character, what is one to make of the fact that, in October 2006, President Bush declared an official "National Character Counts Week," at the very moment he needed to respond to revelations of detainee abuse?[164] This could not be coincidental. His accompanying speech proclaimed, "America's strength is found in the spirit and character of our people. During National Character Counts Week, we renew our commitment to instilling values in our young people and to encouraging all Americans to remember the importance of good character."[165] The speech made no reference, of course, to the contemporaneously raging debate within the U.S. officer corps over the question of "who we are" (i.e., of the nation's moral character in light of its employment of torture). (In reaction to the president's initiative here, the reader may understandably be unsure whether to laugh or cry.)

Four years after 9/11, most Americans were expressing serious doubt about abusive treatment of the country's detainees.[166] Yet this response is still a long way from accepting collective, national responsibility for the rights violations reflected in such mistreatment. Accepting responsibility for war crimes (on a much greater scale, in fact) did eventually become central to national identity in both West Germany and – to a much lesser degree – Japan, decisively influencing their foreign policies after World War II.[167] Anecdotal though they may be, these historical episodes offer seductive hints about how national identities may be partly redefined in light of evolving international norms, giving such countries a solid stake – a self-interest, if one insists – in honoring humanitarian law. The circumstances under which such legal norms may come to influence national identity (at the level of individual self-understanding) have not been well identified[168] nor their causal mechanisms clarified.[169] Though we social scientists are loathe to admit the limits of our methods, that process is all still something of a mystery.

Critical self-assessment clearly plays a central part in this enigmatic process through which we experience shame for having failed to live up to our ideals and then reshape our collective character so that we will be disposed never to repeat our errors. Our national self-respect, like our personal, is injured when we betray identity-forming commitments.[170] We respect ourselves when we identify with what we are doing, see ourselves as realizing purposes embraced as our own, as Bernard Williams writes.[171]

Self-respect is thus a central theme in the JAG memoranda opposing detainee abuse.[172] A rational person or society aspires to self-respect. This does not involve the instrumental rationality of cost-benefit analysis, but rather "value-rationality," as Max Weber called it: the notion that "an action can be rational for a person regardless of its payoff if it expresses attitudes or principles that it would be inconsistent of him not to express . . . given the character which he is generally content to acknowledge as his own. This is what is called being true to oneself."[173] Self-respect hence differs from self-esteem, on some accounts. Writes Walzer, "Self-esteem is a matter of what Pascal called 'borrowed' qualities: we live in the opinion of others. Self-respect is a matter of our own qualities, hence of knowledge, not opinion, and of identity, not relative standing. This is the most profound meaning of Mark Antony's line: 'If I lose mine honor, I lose myself.'"[174] Though, with these words, Antony sets himself apart from others who think differently, he nonetheless invokes the concept of honor, with all it implies about the shared, social nature of the moral commitments in question.

But is it at all meaningful to speak of *national* self-respect, to extrapolate the notion of respecting oneself to the level of the nation-state? What remains constant, and what must change, to extend this concept from individual to collective? Or is it enough to say that our nation-state's conduct is relevant to our self-respect as particular persons? This would surely be the more cautious argument, for any appeal to that collectivity called the nation presents perplexities of its own, even in more homogeneous societies than the United States.

Unlike the self-respect of professional soldiers – rooted in traditions of martial honor – the self-respect of American citizens is not dependent on occupying any particular social position. As democratic citizens *simpliciter*, "we hold ourselves responsible," Walzer writes, "and we are held responsible by our fellow citizens. From this mutual holding, the possibility of self-respect and also of public honor follows."[175] He adds, however, "The experience of citizenship requires the prior acknowledgment that everyone is a citizen – a public form of simple recognition."[176] The current controversy escapes even the reach of citizenship, however, and its correlative notions of public honor. For the persons to whom the pertinent duties may be owed do not share even this collective identity, however defined.

Once we move beyond social commitments shared as citizens, in other words, to moral principles shared and owed as humans, it is unclear how – or even whether – the concept of honor is any longer relevant. For it has always been tied historically to some particular status, first occupational or socioeconomic and more recently national.[177] In this regard, Tocqueville wisely observed the transformation of honor and its social meaning in the America he visited during the 1830s:

> The prescriptions of honor will . . . always be less numerous among a people not divided into castes than among any other. If ever there come to be nations in which it is hard to discover a trace of class distinctions, honor will then be limited to a few precepts, and these precepts will draw continually closer to the moral laws accepted by humanity in general.[178]

In other words, once we regard ourselves as subject to moral laws accepted by humanity in general, the role of honor must either change beyond recognition or become increasingly anachronistic, even superfluous. Until that happens, however, the key question will not be that of what rights in international law we owe the Other as human, but the more confessedly local puzzle of what we owe one another as Americans. The duties we owe to those we have detained as terror suspects should best be understood, on this view, as an inference from the duties we owe our fellow citizens to behave honorably, consistent with our identity as a people constitutively committed to the rule of law.

This is why Senators McCain, Warner, and Graham employed the provincial idiom of national honor, rather than the universalistic rhetoric of human rights, when they criticized Bush administration policy. Their discourse here differs significantly from that of the JAG leaders, with the latter's more prominent invocation, especially in private, of military tradition and professional relations with other Western lawyers. Writing just days after 9/11, Stanley Fish captured a sentiment shared by the JAGs, senators, and apparently some postmodernists alike:

> At times like these, the nation rightly falls back on the record of aspiration and accomplishment that makes up our collective understanding of what we live for. That understanding is sufficient, and far from undermining its sufficiency, postmodern thought tells us that we have grounds enough for action and justified condemnation in the democratic ideals we embrace, without grasping for the empty rhetoric of universal absolutes to which all subscribe but which all define differently.[179]

Even utilitarians like Eric Posner agree that all talk of universal human rights is empty rhetoric,[180] though what they would put in its place differs radically from Fish. Cost-benefit analysis can readily accept the notion that people might acquire a preference against torture, though such an explanation essentially assumes what has to be explained. In conceptualizing this commitment as a mere preference, moreover, economics treats it as just another desire to be balanced against others in a utility function, one that might be overridden at any moment by competing desires because they are all commensurable.[181] Yet there remains the little difference between telling someone, "I love you," and telling her, "You are, for now, an integral parameter in my utility function."[182]

It lies beyond the economic imagination that it may simply be wrong, and that it taints an essential character of the commitment, even to put one's repudiation of torture on the same scale with more mundane, egoistic considerations. Some formal demarcation between them may nonetheless be necessary, symbolically registering the "sacred" quality of one's opposition to this practice, as Waldron put it, even if he is mistaken about torture's "distinctive" brutality.[183]

But to say that two options cannot be compared is not in itself to say anything about which of them is ultimately preferable as grounds for policy. That an option cannot be compared along the same scale with other options does not demand that we ascribe it infinite value. Without more, the "incommensurability" thesis (as philosophers call it) does not aid in making hard choices. In fact, it has no particular implications for action at all.[184] When survey researchers inform Americans and even Europeans of the costs of protection against climate change, for instance, respondents prove unwilling to pay very much at all, though in the abstract they proclaim the environment's value as infinite, overriding all competing claims.

We moderns distinguish ourselves as such on the basis of our legal repudiation of torture, Foucault observed.[185] And so our law – specifically, humanitarian law and the Convention Against Torture[186] – has found it possible to make the prohibition of torture "peremptory" (i.e., insusceptible to derogation by any claim of national emergency). *Jus cogens*/peremptory norms in international law provide "exclusionary reasons," in Raz's terms, in that they eliminate from consideration other reasons for action inconsistent with them.[187]

Still, there would be no need to make certain options utterly unthinkable if we did not know from experience that we will not merely think about them, but will likely adopt them unjustifiably – with the injustice perceptible only too late.[188] *Jus cogens* norms are thus a form of precommitment that our law employs against a cognitive limitation – the propensity to panic.[189] This proclivity we readily acknowledge in ourselves, even as we know that we cannot fully exorcise it,[190] as if it occupied a different and phylogenetically older part of the brain, one not fully under the control of higher, later-evolved portions. Montaigne and Shakespeare observed that even the greatest philosophers have trouble thinking clearly when suffering a toothache.[191] So much more so the rest of us when reasonably fearing the possibility of our imminent extinction. And as Montaigne observed, when our fear of another collides with sympathy for his plight, fear proves the stronger emotion.[192]

The next and final chapter argues that reciprocity needs to be reimagined in ways more consistent with America's aspiration to global leadership and with what social science suggests about how best to advance that end. This requires more comprehensive thinking about how to reconcile the country's national security interests with ethical concerns that the world has raised about how we have pursued the conflict with Al Qaeda.

13

Roots of Antireciprocity:
Transnational Identity and National Self-Respect

Let us begin with an incident from a very different place and time, because the contrasting reactions to it will help deepen our appreciation of the place of reciprocity in the American torture debate and in humanitarian law more generally:

> In Warsaw in the autumn of 1939, shortly after the Germans captured the city and before they had walled up the Jews in a ghetto, a couple of Nazi soldiers were seen harassing a Jewish child on the street. The child's mother ran out of the courtyard, picked up her bruised little boy, placed his cap back on his head, and said to him, "Come inside the courtyard and *za a mentsch.*" The word *mentsch* – which in German means "man" or "human being" – acquires in Yiddish the moral connotation of "what a human being ought to be." In her Polish-inflected Yiddish the mother was instructing her son to become a decent human being.[1]

Two old Jewish men observing the incident were touched and much impressed by the fact that, as Wisse writes, "the mother's instruction to her son was that rather than warn against his tormenters, she warned him not to become like them. . . . The term *mentsch* conveyed to them the essence of Jewishness . . . a commitment to human decency and mutual respect."

A lovely thought, surely, at the very least?

Wisse herself disdains any such sentimentality. For her, the story conveys, on the contrary, everything wrong with how diaspora Jews thought about political power for two millennia. Given the political circumstances at the time, "that little boy in Warsaw could not have done his mother's bidding, because becoming fully human presupposed staying alive." To that end, warning the boy to be more wary of his tormenters would have been the better counsel. Her advice – restated in a more philosophical key – should have been to act justly, but only when in circumstances of justice. The child

362

should learn, above all, to discern when such circumstances are lacking. Then he would not make the mistake of attempting rationally to dissuade his Nazi tormenters by offering them moral arguments that "no reasonable person could reject," a move sure to try their limited patience and place him in further peril.

That the woman could not see this patent fact was no mere personal failing on her part, Wisse emphasizes. Her people, the Jews, "had concentrated on their moral improvement with no political structure in place to defend Jewish civilization or the children who were expected to perpetuate it." The mother was therefore guilty of "moral solipsism," Wisse charges, a phrase "describing a reckoning that is preoccupied with its own performance to the exclusion of everyone else's." The same must be said of the Jewish people as a whole, Wisse laments; that is, until the creation of the state of Israel, with its unabashedly capacious understanding of the requirements of self-defense.

We may readily draw from these opposing responses to the Warsaw incident – by Wisse and by the elderly male observers at the time – two very different views of the place of the reciprocity principle in social life and, by implication, in international relations and the law governing it. For Wisse, the important lesson to impart to the young boy would have been that he must learn to defend himself – evasively or passively where necessary, more actively where possible. Defending oneself entails the capacity to retaliate against aggression and the readiness to display this capacity with a view to deterring hostility. The boy can only hope to honor the principle of treating others as he would have them treat himself if he is also prepared at times to show others that they will pay a stiff price for dishonoring this principle in their relations with him.

Paradoxically perhaps, in the world as we know it, the capacity to reciprocate bad for bad is sometimes a precondition for being able to reciprocate good for good. So too in international relations, Wisse implies: Aggressive states often adopt a "bully" strategy, exploiting the cooperative moves of others rather than returning the favor. Offering a cooperative gesture to such a bully (a Hitler or Saddam Hussein) in the face of his reprehensible behavior only persuades him to take further advantage of one's good nature, as international relations scholars have observed.[2]

For the old Jewish men, however, it was more important that the boy learn how, when feeling resentment or indignation toward others, to be true to himself, to the principle of respect for others, a principle central to the religious civilization in which his mother sought to raise him. He must learn above all to resist the temptation to torment his tormenters and thereby to become his enemy. He must learn more subtle means of avoiding conflict, to avoid the resort to reciprocation. Emmanuel Levinas, himself a Holocaust survivor, articulates similar sentiments. In criticizing the Christian conception of redemption as reward for earthly morality, Levinas once said, "I am responsible for the other, without waiting for reciprocity, even if it should cost me my life. Reciprocation – that is his business."[3]

To avoid unnecessary polemics, we should begin by observing that both reactions to the story, though radically different, are deeply compelling. Neither may be casually dismissed as simply mistaken.

AN ECONOMICS OF SELF-RESPECT?

There is much in human experience and even in international relations that economics, exemplified by what might be called the "rational choice of torture" school of thought (critiqued in Chapter 10), simply cannot apprehend. Conspicuously absent from economic thought, in particular, is how human beings can entirely exclude some desires from consideration, rather than merely subordinating them to others.

An extreme case of such structuring is illustrated by the apparent absence of weighing and balancing even when the costs of one's choice may be lethal. Studies of those who rescued Jews during the Holocaust, for instance, find that surprisingly few experienced any anguish or soul-searching in deciding to risk their lives, because their personal identity – often rooted in religious or political commitments – all but excluded conscious consideration of any other possibility. They scarcely felt themselves to be making any choice at all, they report, much less carefully comparing the costs and benefits of alternative paths.[4] Had they done so, they would likely have behaved differently. The structure of their reasoning was very different. When the anticipation of shame, in particular, provides an exclusionary reason for action, it does so by calling our self-respect into doubt. If there is a social dimension to this process, it consists in the fact that "people have reason to want to act in ways that can be justified to others,"[5] as Scanlon writes, because they care about what respected others think of them.

This is true generally – beyond the particular context of the preceding story, of course. Other peoples are unconvinced by America's rationales for its treatment of Al Qaeda suspects.[6] This is in part because, once humanitarian law becomes part of a larger system of international cooperation, states expect adherence to its norms, such as the prohibition on torture, arbitrary detention, and extrajudicial killing. That expectation is grounded in their citizens' belief that failing to honor these legal commitments is a way of not doing the country's fair share to preserve this larger public good.[7] This belief and attendant expectation find broader support in experimental data: "When they perceive that other individuals are voluntarily contributing to public goods, most . . . are moved by honor, generosity, and like dispositions to do the same. When, in contrast, they perceive that others are shirking or otherwise taking advantage of them, individuals are moved by resentment and pride to withhold their own contributions and even to retaliate if possible."[8]

How these empirical findings about interpersonal relations might play out in international relations – without succumbing to the fallacy of composition[9] – is an open question. If most people display some innate empathy for others, the same cannot be said of states, even though states are composed of people. Nonetheless, an undoubted appeal of reciprocity is that it holds an effective rule of law in international relations hostage neither to a crude "realism" – for which the insatiable, zero-sum lust for power severely limits cooperative possibilities – nor to an airy constructivism in which ideals are expected entirely to transform national identity, rendering material self-interest all but irrelevant. There is much evidence, moreover, that not only individuals but also institutions are highly receptive to reciprocity, particularly tit-for-tat, as a mode of interaction with others.[10]

The JAG memoranda, in opposing detainee abuse on grounds of reciprocity in future wars, are more persuasive if we understand their invocation of that concept in the manner of cultural sociology, rather than as economic tit-for-tat, strictly speaking. The memoranda voice concerns of just this sort, in fact, expressing the view that "such a policy [of detainee abuse] will open America to international criticism that the 'U.S. is a law unto itself.'"[11] This rationale for restraint is not quite the same as choosing to follow the rules conditionally because doing so is in one's long-term interests. States, like individual persons (including the persons who lead states), are sometimes moved by settled dispositions of honor and fair play, rather than merely by material inducement, to contribute to such international public goods as humanitarian law.[12] This occurs when they perceive most others also to be behaving cooperatively most of the time, in the particular issue-area or beyond.[13]

Within most states and their political elites, there exist individuals sensitive to considerations of systemic reciprocity, pressing for its greater appreciation and recognition in foreign policymaking.[14] The transnational professional networks to which they are increasingly tied bolster these inclinations. American JAGs, we have seen, discuss humanitarian law not only among themselves, but increasingly with military lawyers from many other countries. These horizontal linkages are creating a transnational culture underpinning and perhaps reinterpreting the Geneva Conventions.[15] In these professional networks now lie the social foundations of American restraint in the ongoing conflict with Al Qaeda.

In this way, domestic conceptions of martial honor and professional interest are informally leavened by social relations with America's allies, albeit in relatively formal settings. Chivalric forbearance in war relied historically on ties of dynastic aristocratic lineage across the battle lines[16] and shared conceptions of courage and honorable wartime conduct. These ties enabled the victor to respect the vanquished through gestures of magnanimity, as Ulysses S. Grant showed in accepting Robert E. Lee's surrender at Appomattox.[17] As one observer pertinently adds, however, "While the vanquished is the direct beneficiary of magnanimity, such gestures are always performed for the third parties, . . . other sovereign authorities in a world system."[18] Today, restraint relies in a curiously similar way on transnational networks of military lawyers, steeped in a humanitarian law they regard as central to their professional identity. War's gradual transformation from gentlemanly pastime to full-time profession has not reduced the dependence on moral restraint derived from cross-border, "caste" affinities.

In this sense, the "reality" that international relations realists avow – one consisting exclusively of fully autonomous, self-regarding nation-states – is one that nobody has ever really inhabited, certainly not a reality in which anyone today resides. "State practice ultimately reflects the socialization of relevant individuals,"[19] Goodman and Jinks argue, in international relations no less than domestic. These socialized individuals must overcome, to be sure, the often greater power of domestic opponents – the unsocialized, provincially "unwashed," in their view. But it is true that global socialization of this sort increasingly accords importance to international law and the public goods it provides. Through its influence on military lawyers, international human rights have begun to influence prevalent understandings of humanitarian law, particularly the Geneva Conventions.[20] The JAG memoranda opposing detainee abuse reflect their authors' acceptance of this influence in various ways.[21]

For military lawyers who are socialized in this manner, and who interact regularly with like-minded professional peers from allied states, the meaning of vice is altered along with that of vocational virtue. Economics again fails to capture any of these moral and sociological subtleties. The effect of feeling shame for free-riding off an international public good is not, as rational choice would have it, to register a cost that will then be tallied alongside others and balanced against the benefits of failing to honor abiding commitments. That simply does not accurately describe anyone's subjective experience of shame.[22] By contrast, from the rational choice perspective, shame – say, for instance, over the fact that one's country practices torture – can never entail anything more than a fear of social reproach, perhaps a brief loss of self-esteem, another cost to be avoided if possible, like any other.

To be sure, when *homo economicus* practices torture, others may become angry and disillusioned, reducing the esteem in which they hold him. This may raise his costs in relations with them, for a time, and so diminish his utility. He may even learn that "good will" creates value-added, in foreign affairs as in all human "commerce." Yet his honor and virtue have not, on this view, been besmirched in the more grievous and enduring way that professional soldiers have always understood. Such antiquated notions, like the dusty language in which they are rendered, are all but unintelligible to him.

The torturer as imagined by rational choice theory, like the national principal he serves as agent, continues into the future utterly unsullied by his past, however reprehensible, of which he need retain little memory. Constitutionally incapable of remorse,[23] he does not linger for long over lessons to be gleaned, except perhaps on how better to calculate future costs and benefits. He owes the past no debt, as its moral traditions – like the longstanding military understanding giving specific meaning to the prohibition against humiliating and degrading treatment – have no purchase on him. He glides effortlessly from one war to the next, as in Alexander Pope's poem, reveling in the "eternal sunshine of the spotless mind."[24]

Still, apart from the academic community and a few social pockets of the like-minded, deep shame over America's resort to torture and the resulting threat to national self-respect today are most firmly and widely found in the highest reaches of the active-duty officer corps. Even enlisted personnel in the field, especially those experiencing combat stress, have confessed to favoring torture for gathering life-saving information.[25] Yet when the next major attack occurs, a sense of martial honor in the country's professional soldiers, joined to abstract notions of national self-respect not deeply shared in the country at large, is unlikely to provide sufficient counterweight to conflicting popular pressures for "getting tough."

Hence the need to ground further support for such forbearance in national aspirations to soft power. Most critics of U.S. foreign policy see a country imperiled by nationalistic hubris and imperial overreach.[26] Yet it may ironically prove to be America's ambitions to global influence that most effectively induce its martial self-restraint. To most citizens, such influence is more meaningful and widely sought than is virtue in our professional warriors or adherence to pure Kantian principle in the face of genuine security threats. This conclusion will sit uneasily, however, with the many people, on both the left and right, favoring a diminished U.S. concern with international preeminence since the Cold War's end.

REIMAGINING RECIPROCITY

In understanding America's place in the world, soft power displays its true significance only as we reimagine the notion of reciprocity itself. We may here illustrate the distinction between diffuse or systemic reciprocity and its more specific cousin by showing how differently each would respond to one of Posner's claims about the inherent infirmities of humanitarian law. Posner asserts that the United States has no rational self-interest in respecting such law, in its conflict with Al Qaeda, because the latter gains much less by sparing Americans in its possession than the United States would gain by sparing Al Qaeda detainees from sustained detention and coercive interrogation. There would be no symmetry in possible benefits to both sides, in other words, from their mutual respect for the dignity of enemy fighters in their custody. True enough. On this view, reciprocity is meaningful only if it is bilateral and nearly immediate and measured only in the lives and treatment of soldiers, not others.

This analysis altogether ignores, however, likely U.S. gains from forbearance that emerge at the multilateral level over a longer term, gains that the concept of systemic reciprocity is designed to capture.[27] From this broader vantage point, the assessment of potential costs from treating enemy detainees leniently must take several factors into account. It must consider not only the admittedly slight gains from Al Qaeda, in its treatment of U.S. citizens and military personnel, but must also register anticipated benefits in relations with myriad allies in various issue-areas. Such gains resemble the economist's notion of multiplier effects. These occur when a major business decision, for instance, has manifold consequences that ripple widely throughout the environing economy, sometimes in subtle ways not perceptible to the investors themselves, much less readily measurable. These processes also resemble the sort of reciprocity that Lévi-Strauss described in situations of generalized exchange, whereby donors anticipate repayment by someone other than the party on whom they immediately confer their "gift."[28]

Invoking systemic reciprocity may initially seem far too tender-hearted and indistinct a notion for making sense of war, to say nothing of the compositional fallacy in leaping from interpersonal relations to international ones.

Yet no less a proponent and founder of rational choice theory than Thomas Schelling, in his influential analysis of military strategy, found himself curiously drawn at key points to the child psychology of Jean Piaget,[29] much as other leading thinkers in international relations have since relied on Erving Goffman's micro-sociology of face-to-face interaction.[30] As boys develop from age 7 to 11, Piaget noted from his observations of a Geneva schoolyard, they advance from an "expiatory" to a "reciprocal" notion of punishment and its purposes. The younger boys begin with the view that "one must compensate for the offense by [inflicting] proportionate suffering . . . doing to the transgressor something analogous to what he had done himself." Over the next four years, however, these boys come to the view that, in punishing another, "one must make the offender realize, by measures appropriate to the fault itself, in what way he has broken the bond of solidarity."[31]

Schelling quickly concedes, in quoting these words from Piaget, that "'bonds of solidarity' somewhat exaggerates the contractual relationship between Arabs and Israelis, or Americans and North Vietnamese!"[32] In his ensuing analysis of belligerent reprisal, Schelling nonetheless proceeds to reject the expiatory for the reciprocal view (in Piaget's sense) of this military practice. He distinguishes an intelligent reprisal from a dangerously imprudent one on precisely this basis. The "key difference between the expiatory and the reciprocal modes," he concludes, "is . . . between judging the deed and its punishment as an isolated event and viewing them as episodes of a continuing relationship, an essentially bargaining relationship."[33] Just as "the child's developing notion of social contract" eventually draws him or her to this second conception of sanction, Schelling writes, so too our maturing understanding of the relations between military antagonists – of the contractual or bargaining element within these relations – leads us to this same view of war.

Still, a "tragedy of the commons" confronts any such approach.[34] It may be in the interests of the United States, like any state, for all others to obey international law in their relations with it. Yet they will do so only if they believe the United States will do the same in its relations with them. So far, so good, inasmuch as the future shadow of such reciprocal retaliation may keep them all in line. In any particular disagreement with another state, however, it will likely be in the U.S. interest, as for any state, to "free-ride" on this mutually beneficial scheme. A state could be expected to defect from cooperation if the benefits of so doing exceed the costs, unless it considers itself bound to that scheme by way of its national identity or binds itself indirectly by way of the moral-professional identity of its military elite. If restraint is to endure during war's most trying moments, even the hardest bargaining, including that in the dynamics of belligerent reprisal, must not destroy all prospects for Schelling's "bonds of solidarity." Destroying these bonds is all too easy, given their fragility, the anarchy of the international legal system, and its frequent inability to enforce its writ even in peacetime.

If all this is true, then why would any state sign on to the global social contract in the first place (i.e., with the honest intention of respecting its legal duties even when doing so proves disadvantageous)? And so, anticipating this very defection from its contractual counterparts, why would any other state sincerely enter into such an agreement with the first or any of the rest? The third type of reciprocity here proposed necessarily runs aground on these shoals, one might suppose. It often has, in fact. There occurs a gradual slide – by a progression of micro-missteps toward macro-chaos – toward what approximates the world of international relations as we so often know it.

That is where the JAGs and other career officers come in.[35] Their professional ethics, bolstered by networks of like-minded officers in allied Western nations, has helped resist this process of ethical devolution, providing a kind of sociological brake against it. This is precisely what transpired through the memoranda and Senate testimony of leading U.S. military lawyers opposed to torture. One might go so far as to say that the very function of a professional officer corps and its lawyers at such times is precisely to hold the state they represent to its humanitarian law duties, in service of both its identity-defining ideals and its long-term interests.

But institutions very often do not fulfill their intended social purposes, or they develop and pursue different ones of their own. This fact renders unpersuasive any such explanation of these events in functionalist terms.[36] The JAGs' recent role in promoting U.S. compliance with humanitarian law norms, in the face of powerful executive counterefforts, is admittedly not one contemplated by the corps' founders.[37] The JAGs' role as advisers on legal policymaking at the highest levels is historically recent, arising only in the last generation. The lawyers' understandings of long-term U.S. strategic interests may also be mistaken. So we have argued, in fact, on the basis of the best recent social science regarding likely compliance with humanitarian law by probable future adversaries.

It is unclear whether the JAGs' intervention will prove a heartening harbinger of things to come. Certainly, no grand theory of how this could or should occur will be on offer here, in this already immodest meditation. In contrast to domestic social networks,[38] the study of cross-border professional and intergovernmental networks, especially their impact on policy formation, remains in its infancy.[39] That American self-restraint in the conflict with Al Qaeda rests so heavily on the shoulders of a relatively insular and self-perpetuating professional "caste,"[40] which defends standards originating in an aristocratic virtue ethics,[41] must give pause to any modern democrat.[42] For such is indeed a principal societal source of moderation in U.S. counterterrorism policy today.

The implications of this fact for our understanding of the proper relationship among American power, moral principle, and public deliberation are heretical, from the standpoint of democratic theory.[43] More important still is the precariousness of martial honor's influence on public policy within a commercial republic and constitutional democracy governed by principles quite distinct, even at odds with it. As Rhodes observes in reaction to the preceding analysis, it would be wrong for us to

> underestimate the importance of national identity and civic virtue for enabling specialized communities (i.e., the JAGs) to be effective in their efforts to constrain national self-assertion in the face of various [national security] threats. These communities depend upon a broader public context of civic virtue. First, they require national political communities receptive to the forms of moral and legal restraints proposed by military and legal professionals. Second, officers' traditions of martial honor will be unsustainable if the nation is not committed to complementary forms of civic virtue. (MacIntyre could imagine the community of virtue withdrawing to the cloisters to await a new St. Benedict. We have no such option.) Third, and especially in a democratic regime such as ours, the "people" act as a source of responsibility for holding military and political leaders accountable to humanitarian norms. Small groups of far-sighted and conscientious people may save a nation from its vices at crucial points. But they cannot – all by themselves – secure a nation's self-restraint with sufficient constancy to make all wars just. For this, these groups require a broader public commitment to civic virtue.[44]

This is a sobering reminder of the limits of martial virtue as a guard against passing nationalist and populist enthusiasms. Yet the reverse is also true: Democratic publics often depend for their flourishing on what might be called aristocrats of the spirit. As Sharon Krause argues,

> The democratic ideal of intrinsic dignity could not long survive without the aristocratic sense of dignity . . . that rises to defend it when necessary. . . . The intrinsic dignity of humankind sometimes must be vindicated, and for its vindication the universal ideal of intrinsic dignity relies on the presence of qualities of character that are more than merely intrinsic and not at all universal . . . for the ideal of dignity is a normative standard, not a motivation, or a quality of character, or a source of agency. Democratic euphemisms can make remarkable qualities appear to be undistinctive, but they also can make us think that undistinctive or

common qualities are the only ones available to us. Calling honor what it is . . . makes us aware of the aristocratic qualities or capacities in ourselves that have survived the rise of modern man.[45]

Military historian John Keegan writes to similar effect, with perhaps excessive confidence, that "there is no substitute for honour as a medium for enforcing decency on the battlefield, never has been and never will be."[46] More judiciously, Oxford's Adam Roberts cautions that there is reason to "question . . . whether formal legal codification is necessarily superior to notions of custom, honour, professional standards, and natural law"[47] in making for battlefield decencies in the modern era. This may continue to be the case for the foreseeable future with regard to the treatment of captives. Humanitarian lawyer Anthony Dworkin rightly concedes that "the place of honour and custom is likely to be particularly important at times when the nature of conflict is changing – as with the rise of transnational terrorism – and written law may not apply in a clear way or may seem outdated in its assumptions."[48]

There has occurred a major transmutation in the wellsprings and specific requirements of martial honor from its medieval origins in chivalric valor and early modern notions of "civilization," through the humanitarian law of the late nineteenth and early twentieth centuries, and finally into such law's incipient incorporation of human rights law in the present.[49] Yet this intellectual transformation may leave much the same conduct endorsed and reproached as centuries ago. For example, the human right not to be raped in war closely tracks the chivalric duty to respect the honor of enemy womenfolk. But the scope of honor's demands extends much further today, encompassing a wider range of noncombatants and civilian property.[50] The beneficiaries of the current human rights approach are no longer understood, moreover, as mere objects of the chivalric benevolence, but now rather as rights-bearing subjects. This is no small advancement in the rule's social and moral basis. Yet alongside rights, honor retains an indispensable place, if only as the motivating impulse to respect them. The theoretical revision just described is one in which lawyers, including military lawyers, have increasingly played and continue to play a vital part, despite the enduring allure for them – as for other officers – of extralegal modalities of martial restraint.[51]

UNPALATABLE PERMUTATIONS, INCONSIDERATE CONSIDERATIONS: TWO CHEERS FOR RESTRAINT

Those voicing noble sentiments in critique of coercive U.S. practices against Al Qaeda suspects may tacitly assume that any unfair advantage gained by that adversary's unrequited breach of humanitarian law will not really affect who prevails. They may even insist on redefining "winning" to exclude any strictly military triumph obtained by means regarded as shameful. Hence, when asked by Senator Lindsay Graham – himself a reservist Air Force JAG colonel – whether the United States "can win the war [against Al Qaeda] within common Article 3" of the Geneva Convention, JAG Admiral Hutson responds, "I don't think we can win the war *unless* we live within common Article 3."[52] Senator Graham replies, "We can and we must win the war, using our value systems, because if we change who we are to win the war, then I agree with you, Admiral Hutson, we've lost."[53]

A discussion about "who we are" is necessarily an invitation to debate the nature of a national identity, which is rarely a deep preoccupation of American politics. Those who raise the question do not wish to push aside the matter of national self-interest, of course. Rather, they believe – as constructivists of international relations tell us[54] – that a nation has few intrinsic interests apart from how such members choose to interpret them, by way of their shared perceptions, ideals, and consequent identity. President Bush himself repeatedly argued, as in his second inaugural address, for the inseparability of the country's interests and ideals in its conflict with Al Qaeda: "America's vital interests and our deepest beliefs are now one. . . . Advancing these [democratic, rule of law] ideals is the mission that created our Nation. It is the honorable achievement of our fathers. Now it is the urgent requirement of our nation's security, and the calling of our time."[55]

If constructivists are correct that national self-interest really just means how people *think* about their interests, then the door lies open, Keohane notes, to "the possibility that they may be interested in the welfare of others, both from empathy and from principle."[56] An economist might want to respond that we then simply have an "interest" in preserving our identity. But this gets matters rather backward if it is our identity and the moral ideals on which it rests that constitute such interests in the first instance.

One may deny that America faces a true war at all or concede that it would prefer to lose a war than win through morally objectionable methods, assuming that national survival is not at stake.[57] That assumption may require a defense it rarely receives in the heat of public debate, as survival is nothing to be trifled with. The prospect of violent death, and the resulting preoccupation with self-preservation, has always offered the principal appeal of "realism," in its most convincing versions.[58] Even libertarian thinkers, from Adam Smith to Robert Nozick, demand that the state – though it may do little else – must safeguard its citizens against external attack.[59] And it is not difficult to imagine, at least, a hypothetical scenario – no longer mere science fiction – in which jihadist attacks with nuclear or biological weapons ensured that no prospective gains in soft power from the most scrupulous self-restraint could legitimately outweigh attendant costs to national security. At that point, aspirations to soft power would rightly become a self-indulgent frivolity. Only honor and identity – martial and national – would then stand in the path of less inhibited policy, given the very limited restrictions actually imposed by law and morality, as shown in this book's Parts One and Two.

Those who initially seem most high-mindedly absolute in their condemnation of torture often turn out to yield to its temptations in their fine print. The British Law Lords, for instance, decried the practice as inherently "barbaric," repudiating evidence obtained from it as inadmissible before them, regardless of its reliability in the circumstances. The Law Lords nonetheless quietly drop footnotes allowing use of the resulting information for purposes of arrest and of averting future attacks.[60] An ungenerous critic might parse all this as saying simply that torture is acceptable – for certain disagreeable but necessary police purposes – as long as it is not rubbed in the good Lords' faces, at trial.[61] Their ultimate position is hardly *fiat justitia, ruat caelum* – let justice be done, though the heavens may fall.[62]

Evidence of the threat posed by a given detainee will often be inconclusive, the consequences of "turning the other cheek" unknowable. In deciding whom to detain and release, there have been false positives,[63] as well as false negatives,[64] both in nontrivial numbers. A false positive compels an innocent human being to endure long-term detention, under conditions of serious discomfort, whereas a false negative yields the release of a culpable detainee, likely to cause death or extreme suffering to innocents. As indicated, the current legal adviser to the secretary of state claims, in fact, that "ten percent of the people who we have released have gone right back to fighting again."[65] No numbers exist, of course, for released detainees who returned to the fight, but have not been recaptured, which is probably the most important number of all. Provisional findings from an ongoing study of the Guantánamo cases processed by Combatant Status Review Tribunals and Administrative Review Boards suggest that "there is an element of romantic fantasy in the belief that large numbers of . . . detainees are there by mistake." The study also finds that the evidence "cannot possibly support" *The New York Times'* recurrent insistence that the facility has held "hundreds of innocent men."[66]

In any event, the person wrongfully detained who, in response to the experience, joins a terrorist organization, must still count as a "true" positive, for purposes of policy analysis. That an injustice was earlier done to him in no way diminishes the threat he would, *ex hypothesi*, prospectively pose. A just and efficient legal system would provide him a remedy for the error from which he has indubitably suffered, especially if that error was unreasonable. Several recent proposals for U.S. law reform move thoughtfully in this direction.[67] In fact, the Convention Against Torture, to which the United States is a party, requires states to compensate those they have victimized in this way,[68] and the United States has on occasion granted compensation to those wrongfully detained as terrorist suspects.[69] Sometimes, a public policy makes possible large benefits to a majority only by imposing significant costs on a few. At such times, side-payments to those few are widely welcomed as desirable, and demanded not only by justice but also by efficiency itself. Several U.S. states are today seriously considering compensation for innocent convicts who, after years in jail, are later released on the basis of exculpatory DNA evidence.[70] In this spirit, the British government enacted legislation in June 2008 providing 3,000 pounds sterling ($5,900) per diem to terror suspects detained without charge for longer than twenty-eight days.[71]

The possibility of compensation for released terror suspects in most circumstances poses hard moral and legal questions, however, even apart from the apparent political obstacles to enacting such a proposal. David Cole, a vehement critic of administration counterterrorism policy, here asks,

> What about someone detained on a showing that amounted to probable cause of involvement in a terrorist plot, but who then turned out to have been innocent? Under any rational preventive detection scheme, we would want that person, even if ultimately innocent, to have been detained in the first place. But if that is the case, there is nothing "wrong" with his preventive detention, and he should not receive compensation. Just as a search based on probable cause is not rendered unlawful by the fact that it comes up empty, so an arrest based on probable cause does not become illegal if the arrestee ultimately turns out to be innocent . . . and American law generally denies compensation to such persons.[72]

It is also true, Cole adds, that "compensating 'innocents' will deter the detention of apparently dangerous persons who . . . probably ought to have been detained."[73] So writes this seemingly staunchest of civil libertarians.

RISK STATISTICS: FACTS AND VALUES

One need not doubt that fear of a particular detainee, as of terror risk generally, may be exaggerated – in the sense of statistical overestimation[74] – and that it will always be in the political interests of some to do so.[75] The political costs to elected leaders of exaggerating such a risk, moreover, are surely lower than those of unduly assuaging fears of risks that materialize soon thereafter. As sociologists stress, however, "anything can be treated as a risk if a party claims it has the potential to adversely affect their interests and values.... Nothing is inherently risky."[76] Or as Sunstein more plainly puts it, "Consequences do not speak for themselves; human beings have to evaluate them."[77] Yet to say that all risk, including risk of terrorism, is a social construct is not to say that "the only thing we really have to fear is fear itself,"[78] as the *New York Times* sometimes suggests.[79] Anyone who literally and sincerely believes the latter, in fact, is very much among those to be feared, to the extent that he or she aspires to have such views reflected in U.S. counterterrorism law and policy. Even so, if we are going to stoop to policy-by-platitude, there is still some sage counsel in the old French proverb: Fear is a poor adviser.[80]

Once we take to heart the constructivist point about risk evaluation, it nonetheless becomes all but impossible to claim that anyone's assessment of terrorism risk, however self-interested, is truly "exaggerated," in the sense of according it excessive policy weight. Our preferred policies follow from our larger worldviews, which are essentially normative. These views need only satisfy the empirical constraint that "ought implies can." How much higher a risk of death we should be prepared to accept in exchange for how much greater a loss of liberty is simply not an empirical question, the only kind to which "the data" could appositely speak.

Perceptions of terrorism risk vary according to cultural orientations, Kahan and colleagues show.[81] This is one of few major public issues, however, on which people with diametrically opposing orientations – individualists and solidarists, egalitarians and hierarchists – are not far apart.[82] In a highly polarized debate, one here finds notable consensus: The threat is very real, and most Americans agree that many costly measures are warranted.[83] In 2006, 80 percent of Americans ranked defending the country from terrorism as a "top priority," a higher percentage than for any other problem.[84]

Cognitive psychology suggests that we tend to exaggerate the consequences of human actions in comparison with omissions, the results of which we consistently underestimate and therefore undervalue in our decision making.[85] For instance, because the suffering caused by torture entails overt action by the torturer, its wrongfulness is more salient in our minds than the consequences of failing to employ such methods where this omission may cause deaths by terrorism. Terrorists' intended victims are, moreover, only "statistical lives"[86] in that we normally cannot identify *ex ante* any of the particular individuals whose deaths their wrongs would bring about, deaths that their coercive interrogation could *ex hypothesi* prevent. As one Kansas emergency official says, in explaining the need for local counterterrorism preparedness in his rural county, "My job is to tell you things you don't want to hear, asking you to spend money you don't have, for something you don't believe will ever happen."[87]

The terrorist who is interrogated, by contrast, is not a merely statistical life. He is readily identifiable as a flesh-and-blood human being, whose pain is therefore more palpable to us, whether directly through his poetry[88] or indirectly via his lawyers. His suffering will therefore tend to be more prominent in our deliberations than the greater suffering of his more numerous – but more abstract and imponderable – intended victims. There is little to suggest that we can somehow override this cognitive distortion by becoming aware of its subtly unconscious impact on us.

A countervailing source of cognitive distortion here, however, is the fact that people tend systematically to exaggerate the risks associated with "high-visibility" events. The 9/11 attack represents a conspicuous such instance, however low the probability that such events will soon recur.[89] Thus, each side to the contemporary debate can invoke the cognitive psychology suggesting that its opponents are exaggerating their "favored" risks and neglecting more important "underestimated" ones. Social science again fails to resolve the problem, as its undoubted insights are simply absorbed into the ongoing political argument, raising its sophistication without altering its essential terms.

The false negatives might first appear to impose higher aggregate social costs than the false positives. After all, the murder of innocent thousands must count for more, in any consequentialist ethical analysis, than the inconvenience of sustained detention experienced by a few hundred, however considerable their discomfort.[90] This analysis might be in error, however, if the number of false positives – those detained without good grounds – proves to be extremely high, as some military and FBI insiders with interrogation experience report,[91] and if the number of false negatives proves very small (and/or these persons fail to give effect to their destructive desires). The historical experience of several civil wars suggests that the number of false positives resulting specifically from "grudge informing," in particular, can be quite high.[92] This problem has likely been aggravated in Afghanistan by the substantial bounties offered Northern Alliance members for each "terrorist" handed over to U.S. forces.[93] In the conventional conflicts for which humanitarian law was designed, by contrast, the risk of detaining innocents is much less.

Because we lack the most relevant numbers on such questions,[94] however, the upshot for legal policy remains unclear. Any confidently proffered answer, pro or con, to the preceding questions is therefore clearly wrong in one respect: its self-assurance, examples of which are easy to multiply.[95] Policy emphasis on reducing the number of false positives, as through greater judicial protection for detainees (in federal courts or courts-martial, instead of military commissions, for instance), is likely to increase the number of false negatives. And vice versa. There is no certain, *a priori* way to know which type of error will prove the greater. What *can* be said with certainty here is that notions of reciprocity – whether as tit-for-tat or as fair fight – are not particularly helpful in answering the question of what should be done. This study has shown the need to look elsewhere.

Scientific evidence confirming or disconfirming the efficacy of particular interrogation methods does not exist.[96] In fact, it is impossible to obtain.[97] Interrogators themselves regularly report that the credible threat of torture appears at least as effective as the practice itself, and generally more so. But how to give such threat credibility without its periodic practice is anyone's guess. Ideally, there would exist a method for creating the false impression in an enemy's mind of one's willingness to reciprocate its unscrupulous methods, much as that species of butterfly has evolved so that its wings mimic an owl's eyes, continually threatening an attack that augurs only in the feeble mind of a predator. The owl butterfly defends itself by effectively mimicking its predator's predator. America, in threatening illicit methods it was unprepared to employ, would – in theory – decline to mimic its foe's inhumane methods while effectively mimicking a mimicry of them. Under the surveillant gaze of a watchful press and democratic public, however, such dissimulation is impossible in a rule of law regime. How then to obtain the benefits of the signal without incurring the considerable cost – diplomatic and moral – of the substance?

In any event, most experienced interrogators, in explaining "what works," stress their skills at subterfuge,[98] flattery, ingratiation (bordering on seduction), inducing dependency, positive incentivizing, and good-cop/bad-cop cunning, rather than their capacity to instill fear, much less inflict pain.[99] The question is whether adding the last (or last two) of these methods much compromises the efficacy of the preceding ones. No one knows.

Critics of the Bush administration (including one of its former, high-ranking officials) demand hard proof for the efficacy of coercive interrogation.[100] Yet there is no way to prove that information obtained by coercion could not have been obtained eventually by other means.[101] If we were to require that every public policy enjoy unimpeachable scientific support before adopting it, there would be little such policy. Even when there exists good science on a policy question, such findings are rarely the principal basis of legislative action, in any event. Nor should they be, as the leap from "is" to "ought" is always fraught with intervening consider-ations, often entirely legitimate. The appeal to science here, so seemingly high-minded, is thus a red herring.

As Aristotle argued, it is wrong to demand a higher level of exactitude in the analysis of a political question than it properly affords[102]; demanding too much exactitude is no better than expecting too little of this undoubted virtue. To learn which methods of questioning might most effectively elicit confession of sinful secrets from the reticent, one might do better to avoid social science entirely and return instead to the much older humanistic and pastoral literature on this subject since the Hellenistic period,[103] later much elaborated within Christianity. The focus of this literature was always on the frame of mind one must achieve, what sort of person one must become, to hear the truth[104] and appreciatively apprehend it, more than on techniques for its extraction. Listening carefully, in an almost "ethnographic" mode, is sometimes the best military approach as well, leading strategists contend.[105]

How certain should political leaders be before authorizing great coer-cion against potential innocents? "A morally strong leader," Walzer recently argues, "is someone who understands why it is wrong to kill the innocent," as through collateral damage, "and refuses to do so, refuses again and again, until the heavens are about to fall. And then he becomes a moral criminal (like Albert Camus' 'just assassin') who knows that he can't do what he has to do – and finally does." Walzer adds that this stance "conforms to the professional ethic of the soldier as this has evolved over time."[106]

Put aside Walzer's existential pathos, the overwrought *sturm und drang*. The primary weakness of his response to the dilemma is his seeming assump-tion that it is often possible to identify with great clarity, *ex ante*, the point at which it becomes genuinely necessary to dirty one's hands. The "fog of war," as Clausewitz described it, can grow very dense indeed, in this as in so many other respects. "Many intelligence reports in war are contradictory," he wrote, "even more are false, and most are uncertain."[107] Also problem-atic, and closely related, is Walzer's failure to address the possibility that, in a democracy, elected leaders should resolve reasonable doubts about whether that point has been reached in favor of protecting those they represent and whose most fundamental interests they have a constitutional duty to ensure.

PLACING TOO MUCH BURDEN ON BURDENS OF PROOF

The central question for counterterrorism policy in this area might seem a rather microscopic, lawyerly one: Which side should bear the burden of proof on the likely consequences of adhering to humanitarian norms? Torture's defenders rightly proclaim that "there is no relevant evidence that torture cannot work in the circumstances" at hand, as write two Australian law professors.[108] Torture's critics would rightly retort that "it is hardly clear that 'enhanced' interrogation methods are efficacious."[109] Neither side seeks to explain why the burden of proof should lie with the other. The burden should probably lie with anyone favoring the use of methods at odds with basic *jus cogens* norms,[110] adherence to which the rest of the world demands, a world whose good will is essential to American aspirations to soft power in global leadership.[111]

Yet how high to set that evidentiary burden remains unclear, vexingly so. As one military law scholar writes, "To demand perfect evidence of future attacks and their source would be to render victims defenseless."[112] In political argument, no one defends a position chiefly on mere burden of proof grounds, for that matter, unless one recognizes that one's position on the merits is weaker still. This is what leads to such statements as that of former White House spokesman Ari Fleischer: "I think the burden is on those people who think [Saddam Hussein] didn't have weapons of mass destruction to tell the world where they are."[113]

Public discussion of these issues must strive for a higher level. Oral presentations of the present work disclose the current weakness of such deliberation. Often a questioner who publicly proclaims opposition to coercive methods, even the targeted killing of undisputed Al Qaeda leaders, later in private conversation casually acknowledges that such techniques must likely "work" with some regularity; otherwise, they would not be so regularly employed by police departments throughout the world and by even the most modern, professional militaries when resisting armed insurgencies. Such conversational interactions have never moved in the other direction, with the questioner publicly offering extenuating rationales for torture while privately condemning it without equivocation.

It cannot be coincidental that the chronological course of such "preference falsification,"[114] as economists call it, is always one-way. At the very least, such falsification (or simplification, more precisely) suggests that the present terms of public debate, at least in universities and elite media, do not accurately capture the true distribution of private belief.[115] The sociology of "undiscussability" is more complex, however, than any simple notion of political correctness can fully capture.[116] Still, what we generally praise as "tact is but a 'soft' version of taboo."[117] Taboos are not necessarily pernicious, even in liberal societies that pride themselves on their undistorted public communication. Perhaps, the taboo against torture itself is reinforced by the taboo against debating its propriety – one from which in recent years we have all been ambivalently "liberated."

As an ethical matter, it is even difficult for an author to discuss and dissect this change in the respectable parameters of public discourse without also appearing to exploit it; in fact, without *necessarily* exploiting it. Yet it must also be said that it is easier to feign ignorance of discomforting truths and possible truths when no one turns a public spotlight on them, in the knowledge that one will never be forgiven for having forced others to open their eyes to unpleasant possibilities. Intellectuals pride themselves on publicly exposing conspiracies of silence. This is one, however, that no one may take any joy in transgressing.

Bernard Williams was surely correct when he said that, although it is wrong to believe that the material consequences of our actions count for everything, morally speaking, it is no less preposterous to hold that they count for nothing.[118] And no one has yet devised a coherent, convincing account of when consequences should matter and when they should not. Even most deontological defenses of the rule against torture stop short of absolutism.[119] We engage in some form of cost-benefit analysis in most if not all our decision making, at least semi-consciously,[120] differing only in our respective payoff matrices. This is certainly true when we think about how best to prevent terrorist atrocities. These are events that – in terms of Learned Hand's formula – entail catastrophic consequences on a colossal scale, however small the odds of their occurrence at any particular moment or of being directly occasioned by any given Al Qaeda detainee.[121]

Yet there are at least two problems with Hand's approach when applied to preventing jihadist terror. First, if the magnitude of possible harm is high enough, as in the destruction of major U.S. cities, then the probability of its occurrence might be correspondingly low – even extremely low – and still warrant very costly precautions, as Sunstein acknowledges.[122] Learned Hand's influential formula, which Sunstein invokes, provides little effective guidance when one factor in the equation so tremendously overpowers another introduced partly to counter it.[123] This is what leads Vice President Cheney to conclude, "With a low-probability, high-impact event like this . . . if there's a one percent chance that Pakistani scientists are helping Al Qaeda build or develop a nuclear weapon, we have to treat it as a certainty in terms of our response."[124] According to the "precautionary principle," novel risks of catastrophic or irreversible harm need not be absolutely certain to warrant very serious prevention measures. Yet as two scholarly defenders of Bush counterterrorism policy concede, "We still have no idea . . . whether the probability of another 9/11, or worse, is one in ten or one in ten million."[125] A counterterrorism policy that made no effort to distinguish between these two numbers and the situations to which they pertained would be preposterous.

Perhaps the precautionary principle nonetheless offers some guidance here. This is the notion that we should introduce nothing new until its risks have been carefully and fully ascertained. The "something new" could here entail a modest departure from standard conceptions of dignified treatment within humanitarian law, particularly the targeted killing of Al Qaeda leaders and in interpreting Common Article 3 of the Geneva Conventions. As in other areas of law where the precautionary principle has been entertained, however, there often turn out to exist other risks, equally grave, associated with preserving the status quo.[126] In the present context, that would mean treating Al Qaeda detainees as if they were the reluctant World War II conscripts (or homesick World War I "doughboys") that the Geneva drafters chiefly contemplated.

Thus, the precautionary principle is credibly invoked on both sides of the torture debate for it simply tells us: Accept no incalculable novel risk where vital interests are at stake. It does not tell us whether the more relevant new risk, against which such precautions must be taken, is that to national security or that to civil liberty. Such limits to the precautionary principle therefore inexorably lead us back to the morality of consequentialism and its more earthy corollary – cost-benefit analysis – in some form.

As this analysis also suggests, the precautionary principle has no natural political affinity for left or right. Though it tilts left in the environmental context, where it first developed and still receives most attention, it readily veers right, as Jonathan Simon observes, in regard to the risk of crime, where it may be invoked to "demand . . . the state to incarcerate low level criminals who might pose a danger and permanently incapacitate those who committed more serious crimes."[127] Richard Tuck similarly suggests that risk aversion – of the sort encouraged by the precautionary principle – favors restricting liberty whenever so doing will likely reduce terrorist risk. He notes that "a rights theorist might want to minimize risk" (i.e., of destruction through terrorism), "whereas a Utilitarian is prepared to gamble." Regarding jury trials of terror suspects in Northern Ireland, for instance, "a Utilitarian may be willing to risk his own death at the hands of the unconvicted terrorist in return for the wider benefits to himself of the jury system;

the rights theorist will not want to take such a risk,"[128] and will consequently agree to suspend the right to jury trial for such suspects.

Surely pertinent to the present analysis is the fact that, echoing the president himself,[129] former CIA director George Tenet claims that, when employed against "a handful of the worst terrorists," the "most aggressive interrogation techniques" have yielded information that "helped disrupt plots aimed at locations in the United States, the United Kingdom, the Middle East, and Central Asia."[130] These techniques proved, he claims, "worth more than [what] the FBI, the Central Intelligence Agency and the National Security Agency put together have been able to tell us."[131] If this sentence were true, every other one written on the entire subject would be dross.[132] A few other knowledgeable sources have endorsed Tenet's view of intelligence gains.[133] But other sources suggest that informants planted by intelligence agencies within terrorist groups have been more important to date in uncovering most plots in progress than coercive interrogation.[134] However, the cultivation of such informants is impeded by their reasonable belief that those about whom they report their suspicions may be indefinitely detained and tortured.

As Bush administration critic David Cole admits, "There are often difficult trade-offs to be made between liberty and security." He continues, however, that "it does not follow that sacrificing liberties will always, or even generally, promote security."[135] But such language – especially the "always" – raises the bar too high. At the very least, there is surely a rational relationship, in the language of constitutional law, between many recent measures for security enhancement and the freedom from terror attack that Americans demand from their government. Whether the legal test should be more demanding than this is the real question, given the fundamental liberties on the other side of the ledger.[136]

If we apply the Hand formula, the consequences of coercively interrogating even a few hundred detainees would likely be completely drowned out by the repercussions of even a single, additional attack on the scale of 9/11, much less several. This would be especially true if such an attack employed weapons of mass destruction within any major American city. Nonetheless, as one leading security analyst reminds us, "A threat consists of capabilities multiplied by intentions; if either one is zero, the threat is zero."[137] If the threat today is much greater than zero, this is because real capabilities now combine with undoubted intentions.

An honest application of economic methods would require due attention not only to costs and benefits registered by the United States – the focus in the present volume – but also to those of all others concerned.[138]

For the moral theory behind cost-benefit analysis is utilitarianism, which counts equally the happiness and unhappiness of all affected, regardless of nationality.[139] In war, each side normally attaches *negative* value to the other side's utilities, however, including those of the other side's civilians.[140] This may simply be to say that the effort to restrain unnecessary suffering in war will find cold comfort in cost-benefit analysis, if that method is applied in a manner consistent with its own professed presuppositions. As a moral philosophy, utilitarianism is highly cosmopolitan and egalitarian. For that reason alone, it is worthwhile to engage avowedly utilitarian realists in sympathetic dialogue, to hold them to their own professed premises. This book has therefore declined to reject such premises entirely as incoherent, even as it has pointed out their limitations and occasional inconsistencies.[141] Neither has it demonized their defenders as morally obtuse, in the way many others have done.[142] It has shown, in fact, how their own preoccupation with national self-interest points to conclusions they have not yet accepted but could be anticipated to acknowledge, on suitable evidence.

TOWARD A NEW RECIPROCITY: HUMANITARIAN LAW WITHIN AN EMERGENT GLOBAL CONTRACT

In any social contract, parties accept a duty to obey the law "as fair recompense for benefits conferred . . . by others' sacrifices in obeying the law themselves."[143] This is the type of reciprocity that the present study has described as Kantian, though many other major liberal theorists have employed some version of it. If there exists anything resembling such a social contract in international relations, it is incipient at best, covering only discrete issue-areas. Moreover, finding a universally acceptable balance of benefit and burden is even more difficult in the global context than in the domestic, where it was first encountered.

How much in sovereignty costs should the United States give up in exchange for how much "rule of law" benefit from such international institutions as the law of war? Robert Keohane offers an answer that borders dangerously on the stipulative and definitional:

> Each observable material flow *is assumed to have* an intangible counterpart. . . . The U.S. sent material goods to Europe . . . in return, the U.S. gained influence. . . . [If] reciprocity is the underlying principle of a self-help system, when we observe a flow of resources in one direction, there must be a reciprocal flow in the other.[144]

Diffuse reciprocity may nonetheless also become *so* diffuse that it ceases to be identifiable as reciprocity at all. As an empirical assertion, it is no longer susceptible to disconfirmation, a common test of scientific validity. Only through such seeming tautologies as Keohane's can the claim – that interactions adhere to an agreed balance of benefits for burdens – be saved from the charge that it is not a factual claim at all, but merely a normative ideal, if not simply an ideological mystification. States sometimes make precisely this latter claim: that exchange is not truly reciprocal because the terms of trade are unfairly skewed, in application at least if not on the books. In the mid-1980s, for instance, Japan's pervasive evasion of its general "free trade" duties under GATT led its major trading partners to demand a more "specific" variety of reciprocity, by which their national markets would be opened to Japanese goods only in explicit exchange for an agreed percentage of the Japanese domestic market in particular products.[145] Even such short-term retreats from diffuse reciprocity limit the scope and prospects of interstate agreements and emergent global contract they may represent.

By joining civil society, one gives up certain natural rights to receive the security that the law bestows on all members, including security in the exercise of one's rights. To justify disobedience at that point, the imbalance between burdens and benefits must be greater than to warrant departure from a private agreement, reflecting a more specific reciprocity. The legal rules on release from bilateral contracts are therefore much more lenient than those on excuse from more general obligations of criminal law, of which humanitarian law is now largely a part. Withdrawal from the social contract is a retreat to the state of nature, with all this implies not only for increased rights to self-help but also for diminished rights to social protection and other public goods. In Locke's state of nature, for instance, every individual may enforce her natural rights as she understands them.[146]

The terms of a social contract are often somewhat unclear, and always so at the margins, especially insofar as they are not fully codified by law. These terms occasionally become subject to public discussion and open controversy. Veterans returning from Iraq, for instance, regularly comment at the "disconnect" between their personal experiences of self-sacrifice for their country and the seemingly unaffected leisure, comfort, even self-indulgence of their fellow citizens. The implication is that the social contract, in compliance with which these veterans have served abroad, has somehow been breached by the failure of their fellow Americans to incur concomitant burdens, such as greater taxation and diminished consumption.

Whether international society now actually offers threatened states very much collective security, as a well-ordered domestic society provides the individual, is doubtful. If there exists a global social contract of any sort, it consists at the very least in the sum of all successful treaties, plus truly accepted custom. These agreements are not equivalent – in their scope and depth – to the domestic equivalent (i.e., the state, its courts, and police). They do not add up even to an agreement someday to form a state. Still, on the global plane we have not the abstract, hypothetical social contract of the Enlightenment philosophers, but rather a very concrete set of agreements with very particular rights and duties, covering an admittedly limited set of issues.[147]

The contract is "social" in that it is multilateral and its constituent agreements aspire to widespread adoption. It is a contract to manage certain issues collectively, rather than unilaterally, in accordance with specified terms. The scope of the contract will likely enlarge over time in a piecemeal way, as interdependence increasingly creates "circumstances of justice" in new issue-areas.[148] The ideal of voluntary agreement among parties whose altruism is limited remains essential here – and not only for professed "realists." This is a confessedly modest vision of international law's future, if it may be described as a vision at all.

Even so, it is open to question whether the sort of duty to international society described in this chapter and the preceding one may any longer be usefully characterized in terms of reciprocity at all. Perhaps not, if America's forbearance against unnecessary detentions and coercive mistreatment relies less on any sort of recognizable *quid pro quo* than on the antireciprocal ethics and national identity of its officer corps. Virtue ethics of the sort professional soldiers have historically endorsed are intrinsically antireciprocal. For they govern action on the basis of how it reflects on the actor's character, on what kind of person (or country) one is, irrespective of others' views or responses. If virtue is indeed its own reward, then it does not condition conduct on the conferral of rewards by others. It here resembles the Kantian conception of ethics, merely substituting one's practical, human identity as a rational being for the role-identity of a soldier.[149] But there likely are certain qualities of mind and heart generic to virtuosity in any field. Even utilitarians like J. S. Mill manage to find a place for virtue in their accounts of justice, insofar as anyone committed to a given virtue will find some happiness in exercising it.[150]

Just as market society depends on certain antimarket dispositions of character in consumers,[151] so too diffuse reciprocity in international society may depend on traits of national identity and dispositions of professional character best understood as nonreciprocal. A Puritan conception of "calling" was apparently necessary to foster the sustained self-denial that made possible capital accumulation – and its resulting material riches – on a nationwide scale.[152] So too, modern humanitarianism has recently been carried forward by a vocation whose members now understand their calling as harnessed to self-interest, personal or national, in only the most uncertain way. For now, at least, this curiously incongruous set of features is primarily what makes possible such self-restraint as America has exercised in its conflict with Al Qaeda.

For the future, the proper path might lie in a principled antireciprocity based on universal human rights alone. It is questionable, however, whether human rights doctrine will someday successfully "re-enchant" the world for secularists, skeptical of all transcendent creeds, inducing us all to worship at the shrine of Durkheim's "cult of the individual," while it overpowers more overtly religious forms of enchantment in the bargain. Better to preserve a more earthly option. This would lie in a far-sighted form of reciprocity: the expectation of mutual benefit from a more effective international law that permits collective action to provide public goods on an ever wider set of issues. Humanitarianism in war would then no longer rest on social roots in the antireciprocal ethos of a martial caste, concealing the force of this ethos behind unconvincing talk about risks of retaliation in future wars. America can better advance its claims to global stewardship by sponsoring systemic reciprocity of this latter sort than by indulging more specific forms of reciprocity, whether tit-for-tat or fighting fairly by morally abominable rules.

TORTURE AND SUSTAINED DETENTION VS. TARGETED KILLING: LAW LAGS BEHIND MORALITY

Extrajudicial killing stands on no firmer legal grounds than torture or detention without charges. Yet morally speaking, it is a world apart. It withstands the two major criticisms this book makes of these other practices. The targeted killing of terrorist leaders presents little obstacle to maintaining American soft power, because most of the world appears to accept the legitimacy of this practice, unlike torture and sustained detention. For many people, the latter two practices are illegitimate, entirely apart from the simple fact of their international illegality, because the culpability of most of the people subject to these practices has often been unclear. There have been at least a few, well-established instances of false positives, innocents who have been wronged by, and suffered greatly from, these twin policies.

There are also legitimate doubts about the culpability of the significant number of youths among those mistreated and detained for long periods. Many are very young men who must have been recent recruits and are therefore unlikely to possess valuable intelligence. Some may also fairly be described as having simply "fallen in with the wrong crowd." In this respect, they can no more be considered as confirmed, jihadist militants than the seventeen-year-old Bavarian conscripts, indoctrinated from early adolescence by compulsory participation in Hitler Youth, could be fairly called, without qualification, "Nazis." Mistreating those whose culpability is thus ambiguous is not only incompatible with preserving America's positive global image as worthy of emulation. It is also inconsistent with the self-understanding of the country's officer class, its sense of martial honor, which bars the intentional harming of innocents. Such mistreatment should be forsworn for these reasons alone, this book has shown, more than for reasons of law or morality.

Terrorist leaders differ here in all relevant respects from many of their youthful underlings. There is no question about the culpability of such leaders, because they publicly profess it. They expressly proclaim their most reprehensible intentions and celebrate their most sanguinary accomplishments. The chief moral objection to reprisals – that by use of collective responsibility, they punish the innocent – is inapposite when the culpability of those suffering reprisal is clear. The most compelling argument against reprisals has been that, historically, they have almost invariably punished A for B's misconduct. Reprisals against terrorist leaders, by contrast, punish B for B's own mischief. Whatever minor doctrinal extensions are necessary to accommodate this patent moral reality are surely warranted.

Extrajudicial killing of terrorist leaders is consistent with American soft power, because the world has little doubt about their responsibility for mass murder and their active planning for more to come. Targeting them is also congruent with the conception of martial virtue increasingly upheld by the American officer corps, notwithstanding its traditional view of such methods as dishonorable.[153] This is because terrorist leaders, in openly "declaring war" on the United States, willingly assume a prominent spotlight that is the moral equivalent of dressing in military uniform, setting themselves apart from innocent civilians and from less culpable supporters in this way.[154] When leaders announce their violent intentions, they voluntarily identify themselves as belligerents, thereby placing themselves at risk of being killed. If these leaders nonetheless hide from attack in remote mountainous caves, still they affirm a conspicuous public role through their videotaped proclamations and *pronunciamentos*. That they have not been found guilty in a court of law is due largely to their own evasive maneuvers for escaping justice. The evidentiary standards for moral and military judgment are quite different, in any event, from those of criminal prosecution.[155]

For all these reasons, attacks on terrorist leaders, though still amounting to extrajudicial killing – a crime against humanity, at least presumptively – are readily distinguishable in moral terms from the torture and long-term detention without charges of their lowly followers. To be sure, humanitarian law has not yet caught up to this moral reality. The law has not yet discovered, in other words, a way of properly conceptualizing it. This is a failure of international law and its practitioners, however, not of U.S. counterterrorism policy.

Conclusion

There are certain questions in political life for which the right answers are so clear, Bernard Williams once remarked that one would have to wonder about the moral character of anyone who found it necessary to pose them in the first place, to raise them even to the level of consciousness. The impermissibility of torture, extrajudicial killing, and sustained detention without trial was long comfortably considered such a question. Elaine Scarry could hence confidently pronounce in 1985, "An intelligent argument on behalf of torture" (i.e., worthy of careful refutation) "is a conceptual impossibility."[1]

Torture, in particular, has been an essentially *un*contested concept within Western legal and political discourse for some centuries.[2] There was near universal consensus that it is never justified or excused and that it would soon disappear entirely.[3] If it was ever excused on grounds of necessity, its practice would be confined to the colonies and concealed. Today, by contrast, torture is very much contested, both its definition and its permissibility, largely as a result of U.S. policies in the conflict with Al Qaeda and kindred groups.[4] According to Amnesty International and other reliable human rights organizations, there are more than one hundred countries in which the state regularly practices torture.[5] But in essentially none of them is its defensibility publicly debated, much less endorsed. There are several countries, mostly in northwestern Europe, where torture is neither practiced nor debated as a conceivable policy option. And there are, unsurprisingly, no countries where it is seriously debated but not practiced. What is distinctive about America today is that it is the only place where torture is practiced while being publicly debated – and even semi-officially endorsed.[6]

Some may still believe, with Slavoj Žižek, that "those who refuse to advocate torture outright but still accept it as a legitimate topic of debate are more dangerous than those who explicitly endorse it."[7] Yet we have reached a point in the United States where one would now almost have to wonder about the character of anyone who was *not* prepared at least to demonstrate a careful consideration of the question, even if ultimately reaching the conventional answer. In other words, no one of moral seriousness may today afford to regard the matter as all sewn up, neatly and unequivocally settled, as by U.S. ratification of the Geneva Conventions, the Convention Against Torture, and the International Covenant on Civil and Political Rights. Such legal commitments cannot properly mark the end of the conversation, even the legal discussion. As with torture, so too with sustained detention and extrajudicial killings.

The topic has become not merely a legitimate but even an inescapable subject of public and private deliberation. It was introduced into American public debate by voices of the sort to which Žižek refers, voices claiming in the same breath that they themselves actually opposed the practice in virtually all circumstances.[8] Without such tentative opening moves, however, later advocacy of the practice would have been quickly dismissed as beyond serious contemplation. Once the possibility became discursively acceptable, the sheer etiquette of dialogue, with its expectation of reciprocity among conversants,[9] required respectful refutation. One whispered to oneself, "What possible harm can it do merely to discuss the matter – in the abstract, of course?"[10]

None, in fact, as long as there prove to be serious arguments to consider. This book develops and entertains two such arguments – from law and morality – that, though convincing enough on their own terms, are outweighed by further considerations. All these arguments and considerations relate directly to reciprocity: its interpretation, acceptance, rejection, and relevance to a variety of fact-specific situations.

TORTURE AS RECIPROCITY

Both reciprocity and its rejection find expression in various rules of humanitarian and human rights law, as shown in Chapters 1 through 3. Within humanitarian law, reciprocity merits decisive weight in two situations: where necessary to restore a symmetry of relevant risk disrupted by one side's rule violations, and second, where it contributes to the rules' self-enforcement in the absence of other such mechanisms. Exploring the first of these situations led naturally into an application of Kantian-inspired theories of fairness, the second into the workings of tit-for-tat in warfare – by way of reprisal and the more standard, lawful retaliation of retorsion for perceived legal breaches – as assessed by military historiography and recent social science.

The historical and statistical evidence examined in Chapter 10 reveals that tit-for-tat retaliation works passably well for inducing restraint, but only when an adversary is readily susceptible to deterrence because of its internal accountability mechanisms. Such mechanisms hold commanders responsible for subordinates' wrongful acts and elected leaders responsible to democratic voters for misguided policies. These accountability systems do not exist, however, within America's current and possible future opponents – terrorist networks and nondemocratic states. Their control of territory susceptible to invasion – in the cases of Iran, North Korea, and Syria – is insufficient.

There remains the second rationale for reciprocation, as a norm of justice inspired by conceptions of fairness. These are drawn from Rawls (Chapter 5), Kant (Chapter 6), and Aristotle among others (Chapter 7). In this regard, reciprocity demands that both sides be permitted to play by the same rules. When one side gains unfair advantage by departing from the initial rules, the other is entitled to like departures to overcome the resulting unfairness. Al Qaeda gains unfair advantage by targeting U.S. and other Western civilians throughout the world, contrary to long-settled, uncontroversial rules of humanitarian law. Permitting the United States to target Al Qaeda's leaders, rather than only capture and prosecute them, helps overcome this disadvantage. That disadvantage would also justify the United States in holding Al Qaeda members in long-term administrative detention and perhaps even interrogating them in ways unauthorized by Geneva norms. These practices would help restore a fairer fight and are defensible in such terms – regardless of their possible efficacy in saving civilian lives through incapacitation.

America's use of coercive interrogation is defensible if this practice gains actionable intelligence of great value, otherwise unobtainable. Such must be the conclusion of virtually any consequentialist morality. But the evidence of such unique efficacy is decidedly mixed. In addition, the reputational losses that the United States has suffered in global opinion, and the corresponding decline in its soft power, have likely imposed costs higher than any such benefits, even where the numbers and their meaning are debatable, as we have seen.

Thus, "realist" and rationalist approaches to international relations, properly applied to pertinent facts, lead to policy conclusions quite different from those favored by Posner, Vermeule, Goldsmith, Yoo, and others.[11] Whatever unfair advantage Al Qaeda gained through its humanitarian law breaches has hence not been effectively countered by U.S. reciprocation of illicit methods, however fair and lawful the American resort to them may be.

Reciprocity may restore the proverbial level playing field, but at the cost of making others disinclined to play at all, in the belief that we no longer, if you will, "play well with others,"[12] returning to our earlier comparison with Piaget's schoolyard.

If adherence to humanitarian law only works through the two forms of bilateral reciprocity on which this study concentrates (i.e., fair fight, and tit-for-tat), then there will be little forbearance from the United States in its war on transnational jihadist terror. If there is a good argument for self-restraint, it must be found entirely apart from reciprocity in either form. Otherwise, the informal negotiation over rules by which all may fight, and their self-enforcement through response in kind, will surely lead both to greater violence and reduced American influence in the world.

This study has hence focused on the country's professional soldiers, their commitment to a nonconsequentialist ethics and to the development of corresponding identities, martial and national.[13] These commitments are reflected in the JAGs' congressional testimony and legal memoranda questioning the use of coercive interrogation (see Chapter 12). The JAGs are most convincing when they rest the case for national self-restraint in fighting Al Qaeda on their proffered answer to the question of "who we are," as military professionals and as a liberal society, rather than on what fairness permits, law requires, or even what the national interest will demand in future wars. Opposition to a bilateral reciprocity requirement within humanitarian law thus finds its principal wellsprings in the increasing inclination of America's transnationalized military/legal elites toward a more diffuse or systemic variety of reciprocity to guide the country's global relationships, even in armed conflict.

Because it entails equality between opponents, reciprocity is an egalitarian principle, congenial to denizens of a democracy. Hence the expectation that America's military opponents must reciprocate its restraint has been strongest in the democratic branches – Congress and the president. By contrast, antireciprocity is a principle historically rooted in aristocratic notions of honor – first martial, then national. It consequently finds its chief institutional support in the officer class, including its lawyers, and to a lesser extent in an unelected, life-tenured federal judiciary.

Despite its inegalitarian origins, the antireciprocity ideal is today widely invoked in defense of human rights, the most seemingly egalitarian of doctrines. But this invocation does not arise everywhere in equal measure. It is strongest where the traditional notion of personal honor has been strong and has come over time to be democratized, morphing into more congenial, contemporary ideas about dignity and respect: everyman a noble.[14] Herein may even lie the intellectual origins of the West European welfare state.[15] And so it is unsurprising that its West European allies have parted company so vigorously with America on the importance of human rights law to the proper treatment of terror suspects.

The politics of reaction is no monopoly of the right,[16] postmodernist insinuations notwithstanding. And it should not require war with an evil Other – Soviet or jihadist – to summon up our constitutive commitments, to hold ourselves to our own high ethical standards.[17] History suggests that such conflicts just as often lead to the reciprocal reinforcement of each side's worst impulses, rather than to stricter adherence to a state's settled aspirations. Close allies committed to similar civic identities as law-abiding peoples provide a more salutary source of reinforcement.[18] And networks of military lawyers, quietly discussing the meaning of humanitarian law among themselves beneath the radar and high drama of macro-politics, offer one of the vital institutional mechanisms through which such national commitments are continually revised and revived.

A world that perceives U.S. forbearance as calculated merely to curry favor with it may less likely accept the country's influence. So a public argument for restraint, cast only in terms of a national interest in soft power, may prove at least partly self-defeating. If the United States values its good name only for instrumental ends rather than intrinsically, this very feature of American conduct may prove not merely hypocritical, but self-destructive.[19] Still, even an interested gift implicitly invites, and tends to elicit, a countergift as a reciprocal gesture. This is true between states no less than between people, as indicated in Chapter 11 regarding the Marshall Plan and U.S. foreign aid to Pakistan.[20] If gifts and violence so often run in the same grooves, then just as we have been recently disposed to repay terrorism with torture and other illegal coercion, so too much of the world will be inclined to repay, in counterterrorism cooperation and further diplomatic currency, our "gift" of a restored humanitarianism on detention and interrogation issues. At the very least, the world will discern a benevolent signal.

In sum, ideas about reciprocity – often explicit, sometimes *sub rosa* – are vital to both defenders and critics of Bush administration counter-terrorism policy. Defenders believe that, because America's opponents do not respect the rules of war, the reciprocity principle authorizes other, presumptively illicit methods in response, including the sustained detention without prosecution and coercive interrogation of high-ranking detainees believed to possess information that could save lives. The administration's critics worry, however, that in response to such practices, America's future opponents will reciprocate by mistreating its captured soldiers (and perhaps arbitrarily detaining its citizens); such enemies will claim, as does bin Laden in his epigraphs to this book, that we "started it" and – having revealed our true character – cannot be trusted not to do so again.

This book shows that neither argument is convincing. Forbearance through tit-for-tat in modern warfare has worked only under historical conditions that are absent from the conflict with Al Qaeda and kindred jihadist groups (Chapter 10). If it were the only relevant norm, fairness – as uniform rules for all belligerents – would indeed permit the relaxation of U.S. restraints on detainee treatment as a means of restoring the symmetrical balance of benefits and burdens that humanitarian law establishes. For this reason, and because the brutality of torture is not unique to that practice (Chapter 4), there is no absolute moral prohibition on torture (or targeted killing, etc.) any more than there is on the use of a banned weapon system already first employed by a military antagonist.

Suspension or withdrawal from such *prima facie* prohibitions on an adversary's breach of them is the operative rule in the weapons restriction agreements, we have seen, a field no less imbued with humanitarianism than Geneva law. The reciprocity principle thus exerts much gravitational force within humanitarian law, as throughout public international law more generally. Also vital is the fact of reservations and persistent objection by the United States and several other major powers to treaties prohibiting civilian reprisal. State consent is thus qualified, preventing formation of a customary norm against such conduct. The upshot would be a perfectly plausible argument for the defensibility of the three most controversial U.S. practices in the conflict with Al Qaeda.

AGAINST TORTURE AND SUSTAINED DETENTION

The United States should nonetheless eschew torture and arbitrary detention,[21] at least, though targeted killing is another matter. First, there is the instrumental reason, inspired by rational choice "realism": Torture diminishes the country's regard and salutary influence around the world, thereby harming national interests more than it demonstrably helps them. Practicing torture conflicts with the more diffuse reciprocity entailed in an emergent (albeit delimited) social contract at the global level, to which anti-torture norms are universally regarded as integral and from which America greatly profits.

Second, there is the moral reason: Torture is inconsistent with the professional self-understanding of our armed forces, derived from a democratized virtue ethics of martial honor. Torture and arbitrary detention are also incompatible with our national identity, with what we – in the sense of "We the People" – have represented at our best and to which we abidingly aspire (Chapter 8). To this end, humanitarian law – as a way of thinking about how war may be fought – offers a healthy check on the powerful tendency for confrontational rhetoric on both sides to escalate, through a pathological dynamic of differentiation: reciprocity's *doppelgänger*. This unfortunate dynamic tends to exaggerate the distinctions between an impeccable moral self and an implacably unscrupulous Other, ending paradoxically in a mirror imaging of monsters (Chapter 9).

If "who we are" is at stake in how we fight, and if projecting a positive image of national character is essential to winning that fight, then reciprocal mimicry of the enemy leads straight to defeat. If we conclude that we must become more "like them" in order to defeat them militarily, then they will assuredly defeat us politically. If we want the world to mimic us, we cannot very well mimic Al Qaeda, for what may work as military tactics here fails as geopolitical strategy. Just as bin Laden refuses to reciprocate restraint by way of "utilitarian" tit-for-tat, we should decline to reciprocate misconduct through "Kantian" insistence on a risk symmetry of uniform rules. And just as they show their colors by falling so far short of law's requirements, we should show our character by reaching higher than the law of reprisal and its underlying morality of bilateral reciprocity. As they abandon a strict, means-end rationality in their methods of fighting for a value rationality concerned with ultimate ends, so should we – in the service of ends very different from theirs. The logic of law and morality permits the United States to play by the same rules as its adversary. But the logic of interest and identity requires it to play by different and more demanding ones.

Still, the present contribution to America's torture debate has offered up no local villains and few heroes. Unlike other writing on the subject, it is relentlessly anti-Manichaen, displaying a sangfroid seemingly unsuited to the moral ardor that these issues typically elicit. Almost everything written since 9/11 on the legal response to jihadist terror from either the left or right reflects the enhanced Red versus Blue polarization within much of American society.

At the end of his life, Michel Foucault offered a luminous critique of polemics, of the polemical mode of argument. The polemicist's "final objective," he wrote, is "not to come as close as possible to a difficult truth but to bring about the triumph of the just cause he has been manifestly upholding from the beginning." Hence for the polemicist, "the person he confronts is not a partner in search for the truth but an adversary, an enemy who is wrong, who is harmful, whose very existence constitutes a threat."[22] To write a book on a topic like torture *without* engaging heavily in polemics might nonetheless seem perverse. "*Not* to get angry when horrible things take place seems itself to be a diminution of one's humanity," Nussbaum rightly observes.[23] But it has been precisely the intensity of partisan passions that has so often led to remarkably sloppy thinking on all sides of this vital national conversation.[24]

It is axiomatic, much social theory urges, that an inexorable cycle of reciprocal exchange ensures, within all societies, that gifts will soon be met with countergifts from their recipients, that violence and other misdeeds will be repaid in the same currency by their victims. The process may alter in appearance over time, assuming a more subtle and "civilized" form, a more discreet guise. Yet it does not diminish in force, much less disappear, we are sternly warned. Modernity is primitivism – artfully cloaked, elegantly dissimulated. For we remain social beings, and reciprocity is, Lévi-Strauss intones, "the essence of the social."[25] It follows: Do not give unless you are likely to receive, in turn, from your donee, and feel no compunction about repaying your antagonist's mischief in spades. For such is nature's law or at least that of all known societies, human and otherwise.

In the conflict between America and Al Qaeda, much conduct on both sides has been all too readily explicable in these terms. The story cannot end just there, however, for social theory need not be so determinist or fatalistic. Networks of transnational influence will continue to foster American self-conceptions of civilized conduct based in modernized notions of martial honor. This will permit a deepening social contract. And Americans may rationally make a gift of humanitarianism without hope of reciprocation from its immediate beneficiaries as long as other states can be expected to tender repayment, albeit discreetly and without acknowledging it as such. Reciprocal gift-giving of this sort forms a system of generalized exchange that fills the gaps in an incipient contract remaining very patchy at the global level.[26] Both national identity and self-interest in world influence will then counsel the country, though victimized and continually threatened by terror, not to return the favor. Gifts and violence need not always run in precisely the same grooves.

Acknowledgments

As a literary genre, a book's acknowledgments are always a profession of indebtedness to others, hence of humility, and I profess both herein. But truth be told, good scholarship requires an odd mix of modesty and mega-lomania, in uncertain balance. One must forever sit at the feet of greater talents, and not only one's elders, because acknowledging their superior profundity is necessary to improve one's own game. Even as one sends the final draft off to the publisher, one always knows that it would be better yet with still another, more self-critical read-through, however many times – seemingly thousands – one has already reread it all, indeed after one could recite it almost by heart *ad nauseum* (i.e., to the author's nausea – no one else's, he hopes). As a senior scholar, one must also welcome acute criticism of one's lifework from all quarters, embracing the possibility of its demotion, even demolition, in hopes of revivifying its claims for a new generation of readers. One must hold one's mind open to profiting from the most original and difficult thinkers of many persuasions, however seemingly incompatible their premises and insistent their mutual disdain.

Yet one must nonetheless somewhere find the *amour-propre* to believe that one might – if not quite supersede those thinkers, to be sure – nonetheless at least say something at once new, true, and significant. If one is not merely plugging a momentary "gap in the literature" or following fleeting fashion, doing so entails addressing a perennial question to which many have already long applied formidable intelligence and prodigious energies. On what possible basis could such heroic self-confidence rightly rest, especially when starting out? Immodest imaginings are essential to attempting a venturous book, whether it succeeds or fails. Whom does one thank, one wonders, for endowing or implanting them?

In writing a first book, the pull toward modesty is legitimately stronger, given the stakes of failing to find a secure academic cubbyhole. Thereafter,

however, one is rightly expected to aim ever a bit higher, still without
succumbing to pride and thereby embarrassingly exceeding one's reach.
Getting this balance right is difficult, as the line is thin between hubris and
high hopes, realistically placed. Yet one must try – that is, if one has any true
vocation for scholarship. As this is my fifth tome on law's response to mass
atrocity (to 9/11, in this case), its undoubted missteps are not those of the
pusillanimous novice. Junior scholars feel obliged to anticipate all criticisms
of their every assertion, preemptively refuting them, saying nothing that
cannot withstand the closest scrutiny. This risks pedantry. By contrast, the
distinguished academician, with a sober reputation for careful scholarship,
feels rightly emboldened to go out on the occasional limb, sharpening points
of potential disagreement with others, inviting their criticism, occasionally
unburdening himself of the confessedly half-baked suggestion in the hope
that others will develop and qualify it. Here the danger is one of tossing
off an ill-considered provocation on a pressing public controversy, for mere
shock value. This is irresponsible, especially concerning matters of moral
gravity. Whether this book has steered a successful course between these
opposing perils is not for the author to judge.

This brief, potted psychology of the scholarly calling and intellectual
maturation within it must explain the incautious spirit of these pages. The
range of my theoretical ambit here, in particular, has made the guidance of
others especially valuable, demanding a recurrent tacking back and forth
between the modesty and the megalomania. My prior books examine how
to design military law in light of the social sources of mass criminality in war,
whereas the present volume has flipped that question around, addressing
the sources of social restraint on such wrongdoing.

All scholarship also necessarily involves a goodly splash of monomania,
in the passionate, near-obsessive preoccupation one must somehow sustain
for long periods about an often arcane, highly delimited patch of terrain,
necessarily at the expense of a wider worldliness and broader reading. To
justify such single-minded focus, one must acquire a quiet but unfailing confidence – however pretentious this sounds when so unguardedly couched –
that one will ultimately discover a small but elegant truth (perhaps even
something universal and sublime, one dares hope) with larger implications,
far-reaching ramifications even, in what others shall nonetheless insist, one
knows, really *does* remain only a clump of sand.

Thus, despite the unassumingly narrow band of scholars' professional
attention, their monomania betrays a capacious ambition; in their very
modesty lurks a will-to-power, albeit the life-affirming sort. And the reality
of academic life, as opposed to the ideal just rhapsodized, is always of

course decidedly stronger on both manias (mono- and megalo-) – personal qualities distinctly unappealing, albeit indispensable – than on the humility that too remains essential in all good scholarship. To make it harder still, no one quite directly tells you any of this, unless perhaps you had a particularly generous mentor or parent in the racket, who put it in lights. At any rate, no one ever told me, the son of a single stenographer from Carpinteria, a small, simple southern California town. To her, my mother, I express my deepest thanks, especially for her suggestion, when I was thirteen, to apply for a scholarship to Philips Exeter Academy, across the country in New Hampshire (before returning to California, to Berkeley for university).

Having accused my intellectual antagonists of too privileged a distance from the unsavory realities they too confidently pronounce on, it is only fair – in a spirit of reciprocity as rules for all – that I apply such a reflexive sociology of knowledge (in the spirit of Bourdieu) to myself as well, at the admitted risk of appearing too intimate for a study of large and grave concerns. People often imagine the life of the international lawyer/academician to be quite grand and glamorous, in a way surely conducive to megalomania. Human rights law and humanitarian aid work, in particular, are fields that – despite their image (and periodic reality) of self-sacrifice – do paradoxically attract some of the most outsized egos, far more than corporate law, which I practiced for some years, where one must always answer to a more powerful and knowledgeable client. For whom does the humanitarian lawyer claim to speak? Who is the client? Humanity at large? Bit of a principal-agent problem there. Lunch-time interaction with many in the humanitarian field has the omnipresent subtext: I've just been out saving the world, or defending Magna Carta, and what have you been doing this morning? A portentous, reverential air hovers above every conversation.

This book has been written in a decidedly different spirit, of course, though not without some immersion in and sympathetic engagement with that professional world. As a member of it, one does not decline the romantic jaunts to lecture in The Hague and to give the short course in Paris (in May, of course). But these only periodically punctuate the more quotidian reality of microwaved Salisbury steaks in the modest "trailer park" house, in the small Midwestern college town, enduring interminably bitter winters, always hunched over and hunkered down. Globalization and the democratization of intellect it permits have made it possible to combine at once all these into a single life – three parts *Stoner*, one part Morris Zapp (or downmarket simulacrum thereof). An author can only hope that the resulting balance of high and low yields the right measure of intense identification with, and self-critical distance on, the results of his or her thinking.

There is a connection between my primary argument about the central place of reciprocity in the experience of war and my periodic, parenthetical allusions to the diffident remove from this fact maintained by most legal scholarship on humanitarian law. Given the death, sweat, and blood integral to warfare, it is also fair to expect those who write about its regulation to manifest some modicum of interest, at least, in the human experience of armed conflict, its history, organizational mechanics, and political dynamics. No one can emerge from the serious study of such subjects without acknowledging the pervasiveness, the near ubiquity in fact, of reciprocity as a social process within wars, arms races, and arms control agreements.

Legal scholars show almost no such awareness, however, and seem even to take pride in their ignorance of such "petty and pedestrian" affairs as beneath their dignity, on the view that war – like any other human activity – is just another outpost of law's empire and must simply submit to its dominion. The recurrent failings of legal thinking exposed in these pages thus originate in these more personal failings. To observe the latter is hence not to descend to gratuitous *ad homimens*, but simply to help us understand the former. Still, the problem with this body of professional discourse is not, *pace* Foucault, that its spokespeople have too strong a vested stake in preserving control over the activity they purport to govern. In fact, they have little such self-interest or control. They would be happy to see war entirely banished from the planet, even as this did away with any need for their expertise. They may be taken at their word here and surely deserve that much credit. In this spirit of modesty, the ICRC has also been the first to contend that the conflict with Al Qaeda and kindred groups does not constitute an armed conflict, thereby essentially conceding the substantial irrelevance of the law governing armed conflicts, which is the only professional domain over which it may claim any special acumen.

For their conversation and comments on written drafts, I wish to express my gratitude to Khaliq Abdul, Jon Amarilio, Paul Schiff Berman, Jon Carlson, Ken Cmiel, Martin Cook, Lt. Col. Geoffrey Corn, Louise Doswald-Beck, Paul Dubinsky, Zach Falcon, Amna Guellali, Roger Haydon, Dan Kahan, Susanne Karstadt, Benedict Kingsbury, David Koplow, Ken Kress, Martin Lederman, Sanford Levinson, Catherine Lu, Larry May, James Morrow, Lt. Col. Michael Newton, W. Hays Parks, Deborah Pearlstein, Eric Posner, Howard Rhodes, Joel Rohlf, Brad Roth, Johanna Schoen, Lt. Col. Gary Solis, Sanford Thatcher, Robert F. Turner, Benjamin Valentino, Teresa Wagner, Kenneth Winston, Tung Yin, a few confidential military sources, as well as the anonymous reviewers for Cambridge and a number of other presses. Elizabeth Donnelly, David Osipovich, and Benjamin To provided superlative research assistance. I profited enormously from dozens of hours of conversation with David, in particular. I am also particularly grateful to a very critical reviewer for the University of Chicago Press who, while accepting or ignoring all my major arguments, opposed publication by performing an artful but withering postcolonialist deconstruction of me *qua* text, thus affording a welcome opportunity to explain (in Chapter 8) what I find both valuable and deeply misguided in that approach to the questions at hand.

This study also much profited from presentations of my developing ideas in recent years to audiences at the U.S. National Institute for Military Justice, Royal Military College (Canada), U.S. Air War College, U.S. Army War College, Ecole Normale Supérieur (Paris), L'École des Hautes Études en Sciences Sociales (Paris), Australian National University (Canberra), National Law School of India University (Bangalore), the W. B. National University of Juridical Sciences and the Center for Studies in Social Sciences (Kolkata), University of Calcutta, Oñati International Institute for the Sociology of Law (Spain), the T. M. C. Asser Institute (The Hague), the University of Puerto Rico, University of Texas (Austin), University of California (Riverside), Wayne State University, the Iowa Legal Studies Workshop, plus Stanford and Harvard Law Schools. Summer research grants from the University of Iowa, College of Law, facilitated its progress. A lovely summer at Antoine Garapon's Paris Institut des Hautes Etudes sur la Justice permitted some concentrated writing. The author is responsible for all errors. Fernando Botero, the Colombian artist, graciously offered his etching for this book's cover.

Notes

1 This study employs the term "humanitarian law" in reference to all sources of international law concerned with minimizing unnecessary suffering in war. This means particularly the Geneva and Hague Conventions, plus related customary law, as well as certain treaties prohibiting or restricting possession or use of particular types of weapons. Also pertinent are the Rome Statute of the International Criminal Court, the Convention Against Torture, and the Genocide Convention. The last three treaties address forms of violence that occur mostly but not exclusively during war. The last two treaties are generally categorized, however, as part of international human rights law, rather than humanitarian law. The differences between these two fields are described at length in Chapter 3. To simplify discussion and enhance readability, I use the term humanitarian law to encompass legal materials that specialists would often classify under the label international criminal law. The two bodies of law – one concerning the civil liability of states, the other the criminal liability of natural persons – are distinguished in the text only where the context of discussion so requires. The offenses of war crimes, crimes against humanity, and genocide are common to both bodies of law.

2 The scope of "protected persons" under the Fourth Geneva Convention is discussed in some detail herein. That category does not encompass most of those detained by the United States in its conflict with Al Qaeda and kindred groups. Of those captured in Iraq, for instance, only Iraqi citizens would likely count as protected under this Convention, because the state of Iraq, like the United States, would be classified as a party to the pertinent conflict or conflicts. For one analysis, *see* Jack Goldsmith, The Terror Presidency 156, 172 (2007).

3 The term "high-ranking Al Qaeda suspects" would fairly describe, among others, three men currently in U.S. custody. These are Abu Zubaydah, a top Al Qaeda operative involved in many terrorist attacks on Americans; Khalid Sheikh Mohammed, self-declared "mastermind" of Al Qaeda's 9/11 attacks; and Abd al-Rahim al-Nashiri, head of Al Qaeda operations in the Persian Gulf. By the terms "terrorism" or "terrorist," this study refers to the intentional killing of innocent civilians to inspire public fear and gain publicity for a political cause,

with a view to forcing the hand of political leadership. For the groups here in issue, the larger aim of such terror is generally to impose Islamist theocracy and, failing that, to eliminate Western secularizing influence in the Muslim world. When such groups attack Americans, they often do not consider their conduct as terrorism, by this definition, for they generally hold that there are no innocent Americans. "Terrorism" is treated in this book as an ideal-type (i.e., an analytical construct helpful in making sense of particular organizations and their members insofar as they conform to its terms). Max Weber, The Methodology of the Social Sciences 89–103 (1949). Recurrent quotation marks throughout the entire text might highlight the heuristic nature of this usage, but would compromise stylistic felicity.

4 The U.S. government's intention to conduct such operations has been its announced, official policy since the National Security Strategy of 2002, at http://www.whitehouse.gov/nsc/nss/2002/index.html. Killed in one such 2006 operation was Abu Musab al-Zarqawi, a Jordanian militant who founded the group that became Al Qaeda in Iraq. Earlier that year, a similar missile strike was directed, unsuccessfully, at al-Qaeda deputy Ayman al-Zawahiri, in Pakistan. Another strike targeted Saddam Hussein shortly before the 2003 U.S. invasion of Iraq. On more recent targeted killings of Al Qaeda leaders, *see* Eric Schmitt, "Senior Qaeda Commander Is Killed by U.S. Missile," New York Times, Feb. 1, 2008, at A1; Reuters, "Missile Kills 13 in Pakistan," New York Times, Feb. 28, 2008, at A1 ("A missile struck a house in a Pakistani region known as a safe haven for al Qaeda early on Thursday, killing 13 suspected militants including foreigners, intelligence officials and residents said."); Associated Press, "U.S. Says It Hit Somali Target," New York Times, March 3, 2008 ("The U.S. military attacked a 'known al-Qaida terrorist' in southern Somalia, a Pentagon spokesman said Monday."). Eric Schmitt & Jeffrey Gettleman, "Qaeda Leader Reported Killed in Somalia," New York Times, May 2, 2008 (describing "an American missile strike in Somalia [which] apparently killed a militant long identified as one of Al Qaeda's top operatives in East Africa"); Steven Myers, "Bush Praises Pakistan Just Hours after U.S. Strike," New York Times, July 29, 2008 at A6 (referencing a recent missile strike that "destroyed what American and Pakistani officials described as a militant outpost in the region, killing at least six fighters").

These were reported as U.S. military operations of a sort that involve presidential approval. When the CIA conducts such an attack, the director obtains a legal opinion from a CIA lawyer. Eben Kaplan, "Targeted Killing," Council on Foreign Relations, March 2, 2006, at http://www.cfr.org/publication/9627 (quoting former Assistant Secretary of Defense Lawrence Korb). On recent Israeli strikes at Hamas and Hezbollah leaders, *see* Steven Erlanger, "Israeli Strike Kills Three Militants," New York Times, Dec. 19, 2007, at A1. For an early defense of such practice as "peacetime reprisal," *see* Michael Walzer, Just and Unjust Wars 220 (1977). He writes, "If a government literally cannot control the inhabitants of the territory over which it supposedly presides, or police its borders, and if other countries suffer because of this incapacity, then surrogate controlling and policing are clearly permissible. And these may go well beyond the limits commonly accepted for reprisal raids" (i.e., belligerent reprisals during full-scale "armed conflict"). For a recent policy defense of this practice, as a second-best but often necessary alternative to capture and interrogation, *see* Daniel Byman, The Five Front War: The Better Way to Fight Global Jihad 83, 113–30 (2008). The legal scholarship concerning targeted killing of suspected terrorists is almost entirely hostile to the practice, sanctioning it only under the most restrictive conditions, of a sort that can virtually never be satisfied in practice. For a recent summary of this considerable literature, *see* Nils Melzer, Targeted Killing in International Law 44–70 (2008).

5 The "law of armed conflict" is the current term of art for what was once called the law of war. This contemporary wording was adopted to enlarge the law's regulatory reach beyond full-scale "war," which the International Committee of the Red Cross (ICRC) defines as "armed hostilities between two or more states, carried on by their armed forces." Pietro Verri, Dictionary of the International Law of Armed Conflict 123 (1992). But the scope of the new term has not yet received great clarification from legal authorities, several of whose views on the matter are discussed herein.

6 Groups that may fairly be described as "kindred" to Al Qaeda, because of common concerns and methods (notwithstanding differences in local agendas), include Hamas, Palestinian Islamic Jihad, Abu Sayyaf, Ansar al-Islam, the Armed Islamic Group, Asbat al-Ansar, al-Gama'a al-Islamiyya, the Islamic Jihad Group, Jemaah Islamiyah, al-Jihad, Lashkar i Jhangvi, the Salafist Group for Call and Combat, the Moroccan Islamic Combatant Group, the Libyan Islamic Fighting Group, and Al Qaeda in the Islamic Maghreb, among others. For many of these groups, the local political program is closely linked to an international agenda of opposing the United States on the basis of its support for local regimes that oppose Islamist goals.

7 This book employs the term "belligerent" in a generic sense to refer both to states and nonstate actors engaged in armed conflict, as well as individual persons fighting on their behalf. Belligerents will sometimes enjoy the legal privileges of "combatant" status if they meet the requirements of that classification within the Geneva Conventions. If they do not, they will be described in these pages as "unprivileged" belligerents. This is the least controversial of the terminologies now available for the empirical phenomena to be examined. On such issues and the politics of the competing vocabularies, *see* Derek Jinks, "September 11 and the Law of War," 28 Yale J. Int'l L. 1, 20 (2003); Knut Dörmann, "The Legal Situation of Unlawful/Unprivileged Combatants," 85 Int'l Rev. of the Red Cross 45 (2003); Kenneth Watkins, "Warriors without Rights? Combatants, Unprivileged Belligerents, and the Struggle over Legitimacy," Occasional Paper Series, Program on Humanitarian Policy and Conflict Research, Harvard University, Winter 2005.

8 *Hamdan v. Rumsfeld*, 126 S.Ct. 2749 (2006).

9 Third Geneva Convention, Art. 3. The Court did not examine particular interrogation practices under this standard.

10 *Id.* The Court's majority relied on Art. 75 of Geneva Additional Protocol I to interpret the quoted wording, as the United States had officially characterized most of that provision as part of customary international law. The State Department Legal Adviser affirmed this position as late as 2003.

This study deliberately sidesteps a variety of debates over many important issues because they do not immediately concern reciprocity. These include the definition of torture, the quality of the evidence and surveillance/investigatory process by which individuals may be detained, the president's constitutional and statutory war powers, the proper jurisdiction of military commissions, the institutional design of intelligence gathering, and the practical difficulty of confining torture's use to the rare circumstances in which it would be morally justified or excused. Much has been written on all these issues. In the interests of adding something new to the debate, the present focus is on the largely unexamined question of reciprocity in humanitarian law and within the experience of armed conflict itself. Reciprocity is a neglected issue in the larger debate over U.S. counterterrorism policy.

A concern with reciprocity has long been central to social theory, and the present approach is that of a socio-legal theorist focusing (in four prior books) on legal responses to mass atrocity. The sociology of law itself, as a truly interdisciplinary endeavor, has admittedly amounted to very little. The essential challenge, rarely if ever overcome, is that whereas sociological theory aims for the broadest and most ambitious generalizations about the world, the law and any careful thinking about it – especially in the common law world – commit to the view that almost any generalization always borders on overgeneralization, with the energy focused on finding exceptions to the initial suggestion of a rule-like proposition, and then exceptions to those exceptions. Hence, everything said by an intellectually serious sociologist is likely to strike a good lawyer as bloated with flatulent generality, and anything by a careful lawyer strikes the sociological theorist as always at the precipice of the banal. The cast of mind that makes for virtuosity in one field undermines it in the other, though the two must be well joined to do justice at once both to crucial complexities and overarching trends.

On these shoals, the discipline long ago ran aground and ceased to produce ideas nearly as novel or compelling as the promising beginnings offered, now more than a century ago, by Durkheim and especially Weber, who were at once somehow able – in their unique genius – both to generalize and particularize about the relation of law to society. Sociologists now study law through their own professionalized, autopoietic lens, and hence are not truly interdisciplinary, whereas lawyers selectively sample this or that convenient fact as found by sociologists whenever this serves the advocate's momentary needs in litigation, without serious interest in the validity of the methods by which such purported facts were discerned or what larger patterns they may constitute.

It bears mention as well that this study does not propose specific operational approaches for fighting Al Qaeda, matters addressed by specialists in security studies and military strategy. On such issues, *see, e.g.,* Daniel Byman, "U.S. Counter-terrorism Options: A Taxonomy," 49 Survival 121 (2007); David Cortright & George Lopez, "Strategic Counter-Terrorism," *in* Uniting against Terror: Cooperative Nonmilitary Responses to the Global Terrorist Threat, David Cortright & George Lopez, eds. 1 (2007).

11 A series of Executive Orders, beginning in 1976, have embodied this self-imposed national prohibition. None have defined "assassination," however. *See, e.g.,* Executive Order 11905, Feb. 15, 1976. Dissonant with these orders are a number of Presidential National Security Decision Directives since the 1980s, some still partly classified, authorizing covert CIA operations against certain

organizations and their leaders, designated as terrorists. Center for Defense Information, Presidential Orders and Documents Regarding Foreign Intelligence and Terrorism, at http://www.cdi.org/terrorism/presidential-orders-pr.cfm. A "presidential finding" by President Clinton also authorized the CIA to initiate covert operations against Osama bin Laden; this was never formally codified into a Presidential Decision Directive such as those of the 1980s. *Id.* None of the findings or directives yet made public expressly ordered assassination, of course. They did, however, authorize conduct defined in language general enough, by any reasonable inference, to encompass murder. Further, following 9/11 a congressional resolution authorized President Bush "to use all necessary and appropriate force . . . in order to prevent any future acts of international terrorism against the U.S." Authorization for Use of Military Force, Sept. 18, 2001, Pub. Law 107–40 S. J. Res. 23. Yet unless such peacetime operations are authorized by the nation in which the operations take place, international law would consider attacks on foreign soil a violation of sovereignty. It is consistent with international law for a belligerent state to target a commander in chief during, or in imminent anticipation of armed conflict with the state he or she represents, as the U.S. targeted Saddam Hussein in April 2003. But this legal right is irrelevant to the conflict with Al Qaeda and kindred groups. Insofar as the U.S. suffered "armed attack" on 9/11, it could also lawfully employ proportionate force in "self-defense," even if the attack bore no nexus to a larger "armed conflict." UN Charter Art. 51. The legal meaning of "armed attack" in international law, however, has never been authoritatively applied to violence initiated by a nonstate actor; hence, the question of whether the 9/11 events constituted an armed attack was one about which international lawyers did not initially concur. And the right of "self-defense" in international law has always been understood as limited in several ways inconsistent with the scope of many key policies, including the targeted killing of Al Qaeda leaders in Yemen, Pakistan, Iraq, Afghanistan, and elsewhere, that the Bush administration adopted in furtherance of its announced "long war on global terrorism." *See generally* Michael Schmitt, "State-Sponsored Assassination in International and Domestic Law," 17 Yale J. Int'l L. 609 (1992).

12 Belligerent reprisals are wartime acts that would violate humanitarian law, but for the fact that they are directed against an adversary responsible for prior violations, with the intent to force the initial violator to respect the law of armed conflict. They may only be carried out as a last resort, after having given formal notice of the intention to engage in reprisal. They must be proportionate to the original violation and must not continue after the illegal behavior of the initial violator ends. *Naulilaa Case (Port. v. Ger.),* 2 R.I.A.A. 1011 (1928).

The United States has affirmed its right to employ reprisals against enemy civilians in extreme circumstances through its refusal to ratify Geneva Additional Protocol I, with its blanket prohibition of such measures, as well as its persistent objection to the formation of customary law to that effect. *See* II Customary International Humanitarian Law, Jean-Marie Henckaerts & Louise Doswald-Beck, eds. 3420–21 (2005); U.S. Navy, The Commander's Handbook of Naval Operations, NWP-1–14M,¶ 6.2.3.3. (1995) (authorizing reprisals on approval of national command authority). Regarding the "persistent objector" rule, *see* American Law Commission, U.S. Restatement (Third), Foreign

Relations Law, Art. 102, comment D (1987); Antonio Cassese, International Law 162–63 (2005). A reprisal is considered "belligerent" when it occurs during armed conflict. For analysis, *see* Anthony Clark & Robert Beck, International Law and the Use of Force: Beyond the UN Charter Paradigm 42 (1993); Marjorie Whitman, 12 Digest of International Law 148–87 (1971).

13 Accusations of euphemism and Orwellian "newspeak" are frequent in debate over the propriety of terms like "coercive interrogation," "rendition" of terror suspects, and so forth. *See, e.g.,* David Bromwich, "Euphemism and American Violence," 55 N.Y. Rev. of Books, April 3, 2008, at 28; Marguerite Feitlowitz, A Lexicon of Terror: Argentina and the Legacies of Torture 19–62 (1998). Listeners would rightly fear the worst in this regard when, for instance, Secretary of Defense Donald Rumsfeld announced, shortly after 9/11, 2001, that "even the vocabulary of this war will be different." Speech of Sept. 27, 2001, at http://www.defenselink.mil/speeches/s20010927-secdef.html. But it is a mistake to label terms like "coercive interrogation" as necessarily and invariably a euphemism for torture. If a given practice may fairly be described only in highly negative terms, then any other characterization designed to sound less pernicious must indeed be called euphemistic. Such an accusation cannot be the point of departure, however. To start the discussion with a charge of euphemism is to beg the prior question of what is the true nature of the conduct being described. Such charges thus often rely on a naïvely mimetic theory of language according to which there must exist one and only one correct verbal designation for each empirical datum in the world, for translating event into sign. This is not to deny the trenchancy of Orwell's original illustrations of political euphemism. Yet we must also acknowledge that there are many methods of interrogation that must be called "coercive" that nonetheless fall short of torture, as that crime is defined by all pertinent legal authorities. And when two verbal characterizations of the "same" social phenomenon both selectively capture salient features of it, it is perfectly legitimate for a speaker's particular concerns and purposes to govern the choice between them.

14 The term "retaliation" is used in these pages in a generic, nontechnical sense to encompass all unfriendly actions taken by the victim in response to perceived violations against it of humanitarian law. The word hence refers to reprisal, retorsion – terms defined herein – as well as other acts of violent responses not meeting the legal requirements of either.

15 This conclusion admittedly sits uneasily with Art. 75 of Geneva Additional Protocol I, much of which is generally binding as customary law, and endorsed as such by the U.S. Supreme Court in *Hamdan*. But more immediately pertinent is the fact that the United States has persistently objected, for *in extremis* situations, to the formation of any customary rule against civilian reprisal. *See* Customary International Humanitarian Law, *supra* note 12, at 3420–21.

16 *See, e.g.,* Mark Mazzetti, "C.I.A. Allowed to Resume Interrogations," New York Times online, July 20, 2007 ("After months of behind the scenes wrangling, the White House said Friday that it had given the Central Intelligence Agency approval to resume its use of some harsh interrogation methods in questioning terrorism suspects in secret prisons overseas."). Insofar as such methods involve

humiliating and degrading treatment, they would violate Common Art. 3 of the Geneva Conventions, to which the United States is a party.

17 Steven Kull et al., Program on Int'l Policy Attitudes/Knowledge Networks, Americans on Detention, Torture and the War on Terrorism 7 (2004), at http://www.pipa.org/OnlineReports/Terrorism/TortureJul04/TortureJul.04rpt.pdf. Americans are not alone in defending torture of terrorists in certain, limited circumstances. Public opinion in most Western democracies concurs, albeit to a lesser extent. "Poll Finds Broad Approval of Terrorist Torture – Americas," MSNBC.com, at http://www.msnbc.com/id/10345320/print/displaymode/1098.

Many Bush administration critics make the obvious point that the "war on terrorism" is a misnomer, in that one cannot intelligibly be said to wage war against a method of warfare. One may wage war only against a particular belligerent, perhaps one employing an illicit method such as terrorism. The administration cannot be so foolish, however, as to make this simple category error. To evaluate the merits of its favored moniker, one must consider the alternatives. To describe the conflict as a war against "Islamists" would define the enemy with a word that incorporated "Islam" itself, the religion of that name. Adding "ism" to the end of that moniker would not adequately convey the message that the administration is not at war with Muslims. Moreover, several avowedly Islamist political groups, such as Turkey's Justice and Development Party and Egypt's Muslim Brotherhood (on most accounts, for most of its history), have not been violent; they seek state implementation of *shari'a* but by lawful, democratic means. Fawaz Gerges, The Far Enemy: Why Jihad Went Global 2–3 (2005). To describe the conflict as a war against "jihadists" would succumb to a similar problem, incorporating the word "jihad," which many Muslims understand to encompass almost any variety of religiously inspired struggle or personal mission. David Cook, Martyrdom in Islam 147 (2007).

Political prudence thus again precludes such a definition of the adversary. Even active proponents of the martial conception of jihad, moreover, avowedly condemn "terrorism," as they understand the term. And a "war on violent extremism" is obviously overinclusive. The term "war on terrorism" is also overinclusive, of course, as there are many terrorist groups, such as the Basque ETA, with which the current U.S. efforts are not concerned. If one adds "in the Middle East" or "Arab world" to such monikers, then the definition immediately becomes underinclusive, as terrorist groups are well established in other parts of the world, such as Indonesia and the Philippines.

The administration's critics also mistakenly assume that a definition must serve only one purpose: to describe the single feature of reality with maximal precision. Definitions often serve purposes quite different from this. The merit of any definition depends on the larger theory in which it is inserted. John Rawls, A Theory of Justice 130 (1971). The Bush administration's definition of its adversary is embedded in its larger theory of how best to promote liberal democracy in the Middle East, an objective that requires some cultural/linguistic sensitivity of the sort just described, so as not to give unnecessary offense. In short, a scrupulously delimited designation of the adversary would be diplomatically imprudent, whereas a politically prudent characterization would inevitably be imprecise. The Bush administration has chosen the latter.

The further criticism that the "war on terrorism" is not really a "war," regardless of who its putative adversary might be, is an entirely different objection, examined elsewhere herein.

18 Human Rights First, "Human Rights First Expresses Concerns over Republican Debate Discussion of Extreme Interrogation," Law and Security Digest, May 18, 2007.

19 Martha Moore, "Guantánamo Bay Puzzles Candidates," U.S.A. Today, June 22, 2007, at 8A. In a Nov. 28, 2007 debate among Republican presidential candidates, Mitt Romney stated, "I want to make sure these folks are kept at Guantánamo. I don't want the people that are carrying out attacks on this country to be brought into our jail system and be given legal representation in this country. I want to make sure that what happened to Khalid Sheikh Mohammed happens to other people who are terrorists. He was captured. . . . And he turned to his captors and he said, 'I'll see you in New York with my lawyers.' I presume ACLU lawyers. Well, that's not what happened. He went to Guantánamo and he met G.I.s and C.I.A. interrogators. And that's just exactly how it ought to be." Transcript, The Republican Debate, New York Times, Nov. 27, 2007. The Scott Shane, "Inside a 9/11 Mastermind's Interrogation," New York Times, June 22, 2008 ("Mr. Mohammed met his captors at first with cocky defiance, telling one veteran CIA officer, a former Pakistan station chief, that he would talk only when he got to New York and was assigned a lawyer – the experience of his nephew and partner in terrorism, Ramzi Yousef, after Mr. Yousef's arrest in 1995.").

20 Human Rights First, Rights Wire, June 30, 2007 (reporting that Justice Scalia made this statement at a judicial conference in Ottawa, Canada). Homeland Security Secretary Michael Chertoff has said that the program "reflects real life." Former CIA Director James Woolsey similarly remarked that its depictions of security threats are "quite realistic." Former U.S. presidential candidate Rep. Tom Tancredo even publicly stated that if the government captured a would-be suicide bomber, "I'm looking for Jack Bauer at that point, let me tell you!" Clarence Page, "Memo to the Candidates: *24* Is Just a TV Show," *in* Dan Burstein & Arne De Keikzer, Secrets of 24, 149 (2007).

21 These methods included head slapping, exposure to cold and simulated drowning (i.e., so-called waterboarding), and the combination of these. Scott Shane, David Johnston & James Risen, "Secret U.S. Endorsement of Severe Interrogations," New York Times, Oct 4, 1007, at A1. The legal opinions concluded that these methods amounted neither to torture nor to "cruel, inhuman, or degrading" treatment, a category of conduct criminalized by Congress in 2005. On the distinct categories of interrogation methods considered and, in some cases, approved by the U.S. Defense Department for use on suspected terrorists, *see* the several executive memoranda assembled by the National Security Archive, "The Interrogation Documents: Debating U.S. Policy and Methods," at http://www.gwu.edu/~nsarchiv/NSAEBB/NSAEBB127/. The chronology of deliberation and decision within the Bush administration on interrogation methods is reviewed in Philippe Sands, Torture Team: Rumsfeld's Memo and The Betrayal of American Values 21–22, 67–70, 128, 140–41, 150–51, 175–76 (2008).

22 Libby Quaid, "McCain: Bush Should Veto Torture Bill," Associated Press, Feb. 20, 2008.

23 Quoted in Sanford Levinson, "Slavery and the Phenomenology of Torture," 74 Social Research 149, 158 (2007). Senator Hillary Clinton stated, "In the event we were ever confronted with having to interrogate a detainee with knowledge of an imminent threat to millions of Americans, then the decision to depart from standard international practices must be made by the President, and the President must be held accountable. That very, very narrow exception within very, very limited circumstances is better than blasting a big hole in our entire law." During the 2004 presidential campaign, which took place after the revelations of detainee abuse at Abu Ghraib, "the word 'torture' . . . was rarely if ever spoken by John Kerry. Democrats felt it was political suicide to voice concern about human rights abuses when the public was demanding protection from another attack." David Cole, "The Grand Inquisitors," 54 N.Y. Rev. of Books, July 19, 2007, 53, 55. As Senator Dianne Feinstein was poised to become Chair of the Senate Intelligence Committee in January 2009, she told an interviewer that "I think that you have to use the noncoercive standard to the greatest extent possible." The New York Times interpreted that statement as "raising the possibility that an imminent terrorist threat might require special measures." Mark Mazzetti & Scott Shane, "After Sharp Words on C.I.A., Obama Faces a Delicate Task," New York Times, Dec. 3, 2008, at A1. Earlier in the year, Feinstein had sponsored legislation requiring the C.I.A. to follow restrictive Army Field Manual interrogation rules, legislation vetoed by President Bush.

24 Robert Delahunty & John Yoo, "Rewriting the Laws of War for a New Enemy: The Geneva Convention Isn't the Last Word," Los Angeles Times, Feb. 1, 2005, at B11. The authors contend, "The Geneva Conventions make little sense when applied to a terrorist group or a pseudo-state. If we must fight these kinds of enemies, we must create a new set of rules." The existing Conventions "will become increasingly obsolete. Rather than attempting . . . to deny this reality, we should be seeking to address it." *Id. See also* Lt. Col. (ret.) James Zumwalt, "The Laws of War Need to Change to Defeat "Uncivilized" Enemy," Air Force Times, Dec. 25, 2006 (a widely republished piece by the son of U.S. Admiral Elmo Zumwalt arguing that "initiative should be taken to review the [humanitarian] law, with an eye toward providing more liberal interpretations to enhance the capabilities of civilized forces in combating uncivilized ones").

25 Hendrick Hertzberg, "Sparring Partners," New Yorker, Aug. 20, 2007, at 23–24. "When Obama, in a speech on terrorism at the Wilson Center in Washington, said 'If we have actionable intelligence about high-value terrorist targets (in Pakistan) and President Musharraf won't act, we will,' he came under attack not only from Hillary Clinton but also from Senators Joseph Biden and Christopher Dodd. It turned out, though, that their objection was not to what he said – which they agreed with – but to the undiplomatic indiscretion of saying it out loud."

26 I shall employ the term "sustained detention without charge" rather than "arbitrary detention," because to characterize the detention of a particular individual as "arbitrary" is to say that it has been effected without due process. But how much process is actually "due" a given detainee, according to American

constitutional law, always depends on what reasonableness in the particular circumstances requires. Thus, to describe U.S. custody over Guantánamo captives as arbitrary is to assume that U.S. authorities behaved unreasonably given the circumstances of capture. That question must therefore be addressed on its own terms before one may conclude that the resulting detentions do or do not violate due process. *See, e.g.,* Fiona de Londras, "The Right to Challenge the Lawfulness of Detention: An International Perspective on U.S. Detention of Suspected Terrorists," 12 J. J. Conflict & Security L. 223, 238–47 (2007).

27 This standpoint today draws moral sustenance from notions of human rights and finds textual support in Art. 5(3) of the Fourth Geneva Convention (protecting civilians who lose protected status by taking up arms) and Common Art. 3 of the Conventions. Key terms of the latter provision, however, are vague and the scope of its application contested, as Derek Jinks observes in "The Declining Significance of POW Status," 45 Harv. Int'l L.J. 367, 402 (2004).

28 Larry May, War Crimes and Just War 301–02 (2007) (describing a view he does not hold and does not ascribe to anyone). Or perhaps one should say, more precisely, that no one seriously argues this view in print, which is not to deny that it may be widely held and even publicly expressed in certain venues, on occasion; Slavoj Žižek, Iraq: The Borrowed Kettle 53 (2006) (describing the comments of one call-in contributor to a Fox TV discussion).

29 Tit-for-tat is the game strategy by which one cooperates on the first move and thereafter mirrors the other player's previous move.

30 *Hilton v. Guyot,* 159 U.S. 113, 228 (1895) (stating that "international law is founded upon mutuality and reciprocity"); Antonio Cassese, International Law 15 (2005) ("In the present international community traditional rules based on reciprocity still constitute the bulk of international law."); Francesco Parisi & Nita Ghei, "The Role of Reciprocity in International Law," 36 Cornell Int'l L.J. 93, 119, 122 (2003) (describing reciprocity as a "meta-rule" for all of international law and "a basic principle of customary law"); Bruno Simma, "Reciprocity," 7 Encyclopedia of Public International Law, 400, 400 (1985) ("As long as international law lacks a centralized enforcement machinery . . . reciprocity will remain . . . a constructive, mitigating, and stabilizing force, the importance of which can hardly be overestimated."); Elizabeth Zoller, Peacetime Unilateral Remedies 15 (1984) (describing reciprocity as "a condition theoretically attached to every legal norm of international law"); Ingrid Detter de Lupis, The Law of War 339–40 (1987) ("Reciprocity is at the root of the international legal system itself . . . It is a concept particularly important to the Law of War."); Eyal Benvenisti, "The U.S. and the Use of Force: Double-Edged Hegemony and the Management of Global Emergencies," 15 Euro. J. Int'l L. 677, 695 (2004) ("actors that are undeterrable – rogue governments, terrorist groups – undermine the promise of reciprocity, which has long been the foundation of the international legal order"); Ernst Schneeberger, "Reciprocity as a Maxim of International Law," 37 Geo. L. J. 29 (1948) ("Reciprocity has a governing position both in peacetime and wartime. Solely on the constructive basis of reciprocity it was possible to mitigate even the severities of war."); James Turner Johnson, "International Law," *in* The Blackwell Encyclopedia of Political Thought, David Miller, ed. 246, 247 (1987) ("Much international law, particularly the law of war, depends on the deterrent force of . . . the fear of reciprocal reaction."); Ward Thomas,

The Ethics of Destruction 67 (1992) (noting that "the concept of reciprocity seems to be crucial to the idea of the sovereign equality of states that is at the very core of the Westphalian system").

31 Allowing response in kind, as write two legal scholars, "is reasonably designed so to affect the enemy's expectations about the costs and gains of reiteration or continuation of his initial criminal act . . . as to induce its termination." Myres McDougal & Florentino Feliciano, Law and Minimum World Public Order 682 (1961); Edward Kwakwa, The International Law of Armed Conflict 131 (1992) ("Because the international legal order does not provide for a supranational law-enforcement authority, states are traditionally allowed to resort to 'self-help' mechanisms to ensure compliance with the law."); Han Kelsen, Principles of International Law 24 (1952) ("There is nothing to prevent us from calling reprisals sanctions of international law, [because] reprisals are reactions against violations of international law.").

32 Hersch Lauterpacht, "The Limits of the Operation of the Law of War," 30 Brit. Yearbook. of Int'l L. 206, 212 (1953); *see also* Steven Ratner, "The War on Terrorism and International Humanitarian Law," 14 Mich. St. J. Int'l L. 19, 22 (2006) ("We cannot have a legal regime where only one side of combatants benefits from the protection of international humanitarian law."); L. C. Green, The Contemporary Law of Armed Conflict 55 (1993) ("The law of war, particularly the Geneva Law embodying principles of humanitarianism, operates on a reciprocal basis, as is emphasized by Art. 2 common to the Conventions.").

33 Hans Kelsen, "La Technique du Droit International de L'organisation de la Paix," 15 R.D.I.L.C. 16 (1934).

34 Louise Richardson, What Terrorists Want: Understanding the Enemy, Containing the Threat 207 (2006).

35 George Washington, 17 The Writings of George Washington, 1732–1799, quoted in Richardson, *id.*

36 Quoted in David Hackett Fischer, Washington's Crossing 379 (2004).

37 Thus, the Hague Regulations of 1907 prohibit poisoned weapons, "treacherous" attack, deliberate harm to those who have surrendered, denial of quarter, any weapon "calculated to cause unnecessary suffering," pillage, destruction of enemy property not "imperatively demanded by the necessities of war," and so forth. Art. 23(b), at http://www.icrc.org/ihl.nsf/FULL/195.

38 In some respects these latter conventions resemble arms control agreements limiting the number of missiles, for instance, that each side may deploy. Unlike weapons-prohibition agreements, arms control treaties are not primarily concerned, however, with minimizing unnecessary suffering in war, but rather with preserving the peace by balancing power between potential antagonists.

39 This is a rough characterization and slight oversimplification for, as we see in later chapters, there are places within Geneva law, especially as influenced by custom and limited by reservation, where reciprocity is authorized. There are increasingly also places within weapons-prohibitions law where it is not. Instances of the latter include the Biological Weapons Convention, the Chemical Weapons Convention, and the Convention on the Prohibition of the Use, Stockpiling, Production and Transfer of Anti-Personnel Mines and on their Destruction. The terms "Geneva law" and "Hague-type law" are almost misnomers, in that some treaties, from the 1899 and 1907 Hague Conventions

themselves through Geneva Additional Protocol I, cover both sets of issues (i.e., the treatment of *hors de combat* and methods of combat).

40 Nathaniel Berman, "Privileging Combat? Contemporary Conflict and the Legal Construction of War," 43 Colum. J. Transnat'l L. 1, 17 (2004) (describing the law of war as consistently displaying a "strong statist and governmentalist bias" in favoring states over nonstate adversaries).

41 George H. Aldrich, "Review of David Wippman & Matthew Evangelista, New Wars, New Laws? Applying the Laws of War in 21st Century Conflicts," 100 A.J.I.L. 495, 497 (2006) (noting that, with respect to civil wars, the relevant international law "has been structured with great care to avoid giving any recognition or legitimacy to any entity other than the state in which the armed conflict occurs").

42 One cannot do this, that is, if one aspires to logical consistency rather than resting content with partisan point scoring.

43 Third Geneva Convention, Arts. 4(1) and (2). The U.S. Army Center for Military History suggests that the United States, in ratifying the Conventions, assumed the country's wars would display such characteristics. "Prisoners of War and War Crime," at http://www.army.mil/cmh/books/Vietnam/Law-War/law-04.htm, at 1.

44 Olivier Roy notes in this respect that Al Qaeda "has no strategic vision. It fights against Babylon, against what it sees as evil." Olivier Roy, Globalized Islam: The Search for a New Ummah 293–94 (2004). Hence, many of its targets – nightclubs and tourist resorts – have no military or strategic value in the normal sense.

45 William H. Taft, IV, "A View from the Top: American Perspectives on International Law after the Cold War," 31 Yale J. Int'l L. 503, 509 (2006). The initial conclusion that the Geneva Conventions did not apply was based on the view that the conflict with Al Qaeda was neither an interstate war, governed by Common Art. 2, nor a civil war "occurring in the territory of one of the High Contracting [i.e., state] Parties," for which Art. 3 was chiefly intended.

However it is characterized, the conflict with Al Qaeda and kindred jihadist groups is expected to continue long after U.S. withdrawal from Iraq. Bruce Berkowitz, "Strategy for a Long Struggle," 141 Policy Rev. 33, 39–46 (Feb. & Mar., 2007) (comparing the struggle against Al Qaeda with the Cold War, noting that resolution will not occur from a U.S. withdrawal from Iraq); Mark Mazzetti, "New Generation of Qaeda Chiefs Is Seen on Rise," New York Times, April 2, 2007, at A1; Associated Press, "Chertoff Warns of Higher Risks of Terrorism," New York Times, July 11, 2007, at A16 (reporting that U.S intelligence analysts have concluded that Al Qaeda has rebuilt its operating capability to a level not seen since just before the 9/11 attacks); Mark Mazzetti & David Rohde, "Amid Policy Disputes, Qaeda Grows in Pakistan," New York Times, June 30, 2008, at A1.

46 Goldsmith, *supra* note 2, at 146. This answer was embraced because the president and vice president made clear that, as a policy judgment, they believed it would best serve their preeminent concern with preventing another 9/11-scale attack. *See also* Steven Lee Myers, "Bush Uses Veto on C.I.A. Tactics to Affirm Legacy," New York Times, March 9, 2008, at A1 (describing the president's veto of legislation that would have outlawed waterboarding by the CIA).

47 George W. Bush, March 29, 2002, at http://www.whitehouse.gov/news/releases/2002/03/20020328.html.

48 Maj. Jefferson Reynolds, "Collateral Damage on the 21st Century Battlefield," 56 Air Force L. Rev. 1, 79 (2005).

49 Posted by Aaron, April 25, 2008, at http://meganmcardle.theatlantic.com/archives/2008/04/strategy_or_vendetta.php.

50 Moral hazard may be found almost anywhere, but the extent of its influence on given behavior is much harder to establish. On some of the concept's difficulties, *see* Tom Baker, "On the Genealogy of Moral Hazard," 75 Tex. L. Rev. 237 (1996).

51 Steven Ratner, "Predator and Prey: Seizing and Killing Suspected Terrorists Abroad," 15 J. Polit. Phil. 251, 274 (2007).

52 Barbara Fried, "Ex Ante/Ex Post," 13 J. Contemp. Legal Issues 123, 125 (2003). Fried shows how this conclusion is reached not only by "rational expectations" economists, but also – with only minor qualifications – by moral theorists of the "luck egalitarianism" school. Thinkers in both schools conclude that "a just state would equalize the effects of brute luck on individual endowments, but leave individuals to bear the consequences (good and bad) of their choices."

53 The analogous doctrine is that of "concurrent conditions," according to which "tender by each party is a constructive condition of the other party's duty to perform. Each party may claim that he was justified in terminating the contract because of the other's breach." E. Allan Farnsworth, Contracts 610 (1982).

54 John Yoo, War by Other Means 23 (2006). As Oppenheim writes, "Breach of a bilateral treaty by one of the parties . . . entitles the other party to invoke the breach as a ground for terminating the treaty or suspending its operation. This has been accepted as customary international law." 1 Oppenheim's International Law. Sir Robert Jennings & Sir Arthur Watts, eds. 1300 (9th ed. 1992). In the "civil law world," a treaty duty that is contingent on a treaty partner's corresponding compliance is described as "synallagmatic." 17 Oxford Engl. Dict. 468 (2nd ed. 1989).

55 On reprisal, *see* Stefan Oeter, "Methods and Means of Combat," *in* The Handbook of Humanitarian Law in Armed Conflicts, Dieter Fleck, ed. 105, 149 (1995); Christopher Greenwood, "The Twilight of the Law of Belligerent Reprisals," *in* Greenwood, Essays on War in International Law 295, 334 (2006).

56 This study often employs the term "coercive interrogation" instead of torture, because the latter, in addition to having a lay meaning, is also a legal term of art, so that its very invocation can raise irrelevant issues. Also, the present study is equally concerned with coercive forms of interrogation that may fall short of torture in the legal sense. When the word "torture" *is* here employed, then, it is used in a manner consistent with its legal meaning. But unless clearly indicated, the concern here is not to distinguish torture from other forms of cruel, inhuman, and/or degrading treatment during interrogation, as all of these are prohibited by the Convention Against Torture.

57 Kurt Campbell & Michael O'Hanlon, Hard Power: The New Politics of National Security 195 (2006). One may quibble over whether this may accurately be characterized as "power" at all, insofar as it does not involve compelling people to do anything against their will, anything they do not freely choose to do. One could say, more precisely, that soft power arises only as a byproduct of the

more proximate "demonstration effect" entailed in the voluntary emulation of societal models widely perceived as particularly successful in relevant respects. The latter is scarcely a new idea. Ragnar Nurkse, Problems of Capital Formation in Underdeveloped Countries 67–76 (1953); *see also* Thomas Loya & John Boli, "Standardization in the World Polity: Technical Rationality over Power," *in* Constructing World Culture. J. Boli & G. Thomas, eds. 169 (1999).

58 On the distinction between specific and diffuse reciprocity, *see* Robert Keohane, "Reciprocity in International Relations," 40 Int'l Org. 1, 4 (1986). International law employs both varieties. In international trade law, for instance, specific reciprocity is embodied in rules on "most favored nation," whereas diffuse reciprocity finds expression in the rules on "national treatment." *Id.* at 25–27; *see also* Ronald Mitchell & Patricia Keilbach, "Situation Structure and Institutional Design: Reciprocity, Coercion and Exchange," 55 Int'l Org. 891 (2001) (showing that specific reciprocity, without linkage to wider issues, is widely preferred in most multilateral treaties, especially where benefits and burdens can be distributed symmetrically in this way among all party states); Alan Swan, "'Fairness' and 'Reciprocity' in International Trade Section 301 and The Rule of Law," 16 Ariz. J. Int'l & Comp. L. 37, 38, 43–45 (1999). Trade law differs from war law in that when a victim of trade law violations retaliates by imposing duties on products exported by the violator, the costs are not confined to the latter, but very much shared by the former, whose consumers must then pay more than before retaliatory penalties (such as countervailing duties) were imposed. A commitment to such "strong reciprocity," as some call this, often springs as much from a desire to punish wrongdoing as to defend one's immediate interests. Samuel Bowles & Herbert Gintis, "Is Equality Passé? *Homo Reciprocans* and the Future of Egalitarian Politics," Boston Rev. 4, 8 (Jan. 1999).

59 World Trade Organization, Dispute Settlement Gateway, at http://www.wto.org/english/tratop_e/dispu_e/dispu_e.htm (last visited Jan. 28, 2008).

60 Michael Scott, 1 Scott on Information Technology Law 5–63 (2007); Peter Yu, "Currents and Crosscurrents in the International Intellectual Property Regime," 38 Loy. L.A. L. Rev. 323, 339–340 (2004). As a multilateral agreement, however, the Berne Convention seeks to dispense with the need for reciprocity in "national treatment" through bilateral treaty. Even so, under the Convention, "if a Contracting State provides for a term of protection of 70 years after the death of the author (that is, 20 years more than the required minimum under that Convention), such a Contracting State may, in the case of works originating in another Contracting State which grants 50 years, apply to such works a term of protection of 50 years rather than 70 years. Basic Principles of the Multilateral Treaties in the Field of Intellectual Property, Int'l Bureau of the World Intel. Prop. Org. 3 (1989).

61 Jean Piaget, Biology and Knowledge, B. Walsh, trans. 323–24 (1971); *see also* Talcott Parsons, The Social System 300 (1951) (arguing that personality development requires that one acquire "the discipline of refusal to reciprocate," necessary to avoid "a vicious circle-building").

62 C. S. Lewis, The Problem of Pain 93 (1962).

63 States have inherent authority, in virtue of their sovereignty, to establish national law at odds with their international legal duties. They may, for instance,

incorporate mistaken understandings of international legal norms into their internal law. This does not mean, however, that states are the only authoritative arbiters of their duties under international law itself. Other states and international tribunals may differently interpret the scope of a country's duties under an applicable customary or treaty norm.

64 This prevalent attitude within the Bush administration was revealed, for instance, in the executive order establishing Combatant Status Review Tribunals (CSRTs). As one legal scholar notes, these "define so broadly the circumstances justifying detention that, rather than instituting temporal, spatial or other constraints on the scope of application of the law of armed conflict, these procedures simply exploit the absence of such constraints. The CSRT order permits detention for anyone who, before capture, 'was part of or supporting Taliban or al Qaeda forces, or associated forces that are engaged in hostilities against the United States or its coalition partners.'" Monica Hakimi, "International Standards for Detaining Terrorism Suspects: Moving beyond the Armed Conflict-Criminal Divide," 33 Yale J. Int'l L. 369, 407 (2008); *See* Memorandum from Dep. Sec. Def. to Sec. Navy, Order Establishing Combatant Status Review Tribunals (July 7, 2004).

65 In arguing from both customary international law and the jurisprudence of Ronald Dworkin, Chapter 2 adopts legal approaches that Bush administration defenders are loath to employ. Yet Dworkin's methods, we will see, are by no means intrinsically "liberal" or left-leaning in their results, any more than the concept of reciprocity is inherently conservative. One finds no reference to the latter concept, for instance, in any leading, book-length survey of the history of conservative thought. *See, e.g.,* Ted Honderich, Conservatism (1990); Russell Kirk, The Conservative Mind: From Burke to Eliot (1978); Mark Gerson, The Neoconservative Vision: From the Cold War to the Culture Wars (1997); Clinton Rossiter, Conservatism in America (1982).

66 Increased U.S. reliance on reciprocity in this regard "need not involve resort to tit-for-tat reprisals," notes one discussion of this possibility, "but could be a flexible approach whereby the United States takes account of its opponent's compliance record in its own interpretation and application of the treaties." Lee A. Casey & David Rivkin, Jr., "Rethinking the Geneva Conventions," *in* The Torture Debate in America, Karen Greenberg, ed. 203, 204 (2006). These authors do not elaborate, however, on the ways in which this suggestion might be rendered operational nor how it would be in any way legally cabined. *Cf.* Glenn Sulmasy, "The Law of Armed Conflict in the Global War on Terror: International Lawyers Fighting the Last War," 19 Notre Dame J. L. Ethics & Pub. Pol'y 309, 314 (2005) ("A new, modified law of armed conflict against international terrorism needs to be developed in order to regulate . . . the treatment of captured international terrorists. . . . Lawyers must create an adequate code to meet the new threats."); Rosa Ehrenreich Brooks, "War Everywhere: Rights, National Security Law, and the Law of Armed Conflict in the Age of Terror," 153 U. Penn. L. Rev. 675, 761 (2003) (arguing the need for "a new law of war [that] would have to resort to standards rather than rules").

67 Pub. L. No. 109–366, 120 Stat. 2600 (Oct. 17, 2006).

68 On the JAG corps – its organization, history, and advisory role in law of war issues – *see* Frederic Borch, Judge Advocates in Combat: Army Lawyers in

Military Operations from Vietnam to Haiti (2001); U.S. Army Judge Advocate Generals Corps, The Army Lawyer: A History of the Judge Advocate General's Corps, 1775–1975 (1976).

69 Associated Press, "Pentagon Lawyers Warn against Evidence Limits," New York Times, Sept. 7, 2006, at A27; Mark Mazzetti & Neil A. Lewis, "Military Lawyers Caught in Middle on Tribunals," New York Times, Sept. 16, 2006, at A1.

70 Editorial, "A Dangerous New Order," New York Times, Oct. 19, 2006, at A26.

71 Paul Rieckhoff, "Do Unto Your Enemy . . . ," New York Times, Sept. 25, 2006, A25. The JAG memoranda supporting adherence to Geneva norms in treatment of Al Qaeda detainees may be found at http://www.balkin.blogspot.com/ jag.memos.pdf. Many legal scholars have made similar assertions. *See, e.g.,* Jordan Paust, Beyond the Law: The Bush Administration's Unlawful Responses in the "War" on Terror 55 (2007).

72 Kate Zernike, "Rebuff for Bush on How To Treat Terror Suspects," New York Times, Sept. 15, 2006, at A1 (reporting that Republican leaders, including Senator John McCain and former Secretary of State Colin Powell disagreed with President Bush's "redefinition" of the Geneva Conventions, worrying that it would "put [the] troops at risk"). General Richard Myers, Chairman of the Joint Chiefs of Staff during the key period of the Bush administation, expressed similar views regarding the importance of maximizing prospects for reciprocity in future conflicts. Sands, *supra* note 21, at 89. After questioning Attorney General designate Michael Mukasey in October 2007, moreover, ten Democrats on the Senate Judiciary Committee similarly wrote that Mukasey's "unwillingness to state that waterboarding is illegal may place Americans at risk of being subject to this abusive technique." "Senate Committee Democrats Demand Mukasey's Views on Waterboarding," http://www.humanrightsfirst. org/us_law/digest/usls_digest170_102607.html. Human Rights First, Law and Security Digest, Oct. 26, 2007. In a Nov. 2007 CNN opinion poll, nearly 70% of Americans report that they consider waterboarding to constitute "torture," but some 40% thought it should be used on certain terror suspects. Marc Santora, "McCain Finds Sympathy on Torture Issue," New York Times, Nov. 16, 2007, at A1.

73 Peter Singer, The Expanding Circle: Ethics and Sociobiology 136–37 (1981). Singer notes, "The idea crops up independently in quite different . . . traditions, and is, in each case, seized on as something fundamental to ethical living, a foundation from which all else can be derived." *Id.* The Golden Rule is very close in substance to Kant's first formulation of the categorical imperative: "Act only according to that maxim by which you can at the same time will that it should become a universal law." Immanuel Kant, Foundations of the Metaphysics of Morals, Lewis White Beck, trans. 38 (1995) (1785).

74 The two formulations are sometimes combined, as in Leviticus 19:18, "Do not seek revenge or bear a grudge against one of your people, but love your neighbor as yourself." *See also* Leviticus 19:34. "But the stranger that dwelleth with you shall be unto you as one born among you, and thou shalt love him as thyself; for ye were strangers in the land of Egypt."

75 Robert Turner, "Constitutional and International Law Implications of Executive Order 13440 Interpreting Common Art. 3 of the 1949 Geneva Conventions," Testimony, Select Committee on Intelligence, U.S. Senate, Sept. 25, 2007, at 40.

The JAG instructors describe this maxim as their "Modified Golden Rule." The modification consists in the fact that it includes the qualification: "There are things we can do to U.S. soldiers that we CANNOT do to Detainees (SERE training, lack of sleep, mandatory PT)." *Id.* SERE stands for "Survival, Evasion, Resistance, and Escape."

76 Luke 6:27–35; Alan Kirk, "'Love Your Enemies,' the Golden Rule, and Ancient Reciprocity," 122 J. Biblical Lit. 667, 669 (2003). Kirk argues that the "love your enemies" maxim "excludes the principles of reciprocity and equivalence that are crucial to justice. Accordingly, it cannot found an equitable system of ethics; indeed, if applied autonomously, it would create grotesque caricatures of morality." *Id.*; *compare* Paul Ricoeur, "The Golden Rule: Exegetical and Theological Perspectives," 36 New Test. Stud. 392, 392, 396 (1990). Ricoeur distinguishes the "love your enemies" maxim, with its "logic of superabundance," from the Golden Rule, with its "logic of equivalence." He writes, "The one is unilateral. The other is bilateral. The one expects nothing in return. The other legitimates a certain kind of reciprocity." Still, the Golden Rule entails only what might be called a hypothetical or subjunctive reciprocity: Treat the other *as if* the other were to treat you as you treat him, not as he *actually* treats you, which may be quite differently. In several statements in which Osama bin Laden appears to embrace the reciprocity principle, he seems to understand it primarily to mean, Do unto others as they have done unto you, at least when this entails doing harmful things.

77 William Ian Miller, Eye for an Eye 69 (2006) ("One can see the Golden Rule as only a slight modification of the basic moral rule of mandatory reciprocity" among the ancient Greeks and Persians, as well as the medieval Vikings). Miller says nothing about what the "slight modification" may involve.

78 These are Arts. 4 and 5. For their analysis in this regard, *see* Jinks, *supra* note 27, at 370–83.

79 *Id.* at 406.

80 Forcible countermeasures consist of permissible applications of force employed in response to preceding uses of force that, though unlawful, do not constitute "armed attack" within the meaning of UN Charter, Art. 51. Existing judicial discussions of countermeasures, such as those of Judge Simma's Separate Opinion in the *Oil Platforms* case and in *Nicaragua v. U.S.*, both from the ICJ, concern the rules governing such measures as a resort to force. *Oil Platforms (Iran v. U.S.)*, 2003 I.C.J. 161, at 332–33 (Judgment of Nov. 6). Once a state of armed conflict comes into being, the law of belligerent reprisals generally applies. I.L.C., Draft Articles on State Responsibility, Art. 49 (permitting countermeasures "against a State which is responsible for an internationally wrongful act in order to induce that State to comply with its obligations"); *Corfu Channel Case*, Judgment of April 9, 1949, I.C.J. Reports, 1949, 4, 34–35 (recognizing the legality of countermeasures); Restatement (Third), of the Foreign Relations Law of the United States, §905(2), providing that "a state victim of a violation of an international obligation by another state may resort to countermeasures that might otherwise be unlawful, if such measures: (a) are necessary to terminate the violation or prevent further violation, or to remedy the violation; and (b) are not out of proportion to the violation and the injury suffered. (2) The threat or use of force in response to a violation in international law is subject

to prohibitions on the threat or use of force in the United Nations Charter as well as to Subsection (1)."

81 Patterns of implementation, including nonenforcement, may work to qualify the express terms of treaties, in establishing the parties' duties. Vienna Convention on the Law of Treaties, Art. 31(3) ("There shall be taken into account, together with the context . . . (b) any subsequent practice in the application of the treaty."); *see generally* Eric A. Posner, "Terrorism and the Laws of War," 5 Chi. J. Int'l Law 423 (2005).

82 Joel Rohlf, "The Geneva Conventions and the War on Terror: International Legal Reform as a Solution," seminar paper, Univ. of Iowa College of Law, May 2007 (parsing Jinks's scholarship).

83 Fréderic Mégret, "From 'Savages' to 'Unlawful Combatants': A Postcolonial Look at International Humanitarian Law's 'Other,'" *in* International Law and its Others, Anne Orford, ed. 265, 287 (2007).

84 Frits Kalshoven, Belligerent Reprisals 390 (2005).

85 As noted before, however, whereas the act of reprisal reflects the game-theoretic strategy of tit-for-tat, the intention accompanying that act must be to deter future violations of the sort prompting reprisal, rather than retribution or the desire to gain strategic advantage.

86 *See, e.g.,* Stephen Neff, War and the Law of Nations 228–29 (2005). Walzer discusses another such apparent success from World War II, in which French partisans seem to have terminated the German practice of killing ten Frenchmen for every German soldier killed when the partisans killed eighty German POWs. Michael Walzer, Just and Unjust Wars: A Moral Argument with Historical Illustrations 208–09 (1977). Military historians describe many instances of reprisals as successfully stopping an adversary's law of war violations. *See, e.g.,* Geoffrey Parker, "Early Modern Europe," *in* The Laws of War: Constraints on Warfare in the Western World, Michael Howard et al., eds. 40, 55 (1994). Yet it would also be easy to describe many situations in which reprisals were demonstrably unsuccessful in stopping enemy misconduct, as in the Iran-Iraq war, during which both sides frequently bombed each other's civilian population in professed reprisal. Andrew Mitchell, "Does One Illegality Merit Another? The Law of Belligerent Reprisals in International Law," 170 Mil. L. Rev. 155, 171–72 (2001). As neither state had ratified the 1977 Geneva Additional Protocol I, neither was treaty-bound to abjure civilian reprisals on enemy-controlled territory. Many, and probably most, belligerents' invocations of reprisal do not fully satisfy the pertinent legal criteria to be so classified (i.e., advance notice, last resort, proportionality, etc.). The most technically scrupulous account of retaliation in warfare would therefore employ the term "reprisal" within quotation marks in most instances. Stylistic reasons to the contrary are overriding, however.

87 In civil litigation, for example, restoring plaintiffs to their rightful position regularly requires remedies that make the defendants pay for more damage than they caused or that inflict harm on third parties who have done no wrong. Douglas Laycock devotes great attention to this problem in its myriad manifestations throughout his Modern American Remedies (2002, 3rd ed.).

88 As Coleman observes, "If corrective justice requires rectifying wrongful losses but prohibits doing so if doing so creates other wrongful losses, then corrective justice may permit considerable wrongful loss. On the other hand, if corrective justice permits the imposition of wrongful losses in order to eliminate even greater losses, then at least it minimizes the total amount of corrective injustice in the world." This raises the question, "Which is the proper way of understanding the demands of corrective justice?" Jules Coleman, Risks and Wrongs 307 (1992). That question, as it bears on humanitarian law, is addressed in Chapter 7.

89 Jon Elster, Explaining Social Behavior: More Nuts and Bolts for the Social Sciences 104–05 (2007). Elster here adopts the first of the four conceptions of reciprocity outlined in the next few pages of this book.

90 *Id.* at 104.

91 *Id.* at 105.

92 *Id.*

93 Robert Keohane, "The Public Delegitimation of Terrorism," *in* Worlds in Collision: Terror and the Future of Global Order, 141, 143 (2002); *see also* Deborah W. Larson, "Exchange and Reciprocity in International Negotiations," 3 Int'l Negotiation 121, 127 (1998) ("Foreign aid is like a gift which creates an implicit obligation on the part of the recipient to reciprocate. . . . Even aid which appears to be given without expectation of commercial gains may nevertheless be motivated by the desire to gain influence over the recipient countries' policies or acquire markets in the future."); David Baldwin, Economic Statecraft 292–94 (1985); *cf.* Jonathan Schwartz, "Dealing with a 'Rogue State': The Libya Precedent," 101 A.J.I.L. 553, 553 (2007) ("On December 19, 2003, the leaders of Libya, the United States, and the United Kingdom issued parallel announcements confirming a dramatic change of Libyan policy on weapons of mass destruction and a reciprocal willingness of the United States and the United Kingdom to respond positively as that policy was implemented.").

　　The precise terms of trade, of benefits for burdens, that foreign assistance programs impose are registered only in the most approximate manner and are by no means susceptible to precise calculation. As Keohane observes, "It would be hard now, much less in 1947 or 1956, to determine whether the U.S. extracted 'enough' deference to compensate for its aid" to Western Europe in those years. Robert Keohane, "Empathy and International Regimes," *in* Beyond Self-Interest, Jane Mansbridge, ed. 227, 233 (1990). This aid was provided through the Marshall Plan and several trade arrangements facilitating U.S. imports from a slowly recovering Continent. In repayment, the United States soon had occasion to demand considerable deference from its beneficiaries in key crises, such as that over Suez in 1956.

94 William Arkin, "What $10 Billion Has Bought in Pakistan," Wash. Post, Nov. 6, 2007.

95 The word "perceives" is introduced here to suggest a key limitation of game theory, the intellectual tradition that has sought to make the most of this type of reciprocity. Game theory relies on a conception of learning that views persons as stimulus-response automatons, leaving out their perceptions of others' beliefs, motives, and intentions, as well as changes in their preferences and identity

over time, as they interact with one another. Yet the perceived motives of others, including other states in the international arena, often decisively affect whether one party will reciprocate another's gift-like concessions. In particular, parties are more likely to reciprocate favors when they perceive these as given freely and as genuinely costly to the giver. Such perceptions are affected by many considerations other than the simple "facts of the matter." Deborah Welch Larson, "The Psychology of Reciprocity in International Relations," 4 Negotiation J. 281, 282–83 (July 1988). Because game theory has not found a way to handle the complexities mentioned here, this book ultimately relies very little on such theory for its main arguments and is, in fact, generally critical of its value for analyzing the key questions here in issue, unless it were applied very differently than by its current adherents. *See* Chapter 10.

96 Adam Smith, The Theory of Moral Sentiments 160 (1969) (1759).

97 Bronislaw Malinowski, Crime and Custom in Savage Society 47 (1926) (emphasis supplied). He observed that in the villages he studied the give-and-take principle was "well-assessed . . . always mentally ticked off and in the long run balanced." *Id.* at 26. Ten years earlier, Thurnwald was the first ethnographer to employ and develop the concept of reciprocity, in the context of bridal exchange. Richard Thurnwald, Bánaro Society: Social Organization and Kinship System of a Tribe in the Interior of New Guinea 325, 338–43 (1916).

98 For a vivid illustration of how, as a practical matter, nothing more than passions of vengeance sometimes underlie the political demand for reprisal, *see, e.g.,* Mark Neely Jr., The Civil War and The Limits of Destruction 170–79 (2008) (describing vehement demands by northern radicals in Congress for retaliation against Confederate POWs in response to Confederate starvation of Union POWs at Andersonville Prison).

99 Ricoeur, *supra* note 76, at 397 (emphasis in original).

100 Martha Nussbaum, "Seneca on Anger in Public Life," *in* Nussbaum, The Therapy of Desire: Theory and Practice in Hellenistic Ethics 402, 403 (1994).

101 On the prominence of revenge in the express motivations of jihadist suicide bombers and Al Qaeda members, *see* Richardson, *supra* note 34, at 88–94.

102 Reciprocity as tit-for-tat differs from retribution in that it is prospective, not retrospective in its chief concerns; it aims to establish or reestablish cooperation in the present and future. It punishes only to that end and only to the extent that punishment will likely further that end. It does not assume that punishment is morally required by justice or fairness, whether these are conceived as the restoration of balance between benefit and burden or as respecting the victim's rights and the perpetrator's autonomy.

103 As a preferred strategy of interaction with others, tit-for-tat may not be logically entailed by a recognition of our psychological propensity to treat others as they treat us. Yet anyone displaying this propensity would quickly discover an elective affinity for tit-for-tat, finding it highly congenial as an approach to interaction with others.

104 It bears mention here that reciprocity of this variety differs from simple self-defense in that the retaliating belligerent sometimes formally acts as legal agent of the international community, enforcing international law when that community itself is unable to do so by other means.

105 The notion that parties to a conflict are bound by the same set of rules should not be confused with the notion that each party has a duty to respect the other's rights. Some rights are of this nature, others not. Consider an example of each, both drawn from the law of war. When country A initiates an armed attack against country B, B is entitled to defend itself. But this does not mean that A has a duty to prostrate itself before B's counterattack (i.e., a duty not to resist it). Though B acts within its rights, A may nonetheless – once a state of armed conflict exists – lawfully employ force to repel B's actions, as long as A complies with the law on means and methods of fighting. Here, B's rights do not imply correlative duties for A. In contrast, if soldier C has a right to POW status, then enemy soldier D, when accepting C's surrender, has a duty to respect C's right and must treat him accordingly. Here, rights do have correlative duties. On the basis for such distinctions, *see generally* Wesley Hohfeld, Fundamental Legal Conceptions 23–114 (1923) (distinguishing types of rights as liberties, powers, immunities, and permissions).

106 Though normative in nature, this conception of reciprocity requires certain empirical predicates to become effectively operational, as we see in later chapters.

107 Robert Keohane "International Relations: Two Approaches," *in* International Theory: Critical Investigations 279, 289 (1995). Keohane in turn quotes from Martin Wight, System of States 135 (1977).

108 As one avowedly "Third World" author acknowledged in the early 1960s, "international law applied to the relations between the East and West in the sixteenth century and later was a law of reciprocity which accepted the sovereignty of Indian and Asian rulers and communities. Not only Grotius but also Pufendorf, Vattel, and other classical writers testified to this state of affairs. It was only after the establishment of Western colonial rule in Asia that writers on international law began to deny sovereignty to these rulers and communities." R. P. Anand, "Role of the 'New' Asian-African Countries in the Present International Legal Order," 56 Proc. Amer. Soc. Int'l L. 383, 386–87 (1962).

109 Michael Byers, Custom, Power and the Power of Rules: International Relations and Customary International Law 89–90 (1999).

110 More precisely, we should say that the prospect of Kantian generalization *would* limit the advent of new customary rules if powerful states were much worried about the effects of their conduct on custom. Yet consider one illustration of how such states often do not seem to care. International lawyers roundly condemned the Bush administration's 2002 U.S. National Security Strategy for its doctrine of preventive war. The most offensive feature of that doctrine, the lawyers lamented, was the implication that America would more readily resort to force and thereby alter customary international law. This, in turn, would open the floodgates for other states to do the same. That result was entailed, they observed, by the settled norm that all states enjoy equal rights of formal sovereignty, which reflects (our second conception of) the reciprocity principle. Yet "realists" rightly retort that the existence of a right is less significant than the material factors determining whether a state will use it against another. On this view, states' ambitions and the balance of power, not legal doctrine, determine when states resort to force.

111 Immanuel Kant, Foundations of the Metaphysics of Morals, Lewis White Beck, trans. 38 (1995) (1785).

112 Samuel Pufendorf, The Law of Nature and Nations, Basil Kennet, trans. 2.3.13 (1749) (1672); for analysis, *see* Istvan Hont, "The Language of Sociability and Commerce: Samuel Pufendorf and the Theoretical Foundations of the 'Four-Stages' Theory," *in* The Languages of Political Theory in Early-Modern Europe, Anthony Pagden, ed. 253, 268 (1987).

113 "When risks are reciprocally imposed, actors receive implicit in kind compensation for their exposure to risks in the form of a right to impose equivalent risks on others." Gregory Keating, "Fidelity to Pre-existing Law and the Legitimacy of Legal Decision," 69 Notre Dame L. Rev. 1, 46 (1993).

114 Such rules would also surely seek to do many other things, of course.

115 John Gardner, Offences and Defenses: Selected Essays in the Philosophy of Criminal Law 231 (2007).

116 The same promise was once represented, to be sure, by the International Court of Justice. But there only states themselves, not individual officeholders, are potentially liable for war crimes, and the court's jurisdiction is even more strictly voluntary than that of the International Criminal Court.

Beyond war, in other issue-areas like trade and even the natural environment, the enforcement of international law has undergone a considerable strengthening in recent years. This heartening development has awakened new enthusiasm about the prospect of achieving the same in international criminal and humanitarian law. In other areas of public international law, there has been some concern that the extension and strengthening of formal enforcement institutions will have the undesired side effect of "crowding out" more informal cooperative mechanisms that rely on bilateral reciprocity and that continue to have value. Robert Scott & Paul Stephan, The Limits of Leviathan: Contract Theory and the Enforcement of International Law 27, 104 (2007). But that is precisely the central and avowed aim of international criminal tribunals, as the informal methods of inducing cooperation often entail force or the threat of force.

117 Habermas is the preeminent proponent of this species of reciprocity. *See, e.g.,* Jürgen Habermas, The Philosophical Discourse of Modernity 107 (1987) (seeking to ground moral duties in the principle of reciprocity that is implicit in intersubjective discourse).

118 The four conceptions of reciprocity just identified may share a certain family resemblance, but identifying it convincingly with any care would involve a more strictly philosophical discussion than warranted in a book on institutional political theory.

119 Stephen Neff, War and the Law of Nations 126 (2005).

120 David Glazier, "Ignorance is Not Bliss: The Law of Belligerent Occupation and the U.S. Invasion of Iraq," 58 Rutgers L. Rev. 121, 151 (2005) (quoting Henry W. Halleck, International Law 791, 795 [1861]); *see also* H. Droop, "On the Relations between an Invading Army and the Inhabitants, and the Conditions under which Irregular Troops are Entitled to the Same Treatment as Regular Soldiers," *in* Transactions of the Grotius Society 713 (1871) ("The rights of the non-combatant population to protection for their persons and property . . . necessarily involves . . . a corresponding duty of abstaining from all

further hostilities against the invaders."). Today, the international legal regime of belligerent occupation is regulated by the 1907 Hague Regulations and the Fourth 1949 Geneva Convention. Both also apply as customary law.

It may first seem unconvincing, even bizarre, to classify the relation between military occupier and subject population as contractual, given the centrality of coercion in the relationship. But such a social contract is simply more of the Hobbesian than Lockean variety (i.e., in which the citizen is promised public order and personal security, not democracy or even the rule of law).

121 Law Reports of Trials of War Criminals, Vol. VIII, 1949, (Hostages Trial of Wilhelm List and Others), Int'l Military Tribunal, 15 AD, 632, 637 (1948). *But see* Trial of Hans Rauter, 8 War Crimes Reports 123 (1949). In this latter case, "the defendant was accused of war crimes against the inhabitants of The Netherlands during the German occupation. His main defense was that his actions were justified as reprisals for violations of the rules of war committed by the Dutch. The Netherlands Special Court of Cassation rejected this defense on the theory that since the original wrong lay with Germany as the initator of an unprovoked war of aggression against The Netherlands, The Netherlands was entitled to resort to reprisals against Germany, but that Germany had no right to take counter-reprisals against the The Netherlands." A.R. Albrecht, "War Reprisals in the War Crimes Trials and in the Geneva Conventions of 1949," 47 A.J.I.L. 590, 593 (1953). Albrecht rejects this conclusion. *Id.* at 594.

122 Though initially appealing, this result poses serious problems of its own. Kalshoven, *supra* note 84, at 204–06, 363; René Provost, International Human Rights and Humanitarian Law 175 (2002).

123 German reprisal policy was no more restrained on the Eastern front, often less so. Alexander Rossino, Hitler Strikes Poland: Blitzkrieg, Ideology, and Atrocity 126–52 (2003).

124 Int'l Comm. of the Red Cross, The Geneva Conventions of the 12 August 1949, Commentary, Jean S. Pictet, ed. 454 (1958) ("It is absolutely forbidden for [the POW] to commit any belligerent act, to carry weapons, or to engage in armed resistance, otherwise he will be liable to be treated as a sniper or saboteur."), at http://www.icrc.org/ihl.nsf/COM/375–590113. Geneva Additional Protocol I, Art. 41 defines an *hors de combat* as a person who may not be attacked "provided that . . . he abstains from any hostile act." This same provision in the Protocol, like the Third 1949 Geneva Convention, nonetheless anticipates that POWs will attempt to escape. Third Geneva Convention, Arts. 91-92. Even so, POW escape attempts that employ force may be punished more stringently than nonviolent attempts. *Id.* Art. 93.

125 Max Hastings, Retribution: The Battle for Japan, 1944–45, 54 (2008).

126 For analysis, *see* Antonio Cassese, "On Some Merits of the Israeli Judgment on Targeted Killings," 5 J. Int'l Crim. Justice 339 (2007). The proper scope of the quoted wording is disputed in key respects. Some support the narrow view that targeted killing is not legal because it kills civilians who are not actually carrying weapons or directing troops at the moment they are targeted. Others prefer a broader view, maintaining that targeted killing is lawful insofar as those targeted are regularly engaged in planning, conducting, or dispatching others to commit acts of terror, even if not performing any of these activities at the instant they are targeted. In 2007, the Israel Supreme Court adopted the latter view. H.C.J.

769/02 *The Public Committee against Torture in Israel v. Government of Israel et al.* (at http://elyon1.court.gov.il/files_eng/02/690/007/a34/02007690.a34.pdf). In the absence of a state of "armed conflict," the applicable international law would be that of human rights, rather than humanitarian law, in which case targeted killing would be incompatible with the "inherent right to life" protected in Art. 6(1) of the International Covenant on Civil and Political Rights.

127 Louise Doswald-Beck, "The Right to Life in Armed Conflict: Does International Humanitarian Law Provide All the Answers?" 88 Int'l Rev. of the Red Cross 881, 894 (Dec. 2006).

128 James Kent, Commentaries, *in* 3 The Founders' Constitution, Phillip B. Kurland & Ralph Lerner, eds. 87 (1987) (observing that "every nation has a right to attack and exterminate" pirates); Ingrid Detter, "The Law of War and Illegal Combatants," 75 Geo. Wash. L. Rev. 1049, 1098–99 (2007) ("In earlier days, the pirate was not even entitled to any form of trial but could, if caught *in flagrante delicto*, be summarily executed; he would normally be immediately hanged by the mast of the ship or drowned by the captor."); Eugene Kontorovich, The Piracy Analogy: Modern Universal Jurisdiction's Hollow Foundation, 45 Harv. Int'l L. J. 183, 190 (2004) ("The law of nations also permitted any nation that caught a pirate to summarily execute him at sea.").

129 Mikkel Thorup, "The Horror of the 'Enemy of Humanity' – on Pirates, Terrorists and States," paper for Conference on "Fear, Horror & Terror," Mansfield College, Oxford Univ. (2007); Douglas Burgess Jr., "The Dread Pirate bin Laden: How Thinking of Terrorists as Pirates Can Help Win the War on Terror," Legal Affairs, July/Aug. 2005. The similarities in how and why international law condemns terrorism and piracy are mirrored in how the left critique of international law sometimes rhapsodizes about common features of both, viewing them equally as latent expressions of resistance to global capitalism, early and late, respectively. Marcus Rediker, Villains of All Nations: Atlantic Pirates in the Golden Age 5–6, 61, 70, 112–20, 136, 143, 159–60, 205–06 (2004); Jean Baudrillard, The Spirit of Terrorism and Other Essays, Chris Turner, trans. 70–71 (2003); Slavoj Žižek, Iraq: The Borrowed Kettle 48–49 (2006).

130 International Covenant on Civil and Political Rights, Art. 6.

131 The term generally preferred in international law would be "unprivileged belligerent," but the term "unlawful combatant" has been employed in U.S. law since *Ex Parte Quirin* and codified in the Military Commissions Act of 2006. Richard R. Baxter, "So-Called 'Unprivileged Belligerency': Spies, Guerrillas, and Saboteurs," 28 B.Y. Int'l L. 1951 321, 328 (1952) ("International law deliberately neglects to protect unprivileged belligerents because of the danger their acts present to their opponents.").

132 There is some disagreement, irrelevant for present purposes, over whether unprivileged belligerency is a distinct crime within international law or whether such law merely authorizes states to prosecute this conduct under domestic law. A. P. V. Rogers, "Unequal Combat and the Law of War," 7 Yearbook of Int'l Humanitarian L. 3, 25 (reviewing conflict among authorities on the question).

133 The authority for this position is not well established in international law, however.

134 Jane Mayer, "The Black Sites," New Yorker, Aug. 13, 2007, at 46, 50. The program was disclosed publicly only in late 2006, "Remarks on the War on Terror," 42 Weekly Comp. Pres. Doc. 1569 (Sept. 6, 2006).

135 "C.I.A. Killed al-Qaeda Suspects in Yemen," BBC News, Nov. 5, 2002, at http://news.bbc.co.uk/2/hi/middle east/2402479.stm. The special rapporteur for the UN Commission on Human Rights characterized the incident as "a clear case of extrajudicial killing." *See* "Civil and Political Rights, Including the Questions of Disappearances and Summary Executions – Extrajudicial, Summary and Arbitrary Executions," Report of the Special Rapporteur, Asma Jahangir (E/CN.4/2003/3) submitted to the UN Economic and Social Council Commission on Human Rights (January 2003), ¶ 39.

136 Center for Defense Information, Presidential Orders and Documents Regarding Foreign Intelligence and Terrorism, at http://www.cdi.org/terrorism/presidential-orders-pr.cfm.

137 Evelyn Colbert, Retaliation in International Law 2 (1948).

138 Ingrid Detter, The Law of War 148 (2000) ("Unlawful combatants... are a legitimate target for any belligerent action."); John C. Yoo & James C. Ho, "The Status of Terrorists," 44 Va. J. Int'l L. 207, 222 (2003).

139 Punishment and detention are the only remedies expressly afforded by the Fourth Geneva Convention. On civil detention under U.S. domestic law, *see* Stephen Dycus et al., Counter terrorism Law 302–10 (2007); *Ex parte Quirin*, 317 U.S. 1, 30–31 (1942) ("Unlawful combatants... are subject to trial and punishment... for acts which render their belligerency unlawful.").

140 Richard Baxter, "The Geneva Conventions of 1949 and Wars of National Liberation," *in* International Terrorism and Political Crimes, M. Cherif Bassiouni, ed. 120, 131 (1973).

141 Yoo & Ho, *supra* note 138, at 217. Though generally rejecting reciprocity within humanitarian law, Kalshoven admits as "psychologically understandable" the persistent question: "How... can one expect a party to respect and protect the prisoners of war which he captures when the enemy refuses even to grant quarter to his soldiers." Kalshoven, *supra* note 84, at 303. That position, though "fallacious," displays "a semblance of reasonableness," he admits. *Id.* He offers no explanation for its fallaciousness.

142 The point may nonetheless be resisted insofar as it entails classifying the present conflict as a "war," rather than a novel challenge to law enforcement. On the blurry line between situations that international law characterizes as armed conflict rather than crime, susceptible to law enforcement measures, *see* Kenneth Roth, "The Law of War in the War on Terror," Foreign Affairs (Jan./Feb. 2004) at 2, 3 ("There is little law... to explain exactly when one set of rules should apply instead of the other."); Noah Feldman, "Choices of Law, Choices of War," 25 Harv. J. L. & Pub. Pol'y 457, 457–58 (2002) (contending that "international terrorism can plausibly be characterized as both crime and war" and that the distinction's "reexamination [is] perhaps long overdue"); *cf.* David Luban, "The War on Terrorism and the End of Human Rights," 22 Phil. & Publ. Pol'y Quart. 9 (Summer 2002). Luban charges that "the U.S. has simply chosen the bits of the law model and the bits of the war model that are most convenient for American interests, and ignored the rest." He rejects without argument

the notion that even "under circumstances of ... dire menace, it is appropriate to treat terrorists as though they embody the most dangerous aspects of both warriors and criminals" in a kind of "hybrid war-law model." *Id.* at 12.

143 Mégret, *supra* note 83, at 303. Mégret writes, "The case that Al Qaeda members should not be entitled to POW status is hard to defeat, and on that specific point one would have to be in bad faith not to agree with the likes of Bybee, Yoo and Rumsfeld. . . . There are . . . very good normative reasons why this should be so: failure by combatants to distinguish themselves, after all, is the single biggest risk to civilians in combat."

But since he is so clearly uncomfortable in such political company, Mégret is not content to let the matter rest there and feels impelled to add that the administration's legal interpretation here, though professionally unobjectionable, is nonetheless a "strict, almost legalistic . . . one that [does] not partake of the relatively benign background understanding of the 'invisible college' of international humanitarian lawyers," whose company he clearly finds more congenial. *Id.* at 302. This is mere posturing, however, because he has already conceded the legal point to his opponents. And having conceded, in particular, "good normative reasons" (i.e., noncombatant protection) for requiring combatants to distinguish themselves from noncombatants, to then describe the law's insistence that fighters wear uniforms as "a barely repressed homoerotic fetishism" can only be a gratuitous slur. *Id.* at 306.

144 Robert Delahunty & John Yoo, "Statehood and the Third Geneva Convention," 46 Va. J. Int'l L. 131 (2005); *see also* John Yoo, "The Status of Soldiers and Terrorists under the Geneva Conventions," 3 Chin. J. Int'l L. 135 (2005). Critics of the Bush administration often profess particular dismay that its most notable legal defenders (i.e., John Yoo, David Addington, Jay Bybee, Douglas Feith, and William J. Haynes) studied and sometimes teach at the country's most elite law schools, whose graduates could presumably be expected to "know the law," especially those, like Bybee, who now sit as judges on its most distinguished tribunals. *See, e.g.,* Sands, *supra* note 21, at 227. In fact, it is only at such institutions that one learns the extent to which sophisticated legal analysis consists precisely in one's ability to discover elements of indeterminacy in legal authorities, ambiguities that may be put to a client's advantage. Laypeople call these "loopholes." Sophisticated lawyers call them simply "the law." When the client's case initially appears unpromising, legal uncertainties of this sort, invisible to the naked eye (of the average lawyer and layperson), permit a sympathetic judge to rule in the client's favor if so disposed – for whatever reason, presumably extraneous to "the law." This is a central tenet of the elite curriculum even if rarely stated so baldly (i.e., except by in-house critics). *See, e.g.,* Duncan Kennedy, "Freedom and Constraint in Adjudication: A Critical Phenomenology," 36 J. Legal Ed. 518 (1986).

Only at less distinguished law schools do most students come to regard their education as consisting primarily in mastering, even memorizing, a settled body of rules simply to be straightforwardly "applied" to client matters they will later encounter in legal practice. When military lawyers condemn "lawfare" as "enemy exploitation of the law of armed conflict," they betray the limits of their legal education in this regard. *See, e.g.,* Jefferson Reynolds, "Collateral Damage on the 21st Century Battlefield: Enemy Exploitation of the Law of

Armed Conflict, and the Struggle for a Moral High Ground," 56 Air Force. L. Rev. 1 (Winter 2005); Col. Kelly Wheaton, "Strategic Lawyering: Realizing the Potential of Military Lawyers at the Strategic Level," Army Lawyer 1, 5-7 (Sept. 2006) (warning of the "use of lawfare against the U.S. . . . . cynically manipulating the law of armed conflict to undermine U.S. and international support for a military operation, potentially restricting or completely stopping the military effort."). What such officers decry as the exploitation of humanitarian law or as "warfare by legal means" is simply the adroit identification and cultivation of law's latent ambiguities by means of professional skills routinely imparted at elite universities. These are the very skills enlisted on behalf of the Bush administration by John Yoo and Keith Bybee in their notorious "torture memos." One could scarcely imagine most graduates lesser law schools authoring such memoranda, whatever the deficiencies of these documents as *ex ante* counsel on the larger range of relevant legal and political risks. Such weaknesses notwithstanding, no one could gainsay the tactical acumen of these analyses, precisely in their artfully selective use of sources for defense of the president's already chosen path. This is not to prejudge the issues of professional responsibility such memoranda necessarily raise, issues which are more complex than any published discussion has yet suggested. *But see* Kathleen Clark, "Ethical Issues Raised by the OLC Torture Memorandum," 1 J. Nat. Security L. & Policy 455 (2005). These complexities include the fact that Yoo acted in professional good faith inasmuch as he clearly and sincerely believed the law to be as he represented it. This is apparent from his scholarly writings on executive power, for instance, published before appointment to the OLC. In other words, one may question his professional competence here more than his professional ethics, except perhaps insofar as competence is the first duty of legal ethics. Model Rules of Professional Conduct, Rule 1(1) (1983).

All of the Bush administration attorneys mentioned above will face criminal charges if they travel abroad. Scott Horton, "Travel Advisory," New Republic, June 19, 2008, at 25 (describing how magistrates in several European countries are preparing files to prosecute these people after January 20, 2009, when President Bush leaves office and loses certain immunities). The Nuremberg *Alstoetter* case will be a pertinent precedent here. Sands, *supra* note 21, at 191–202. *See generally* Ramsey Clark, Samir Amin, et al., International Justice and Impunity: The Case of the United States (2008). However, *Alstoetter* is readily distinguishable in that the defendants there were not simply legal advisers but exercised political authority in formulating Nazi Party policy regarding the Night and Fog decrees, which they also implemented. Kevin Jon Heller, "John Yoo and the Justice Case," May 1, 2008, Balkinization Blog, at http://balkin.blogspot.com/2008/05/john-yoo-and-justice-case.html ("The only specific discussion of legal advice in the Justice Case seems to imply that 'merely' giving such [legal] advice, no matter how erroneous or damaging, does not give rise to criminal responsibility."). Yoo and Bybee had no such active role in policy formation or implementation, according to all currently available accounts. The more recent doctrine of "joint criminal enterprise" may have some footing here, however, as well as longstanding rules on aiding and abetting.

145 Lt. Col. Joseph P. Bialke, "Al-Qaeda & Taliban Unlawful Combatant Detainees, Unlawful Belligerency, and the International Laws of Armed Conflict," 55 A.F. L. Rev. 1, 29–34 (2004) (documenting extensive Taliban noncompliance); Lt. Col Michael Newton, "Unlawful Belligerency after September 11," *in* New Wars, New Laws?, David Wippman & Matthew Evangelista, eds. 76 (2005).

146 Yoo & Ho, *supra* note 138, at 218–20.

147 George Aldrich, "The Taliban, Al Qaeda, and the Determination of Illegal Combatants," 96 A.J.I.L. 891, 895–96 (2002).

148 Yoo & Ho, *supra* note 138, at 221–22. They write, "Only those combatants who comply with the four conditions are entitled to the protections afforded to captured prisoners of war under the laws and usages of war. Indeed, denial of protected status under the laws of war has been recognized as an effective method of encouraging combatants to comply with the four conditions." The Military Commissions Act of 2006, in fact, defines an "unlawful enemy combatant" as one who does not meet the four requirements of the Third Geneva Convention, Art. 4. Yoo elsewhere states forcefully, "The primary enforcer of the laws of war has been reciprocal treatment." John Yoo, "Terrorists Have No Geneva Rights," Wall St. J., May 26, 2004, at A16; *see also* Jane Stromseth, "Law and Force after Iraq: A Transitional Moment," 97 A.J.I.L. 628, 634 (2003) ("Terrorist networks are not constrained by the norms of reciprocity so central to the international legal system.").

149 *Ex Parte Quirin,* 317 U.S. 1 (1942).

150 Anthony Dworkin, "The Laws of War and the Age of Asymmetric Conflict," *in* The Barbarisation of Warfare, George Kassimeris, ed. 220, 235 (2006).

151 Kelly Wallace et al., "Bush Officials Defend Military Trials in Terror Cases," Nov. 15, 2001, at http://archives.cnn.com/2001/LAW/11/14/inv.military.court/ (quoting Vice President Richard Cheney).

152 Michael Hoffman, "Rescuing the Law of War: A Way Forward in an Era of Global Terrorism," 34 Parameters 18, 126 (2005).

153 *Boumediene v. Bush,* No. 06–1195 (argued Dec. 5, 2007), at http://www.oyez.org/cases/2000–2009/2007/2007_06_1195/argument/.

154 Jeremy Waldron, "Torture and Positive Law: Jurisprudence for the White House," 105 Colum. L. Rev. 1681, 1694 (2005); Mégret, *supra* note 83, at 302 (describing the administration's legal interpretation of Art. 4 of the Third Geneva Convention, which he acknowledges to be professionally compelling, as "legalistic"). Nonlawyers should appreciate here that no lawyer ever accuses another of being "legalistic" or finding "loopholes" unless believing that his or her own legal position is the weaker one, by professional standards. These terms are virtually out of bounds in conventional lawyerly discourse, as they amount to accusing a fellow lawyer of being lawyerly.

155 Waldron, *id.* at 1695. In contrast, Noah Feldman, though equally opposed to Bush administration policy here, concedes its principled basis in the morality of reciprocity. "Ugly Americans," *in* The Torture Debate in America, Karen Greenberg, ed. 267, 275–76 (2006).

156 This move, it has rightly been observed, "can so easily be abused, as it was by North Korea and North Vietnam, to deny POW treatment to all members of a state's armed forces on the grounds that their state was an aggressor or that

some of the members of its armed forces allegedly committed war crimes." Aldrich, *supra* note 147, at 895–96.

157 For that matter, unprivileged belligerents, though lawfully denied POW status, enjoy key legal protections under Geneva Common Art. 3. The UN Report on Guantánamo Detainees concluded that the detention regime must be identical for lawful and unlawful belligerents, grounding this conclusion in the International Covenant for Civil and Political Rights, Art. 9. *See* Situation of Detainees at Guantánamo Bay, E/CN.4/2006/120, at ¶¶ 19–22. One leading scholar even invokes a species of reciprocity in explaining the *ad bellum/in bellum* bifurcation. In agreeing to humane treatment for the enemy soldier though he fights for an aggressor, states act in recognition of the possibility "that they might, after all, be the aggressor one day." Steven Ratner, "The War on Terrorism and International Humanitarian Law," 14 Mich. St. J. Int'l L. 19, 21 (2006). This is unconvincing, however, as there is little evidence that states – or their rulers, more precisely – think that far in advance on such matters.

158 Anita Bernstein, "Reciprocity, Utility, and the Law of Aggression," 54 Vand. L. Rev. 1, 26 (2001). Bernstein is concerned with reciprocity primarily in the domestic context.

159 Dennis Thompson, Just Elections: Creating a Fair Electoral Process in the United States viii–ix (2002).

160 *Id.* at ix.

CHAPTER 1. RECIPROCITY IN THE LAW OF WAR: AMBIENT SIGHTINGS, AMBIVALENT SOUNDINGS

1 Xenophon, Anabasis I.9.II.

2 Stephen Neff, War and the Law of Nations 225 (2005). He continues, "Such a sanguinary assessment would, however, be proved very wrong, for the 19th century actually witnessed a dramatic rebirth of reprisals." *Id.*

3 William Ian Miller, Humiliation 50 (1993).

4 Jonathan Haidt, The Happiness Hypothesis 52 (2006).

5 Alan Sanfey, James Rilling et al., "The Neural Basis of Economic Decision-Making in the Ultimatum Game," 300 Science 1755, 1756 (2003) (contending that the impulse to exact retributive punishment may be driven by phylogenetically old mechanisms in the human brain); Martin Nowak & Sebastien Roch "Upstream Reciprocity and the Evolution of Gratitude," 274 Proc. R. Soc. B. 605, 605 (2007) (concluding that "gratitude . . . which increases the willingness to help others, can evolve in the competitive world of natural selection").

6 Osama bin Laden, "To the Peoples of Europe," April 15, 2004, *in* Messages to the World: The Statements of Osama bin Laden, Bruce Lawrence, ed., James Howarth, trans. 233, 243 (2005). *See generally* Al Qaeda in its Own Words, Gilles Kepel & John-Pierre Milelli, eds., Pascale Ghazaleh, trans. (2008).

7 The implicit question here is whether, as Hume argued, reason – especially philosophy, reason's most ambitious form – is really just a slave to passion, that of revenge in this case. Susan Jacoby, Wild Justice: The Evolution of Revenge 4 (1983); Ernst Fehr & Simon Gächter, "Fairness and Retaliation," *in* The Economics of Reciprocity, Giving and Altruism, L.-A. Gérard-Varet, et al., eds. 153 (2000).

8 Thucydides, History of the Peloponnesian War, Benjamin Jowett, trans. 3.52, 3.56 (1998); Adriaan Lanni, "The Laws of War in Ancient Greece," 26 L. & Hist. Rev. 469, 473 (2008). There is sparse evidence that reprisals were not permitted, however, against religious shrines. Lanni, *id.* at 473–74, 477.

9 David Bederman, International Law in Antiquity 122–24 (2001) (describing the Greek practice of *androlepsia*).

10 The Magna Carta, (June 12, 1215), Art. 41, *in* Sources of Our Liberties, Richard Perry & John Cooper, eds. 11, 17 (1959). The provision read, "All merchants, unless they have been previously and publicly forbidden, are to have safe and secure conduct in leaving and coming to England and in staying and going through England both by land and by water to buy and to sell, without any evil exactions, according to the ancient and right customs, save in time of war, and if they should be from a land at war against us and be found in our land at the beginning of the war, they are to be attached without damage to their bodies or goods *until it is established by us or our chief justiciary in what way the merchants of our land are treated who at such a time are found in the land that is at war with us, and if our merchants are safe there, the other merchants are to be safe in our land.*" (emphasis supplied).

11 Alberico Gentili, De Iure Belli Libri Tres 253–54 (1933).

12 Emmerich de Vattel, The Law of Nations, Joseph Chitty, ed. 348–49 (1852) (1758). He propounds that enemy prisoners may be killed "when the enemy has been guilty of some enormous breach of the law of nations, and particularly when he has violated the laws of war. . . . When we are at war with a savage nation, who observe no rules, and never give quarter, we may punish them in the persons of any of their people whom we take (these belonging to the number of the guilty,) and endeavour, by this rigorous proceeding, to force them to respect the laws of humanity." Vattel proceeds, however, to laud several examples from Greek and Roman military history, including decisions of Scipio and Alexander the Great, of magnanimous commanders who declined to employ such retaliation where it was ethically permissible. "He who has even the most just cause to punish a sovereign with whom he is in enmity, will ever incur the reproach of cruelty, if he causes the punishment to fall on his innocent subjects. There are other methods of chastising the sovereign." When retaliation is called for, a good leader "would not avenge it on an unarmed enemy, but on those who should be found in arms" (i.e., when the sovereign himself cannot be punished directly).

13 David Hume, A Treatise of Human Nature, 2nd ed., L. A. Selby-Bigge, ed. 521 (1978) (1739). Much earlier, Aristotle did make a similar point regarding what he called "utilitarian friendship" but confined it to the patron-client relationship: "For what use is it to be the friend of an excellent or powerful man if you are not going to gain anything by it?" Nicomachean Ethics, 1163a33–35.

14 David Hume, An Enquiry Concerning the Principles of Morals §3, pt. 1 (1777).

15 The Lieber Code of 1863, Art. 62, Gen. Order 100, U.S. War Dept. In practice, however, the Lincoln administration did not retaliate against Confederate POWs after Confederate officials refused to accord POW status to African American soldiers. These officials had even authorized the murder of such POWs in several instances. James M. McPherson, Battle Cry of Freedom: The

Civil War Era 793–96 (1998). Lieber limited his general approval of the legality of reprisal and did not favor its use against POWs. Mark Neely Jr., The Civil War and The Limits of Destruction 181 (2008). In a discussion of Bush administration policy toward the Guantánamo detainees, Scott Horton praises the Lieber Code for its author's decision "to eschew niggling distinctions that could be made to justify mistreatment." Horton, "Military Necessity, Torture, and the Criminality of Lawyers," *in* International Prosecution of Human Rights Crimes, Wolfgang Kaleck et al., eds. 169 (2007). The Code expressly provides, however, that guerrillas "are not entitled to the privileges of prisoners of war, but shall be treated summarily as highway robbers or pirates," who "suffer death." Arts. 82–83. The same fate is promised saboteurs and civilians who take up arms within occupied territory. Arts. 84–85.

16 In German, the term is *allbeteiligungsklausel.*

17 *See, e.g.,* Laws and Customs of War on Land (Hague IV), Oct. 18, 1907, Art. 2; Convention Respecting the Rights and Duties of Neutral Persons in Case of War on Land, The Hague, Oct. 18, 1907, into force Jan. 26, 1910, 36 Stat. 2310. *See also* Hague V, Art. 20; Hague VI, Art. 6; Hague VII, Art. 7; Hague VIII, Art. 8; Hague IX, Art. 8; Hague X, Art. 18; Hague XI, Art. 9; Hague XIII, Art. 28. Several of the Hague treaties and Regulations have a term providing that these agreements "will . . . cease to be compulsory from the moment when, in a war between Contracting or Acceding Parties, a non-Contracting Party or a non-Acceding Party shall join one of the belligerents." *See, e.g.,* Declaration Renouncing the Use, in Time of War, of Certain Explosive Projectiles (1868). In 1929, however, the Geneva Conventions first adopted the contrary position: that state parties in an armed conflict should remain bound to treaty duties vis-à-vis all belligerents who had also ratified (i.e., despite the simultaneous belligerency of a nonratifying state).

18 This was the case, for instance, with the Nuclear Test Ban Treaty of 1963. Egon Schwelb, "The Nuclear Test Ban Treaty and International Law," 58 A.J.I.L. 642, 664–68 (1964); Vienna Convention on the Law of Treaties, Art. 60(2)(b).

19 The reference here to China is hypothetical, as that country did not explode an atom bomb until late 1964 and never signed the 1963 Limited Test Ban Treaty.

20 For a recent statement of this view, *see, e.g.,* U.K. Ministry of Defense, British Manual of Military Law, 16.14 (2005), at 419 ("Reprisals . . . may sometimes provide the only practical means of inducing the adverse party to desist from its unlawful conduct.").

21 Frits Kalshoven, Belligerent Reprisals 24, 92, 102 (1986). Appeal to the UN Security Council is the only remedy expressly provided, for instance, by the Convention on the Prohibition of the Development, Production and Stockpiling of Bacteriological (Biological) and Toxin Weapons and on Their Destruction (1972), Art. VI. Additional Protocol I to the Geneva Conventions provides only for establishing an international fact-finding commission to investigate allegations of grave violations.

22 Cassese is the former chief judge of the International Criminal Tribunal for the former Yugoslavia.

23 Antonio Cassese, International Criminal Law 220 (2003).

24 Simon Caney, Justice beyond Borders: A Global Political Theory 218 (2005).

25   Col. Morris Davis, quoted in Human Rights First, Law and Security Digest, Feb. 22, 2008.

26   Sahr Conway-Lanz, Collateral Damage: Americans, Noncombatant Immunity, and Atrocity after World War II 223 (2006). On the origins of this contemporary legal rule in the medieval Catholic just war doctrine of "double effect," *see* Shannon French, "Murderers, Not Warriors," in Terrorism and International Justice, James Sterba, ed. 31, 38–39 (2003).

27   Reprisals entail the harsh treatment of one member of a group on account of misconduct by another member. As such, they are a form of collective responsibility, which liberal law generally strives to abjure, in preference for punishment of the culpable member. Stanislaw-Edward Nahlik, "From Reprisals to Individual Penal Responsibility," *in* Humanitarian Law of Armed Conflict, A. J. M. Delissen & Gerard Tanja, eds. 165, 167, 173 (1991). That they punish the innocent is surely the strongest argument against reprisals. As Schmitt writes, "An approach which refuses to release one side from its full obligations under humanitarian law when the other violates it is consistent with the underlying purpose of that body of law – protection of those . . . not engaged in the conflict from its effects." Michael N. Schmitt, "Targeting and Humanitarian Law: Current Issues," 34 Israel Yearbook on Human Rights 59, 89 (2004).

28   Theodor Meron, "The Humanization of Humanitarian Law," 94 A. J. I. L. 239, 250 (2000).

29   Third Geneva Convention, Art. 2, outlawing reprisals against prisoners of war; Frits Kalshoven, "Belligerent Reprisals Revisited," *in* Kalshoven, Reflections on the Law of War 759 (2007).

30   British Manual of Military Law (1958), ¶ 121, at 44.

31   Hugo Grotius, De Jure Belli Ac Pacis Libri Tres, Francis W. Kelsey, trans. 447 (1964) (1625); Theodor Meron, Henry's Wars and Shakespeare's Laws: Perspectives on the Law of War in the Later Middle Ages 176 (1993).

32   Kalshoven, *supra* note 21, at 24, 362.

33   *Legality of the Threat or Use of Nuclear Weapons*, Advisory Opinion, 1996 I.C.J. 226, 328 (July 8).

34   *Id.* For scholarly endorsements of this view, *see, e.g.*, Shane Darcy, "The Evolution of the Law of Belligerent Reprisals," 175 Mil. L. Rev. 184, 209 (2003) ("In a limited number of situations, the treaty law is silent on reprisals, thus inferring that their use in such instances would be lawful."); Christopher Greenwood, "The Twilight of Belligerent Reprisals," Neth. Y.B. Int'l L. 35, 53–54 (1989) (contending that Protocol I's prohibition on reprisals "do not apply to ship-to-ship, ship-to-air, or air-to-air combat," and that enemy merchant ships are also subject to belligerent reprisal); S.E. Nahlik, "Belligerent Reprisals as Seen in the Light of the Diplomatic Conference on Humanitarain Law, Geneva, 1974–1977," 42 L. & Contemp. Prob. 3, 56–57 (1978).

35   Christopher Greenwood, Essays on War in International Law 310, 344–45 (2006) (quoting the 1956 U.S. Army Field Manual, the 1999 U.S. Naval Commander's Handbook on the Law of Naval Operations, and the 1958 U.K. Military Field Manual).

36   *Id.* at 310.

37 Countermeasures entail justified violation of a norm that continues to be binding, whereas reprisals involve suspension of the norm. René Provost, International Human Rights and Humanitarian Law 165, 182–83 (2002). Both must be intended to induce cessation of wrongful conduct and/or its reparation and must be commensurate with past injury. Int'l L. Commission, Draft Articles on Responsibility of States for Internationally Wrongful Acts (2001), Arts. 22, 49–52. A common countermeasure is the levying of trade sanctions in response to violation of WTO obligations; Edward Kwakwa, The International Law of Armed Conflict 132 (1992) (noting that "recent trends in state practice indicate a continued resort to reprisal in peace-time, euphemistically referred to as 'counter-measures'").

38 Suspension or termination is a permissible remedy for material breach of a treaty, whereas countermeasures are a remedy for a "wrongful act," the illegality of which may derive from *any* source of international law, including a source other than a treaty between the wrongdoing state and the victim of such wrong. This is admittedly a legally complicated state of affairs, but a sensible one, as the International Court of Justice has convincingly shown. *Gabcikovo-Nagymaros Project (Hung. v. Slovk.)*, 1997 I.C.J. 7, 53–55 (Sept. 25); René Lefeber, "The *Gabčikovo-Nagymaros Project* and the Law of State Responsibillity," 11 Leiden J. Int'l L. 609, 611 (1998).

39 *See, e.g.,* Sanford Levinson, "Constitutional Norms in a State of Permanent Emergency," 40 Ga. L. Rev. 699 (2006); Giorgio Agamben, State of Exception, Kevin Attell, trans. (2005).

40 This is true to widely differing degrees in various countries, of course.

41 This is a generic term employed to describe a state of affairs historically called in French law a "state of siege," in Anglo-American "martial law," and in German law "emergency powers." At such times, the writ of *habeas corpus* or its equivalent may be suspended and the administration of justice transferred from civilian to military courts. Other details vary, often significantly.

42 Jodi Dean, Žižek's Politics 74 (2006). The words that Dean quotes are from Agamben. Benjamin was the first such literary intellectual to give importance to the state of exception in understanding twentieth-century politics. Walter Benjamin, "Theses on the Philosophy of History," *in* The Critique of Violence, Harry Zohn, trans. (1940).

43 Most of Agamben's many books concern aesthetics and philosophy.

44 Giorgio Agamben, Homo Sacer: Sovereign Power and Bare Life, Daniel Heller-Roazen, trans. 173 (1995).

45 Margaret Kohn, "Bare Life and the Limits of the Law," 9 Theory & Event 2 (2006) (reviewing Giorgio Agamben, State of Exception, 2005).

46 Though this view has in recent years been argued by some on the left, the thesis was first proposed by Nazi jurist Carl Schmitt, in his Political Theology (1985) (1934). Assessing this position would stray too far beyond this book's chief concerns. *See generally* William Scheuerman, Between the Norm and the Exception: The Frankfurt School and the Rule of Law (1997).

47 Karl Marx, "On the Jewish Question," *in* The Marx-Engels Reader, Robert Tucker, ed., 26 (1978); Marx, "The Communist Manifesto," *id.* at 482 (arguing

that all talk of rights, justice, and morality is just "so many bourgeois prejudices behind which lurk in ambush just so many bourgeois interests.").

48 Michael Walzer, Arguing about War 50 (2004).

49 This was the position of H. L. A. Hart in the famous 1958 Hart-Fuller debate. For an assessment of the question and of that debate in relation to recent authoritarian rule in South America, *see* Mark Osiel, "Dialogue with Dictators: Judicial Resistance in Argentina and Brazil," 20 Law & Soc. Inquiry 481 (1995).

50 *Id.* at 44–45.

51 Philippe Sands, Torture Team: Rumsfeld's Memo and The Betrayal of American Values 189 (2008) (quoting Feith). *See also id.* at 103–04. Rabkin elaborates the reasoning: "Islamist radicals do not think of war as a conflict between states from which ordinary humanity should, as much as possible, be spared. They think of war as an all-out contest between peoples, so that American civilians (or, in the counterpart struggle in the Middle East, Israeli civilians) are no less legitimate targets than uniformed soldiers. Neither age nor sex nor disability makes any difference. The aim is simply to punish a whole society for its sins. The preconditions for reciprocal restraint are wholly absent." Jeremy Rabkin, "After Guantánamo: The War over the Geneva Convention," The National Interest, Summer 2002, at 15, 23.

52 On the recent debate within Al Qaeda, suggesting that Feith's conclusion may exaggerate the movement's ideological uniformity and rigidity, *see* Peter Bergen & Paul Cruickshank, "The Unraveling: Al Qaeda's Revolt Against bin Laden," New Republic, June 11, 2008, at 16, 18; Lawrence Wright, "The Rebellion Within: An Al Qaeda Mastermind Questions Terrorism," New Yorker, June 2, 2008, at 37, 44.

53 Benjamin, *supra* note 42. It is natural that such literary forays into the state of legal exception often proceed by way of Kafka. Giorgio Agamben, Homo Sacer: Sovereign Power and Bare Life, Daniel Heller-Roazen, trans. 49–58 (1995) (describing, at 57, Kafka's vision as one in which "it is impossible to distinguish transgression of the law from execution of the law").

54 Oren Gross & Fiounnuala Ní Aoláin, Law in Times of Crisis: Emergency Powers in Theory and Practice 334–39 (2006).

55 Christopher Kutz, "Torture, Necessity and Existential Politics," 95 Cal. L. Rev. 235, 266 (2007). Kutz's deontological stance against Bush administration interrogation policy holds, as Brad Roth parses it, that "we do better simply to acknowledge the contradiction" – between wrongful means (that remain wrongful) and the just consequences they secure – "than to adjust our moral views so to render them capable of meaningfully addressing the awful realities that we face." Roth himself rightly responds, however, that this "proposition . . . defies the whole purpose of engaging in moral discussion of such dilemmas, and worse, abandons the field to those with precisely the wrong sensibilities. We are speaking here of acts that are asserted to be practically necessary from a moral point of view, and either this assertion" – that these acts are moral – "is right or it is wrong." Correspondence with author, Dec. 2007.

56 Richard Pildes rightly stresses this fact in his "Conflicts Between American and European Views of Law: The Dark Side of Legalism," 44 Va. J. Int'l L. 145, 162–64 (2003).

57 Though rule by executive decree, lawful or otherwise, often seems an usurpation of power from other branches of government, it is frequently effected with legislative indulgence and sometimes outright approval. *See, e.g., Executive Decree Authority*, John Carey & Matthew Shugart, eds. 16–18, 109–10, 120, 256–57 (1998).

58 *See, e.g.,* Gross & Ní Aoláin, *supra* note 54, at 35–72, 146–62; Alan Dershowitz, Why Terrorism Works: Understanding the Threat, Responding to the Challenge 156–60 (2003) (arguing that if torture is not made subject to a system of legal warrants, it will simply go underground and free itself from legal restraint altogether); Bruce Ackerman, "The Emergency Constitution," 113 Yale L.J. 1029 (2004); Mark Tushnet, "Emergencies and the Idea of Constitutionalism," *in* The Constitution in Wartime, Mark Tushnet, ed. 39 (2005); Leonard Feldman, "Judging Necessity: Democracy and Extra-Legalism," 36 Polit. Theory 500, April 24, 2008, at http://ptx.sagepub.com/cgi/rapidpdf/0090591708317900v1.pdf.

59 National Security Strategy of the United States, March 2006, at http://www.whitehouse.gov/nsc/nss/2006 ("The United States can no longer simply rely on deterrence to keep the terrorists at bay or defensive measures to thwart them at the last moment. The fight must be taken to the enemy, to keep them on the run.").

60 Quoted in CNN.com, "Top Bush Officials Push Saddam Hussein," Sept. 8, 2002, at http://archives.cnn.com/2002/ALLPOLITICS/09/08/iraq.debate.

61 Lawrence Freedman, "The Coming War on Terrorism," *in* Superterrorism: Policy Responses, Lawrence Freedman, ed. 40 (2002). One distinguished international lawyer, M. Cherif Bassiouni, nonetheless claims that the international community could readily incentivize Al Qaeda members to obey humanitarian law by simply ceasing to support the repressive national regimes (the "near enemy," in jihadist discourse) against which these militants harbor their proximate grievances. "Summary of the Proceedings," Third Hague Colloquium on Fundamental Principles of Law, "Jihad and the Challenges of International and Domestic Law," Oct. 3, 2008. But if these repressive regimes no longer received support – primarily lawful arms sales by trading partners in exchange for petroleum purchases – such militants would then cease to have any basis for warring against these foreign states in the first place, not merely for directing their attacks at civilians. Questions of humanitarian law (i.e., in relations between domestic militants and foreign states) would hence scarcely arise. Bassiouni's is thus not really an argument about the willingness of jihadist militants to reciprocate restraint within an armed conflict, but rather an argument that the West should acknowledge the justice of their underlying cause, at which point they will abandon their arms, both those permitted and prohibited. This is rather beside the point, of course.

Also, since public international law prohibits "regime change" as an objective of foreign policy, trading partners cannot lawfully take very effective measures to reduce severe repression in the Muslim countries now spawning so many militants.

Finally, some of the states that are most repressive of domestic jihadist groups, such as Algeria, receive virtually no military or political support whatever from the "far enemy," especially the U.S., which their militants nonetheless regard as a principal adversary. And many of the world's most abusive states, such as Myanmar, manage to oppress their ethnoreligious minorites without any foreign aid from, or even significant trade with the U.S. Egyptian authorities, for that matter, have reasons of their own to monitor and restrain the activities of radical Islamist groups there, entirely apart from American endorsement of such efforts. This second feature of Bassiouni's argument is hence also without merit, though it is widely recited among prominent Muslim intellectuals. *See, e.g.*, Tariq Ramadan, "Regime Change in the Middle East: The Expansion of Political Islam in the Modern Era," Third Hague Colloquium, *id.*

62 Albert Wohlstetter, "The Delicate Balance of Terror," (1958), at http://www. rand.org/publications/classics/wohlstetter/P1472/P1472.html; Robert Ayson, Thomas Schelling and the Nuclear Age 60–90 (2004).

63 Thomas Schelling, The Strategy of Conflict 232 (1960); *see also* Bernard Brodie, Strategy in the Missile Age 331 (1959); Wohlstetter, *supra* note 62.

64 It is very difficult to prevent the financing of terrorist operations through money-laundering regulation, national and international, because the two forms of criminal finance, though similar in general purpose – the sustenance of illegal activity – are diametrically different in form. Money-laundering legislation seeks to prevent resources garnered from criminal conduct from finding their way into lawful economic enterprise, whereas terrorist finance generally involves exactly the opposite: preventing the movement of assets earned from lawful activities, such as the bin Laden family's construction business or charitable donations from jihadist sympathizers throughout the world, into unlawful ones. The rules against money laundering hence concentrate on the point of entry into the financial system, when money is first deposited, for this is the place at which the "dirty" origin of the funds is most readily subject to detection, if at all.

This approach cannot much constrain terrorist finance, as its resources when first deposited are clean. They are eventually put to criminal ends only by their subsequent movement through and withdrawal from the financial system. Hence, most of the major terrorist attacks against Western interests have been financed by assets flowing not through the informal Islamic Halawi networks but rather through large, formal, and fully regulated Western banks. Victor Comras, "Al Qaeda Finances and the Funding to Affiliated Groups," in Terrorism Financing and State Responses, Jeanne Giraldo & Harold Trinkunas, eds. 115, 127–30 (2007); *see generally* Kathryn Gardner, "Terrorism Defanged: The Financial Action Task Force and International Efforts to Capture Terrorist Finances," in Uniting against Terror: Cooperative Nonmilitary Responses to the Global Terrorist Threat, David Cortright & George Lopez, eds (2007).

65 Marc Sageman, Leaderless Jihad: Terror Networks in the 21st Century 109–46 (2008).

66 W. Michael Reisman, "Assessing Claims to Revise the Laws of War," 97 A.J.I.L. 82, 89 (2002).

67 Even this feature is not entirely unique insofar as it also describes the conduct of Japan's *kamikaze* pilots during World War II, of course. But this method of fighting was never central to Japan's wartime strategy; in most other respects,

that conflict was a conventional interstate war, one to which standard notions of deterrence and tit-for-tat could apply. Such pilots fought for a bureaucratically organized armed force and wore uniforms, moreover.

68 The desire to eliminate all Western, secularizing influence from the Middle East, in particular, is an objective that knows no fixed, chronological endpoint, as it clearly encompasses much more than the removal of Western military forces from the region. In fact, it is an objective largely beyond the capacity of any Western state, or coalition of states, to secure (i.e., consistently with their constitutional law).

69 Lt. Col. Michael H. Hoffman, "Rescuing the Law of War: A Way Forward in an Era of Global Terrorism," 35 Parameters 18, 22 (Summer 2005) (observing that "though terrorism presents unfamiliar legal issues, these aren't quite as novel as they seem"). Historical precedents for the use of guerrilla insurgency methods are many. On their use in the U.S. Civil War alone, for instance, *see, e.g.,* Noel Fisher, War at Every Door: Partisan Politics and Guerrilla Violence in East Tennessee, 1860–1869 (1997); Sean Michael O'Brien, Mountain Partisans: Guerrilla Warfare in the Southern Appalachians, 1861–1865 (1999); Thomas Goodrich, Black Flag: Guerrilla Warfare on the Western Border, 1861–1865 (1995); Robert Mackey, The Uncivil War: Irregular Warfare in the Upper South, 1861–1865 (2004). *See generally* Rod Thornton, Asymmetric Warfare: Threat and Response in the Twenty-First Century (2007).

70 William Polk, Violent Politics: A History of Terrorism, Insurgency, and Guerrilla War 5–11 (2007); Harold Selesky, "Colonial America," *in* The Laws of War: Constraints on Warfare in the Western World, Michael Howard et al., eds. 59, 80–82 (1994).

71 For recent accounts, *see* Charles Esdaile, Fighting Napoleon: Guerrillas, Bandits, and Adventurers in Spain, 1808–1814 (2004); Ronald Fraser, Napoleon's Cursed War: Popular Resistance in the Spanish Peninsular War 393–431 (2007).

72 Hanson stresses the Attic warriors' "primitive animality," the "savagery in the fighting between armored men . . . an experience unrivaled in its brutality by the modern firefight in the jungle, or the weeks of shelling in the trenches." Victor Davis Hanson, The Western Way of War: Infantry Battle in Classical Greece 226, 225 (1989). Massacres were common. Their victims and perpetrators were both "Western." Yet because it involved face-to-face confrontation, such savagery was universally considered honorable.

73 On this and other similarities between the Cold War and the conflict with Al Qaeda/militant jihad, *see* Timothy Lynch & Robert Singh, After Bush: The Case for Continuity in American Foreign Policy 11–15 (2008).

74 John Gray, Heresies 85 (2004). On the features of their political institutions and social structure that make industrially advanced democracies so vulnerable in this respect, *see* Donald Black, "The Geometry of Terrorism," 22 Sociological Theory 14 (March 2004); Alan Krueger, What Makes a Terrorist: Economics and the Roots of Terrorism 4 (2007).

75 David Wippman & Matthew Evangelista, "Introduction," *in* New Wars, New Laws? Applying the Laws of War in 21st Century Conflicts, David Wippman & Matthew Evangelista, eds. 1, 6 (2005).

76 In the term's more contemporary meaning – if the reader will forgive the *double entendre* – ground zero may indeed offer precisely the place to begin. On the

etiology of the term, *see* "Listening with the Third Ear: Echoes from Ground Zero," *in* Gene Ray, Terror and the Sublime in Art and Critical Theory 135, 137–38 (2005). The term was first employed in reference to Hiroshima after its nuclear destruction.

77   Laura A. Dickinson, "Public Law Values in a Privatized World," 31 Yale. J. Int'l L. 383, 400–01 (2006); P. W. Singer, Corporate Warriors: The Rise of the Privatized Military Industry 233 (2003); Paul Verkuil, Outsourcing Sovereignty (2007); From Mercenaries to Market: The Rise and Regulation of Private Military Companies, Simon Chesterman & Chia Lehnardt, eds. (2007).

78   Such contractors generally are not subject to the Uniform Code of Military Justice, for instance, though the full scope of this exclusion is the subject of pending litigation. Criticism of today's military contracting focuses on how such privatization appears to prejudice the protection of human rights in war zones. Human rights advocates are hence highly skeptical of privatization. This skepticism leads them in turn to endorse the state's continued monopoly over the right to employ violence and to oppose its delegation to private parties.

     Yet the state's monopoly of force follows directly from how international law privileges the state and its interests over the rights of private individuals residing in its territory. The state-centrism of international law, so often condemned by human rights advocates for its contribution to human rights abuse, here suddenly becomes essential to human rights protection, when the issue is private military contracting. Whether we can truly have it both ways – foreclosing the outsourcing of repression without strengthening the state's own powers to oppress – is open to question at least and worthy of careful consideration.

79   Many other developments in U.S military structure and posture, such as lily-pad basing, are similarly aimed at enhanced operational flexibility. On lily-pad basing, *see* http://www.almc.army.mil/ALOG/issues/MarApr05/lilypad.html.

80   Anyone who has visited the U.S. Embassy in Bogotá will see how ingeniously this challenge has been met by some contemporary architects. *See generally* Paul Hirst, Space and Power: Politics, War and Architecture 179–223 (2005).

81   U.S. Constitution, Art. I, §. 8. A letter of marque was an official warrant or commission to a private party – hence, the term privateering – from a government authorizing the designated agent to search, seize, or destroy specific assets or personnel belonging to a party that has committed some offense under the law of nations against the assets or citizens of the issuing nation. Such commissions were usually employed to authorize private parties in raiding and capturing the merchant ships of an enemy nation.

82   Laura Dickinson, "Filartiga's Legacy in an Era of Military Privatization," 37 Rutgers L.J. 703, 703 (2006).

83   In some ways, private contractors may actually be more legally vulnerable than public entities, with their panoply of immunities, both for individual officials and the sovereign itself. *Id.* at 704, 710. Tim Weiner, "A Security Contractor Defends His Team, Which, He Says, Is Not a Private Army," New York Times, April 29, 2007, Week in Rev. 4 (quoting Gary Jackson, President of Blackwater USA, noting that "the Military Extraterritorial Jurisdiction Act creates jurisdiction for federal court trials, and the wrongdoing itself is covered under statutes like the War Crimes Act, The Victims of Trafficking and Violence Protection

Act, the Anti-Torture Act, the Defense Base Act, and a whole raft of other domestic regulations, not to mention international prohibitions."). The statement is at least partly deceptive in that the Military Extraterritorial Jurisdiction Act covers civilians employed by the Defense Department, whereas Blackwater guards were employed by the State Department. In October 2007, Congress debated several bills designed to increase U.S. judicial authority over such companies. *See generally* Jeremy Scahill, Blackwater: The Rise of the World's Most Powerful Mercenary Army (2007); Robert Young Pelton, Licensed to Kill: Hired Guns in the War on Terror (2006).

84 For example, many detained Al Qaeda members have acknowledged familiarity with the organization's so-called Manchester Manual, instructing them on how to resist particular interrogation techniques likely to be applied to them on capture. Sands, *supra* note 51, at 82. To similar effect, domestic jurisdictional limits also present a perennial problem for law enforcement, one that terrorist groups long ago learned to exploit. In the 1970s, for instance, the Baader-Meinhof group often made a point of crossing West German provincial borders in the course of their operations, as the legal structure of German federalism – which restricted the surveillance powers of federal police – limited the state's responsive capacity. Today, Taliban forces similarly flee into Pakistan after conducting operations across the border in Afghanistan, just as Hezbollah guerrillas in southern Lebanon have regularly entered UN refugee camps after launching rockets into northern Israel.

85 Scott Shane, "Inside a 9/11 Mastermind's Interrogation," New York Times, June 21, 2008, at A1.

86 I here paraphrase Nancy Sherman, Stoic Warriors: The Ancient Philosophy behind the Military Mind 172 (2005).

87 Geoffrey Best, War and Law since 1945, at 59 (1994).

88 *See, e.g.*, Jeremy Rabkin, Law without Nations?: Why Constitutional Government Requires Sovereign States 25–32, 178–92, 258–63 (2005). For analysis of the range of views among those who oppose strengthening the international law of armed conflicts, *see* Gerry Simpson, Law, War & Crime: War Crimes Trials and the Reinvention of International Law 152–56 (2007).

89 Michael Howard, "War as an Instrument of Policy," *in* Diplomatic Investigations, Herbert Butterfield & Martin Wight, eds. 193 (1968).

90 Carl Von Clausewitz, On War, Michael Howard & Peter Paret, eds. & trans. 75–76 (1976) (1832) ("War is . . . an act of force to compel our enemy to do our will . . . To introduce the principle of moderation into the theory of war itself would always lead to logical absurdity.").

91 René Descartes, 4 Oeuvres Complctes 357 (1910) ("La principale finesse est de ne vouloir point de tout user de finesse.").

92 William T. Sherman, Memoirs of General William T. Sherman, vol. 2, 126 (1972) (1875).

93 Robert Cover, "*Nomos* and Narrative," 97 Harv. L. Rev. 4, 40, 46, 48 (1983).

94 *See, e.g.*, Nathaniel Berman, "Privileging Combat? Contemporary Conflict and the Legal Construction of War," 43 Colum. J. Transnat'l L. 1 (2004); David Kennedy, Of War and Law 167 (2006) ("Our fabric of norms focuses the attention of the world on this or that excess, while armoring the most heinous human suffering in legal privilege, redefining terrible injury as collateral damage,

self-defense, proportionality, or necessity."). Talal Asad, "On Torture, or Cruel, Inhuman, and Degrading Treatment," 63 Soc. Research 1084, 1096 (1996) ("The Geneva Convention (sic), it is true, seeks to regulate conduct in war. But, paradoxically, this has the effect of legalizing most of the new kinds of suffering endured in modern war . . ."). There is nothing uniquely postmodernist in this perfectly accurate observation, of course. For its assertion by a deontologist, for instance, *see* Kutz, *supra* note 55, at 261.

95 Alexander Wendt, Social Theory of International Politics 266 (1999).

96 John Searle, Mind, Language, and Society 120 (1998). On the "social" aspects of war, *see* Hedley Bull, "Society and Anarchy in International Relations," *in* Butterfield & Wight, *supra* note 89, at 35, 43–45.

97 Elaine Scarry, The Body in Pain: The Making and Unmaking of the World 85 (1985). Her full description of war is "the reciprocal activity of injuring for a non-reciprocal outcome" (i.e., for winning and losing).

98 On such efforts and their difficulties, *see* Cortright & Lopez, *supra* note 64, *passim*.

99 Derek Jinks, "September 11 and the Laws of War," 28 Yale J. Int'l L. 1, 31–38 (2003); Monica Hakimi, "International Standards for Detaining Terrorism Suspects: Moving beyond the Armed Conflict-Criminal Divide," 33 Yale J. Int'l L. 369, 376–77 (2008). This view has a long history. *See, e.g.,* A.D. McNair, "The Legal Meaning of War and the Relations of War to Reprisals," 11 Trans. Grotius Soc. 45 (1925).

100 In qualification, it must be noted that neither the Sept. 19, 2001 Authorization for Use of Military Force nor the USA Patriot Act employ the term "armed conflict." The word "war" appears only in the first of these statutes, and only with reference to the War Powers Act, not the conflict with Al Qaeda. *But see* Eric Lichtblau, "Administrtation Calls for Action on Detainees," New York Times, July 22, 2008, at A1 (describing a request by President Bush to Congress to "reaffirm" that the United States "remains engaged in an armed conflict with al Qaeda" and terrorist groups).

101 In the present conflict, the United States has not formally declared war, in the manner that the Constitution would require, though Congress authorized the use of force in response to the 9/11 attacks. The law of armed conflict may nonetheless apply to the dispute between the United States and Al Qaeda without the need to characterize it formally as a "war," which international law historically understood as involving sustained violence between states. Today, this body of law is broader in scope, governing other forms of violent hostilities as well, notably noninternational armed conflicts.

102 The 1949 Geneva Conventions, however, allow the possibility that an armed conflict may exist though not recognized as such by one of the belligerents. *See* Common Article 2.

103 Christopher Greenwood, "The Concept of War in Modern International Law," 36 Int'l & Comp. L. Q. 283, 302 (1987) (quoting from Ian Brownlie, International Law and the Use of Force by States 368, 1963).

104 It may sometimes be true that "globalization creates problems that can be solved only by stronger, deeper, and more effective forms of international cooperation." Andrew Hurrell, "Order and Justice in International Relations:

What Is at Stake?" *in* Order and Justice in International Relations, Rosemary Foot et al., eds. 24, 33 (2003). It is often unclear how much cooperation will prove to be necessary and possible in a given situation, however, or whether such cooperation would best be formalized into such "hard" legal instruments as treaties.

105 Ryan Goodman & Derek Jinks, Extended Book Prospectus – Socializing States: Promoting Human Rights through International Law 8-11, Oxford University Press, 2008, forthcoming.

106 Stanley Cohen, "Crime and Politics: Spot the Difference," 47 Brit. J. Soc. 1, 13 (1996).

107 The aspect of legal realism most pertinent here is not its common claim that formalistic modes of legal reasoning cannot decide actual cases, but that they should not, because legal interpretation and decision making will yield results superior in both principle and policy if approached more instrumentally, as a means for realizing these purposes. This regularly requires a willingness to depart from the binary classifications with which formal legal sources often seek to carve up human experience – in the present context, for distinguishing war from peace, civilian from combatant, belligerent from neutral. Legal realists would contend that an "essentialist" conception of these distinctions, as defined by a set of necessary and sufficient conditions, is useful only when they are employed heuristically, as ideal-types, leaving open the question of their usefulness in making sense of any particular factual configuration. Max Weber, The Methodology of the Social Sciences, Edward Shils, trans. 89–103 (1949).

108 Michael Ignatieff, Isaiah Berlin: A Life 250 (1998) (citing Berlin).

109 *See* Judith N. Shklar, "The Liberalism of Fear," *in* Liberalism and the Moral Life, Nancy Rosenblum, ed. (1989).

110 John Gray, Straw Dogs: Thoughts on Humans and Other Animals 37–38 (2002).

111 Robert Keohane adopts a similar stance in "The Contingent Legitimacy of Multilateralism," *in* Multilateralism Under Challenge? Power, International Order, and Structural Change, Edward Newman, et al., eds. 56, 67 (2006) (contending that certain global problems are too urgent to permit the delays associated with coordinating a multilateral response). This position does not deny that once humanitarian law addresses a particular question, a satisfactory answer must be consistent with the rest of international law, including human rights law and international environmental law. On this general problem, *see* International Law Commission, "Fragmentation of International Law: Difficulties arising from the Diversification and Expansion of International Law," June 30, 2005, at http://untreaty.un.org/ilc/summaries/1_9.htm#_ftn1.

112 Andrew Hurrell, "International Law and the Making and Unmaking of Boundaries," *in* States, Nations, and Borders: The Ethics of Making Boundaries, Allen Buchanan & Margaret Moore, eds. 275, 277 (2003). Hurrell is a scholar of international relations. He contends that international society is no longer simply a minimum structure for basic order, but has developed more extensive legal needs on account of its more purposive goals and deeper solidarities. Andrew Hurrell, "International Society and the Study of Regimes: A Reflective Approach," *in* Regime Theory and International Relations, Volker Rittberger, ed. 49 (1993).

113 As Pildes contends, "What is needed is a comparative and pragmatic analysis of the advantages and disadvantages of different modes and tools of checking power." Pildes, *supra* note 56, at 165–66. He encourages European legal thinkers, in particular, to question their common "premise – that if the law is absent in the regulation of international affairs, it must be that there are no meaningful checks on power at all. Instead, law should be understood as only one tool or mode of checking power in the international context, just as it is in the domestic context." *Id.* He discusses several features of recent American legal experience, counseling caution about any effort to "depoliticize" inherently controversial aspects of governance by "juridifying" them. *See also* Mark Tushnet, "Skepticism about Judicial Review: A Perspective from the U.S.," *in* Skeptical Essays on Human Rights, Tom Campbell, et al., eds. 359 (2008). "Based on the more realist sensibility of American legal cultures, informed by our experience with efforts to legalize other problems at the intersection of law and politics," Pildes continues, "Americans are likely to approach issues like the International Criminal Court with more concern about the limitations of law than Europeans currently are.... A wholly legal mechanism for trying war crimes tries to suppress the inevitable judgments of political morality that must be made. But sound institutional design should perhaps seek, not to deny that reality, but to incorporate it in various ways into the institutional structures for holding responsible those who have committed these kinds of acts." *Id.* at 160–61. For an extended proposal to this effect, *see* Mark Osiel, Mass Atrocity, Collective Memory and the Law (1997). The Europeans to whom Pildes alludes would be quick to observe, however, that although the alternative to judicialization at the national level may be greater reliance on more democratic institutions, at the international level the alternative is likely to give priority to raw power politics (i.e., to military and economic prowess).

114 "The doctrine that a wrong may not be answered with a 'wrong' would in practice lead to unsatisfactory consequences. The malefactor would be overly spared and the victim forsaken. This would undermine confidence in international law." Ernst Schneeberger, "Reciprocity as a Maxim of International Law," 37 Geo. L. J. 29, 31 (1948). So would the alternative scenario, in which such a victim must violate the law to restore a defensible balance in relations with its enemy.

115 Schneeberger, *supra* note 114, at 32 (1948); *see also* Max Huber, "Die Kriegsrechtlichen Verträge und die Kriegsraison," VII Zeitschrift für Völkerrecht 365 (1913).

CHAPTER 2. RECIPROCITY IN HUMANITARIAN LAW:
ACCEPTANCE AND REPUDIATION

1 Kenneth Roth, "After Guantánamo: The Case against Preventive Detention," Foreign Affairs, May/June 2008, at 9; John Burns, "Terror Bill Passes Narrowly in Britain," New York Times, June 12, 2008, at A6. The British legislation extended from twenty-eight to forty-two days the period during which the state may lawfully hold terror suspects without filing criminal charges. In exchange for votes from wavering Labor representatives, the government of Gordon Brown amended the bill to provide 3,000 pounds sterling ($5,900) per

diem to detainees held longer than twenty-eight days who are not thereafter charged. In the United States detention of this sort is lawful only for forty-eight hours, a rule Britain retained until 2003.

2 First Geneva Convention, Art. 46 (barring reprisal against the wounded and sick, medical personnel, buildings or equipment); Second Geneva Convention Art. 47 (barring reprisal against the shipwrecked and vessels for the amelioration of the condition of the wounded and sick in the field and at sea); Third Geneva Convention, Art. 13 (barring reprisal against POWs); Fourth Geneva Convention, Art. 33 (barring reprisal against civilian persons and their property); Hague Convention on Cultural Property, Art. 4 (1954) (barring reprisal against cultural heritage); Geneva Additional Protocol I, Art. 51(6) (barring reprisal against civilians). The prohibition on reprisals is even clearer with respect to periods of "peace" (i.e., when violence has not reached a level fairly classified as "armed conflict"). UN Charter 2(4); *Legality of the Threat or Use of Nuclear Weapons*, Advisory Opinion, 1996 I.C.J. 226, 246 (July 8) (concluding that "armed reprisals in time of peace . . . are considered to be unlawful").

3 *Prosecutor v. Kupreskić*, Case IT-95-16-T (Judgment of Jan. 14, 2000), ¶¶ 511, 517, 518. Though this chapter focuses on international humanitarian law, the lay reader may find helpful a brief summary of how the American legal system has recently positioned itself vis-à-vis the claims of international law. A cursory glance at the headlines in recent years would leave one with the impression that the president and Congress had come to endorse a reciprocity requirement – in restricting the scope of Geneva protections to be enjoyed by those repudiating humanitarian norms – whereas the Supreme Court had entirely rejected one. Though this is an oversimplification, it does roughly reflect a major political fault line. The contours of the disagreement are somewhat more complex, to be sure, and worthy of brief delineation here before looking to international law itself.

The Authorization for Use of Military Force Act, Sept. 21, 2001, Public Law 107-40, S. J. Res. 23, identified those responsible for the 9/11 attacks as an enemy and classified the situation as one of armed conflict, to which humanitarian law (rather than international human rights, with its greater rejection of reciprocity) therefore pertained. This executive and legislative decision implicitly imposed reciprocity requirements as a condition of favorable treatment of the enemy (i.e., to the extent that humanitarian law – especially as adopted by the United States – imposes them). The upshot was that Al Qaeda members, once determined to be taking part in hostilities, could be killed outright, rather than having to be arrested and criminally prosecuted. On the antireciprocity side of the ledger, however, fifty-six Senators voted in 2007 to provide an alternative route to *habeas* jurisdiction for Guantánamo detainees, rather than eliminating it entirely. Their efforts failed, however. Both the Military Commissions Act and the Detainee Treatment Act retain certain, longstanding limits on war's conduct even where the enemy does not reciprocate U.S. restraint. The executive, including the White House and Department of Defense, has long similarly recognized certain nonreciprocal restraints on how the United States wages war.

It would hence be wrong to imply that the officer corps has been the only source of forbearance in U.S. interrogation policy, though its opposition to torture has been vital, even indispensable, and hence the focus of Chapter 12. Whereas Congress and the executive have sought to condition full Geneva protections on satisfying a reciprocity requirement, the D.C. Circuit retains jurisdiction to hear appeals from Guantánamo detainees convicted by military tribunals. But detainees not convicted of any crime and being held solely as enemy combatants during ongoing hostilities enjoy more limited rights. The D.C. Circuit's jurisdiction is limited to reviewing the adequacy of the procedures used by the Combatant Status Review Tribunals when determining that a given detainee is, in fact, an enemy combatant. The Circuit Court does not have authority to review the accuracy of the enemy-combatant designation itself. Still, the detainees are allowed to present the substance of their Geneva Conventions claims under this scheme, so long as the source of the particular right invoked is also established in a federal statute or regulation. Department of Defense regulations, White House orders, and various congressional statutes have incorporated some of the very requirements of the Geneva Conventions into U.S. law.

In providing some appellate review, the Detainee Treatment Act does not entirely obstruct federal courts from exercising their duty to ensure that Guantánamo detentions remain consistent with these sources of U.S. law. Thus, even if the detainees may not expressly invoke the Conventions as a formal source of rights, the executive is bound to observe many of the same rights recognized in those treaties under a different label. The rationales publicly offered for such continued legislative forbearance generally follow the "soft power" argument developed in Chapter 11, as well as a generic rule of law rationale: the necessity to bring legislation and executive practice into closer conformity with recent Supreme Court rulings.

4 Whereas treaties require states' express consent to be bound, a developing rule of customary law will obligate states unless they expressly resist it. The objecting state must hence act affirmatively, thereby conspicuously placing itself outside an emerging consensus of other states. This raises to some extent the reputational cost of remaining free from constraint by the incipient rule. This approach to rule design seeks to establish a default norm conducive to social cooperation. It resembles in this respect the domestic law of several, liberally oriented U.S. states that presume tacit consent to organ donation on death, unless the citizen takes the initiative to specify the contrary when seeking renewal of a driver's license. Semi-covert stratagems of this sort are central to contemporary policy efforts in several areas. *See generally* Richard Thaler & Cass Sunstein, Nudge: Improving Decisions about Health, Wealth, and Happiness 3–13, 81–87 (2008).

5 *See, e.g.,* Antonio Cassese, "Expert Opinion on Whether Israel's Targeted Killings of Palestinian Terrorists is Consonant with International Humanitarian Law" (2002), at http://www.stoptorture.org.il/files/cassese.pdf at 20; Nils Melzer, Targeted Killing in International Law 433 (2008) (dismissing without elaboration as "almost inherently doubtful . . . the lawfulness of attacks directed against civilians based on the claim that they are directly participating in hostilities").

But see the position adopted by Israel's Supreme Court in *Public Committee against Torture in Israel vs. Palestinian Society for the Protection of Human Rights and the Environment* (Israel HCJ, Sept. 5, 2005), at ¶ 39; Kristen Eichensehr, "On Target? The Israeli Supreme Court and the Expansion of Targeted Killings," 116 Yale L. J. 1873 (2007); ICRC, Clarification Process on the Notion of Direct Participation in Hostilities under International Humanitarian Law (forthcoming 2009).

6 The pertinent wording provides, "The present Convention shall apply to all cases of declared war or of any other armed conflict which may arise between two or more of the High Contracting Parties."

7 The relevant language in Art. 4 is, "Nationals of a neutral State who find themselves in the territory of a belligerent State, and nationals of a co-belligerent State, shall not be regarded as protected persons while the State of which they are nationals has normal diplomatic representation in the State in whose hands they are."

8 Geneva Additional Protocol I provides, in Art. 43, "1. The armed forces of a Party to a conflict consist of all organized armed forces, groups and units which are under a command responsible to that Party for the conduct or its subordinates, even if that Party is represented by a government or an authority not recognized by an adverse Party. Such armed forces shall be subject to an internal disciplinary system which, inter alia, shall enforce compliance with the rules of international law applicable in armed conflict. 2. Members of the armed forces of a Party to a conflict (other than medical personnel and chaplains covered by Art. 33 of the Third Convention) are combatants, that is to say, they have the right to participate directly in hostilities." *See also* Avril McDonald, "*Hors de Combat*: Post-September 11 Challenges to the Rules," in The Legitimate Use of Military Force: The Just War Tradition and the Customary Law of Armed Conflict, Howard M. Hensel ed., 219, 232 (2008) (concluding that "it is difficult to consider Al Qaeda as an armed force within the meaning of Common Article 3").

9 The applicable textual wording is, "A. Prisoners of war, in the sense of the present Convention, are persons belonging to one of the following categories, who have fallen into the power of the enemy: 1. Members of the armed forces of a Party to the conflict as well as members of militias or volunteer corps forming part of such armed forces. 2. Members of other militias and members of other volunteer corps, including those of organized resistance movements, belonging to a Party to the conflict and operating in or outside their own territory, even if this territory is occupied, provided that such militias or volunteer corps, including such organized resistance movements, fulfil the following conditions: (a) That of being commanded by a person responsible for his subordinates; (b) That of having a fixed distinctive sign recognizable at a distance; (c) That of carrying arms openly; (d) That of conducting their operations in accordance with the laws and customs of war."

10 POW status entitles one to legal immunity from prosecution for ordinary acts of belligerence, which would otherwise constitute crimes. Practically speaking, this is the most important consequence of granting such status to a detainee.

11 1949 Geneva Conventions, Common Art. 2. Since Common Art. 2 applies only to interstate conflicts, Al Qaeda would not formally be entitled to Geneva protections even if it chose to accept and sought to apply them to its followers.

So the argument for allowing the organization Geneva protections on this basis would have to proceed by way of customary international law. But the prevailing practice of insurgent and terrorist groups has clearly been one of not enforcing Geneva duties on their forces, notwithstanding occasional, rhetorical protestations to the contrary.

12 A common view among specialists in humanitarian law, however, is that such a conclusion would require a competent tribunal to assess Taliban legal compliance on a unit-by-unit basis (i.e., before denying POW status to any given fighter). This view stresses that a court-martial for war crimes, rather than denial of POW status, is the principal remedy contemplated by the Geneva Conventions for such misconduct. The United States itself strongly endorsed this position in the negotiations leading to Geneva Additional Protocol I.

13 Until the U.S. Supreme Court's 2006 decision in *Hamdan v. Rumsfeld*, 548 U.S. 557 (2006), the executive branch was in the process of rewriting the Army Field Manual to clarify that suspected Al Qaeda detainees were not entitled to Common Art. 3 protections. Julian E. Barnes, "Army Manual to Skip Geneva Rule," L.A. Times, June 5, 2006, at A1.

14 Jack Goldsmith faults John Yoo's "torture memos" for lacking the professional independence that has generally characterized the Office of Legal Counsel. Yet Goldsmith himself acknowledges that he viewed his own job, as head of that very office, to be the discovery of any argument "right up to the chalk line of legality" that might support the president's desired policies. Jack Goldsmith, The Terror Presidency 78 (2008). Goldsmith is unclear here about whether by this colloquial metaphor he means any meritorious legal argument (i.e., likely to prevail in court if challenged and therefore the legitimate basis for conduct *ex ante*) or simply any argument that is nonfrivolous (i.e., not subject to judicial sanction for being raised *ex post* – a much lower standard). The latter meaning would be highly controversial in this context, the former not at all so. Entering this discussion, several former Justice Department lawyers have offered one formulation of the Office of Legal Counsel's ethical responsibilities. *See* "Principles to Guide the Office of Legal Counsel," Dec. 21, 2004, at http://www.acslaw.org/files/2004%20programs_OLC%20principles_white%20paper.pdf. This "white paper" concludes, "When providing legal advice to guide contemplated executive branch action, OLC should provide an accurate and honest appraisal of applicable law, even if that advice will constrain the Administration's pursuit of desired policies. The advocacy model of lawyering, in which lawyers craft merely plausible legal arguments to support their clients' desired actions, inadequately promotes the President's constitutional obligation to ensure the legality of executive action." *Id.* at 1.

15 Lindsay Moir, The Law of Internal Armed Conflict 85 (2005).

16 Vienna Convention on the Law of Treaties, Art. 31(3)(b).

17 Moir, *supra* note 15, at 86, 107–08. The court's conclusion that Art. 75 has become part of customary international law binding on the United States is relevant to American treatment of Al Qaeda and other jihadist suspects only insofar as the Protocol applies to a conflict of this variety in the first place. Generally, it does not. Art. 1 expressly provides that the treaty pertains only to armed conflicts "which take place in the territory of a High Contracting Party

between its armed forces and dissident armed forces or other organized armed groups which, under responsible command, *exercise such control over a part of its territory as to enable them to carry out sustained and concerted military operations and to implement this Protocol.*" (Emphasis supplied.) This is a high predicate to meet (i.e., in order to trigger the Protocol's very application). The jihadist groups at issue do not generally satisfy these criteria, except perhaps with respect to certain of their confrontations with the government forces of Pakistan, Afghanistan, and Iraq.

18 *Hamdan v. Rumsfeld*, 126 S. Ct. 2749, 2796. The Supreme Court majority concluded, "Although the official commentaries accompanying Common Art. 3 indicate that an important purpose of the provision was to furnish minimal protection to rebels involved in one kind of 'conflict not of an international character'" (i.e., a civil war), *see* GCIII Commentary 36–37, the commentaries also make clear "that the scope of the Article must be as wide as possible," *id.* at 36, note 63. In fact, limiting language that would have rendered Common Art. 3 applicable "especially [to] cases of civil war, colonial conflicts, or wars of religion," was omitted from the final version of the Article, which coupled a broader scope of application with a narrower range of rights than did earlier proposed iterations. *See* Geneva Convention III Commentaries 42–43. In dissent, Justice Thomas – joined by Justices Scalia and Alito – acknowledged that such a reading was plausible, but concluded that the majority should have deferred to the executive's interpretation, given that the treaty provision was ambiguous. *Hamdan* at 2846. The Court's majority also held that, to count as a noninternational armed conflict, the confrontation need not occur exclusively "in the territory of one of the High Contracting Parties," but might take place within more than one such state.

19 Reciprocity comes further to the fore, moreover, insofar as murder in war is likely to be prosecuted increasingly in national courts as an international war crime, rather than as a domestic "service offense" (i.e., an ordinary crime). This is because though considerations of reciprocity play no role whatever in domestic prosecutions for murder, they undoubtedly continue to occupy a central place within the international law of armed conflict and hence in the recent extension of that law into the domain of individual criminal liability. On the increasing salience of international criminal law in national prosecutions of soldiers for murder during war, *see* Nobuo Hayashi, "Branding One's Own Soldiers as War Criminals: Can National Jurisdictions Be Trusted to Enforce International Criminal Law vis-à-vis Members of Their Own Armed Forces?" Conference presentation, International Criminal Law and the Military, International Peace Research Institute, Oslo, Sept. 12, 2008.

20 To be sure, the ambiguity concerning Common Art. 3 concerned whether its coverage of "conflicts not of an international character" extends beyond civil wars to other types of armed conflict that, like civil wars, are not between sovereign states. Once found applicable to the conflict between the U.S. and Al Qaeda, there was no real ambiguity, however, over whether several American interrogation practices would have to be classified as "degrading," and hence in violation of this provision.

21 Moir, *supra* note 15, at 239.

22 Vienna Convention on the Law of Treaties, Art. 31(3)(b).
23 Anthony D'Amato, "Trashing Customary International Law," 81 A.J.I.L. 101, 105; *see also* Michael Glennon, Limits of Law, Prerogatives of Power: Interventionism After Kosovo 49 (2001). This same state practice of humanitarian intervention is pertinent both to interpreting the UN Charter itself and to the formation of customary law potentially at odds with it. International law also accepts the possibility that unenforced treaty provisions may fall into desuetude and thereby cease to be legally binding. Restatement (Third) of the Foreign Relations Law of the U.S., §102, Reporter's Note 4 (1987). Morrow's data, examined in Chapter 10, suggest that treaty prohibitions against civilian reprisals may indeed have succumbed to such desuetude. James D. Morrow, "When Do States Follow the Laws of War?" 101 Amer. Polit. Sci. Rev. 559, 562–633 (2007).
24 It is admittedly an indirect inference from known facts to speak of the pervasiveness of reprisal and professed reprisal here. The data on states' responses to their perceived victimization by war crimes, examined in Chapter 10, clearly suggest a general and persistent practice of retaliation, but they do not permit one to discern in which cases such retaliation was publicly defended by reference to the legal doctrine of reprisal, retorsion, self-defense, or something else. That latter data would be pertinent to determining *opinio juris*, and hence the ultimate implications of such state practice for customary law. There is good reason to believe that the law of reprisal would have been invoked in many such cases, because it is generally the most plausible basis for justifying acts that are otherwise inconsistent with humanitarian law. Still, the data themselves, as Morrow coded them, speak only of retaliation, not reprisal; the latter consists of retaliation only for certain ends (deterrence of further war crimes through restoring a level playing field), by certain (proportionate) means, and in certain circumstances (last resort, after advance warning). The formalities of *opinio juris* merit respect here, for it is this requirement alone that prevents repellent but pervasive practices like torture from becoming permissible as custom, and are pertinent even to interpreting treaty provisions seeking to ban them.
25 Like treaty law, customary law may not contravene a *jus cogens* norm, such as that against torture or arbitrary detention, though in a given dispute there will sometimes be doubts about whether an interested state has accepted a particular norm as peremptory. At this point, the key questions therefore become ones beyond the scope of the present book: Which, if any, coercive American interrogation practices amount to "torture" within the legal meaning of that term, and which detentions of terror suspects at Guantánamo and elsewhere must be considered "arbitrary" (i.e., in light of how much process would be legally "due" to these persons)?
26 Custom was for centuries the principal means of creating international law. All central principles of the law of armed conflict originated in this way. In ascertaining custom, it is mistaken to assume that, where states insist that a given prohibition does not precisely pertain to the facts of their situation, this necessarily implies that they affirm the rule's validity. Glennon, *supra* note 23, at 44 (identifying several other, more credible reasons why states do not challenge the rule's validity when seeming to breach it).
27 For instance, several treaties in international criminal and humanitarian law require states to prosecute (or extradite for prosecution elsewhere) those found

on their territory who are guilty of genocide, crimes against humanity, and the most serious war crimes. Yet the vast majority of states confronting this situation, which generally arises after civil war or during a transition from authoritarian rule, have preferred some combination of very different remedies: truth commissions, vetting of former officials, civil compensation of victims, official apologies, public memorials, and so forth. When states take this noncriminal road, few if any other states criticize them for so doing – even publicly, much less privately. Thus, state practice and accompanying *opinio juris* combine to establish that customary law permits behavior largely foreclosed by treaty law. On this disparity, *see* Mark Osiel, "Modes of Participation in Mass Atrocity," 38 Cornell J. Intl'l L. 793, 818 (2005).

28 Geoffrey Best, War and Law since 1945, 360 (1994). *But see* McDonald, *supra* note 8, at 244 ("If an expectation of reciprocity provides the most powerful incentive to comply with the law, a lack of reciprocity does not provide an excuse for breaking it.").

29 One influential view, in particular, "suggests that a separate enquiry into the existence of the subjective element [i.e., *opinio juris*] may be necessary only when the amount of international practice leaves doubts as to the legally binding [or presumably, permissible] character of the rule involved." Emmanuel Voyiakis, "A Theory of Customary International Law," 15, at http://papers.ssrn.com/sol3/papers.cfm?abstract_id=895462.

30 Hans Kelsen, "Théories du Droit International Coutumier," Rev. Int'l de la Théorie du Droit 248, 253 (1939); *see also* Anthony D'Amato, The Concept of Custom in International Law 73 (1971); Paul Guggenheim, "Les Principes de Droit International Public," 80 Recueil des Cours 36, 70–72 (1952).

31 The formalities of *opinio juris* merit respect here, for it is this requirement alone that prevents repellent but pervasive practices like torture from becoming permissible as custom, and pertinent even to interpreting treaty provisions seeking to ban them.

32 International Law Association, "Statement of Principles Applicable to the Formation of General Customary International Law," 34 (2000).

33 Steven Ratner, "Predator and Prey: Seizing and Killing Suspected Terrorists Abroad," 15 J. Polit. Phil. 251, 267 (2007); W. Michael Reisman & James Baker, Regulating Covert Action 69–71, 126–27 (1992).

34 Noted in David Kretzmer, "Targeted Killing of Suspected Terrorists: Extrajudicial Executions or Legitimate Means of Defense?" 16 Euro. J. Int'l L. 171, 173 (2005).

35 II Customary International Humanitarian Law, Jean-Marie Henckaerts & Louise Doswald-Beck, eds. 3420–21 (2005). The ICTY acknowledges as much in its *Krupeskić* judgment, at ¶ 532: "In his report to the U.S. Secretary of State, the U.S. Deputy Legal Adviser and Head of the U.S. Delegation to the Geneva Diplomatic Conference of 1974–77 stated that in his view the Geneva Conference had 'gone unreasonably far in its prohibition of [reprisals]' (text in 72(2) American Journal of International Law, 1978 at p. 406) and added: 'It is unreasonable to think that massive and continuing attacks directed against a nation's civilian population could be absorbed without a response in kind. By denying the possibility of response and not offering any workable substitute, Art. 51 [of the First Additional Protocol] is unrealistic and cannot be expected

to withstand the test of future conflicts. On the other hand, it will not be easy for any country to reserve, explicitly, the right of reprisal against an enemy's civilian population, and we shall have to consider carefully whether such a reservation is indispensable for us'" (*ibid*). Furthermore, it has been reported that the U.S. JCS (Joint Chiefs of Staff), faced with the possibility that other States would not accept individual monitoring mechanisms, expressed misgivings about the acceptance of the prohibition of reprisals against civilians. J. A. Roach, in ICCR Review, 1991, 67 at p. 183, note 7: "If the U.S. cannot rely on neutral supervision to ensure compliance with humanitarian law, then the threat of unilateral retaliation retains its importance as a deterrent sanction to ensure at least a minimum level of humane behaviour by US adversaries".

36 On the "persistent objector" rule, *see* American Law Commission, Restatement Third, of Foreign Relations Law, Art. 102, comment D (1987); Antonio Cassese, International Law 162–63 (2005); Ted L. Stein, "The Approach of the Different Drummer: The Principle of the Persistent Objector in International Law," 26 Harv. Int'l L.J. 457, 457 (1985).

37 *Case concerning Military and Paramilitary Activities in and against Nicaragua (Nicaragua v. U.S.)*, Merits, Judgment, 27 June 1986, ICJ Reports 1986, § 184–186; *North Sea Continental Shelf, Fed. Rep. of Germany v. Denmark*, I.C.J. (Feb. 20, 1969), Gen. List 51, 52.

38 Vienna Convention on the Law of Treaties, Art. 53 (emphasis supplied). This requirement also implies that the proximate source of peremptory norms is not truly "natural law," after all. State consent remains indispensable, as "positivists" within international law have long claimed.

39 Glennon, *supra* note 23, at 44–45 (identifying several other, more credible reasons why states do not publicly challenge the rule's validity in such circumstances).

40 *Id.* at 48.

41 The ICRC seeks to finesse this problem by describing its intellectual contribution to humanitarian law as one of clarifying custom rather than making it, but because clarification often involves a choice between contestable interpretations, the organization's activities cannot accurately be described in such innocuous or simple terms. *See* "U.S. Initial Reactions to ICRC Study on Customary International Law, Nov. 3, 2006, at http://www.state.gov/s/l/rls/82630.htm (challenging several key ICRC assertions that particular norms have crystallized as customary law). As this chapter and Chapter 10 together show, one may credibly interpret the empirical evidence of custom concerning rights of reprisal, for instance, in a manner very different from how the ICRC has done.

Though its experience of fighting wars has been scarce in modern times, Switzerland has long been a major power in international banking. Its "state practice" in that domain – including its handling of dormant Jewish accounts and Nazi gold – bears much more heavily on customary international norms than its views regarding the proper conduct of military hostilities. One might therefore naively suppose that when such a state and its legal servants offer broad guidance to the international community, they would concentrate their efforts in greater measure on issues about which their national conduct (and its moral scrutiny) would provide a more pertinent basis for global exhortation. *See generally* Stuart Eizenstat, Imperfect Justice: Looted Assets, Slave Labor, and the Unfinished Business of World War II (2003).

42 This formulation assumes that all three practices are contrary to international law, as accepted by U.S. law, unless their *prima facie* prohibition may be rebutted by a legal justification or excuse.

43 Ronald Dworkin, Law's Empire 47 (1986).

44 In reality, of course, motives are often mixed. Even if it were agreed that the "primary" motive for an lawful act of reprisal must be deterrence (and if such motive in a given case was actually retributive or strategic), it is extremely difficult for outsiders, including courts, to determine which, among several present motivations, is actually the primary one.

   To be sure, cultivated connoisseurs of customary international law who are uncomfortable with my substantive conclusions about the continuing relevance of reprisal doctrine for the conflict with Al Qaeda will retort that I have misunderstood the method for ascertaining and applying customary rules. There exist several widely respected theories of customary international law, however, offering very different views of such methodological questions. Each has some textual footing in authoritative materials. And such legal materials do not help one decide among these competing theories for understanding those methods. *See generally*, Voyiakis, *supra* note 29, at 36 (critically reviewing competing theories of CIL and concluding that "any account of customary international law that relies solely on information about what international agents do and believe will lack the resources to arbitrate some of the commonest and politically pressing disagreements about the proper interpretation of customary practices"). In the face of such critiques, there is reason to question the practical value of the very notion of CIL in almost any form or at least to be much more chary about invoking it until some defensible method is found to distinguish workable and worthy appeals to custom from other, undeserving claimants to that legal status. For recent skepticism to this effect, *see, e.g.,* Susan Estreicher, "Rethinking the Binding Effect of Customary International Law," 44 Va. J. Int'l L. 5 (2003); Eugene Kontorovich, "Inefficient Customs in International Law," 48 William & Mary L.R. 859 (2006); Jack Goldsmith & Eric Posner, "A Theory of Customary International Law," 66 U. Chi. L. Rev. 1113 (1998); Goldsmith & Posner, "Understanding the Resemblance between Modern and Traditional Customary International Law," 40 Va. J. Int'l L. 639 (2000). Still others have questioned whether the doctrine of CIL is consistent with the essential requirements of democratic legitimacy. Jed Rubenfeld, "Two World Orders," 27 Wilson Q. 22 (Autumn 2003); William Dodge, "Customary International Law and the Question of Legitimacy," 120 Harv. L. Rev. 19 (2007).

45 Elizabeth Zoller, Peacetime Unilateral Remedies: An Analysis of Countermeasures 95 (1984) ("The purpose for which international law exceptionally grants states a coercive power," i.e., in employing reprisals against a state that has violated such law, is "to re-establish an equality between the parties.").

46 Similarly, there would be no need to resort to the right of reprisal if the retaliatory acts did not rise to the level of prohibited "outrages upon personal dignity" within the meaning of Geneva Common Art. 3(1)(c). When such acts

are intended to thwart further terror attack rather than seeking retribution or humiliation, this could weigh significantly in any objective assessment of their outrageousness. Mark Mazetti, "Letters Give C.I.A. Tactics a Legal Rationale," New York Times, April 27, 2008, at A1.

47　There is by now a voluminous literature on the legal definition of torture and its scope, none of which this study addresses. *See, e.g.,* Gail Miller, Defining Torture (2005). It is sufficient for present purposes to acknowledge that reasonable disagreement exists over whether the term, properly understood, applies to certain interrogation techniques that the U.S. has recently employed against Al Qaeda suspects. A leading Justice Department lawyer contends, "Something can be quite distressing, uncomfortable, even frightening.... [But] if it doesn't involve severe physical pain, and it doesn't last very long, it may not constitute severe physical suffering. That would be the analysis." Steven Bradbury, Acting Chief of the Office of Legal Counsel, Feb. 14, 2008, testimony before a House Judiciary Subcommittee, quoted in Human Rights First, Law and Security Digest, Issue 186, Feb. 22, 2008.

48　Jordan Paust, Beyond the Law: The Bush Administration's Unlawful Responses in the "War" on Terror 3 (2007) ("Under the Geneva Conventions, any person who is not a prisoner of war has rights under the Geneva Civilian Convention"); McDonald, *supra* note 8, at 237, 239.

49　For this view, *see* Mary Ellen O'Connell, "The Criteria of Armed Conflict," Int'l L. Assoc., Study Committee on the Meaning of War, Spring 2007; Nathaniel Berman, "Privileging Combat: Contemporary Conflict and the Legal Construction of War," 42 Colum. J. Transnat'l L. 1, 32–33 (2004).

50　Philip Bobbitt, The Shield of Achilles 820 (2002).

51　Randal Archibold, "Diverging View of Californian at Terror Trial," New York Times, Feb. 17, 2006, at A14 (describing Californian Hamid Hayat, who admitted to investigators having attended Al Qaeda training camps and was recorded discussing methods for planned attacks on U.S. hospitals and supermarkets).

52　On the development of this legal doctrine, *see* Mark Osiel, "The Banality of Good: Aligning Incentives Against Mass Atrocity," 105 Colum. L. Rev. 1751, 1783–1805 (2005).

53　Benedict Carey, "Close Doesn't Always Count in Winning Games," New York Times, March 7, 2005, at A1 (describing results of research on what sociologists have come to call the "strength of weak ties"); *see generally* Mark Granovetter, "The Strength of Weak Ties: A Network Theory Revisited," 1 Sociological Theory 201 (1983).

54　It bears emphasis, however, that the 9/11 attacks and similar actions are already susceptible to prosecution in many cases as crimes against humanity, i.e., without need to establish the existence of an armed conflict.

55　Michael Moss, "In Algeria, Insurgency Gains a Lifeline From Al Qaeda," New York Times, July 1, 2008, at A1 ("The transformation of the group from a nationalist insurgency to a force in the global jihad is a page out of Mr. Bin Laden's playbook: expanding his reach by bringing local militants under the Qaeda brand.") *See also* John Simpson, "Battling the Al Qaeda Francise," B.B.C. News, Oct. 3, 2005, at http://news.bbc.co.uk/2/hi/asia-pacific/4304516.stm (developing the franchise analogy).

56 Black's Law Dictionary, 7th ed., 668 (1999).

57 Ilan Alon, Service Franchising: A Global Perspective (2005).

58 *Id.* at 1515; Douglas Laycock, Modern American Remedies 689–90 (2002).

59 ICTY *Prosecutor v. Delalic et al.,* Case No. IT-96-21-A, Judgment, ¶¶ 248–268 (Feb. 20, 2001), at http://www.un.org/icty/celebici/appeal/judgement/cel-aj010220.pdf, at 193. For discussion, *see* Osiel, *supra* note 52, at 1776, 1804.

60 William Killion, "Franchisor Vicarious Liability – The Proverbial Assault on the Citadel," 24 Franchise L.J. 162, 166–67 (Winter 2005) (noting that the majority rule is that the franchisor is liable for the acts of the franchisee when the franchisor exercises control over the instruments of injury).

61 On peacetime reprisal, *see* Yoram Dinstein, War, Aggression and Self-Defence 193–204 (2001) (contending that "defensive armed reprisals" are admissible in the Charter era); Lawrence T. Greenberg et al., Information Warfare and International Law 26–27 (1997) (concluding that forceful reprisals are admissible); D. W. Bowett, "Reprisals Involving Recourse to Armed Force," 66 A.J.I.L. 1, 3 (1972) ("Within the whole context of a continuing state of antagonism . . . with recurring acts of violence, an act of reprisal may be regarded as being at the same time both a form of punishment and the best form of protection against future acts of violence by the other party."); Maj. Philip Seymour, "The Legitimacy of Peacetime Reprisal as a Tool against State-Sponsored Terrorism," 39 Naval L. Rev. 221 (1990); William O'Brien, "Reprisals, Deterrence and Self-Defense in Counter-Terror Operations," 30 Va. J. Int'l L. 421 (1990) (arguing that in a situation of continuing low-level conflict, between peace and outright war, it is often pointless in practice to attempt distinguishing retrospective "punitive" measures from those designed for current self-defense and/or prospective deterrence); *see also* Remigiusz Bierzanek, "Reprisals as a Means of Enforcing the Laws of Warfare: The Old and the New Law," *in* The New Humanitarian Law of Armed Conflict, Antonio Cassese, ed. 232 (1980); R. Barsotti, "Armed Reprisals," *in* The Current Legal Regulation of the Use of Force, Antonio Cassese, ed. 79 (1986).

62 *See infra* note 164. The United States sought to lay the basis for such an argument of lawful peacetime reprisal/forcible countermeasures in how it initiated its attack on Afghanistan after 9/11. Michael Kelley, "Time Warp to 1945 – Resurrection of the Reprisal and Anticipatory Self-Defense Doctrines in International Law," 13 J. Transnat'l L. & Policy 1, 2, 21 (2003). Kelley observes, "President Bush . . . was careful to match his responsive form [after the 9/11 attacks] to the requirements of customary reprisal doctrine. After suffering an injury from Afghanistan's breach of international law during peacetime, an ultimatum was issued that was not complied with, the Taliban regime was toppled, and the Al Qaeda terrorist network disrupted as a necessary and proportional response to the prior injury. . . . Thus, the argument for the return of reprisal doctrine, at least in the context of responding to terrorist attacks, has found a mooring in the current Administration." *Id.* at 2, 21.

63 As Kelsen noted, "One of the norms of international law created by custom authorizes states to regulate their mutual relations by treaty. The reason for the validity of the legal norms of international law created by treaty is this custom-created norm . . . *pact sunt servanda.*" Hans Kelsen, "The Pure Theory

of Law," *in* International Law: Cases and Materials, Louis Henkin, ed. 20 (1993). Glennon plausibly infers from this fact, "Thus, it would seem strange if the Charter or any other treaty were deemed resistant to supersession by custom." Glennon, *supra* note 23, at 40.

64 UN Charter, Arts. 2(4), 2(3), and 33(2).

65 Ingrid Detter de Lupis, The Law of War 352 (1987) (observing that some "rules of war . . . are subjected to ordinary requirements of reciprocity and others . . . do not seem to be subject to reciprocity"). By their words and deeds, states may also bind themselves unilaterally (i.e., nonreciprocally) in a variety of undertakings, the World Court has concluded in other contexts. This is especially so where other states reasonably rely on such representations, creating a situation of equitable or promissory estoppel.

66 To identify every place where humanitarian law accepts or rejects any conception of reciprocity would require a much longer book that would be written for a readership of specialists only.

67 Third Geneva Convention, Art. 118.

68 Convention for the Protection of Cultural Property in the Event of Armed Conflict, Arts. 4, 5, *adopted* May 14, 1954, 249 U.N.T.S. 240. The Contracting Parites "shall refrain from any act directed by way of reprisals against cultural property." Art. 4(4).

69 Geneva Additional Protocol I, Art. 51(8).

70 *Id.* Art. 44(4).

71 Fourth Geneva Convention, Art. 5.

72 United Nations Charter, Art. 51.

73 *Military and Paramilitary Activities in and against Nicaragua (Nicar. v. U.S.)*, Jurisdiction and Admissibility, 1986 I.C.J. 14, 103–04 (June 27) (defining "armed attack" as activity carried out either directly or "on behalf" of the state, but excluding state, "assistance . . . in the form of provisions . . . weapons . . . logistical or other support"). *Contra, id.* at 345–47 (dissenting opinion of Judge Schwebel) (arguing that "large-scale" state support – provisions, planning, facilities, and communications – is "legally tantamount" to an "armed attack" and must be included in its definition).

74 On this basis, one leading scholar concludes that "reciprocity . . . is a false and even dangerous concept when made the overriding principle of the law of war." Frits Kalshoven, Belligerent Reprisals 253 (1986). This view has a long pedigree and draws on examples throughout the history of Western warfare. *See, e.g.,* Theodore Woolsey, Introduction to the Study of International Law 183–83 (6th ed. 1892).

75 Collective security treaties nonetheless themselves rely upon a species of reciprocity, by establishing a mutually acceptable balance of burden and benefit among their parties. Such agreements rest on the *quid pro quo* exchange, after all, that "we will agree to defend you against attack, if you agree to help defend us in such an event."

76 Geneva Additional Protocol I, Art. 44(7).

77 Additional Protocol I, in Art. 1(4) defines these conflicts as ones "in which peoples are fighting against colonial domination and alien occupation and against racist regimes in the exercise of their right of self-determination." Several of the terms within this legal formulations, however, themselves lack widely-accepted

definitions, rendering its application to many cases highly contestable. On these difficulties, *see, e.g.,* Heather Wilson, International Law and the Use of Force by National Liberation Movements 1–2 (1988). On the challenge the law faces in differentiating such movements from contemporary terrorist groups claiming their mantle, *see* Lucia Aleni, "Distinguishing Terrorism from Wars of National Liberation in the Light of International Law: A View from Italian Courts," 6 J. Int'l Crim. Just. 525 (2008).

78 *Id.* Art. 44(3) provides that a fighter enjoys combatant privileges only insofar as "he carries his arms openly . . . during such time as he is visible to the adversary while he is engaged in a military deployment preceding the launching of an attack in which he is to participate." *See also* Art. 51(3) providing that "civilians shall enjoy the protection afforded by [the Geneva Conventions] unless and for such time as they take a direct part in hostilities." Françoise J. Hampson, "Detention, the 'War on Terror' and International Law," *in* The Law of Armed Conflict: Constraints on the Contemporary Use of Military Force, Howard Hensel, ed. 131, 148 (2005) ("Whilst combatants can be attacked at any time, civilians who take direct part in hostilities can only be attacked at the time when they are so participating."). The lack of reciprocity in this provision provided a major reason for U.S. rejection of the Protocol. There is considerable disagreement, moreover, regarding the meaning of the quoted treaty wording. *Compare* Curtis Bradley & Jack Goldsmith, "Rejoinder: The War on Terrorism," 118 Harv. L. Rev. 2683, 2687–90 (2005) (arguing that such wording permits targeting of all Al Qaeda members at all times, even if they have only trained for but not yet participated in armed attacks, or are at the time of their attack engaged in nonmartial activities); Robert Goldman & Brian Tittemore, "Unprivileged Combatants and the Hostilities in Afghanistan: Their Status and Rights under International Humanitarian and Human Rights Law," Amer. Soc. Int'l L. Task Force on Terrorism, 20–21 (Dec. 2002) (same), and Moir, *supra* note 15, at 59 (same), *with* Ryan Goodman & Derek Jinks, "International Law, U.S. War Powers, and the Global War on Terrorism," 118 Harv. L. Rev. 2653, 2655–58 (2005) (rejecting this view).

79 Marcus Rediker, Villains of All Nations: Atlantic Pirates in the Golden Age 83, 102, 162–68 (2004); David Cordingly, Under the Black Flag: The Romance and the Reality of Life among the Pirates 114–19 (1995). Such a flag was raised imminently on attacking a merchant ship, not with the intention of providing fair warning of one's criminal intentions, but simply to strike fear into hearts, with a view to eliciting quick surrender. Such piracy constituted an international crime, regardless of whether the flag was or was not raised at any point.

    The analogy to contemporary terrorists may be questioned on many grounds, of course, not least the fact that those employing terrorism today often do not disclose their belligerent status and intentions even while engaged in operations, as when a suicide bomber explodes himself in a crowd without warning.

80 Under Art. 37(1) of Geneva Additional Protocol I, "Acts inviting the confidence of an adversary to lead him to believe that he is entitled to, or is obliged to accord, protection under the rules of international law applicable in armed conflict, with intent to betray that confidence, shall constitute perfidy," including "(c) the feigning of civilian, non-combatant status."

81 This was one reason why the United States declined to sign or ratify the Protocol. President Reagan explained that it would "give recognition and protection to terrorist groups" by permitting them to claim that they were fighting "wars of national liberation," which the treaty expressly endorses. Message from the President of the U.S. Transmitting the Protocol II Additional to the Geneva Conventions of August 12, 1949, and Relating to the Protection of Victims of Non-International Armed Conflicts, Concluded at Geneva on June 10, 1977, S. Treaty Doc. No. 2, 100th Cong., 1st Sess. (1987).

82 Clive James, Cultural Amnesia 653 (2007).

83 Waldemar Solf, "A Response to Douglas J. Feither's Law in the Service of Terror – The Strange Case of the Additional Protocol," 20 Akron L. Rev. 261, 269–71 (1987).

84 Hague Convention Respecting the Laws and Customs of War on Land, Oct. 17, 1910, Art. 35; Ernst Schneeberger, "Reciprocity as a Maxim of International Law," 37 Geo. L. J. 29, 32 (1948).

85 Convention (IV) Respecting the Laws and Customs of War on Land; Annex: Regulations Concerning the Laws and Customs of War on Land. The Hague, 18 October 1907, Art. 2 (emphasis supplied).

86 Geneva Additional Protocol I, Art. 4(A)(1) and (2).

87 *See, e.g.,* Pietro Verri, Dictionary of the International Law of Armed Conflict 30–31 (1992) (defining "civilian" only by process of elimination). The Fourth Geneva Convention includes the word "civilian" in its very name, but offers no definition of the term. Geneva Convention Relative to the Protection of Civilians in Time of War, entry into force Oct. 21, 1950.

88 Though they are not "protected persons" within the Fourth Geneva Convention, such people may nonetheless enjoy some of the longstanding rights of aliens under customary law. These rights are today codified in many bilateral treaties of "Friendship, Commerce, and Navigation." That legal regime, though partly eclipsed by the burgeoning of human rights law, rests squarely on the reciprocity principle: the appreciation by each state that its own nationals could expect treatment only as good as it agreed, on its home territory, to treat the other's nationals. Critics of Bush administration policy did not much develop this line of legal analysis in arguing for heightened protection of detained terror suspects, perhaps because many countries do not afford a very high level of protection even to their own nationals.

89 The Land Mines Protocol is an exception, but only in situations where such weapons are intentionally directed against the civilian population. Art. 3, ¶ 2, 19 Int'l Legal Materials 1534 (1980); Protocol on Prohibitions or Restrictions on the Use of Mines, Booby-Traps and Other Devices, Art. 3, ¶ 2, 19 Int'l Legal Materials 1534 (1980); Amended Protocol on the Use of Mines, Booby-Traps and Other Devices, Art. 3(7) (1996).

90 Christian Tams, Enforcing Obligations *Erga Omnes* in International Law 57 (2005); Lalgosia Fitzmaurice & Olufemi Elias, Contemporary Issues in the Law of Treaties 148, 163 (2005).

91 These include, for instance, the Hague Conventions of 1899 and 1907. Kalshoven, *supra* note 74, at 24–5, 92. Hence, when a state claiming neutrality in an armed conflict breaches duties attendant to that status, as by selling

contraband to one of the belligerents, the remedies available to the opposing belligerent include a right to proportionate countermeasures and, on some accounts, to treat the professed neutral thereafter as itself an enemy belligerent. Hague Convention Respecting the Rights and Duties of Neutral Powers and Persons in Case of War on Land, 1907 (providing in Art. 17 that "A neutral cannot avail himself of his neutrality (1) if he commits hostile acts against a belligerent. . . . ").

92 *See infra* text accompanying notes (on Morrow's data).

93 Geneva Convention I for the Amelioration of the Condition of the Wounded and Sick in Armed Forces in the Field, Art. 63.

94 Theodor Meron, "The Humanization of Humanitarian Law," 94 A.J.I.L. 239, 250 (2000). Meron reports that the steering committee of ICRC experts on customary rules of international humanitarian law concluded that the ban on reprisals against civilian objects and persons in the power of the opposing belligerent is contentious and has not matured into customary law (Apr. 1998).

95 *Id.* at 251. *See also* Moir, *supra* note 15, at 86 (noting that in civil wars states are unlikely to honor obligations under Common Art. 3 when opposing insurgents fail to, and vice versa); George Aldrich, "Compliance with the Law: Problems and Prospects," *in* II Armed Conflict and the New Law: Effecting Compliance 3 (1993) (observing that in ratifying Additional Protocol I, "states are agreeing to sweeping prohibitions of reprisal which they will find it impossible to respect when faced with serious violations of the law by an enemy"); Detter, *supra* note 65, at 344 ("Yet in practice considerations of reciprocity may still be decisive.").

96 Meron, *supra* note 94, at 250.

97 The International Court of Justice developed an elaborate schema, based on the reciprocity norm, to resolve the question of what happens to the respective duties of multiple parties when a state enters a reservation to a multilateral human rights treaty, a reservation that some states reject as incompatible with the treaty's object and purpose, while other states accept the reservation. Advisory Opinion, *Reservations to the Convention on the Prevention and Punishment of Genocide,* I.C.J., 28 May 1951, at 12.

98 On North Vietnamese torture of U.S. POWs, *see* Stuart Rochester & Frederick Kiley, Honor Bound: The History of American Prisoners of War in Southeast Asia, 1961–1973, at 144–65, 330–38 (1998).

99 Documents on the Laws of War, Adam Roberts & Richard Guelff, eds. 507–11 (2000); U.K. Ministry of Defense, The Manual of The Law of Armed Conflict 19.19.1, at 420–21 (2005); Dept. of the Navy, The Commander's Handbook of the Law of Naval Operations 6–4 (July 2007) ("Reprisals may be taken against enemy armed forces, enemy civilians other than those in occupied territory, and enemy property."); Christopher Greenwood, "The Twilight of the Law of Belligerent Reprisals," *in* Greenwood, Essays on War in International Law 295, 336–37 (2006).

100 Manual of The Law of Armed Conflict, *id.* at 421.

101 *Legality of the Threat or Use of Nuclear Weapons,* Advisory Opinion, 1996 I.C.J. 226, 246 (July 8).

102 *Id.* at 328 (July 8), J. Schwebel (arguing that "had Iraq employed chemical or biological weapons . . . against coalition forces [in 1991], that would have been a wrong in international law giving rise to the right of belligerent reprisal"). Schwebel represented the United States on the court. The later Chemical Weapons Convention, which entered into force in 1997, prohibits reprisal in Art I(1) – barring the use of such weapons "in all circumstances" – and permits no reservations (Art. 22). Iraq never ratified this treaty during the rule of Saddam Hussein. On the history of U.S. concern over the humanitarian repercussions of tactical nuclear weapons, *see* Sahr Conway-Lanz, Collateral Damage: Americans, Noncombatant Immunity, and Atrocity after World War II 123–49 (2006).

103 Schwebel, *id.* at 211 (describing the U.S.'s "most recent and effective threat of the use of nuclear weapons – on the eve of 'Desert Storm'").

104 Paula McCarron & Cynthia Holt, "A Faustian Bargain: Nuclear Weapons, Negative Security Assurances, and Belligerent Reprisals," 25 Fletcher Forum of World Affairs 203, 217 (2001) (describing the 1996 threat by Secretary of Defense William Perry to consider "all options" in response to a chemical weapons attack on the U.S. or its armed forces; the U.S. response to such attack, he added, would be "absolute, overwhelming and devastating"). Presidential Decision Directive 60 authorized U.S. forces to target nuclear weapons against "rogue" states in retaliation for their use of weapons of mass destruction. Patrick Sloyan, "New Nuke Policy by Clinton Directive Allows Atomic Retaliation," Newsday, Feb. 1, 1998, at A7.

105 Greenwood, *supra* note 99, at 344–45 (quoting the 1956 U.S. Army Field Manual, the 1999 U.S. Naval Commander's Handbook on the Law of Naval Operations, and the 1958 U.K. Military Field Manual). The statement in the text assumes, of course, that the other conditions required for lawful belligerent reprisal would have been satisfied.

106 Marc Sageman, "Does Osama Still Call the Shots? Debating the Containment of al Qaeda's Leadership," Foreign Affairs, July/Aug. 2008, at 165 (contending that "al Qaeda had reconstituted itself in Pakistan's Pashtun-tribal frontier areas and from that base was again actively directing and initiating international terrorist operations on a grand scale"); Thomas Johnson & M. Chris Mason, "No Sign until the Burst of Fire: Understanding the Pakistan-Afghanistan Frontier," 32 Int'l Security 41, 41 (2008) (citing several recent intelligence assessments describing the region as "a locus for a regenerating Al Qaeda network").

107 Third Geneva Convention, Art. 5.

108 Such measures would have to meet the standard doctrinal requirements of reprisal, including proportionality and advance notice. *See, e.g.,* U.K. Ministry of Defense, British Manual, The Law of War on Land 184, ¶ 644 (1958) (prohibiting civilian reprisals only "against prisoners of war, against sick and wounded, and against shipwrecked members of the enemy armed forces, against buildings, equipment, and vessels protected by the Wounded and Maritime Convention, as well as against civilian protected persons and their property in occupied territory and in the belligerent's own territory"). Very few detained Al Qaeda suspects are covered by these categories of protection, for reasons discussed in the text. *See also* the Austrian Manual (*Truppenführung*), Bundesministerium

für Landesverteidigung 255 (1965), listing similar categories of persons and objects against whom reprisals are prohibited by the Geneva Conventions.

109 Charles Dickens, Oliver Twist 489 (1970) (1838).

110 Gary Solis, The Law of Armed Conflict, (Cambridge University Press, forthcoming 2009); *see generally* Gen. Charles Dunlap, "Legal Issues in Coalition Warfare: A U.S. Perspective," *in* The Law of War in the 21st Century, Anthony Helm, ed. 221 (2006); Dale Stephens, "Coalition Warfare: Challenges and Opportunities," *id.* at 245.

111 John Burns, "Britain Joins Draft Treaty on Cluster Munitions," New York Times, May 29, 2008, A13 (indicating that, after some controversy over the question, "the draft treaty contains a permissive provision stating that the troops of signatory nations 'may engage in military cooperation and operations with states not party to this convention that might engage' in the use of cluster munitions").

112 George Aldrich, "The Laws of War on Land," 94 A.J.I.L. 42, 46–48 (2000); Theodor Meron, "The Time Has Come for the U.S. to Ratify Geneva Protocol I," 88 A.J.I.L. 678, 682–84 (1994).

113 André Durand, History of the International Committee of the Red Cross: From Sarajevo to Hiroshima, vol. 2, 521 (1978).

114 As an enforcement mechanism, reciprocity "occupies a more central place . . . in pre-modern and especially in pre-state societies than in modern industrial societies." Richard Seaford, "Introduction," *in* Reciprocity in Ancient Greece Christopher Gill et al., eds. 1, 4 (1998). Kohlberg locates reciprocity at the second of his five stages of moral development. Lawrence Kohlberg, "From Is to Ought: How to Commit the Naturalistic Fallacy and Get Away with it in the Study of Moral Development," *in* Cognitive Development and Epistemology, T. Mischel, ed. 164, 165 (1971); Lawrence Kohlberg, "Justice as Reversibility," *in* Kohlberg, Essays on Moral Development, vol. 1, 194 (1981).

115 Keohane characterizes this transition as a change from "specific" to "diffuse" reciprocity, Provost as one from "immediate" to "systemic" reciprocity. Claude Lévi-Strauss much earlier distinguished "mutual" from "univocal" reciprocity in very similar terms. Lévi-Strauss, "The Principle of Reciprocity," *in* Sociological Theory: A Book of Readings, Lewis Coser & Bernard Rosenberg, eds. 84, 84 (1957); Robert Keohane, "Reciprocity in International Relations," 40 Int'l Org. 1, 4 (1986); René Provost, International Human Rights and Humanitarian Law 153–81 (2002); *cf.* Pierre Bourdieu, Outline of a Theory of Practice 3–10 (1977) (arguing that formal, atemporal models of reciprocal exchange often overlook how such reciprocity is actually "a scheme which works itself out only in and through time"). On all these accounts, reciprocity tends to develop and evolve over time from short-term, bilateral exchange to longer term, multilateral exchange.

116 Chapters 5 to 7 explore the meaning of this concept in depth.

117 Vienna Convention on the Law of Treaties, Art. 60(a). *See also* Restatement (Third), Foreign Relations Law of the U.S., §335(2)(b) (1987).

118 Eric A. Posner, "Terrorism and the Laws of War," 5 Chi. J. Int'l Law 423, 433 (2005).

119 Geoffrey Best, *supra* note 28, at 420 (1994).

120 Keohane, *supra* note 115, at 19. In tit-for-tat, players always meet cooperation with cooperation, defection with defection. The robustness of tit-for-tat in accounting for much of social life was first discovered by Robert Axelrod, The Evolution of Cooperation 21, 57–62 (1984) (describing, at 21, reciprocity as "the most effective strategy for maintaining cooperation among egoists"). *See also* Ernst Fehr & Simon Gaechter, "Fairness and Retaliation: The Economics of Reciprocity," 14 J. Econ. Perspectives 159, 165 (2000).

121 Consequentialism refers to a class of moral theories that judge actions and institutions by their consequences in the world, rather than by their adherence to general principles of conduct. The latter view goes by the name of deontology.

122 Inasmuch as law abidingness can be here equated with rights-respecting conduct, this stance rests on the position called rights-consequentialism. Amartya Sen, "Rights and Agency," 11 Phil. & Pub. Affairs 3, 15–19 (1982); T.M. Scanlon, "Rights, Goals, and Fairness," *in* Consequentialism and its Critics, Samuel Scheffler, ed. 74 (1988).

123 *Air Services Agreement Case, France v. U.S.* (1978) 18 R.I.A.A. 416, ¶ 92. "It goes without saying that recourse to counter-measures involves the great risk of giving rise, in turn, to a further reaction, thereby causing an escalation which will lead to a worsening of the conflict. Counter-measures therefore should be a wager on the wisdom, not on the weakness of the other Party. They should be used with a spirit of great moderation."

124 Vienna Convention on the Law of Treaties, Art. 60(5). Hence a peremptory/*jus cogens* norm embodied within a treaty cannot be set aside in response to its breach. *Prosecutor v. Kupreskic*, Judgment, 14 Jan. 2000, IT-95-16-T, ¶ 520, ICTY; Bruno Simma, "Reflections on Article 60 of the Vienna Convention on the Law of Treaties and its Background in General International Law," 20 Österreichische Zeitschrift für öffentliches Recht 5, 20–21 (1970); *see generally* Reservations to Human Rights Treaties and the Vienna Convention Regime, Ineta Ziemele, ed. (2004).

125 Advisory Opinion, *supra* note 97, at 23.

126 One major exception to this proposition concerns refugee flows from country X to country Y resulting from human rights abuse by the government of X. Country Y would then have a significant and legitimate concern with X's treatment of X's citizens. In fact, cases involving even the serious possibility of major cross-border refugee flows pose a "threat to international peace and security," thereby legally authorizing UN intercession on behalf of the wider international community. A less obvious example concerns labor rights as a species of human rights; if country A allows its employers to violate employees' internationally recognized labor rights, this may give A's manufacturers unfair advantage in international trade competition with those of country B, which holds its employers to international treaty commitments on labor rights.

127 Alan Sykes, "International Law," *in* Handbook of Law and Economics, Mitchell Polinsky & Steven Shavell, eds. 757, 815 (2007).

128 There was some confusion and disagreement among the drafters concerning the meaning of the word "humanitarian." United Nations Conference on the Law of Treaties, First Session, Vienna Austria, Mar. 26–May 24, 1968, Summary Records of the 61st Meeting of the Committee of the Whole, 83, UN Doc

A/CONF.39/11 (1969). The Swiss delegation, which proposed the exemption, believed that it would cover treaties like the Geneva Conventions, as well as "conventions concerning the status of refugees, the prevention of slavery, the prohibition of genocide and the protection of human rights in general." *Id.* at 12.

129 As an empirical matter, it is probably safe to say that most Westerners accept such reciprocity. Despite the innumerable apologies from various governmental bodies, throughout the country, for past unethical conduct dating back to slavery, Americans' moral views do not lead them to demand that the U.S. government apologize for firebombing Japan's largest cities at the end of World War II, though more than 330,000 civilians were thereby killed. Edwin P. Hoyt, Inferno: The Firebombing of Japan 137 (2000); Conway-Lanz, *supra* note 102, at 227 (concluding from historical research that, since the end of World War II, "Americans have never had sustained public discussions over the potential conflict between the lives of [U.S.] soldiers and the lives of noncombatants"). On the comparable British and American firebombing of German cities, *see* Jörg Friedrich, The Fire: The Bombing of Germany, 1940–1945, trans. Allison Brown (2006). Firebombing of civilian population centers clearly seemed excusable, even justified, after earlier Axis bombing of British cities. Noble Frankland, Bomber Offensive: The Devastation of Europe 25 (1970). In fact, at the war's end most Americans endorsed still more punitive policies toward Japan, according to opinion surveys at the time. John Dower, War without Mercy: Race and Power in the Pacific War 52–53 (1986). Dower attributes the targeting of Japanese civilians to America's racism. But the Allied bombardment of Germany killed comparable numbers of German civilians. Michael Sherry, The Rise of American Air Power 260, 314 (1987). Anti-German stereotypes and dehumanizing epithets were also common among Americans at the time, despite the fact that Germans are white. One statistical study finds that differences of race or ethnicity between belligerents does not affect whether civilians are directly targeted. Alexander Downes, Targeting Civilians in War 248–50 (2008).

Evidence of the moral insignificance still widely attached to Allied civilian bombing may be found almost anywhere at hand. In even an airline magazine, for instance, one encounters a casual comparison of J. Robert Oppenheimer's exhilaration before testing the first atomic weapon with the article author's exhilaration before tasting a new flavor of coffee. Josh Ozersky, "Food Hackers," American Way, April 1, 2007, at 56. To this day, Americans express no great regret about their government's conduct at that time. This may be at least partly because the ethics of reciprocity makes sense to them. To be sure, another factor was the belief that an unequivocally just war against a regime like the Third Reich and its allies justified measures otherwise excessive, in order to achieve an overriding goal. The moral "wrong" of responding in kind, to the extent it was at all perceived as such, was simply outweighed in many minds by the potential political consequences of nonreciprocation. Retribution for past harm provided still a third rationale for Western conduct.

130 The *travaux préparatoires* to the Vienna Convention on the Law of Treaties disclose nothing inconsistent with this reading. United Nations Conference on the Law of Treaties, Vienna, Austria, Mar. 26–May 24, 1968 & Apr. 9–May 22,

1969, Reports of the Committee of the Whole on its work at the first session of the Conference, ¶ 524, UN Doc A/CONF.39/14 (May 1, 1969).

131 Sir Gerald Fitzmaurice, Second Report on the Law of Treaties, 1957 2 Y.B. Int'l L. Comm'n 16, 54, UN Doc. A/CN.4/107. One author nonetheless claims that Art. 60(5) exempts from reciprocity even weapons and disarmament treaties. Mohammed Gomaa, Suspension or Termination of Treaties on Grounds of Breach 110–11 (1966). But such a reading goes well beyond the scope of what the exception's drafters contemplated; they anticipated that it would encompass treaties regarding labor conditions, maritime conventions on safety standards at sea, and the Geneva Conventions. *Id.* at 54.

132 *Id.* Early drafts of the Geneva Conventions covering civil war themselves had included express reciprocity requirements. Moir, *supra* note 15, at 23; Anton Schlögel, "Civil War," 108 Int'l Rev. of the Red Cross 123, 127 (1970).

133 Sir Humphrey Waldock, Summary Records of the 831st Meeting, 1966 pt. 1, 1 Y.B. Int'l L. Comm'n 57, 59, 66, UN Doc. A/CN.4/SER.A/1966.

134 Bruno Simma, "Bilateralism and the Community of Interest in the Law of State Responsibility," *in* International Law at a Time of Perplexity, Yoram Dinstein & Mala Taboury, eds. 821, 825 (1989).

135 Int'l Covenant on Civil and Political Rights, Art. 4(2). This statement is complicated by the fact that the United States has never officially accepted any case-specific application of the *jus cogens* doctrine, the doctrine that could render such rights nonderogable.

136 Fourth Geneva Convention, Art. 148.

137 In *Hamdan*, the U.S. Supreme Court ruled that all detainees in American captivity must be treated in accordance with Common Art. 3 of the Geneva Conventions, which prohibits humiliating and degrading treatment. *Hamdan v. Rumsfeld*, 126 S.Ct. 2749, 2757 (2006) ("[Article 3's] requirements are general ones, crafted to accommodate a wide variety of legal systems. But requirements they are nonetheless. The commission that the President has convened to try Hamdan does not meet those requirements.")

138 On such irrelevance, *see* Kim Rubinstein, "Rethinking Nationality in International Humanitarian Law" *in* The Challenge of Conflict: International Law Responds, Ustinia Dolgopol, Judith Gardam, eds. (2006).

139 Unless the agreement expressly provides otherwise, a state may withdraw from or suspend its duties under a bilateral treaty on the other state's material breach. Vienna Convention on the Law of Treaties, Art. 60(1). With multilateral treaties like the Geneva Conventions, however, a party specifically affected by another's breach may suspend its operation in relation to the defaulting state, but duties to other state parties remain unaffected. *Id.* Art. 60 (2).

140 John Yoo & Will Trachman, "Less than Bargained For: The Use of Force and the Declining Relevance of the United Nations," 5 Chi. J. Int'l L. 379, 394 (2005).

141 Frank Easterbrook, "The Supreme Court, 1983 Term-Foreword: The Court and the Economic System," 98 Harv. L. Rev. 4, 15 (1984).

142 Laurence Helfer, "Constitutional Analogies in the International Legal System," 37 Loyola L.A. L. Rev. 193, 213–14 (2003); on *jus cogens* norms, *see* Restatement (Third) of the Foreign Relations Law of the U.S., §702, Comment K (1987).

143 Hanna Beate Schöpp-Schilling, "Reservations to the Convention on the Elimination of All Forms of Discrimination against Women," *in* Reservations

to Human Rights Treaties and the Vienna Convention Regime: Conflict, Harmony or Reconciliation?, Ineta Ziemele, ed., 3, 8, 10, 12 (2004). Muslim countries have entered similar reservations to the Convention on the Rights of the Child.

144 No definitions are offered, in particular, for the terms "cruel, inhuman, or degrading." Even the definition of torture is quite imprecise, by conventional standards of statutory drafting.

145 *Barcelona Traction, Light and Power Co., Ltd., Second Phase (Belg. v. Spain)*, 1970 I.C.J. 3, 32 (Feb. 5). The "importance of the rights involved" traditionally derived simply from a "joint interest" in their enforcement against a common danger, as initially represented by pirates, for instance. In the last half-century, however, *erga omnes* duties increasingly sought to vindicate "fundamental values of the international community" as such, understood as an indivisible entity. On this distinction and its emergence, *see* Antonio Cassese, International Law 15–16 (2005). On how *erga omnes* and other multilateral duties confer standing to challenge a state's misconduct, including standing in those not immediately prejudiced by such misconduct, *see* James Crawford, "Standing to Claim for Breaches of Multilateral Obligations," *in* Académie de Droit International, Collected Courses of the Hague Academy of International Law 2006, 421–451 (2007).

146 International Law Commission, Draft Articles on the Law of State Responsibility, Art. 42, ¶ 2(a), II YbILC, 204 (1963); Simma, *supra* note 124, at 68; Tams, *supra* note 90, at 59.

147 André de Hoogh, Obligations *Erga Omnes* and International Crimes 53–54 (1996).

148 Alexander Orakhelashvili, Peremptory Norms in International Law 269 (2007).

149 Invoking both Kantian and biblical themes, Feldman supports the view taken by most human rights NGOs that "the universally true and indefeasible value of human dignity" requires U.S. adherence to Geneva norms in treatment of Al Qaeda detainees, irrespective of nonreciprocity by adversaries and regardless of consequences. Noah Feldman, "Ugly Americans," *in* The Torture Debate in America, Karen Greenberg, ed. 267, 275–76 (2006).

150 ICRC, Commentary on the Geneva Conventions of 12 Aug. 1949, Gen. Con. III, 18 (1960). The ICRC acknowledges, however, that though this is how the Conventions "are coming to be regarded," it was not their prevalent understanding when drafted. *Id.* at 20. Admittedly, Common Art. 1 of the Conventions requires parties "to respect and ensure respect for" the treaties "in all circumstances." But this surely refers to all circumstances in which these treaties pertain. They do not apply at all when there is no "armed conflict" and the existence of such a conflict may be subject to dispute. There is certainly such a dispute on whether "the global war on terror" in all of its elements and aspects constitutes a single "armed conflict" within the meaning of humanitarian law. Moreover, certain Geneva provisions expressly contemplate reciprocity, such as the requirement of Common Art. 2 that prisoners of a nonparty state receive POW protection only if that state "accepts and applies" the Conventions, i.e., gives evidence of its willingness to reciprocate its adversary's compliance. Admittedly, Common Art. 1 of the Conventions requires parties "to respect and ensure respect for" the treaties "in all circumstances." But because the treaties themselves endorse reciprocity in key places, "the statement in the Geneva Conventions that the

obligations assumed under them will be binding 'in all circumstances' is not necessarily any indication that the condition of reciprocity is abandoned." Detter, *supra* note 65, at 342–43; Fritz Kalshoven, "Reprisals and the Protection of Civilians: Two Recent Decisions of the Yugoslavia Tribunal," *in* Man's Inhumanity to Man: Essays on International Law in Honour of Antonio Cassese, Lai Chand Vohrah, et al., eds. 481, 491, 502 (2003).

The capacious "all circumstances" wording does not even appear, moreover, in Geneva Additional Protocol II, which is the most relevant source of customary law on the matter, relating to noninternational armed conflicts and having been ratified by the vast majority (165) of states. For these reasons, it is mistaken to conclude summarily, as does Geoffrey Best, that Art. 1 "announces the death of reciprocity." Best, *supra* note 119, at 146. Similarly exaggerated, as we shall see, is Dworkin's claim that "at a stroke, Article 3 severed the link between the international law of armed conflict and the concept[] of reciprocity." Anthony Dworkin, "The Laws of War and the Age of Asymmetric Conflict," *in* The Barbarisation of Warfare, George Kassimeris, ed. 220, 226 (2006).

151 There is reason to question the legal significance properly accorded the ICRC's occasional pronouncements suggesting the much diminished scope and recognition of reciprocity within humanitarian law. *See, e.g.,* Jean Pictet, I Commentary on the Geneva Conventions of 12 Aug. 1949, 51 (1952). "The obligation [of Common Art. 3] is absolute for each of the parties [to an armed conflict], and independent of the obligation of the other party. The reciprocity clause has been omitted intentionally." Pictet, IV Commentary on the Geneva Conventions of 12 Aug 1949, 39–40 (1958). I Customary International Humanitarian Law, Jean-Marie Henckaerts & Louise Doswald-Beck, eds., Rule 140, at 498 ("The obligation to respect and ensure respect for international humanitarian law does not depend on reciprocity."); vol. II, Part 2, at 3195 (announcing "the general erosion of the role of reciprocity in the application of humanitarian law over the last century"). This is especially true with respect to those sources of humanitarian law beyond the organization's limited mandate. As Meron notes, the ICRC "is not a direct participant in the making of international law, which under the prevailing theory of sources is reserved to states." Theodor Meron, "The Continuing Role of Custom in the Formation of International Humanitarian Law," 90 A.J.I.L. 238, 245 (1949). The ICRC's legal personality derives from the Swiss Civil Code, Art. 60, and it is only Swiss law that accords it a role in "the preparation of the development" of humanitarian law. ICRC, Statutes and Rules of Procedure of the International Red Cross Movement, Art. 5(2)(g). The role expressly granted by the Geneva Conventions is confined to "visiting prisoners, organizing relief operations, re-uniting separated families and similar humanitarian activities during armed conflict." At http://www.icrc.org/Web/Eng/siteengO.nsf/htmlall/section_mandate? The ICRC Statutes are revised every four years. In that process, though a matter of Swiss law, other states that are party to the Geneva Conventions may "take part, thereby conferring a quasi-legal or 'soft law' status on the Statutes," according to the organization's Web site. The latter assertion would be subject to considerable contention by many international lawyers, however, even among those who accept the very notion of "soft law," which is controversial in its

own right. The organization's quoted assertion also betrays a whiff of self-appointed bootstrapping, even if much of the international community has apparently decided to indulge this "mission creep" or, less generously, seeming self-aggrandizement.

The Geneva Conventions do not expressly accord the ICRC any role in interpreting these agreements. The international community has acquiesced in the organization's assumption of such a role, to be sure, which it has performed assiduously. Yet the ICRC's claim to authority in this regard requires a circuitous legal argument, to say the least. Common Article 8 of the 1949 Geneva Conventions and Art. 5 of the 1977 Additional Protocol I provide that these treaties should be implemented "with the cooperation and under the scrutiny" of the "Protecting Powers." Only if there are no states willing to assume this function may the ICRC do so, these provisions indicate. Because this contemplated system of protecting powers has virtually never functioned, however, the ICRC plausibly concludes that it "has had to bear the whole burden of this role of scrutiny." Yves Sandoz, "The International Committee of the Red Cross as Guardian of International Humanitarian Law," Dec. 31, 1998, at http://www.icrc.org/Web/Eng/siteeng0.nsf/html/about-the-icrc-311298. Moreover, to instruct a state as to its duties under these treaties, the pertinent provisions must first be interpreted. Such interpretive authority as the ICRC formally enjoys derives only from this fact. The extensive authority now exercised in this regard was not initially contemplated by the drafters of these Conventions, in other words, but has been widely welcomed by most states, especially in ascertaining customary international law, for which there exists no single, canonical text.

Neither do the Hague Conventions nor most weapons-prohibition protocols grant the organization any special interpretive authority. Its representatives did not attend the key international conferences at which The Hague treaties were negotiated and drafted, for that matter. Francois Bugnion, "The International Committee of the Red Cross and the Development of International Humanitarian Law," 5 Chi. J. Int'l L. 191, 200 (2004); *see also* Sandoz, *id.* Its influence has nonetheless expanded in recent years beyond "Geneva" matters of war victims' protection to the conduct of hostilities more broadly. This influence has little basis in treaty law. The organization itself acknowledges that its proper contribution to Hague law remains "much more modest," as writes one high-ranking ICRC official. *Id.* Bugnion was, at the time of this writing, the ICRC's Director for International Law and Cooperation.

152 Fourth Geneva Convention, Art. 4, ¶ 2.

153 Derek Jinks, "The Applicability of the Geneva Conventions to the 'Global War on Terrorism,'" 46 Va. J. Int'l L. 165, 192 (2005). Such first-order reciprocity may be found, for instance, in the Third Geneva Convention, Art. 2, 6 U.S.T 3316, 3318, 75 U.N.T.S 135, 136; Art. 2, 6 U.S.T. at 3320, 75 U.N.T.S at 138.

154 Lassa Oppenheim, International Law 341 (8th ed. 1955).

155 Reciprocity, in the present sense, might be analogized to the legal concept of "waiver." Larry May, War Crimes and Just War 311 (2007) (entertaining "the idea that terrorists," like eighteenth-century pirates, "have waived whatever

protections they might otherwise have by refusing to conform to the rules of war"). But the term "waiver" is here employed only by analogy. The concept uncontroversially applies only to the voluntary relinquishment of known rights. Whether Al Qaeda detainees could be said to have done so would be highly contested. A second, frequent basis for a finding of waiver arises when one party detrimentally relies on the other's failure to assert a right. This too is not material to the present circumstance. Neither has there ever been any detrimental reliance by the United States on Al Qaeda representations of law abidingness, of which there have been none. Finally, the concept of waiver does not apply to rights that are unalienable. Yet the scope of that class of rights is precisely the chief question here in issue. The right to POW status, for instance, may be forfeited by conduct inconsistent with its corresponding duties. Some might wish to contend that, though the right not to be tortured is nonreciprocal, the right to freedom from cruel, inhuman, and degrading treatment is contingent on like treatment of an adversary's combatants. It is impossible to find any basis for this distinction, however, in the language of the pertinent treaties, their *travaux préparatoires*, American legislative incorporation, or, for that matter, in the moral theories implicitly informing any of these. It is true that American law once distinguished between the two categories of mistreatment in criminalizing only torture, but the 2006 Military Commissions Act criminalizes the second category as well, albeit only where the degrading treatment approximates torture, as defined in 18 USC § 2340.

156 J.P. Bialke "Al-Qaeda and Taliban Unlawful Combatant Detainees, Unlawful Belligerency, and the International Laws of Armed Conflict," 55 A.F.L. Rev. 16, 29–34 (2004); John C. Yoo & James C. Ho, "The Status of Terrorists," 44 Va. J. Int'l L. 207, 221–22 (2003).

157 *U.S. v. Lindh*, 212 F. Supp. 2nd 541, 553 (E.D. Va. 2002) (concluding that, according to Art. 4, the Taliban were not covered by the Third Geneva Convention because that organization had an insufficient internal system of military command, wore no distinctive sign, and regularly targeted civilian populations).

158 Joel Rohlf, "The Geneva Conventions and the War on Terror: International Legal Reform as a Solution," seminar paper, Univ. of Iowa College of Law, May 2007, at 61. *See generally* Anthony D'Amato, "International Law as an Autopoietic System," *in* Developments of International Law in Treaty Making, Rüdiger Wolfrum, Volker Röben, eds. 335, 374 (2005) ("The denial of reciprocity leads to anarchy as states carve out special privileges for themselves that they wish to deny to their intended victims."); Detter, *supra* note 65, at 348 ("if one abandons the condition of reciprocity there is little remedy for a State party to a conflict if the insurgent group resorts to practices which violate the Law of War. . . . Either the non-State party has to be recognized and is then under similar duty as the State party, or, if it is not given that right, it cannot be bound by any duties under these instruments."); Ernst Schneeberger, "Reciprocity as a Maxim of International Law," 37 Geo. L. J. 29, 31, 35 (1948) ("Denial of the right to resort to reciprocity in answer to a wrong would constitute a grotesque encouragement to enter treaties with the mental reservation to disregard obligations to self and to bind merely the other party.").

159 Many states do not regard the Geneva Conventions as self-executing, in the sense of requiring no implementing legislation to allow private legal claims

on their basis in a country's courts. The Third Convention obligates states "to undertake to enact any legislation necessary to provide effective penal sanctions for persons committing … any of the grave breaches of the present Convention." Art. 129. Whether such legislation is "necessary" is a matter of domestic constitutional law. Lower U.S. courts have differed over whether particular Geneva provisions are self-executing. Ronda Cress, "Automatic Rights or Permissive Ones: The Status of Article 4 and 5 of the Third Geneva Convention Relative to the Treatment of Prisoners of War," 74 U. Cinn. L. Rev. 191, 193 (2005). The Supreme Court did not directly address the issue in its 2006 *Hamdan* opinion. But the D.C. Circuit Court of Appeals in that case found the pertinent Geneva provisions not to be self-executing and hence ruled for the government, concluding that Hamdan had no right to invoke these treaties. 415 F.3d 33, 38–40 (2005). For a useful analysis, *see* Carlos Vazquez, "*Hamdan* and the Geneva Conventions," Georgetown Law Faculty Blog, June 30, 2006, at http://gulcfac.typepad.com/georgetown_university_law/2006/06/hamdan_and_the_.html.

160 For example, some have argued that the British Act of 1957 implementing the Geneva Conventions departed in places from the protections of the Conventions, particularly in regard to the due process protections of the POW Convention in Art. 102. Gerald Draper, The Red Cross Conventions 62 (1958).

161 The burdens of accommodating legal differences resulting from disparate nationalities could, of course, be resolved by according common treatment to all detainees at the highest level required by any country represented among their number. There is no legal duty to do so, however. To be sure, Geneva Additional Protocol I provides in Art. 75 that all "persons who are in the custody of a Party" (i.e., regardless of nationality) "shall be treated humanely in all circumstances." Above the acceptable minimum thereby established, this wording is entirely consistent with affording varying degrees of comfort and convenience on the basis of a detainee's nationality. Though the United States has not ratified this Protocol, for many years elements of it have been acknowledged as binding custom. The Supreme Court in *Hamdan* relied on this provision as evidence of customary law to which the United States had not expressly and persistently objected. The provision was then read *in pari materia* with Common Art. 3 of the 1949 Conventions, which similarly makes no reference to a detainee's nationality in defining how he or she may be treated and which the United States has ratified.

162 Tung Yin, "Enemies of the State: Rational Classification in the War on Terrorism" 11 Lewis and Clark L.R. 903, 916 (2007) (opposing treason prosecution where "the citizenship at issue arose by happenstance and was not tempered through cultural upbringing or link to a national identity").

163 Moir, *supra* note 15, at 52; *see also* Detter, *supra* note 65, at 342; Liesbeth Zegveld, Accountability of Armed Opposition Groups in International Law 14–20 (2002); Eve La Haye, War Crimes in Internal Armed Conflicts 119 (2008). Moir's and Detter's analyses find no satisfactory normative basis for holding rebel groups bound to Geneva Common Art. 3, and hence diverge here from that of ICRC Commentary 37 to the Third Geneva Convention, which contends that a belligerent is bound by Common Art. 3 as a "Party" to the armed conflict

even if it is neither a signatory to the Convention nor "even . . . a legal entity capable of undertaking international obligations." The U.S. Supreme Court endorsed the ICRC's view in *Hamdan v. Rumsfeld*, at 2795.

164 Vienna Convention on the Law of Treaties, Arts. 34–36, provide that treaties may impose duties on nonparty states if this was the drafters' intent and if such nonparty states assent to such duties. But the provisions refer only to nonparty *states,* rather than to all nonparties, including nonstate actors.

165 Moir, *supra* note 15, at 53.

166 One may be tempted nevertheless to describe this situation as one of quasi-contract or quantum meruit, in that the insurgents and terrorists are otherwise "unjustly enriched" by the law.

167 E. Allan Farnsworth, Contracts 98–99 (1982).

168 ICRC, Commentary 37, Third Geneva Convention.

169 *Hamdan v. Rumsfeld*, at 2795.

170 Report of the Secretary-General, UN Doc.S/2001/331 (30 March 2001), ¶ 48.

171 UN Commission on Human Rights, E/CN.4/1985/18, p. 37.

172 Inter-American Commission on Human Rights, "Third Report on the Situation of Human Rights in Colombia," O.A.S. Doc.OEA/Ser.L/V, doc.102 (1999).

173 The tribunals here mentioned offer only "subsidiary" sources of international law, according to the Statute of the International Court of Justice. Art. 38(1)(d). International law traditionally accords little weight to precedent in any event, strictly speaking.

174 Statute of the International Court of Justice, Art. 59.

175 No authority for the contentious proposition in question is cited by the UN Secretary General, the UN Human Rights Commission, or the Inter-American Commision for Human Rights. The U.S. Supreme Court simply cited to Art. 3 of the Geneva Conventions, as incorporated into U.S. law, without reference to its drafting history. So did the ICTY in the *Tadić* case. Yet Art. 3, unlike Art. 2 (for interstate conflicts), does not entitle nonstate parties to acquire Geneva rights by "accepting and applying" Geneva duties. And in any event Al Qaeda leaders have not sought to do so.

176 On this effort *see supra* Chapter 3, at 111–12, 126–29, 138–40.

177 The legal requirement of consent to be bound applies not only to treaties but also to customary law, which states are free to disavow through "persistent objection" while the particular norm is developing.

178 This is not to deny, of course, the centrality of bargaining and "horse trading" in developing any complex piece of domestic legislation, as emphasized by public choice theorists among others.

179 For discussion of this question, *see supra* Chapter 3, at 133–42.

180 Marco Sassòli, "Transnational Armed Groups and International Humanitarian Law," Occasional Paper, Program on Humanitarian Policy and Conflict Research, Harvard, Winter 2006, at 41–42, at http://www.hpcrresearch.org/pdfs/OccasionalPaper6.pdf.

181 Their state of nationality might choose to bind its citizens by domestic legislation, of course, as the U.S. has done in its War Crimes Act. But this basis for jurisdiction would not extend to the courts of other states that might wish to prosecute the individual for international crimes. Fighting on the territory of

a state that had incorporated international law in this way would also create jurisdiction, but only in the courts of that particular state.

182 The Ninth Circuit described this aspect of *jus cogens* in some detail, concluding that it "is derived from values taken to be fundamental by the international community, rather than from the fortuitous or self-interested choices of nations. . . . The fundamental and universal norms constituting *jus cogens* transcend such consent." *Siderman de Blake v. Rep. of Argentina*, 965 F.2d 699, 715 (1991). The Vienna Convention on the Law of Treaties nonetheless codifies the *jus cogens* concept into positive law, to which states consent by their ratification of that treaty and of the Statute of the International Court of Justice, Art. 38(1)(c).

183 Edward McWhinney, United Nations Law Making: Cultural and Ideological Relativism and International Law Making for an Era of Transition 74 (1984).

184 Digest of the U.S. Practice in International Law 312–13, 440–43 (2001) (describing the U.S. official statement of interest in *Michael Domingues v. U.S.*, before the Inter-American Commission on Human Rights); A. Mark Weisburg, "American Judges and International Law," 36 Vand. J. Transnat'l L. 1475, 1488–1528 (2003).

185 Stefan Kadelbach, "The Identification of Fundamental Norms," *in* The Fundamental Rules of the International Legal Order, Christian Tomuschat, et al., eds. 21, 34 (2006) ("the obligations which derive from *jus cogens* must be respected not in the interest of parties to a treaty on the basis of reciprocity, but as a result of their common interest character.").

186 John Yoo's writings, as quoted in this book's introduction, come closest to such straightforwardness in their frequent invocation of the analogy to private contract. More often, however, the expectation of reciprocity from military adversaries is defended somewhat more circuitously. American diplomats sometimes prefer, for instance, to speak of *ex ante* deterrence than of *ex post* fairness. *See, e.g.*, Abraham Sofaer, "The Rationale for the United States Decisions," 82 A.J.I.L. 784, 785 (1988). Sofaer, as State Dept. Legal Adviser, represented the United States in negotiations over the 1977 Protocols. "The total elimination of the right of reprisal . . . would hamper the ability of the United States to respond to an enemy's intentional disregard of the limitations established in the Geneva Conventions of 1949 or Protocol I, for the purpose of deterring such disregard."

187 Art. 1(1) of the Statute for the Special Court for Sierra Leone provides, "The Special Court shall . . . have the power to prosecute persons who bear the greatest responsibility for serious violations of international humanitarian law and Sierra Leoncan law committed *in the territory of Sierra Leone* since 30 November 1996, including those leaders who, in committing such crimes, have threatened the establishment of and implementation of the peace process in Sierra Leone." (emphasis supplied) The International Criminal Tribunal for Rwanda invokes both territorial presence and nationality as bases for jurisdiction over defendants. Its statute accords it "the power to prosecute persons responsible for serious violations of international humanitarian law committed in the territory of Rwanda and Rwandan citizens responsible for such violations committed in the territory of neighbouring States

between 1 January 1994 and 31 December 1994." ICTR Statute, Art. 1. at http://69.94.11.53/ENGLISH/basicdocs/statute.html.

188 *See, e.g.,* Gerald Draper, "Humanitarian Law and Internal Armed Conflicts," 13 Georgia J. Int'l & Comp. L. 253, 254 (1983).

189 *Hamdan v. Rumsfeld,* at 2846 (J. Thomas dissenting). This interpretation of the word "international," though plausible enough when Art. 3 is examined in isolation from the rest of the Conventions, is inconsistent with the meaning universally ascribed to the same term in Common Art. 2, which is clearly intended to govern only interstate conflicts.

190 As of April 2008, no trial had yet begun within the troubled American military commission system, still under challenge in the Supreme Court on constitutional grounds. William Glaberson, "New Roadblocks Delay Tribunals at Guantánamo," New York Times, April 10, 2008, at A1. Virtually all prosecutions of accused terrorists had taken place in federal courts, based on U.S. law charges either entirely unrelated to terrorism (e.g., mail and wire fraud, immigration violations) or under fraud, conspiracy, and material support statutes, none of which derive from the international law. International law does not even encompass the offense of conspiracy to commit war crimes, as the Supreme Court ruled in *Hamdan. Hamdan v. Rumsfeld,* at 2779–85.

The international law most pertinent in these domestic trials is that regarding jurisdiction. Such law permits states to assert extraterritorial jurisdiction on the basis of a defendant's acts, though taking place abroad, when these are likely to have "objective" effects in the United States. American Law Institute, Restatement (Third), Foreign Relations Law of the U.S., §402(1)(c) and §402(3) (1987). The Geneva Conventions thus played little role in America's approach to prosecuting jihadist terrorists until the first military commissions of 2008. There has hence been no need to acknowledge the Geneva rights of such defendants in order to detain and try them for major federal offenses.

191 Alberto Gonzales, "Decision RE: Application of the Geneva Convention," Memorandum dated 2002, at http://www.gwo.edu/~nsrchiv/NSAEBB/NSAEBB127/02.01.25,pdf. The term "jihad," and therefore also "jihadist," is controversial among some when associated with jihadist terrorism, because as indicated before, the word does have a secondary meaning as a struggle within the individual soul to live the virtuous life demanded by the Koran. David Cook, Understanding Jihad 32–48 (2005); *see generally* Tariq Ramadan, Islam, the West, and the Challenges of Modernity 59–69 (2001); John Esposito, Unholy War: Terror in the Name of Islam 56–70 (2002). No single word exists, however, for the empirical phenomenon of chief concern to this book: contemporary, radical, "fundamentalist," Islamist groups employing terror by attacking civilians. That is a mouthful, so in the interests of brevity the term "militant jihadist" is here employed exclusively in that sense. I acknowledge that some will object to this terminology. It is a usage widely accepted, however, in the leading scholarly literature. *See, e.g.,* Gilles Kepel, Jihad: The Trail of Political Islam, Anthony Roberts, trans. 217–36, 308–13 (2002).

The term "global jihad" is even more controversial and is employed by few scholars. *But see* Ahmed Rashid, "Jihadi Suicide Bombers: The New Wave," N.Y. Rev. of Books, June 12, 2008, at 17, 17 (employing this term); Jalil Roshandel

& Sharon Chadha, Jihad and International Security 37 (2006) (arguing that though "jihads generally start out as local battles ... since the creation of al Qaeda in 1988, these local struggles are eventually co-opted by what can be described as a global jihad movement"); Brynjar Lia, Architect of Global Jihad: The Life of al-Qaida Strategist Abu us'ab al-Suri (2008). This expression remains questionable if taken to imply that the world's myriad Muslim movements employing violence against civilians constitute a single enterprise, even where local grievances predominate over broader, pan-Islamic aims. The degree of commonality among such geographically disparate movements is an empirical question, so no answer may be assumed by sheer stipulation, as Soshnadel and Chadha appear to do. Such commonality would here involve a shared ideal – state enforcement of a literalist reading of *shari'a* – joined to a shared method of attaining it (i.e., attacks intentionally targeting civilian persons and property). Ominously, the American prosecutor's indictment in *United States v. Hassoun* evoked the notion of a global jihad movement in defining the scope of the conspiracy that the defendants had allegedly joined. 04-cr-60001 (S.D. Fla.) (superseding indictment) (Nov. 17, 2005), ¶¶ 1–5.

192 *Cf.* Gabor Rona, International Legal Director, Human Rights First, "Challenges to International Humanitarian Law Posed by Transnational Armed Groups and by the States that Fight Them," Third Hague Colloquium on Fundamental Principles of Law, Oct. 3, 2008 ("acts of terrorism that target civilians are war crimes. In this, the most critical sense, there is nothing about terrorism that presents any particular challenge to international humanitarian law").

193 Sassòli, *supra* note 180, at 9; Zegveld, *supra* note 163, at 136.

194 Italics added.

195 Richard Oppel, "Foreign Fighters in Iraq Are Tied to Allies of U.S.," New York Times, Nov. 22, 2007, at A1. On the international law of neutrality, *see generally* Stephen Neff, The Rights and Duties of Neutrals: A General History (2000).

196 The Fourth Geneva Convention, though concerned with "the protection of civilian persons in time of war," offers no definition of "civilian," preferring instead to speak throughout of "protected persons," who constitute a distinct subset of civilians.

197 The purpose of this designation, rather than "unprivileged combatant," was apparently to suggest that this status constitutes an international crime. This proposition is contentious, however. An alternative view is that unprivileged belligerency speaks solely to the absence of a defense, within international law, to charges of criminal acts under domestic law. On this second and widely held view, unprivileged participation, without more, is not an international crime, though those failing to meet the requirements for POW status within GCIII, Art. 4, are often guilty of perfidy – in that they carry out attacks in civilian guise – which is an international war crime.

198 This paragraph is informed by Mary Douglas, Purity and Danger 140–79 (1966).

199 Geneva Additional Protocol I, Art. 43.

200 David Luban, "The War on Terrorism and Human Rights," 22 Phil. & Public Polc'y Q. 13 (2002). Like the Clinton administration before it, the Bush

administration took recourse to military means when it concluded that law enforcement cooperation would be ineffective in taking necessary precautions against terrorist attack. On the enormous practical obstacles to successful prosecution of suspected terrorists involved in complex plots, *see, e.g.,* John Burns & Elaine Sciolino, "No One Convicted of Terror Plot to Bomb Planes," New York Times, Sept. 9, 2008, at A1. "The case was hampered ... prosecutors said, by an investigation that was cut short," when one member of the conspiracy was arrested abroad on unrelated charges, "by the conflicting demands of intelligence agencies" in several countries, "and by problems of introducing evidence in the courtroom. To protect sources and methods, the prosecution was unable to introduce material from British or foreign intelligence agencies. In addition, Britain does not allow information in court that has been gathered from domestic wiretaps." Jurors also reported that the decision of British police to abbreviate the investigation, for fear that the conspirators would expedite their criminal plans, left the jury unpersuaded that the defendants "were prepared to strike immediately." *Id.*

201 Primo Levi introduced this term, in The Drowned and the Saved, Raymond Rosenthal, trans. (1988), in reference to the ethical compromises with the Nazi system by which many Jews sought to increase their chances of survival. For elaboration of the phenomenon's many manifestations, *see* Gray Zones: Ambiguity and Compromise in the Holocaust and Its Aftermath, Jonathan Petropoulos & John Roth, eds. (2005).

202 Joseba Zulaika & William Douglass, Terror and Taboo 153 (1996).

203 Alan Dershowitz, "Worshippers of Death," Wall St. J., March 3, 2008, editorial, at A17.

204 *But see* David Cohen & Richard Saller, "Foucault on Sexuality in Greco-Roman Antiquity," *in* Foucault and the Writing of History, Jan Goldstein, ed. 35 (1994) (contending, as have several ancient historians, that Foucault exaggerates the freedom of sexual life as represented within Greco-Roman texts, understating enduring constraints on the range of acceptable sexual experience in that epoch); David Halperin, "Forgetting Foucault: Acts, Identities, and the History of Sexuality," *in* The Sleep of Reason: Erotic Experience and Sexual Ethics in Ancient Greece and Rome, Martha Nussbaum & Juha Sihvola, eds. 21, 27 (2002) (disputing Foucault's account of the relevant chronology in changing sexual mores).

205 *See, e.g.,* John Updike, Due Considerations: Essays and Criticism 413 (2007); Susan Sontag, At the Same Time 111 (2007); Chris Hedges & Leila Al-Arian, Collateral Damage: America's War against Iraqi Civilians (2007); Talal Asad, "Thinking About 'Just War,'" July 17, 2007, at http://www.huffingtonpost.com/talal-asad/thinking-about-just-warb56605.html posted July 11 2007.

206 Hilary Charlesworth, "Alienating Oscar? Feminist Analysis of International Law," *in* Reconceiving Reality: Women and International Law, Dorinda Dallmeyer, ed., 1, 9–11 (1993) (contending that international law's traditional preoccupation with the behavior of states has led it to neglect the human rights of women, the obstacles to which often reside largely in the nonstate realm of social and cultural practices); Karen Engle, "International Human Rights and Feminisms," *in* International Law: Modern Feminist Approaches, Doris Buss & Ambreena Manji, eds. 47, 53–54 (2005) (same).

207 *Id.*; Christine Chinkin, "A Critique of the Public/Private Distinction," 10 Euro. J. Int'l L. 387 (1999); Carole Pateman, "Feminist Critiques of the Public/Private Dichotomy," *in* Public and Private in Social Life, S. I. Benn & G. F. Gaus, eds. (1983). For a leftist critique of the dichotomy, *see generally* Morton Horwitz, "The History of the Public/Private Distinction," 130 U. Penn. L. Rev. 1423 (1982); Duncan Kennedy, "The Stages of the Decline of the Public/Private Distinction," 130 U. Penn. L. Rev. 1349 (1982).

208 Marc Sageman, Leaderless Jihad: Terror Networks in the 21st Century 52–58, 84–88, 91, 101–03, 110–11, 116, 158–59 (2008).

209 *See generally* P.W. Singer, Children at War 101–06 (2005).

210 Rome Statute of the International Criminal Court, Art. 8; *Prosecutor v. Dyilo*, Case No. ICC-01/04-01/06, Warrant of Arrest (Feb. 10, 2006), at http://www.icc-cpi.int/library/cases/ICC-01-04-01-06-2_tEnglish.pdf; *Prosecutor v. Dyilo*, Case No. ICC-01/04-01/06; Prosecution's Submission of Further Information and Materials (Jan. 27, 2006), at http://www.icc-cpi.int/library/cases/ICC-01-04-01-06-39-AnxD_English.pdf. *See generally* International Criminal Accountability and the Rights of Children, Karen Arts & Vesselin Popovski, eds. (2006).

211 Convention on The Rights of The Child, Art. 38(2) and (3).

212 *See generally* Jenny Kuper, International Law Concerning Child Civilians in Armed Conflict (1997); Kuper, Military Training and Children in Armed Conflict (2005).

213 Rome Statute of the International Criminal Court, Art. 26 (providing that the Court will not have jurisdiction over those under age eighteen at the time of the alleged crime).

214 This would be most clearly applicable to boys under age 10, on Piaget's account. Jean Piaget, The Moral Judgment of the Child 319–20 (1932).

215 This statement presumes that noncombatants who take up arms may continue to be characterized as civilians, despite the unprivileged character of their belligerency. This would be because, in noninternational armed conflicts, nonstate fighters cannot be "combatants," given the accepted definition of that term in international law as limited to those fighting on behalf of sovereign states or their proxies, as the appellate court has concluded in *Al-Marri v. Wright*, 487 F.3d 160, 186 (4th Cir. 2007).

216 At the margins, at least, our moral convictions may not even be so settled here. The decision to limit the ICC's jurisdiction to those of age eighteen and older was controversial in some respected quarters. *Compare* Geoffrey Robertson, Crimes against Humanity 343 (2000) (arguing for possible international prosecution of boy soldiers of age sixteen and seventeen) *with* Roger Clark & Otto Trifferer, "Article 26: Exclusion of Jurisdiction over Persons under Eighteen," *in* Commentary on the Rome Statute of the International Criminal Court 493 (1999) (contending that even national criminal courts should not prosecute boys of this age for war crimes, on the grounds that "they should not be victimized a second time").

217 Jordan Paust, Beyond the Law: The Bush Administration's Unlawful Responses in the "War" on Terror 55 (2008).

218 Richard Pildes, "Conflicts between American and European Views of Law: The Dark Side of Legalism," 44 Va. J. Int'l L. 145, 162 (2003).

219 Kalshoven, *supra* note 150, at 491, 502.
220 Shane Darcy, "The Evolution of the Law of Belligerent Reprisals," 175 Mil. L. Rev. 184, 218 (2003); Stanislaw-Edward Nahlik, "Belligerent Reprisals as Seen in the Light of the Diplomatic Conference on Humanitarian Law, Geneva, 1974–1977," 42 L. & Contemp. Prob. 3, 63–64 (1978).
221 *See, e.g.,* Alfred Rubin, The Law of Piracy (1997); Jenny Martinez, "Antislavery Courts and the Dawn of International Human Rights Law," 117 Yale L.J. 552 (2007).
222 Frontline, "Interview with John Yoo", October 18, 2005, at http://www.pbs.org/wgbh/pages/frontline/torture/interviews/yoo.html.
223 Even some of the Bush administration's sharpest critics have had to acknowledge that the law and its standard classifications suffer a serious gap in this respect. The Conventions display "the absence of any clear provision for preventive detention of fighters who view themselves as adherents of networks that spawn terrorist plots (and who therefore might reasonably be considered . . . more dangerous than the traditional prisoner taken captive on the battlefield,") as one leading critic puts it. Joseph Lelyveld, "No Exit," 54 N.Y. Rev. of Books, Feb. 15, 2007, at 12, 16; *see also* Rosa Ehrenreich Brooks, "War Everywhere: Rights, National Security Law, and the Law of Armed Conflict in the Age of Terror," 153 U. Penn. L. Rev. 675, 761 (2003) (acknowledging that "we simply lack an adequate legal paradigm for thinking about the changes brought about by the rise of global terrorism," because "the core distinctions drawn by the laws of armed conflict have broken down," such as that "between combatant and noncombatant"); Laura Donohue, The Cost of Counterterrorism: Power, Politics, and Liberty 9, 10 (2008) (contending, "Neither the war nor the crime model holds wholly true" of the conflict with Al Qaeda; "the reason neither model fits is because terrorism is neither war nor crime"). A better view is that terrorism may at once entail both crime and war. And as Ratner observes, "The two paradigms are not mutually exclusive as a factual or legal matter. . . . [T]he U.S. government can and does act through both methods. U.S. policy since September 11 still relies on law enforcement cooperation, both because of its efficacy in individual cases and because many states object to the alternative paradigm." Steven Ratner, "Predator and Prey: Seizing and Killing Suspected Terrorists Abroad," 15 J. Polit. Phil. 251, 256 (2007).
224 Lt. Col. Thomas Ayres, "'Six Floors' of Detainee Operations in the Post–9/11 World," 35 Parameters 33, 38 (Autumn 2005).
225 Lelyveld, *supra* note 223.
226 Confidential sources, interviews with author. On U.S. efforts to address the question unilaterally, *see* Mark Mazzetti, "C.I.A. Awaits Rules on Terrorism Interrogations," New York Times, March 25, 2007, at A14 (noting that "much of the debate over the interrogation rules has not been made public").
227 Richard Norton-Taylor & Clare Dyer, "Defense Secretary Calls for Geneva Conventions to be Redrawn: International Law Hinders U.K. Troops – Reid," The Guardian, April 4, 2006, at 1 (paraphrasing Minister John Reid's contention that "existing rules, including some of the Conventions . . . were out of date and inadequate to deal with international terrorists").
228 Monica Hakimi, "International Standards for Detaining Terrorism Suspects: Moving beyond the Armed Conflict-Criminal Divide," 33 Yale J. Int'l L. 369,

407–08 (2008) (describing interest among certain U.S. allies in the possibility of a treaty authorizing and establishing acceptable procedures for administrative detention and renditions); David Ignatius, "A Way Out of Guantánamo Bay," Wash. Post, July 7, 2006, at A17 (editorial).

229 Interviews with confidential JAG sources.

230 McDonald, *supra* note 8, at 219, 232. In speaking of the inability of jihadist groups to apply rules of warfare, McDonald is referring particularly to their frequent lack of formal organization sufficient to enforce a chain of command.

231 David Wippman, "Introduction: Do New Wars Call for New Laws?" *in* New Wars, New Laws?, David Wippman & Matthew Evangelista, eds. 1, 10 (2005).

232 Vienna Convention on the Law of Treaties, Art. 53. In fact, the Vienna Convention's effort to interject the concept of *jus cogens* into international law was the principal source of U.S. objection to the treaty. American representatives were concerned about the Convention's vagueness over how particular *jus cogens* norms were to be identified and established, and by whom.

233 10 U.S.C. §948a(1)(a)(i). The statute defines the term even more broadly, in fact. Jack M. Beard, "The Geneva Boomerang: The Military Commissions Act of 2006 and U.S. Counter-terror Operations," 101 A.J.I.L. 56, 60 (2007).

234 *See, e.g.,* Hakimi, *supra* note 228; Tung Yin, "Ending the War on Terrorism One Terrorist at a Time: A Noncriminal Detention Model for Holding and Releasing Guantanamo Detainees," 29 Harv. J.L. & Pub Pol'y 149, 206 (2005); Jack Goldsmith & Neal Katyal, "The Terrorists' Court," New York Times, July 11, 2007, at A19 (recommending that Congress enact legislation creating "a comprehensive system of preventive detention that is overseen by a national security court composed of federal judges with life tenure"); Matthew Waxman, "Administrative Detention of Terrorists: Why Detain, and Detain Whom?" Colum. Law School, Public Law and Legal Theory Working Paper, No. 08–190.

235 *See generally* Michael E. Guillory, "Civilianizing the Force: Is the U.S. Crossing the Rubicon?," 51 A.F.L. Rev. 111, 116–20 (2001); Lisa L. Turner & Lynn G. Norton, "Civilians at the Tip of the Spear," 51 A.F.L. Rev. 1, 28 (2001).

236 Conrad Crane, "'Contrary to Our National Ideals:' American Strategic Bombing of Civilians in World War II," *in* Civilians in the Path of War, Mark Grimsley & Clifford Rogers, eds. 219, 232 (2002) (distinguishing U.S. from British targeting in strategic bombing).

237 Geneva Additional Protocol 1, Art. 52(2).

238 On these difficulties, *see* Ben Saul, Defining Terrorism in International Law 168–90 (2006). The seven multilateral conventions directed at various aspects of terrorism all focus on more particular expressions of the phenomenon, such as airline hijacking, rather than the sowing of terror *per se.*

Jacques Derrida offers a careful account of why the term is so difficult to define, especially to the satisfaction of those sympathetic with some of the causes on behalf of which the disputed methods are employed, *in* Philosophy in a Time of Terror: Dialogues with Jürgen Habermas and Jacques Derrida, Giovanna Borradori, ed. 100–09 (2003).

239 Human Rights First, Private Contractors at War: Ending the Culture of Impunity 7–9, 11 (2008), at http://www.humanrightsfirst.info/pdf/08115-usls-psc-final.pdf

240 *See* II Customary International Humanitarian Law, Jean-Marie Henckaerts & Louise Doswald-Beck, eds. 3420–21 (2005). This volume documents official U.S. assertions in recent decades of a right to belligerent reprisal against civilians in enemy-controlled territory. *Id.* In this way, the U.S. has persistently objected to the emergence of such a customary norm. The American explanation for this stance has been that "massive and continuing attacks against a nation's civilian population could not be absorbed without a response in kind." *Id.* at 3420, ¶ 757. The Fourth Geneva Convention, in Art. 33, did not prohibit such reprisals. The 1956 Army Field Manual 27-10, §497(c) prohibited reprisals only against POWs and protected persons under the Fourth or "Civilian" Convention. Al Qaeda leaders generally qualify as neither. The Fourth Convention, again, protects only civilians who are nationals of a belligerent state (i.e., one party to the armed conflict), and few detained jihadists can be categorized in this way. Additional Protocol I prohibits reprisals against civilians and civilian property regardless of their nationality or location. But the United States has declined to ratify that Protocol. Even so, it has never expressly reserved a right to employ reprisals against unprivileged belligerents in its custody – those who are neither POWs under the Third Convention nor civilian "protected persons" under the Fourth.

The Geneva Conventions limit reprisal only during armed conflict, moreover. In peacetime, their restrictions do not apply. State practice suggests that forcible countermeasures are commonplace and regarded as lawful by the states who have employed them, as well as their allies. President Clinton ordered such reprisals, for instance, by missile strikes on targets in Afghanistan and Sudan in response to the 1998 Al Qaeda bombings of U.S. embassies in Kenya and Tanzania. Several legal scholars endorse forcible countermeasures as consistent with customary law. D.W. Bowett, "Reprisals Involving Recourse to Armed Force," 66 A.J.I.L. 1, 3 (1972); Maj. Philip Seymour, "The Legitimacy of Peacetime Reprisal as a Tool against State-Sponsored Terrorism," 39 Naval L. Rev. 221 (1990); William O'Brien, "Reprisals, Deterrence and Self-Defense in Counter-Terror Operations," 30 Va. J. Int'l L. 421 (1990). Most readings of the UN Charter, Art. 2(4) and Art. 51, reject this position, however. The doctrine of anticipatory self-defense is also pertinent here, but slightly beyond the scope of this book's concerns.

241 Louise Doswald-Beck, "Developments in Customary International Humanitarian Law," 3 Swiss Rev. Int'l & Euro. L. 471, 482 (2005).

242 Osama bin Laden, "Declaration of War against the Americans Occupying the Land of the Two Holy Places," Al-Quds Al Arabi, Aug. 1996, at http://www.pbs.org/newshour/terrorism/international/fatwa_1996.html.

243 Al Qa'eda Declaration of War, 23 Feb. 1998, at http://www.fas.org/irp/world/para/docs/980223-fatwa.htm.

244 In public explanation of his 1996 declaration of war, Osama bin Laden explained that "[t]he reaction came as a result of the aggressive U.S. policy toward the entire Muslim world, not just the Arabian Peninsula" and that the U.S. needed to stop interfering "against Muslims in the whole world." Lawrence Wright, The Looming Tower: Al-Qaeda and the Road to 9/11, 247 (2006).

245 Michael Byers, Custom, Power and the Power of Rules: International Relations and Customary International Law 103 (1999).

246 After leaving public office, Under Secretary of Defense Douglas Feith did privately acknowledge that, in denying Geneva protections to members of jihadist groups that disregard humanitarian law, his legal interpretation would leave any American soldier open to abusive treatment if that soldier, as an individual at least, had done the same. Philippe Sands, Torture Team: Rumsfeld's Memo and the Betrayal of American Values, 104 (2008) (quoting Feith). The depth of Feith's commitment to the reciprocity principle within humanitarian law was apparent as early as the mid-1980s, in his article, "Law in the Service of Terror: The Strange Case of the Additional Protocol," 1 The National Interest 36 (1985). Sands contends that Feith's interpretation of humanitarian law, predicated almost entirely on the bilateral reciprocity principle, greatly influenced Bush administration policy.

247 Elaine Scarry, "Rules of Engagement," *in* The Best American Essays 2007, David Foster Wallace, ed. 234, 252 (2007). Referring to the Bush administration's call for Osama bin Laden's body "dead or alive," she writes, "What judgments would we make if we altered the location and agent of these acts? Were we to look at Al Qaeda's literature and find there "wanted, dead or alive" postings for Western leaders or Western citizens . . . If a Saudi billionaire offered $30 million to any American who could identify a place in which an American leader or ordinary citizen could be captured or killed, what would we think?"

248 Feldman, *supra* note 149, at 267, 275–76.

249 Steven Erlanger & Isabel Kershner, "Gunman in Jerusalem Attack Identified," New York Times, March 7, 2008; Isabel Kershner, "Israel Approves Home Building in West Bank," New York Times, March 10, 2008, at A3.

250 John Kifner, "Death on the Campus: Hamas Says It Regrets American Toll in Attack, But Hails Bombing as a Success," New York Times, Aug. 2, 2002, at A10.

251 For discussion of this issue, *see* Natalino Ronzitti, "The Expanding Law of Self-Defense," 11 J. Conflict & Sec. L. 343, 348–52 (2006).

252 *U.S. v. Rahman*, 189 F.3d 88 (2nd Cir. 1999).

253 18 U.S.C. §2384, reenacted from 37 Cong. Ch. 33, July 31, 1861, 12 Stat. 284.

254 Best, *supra* note 28, at 232. The Lieber Code is a significant exception, having been drafted during the American Civil War. But it was not a treaty between North and South, simply a unilateral undertaking by Union forces and often disregarded by them in practice, as in General Sherman's march through Georgia. Mark Grimsley, The Hard Hand of War: Union Military Policy toward Southern Civilians, 1861–1865 83–85, 151–203, 180–82 (1995).

255 On the weaknesses of this legal analysis, *see* David Caron, "If Afghanistan Has Failed, Then Afghanistan Is Dead: 'Failed States' and the Inappropriate Substitution of Legal Conclusion for Political Description," *in* The Torture Papers: The Road to Abu Ghraib, Karen Greenberg & Joshua Dratel, eds. 214 (2005).

256 *Id.* at 219. Caron observes that "the failed state doctrine not only removes the rights of the failed states (such as protections under the Geneva Conventions), it removes all of the obligations of the failed state." It is therefore "the closest thing to an international bankruptcy regime yet imagined," one that would be of greatest appeal to "the poorest states of the world." *Id.*

257 A postcolonial theorist would be quick to observe the resemblance here to the legal rationales offered by Western colonizers: that because non-Western

peoples lacked civilized (i.e., Christian) states, their lands were *terra nullius* and hence open to conquest. The Bush administration did not offer this "failed state" argument to justify the invasion of Afghanistan, but to explain why Taliban soldiers detained thereafter were not entitled to treatment as POWs. This argument is nonetheless quite weak, for reasons Caron offers.

258 The rule of law sits uneasily, after all, with perennial practices and the settled expectations these have established. By insisting that power over a large territory be concentrated in a single administrative apparatus, the very notion of the modern state has aggravated conflicts over which subgroup within that territory, often defined quite arbitrarily, will control this apparatus and its considerable resources – conflicts that had hitherto been more readily manageable on the basis of more modest land claims and assertions of institutional control.

259 This is certainly not to deny the reality of problems to which that politically uncomfortable and perhaps unfortunate term refers. Robert Bates, When Things Fall Apart: State Failure in Late-Century Africa (2008).

260 Geoffrey Best, Humanity in War: The Modern History of the International Law of Armed Conflicts (1980), *passim*. The Red Cross Convention of 1864 was the first in the history of such treaties.

261 *Al-Marri v. Wright,* 487 F.3d 160, 186 (4th Cir. 2007). The court also concluded that because states do not confront "enemy combatants" at all in a "conflict not of an international character," there simply cannot exist any "unlawful enemy combatants" in such a war.

262 UN Charter, Art. 2(4).

263 Jeremy Waldron, "Torture and Positive Law: Jurisprudence for the White House," 105 Colum. L. Rev. 1681, 1694 (2005) (accusing John Yoo of "narrow textualism" for refusing to apply the underlying principle of nonbrutality, reflected in several Geneva Convention articles, beyond their textual scope). Whereas Waldron finds law's central principle to be "non-brutality," Dworkin considers it "equal concern and respect."

264 John Gray, Heresies 112 (2004).

265 *See, e.g.,* Col. Edbridge Colby, "How to Fight Savage Tribes," 21 A.J.I.L. 279 (1927).

266 David Dudley Field, Amelioration of the Laws of War Required by Modern Civilization: Memoir Presented to the Institute of International Law, Heidelberg 10 (1887) ("The savage tortures his victims, tomahawks the children, scalps the men."); Brett Bowden, "Civilization and Savagery in the Crucible of War," 19 Global Change, Peace & Security 9 (2007); *see generally* Gerrit W. Gong, The Standard of "Civilization" in International Society 54–96 (1984).

267 The military manuals of several Western powers, including the United States, expressly authorize reprisal in response to use of prohibited weapons. Greenwood, *supra* note 99, at 321, 344. *See generally* Provost, *supra* note 115, at 193, 210; Cassese, *supra* note 145, at 219; Ann Van Wynen Thomas & A.J. Thomas, Jr., Legal Limits on the Use of Chemical and Biological Weapons 87–93, 163–65 (1970); Stanisław Nahlik, "Le problème des sanctions en droit international humanitaire," *in* Etudes et essais sur le droit international humanitaire et sur les principes de la Croix-Rouge en l'honneur de Jean Pictet 469–81 (1984). Many

would contend, however, that with regard to nuclear weapons there must be an exception to this exception on unspecific *jus cogens* grounds: "Here the idea of law enforcement has to give way to the sheer inhumanity inherent in such reprisals." Kalshoven, *supra* note 74, at 376.

268 *Prosecutor v. Kupreskic*, Judgment, 14 Jan. 2000, IT-95-16-T, ¶ 532, ICTY.

269 Alvin Gouldner, "The Norm of Reciprocity: A Preliminary Statement," 25 Amer. Sociol. Rev. 161 (1963). Simmel observed long before, "all contacts among men rest on the schema of giving and returning the equivalence." The law often "enforces and guarantees the reciprocity of service and return of service – social equilibrium and cohesion do not exist without it." Georg Simmel, The Sociology of Georg Simmel, Kurt Wolff, ed. 387 (1950). More recent sociology, however, has viewed such reciprocity as consistent with exploitation. Pierre Bourdieu, Outline of a Theory of Practice, Richard Nice, trans. 192 (1977) (observing how Islamic charity in Algeria served to effect domination over the poor); Gloria G. Raheja, The Poison in the Gift: Ritual, Prestation, and the Dominant Caste in a North Indian Village (1988).

270 Greenwood, *supra* note 99, at 319.

271 Winston Churchill, The Hinge of Fate 770 (1962); G. Douhet, Command of the Air 196 (1942). Walzer even regards the British bombing of German cities in 1940–41 as morally justified by the "extreme emergency" created by the magnitude of the Nazi threat at that point. Michael Walzer, Arguing about War 46 (2004).

272 Jeff W. Legro, Cooperation under Fire: Anglo-German Restraint during World War II 128 (1995); Malcolm Smith, British Air Strategy between the Wars 224 (1984); George Quester, "Strategic Bombing in the 1930s and 1940s," *in* The Use of Force, Robert Alt & Kenneth Waltz, eds. 253 (2nd ed. 1983). Even the term "retaliation in kind" is somewhat redundant, as the word "retaliation" derives from the Latin *talio*, which means "of the same kind, of the same nature."

273 Geneva Additional Protocol I, Art. 56.

274 Hague Declaration on Expanding Bullets, No. 3, 1899, 187 CTS 549, *in* The Law of Armed Conflict: A Collection, D. Schindler & J. Toman, eds. 109 (2004).

275 Detlev Vagts, "The Hague Conventions and Arms Control," 94 A.J.I.L. 31, 38 (2000).

276 Michael Walzer, Just and Unjust Wars 215 (1977).

277 Van Wynen Thomas & Thomas, *supra* note 267, at 165, 298.

278 The Laws of Armed Conflict, Dietrich Schindler & Jiri Toman, eds. 121–27 (1988); John Norton Moore, "Ratification of the Geneva Protocol on Gas and Bacteriological Warfare: A Legal and Political Analysis," 58 Va. L. Rev. 419, 453 (1972). France's reservation provided, for instance, that "said protocol shall automatically cease to be binding on the Government of the French Republic with respect to any enemy State whose armed forces or whose allies fail to respect the interdictions which form the subject of this protocol."

279 Detter, *supra* note 65, at 340 ("One could even suggest that reservations to treaties regarding reciprocity, i.e., stipulating that the treaty will apply only on such basis, are unnecessary.").

280 Moore, *supra* note 278, at 482.

281 For similar reasons, one cannot distinguish Geneva from Hague/weapons law on the basis that the first's prohibitions are *mala in se* (wrong in themselves, apart from the law so declaring), whereas the second's are merely *mala prohibita* (wrong only because the law says so), as is sometimes argued. Walzer, *supra* note 276, at 215. This distinction does explain some of the difference between the two bodies of humanitarian law, but by no means all of it. Many today would presumably say, for instance, that it is inherently wrong to kill even an enemy's combatants by means of chemical, biological, or nuclear warfare, regardless of whether one's adversary has first employed such methods. Yet the reasons for that conclusion rely implicitly on human rights or proportionality arguments – about causing more harm than good, or than necessary – that sound in Geneva and human rights law more than in the law of weapons regulation. Geneva Additional Protocol I, Art. 5(b), prohibiting "indiscriminate" attack, defined as one "which may be expected to cause incidental loss of civilian life, injury to civilians, damage to civilian objects, or a combination thereof, which would be excessive in relation to the concrete and direct military advantage anticipated."

282 Kalshoven, *supra* note 74, at 364; Bruno Simma, "Reciprocity," 7 Encyclopedia of Public International Law, 400, 403 (1985); Sienho Yee, "The *Tu Quoque* Argument as a Defense to International Crimes, Prosecution, or Punishment," 3 Chinese J. Int'l L. 87, 98 (2004) (observing that "*tu quoque* as a defense to crime . . . is chiefly an argument from reciprocity").

283 Once they decided formally to reject *tu quoque* entirely, to deny its very existence as a cognizable defense, the Nuremberg judges did not need to confront the issue of whether the temporal sequence of violations should matter to its availability. This inattention to chronology is also an artifact of how the court came to admit evidence of America's use of unrestricted submarine warfare. Defense counsel for the German admirals sought to justify his motion for such admission not by reference to *tu quoque*, realizing that his request would surely be denied. Instead, he shrewdly argued that such evidence was relevant simply to establishing the state of current law on the subject (i.e., to indicate state practice and how other states [besides Germany] understood their duties under the pertinent treaty as well as customary law). Yee, *id.* at 105–07. For that purpose, it was immaterial whether the United States and Britain or Germany and Japan had been first to employ unrestricted submarine warfare. Yet once the evidence of American practice had been admitted, the judges quickly recognized the deeper and more challenging issue it posed for the legitimacy of their entire endeavor (i.e., the question of whether the proceedings were merely "victors' justice"). German unrestricted submarine warfare originated in Hitler's Nov. 1939 War Order No. 154. Exhibit Number GB-196-Trials of German Major War Criminals: Volume 13 Thursday, 9 May 1947.

284 Chronology is more relevant to reciprocity as tit-for-tat than as "Kantian" common rules, because "tit" necessarily responds interactively to a prior "tat," whereas rules for all – once decided on – are simply applied to both belligerents equally, regardless of which first violated the *prima facie* norms governing both.

285 The right of reprisal is also cabined by the further requirements of last resort, advance warning, proportionality, and termination on cessation of misconduct by the party targeted for reprisal.

286 Alan Cowell, "German Ruling Absolves Spies of Former East," New York Times. May 24, 1995, A1. The Court thus found Wolf's prosecution to violate the principle of "proportionality." GER-1995-2-018 (May 15, 1995), BVerfG, Beschluß vom 15.5.1995 AZ 2 BvL 19/91 u.a., BVerfGE 92,277 ff., at www.codices. coe.int; *see also* War Crimes (Preventive Murder) case, Federal Supreme Court, Federal Republic of Germany (1960), 32 ILR 564 (1966) ("No state may accuse another state of violations of international law and exercise criminal jurisdiction over the latter's citizens in respect of such violations if it is itself guilty of similar violations against the other state or its allies.").

287 The International Military Tribunal for the Far East rejected a tu quoque-type argument invoked by one Japanese defense counsel. He had sought exculpation of his client, accused of authorizing rape and murder of Chinese women, on grounds that Chinese military forces had done much the same. Yuma Totani, The Tokyo War Crimes Trial: The Pursuit of Justice in the Wake of World War II 124–25 (2008).

288 Provost, *supra* note 115, at 227–235.

289 Francis Biddle, In Brief Authority 452, 455 (1962).

290 Provost, *supra* note 115, at 229. *See also* Moore, *supra* note 278, at 479, 481–85 (describing "reciprocity" in arms control agreements like the Geneva Gas Protocol as equivalent to "no first use").

291 Provost, *supra* note 115, at 228.

292 In this game, a single departure from cooperation leads to defection in perpetuity, rather than the return to cooperation after the punishment of defection, as in tit-for-tat, or to renegotiation of the violated rule, as in a "penance" game. Robert Axelrod, The Evolution of Cooperation 36 (1984); Drew Fudenberge & Eric Maskin, "The Folk Theorem in Repeated Games with Discounting or with Incomplete Information," 54 Econometrica 389 (1986).

293 Julius Stone, Legal Controls of International Conflict 355 (1954).

294 *Kupreskic*, Judgment, *supra* note 268, at ¶¶ 515–520, ICTY (concluding at ¶ 517 that "individual criminal responsibility for serious violations of that law may not be thwarted by recourse to arguments such as reciprocity"); *see also Prosecutor v. Martić*, Judgment, 8 March 1996, IT-95-11-R61, 108 ILR 39, ICTY, ¶¶ 15–18. In both judgments the tribunal finds reprisals prohibited by customary international law, a conclusion persuasively refuted by two leading scholars, however. Greenwood, *supra* note 99, at 341–47; Frits Kalshoven, "Reprisals and the Protection of Civilians: Two Recent Decisions of the ICTY," *in* Kalshoven, Reflections on the Law of War 809, 819, 830, 833 (2007). Kalshoven observes, in particular, that a prohibition on civilian reprisal was deliberately excluded from the 1977 Geneva Additional Protocol II. Even the ICTY itself, in *Kupreskic* at ¶ 527, expressly admits that state practice, an essential component of customary international law, does not support the view that belligerent reprisals are illegal. The court instead chooses to rely entirely on *opinio juris* in ascertaining custom, a professionally dubious move. The actual practice of states, in other words, reflects a much deeper commitment to the reciprocity principle than does learned juridical opinion.

295 Yee emphasizes the difference between *tu quoque* as a complete defense to any punishment and as grounds for mitigation of sanction. He also mentions the concept's possible use as a defense to prosecution and to conviction, i.e., to

criminal liability, uses that international law has never endorsed. Yee, *supra* note 280, at 100.

296 Yee, *supra* note 280, at 131. Yee even finds *tu quoque*, as a basis for nonpunishment, "sound as a moral principle." *Id.* So did Francis Biddle who, by his own account, was the most influential Nuremberg judge on this issue. *Supra* note 287, at 452.

297 Meir Dan-Cohen, "Decision Rules and Conduct Rules: On Acoustic Separation in Criminal Law," 97 Harv. L. Rev. 625, 630 (1984).

298 This assumes that multilateral judicial institutions like the International Criminal Court will not be dominated by great powers on the Security Council.

A problem similar to *tu quoque* often arises in civil litigation, but was largely resolved nearly a half-century ago with the introduction of "comparative negligence" – contrasting the defendant's greater fault with the plaintiff's lesser. This enabled plaintiffs to recover the share of their damages attributable to the defendant's wrong, even when they themselves bore some responsibility for their injury. Yet criminal law, and hence international criminal law, has never found it necessary to embrace even the idea of comparative fault, presumably because the accuser is always the state, representing society at large, rather than a joint participant in the alleged wrong. If state officers shared criminal responsibility, they would be in the dock along with the defendants from civil society. But the state itself is not subject to criminal liability.

299 David Koplow, "Back to the Future and Up to the Sky: Legal Implications of 'Open Skies' Inspection for Arms Control," 79 Cal. L. Rev. 421, 433, 441 (1991) ("Reciprocity is an indispensable aspect of any arms control arrangement, and under an Open Skies regime, each nation would serve as both inspector and host. . . . The principle of reciprocity provides an important protection against abuses, because each state knows that if it misbehaves (as either inspector or host) and frustrates the purposes of the Open Skies regime, then it will likely be treated poorly in return inspections."); *see also* Louis Henkin, Arms Control and Inspection in American Law 22–24 (1958); Oliver Meier, "The U.S. Rejection of Bioweapons Verification and Implications for Future Negotiations," Int'l Network of Engineers and Scientists Against Proliferation, Bulletin 21, 2003, at http://www.inesap.org/bulletin21/bul21art26.htm ("Reciprocity and the acceptance of equal obligations are preconditions for arms control.").

300 Guido Den Dekker, The Law of Arms Control 69, 333–34, 351 (2001).

301 *Id.* at 369.

302 *Id.*

303 This is the type of move Fried unpersuasively makes to sustain his argument that the entire law of contract can be satisfactorily explained and justified by reference to the single moral principle of promise keeping. The several important doctrines insusceptible to this explanation are then simply relegated to other legal fields, as if the practice of promise keeping occupied a social domain that was naturally bounded and hermetically sealed off from competing considerations. Charles Fried, Contract as Promise 103–09 (1981).

304 Dekker, *supra* note 298, at 352.

305 Ronald Dworkin, Law's Empire 214–17, 442–44 (1986) (condemning statutes not organized in service of a coherent system of moral principle as lacking

integrity and thus as checkerboard quilts); Roberto Mangabeira Unger, "The Critical Legal Studies Movement," 96 Harv. L. Rev. 561, 571 (1983) (describing the moral incoherence evident in a given body of law as resembling a patchwork quilt).

306 Duncan Kennedy, "Form and Substance in Private Law Adjudication," 89 Harv. L. Rev. 1685, 1766 (1976).

307 William Galston, The Practice of Liberal Pluralism 2, 11–12 (2005); Isaiah Berlin, Four Essays on Liberty 169 (1969).

308 John Rawls, Political Liberalism 217 (1993).

309 Dworkin, *supra* note 305, at 443; Ronald Dworkin, "A Reply by Ronald Dworkin," *in* Ronald Dworkin and Contemporary Jurisprudence, Marshall Cohen, ed. 247, 266 (1983).

310 Don Herzog, "As Many as Six Impossible Thing before Breakfast," 75 Cal. L. Rev. 609, 610 (1987) (saying much the same of water: that one needs it to survive, but too much of it will cause drowning). Yet such jocular analogies do not capture the full difficulty of the problem and are hence ultimately inapposite in that we are concerned not simply with how much bilateral reciprocity – like how much wine – is desirable, but more precisely with where to situate the reciprocity principle within a complex body of legal rules. There should be some rationale, in other words, for the decision to introduce it prominently in one place but not in another, i.e., across the panorama of humanitarian law (and international criminal law) as a legal field.

The variety of coherence sought here does not require that any single principle – e.g., that restraint must always (or need never) be reciprocated – will suffuse and dominate an entire legal field, resolving all uncertainties at the level of its more specific rules. Only a less demanding species of coherence is apposite and desirable. For as Duncan Kennedy recently writes (in a more sober spirit than his influential early, but more extravagent work on the subject), "it is understood that many concrete rules of the system may be inconsistent with the principles that should govern them and that there may be conflicts, and that gaps may appear as new cases arise . . . There can be deep and long-standing disagreement about the correct application of the principles, and even about what exactly the principles are, without putting into question the idea that the system is coherent, albeit in this more modest mode." Duncan Kennedy, "Thoughts on Coherence, Social Values, and National Tradition in Private Law," *in* The Politics of a European Civil Code, Martijn Hesselink, ed. 9, 11 (2006). Thus, humanitarian law could be considered coherent if there were some meta-principle determining when the reciprocity principle pertained and when it didn't, as contrasted with applying the principle in a largely *ad hoc* fashion to this rule-specific issue but not to that. In this sense, the present chapter shows humanitarian law to be incoherent, since no such metaprinciple may be found within the authoritative legal materials. A body of law might be incoherent in this way though nonetheless perfectly predictable in its results, i.e., in providing advance warning to a potential defendant about how particular conduct will later be judicially treated.

311 Isaiah Berlin, The Crooked Timber of Humanity: Chapters in the History of Ideas 8–12, 79–87 (1990).

312 On the nature and possibility of principled compromise, *see* J. Patrick Dobel, Compromise and Political Action 79–100 (1990); Compromise in Ethics, Politics, and Law, J. Roland Pennock & John Chapman, eds. (1979).

313 Pierre Schlag, The Enchantment of Reason 68 (1998).

314 Andrew Altman, Critical Legal Studies 117–26 (1990).

315 Kennedy himself says the same of any legal system that tried to live by rules based entirely on individualism or altruism. *Supra* note 306, at 1685, 1776.

316 William Stuntz, "Local Policing After the Terror," 111 Yale. L. J. 2137, 2138–39 (2002); Oren Gross & Fiounnuala Ní Aoláin, Law in Times of Crisis: Emergency Powers in Theory and Practice 74–75 (2006).

317 On this basis, the reader might even find it helpful to revisit each of the more specific doctrines and factual scenarios assayed in the preceding pages to see exactly how this species of balancing test would pertain to them.

318 *See, e.g.,* David Cole, "The Poverty of Posner's Pragmatism: Balancing away Liberty after 9/11," 59 Stan. L. Rev. 1735, 1745–46 (2007) (review of Richard Posner, Not a Suicide Pact: The Constitution in a Time of National Emergency); Vincent-Joël Proulx, "If the Hat Fits, Wear It, If the Turban Fits, Run For Your Life: Reflections on the Indefinite Detention and Targeted Killing of Suspected Terrorists," 56 Hastings. L.J. 801, 894–98 (2005) (rejecting balancing as a means of resolving tensions between civil liberties and national security); Melzer, *supra* note 5, at 54, 55, 67, 69 (dismissing, without elaboration, the balancing metaphor and associated proportionality reasoning as used by several international law scholars and foreign courts as "unsophisticated").

319 In the academic echo chamber where such views are almost exclusively defended, one may even encounter such candid admissions as the following, couched as a critique of an empirical study concluding that Muslim airport profiling may not effectively reduce terrorist risk; its empirical methods are suspect, an Oxford don warns us, despite their reassuring conclusions in the particular case, because "there is always the danger that by accepting that effectiveness matters, we might be forced to concede that some new security measure that undermines rights, even torture, actually works and cannot therefore be resisted." Liora Lazarus & Benjamin Gould, "Introduction: Security and Human Rights: The Search for a Language of Reconciliation," *in* Security and Human Rights, Benjamin Gould & Liora Lazarus, eds. 1, 11 (2007). Nonconsequentialists mercifully face no such peril, for they know what justice requires without having to confront such unsettling, disconcerting questions. They readily reach the answer they wish, in fact, without raising themselves from the professorial armchair, to immerse themselves in any messy empirical complexities beyond their comfortably specialized cubbyhole of the academic world. Better not to ask hard questions than to risk hearing answers one did not desire. This stance not only leads to poor public policy, but more important, – since academicians don't make much policy – is inconsistent with first principles of the scholarly calling, which demand one's confrontation with "inconvenient facts," as Max Weber famously put it. Max Weber, "Science as a Vocation," *in* From Max Weber, H. H. Gerth & C. Wright Mills, eds. 129, 147 (1948) ("The primary task of a useful teacher is to teach his students to recognize 'inconvenient' facts – I mean facts that are inconvenient for their party opinions.").

In moral reasoning, an inattention to consequences in the world as we know it can also lead to efforts to derive meaningful answers to humanitarian law issues from such otherworldly hypotheticals as the following, all offered by a leading Harvard moral theorist. She asks us to consider the moral implications of such military activities as (1) we "consider releasing a flock of butterflies over an opponent's population when we know they are irrationally frightened of butterflies," (2) "some U.S. bombardier intended to hit the munitions site as a mere means to killing children," (3) "a pilot" seeks only "to bomb a building to harm some cows in order to terrorize other cows into trampling the munitions site," (4) "We bomb some trees because we know that people will think we are trying to kill them and they then become terrorized and pressure for a change of policy," and (5) whether it "is terrorism when Baby Killer Nation bombs militarily useful Nazi targets in a manner that is no different from how the Resistance would do this?" Frances M. Kamm, "Terrorism and Several Moral Distinctions," 12 Legal Theory 19, 30, 42, 52, 55 (2006); *see also* Kamm, "Making War (and its Continuation) Unjust," 9 Euro. J. Phil. 328 (2001). These statements are referenced here not to ridicule their author, nor even to reproach their lack of moral seriousness regarding subjects demanding greater *gravitas*, but only to indicate how far the theoretically informed discussion of humanitarian law has strayed from the empirically informed and policy-oriented discussion, to the extent that such bizarre hypotheticals are apparently considered illuminating by cognoscenti. Kamm's uninterest in the world of empirical consequences is representative of most work on war in the deontological tradition purporting to concern "practical ethics." *See, e.g.,* David Rodin, War and Self-Defense (2002) (arguing that nation-states do not possess any moral right to self-defense).

320 Nancie Prud'homme, "*Lex Specialis*: Oversimplifying a More Complex and Multifaceted Relationship?" 40 Israel L. Rev. 355, 390–93 (2007).

321 This is a recurrent enigma within humanitarian law. Its key doctrine of proportionality, for instance, generally adds little further constraint on the use of force beyond that already imposed by the longstanding military doctrine known as "economy of force," i.e., imposed by strictly martial-professional considerations. Carl von Clausewitz, On War, Michael Howard & Peter Paret, eds., chap. IX (1989).

322 McDonald, *supra* note 8, at 247.

CHAPTER 3. HUMANITARIAN VS. HUMAN RIGHTS LAW: THE COMING CLASH

1 The centrality of bilateral reciprocity to human relations at all levels, micro and macro, is a recurrent theme in the theoretical work upon which this book draws throughout, i.e., in legal theory, moral philosophy, anthropology, economics, biology, and international relations.

2 For an especially ardent defense of the primacy of human rights law over humanitarian law, *see, e.g.,* Michael Dennis, "Application of Human Rights Treaties Extraterritorially in Times of Armed conflict and Military Occupation," 99 A. J. I. L. 119, 139, 141 (2005).

3 *Case Concerning Armed Activities on the Territory of the Congo (DRC v. Uganda),* 2005 I.C.J. 116 (Dec. 19), at 216.

4 In dissent, Judge Buergenthal observes as much. Legal Consequences of the Construction of a Wall in the Occupied Palestinian Territory, 2004 I.C.J. 131, P 6 (July 9) (declaration of Judge Buergenthal) (noting that such issues of Israeli security raised by the regular Palestinian attacks launched from the Occupied Territories "are never really seriously examined by the Court, and the dossier provided the Court by the UN on which the Court to a large extent bases its finding barely touches on that subject."). Even an ardent, scholarly supporter of the World Court's Israeli Wall decision admits that "the Court surprisingly offers no substantive reasoning to support its finding that Israel's construction of the wall cannot be justified by military necessity." Ardi Imseis, "Critical Reflections on the International Humanitarian Law Aspects of the ICJ Wall Advisory Opinion," 99 A.J.I.L. 102, 110 (2005). In a word, the Court's assertion to this effect is entirely conclusory.

5 Lindsay Moir, The Law of Internal Armed Conflict 194 (2002).

6 Robert Kolb, "The Relationship between International Humanitarian Law and Human Rights Law," 80 Int'l Rev. of the Red Cross 409, 411–16 (1998); Nancie Prud'homme, "*Lex Specialis*: Oversimplifying a More Complex and Multi-faceted Relationship?," 40 Israel L. Rev. 355, 363 (2007).

7 International Covenant on Civil and Political Rights, Art. 4(1)(1966); European Convention on Human Rights, Art. 15 (1950).

8 This chapter examines the clash between humanitarian and human rights law only as it concerns reciprocity in America's conflict with Al Qaeda. The dissonance between these two bodies of law likely takes different forms in other species of armed confrontation.

9 Jack Goldsmith, The Terror Presidency 111 (2007). In declining to submit Protocol I for ratification, the president wrote to the Senate's resident that Art. 44 "would grant combatant status to irregular forces even if they do not satisfy the traditional requirements to distinguish themselves from the civilian population and otherwise comply with the laws of war. This would endanger civilians among whom terrorists and other irregulars attempt to conceal themselves."

10 Prud'homme, *supra* note 6, at 358.

11 David Kennedy, Of War and Law 113–14 (2006).

12 Secretary-General's Bulletin, ST/SGB/1999/13, 6 August 1999. s. 1.1.

13 Mary Ellen O'Connell, "The Criteria of Armed Conflict," Int'l L. Assoc., Study Committee on the Meaning of War, Spring 2007, at 25. She pronounces: "Armed conflict ends when the intense fighting ends." *Id.*

14 *Id.* at 31.

15 *Legality of the Threat or Use of Nuclear Weapons*, Advisory Opinion, I.C.J. 226, 257, 259–60 (July 9, 1996).

16 If not effected *post facto*, i.e., after the event to be judged, such enlargement of the conceptual scope of "armed conflict" is consistent with the lenity principle, requiring that criminal statutes be strictly construed.

17 Hedley Bull, The Anarchical Society: A Study of Order in World Politics 184 (1977).

18 Carl von Clausewitz, On War, Michael Howard & Peter Paret, eds. and trans. 75 (1976) (1832).

19 Fourth Geneva Convention, Art. 31(1); Additional Protocol I, Art. 51(2); Additional Protocol II, Art. 4(2)(d). In several cases, the ICTY has treated terrorizing of civilian populations as a war crime. *See, e.g., Prosecutor v. Blagojevic and Jokic,* Case No. IT-02-60, Judgment, ¶ 214, 588–592, 755 (Jan. 17, 2005); *Prosecutor vs. Krajišnik,* Case No. IT-00-39/40, Judgment, ¶ 309 (Sept. 27, 2006); *Prosecutor v. Galić,* Case No. IT-98-29, Judgment, ¶ 85–87 (Jan. 27, 2005).

20 This language does not appear, however, in any official formulations of the Martens clause itself. Such wording also risks distorting the intended purpose of that clause insofar as many "gaps" in treaty coverage, as in contracts and statutes, are often quite intentional. Drafters did not wish to see them "filled," in other words, much less by reference to a body of law – on human rights – conceived as differing significantly in its central ends and means.

21 There is some basis in precedent for such a conclusion. In at least two postwar Nuremberg judgments (*Von Leeb* and *Alstoetter*), the Tribunal held that despite the prohibition on retroactive penal legislation, a German defendant had fair warning that he could be found criminally liable for violating a particular duty under international law – a duty arguably ambiguous in scope and potential application to his conduct – because the Martens clause exhorts courts to fill gaps in humanitarian law treaties in light of "the principles of humanity and the dictates of public conscience." The defendant hence had reason to anticipate that doctrinal ambiguities could be resolved against him. For brief discussion, *see* Theodor Meron, "The Martens Clause, Principles of Humanity, and Dictates of Public Conscience," 94 A.J.I.L. 78, 80 (2000).

22 Malise Ruthven, "The Rise of the Muslim Terrorists," N.Y. Rev. of Book, May 29, 2008, at 33, 33 (summarizing the conclusions of Marc Sageman's respected research).

23 Marc Sageman, "Does Osama Still Call the Shots? Debating the Containment of al Qaeda's Leadership," Foreign Affairs, July/Aug. 2008, at 165, 165.

24 Timothy Lynch & Robert Singh, After Bush: The Case for Continuity in American Foreign Policy 260 (2008).

25 O'Connell, *supra* note 13, at 14–20.

26 *Juan Carlos Abella v. Argentina,* Case 11.137, Inter-Amer. C.H.R. Report No. 55/97 OEA/Ser.L/V/II.95 Doc. 7 rev (1997). The ICTY has also found a state of armed conflict to exist during a period of violence lasting only three days. *Prosecutor v. Boskoski, Tarculovski,* IT-04-82-PT, Aug. 22, 2005; *Prosecutor v. Limaj, Bala, Musliu,* IT-03-66-T, Nov. 30, 2005.

27 It is arguable that the scope of "armed conflict" should be broader when the issue, as before the Inter-American Commission, is civil compensation of victims by the state responsible for human rights abuse than when the issue is criminal prosecution of an individual official, soldier, or insurgent. Interpretive maxims enjoin that human rights treaties are to be construed broadly, criminal statutes strictly. As applied here, this would limit the relevance of the Commission's holding beyond the context of compensation. "Armed conflict" would then mean something different for purposes of international criminal law than for human rights law. This introduces greater complexity

than would normally be desirable. And a state is generally liable for violating the human rights of its residents in any event, i.e., irrespective of whether it was at war and therefore without need for a broad reading of "armed conflict."

28 O'Connell, *supra* note 13, at 24. Such analysis, though proffered as scholarship, more closely resembles a litigation brief in its adversarial modality and attendant posture toward issues of professional responsibility.

29 Marco Sassòli, "Transnational Armed Groups and International Humanitarian Law," Occasional Paper, Program on Humanitarian Policy and Conflict Research, Harvard, Winter 2006, at 3.

30 O'Connell, *supra* note 13, at 10; *see also* O'Connell, "The Legal Case Against the War on Terror," 37 Case W. Res. J. Int'l L. 349, 357 (2005).

31 O'Connell, *supra* note 13, at 26–31. The Taliban and associated elements of Al Qaeda do, of course, presently control significant portions of Afghanistan and border areas of Pakistan.

32 *Id.* at 26.

33 *Prosecutor v. Dusan Tadić*, Decision on the Defense Motion for Interlocutory Appeal on Jurisdiction, Oct. 2, 1995, Case IT-94-1-AR72, ¶ 70; *Prosecutor v. Ramush Harandinaj, Idriz Balaj and Lahi Brahimaj*, Judgment, April 3, 2008.

34 *Harandinaj, id.* at ¶¶ 91–98.

35 Victor Davis Hanson, "Re-Rethinking Iraq: Nothing Succeeds like Success," Commentary, April 2008, 19, at https://www.commentarymagazine.com/viewpdf.cfm?article_id=11274.

36 François Hampson, "Human Rights Law and International Humanitarian Law: Two Coins or Two Sides of the Same Coin," 91 Bull. Human Rights 46, 49 (1992)

37 Giorgio Agamben, Homo Sacer: Sovereign Power and Bare Life, Daniel Heller-Roazen, trans. (1998). The very opposite is closer to the truth, in fact, for as this and the preceding two chapters have shown, "war today takes place on a terrain that is intensely governed – not by unified global institutions, but by a dense network of rules and shared assumptions among the world's elites," both military and civilian. Kennedy, *supra* note 11, at 25. And, of course, even the Bush administration did not contend that it was entitled simply to murder the Guantánamo detainees, as the Roman law of *homo sacer* – to which Agamben analogizes Bush administration policies – would have allowed.

38 This is not to deny that some Western military lawyers view the simultaneous application of humanitarian and human rights law as potentially practicable, in certain contexts. *See, e.g.,* Kenneth Watkin, "Controlling the Use of Force: A Role for Human Rights Norms in Contemporary Armed Conflict," 98 A.J.I.L. 1, 34 (2004).

39 Reply of the Government of the United States of America to the Report of the Five UNCHR Special Rapporteurs on Detainees in Guantanamo, March 10, 2006, at http://www.usmission.ch/Press2006/USFinalReplytoGITMOreport2006.pdf; Oral Statements by the United States Delegation to the Committee against Torture, May 8, 2006, at http://www.usmission.ch/Press2006/CAT-May8.pdf; United States Statement on the Draft Convention on Enforced Disappearances, June 27, 2006, at http://www.usmission.ch/Press2006/0627United StatesStatementonForced-Disappearances.html.

40 That the conflict could fairly be classified in legal terms as an armed conflict is not to deny the possibility that, as a matter of policy, it would be better managed through institutions of law enforcement and attendant diplomacy. The Bush Administration itself acknowledged that though it considered America to be in an armed conflict with Al Qaeda, the Taliban, and "associated forces," it did not believe the country to be "engaged in a legal state of armed conflict at all times with every terrorist group in the world," according to the State Department Legal Adviser. John Bellinger, "Armed Conflict with Al Qaeda?" Opinio Juris Feb. 28, 2007, at www.opiniojuris.org.

In defining war, the parties' self-characterization is only one element in a multifactor test. Theodor Meron, Human Rights in Internal Strife: Their International Protection 76 (1987) (explaining that armed conflicts should be distinguished from violent disturbances based on the parties' intentions, their level of organization of the actors, in addition to the duration and intensity of the hostilities). Certain of these factors suggest an affirmative answer to the question of whether the conflict with Al Qaeda constitutes an "armed conflict," whereas other factors suggest a negative answer. One careful, recent study concludes that this body of law, as applied to the current conflict, is indeterminate on the question of whether an armed conflict exists. Monica Hakimi, "International Standards for Detaining Terrorism Suspects: Moving beyond the Armed Conflict-Criminal Divide," 33 Yale J. Int'l L. 369, 379 (2008).

41 For arguments that this is the proper line of legal analysis, *see, e.g.,* Mary Ellen O'Connell, "The Legal Case against the Global War on Terror," 36 Case W. Res. J. Int'l L. 349, 350 (2004); Jordan J. Paust, "Anti-terrorism Military Commissions: Courting Illegality," 23 Mich. J. Int'l L. 1, 8 (2001); Anthony Dworkin, "Military Necessity and Due Process: The Place of Human Rights in the War on Terror," *in* New Wars, New Laws? Applying the Laws of War in 21st Century Conflicts, David Wippman & Matthew Evangelista, eds. 53 (2005).

42 Thom Shanker & David E. Sanger, "New to Job, Gates Argued for Closing Guantánamo," New York Times, Mar. 23, 2007, at A1 (quoting Defense Secretary Gates as acknowledging that the detention facility at Guantánamo Bay has "become so tainted abroad"); Alan Cowell, "Briton Wants Guantánamo Closed," New York Times, May 11, 2006, at A24 (quoting the British attorney general as asserting that "the existence of Guantánamo remains unacceptable" and that it has become "a symbol to many – right or wrong – of injustice"). In the *Rasul* case, the Supreme Court declined to address the question of whether the law of armed conflict applies to detainees not captured on an active battlefield. For discussion, *see* W. Michael Reisman, "Guantánamo Disentangled? The US Supreme Court Step in *Rasul v. Bush*: A Failure to Apply International Law," 2 J. Int'l Crim. Just. 973 (Dec. 2004).

43 Anthony Dworkin, "The Laws of War and the Age of Asymmetric Conflict," *in* The Barbarisation of Warfare, George Kassimeris, ed. 220, 231 (2006).

44 "Media reports suggest that Yemen allowed the Predator drone to strike there in 2002; the protests of the Pakistani government following the 2006 raids were so ambiguous as to suggest that the government probably knew and approved the attacks. At least some European governments appear to have given their permission, indeed actively cooperated, in irregular renditions . . ." Steven Ratner,

"Predator and Prey: Seizing and Killing Suspected Terrorists Abroad," 15 J. of Polit. Phil. 251, 273 (2007). In late 2008, however, the United States abandoned its longstanding policy of seeking consent from Pakistani security authorities before conducting targeted killings in that country, after links between such security services and militant jihadists involved in an attack upon the Indian Embassy in Afghanistan were convincingly established. Eric Schmitt & Mark Mazetti, "Bush Said to Give Orders Allowing Raids in Pakistan," New York Times, Sept. 11, 2008, at A1.

45 Ratner, *id.* at 273.

46 The United States's formal "interpretation" of the meaning of "substantial" is "a greater likelihood than not." Multilateral Treaties Deposited with the Secretary-General, Convention Against Torture, Declarations and Reservations, U.S. at http://untreaty.un.org/ENGLISH/bible/englishinternetbible/partI/chapterIV/treaty14.asp.

47 International Covenant on Civil and Political Rights, Art. 7; Convention Against Torture, Art. 4; Congressional Research Service, Report to Congress, The UN Convention Against Torture: Overview of U.S. Implementation Policy Concerning the Removal of Aliens, Jan. 16, 2007.

48 *See generally* Ethan Nadelmann, "The Evolution of U.S. Involvement in the International Rendition of Fugitive Criminals," 25 N.Y.U. J. Int'l L. & Pol. 813, 858–81 (1993) (reviewing the history of informal rendition as an alternative to extradition); John Bassett Moore, Treatise on Extradition and Interstate Rendition 281 (1891).

49 The Third Geneva Convention, covering POWs, does not call for hearings to justify their detentions, unless the detaining state wishes to deny POW status and there is doubt about this non-entitlement. Art. 5. The Convention does provide certain right of process when a POW is prosecuted for war crimes. Art. 105.

50 This is part of a broader concern over increasing judicial scrutiny of military and intelligence decision-making. *See, e.g.,* Andrew McBride, "Opinion: We'll Rue Having Judges on the Battlefield," Wall St. J., June 21, 2008 (arguing that Justice Kennedy's *Boumediene* judgment "is a watershed of judicial hubris, and in the continuing trend in our society to convert every form of decision making into a lawsuit" and to "confuse the civilian criminal justice system and the waging of war"); Matthew Continetti, "The Gitmo Nightmare: What the Supreme Court Has Wrought," Weekly Standard, June 23, 2008, at 5.

51 Noam Lubell, "Challenges in Applying Human Rights Law to Armed Conflict," 87 Int'l Rev. of the Red Cross 737, 745 (2005).

52 George Andreopoulos, "The Impact of the War on Terror on the Accountability of Armed Groups," *in* The Law of Armed Conflict: Constraints on the Contemporary Use of Military Force, Howard Hensel, ed. 170, 173 (2005). For evidence of the intense antipathy aroused in certain military law circles by the suggestion that human rights law applies on the battlefield, *see* Lt. Col. Michael Hoffman, "Rescuing the Law of War: A Way Forward in an Era of Global Terrorism," 34 Parameters 18, 18, 26 (2005).

53 Stefanie Schmahl, "Der Menschenrechtsschutz in Friedenszeiten im Vergleich zum Menschenrechtsschutz im Krieg," *in* Menschenrechte: Bilanz und Perspektiven, Jana Hasse et al., eds. 41–42, 53 (2002).

54 I.C.J. Advisory Opinion, *supra* note 15, at 226, 240 (8 July 1996). "The Court observes that the protection of the International Covenant on Civil and Political Rights does not cease in times of war, except by operation of Article 4 of the Covenant whereby certain provisions may be derogated from in a time of national emergency. Respect for the right to life is not, however, such a provision. In principle, the right not arbitrarily to be deprived of one's life applies also in hostilities. The test of what is an arbitrary deprivation of life, however, then falls to be determined by the applicable *lex specialis*, namely, the law applicable in armed conflict which is designed to regulate the conduct of hostilities. Thus whether a particular loss of life, through the use of a certain weapon in warfare, is to be considered an arbitrary deprivation of life contrary to Article 6 of the Covenant, can only be decided by reference to the law applicable in armed conflict and not deduced from the terms of the Covenant itself."

55 This clause was introduced into a number of early humanitarian law treaties, beginning in 1899. In various formulations, it exhorts in very broad terms that where gaps in existing legal protections may be found, the civilian "inhabitants and the belligerents remain under the protection and the rule of the principles of the law of nations, as they result from the usages established among civilized peoples, from the laws of humanity, and the dictates of the public conscience." Preamble, Laws and Customs of War on Land (Hague IV), 18 Oct., 1907. Public opinion, it should be emphasized, is one central and acknowledged component of "public conscience." Meron, *supra* note 21, at 83. Opinion surveys in many countries regularly disclose that people accord greater weight to security – national and personal – than to the rights claims of criminal suspects, particularly those accused of terrorism. Following the Supreme Court's June 2008 decision in *Boumediene* to the contrary, for instance, a Washington Post-ABC News poll found that 61 percent of Americans believe noncitizens suspected of terrorism should not have a constitutional right to challenge their incarceration in civilian courts. Washington Post, at http://www.washingtonpost.com/wp-srv/politics/documents/postpoll_061608.html?sid=ST2008061700079; *see also* Lydia Saad, "Few Americans Object to Treatment of Guantanamo Bay Captives," Gallup News Service, Feb. 7, 2002, at http://www.gallup.com/poll/5302 (finding that only 4% of Americans at that date considered the treatment of such detainees unacceptable).

In short, the "dictates of public conscience," as the public itself understands these, may often be more welfarist than deontological in spirit. Even on Kantian grounds, the Martens clause could readily be invoked to resolve uncertainties in legal doctrine to expand the scope of protections for terrorism's victims and potential victims, whose vital interests "the laws of humanity" in warfare seek to secure. Yet empirical facts about public opinion, as a component of "public conscience," are generally ignored by international jurisprudence, which prefers to rely upon the more formal indicia of a state's official *opinio juris*. This preference requires some justification, which has not been provided. One might retort that the public's conscience is sometimes unconscionable and must be dictated to – presumably when, as here for many readers perhaps, it is at odds with one's own. But this is also to make the Martens clause effectively meaningless as anything but a façade for judicial law-making, in light of the judge's personal predilections.

56 *Prosecutor v. Kupreskić*, Case IT-95-16-T (Judgment of Jan. 14, 2000), at ¶ 525; *Prosecutor v. Furundzija*, Case No. IT-95-17/1-T, Judgment, ¶¶ 159–164 (December 10, 1998) (using human rights law, specifically Article 1 of the 1984 Convention against Torture and Other Cruel, Inhuman or Degrading Treatment or Punishment, to determine that the elements of torture in a situation of armed conflict); *but see Prosecutor v. Kunarac et al.,* Case No. IT-96-23-T & IT-96-23/1-T, Judgment, ¶ 466–497 (February 22, 2001) (declining to accept that the definition of torture under international humanitarian law has the same elements as the definition of torture generally applied under human rights law).

57 The Latin term for this rule of priority among conflicting norms is *lex specialis derogat legi generali.*

58 Amna Guellali, *"Lex Specialis,* Droit International Humanitaire et Droit de L'Homme: Leur Interaction Dans Les Nouveaux Conflits Armes," 111 Revue Générale de Droit International Public 539 (2007) (noting the ICJ's departure, since the Nuclear Weapons case, from reliance on the priority of *lex specialis* over *lex generalis,* particularly in the Israeli "Wall" Advisory Opinion).

59 Int'l Court of Justice, Advisory Opinion, *Legal Consequences of a Wall in the Occupied Palestinian Territory,* July 9, 2004, General List No. 131. Even if the *lex specialis* does not displace the *lex generalis,* the relevant general international law in this case would be not only that of human rights, but also of state responsibility. Int'l L. Commission, Draft Articles on Responsibility of States for Internationally Wrongful Acts, Arts. 22, 49–53 (2001); Bruno Simma & Dirk Pulkowski, "Of Planets and the Universe: Self-Contained Regimes in International Law," 17 Euro. J. Int'l L. 483, 485, 493 (2006). This latter body of law provides for countermeasures as a remedy for violations of international law, and countermeasures are the functional equivalent of belligerent reprisals during war, e.g., when a military confrontation has not attained the level of "armed conflict."

60 Alexander Orakhelashvili, "Legal Consequences of the Construction of a Wall in the Occupied Palestinian Territory: Opinion and Reaction," 11 J. Conflict & Security L. 119, 125 (2006).

61 The conflict between humanitarian and human rights law reflects the still broader problem of "fragmentation" within public international law. Legal thinkers from Europe and the United States today offer very different answers to the question of whether such law urgently demands greater hierarchical unity in order to function satisfactorily. The predominant European view is that serious problems now arise from the way in which particular conduct may be conceived and treated somewhat differently under distinct bodies of law and by their specialized enforcement institutions. *See, e.g.,* Mireille Delmas-Marty, Global Law: A Triple Challenge 74 (2003) (contending that all law, including international law, "does not like multiplicity; it represents order, unified through hierarchy and symbolized by Kelsen's pyramid of norms, built for eternity ... "); Pierre-Marie Dupuy, "A Doctrinal Debate in the Globalisation Era: On the 'Fragmentation' of International Law," 1 Euro. J. Legal Stud. (contending that international law must consist of a formally unified intellectual

structure, with jus cogens rules at the top of an orderly normative hierarchy, overriding other legal sources inconsistent with them).

By contrast, a common American view (shared by the two Europeans quoted below) is that the present international situation would be better described as one of "legal pluralism." Such pluralism, on this view, "is unavoidable and might even sometimes be desirable, both as a source of alternative ideas and as a site for discourse among multiple community affiliations." Paul Schiff Berman, "Global Legal Pluralism," 80 USC L. Rev. 1155, 1155 (2007). Such arguments are, to be sure, sometimes simply euphemisms for forum-shopping by nongovernmental organizations seeking out the particular venue most congenial to their cause. *See generally,* Laurence Helfer, "Regime Shifting: The TRIPs Agreement and New Dynamics of International Intellectual Property Lawmaking," 29 Yale J. Int'l L. 1 (2004). Even apart from such political motivations, however, it may be that any attempt to impose a single hierarchy among now-separate legal domains is premature at best, because "legal fragmentation is merely a . . . reflection of a more fundamental, multi-dimensional fragmentation of global society itself." Andreas Fischer-Lescano & Gunther Teubner, "Regime-Collisions: The Vain Search for Legal Unity in the Fragmentation of Global Law," 25 Mich. J. Int'l L. 999, 1004 (2004). From this perspective, if most global regulatory regimes are still largely "self-contained," this is because each "is closely coupled with a sectoral system dedicated to maximizing a particular rationality," e.g., free trade, environmental protection, preventing unnecessary suffering in war. Id. at 1008. Global society is apparently prepared to allow most of its legal domains to operate consistently with the reciprocity principle, other domains somewhat less so. But since "human rights" is not an isolable domain in the fashion of, say, the law of the sea, the rejection of reciprocity by human rights law necessarily affects the operation of the several legal domains upon which its concerns consistently impinge.

62 On this general problem, *see* David Kaye, "Complexity in the Law of War," *in* Progress in International Law, Russell Miller & Rebecca Bratspies, eds. 681 (2008). More than in humanitarian law, rule-makers in domestic lawmaking (both legislative and judicial) commonly consider the relative calculability of alternative legal standards in deciding which should govern a given type of situation. Modern legislators thus regularly take into account the fact that a high degree of legal calculability is more important to attain (also sometimes harder to achieve) in some circumstances than in others. Duncan Kennedy, "The Disenchantment of Logically Formal Legal Rationality, or Max Weber's Sociology in the Genealogy of the Contemporary Mode of Western Legal Thought," 55 Hastings L.J. 1031, 1075 (2004).

The concern with avoiding unnecessary complexity sometimes leads organizations to impose even higher standards on their members than the law requires. For instance, in the interests of avoiding undue complexity, the U.S. military does not train its personnel, when taking prisoners, to distinguish between lawful and unlawful combatants or between international and noninternational armed conflicts, though international rules vary in each such circumstance. (The current regulation to this effect is Dept. of Defense Directive 2311.01E, May 9, 2006.) Thus, the demand for ready calculability and attendant rule-simplicity does not necessarily reduce regulatory standards to some "lowest common denominator." In fact, in this case the U.S. military's interest in ease of training and smoothly administered field operations (minimizing the need for fine-grained situational judgment by soldiers) has actually led to raising humanitarian expectations of personnel in ways congenial to human rights considerations. Kaye, *id.* at 706.

63 Nils Melzer, Targeted Killing in International Law 435 (2008) ("As targeted killings, by definition, are directed against selected individuals, they constitute the conceptual antithesis of depersonalized, inter-collective warfare and often come dangerously close to the denial of quarter.").

64 *Id.* at 56–57.

65 There are important exceptions, however. For instance, the United States had managed to film, with the aid of an unmanned U.S. reconnaissance aircraft, the Nov. 4, 2002, summary execution of captured Navy SEAL Neil Roberts by three jihadists. BBC.com, Mar. 6, 2002, at http://news.bbc.co.uk/1/hi/world/south_asia/1857599.stm. When these three people were later captured and identified as Roberts's murderers, the U.S. was morally correct in refusing POW status to them. In fact, as a general rule, it is surely preferable to treat a captured fighter on the basis of his own past conduct – good or bad – wherever this can, as in this case, be credibly ascertained.

66 For discussion of this question, *see* Frits Kalshoven, Belligerent Reprisals 56–62 (2005); René Provost, International Human Rights and Humanitarian Law 150, 187–92 (2002); Yoram Dinstein, The Conduct of Hostilities under the Law of Armed Conflict 43–44 (2004); Kenneth Watkin, "Humans in the Cross-Hairs: Targeting and Assassination in Contemporary Armed Conflict," *in* Wippman & Evangelista, *supra* note 41, at 139–51. The Fourth Convention uses the terms "person" or "persons" in describing the requirements for protective treatment, whereas the Third Convention – in Art. 4(2) – classifies persons by characteristics of the group for which they fight. Derek Jinks, "The Declining Significance of POW Status," 45 Harv. Int'l L. J. 367, 389–90 (2004).

67 Geneva Additional Protocol I, Art. 51(3); Geneva Additional Protocol II, Art. 13.

68 Watkin, *supra* note 68, at 147–48.

69 Thomas Nagel, "The Problem of Global Justice," 33 Phil. & Pub. Aff. 113, 114 (2005) (expressing doubts "whether we can even form an intelligible ideal of global justice" encompassing the "socio-economic" realm).

70 *Legal Consequences of the Construction of a Wall, supra* note 59, at ¶ 106; *Case Concerning the Armed Activities on the Territory of the Congo (Democratic Republic of the Congo v. Uganda),* Judgment of 19 December 2005, General List No. 116, ¶ 216; European Union Guidelines on Promoting Compliance with International Humanitarian Law, 2005/C327/04, ¶ 12, *Official Journal of the European Union,* 21.12.2005; UN, Situation of Detainees at Guantánamo Bay, E/CN.4/2006/120, at 10; Alexander Orakhelashvili, "The Interaction between Human Rights and Humanitarian Law: A Case of Fragmentation," N.Y.U. Int'l L. & Justice Colloquium, Feb. 26, 2007, at 13.

71 Int'l Comm. of the Red Cross, The Geneva Conventions of the 12 August 1949, Commentary, Jean S. Pictet, ed. 140 (1958), at http://www.icrc.org/ihl.nsf/COM/375-590017?OpenDocument.

72 *Busic v. U.S.*, 446 U.S. 398, 406 (1980); *Edmund v. U.S.*, 520 U.S. 651, 657 (1997);
    But see Prud'homme, *supra* note 6 (disputing the moral relevance of the *lex specialis* doctrine to establishing the proper relationship between humanitarian and human rights law).

73 *Legality of the Threat or Use of Nuclear Weapons, supra* note 15, at 240.

74 Heike Krieger, "A Conflict of Norms: The Relationship between Humanitarian Law and Human Rights Law in the ICRC Customary Law Study," 11 J. Conflict & Security L. 265, 270 (2006).

75 The U.S. officially takes the position that humanitarian law, where applicable, displaces human rights law. Rule of Law Handbook: A Practitioner's Guide for Judge Advocates, Lt. Vasilios Tasikas et al., eds. 65 (July 2007) ("During combat operations, the U.S. regards the law of war as the exclusive legal regime or a *lex specialis*... [which] operates to the exclusion of... human rights law."); Michael Dennis, "Application of Human Rights Extraterritorially in Times of Armed Conflict and Military Occupation," 119 A.J.I.L. 119 (2005).

76 The European Court of Human Rights has introduced some qualifications to this proposition (i.e., with respect to the European Convention on Human Rights). *Banković and Others v. Belgium and 16 Other Contracting States*, Euro. Ct. of H.R., Human Rights Case Digest, Vol 12, Numbers 11–12, 1121–24(4) (2001); *Al-Adsani v. the U.K., Secretary of Defense* (2007), Opinions of the Lords of Appeal for Judgment, House of Lords.

77 John Rawls, A Theory of Justice 136–42 (1971).

78 Frans de Waal, "The Animal Roots of Human Morality," 192 New Scientist 60, 61 (2006). "Reciprocity can be seen in our... experiments of captive chimpanzees," the author writes. "We found that if one chimpanzee had groomed another, this greatly improved his chances of getting a share of the food from the groomee. In other words, chimpanzees remember who has groomed them, and return the favour later. Like humans, they seem to keep track of incoming and outgoing services." *See also* Kristin Bonnie & Frans B.M. de Waal, "Primate Social Reciprocity and the Origin of Gratitude," *in* The Psychology of Gratitude, Robert Emmons & Michael McCullough, eds. 213, 218–19 (2004) (concluding, on the basis of food-sharing behavior among advanced primates, that "reciprocity is not a uniquely human attribute"); Frans de Waal & Sarah Brosnan, "Simple and Complex Reciprocity in Primates," *in* Cooperation in Primates and Humans, Peter Kappeler & Carel van Schaik, eds. 85 (2006). Species of animals with lesser brain capacity are abundantly capable of contemporaneous cooperation, but not necessarily reciprocity, properly speaking. For as one scientist notes, "although seemingly quite straightforward, reciprocity requires substantial psychological machinery, including the capacity to quantify costs and benefits, store these in memory, recall prior interactions, time the returns, detect and punish cheaters, and recognize the contingencies between giving and receiving." Marc Hauser, Moral Minds 180 (2006).

79 John Gray, Straw Dogs: Thoughts on Humans and Other Animals 37–38 (2002).

80 Donald McNeil Jr., "When Human Rights Extend to Nonhumans," New York Times, July 13, 2008, Weekin Review (describing recent Spanish legislation, inspired by Princeton philosopher Peter Singer, extending certain human rights to the higher species of apes).

81 Marian Stamp Dawkins, "The Scientific Basis for Assessing Suffering in Animals," *in* In Defense of Animals: The Second Wave, Peter Singer, ed. 26, 28–29, 36–38 (2006).

82 The notion of human rights and the rules embodying it cannot really lie at the center of our intuitions here, of our impulse to limit the scope of reciprocity in our relations with others. Many of the situations in which our considered judgments insist on such limits do not involve human beings at all or members of our species who lack its most characteristic and defining feature (i.e., the severely retarded or persistently vegetative); Henry Richardson, "Rawlsian Social-Contract Theory and the Severely Disabled," 10 J. Polit. Phil. 419, 435–30 (2006). In any event, it is certainly not their vestigial humanity that elicits the sense of obligation to them that we feel, since we feel the same way toward many other animal species. Brian Barry, Justice as Impartiality 28–51, 60 (1995); Allen Buchanan, "Justice as Reciprocity versus Subject-Centered Justice," 19 Phil. & Pub. Aff. 227, 252 (1990).

83 Humane Methods of Slaughter Act, 7 United State Code §§ 1901–1907 (2002); 9 C.F.R. 313 et seq.

84 Roger Scruton, "A Carnivore's Credo," *in* The Best American Essays 2007, David Foster Wallace, ed. 263 (2007).

85 To be sure, mothers and, after awhile, fathers too are rewarded with such mimicked behavior as smiles, plus satisfaction from the knowledge that another is completely dependent on one's care and attention.

86 One might juxtapose two radically different thinkers to suggest the pervasiveness of the martial metaphor at the foundations of Western social thought. Like many early modern political thinkers, Thomas Hobbes derived his view of relations between individuals in a state of nature from his understanding of relations between states in the international arena, which he viewed as war-like in essence. Richard Tuck, The Rights of War and Peace: Political Thought and the International Order from Grotius to Kant 109–39 (1999).

For the later Foucault, even within civil society, the ubiquity of repressed social conflict preserved many features of interstate war. Michel Foucault, "Society Must Be Defended": Lectures at the Collège de France, 1975–77, 18–23 (2003) (arguing, over several lectures, that life within the modern West closely resembles a state of war in involving latent but passionately intense social conflicts). *See generally* Randall Collins, Conflict Sociology: Toward an Explanatory Science 59, 60 (1975) ("Life is basically a struggle for status in which no one can afford to be oblivious to the power of others around him . . . there is conflict because violent coercion is always a potential resource and it is a zero-sum sort. . . . The availability of coercion as a resource ramifies conflicts throughout the entire society.").

87 John Gray, Heresies 32–40, 77–79 (2004).

88 Bruno Tertrais, War without End 88–96 (2001); Susan Sontag, At the Same Time 119 (2007) ("The war that has been decreed by the Bush Administration will never end."); Antony Anghie, Imperialism, Sovereignty, and the Making of International Law 298 (2005) ("The new imperial imperative created in these circumstances," i.e., the American global war on terror, "while promising to establish perpetual peace, may very well instead result in endless war."); Rosa Ehrenreich Brooks, "War Everywhere: Rights, National Security Law, and the

Law of Armed Conflict in the Age of Terror," 153 U. Penn. L. Rev. 675, 720 (2003); *Cf.* Bruce Ackerman, "This is Not a War," 113 Yale L. J. 1871, 1872–73 (2004) (arguing that the Bush administration was wrong to conceive the terrorist threat in terms of war, because the 9/11 attacks gave rise to what would more accurately be described as a state of emergency, of the sort amply provided for by the law of many democracies); David Rieff, "Policing Terrorism," New York Times, July 22, 2007, at A13. Rieff follows British Prime Minister Gordon Brown in favoring the treatment of terrorism as a matter of criminal law enforcement, rather than war. But this argument conflates two quite different questions: (1) what is the actual nature of the conflict and how should it therefore be managed with (2) by what name is it most prudent to describe this conflict publicly, in the interests of minimizing offense to moderate Muslims throughout the world, especially those within Western democracies? The two questions need not receive a single answer, unless one adopts the most stringent understanding of the requirements of public transparency, a stringency that foreign policy vis-à-vis violent adversaries has never been thought to require. On the other hand, there are often grave dangers in declining to categorize a *de facto* situation of war in corresponding *de jure* terms. Legal advisers to the German armed forces, for instance, counseled civilian leaders in late 2008 that the measure of military confrontation in northern Afghanistan had reached a point that could only be called armed conflict. Yet civilian leaders were unwilling publicly to acknowledge that German troops were no longer engaged in constabulatory "stabilization," to which human rights law rather than humanitarian law applied. Ulf-Peter Häußler, Bundeswehr, "Incorporating International Criminal Justice into Command and Control." Conference presentation, International Criminal Law and The Military, International Peace Research Institute, Oslo, Sept. 11, 2008. To acknowledge a state of armed conflict would have required German leaders to afford their soldiers rules of engagement more permissive of resort to lethal force. That change would in turn have made a continued presence in Afghanistan more controversial at home in Germany. And "Germany at War" would not have made an appealing headline anywhere on earth. Acknowledging realities would likely also have required provisioning German troops with heavier weapons than suitable for a peace operation – a further controversial step. Yet to refrain from confronting an actual state of war necessarily exposed German soldiers to significantly greater risk than admitting and accommodating the deteriorating operational facts on the ground.

But this vexing situation raises moral and political concerns quite different from the question of whether the conflict between the U.S. and Al Qaeda may accurately be called a war and, if so, whether it should be formally acknowledged as such. Even so, Philip Bobbitt – one of the very few legal scholars with serious knowledge of military history and strategey – insists on this designation: 'I think it is important to look this [conflict with Al Qaeda and related groups] straight in the face, clearly, and see it for what it is, and not to believe that by changing the name we can change reality. I don't call this "warfare" because I think that it will be beneficial to do so, although I do believe that on balance. I call it "warfare" because that's what it is. That's what war is becoming. Therefore, I don't think we have the option of saying, "If I withhold the name,

I can somehow transform the reality.'" Philip Bobbitt, "Terror and Consent: The Wars of the 21st Century," at http://www.cceia.org/resources/transcripts/0057.html.

89 Louise Richardson, What Terrorists Want: Understanding the Enemy, Containing the Threat 175 (2006) (citing data indicating that most Americans believe their country to be at war); Stuart Croft, Culture, Crisis and America's War on Terror 10–14 (2007) (tracing the successful diffusion of the "war on terror" narrative into many forms of U.S. popular culture).

90 Whereas human rights treaties allow derogation of many of their protections in time of national emergency, humanitarian law conventions are designed specifically for such emergencies (i.e., those involving war) and hence do not permit such derogation. Moir, *supra* note 5, at 87, 194–95, 207; Aeyal M. Gross, "Human Proportions: Are Human Rights the Emperor's New Clothes of the International Law of Occupation?," 18 Eur. J. Int'l L. 1, 4–5 (2007) (arguing that when the humanitarian law of occupation is interpreted in light of kindred concepts from human rights law, the legal position of those in occupied territories is weakened).

91 Hakimi, *supra* note 40. As she notes, "Even under the most protective regime for armed-conflict detentions – the regime governing the detention of protected civilians in enemy territory – a state has broad discretion to detain where it has 'good reason to think' the suspect poses a security threat, for instance that he is engaged in sabotage or is a member of an organization whose object is to cause disturbances." *See* Commentary: IV Geneva Convention, Jean Pictet, ed. (1958), at 258.

92 UN Situation of Detainees, *supra* note 70, at 5.

93 The ICRC's 2005 three-volume publication on customary international law has no entry for "armed conflict," and its much shorter dictionary, published in 1992, does not attempt to define the term apart from indicating that it refers to "confrontations" between certain types of parties (i.e., states, non-state actors, ethnic groups, etc.). Pietro Verri, Dictionary of the International Law of Armed Conflict 34 (1992). The principal obstacle to agreement on a definition arises from the difficulty, in the context of internal conflict, of distinguishing genuine civil war from lesser forms of organized and semi-organized violence. States are unwilling to accord any rights of belligerency in the latter context, which would therefore need to be clearly distinguishable from the former.

94 The ICTY has described the antitorture norms as similar to "the other general principles protecting human rights." *Prosecutor v. Anto Furundzija*, Judgment of 10 December 1998, case no. IT-95-17/I-T, ¶¶ 147–155. The Tribunal continues, "The general principle of respect for human dignity is the basic underpinning and indeed the very *raison d'etre* of international humanitarian law and human rights law." ¶ 183. *See also Prosecutor v. Delalic*, Judgment of 16 November 1998, case no. IT-96-2-T, ¶ 466; *Prosecutor v. Kunarac*, Judgment of 22 February 2001, case No. IT-96-23-T, ¶ 454; Orakhelashvili, *supra* note 70, at 2; H.P. Gasser, "International Humanitarian Law and Human Rights Law in Non-International Armed Conflicts: Joint Venture or Mutual Exclusions?" 45 German Yearbook of International Law 149 (2002).

95 European Court of Human Rights, *Güleç v. Turkey* Judgment of 27 July 1998, *Reports* 1998-IV, ¶ 71 (finding excessive force in police conduct while breaking

up a demonstration); *Khashiyev and Akayeva v. Russia*, Judgment of 24 February 2005, Nos. 57942/00 & 57945/00, ¶ 16ff (finding arbitrary deprivation of life by the Russian military in Chechnia, in violation of Art. 2 of the European Convention on Human Rights); *Democratic Rep. of the Congo v. Uganda, Armed Activities on the Territory of the Congo*, I.C.J. Dec. 19, 2005 (finding violations of the International Covenant on Civil and Political Rights during armed conflict in the Democratic Republic of Congo).

96 Israel's Supreme Court so held in *The Public Committee Against Torture in Israel and the Palestinian Society for the Protection of Human Rights and the Environment v. The Government of Israel, et al.*, Judgment of Dec. 11, 2005, §40; Louise Doswald-Beck, "The Right to Life in Armed Conflict: Does International Humanitarian Law Provide All the Answers?" 88 Int'l Rev. of the Red Cross 881, 895–96 (Dec. 2006) (describing and defending the same position as reached in 2003 by the UN Human Rights Committee). A leading Canadian military lawyer acknowledges, "Under the law of armed conflict, a sleeping combatant is a lawful target and can be killed. The situation might be different under human rights law where the first question asked might be whether some lesser use of force, even capture, might be appropriate." Col. Charles Garaway, "Occupation Responsibilities and Constraints," *in* The Legitimate Use of Military Force, Howard Hensel, ed. 263, 277 (2008).

97 ICTY, *Kunarac*, Judgment, *supra* note 94, at ¶¶ 467, 482; ICTY, *Furundzija*, Judgment, *supra* note 94, at ¶ 159 (employing human rights law to interpret the meaning of "torture" as a war crime); Doswald-Beck, *id.* at 881; Orakhelashvili, *supra* note 70, at 14; Moir, *supra* note 5, at 203–04 (contending that the Geneva Art. 3 requirement of "judicial guarantees which are recognized as indispensable by civilized peoples" should be interpreted to incorporate the more specific due process provisions of the ICCPR and regional human rights treaties).

98 David Kretzmer "Targeted Killing of Suspected Terrorists: Extra-Judicial Executions or Legitimate Means of Defence?" 16 Eur. J. Int'l L. 171, 200 (2005); Lubell, *supra* note 51, at 749; Meron, *supra* note 21, at 47.

99 Lubell, *supra* note 51, at 749.

100 F.F. Martin, "Using International Human Rights Law for Establishing a Unified Use of Force Rule in the Law of Armed Conflict," 64 Saskatchewan L. R. 347, 373 (2001).

101 David Rodin, War and Self-Defense 189 (2003).

102 Douglas Laycock, Modern American Remedies 794–802 (2002).

103 Doswald-Beck, *supra* note 96, at 903.

104 Optional Protocol to the Covenant on Civil and Political Rights, Art. 41. Both parties, complainant and defendant, must be parties to the Protocol for either one of them to invoke it against the other.

105 For multivariate statistical analysis of the ratification patterns for this Protocol, *see* Wade Cole, "Sovereignty Relinquished? Explaining Commitment to the International Human Rights Covenants, 1966–1999," 70 Amer. Sociol. Rev. 472, 474, 492 (2005).

106 In the European Court of Human Rights, there have been only eight complaints filed by states, and these have arisen only in the aftermath of armed conflict, as between Cyprus and Turkey. David Forsythe, Human Rights in International Relations 126 (2006). Forsythe's explanation: "Under the principle of

reciprocity, my complaint against you today may lead you to complain about me tomorrow." Also significant here is the fact that, as indicated earlier, no state has a very strong self-interest in how other states treat their own nationals.

107 Strictly speaking, human rights courts, such as the European and Inter-American, have jurisdiction to apply human rights law, not the law of war. Yet they have sometimes applied human rights law to military conduct during armed conflict. *See, e.g.,* ECHR, *Isayeva v. Russia*, Judgment of 24 February 2005, No. 57950/00, ¶¶ 13ff., 103; *Khashiyev* Judgment, *supra* note 95; Inter-American Court of Human Rights, *Las Palmeras*, Judgment of December 6, 2001, Ser. C, No. 90 (2001).

108 *See, e.g.,* James Harrison, The Human Rights Impact of the World Trade Organization (2007); Holger Hestermeyer, Human Rights and the WTO: The Case of Patents and Access to Medicines (2007).

109 Orakhelashvili, *supra* note 67, at 22.

110 Allison Danner, "When Courts Make Law: How the International Criminal Tribunals Recast the Laws of War," 59 Vand. L. Rev. 1, 61 (2006) (showing how "the ICTY has substantially broadened the rules governing civil war, and it has lowered the thresholds for the triggering of the rules on international conflicts").

111 ICCPR, Art. 4; European Convention on Human Rights, Art. 15.

112 "Detention, Treatment, and Trial of Certain Non-Citizens in the War Against Terrorism," White House new release, Nov. 13, 2001, at http://www.state.gov/coalition/cr/prs/6077.htm. President Bush defended this proclamation on the grounds that further attacks could "place at NSL the continuity of the United States government." But such a proclamation of "national emergency" would have only a very questionable legal status.

113 The prohibitions against torture and arbitrary detention are generally considered peremptory. Vienna Convention on the Law of Treaties, Art. 53; *Khashiyev*, Judgment, *supra* note 95, ¶¶ 131–32; Orakhelashvili, *supra* note 67, at 6, 8, 15 (citing several sources to this effect).

114 *Prosecutor v. Krupeskic*, Judgment, ICTY (Jan 14, 2000), ¶ 520. Orakhelashvili, *supra* note 67, at 11.

115 Confirmation Hearing on the Nomination of Alberto R. Gonzales To Be Attorney General of the U.S.: Hearing Before the S. Judiciary Comm., 109th Cong. 121 (2005). Its reservations to the Convention Against Torture specified that America accepts the duty to prevent cruel, inhuman, or degrading treatment only insofar as already prohibited by the Fifth, Eighth, and Fourteenth Amendments to the U.S. Constitution. Whether those amendments even apply to aliens, especially those held outside U.S. territory, was long unclear and remains partly unsettled (in pending litigation) as of this writing.

116 Michael J. Matheson, Deputy Legal Adviser, U.S. Dep't of State, Remarks of Michael J. Matheson at The Sixth Annual American Red Cross-Washington College of Law Conference on International Humanitarian Law: A Workshop on Customary International Law and the 1977 Protocols Additional to the 1949 Geneva Conventions (Jan. 22, 1987), 2 Amer. Univ. J. Int'l L & Pol'y 415, 426 (1987).

117 Geoffrey S. Corn, "*Hamdan*, Fundamental Fairness, and the Significance of Additional Protocol II," Army Lawyer 1, 5–6 (Aug. 2006).

118 Mathasen, *supra* note 118, at 425. A key provision is Geneva Additional Protocol I, Art. 44(4). The United States nonetheless regards Arts. 45 and 75, at least, to be "acceptable practice." United States Army, Operational Law Handbook (2002), ch. 2–5. These provisions prohibit torture and "outrages upon personal dignity, in particular humiliating and degrading treatment." At least since *Erie R. Co. v. Tompkins* (304 U.S. 64, 1938), in which the Supreme Court greatly limited the scope of general federal common law, customary international law cannot be described as already automatically "part of our law," in the century-old language of *The Paquete Habana* (175 U.S. 677, 1900). Rather, elements of customary international law may enter U.S. law when they meet a level of clarity and widespread acceptance comparable to that displayed by the international prohibition of piracy and the protection of ambassadors at the time of the first Federal Judiciary Act. The Supreme Court so concluded in *Sosa vs. Alvarez-Machain* 542 U.S. 692, 724–32 (2004).

119 Mao Tse-tung, On Guerrilla Warfare 80–81 (1961).

120 Brooks, *supra* note 88, at 677; Gen. Wesley K. Clark & Kal Raustiala, "Why Terrorists Aren't Soldiers," New York Times, Aug. 8, 2007, at A19 ("Critics have rightly pointed out that traditional categories of combatant and civilian are muddled in a struggle against terrorists.") Yet another outspoken opponent of Bush administration legal policies in the war on terrorism, Oxford legal scholar Adam Roberts, acknowledges that most detainees are unlawful combatants, a category "whose existence can be inferred from numerous legal provisions, including those setting out criteria for who is to qualify for the status of either prisoner of war or civilian. The critical issue," he continues, "is not whether this category exists, but rather what legal rules govern the treatment of those persons in this category." To this end, Roberts invokes Art. 75 of the 1977 Geneva Additional Protocol I, as did the Supreme Court in *Hamdan*, though the United States did not ratify this Protocol. 'Torture and Incompetence in the "War on Terror,"' 49 Survival 199, 204 (Spring 2007).

121 Doswald-Beck, *supra* note 96, at 899.

122 Orakhelashvili, *supra* note 70, at 39. In other words, the controlling body of law is whichever affords the greater measure of protection to potential victims. This is precisely the political strategy that David Kennedy describes, now with seeming self-derision, as the effort "to regulate swords into plowshares." Kennedy, *supra* note 11, at 31.

123 For a rare exception, *see* Richard Butler, "Modern War, Modern Law, and Army Doctrine: Are We in Step For the 21st Century?," 32 Parameters 45 (2002); and in a similar spirit, Mark Osiel, Obeying Orders: Atrocity, Military Discipline, and the Law of War (1999).

124 Geneva Additional Protocol I, Art. 57.

125 Kennedy, *supra* note 11, at 32–36. In addition to this lack of curiosity about the pertinent knowledge of other fields, the legal scholarship shows no interest even in the human experience of combat, apart from a current focus on the victimization of women civilians through sexual violence.

126 Dissenting Opinion of Judge Weeramantry, *Legality of the Threat or Use of Nuclear Weapons,* Advisory Opinion, 1996 I.C.J. 226, 429 (July 8).

127 This precious juristic insistence on remaining high "above the battle" cannot arise from a humanistic sensibility averse to the cold calculation of military

maneuver and the ugliness of bloodshed. Authors of the greatest world literature have often extravagantly immersed their characters in precisely such unsavory details. One finds this not only in the battle epics of Homer and Tolstoy, of course, but even from so intimate and pacific a soul as Marcel Proust, who lovingly expatiates on the "artistry" inherent in any great military campaign and the subtle savoir-faire of distinguished martial strategists throughout history. Marcel Proust, In Search of Lost Time, vol. 3, The Guermantes Way, C.K. Scott Moncrieff et al., trans. 140–151 (2003). The world's greatest humanists have thus seen no obstacle to the most fine-grained evocation and exploration either of war's intellectual heights or its depraved moral depths. But perhaps the appreciation of humanity's rougher edges entailed in being a great humanist is considered ethically or aesthetically "beneath" that involved in being a humanitarian, e.g., a practitioner of humanitarian law.

128 Rule of Law Handbook: A Practitioner's Guide for Judge Advocates, Center for Law and Military Operations, Judge Advocate General Legal Center, July 2007; Counterinsurgency, FM 3-24, MCWP, Appendix D, ii (Dec. 15, 2006).

129 He adds that this now-prevalent partisan strategy effectively "turns the rule of law into its opposite." Brad Roth, correspondence with author, Aug. 2008.

130 Universal Declaration of Human Rights, Art. 24.

131 Michael Burawoy, "Public Sociology vs. The Market," 5 Socio-Economic Rev. 356, 362–63 (2006) (decrying the invocation of the human rights ideal, and particular long-codified rights of this variety, on behalf of political causes to which Burawoy does not subscribe); Perry Anderson, "Arms and Rights: The Adjustable Center," *in* Anderson, Spectrum 140, 155–56 (2005) (parsing Norberto Bobbio).

132 *See generally* Joost Pauwlyn, Conflict of Norms in Public International Law: How WTO Law Relates to other Rules of International Law (2003).

133 On such exceptions in the European context, *see* George Letsas, A Theory of Interpretation of the European Convention on Human Rights 13–15 (2007) (describing "protection of public morals" as such a limitation clause within this regional human rights treaty).

134 None of this is to belittle in any way the invaluable contribution, of course, of human rights advocates throughout the world, especially in the numerous, politically repressive countries.

135 Universal Declaration of Human Rights, Art. 3; International Covenant on Civil and Political Rights, Art. 9; European Convention of Human Rights, Art. 5. All three documents, as well as the International Covenant of Economic, Social, and Cultural Rights in Art. 8(1)(a), also provide exceptions to certain human rights there codified "when necessary . . . in the interests of national security."

136 Jeremy Waldron, "Security and Liberty: The Image of Balance," 11 J. Polit. Phil. 191, 198–99 (2003).

137 *See especially* Richard Pildes, "Why Rights are Not Trumps: Social Meanings, Expressive Harms, and Constitutionalism," 27 J. Leg. Stud. 725, 733–36 (1998).

138 Vienna Convention on the Law of Treaties, Art. 53. *See also* European Court of Human Rights, *Al-Adsani v. U.K.*, App. No. 35763/97, at http://www.echr.coe.int/Eng/Judgments.htm, Dissenting Opinion, ¶¶ 1, 3.

139 UN Charter, Art. 103.

140 Rome Statute of the International Criminal Court, Art. 17(b)1. State parties commit themselves to investigating such offenses with a view to their domestic prosecution or, where they are unable to do so, then to refer the matter to the ICC for possible prosecution in the Hague. Though the United States has not ratified the Statute and joined the ICC, its War Crimes Act of 1996 makes grave breaches of the Geneva Conventions into felonies. The Conventions define grave breaches to include "torture or inhuman treatment" of persons protected by theses treaties. 18 U.S. §2441.

141 Even *jus cogens* norms do not always override other, non-jus cogens rights in international law. The prohibitions against crimes against humanity and the most severe breaches of the Geneva Conventions are widely thought to be *jus cogens.* Yet the World Court has held these legal claims subordinate to those of official immunity. Int'l Court of Justice, *Case Concerning the Arrest Warrant of 11 April 2000 (Democratic Republic of the Congo v. Belgium).* At least when the prospective defendant acts in an official capacity or still occupies high office, protection from prosecution abroad has been considered weightier because it derives from international law's first principle of national sovereignty. But rights of sovereignty are not considered *jus cogens,* and *jus cogens* norms are said to occupy the highest echelon in such law's normative hierarchy.

142 Thomas Hobbes, Leviathan 186 (1985 ed.); *see also* Jeremy Bentham, "The Principles of Civil Life," *in* The Works of Jeremy Bentham, John Bowring, ed. vol. 1, 302 (1837).

143 Philip Ruddock, "Australia's Legislative Response to the Ongoing Threat of Terrorism," 27 U. New S. Wales L.J. 254, 254 (2004); Günther Jakobs, "Bürgerstrafrecht und Feindstrafrecht," Hochstrichterliche Rechtsprechung im Strafrecht 88 (2004) (deducing a robust counterterrorism policy from the state's duty to protect the individual security of its nationals). *But see* Stephen Bottomley & Simon Bronitt, Law in Context 414 (2006) (arguing that this view of the treaty language is inconsistent with the case law interpreting it, which focuses on the "right of security" against a state's coercive activities); Greg Carne, "Reconstituting 'Human Security' in a New Security Environment: One Australian, Two Canadians and Article 3 of the Universal Declaration of Human Rights," *in* 25 The Australian Yearbook of International Law 1 (2006); Christopher Michaelsen, "National Security versus Civil Liberties: Rights-Based Objections to the Idea of Balance," *in* Ethics of War in a Time of Terror, Christian Enemark, ed. 41 (2006).

144 Amitai Etzioni, Security First: For a Muscular, Moral Foreign Policy 6 (2007).

145 William F. Schulz, "Security is a Human Right, Too," New York Times Magazine, April 18, 2004, A20.

146 Bottomley & Bronitt, *supra* note 143, at 414.

147 *See generally* William Eskridge, Dynamic Statutory Interpretation 56 (1994) (arguing that legislation may be interpreted in light of "the evolution of statute" and "current values").

148 Kendall W. Stiles, "The Power of Procedure and the Procedures of the Powerful: Anti-Terror Law in the United Nations," 43 J. Peace Res. 37, 45–48 (2006) (describing the background to the adoption of Security Council Resolution

1373 and domestic legislative responses to it); Paul Szasz, "The Security Council Starts Legislating," 96 A.J.I.L. 901 (2002).

149 Liora Lazarus, "Mapping the Right to Security," *in* Security and Human Rights, Benjamin Gould & Liora Lazarus, eds. 325, 329. (2007).

150 Ian Loader & Neil Walker, Civilizing Security 13 (2007).

151 Mark Tushnet, Weak Courts, Strong Rights: Judicial Review and Social Welfare Rights in Comparative Constitutional Law 205–34 (2008); *see also* Dieter Fleck, "International Accountability for Violations of the *Ius in Bello*: The Impact of the ICRC Study on Customary International Law," 11 J. Conflict & Security L. 179, 192 (2006) ("Some human rights have a clear horizontal effect, obliging the state to provide for legal protection from homicides and intrusions into privacy by private entities."); Alastair Mowbray, The Development of Positive Obligations Under the European Convention on Human Rights by the European Court of Human Rights (2004).

152 *See generally* Barbara von Tigerstrom, Human Security and International Law: Prospects and Problems (2007).

153 Waldron further observes that most conflicts of rights may be avoided by making all rights "negative," in this sense, so that they do not generate active duties for others, duties very likely to conflict with one another. Jeremy Waldron, Liberal Rights 203 (1993).

154 Sandra Fredman, "The Positive Right to Security," *in* Gould & Lazarus, *supra* note 149, at 307, 359; Loader & Walker, *supra* note 150, at 14–15.

155 Brad Roth, "Retrieving Marx for the Human Rights Project," 17 Leiden J. Int'l L. 31, 46 (2004).

156 The Responsibility to Protect: Report of the International Commission on Intervention and State Sovereignty, at http://www.iciss-ciise.gc.ca/report2-en.asp.

157 For an argument to this effect, *see* Shlomi Wallerstein, "The State's Duty of Self-Defense," *in* Security and Human Rights, Benjamin Gould & Liora Lazarus, eds. 277, 280–81 (2007).

158 Richard Tuck, "The Dangers of Natural Rights," 20 Harv. J. L. & Pub. Pol'y 683, 684 (1997).

159 *Id.* at 683–84.

160 *Id.* at 686.

161 *Id.* at 687, 692.

162 Bernard Williams, In the Beginning Was the Deed: Realism and Moralism in Political Argument 3 (2005). The state's provision of such basic physical security, he continues, "is particularly important because, a solution . . . being required *all the time*, it is affected by historical circumstances; it is not a matter of arriving at a solution to the first question at the level of state-of-nature theory and then going on to the rest of the agenda." (emphasis in original).

163 Once the claim to personal security enters positive law as a human right, then "natural rights can undermine civil liberties," Tuck stresses. Tuck, *supra* note 158, at 691. He points to Britain's suspension on this basis of trial by jury for terrorism cases in Northern Ireland during the 1970s. "It is hard to see how to avoid giving priority to the ancient right to life. Once we accept a hierarchy [of rights] then the more fundamental will trump the less fundamental, and the subversion of civil liberties in the interests of natural rights will once more

be possible." *Id.* at 693. Thus, the more recent effort to invoke the international human right to personal security, in defense of limits on civil liberty, is of a piece with the history of natural/human rights thinking.

164 Clifford Rogers, "By Fire and Sword: Bellum Hostile and Civilians in the Hundred Years War," *in* Civilians in the Path of War, Mark Grimsley & Clifford Rogers, eds. 33 (2002) (describing English strategy against the French in the Hundred Years War).

165 Mark Grimsley & Clifford Rogers, "Introduction," *in* Grimsley & Rogers, *Id.* at ix, xiii.

166 Michael Taylor, Community, Anarchy and Liberty 12–19 (1982) (describing such a combined threat/offer as a "throffer").

167 In the U.S. Civil War, General William T. Sherman made this threat/offer explicit when expelling the civilian population of Atlanta. Mark Grimsley & Clifford Rogers, "Introduction," *in* Grimsley & Rogers, *supra* note 164, at ix, xiii, ix, xiii (2002).

168 Leading contemporary thinkers of diverse perspectives who defend this view include Judith Jarvis Thomson, The Realm of Rights 87–93, 158–66 (1990); Waldron, *supra* note 153; Alasdair MacIntyre, After Virtue 2nd ed. (1981) (contending that different human rights have been drawn from disparate traditions of moral thought and therefore rest on incompatible premises); Michel Villey, Le Droit et les Droits de l'Homme 13 (1983) ("Each of the so-called human rights is the negation of other human rights."); *see generally* Symposium on Conflicts of Rights, 7 Legal Theory 235 (2001).

169 Frederick Schauer, "The Exceptional First Amendment," KSG Working Paper No. RWP05-021, Feb. 2005, at http://papers.ssrn.com/sol3/papers.cfm?abstract_id=668543; Adam Liptak, "American Exception: Unlike Others, United States Defends Freedom to Offend," New York Times, June 12, 2008 (contrasting broad U.S. legal protections for hate speech with its prohibition in most Western democracies).

170 Dworkin unabashedly describes his ideal judge as god-like, a Hercules, in the power to synthesize coherently the vast mass of legal materials relevant to resolution of a hard case. Ronald Dworkin, Taking Rights Seriously 186 (1977) (arguing that "taking rights seriously" requires that judges "follow a coherent theory of what these rights are, and act consistently with their own professions").

171 John Rawls defends the "lexicographical priority" of his "equal liberty" principle, for instance. Rawls, *supra* note 77, at 43.

172 Ronald Dworkin, "Do Values Conflict? A Hedgehog's Approach," 43 Ariz. L. Rev. 251 (2001).

173 William Galston, "Realism in Political Theory," Yale Legal Theory Workshop, Aug. 2007 draft, at http://www.law.yale.edu/intellectuallife/ltw.htm, at 9; *see also* John Gray, Two Faces of Liberalism 69–104 (2000) (observing that liberalism's central moral commitments regularly run afoul of one another).

174 Gray, *supra* note 87, at 113.

175 Pew Research Ctr. for People & the Press, Americans Taking Abramoff, Alito and Domestic Spying in Stride, (Jan. 11, 2006), at http://peoplepress.org/reports/display.php3?ReportID=267 (finding that a 46% plurality believe that government counterterrorism policies have not gone far enough, compared to

33% of respondents who believe that policies have gone too far in restricting civil liberties); The Gallup Org., The Patriot Act and Civil Liberties, (May 12–13, 2005), at http://institution.gallup.com.proxy.lib.uiowa.edu/content/ ?ci=5263 (stating that, when asked whether the Bush administration has gone too far in restricting civil liberties in order to fight terrorism, 34% of respondents stated that the administration had not gone too far and a further 19% said that the administration had not gone far enough); The Gallup Org., The Patriot Act and Civil Liberties, (Dec. 16–18, 2005), at http://institution. gallup.com.proxy.lib.uiowa.edu/content/?ci=5263 (concluding that, when asked whether the government should take all steps necessary to prevent additional acts of terrorism in the United States even if doing so means violating civil liberties, 31% of respondents said that all steps should be taken even if they violate civil liberties, and 65% said that steps should be taken but none that violate civil liberties). *See also* W. Kip Viscusi & Richard J. Zeckhauser, "Recollection Bias and the Combat of Terrorism," 34 J. Legal Studies 27 (2005) ("Respondents were generally willing to support airplane passenger profiling when the time costs of alternative policies were great and were supportive of strengthened surveillance policies to address terrorism risks as well.").

176 In 2005, three-quarters of the British public expressed the view that when terror suspects could not be prosecuted but intelligence suggested their involvement in terrorist groups, their liberty of movement could be restricted. Only one-third of respondents sought a judicial role in such determinations prior to executive action. Richardson, *supra* note 89, at 67.

177 *Barcelona Traction, Light and Power Co., Ltd., Second Phase (Belg. v. Spain)*, 1970 I.C.J. 3, 32 (Feb. 5), at ¶¶ 33–35.

178 On the legal issues raised by such a characterization, *see* William Schabas, "Punishment of Non-State Actors in Non-International Armed Conflict," 26 Fordham Int'l L. J. 907, 923 (2003) (citing many legal authorities describing the 9/11 attacks in these terms).

179 Charles Beitz, "What Human Rights Mean," Daedalus, Winter 2003, at 36, 37.

180 For the best recent efforts, *see* Joseph Raz, On Human Rights (2008); Joshua Cohen, "Minimalism about Human Rights: The Most We Can Hope For,"12 J. Pol. Phil. 190 (2004).

181 For a particularly fatuous statement of this stance, *see, e.g.,* UN Vienna Declaration and Programme of Action, Second World Conference on Human Rights, 1993, ¶5: "All human rights are universal, indivisible, and interdependent and interrelated. The international community must treat human rights globally in a fair and equal manner, on the same footing, with the same emphasis."

182 Neither does virtue ethics offer any easy answer here, however, for virtues too, like rights, may conflict. The soldier's courage quickly begins to run up against the virtue of prudence, in much the same way that, in civilian life, the virtue of benevolence often constrains that of truth telling. Lawrence Becker, Reciprocity 145 (1990).

183 Leading political theorists have nonetheless sought to profit from the enormous public currency of human rights discourse by insisting on reading the most ambitious claims of their vocation (as they understand it) – the advancement of "global justice" – into the center of that discourse. *See, e.g,* Beitz, *supra* note 179, at 38, 41, 43 (arguing that human rights should be understood not as

"natural" and pre-social but "as rights that arise out of people's relationships in a global political economy"); Cohen, *supra* note 180, at 196 (endorsing Beitz's stance). An understanding of human rights limited to a least-controversial moral minimum, by contrast, would stop well short of a full-blown theory of global justice.

184 *See, e.g.,* Michael Ignatieff, Human Rights as Politics and Ideology 56 (2001).

185 Rawls's list, for instance, includes only the "right to life . . . ; to liberty (to freedom from slavery, serfdom and forced occupation, and to a sufficient measure of liberty of conscience to ensure freedom of religion and thought); to property (personal property); and to formal equality as expressed by rules of natural justice (that is, that similar cases be treated similarly)." Rawls, *supra* note 77, at 65.

186 Michael Sandel, Liberalism and the Limits of Justice 151 (1979).

187 David Kinley, "Human Rights Fundamentalism," Legal Studies Research Paper, Univ. of Sydney, Feb. 2007, at 20. Kinley continues, "There is an ever-present temptation to justify any proselytizing designs by relying on the apparent unimpeachability of human rights, which like any claims of 'a cause that is above justifying itself,' invites an inevitable and debilitating backlash." *Id.* at 26. *See also* Jeremy Waldron, "A Rights-Based Critique of Constitutional Rights," 13 Oxford J. Leg. Stud. 18, 27 (1993); George Letsas, A Theory of Interpretation of the European Convention on Human Rights 126–30 (2007) (identifying and criticizing a process of "rights inflation" as distorting and overburdening the docket of the European Human Rights Court). This species of skepticism about human rights begins in Edmund Burke. Peter Jones, "Human Rights," *in* The Blackwell Encyclopaedia of Political Thought, David Miller et al., eds. 222, 224–25 (1987) ("The more one conceives political decisions as calling for the balancing of complex and conflicting considerations, the less sympathetic one is likely to be towards theories which demand the honouring of a list of more or less inviolable rights.").

188 Eric Posner, "Human Welfare, Not Human Rights," Human Rights and the New Global Order: An Interdisciplinary Conference, Harvard University, April 18, 2008.

189 Robert Kagan, Of Paradise and Power, America and Europe in the New World Order (2003). Though an American, Kagan's views on international issues are more nuanced than this stark contrast between American and European stances would imply. He recently writes, for instance: "The United States, as the strongest democracy, should not oppose but welcome a world of pooled sovereignty. It has little to fear and much to gain in a world of expanding laws and norms based on liberal ideals and [institutions] designed to protect them." Robert Kagen, "The September 12 Paradigm: America, the World, and George W. Bush," Foreign Affairs, Sept./Oct. 2008.

190 Başak Çali & Saladin Meckled-García, "Introduction: Human Rights Legalized – Defining, Interpreting, and Implementing the Ideal," *in* The Legalization of Human Rights: Multidisciplinary Perspectives on Human Rights and Human Rights Law, Saladin Meckled-García & Başak Çali, eds. 11, 12–24 (2006).

191 *Id.* at 26.

192 Ronald Dworkin, Law's Empire 258 (1986). The upshot is that "it would be wrong to conclude . . . that the discrepancies" – between human rights

principles and their juridification – "are due to imperfect laws and that the continuing project of codification can fill in the gaps." Çali & Meckled-García *supra* note 190, at 25.

193 *Krupeskic*, Judgment, *supra* note 114, at ¶ 518. "The absolute nature of most obligations imposed by rules of international humanitarian law reflects the progressive trend toward the so-called 'humanisation' of international legal obligations, which refers to the general erosion of the role of reciprocity in the application of humanitarian law over the last century. . . . This trend makes the translation into legal norms of the 'categorical imperative' formulated by Kant in the field of morals: one ought to fulfill an obligation regardless of whether others comply with it or disregard it." Other strands of Kantian moral theory may be invoked on the opposite side of this debate, however, as shown in Chapter 6. Some have detected a retreat by Meron, once appointed on the international criminal bench, from his early, academic enthusiasm for infiltrating humanitarian law with human rights thinking. In correspondence, he wonders about whether this tendency may have begun to confront certain inherent limits. "Are there some contradictions in goals and methods which compel the survival of divisions?," he asks.

194 Mary Kaldor, New and Old Wars 9 (2001) (citing no source for this data, however); *see generally* Alexander B. Downes, "Desperate Times, Desperate Measures: The Causes of Civilian Victimization in War," 30 Int'l Security 152, 152 (Spring 2006); Kristine Eck & Lisa Hultman, "One-Sided Violence against Civilians in War," 44 J. Peace Res. 233 (2007); *see generally* The True Cost of Conflict, Michael Cranna, ed. (1994).

195 Mary Kaldor, "Beyond Militarism, Arms Races and Arms Control," Soc. Sci. Res. Council, After Sept. 11, at http://www.ssrc.org/sept11/essays/kaldor.htm.

196 For arguments to this effect, *see* Chris Jochnick & Roger Normand, "The Legitimation of Violence: A Critical History of the Law of War," 35 Harv. Int'l L.J. 49 (1994); Kennedy, *supra* note 11, at 8, 22, 32–33.

197 Michel Foucault, Discipline and Punish: The Birth of the Prison, Alan Sheridan, trans. 148–51 (1991).

198 Michel Foucault, The History of Sexuality: Volume 1, An Introduction, Robert Hurley, trans. 136–37 (1990).

199 Mark Grimsley, "Rebels" and "Redskins": U.S. Military Conduct toward White Southerners and Native Americans in Comparative Perspective," *in* Grimsley & Rogers, *supra* note 164, at 137, 144 (2002).

200 Kennedy, *supra* note 11, at 167.

201 *Id.* at 8. Walzer has made the same observation regarding the U.S. military's increasing study and invocation of just war theory. Michael Walzer, Arguing about War 3–22 (2004). In fact, his own classic text on the subject, Just and Unjust Wars (1977), has long been required reading at the U.S. military service academies and war colleges.

202 James Dawes, The Language of War: Literature and Culture in the U.S. From the Civil War Through World War II 216 (2002).

203 Jean-François Lyotard, The Postmodern Condition: A Report on Knowledge 10, 16, 60–66 (1984); Catherine MacKinnon, Only Words 105, 109 (1993).

204 Dawes, *supra* note 202, 199.

205 *Id.* at 205, 207.

206 Roth, *supra* note 155, at 31, 66 (parsing Marx).

207 Genuine uncertainty about the actual scope and applicability of relevant rules admittedly plays some role as well.

208 Michel Foucault, *supra* note 86, at 18–23. It may even be that Durkheim has the better of the argument with Foucault over modern society (and especially international society), the condition of its normative order in peacetime: as morally underdisciplined, not overdisciplined – or at least underdisciplined in key respects, albeit perhaps overdisciplined in others. If so, then contemporary warfare throughout the world is very much of a piece with domestic disorder and war-like home-grown conflict – as Foucault himself briefly hypothesized in his later years. The differences between the two theorists are the more marked, to be sure.

209 On the various efforts of international humanitarian law, through treaty and recent cases, to limit the scope of violence defensible in terms of "military necessity," *see* Mika N. Hayashi, "The Martens Clause and Military Necessity," *in* The Legitimate Use of Military Force, Howard Hensel, ed. 135, 138–44 (2008); Alexander Zahar & Göran Sluiter, International Criminal Law: A Critical Introduction 149–52 (2007).

210 *See, e.g.,* Geneva Additional Protocol I, Arts. 41, 56–58, 76–78, 86.

211 Such reviews involve a comparison between the intended and actual results attained from particular military operations, especially those that have faired poorly, with a view to improvement. *See, e.g.,* A Leader's Guide to After-Action Reviews, Training Circular, TC-25-20, Dept. of the Army (1993). The U.K. armed forces perform similar evaluations in what they call "patrol reports."

212 Scott Veitch, Law and Irresponsibility: On the Legitimation of Human Suffering 138 (2008).

213 For summaries of judicial and scholarly sources supporting this conclusion, *see* Guénaël Mettraux, International Crimes and the *ad hoc* Tribunals 77–81 (2005); A.P.V. Rogers, Law on the Battlefield 3–6 (2004).

214 Because this chapter argues for strengthening humanitarian considerations within humanitarian law by taking such law more seriously on its own terms, I will not devote further attention to how human rights law might be applied during armed conflict to contribute to this same objective. *But see, e.g.,* Daniel Moeckli, Human Rights and Non-Discrimination in the 'War on Terror' (2008). This is not to deny altogether, however, the potential value of the latter approach, though that value is largely left to be demonstrated. It would not be difficult to show, however, that whether detention of a terrorist suspect after a certain period may be categorized as "arbitrary," within the meaning of various human rights conventions, could turn on the special challenges of gathering evidence on an active battlefield. In fact, there would be no need to find that a state of armed conflict existed in order to interpret the meaning of "arbitrary" in light of such practical evidentiary challenges.

215 Kennedy, *supra* note 11, at 31.

216 This is not to claim that such law has had no effect at all. Chapter 10 is largely concerned with showing the ways and circumstances in which humanitarian law does sometimes exercise genuine influence over events, according to the

best recent social science. But such studies suggest that humanitarian law is most effective when enforced by retaliation (i.e., an expression of the reciprocity principle), rather than by suppressing the workings of that principle.

217 David Rieff, A Bed for the Night: Humanitarianism in Crisis 70 (2002).

218 This reflects the economics of substitution: when counterterrorism policy increases the costs to terrorists of certain methods, terrorist organizations find new ones. Bernard Harcourt, Against Prediction: Profiling, Policing and Punishing in an Actuarial Age 232 (2007) (arguing that recurrent profiling of Arab travelers by airport security might well induce terrorist organizations to devote greater efforts to recruiting non-Arab Muslims for suicide missions). In fact, the averted Al Qaeda plan, disclosed in February 2006, to fly a jetliner into Los Angeles's tallest skyscraper, involved Malaysian Muslims apparently recruited for this reason. Elisabeth Bumiller & David Johnston, "Bush Gives New Details of 2002 Qaeda Plot to Attack Los Angeles," New York Times, Feb. 10, 2006. On the increasing incidence of non-Arabs among jihadist suicide bombers, *see* Malcolm Nance, "How (Not) To Spot a Terrorist," Foreign Policy, June 8, 2008, at 18. On the equal protection issues raised by "profiling" of Arabs for counterterrorism scrutiny, *see* Daniel Moeckli, Human Rights and Non-Discrimination in the "War on Terror" (2008). On the role of the economic principle of substitution within military strategy, *see generally* Jurgen Brauer & Hubert Van Tuyll, Castles, Battles & Bombs: How Economics Explains Military History 292–95 (2008).

219 Robert Mandel, "The Wartime Utility of Precision versus Brute Force in Weaponry," 30 Armed Forces & Society 171, 196 (2007) ("Exactly when precision weaponry seems . . . to be most needed, such as in fighting non-state terrorist or insurgent groups in urban settings, its effectiveness may end up being low because some targeting discriminations are not simply a function of advanced technology."); Nathan Canestaro, "Legal and Policy Constraints on the Conduct of Aerial Precision Warfare," 37 Vand. J. Transnat'l L. 431 (2003). Contrasting America's "smart" weaponry with the methods employed against it on 9/11, Baudrilland writes, "As soon as they combine all the modern resources available to them with this highly symbolic weapon [i.e., their own death as martyrs, through public spectacle], everything changes. The destructive potential is multiplied to infinity. It is this multiplication of factors (which seem irreconcilable to us) that gives them such superiority. The 'zero-death' strategy, by contrast, the strategy of the 'clean' technological war, precisely fails to match up to this transfiguration of 'real' power by symbolic power." Jean Baudrillard, The Spirit of Terrorism and Other Essays, Chris Turner, trans. 21(2003).

CHAPTER 4. IS TORTURE UNIQUELY DEGRADING? THE UNPERSUASIVE ANSWER OF LIBERAL JURISPRUDENCE

1 Waldron himself has generally defended a theory of judging that is quite different from Dworkin's, emphasizing the depth and ubiquity of moral disagreement and thus the practical impossibility of anything approximating a "natural law" view of judicial interpretation, even if correct answers to disputed moral questions do in fact exist. Jeremy Waldron, Law and Disagreement (1999).

2 *See, e.g.,* Dworkin and His Critics, Justine Burley, ed. (2004); Ronald Dworkin and Contemporary Jurisprudence, Marshall Cohen, ed. (1983).

3 Brian Leiter, "Classical Realism," 11 Philosophical Issues 244, 258 (2001).

4 Ronald Dworkin, Taking Rights Seriously 111 (1977); Jeremy Waldron, "Torture and Positive Law: Jurisprudence for the White House," 105 Colum. L. Rev. 1681, 1725 (2005).

5 Waldron, *id.* at 1722–23.

6 *Id.* at 1723.

7 *Id.* at 1721. From this "whole," Waldron maintains, "we understand both the overarching aim of the statute and the organization of the elements that go into achieving that aim."

8 *Id.* at 1724; Dworkin, *supra* note 4, at 26.

9 Ronald Dworkin, Law's Empire 444 (1986). For a refutation of this view, *see* Gregory Keating, "Fidelity to Pre-existing Law and the Legitimacy of Legal Decision," 69 Notre Dame L. Rev. 1, 44–48 (1993) "Different ideal conceptions can, and frequently do, assign different weights to competing principles" embedded within the relevant authoritative materials. "Proponents of different ideals may [then] disagree over cases not because they view those cases as virtual 'ties' and take positions on opposite sides of a fine line, but because they assign priority to different principles which endorse very different conclusions." *Id.* at 45.

10 It should perhaps go without saying that Dworkin's plea for a vastly empowered judiciary appeals still less to the executive power (e.g., the White House), regardless of its partisan affiliation at a particular time.

11 He here employs the Rawlsian method of "reflective equilibrium." John Rawls, A Theory of Justice 48–51 (1971).

12 Most of the field's leading lights festoon his lengthy acknowledgments, in fact. No specialist in national security law and policy, much less in interrogation or intelligence gathering, is acknowledged.

13 Waldron, *supra* note 4, at 1721.

14 *Id.* at 1721, citing Joseph Raz, Practical Reason and Norms 107–48 (1975).

15 Waldron, *supra* note 4, at 1735–39.

16 This may not be entirely fair to Arendt, for she did emphasize that even the most banal evil remains evil. That evil consists specifically in the perpetrator's failure to think (i.e., to rehearse in mind the implications of contemplated actions), especially how he or she may anticipate feeling about these thereafter, when their full consequences are apprehended. Arendt here apparently understands "thinking" to be a process independent of any direct examination of one's conscience, as such. Waldron himself offers a useful recent parsing of Arendt's views in this regard. Jeremy Waldron, "What Would Hannah Say?" 54 N.Y. Rev. of Books, March 15, 2007, at 8.

17 Eric Posner and Adrian Vermeule offer a powerful criticism of Waldron on this point, in their "Should Coercive Interrogation Be Legal?" 104 Mich. L. Rev. 671, 691–92 (2006). Vermeule makes much the same argument for the death penalty that he makes for coercive interrogation: that abjuring the admitted brutality of capital punishment simply permits greater brutality (i.e., more numerous murders by those who could be deterred by the law's threat of capital punishment). Cass Sunstein & Adrian Vermeule, "The Ethics and Empirics of Capital

Punishment: Is Capital Punishment Morally Required? Acts, Omissions, and Life-Life Trade-Offs," 58 Stan. L. Rev. 703 (2005).

18 Chapter 3 explores the far-reaching repercussions of this fact.

19 Joanna Bourke, An Intimate History of Killing: Face-to-Face Killing in 20th Century Warfare 67 (1999).

20 There is no entry for this key term, for instance, in the most widely cited source on the subject: Customary International Humanitarian Law, Vols. I–III, Louise Doswald-Beck & Jean-Marie, Henckearts (2005).

21 Convention against Torture and Other Cruel, Inhuman or Degrading Treatment or Punishment, 1465 U.N.T.S. 85 (1984), Art. 1(1). The U.S. implementing legislation preserves many exceptions to the treaty's prohibitions, however. This legislation does not, for instance, criminalize "cruel, inhuman, and degrading treatment," not even all acts causing pain and suffering, but only those "specifically intended" to cause "severe" physical or mental harm that is "prolonged." 18 U.S.C., §§2340, 2340(A).

22 *Id.*

23 Elaine Scarry, The Body in Pain: The Making and Unmaking of the World 61 (1985) (contending that war "is the most obvious analogue to torture").

24 Terror, too, is an integral feature of war and is generally indispensable to it, in fact. After all, a belligerent must be made to fear for its life – to live in terror of death and destruction – if it is to surrender to the will of a violent enemy. The law of war permits this infliction of fear as long as it is proximately directed against only the enemy's combatants. The terror of war differs from that of contemporary "terrorism" chiefly in this respect. Yet increasing numbers of people appear to question the moral significance of this difference, as we see in examining the doctrine of "collateral damage" or "double effect." Bin Laden himself nonetheless invokes the doctrine occasionally, albeit selectively and opportunistically, as in response to criticism for killing fellow Muslims in many Al Qaeda attacks. "If the enemy occupies an Islamic land and uses its people as human shields, a person has the right to attack the enemy. In the same way, if some thieves broke into a house and took a child hostage to protect themselves, the father has the right to attack the thieves, even if the child gets hurt." Osama bin Laden, "The Example of Vietnam," Nov. 12, 2001, *in* Messages to the World: The Statements of Osama bin Laden, Bruce Lawrence, ed., James Howarth, trans. 139, 140 (2005).

25 The administration sometimes also employed the terms "the long war" and even – unabashedly quoting Osama bin Laden – the "third world war." At http://www.whitehouse.gov/news/releases/2005/06/20050628-7.html.

26 Waldron, *supra* note 4, at 1727.

27 *Id.* at 1702.

28 *Id.* at 1702.

29 *Id.* at 1726.

30 James Whitman, Harsh Justice: Criminal Punishment and the Widening Divide between America and Europe 24 (2003). *But see* Jean Hampton, "An Expressive Theory of Retribution," *in* Retributivism and its Critics, W. Clegg, ed. 14, 16 (1992) (contending that "punishment aims at resubjugating the subjugator").

31 Habermas accepts Kant's conclusion here and employs it in developing his own theory of international law. Jürgen Habermas, "Kant's Idea of Perpetual Peace, with the Benefit of Two Hundred Years' Hindsight," *in* Perpetual Peace: Essays in Kant's Cosmopolitan Ideal, James Bohman & Matthias Lutz-Bachmann, eds. 113, 147 (1997).

32 I owe this last thought to David Osipovich.

33 Whitman, *supra* note 30, at 8; *see also* Habermas, *supra* note 31, at 20–21.

34 Whitman, *supra* note 30, at 20; *see also* Habermas, *supra* note 31, at 30–31 (parsing the arguments of Gustav Radbruch and Friedrich Nietzsche that status degradation is the central feature of all serious punishment); Friedrich Nietzsche, The Birth of Tragedy and the Genealogy of Morals, Francis Golffing, trans. 196–97 (1956) (1887).

35 On the aesthetics of surrender, *see* Robin Wagner-Pacifici, The Art of Surrender: Decomposing Sovereignty at Conflict's End (2005).

36 Harold Garfinkel, "Conditions of Successful Degradation Ceremonies," 61 Amer. J. Sociol. 420 (1956) (defining a "status degradation ritual" as "any communicative work between persons whereby the public identity of an actor is transformed into something looked on as lower in the local scheme of social types"); *see also* Erving Goffman, Asylums (1961).

37 *See generally* Erving Goffman, Stigma: Notes on the Management of Spoiled Identity (1963).

38 The leading theoretical defenses of "shaming" as punishment are John Braithwaite, Crime, Shame and Reintegration (1989), and Daniel Kahan, "What Do Alternative Sanctions Mean?" 63 U. Chi. L. Rev. 591 (1996) (articulating views later abandoned in "What's Really Wrong with Shaming Sanctions," Yale Law School, Public Law Working Paper, No. 125, July 2006). On the popularity of shaming sanctions for misdemeanors, *see, e.g.,* Pam Belluck, "Forget Prisons, Americans Cry Out for the Pillory," New York Times, Oct. 4, 1998, at A5.

39 Durkheim would here respond, to be sure, that the pleasure that law-abiding people take in the punishment of criminals is simply the satisfaction we feel in affirming the collective conscience (i.e., the basic moral values shared among members of our community and enshrined in its criminal law). The sentiments one experiences when participating in a religious ritual are no different, for in both cases the enhanced feeling of solidarity with one's fellows is the true source of satisfaction. That punishment may sometimes require "putting down" another member of the community, because of his willful breach of its most sacred norms, is an unfortunate byproduct.

40 In a criminal prosecution, the process of degradation begins well before the defendant is incarcerated and may even be hardest on the white-collar offender. As one federal judge observes, "Pronouncing the sentence is not as injurious to the person, his relationship to the community, to his family, as the return of the indictment. A loss of credit, a loss of bank credit, a loss of friends, social status, occasionally loss of wife, members of family, children around the father." Kenneth Mann, Defending White Collar Crime 224 (1985) (quoting a federal judge).

41 David Garland, Punishment and Modern Society: A Study in Social Theory 227, 237 (1990).

42 *Id.* at 242 (summarizing a central theme in the work of Norbert Elias, Marja Spierenburg, Lawrence Stone, Keith Thomas, and John Beattie).

43 Amos Tversky & Daniel Kahneman, "Availability: A Heuristic for Judging Frequency and Probability," 5 Cognitive Psych. 207 (1973).

44 The elimination of torture may be partly explained in similar terms. Torture elicits a salient emotional response because of the immediate and severe pain it produces. One can easily picture it, even if Hollywood movies and television programs did not regularly do so. This salience would presumably lead people to overestimate the statistical frequency of the practice, which would in turn contribute to pressures for its legal prohibition. On the other hand, equally vivid in its mental imagery – for anyone who has seen them – are the x-ray photographs of the suicide bomber's victim, her thorax penetrated by dozens of nails. The mental image of the latter tends to reduce opposition to coercive interrogation, whereas the former image tends to increase it.

45 Garland, *supra* note 41, at 235.

46 *Id.* at 243.

47 *Id.* at 241.

48 "A man may have been lingering in prison for a month or two," Bentham wrote, "before he would make answer to a question which at the worst with one stroke of the rack, and therefore almost always with only knowing that he might be made to suffer the rack, he would have answered in a moment." Bentham and Legal Theory, M. H. James 45 (1973).

49 *Id.*

50 William Ian Miller, Humiliation 68 (1993).

51 Garland, *supra* note 41, at 244.

52 *Id.* at 227.

53 Convention Against Torture and Other Cruel, Inhuman, and Degrading Treatment and Punishment, 1465 U.N.T.S. 85 (1984), Art. 16.

54 Oxford English Dictionary Online, entry for the verb "degrade." *See also* Black's Law Dictionary, 7th ed. 435 (1999) (offering as the first of several definitions of degradation: "a reduction in rank, degree, or dignity").

55 O.E.D., *id.* Entry for "brutal."

56 Whitman, *supra* note 30, at 69–95.

57 Laurence Helfer, "Overlegalizing Human Rights: International Relations Theory and the Commonwealth Caribbean Backlash against Human Rights Regimes," 102 Colum. L. Rev. 1832 (2002).

58 The difficulties of devising such a form of punishment are discussed by Thomas Hill, Respect, Pluralism, and Justice: Kantian Perspectives 114–17 (2000).

59 A good place to begin such an argument would be a close examination of incarceration practices in the wealthiest Western European countries. Whitman, *supra* note 30, at 97–150 (describing *inter alia*, at 8 and 89, the one-month paid annual vacation from their jobs enjoyed by felons in Germany). Yet even Western Europe continued to practice torture in its colonies well into the twentieth century, as late as the Algerian War. Rita Maran, Torture: The Role of Ideology in the French-Algerian War (1989); *see generally* Ranabir Samaddar, Terror and the Materiality of Colonial Rule (2005); David Anderson, Histories of the

Hanged: Britain's Dirty War in Kenya and the End of Empire 292–93 (2005); Caroline Elkins, Imperial Reckoning: The Untold Story of Britain's Gulag in Kenya 244–59, 285–95, 312–32 (2005). Moreover, according to Whitman, the European effort to eliminate all social degradation from punishment apparently originates in some very hierarchical, statist, almost theocratic ideas – the *seigneur's* grace – that Americans could never endorse. Whitman, *supra* note 30, at 150.

60 *See* Douglas Laycock, Modern American Remedies 784–800 (2002).

61 Waldron, *supra* note 4, at 1728.

62 *See, e.g.,* Human Rights Watch, "Cruel and Degrading: The Use of Dogs for Cell Extractions in U.S. Prisons" (2006); Human Rights Watch, "Shielded from Justice: Police Brutality and Accountability in the U.S.," (1998); Amnesty International, U.S., "Ill-Treatment in Jails and Police Custody, at http://thereport. amnesty.org/eng/Regions/Americas/United-States-of-America; David Klinger, "The Micro-Structure of Nonlethal Force: Baseline Data from an Observational Study," 20 Crim. Justice Rev. 169 (1995); Anthony Pate & Lorie Fridell, "Toward the Uniform Reporting of Police Use of Force: Results of a National Survey," 20 Crim. Justice Rev. 123 (1995); Jerome Skolnick & James J. Fyfe, Above the Law: Police and the Excessive Use of Force (1993); for ethnographic accounts, *see* Robert Jackall, Wild Cowboys: Urban Marauders and the Forces of Order (1997); Robert Jackall, Street Stories: The World of Police Detectives (2005); Jamie Fellner, "Torture in U.S. Prisons," *in* Torture, Kenneth Roth et al., eds. 173 (2005).

63 Richard Leo, Police Interrogation and American Justice 15–16, 22–24, 41–77, 196, 237–273, 319 (2008); G. Daniel Lassiter & Jennifer Ratcliff, "Exposing Coercive Influences in the Criminal Justice System: An Agenda for Legal Psychology in the Twenty-First Century," *in* Interrogations, Confessions, & Entrapment, G. Daniel Lassiter, ed. 1 (2004); Richard Leo, "Inside the Interrogation Room," 86 J. Crim. L. & Criminology 266, 270, 282–84 (1996); Robert Jackall, Street Stories, *supra* note 62, at 47, 79–80, 109–17, 274–77, 314–15.

64 *See, e.g.,* Human Rights Watch, "'The Perverse Side of Things': Torture, Inadequate Detention Conditions, and Excessive Use of Force by Guinean Security Forces," Vol. 18, No. 7(A), Aug. 2006; Human Rights Watch, "'Rest in Pieces': Police Torture and Deaths in Custody in Nigeria," Vol. 17, No. 11(A), July 2005; Human Rights Watch, "Making Their Own Rules: Police Beatings, Rape, and Torture of Children in Papua New Guinea," Vol. 17, No. 8(C), Sept. 2005; Kenya Human Rights Commission, Mission to Repress: Torture, Illegal Detentions and Extra-Judicial Killings by the Kenyan Police 15–45 (1998).

65 Waldron here cites, as defending such a view, a single essay, by Austin Sarat & Thomas R. Kearns, "A Journey through Forgetting: Toward a Jurisprudence of Violence," *in* The Fate of Law, Austin Sarat & Thomas R. Kearns, eds. 209, 268–69 (1993).

66 Waldron, *supra* note 4, at 1727.

67 *Id.* at 1726–27.

68 *Id.* at 1728.

69 This is a Dworkinian term of art, describing a major goal of all legal interpretation.

70 An important statement of this position is Austin Sarat, "Legal Effectiveness and Social Studies of Law: On the Unfortunate Persistence of a Research Tradition," 9 Legal Studies Forum 23, 28 (1985). He argues, "Gap studies remystify the law by implying that the ideals of the law are indeed realizable. . . . By aiming to make the law more efficacious, they make it less resistible. . . . Having exposed the play of power, interest, or necessity in legal behavior and policy, they act as if power and interest are defects that can, with proper strategic thinking, be avoided."

71 He says only that those holding such views "will be unimpressed by the distinctions I am making." Waldron, *supra* note 4, at 1727. Quite. But this is hardly a response to those views, for it offers no reasons for his belief that they are misguided.

72 Waldron, *supra* note 4, at 1692.

73 This is admittedly a different variety of formalism than that of which Waldron accuses John Yoo.

74 Mike Allen, "A Stain on Our Country's Honor and Our Country's Reputation," Wash. Post, May 7, 2004, at A1 (quoting President Bush).

75 Susan Sontag, At the Same Time 136 (2007).

76 http://parenting.ivillage.com/familyentertainment_csm/games/0,,bom54kv 7,00.html;http://www.amazon.co.uk/Microsoft-Die-Hard Vendetta/dp/ B000065VUW; http://www.gamerwithin.com/index.php?view=article& article=1121&cat=5.

77 Sontag, *supra* note 75, at 136.

78 Whether these fantasies are unleashed or engendered is a point of disagreement, respectively, between Freud and Foucault. In a Freudian key, one would say that civilization entails not the elimination of aggressive impulses, which is impossible, but their sublimation. Impulses that could readily take criminal form and that we struggle successfully to purge from overt expression in our social behavior are nonetheless sometimes manifest in a "return of the repressed." The extraordinary popularity of violent video games – popular not just in the United States, by any means – may offer a telling illustration. *Cf.* Garland, *supra* note 41, at 239 ("The fact that criminals sometimes act out wishes which are present in the unconscious of law-abiding citizens may account for the deep fascination which crime holds for many, and for the widespread appeal of crime literature, crime news."). An effort to link such psychoanalytic concepts of instinctual repression to Foucault's account of "subject formation" in the modern liberal individual is offered by Judith Butler, The Psychic Life of Power 83–105 (1997).

79 Waldron, *supra* note 4, at 1703, 1710 (suggesting "that something sacred is being violated in the Bybee memorandum, in John Yoo's arguments, and in the proposal Alan Dershowitz invites us to consider").

80 *See, e.g., Syriana*, Warner Brothers Inc. (2005).

81 *See, e.g., The World Is Not Enough: James Bond*, Metro-Goldwyn- Mayer (1999).

82 Senator Joseph Lieberman, Feb. 14, 2008, quoted in Human Rights First, Law and Security Digest, Feb. 15, 2008. In a similar spirit, Steven Bradbury, Acting Chief of the Justice Department's Office of Legal Counsel remarked concerning waterboarding, "Something can be quite distressing, uncomfortable, even

frightening . . . [but] if it doesn't involve severe physical pain, and it doesn't last very long, it may not constitute severe physical suffering" as encompassed by legal definitions of torture. Human Rights First, Law and Security Digest, Feb. 22, 2008.

83 Morton Horwitz, The Transformation of American Law: The Crisis of Legal Orthodoxy 193–212 (1992); Mark Osiel, "Dialogue with Dictators: Judicial Resistance in Argentina and Brazil," 20 Law & Soc. Inquiry 481, 506–10 (1995) (illustrating the use of realist modes of legal reasoning by judicial apologists for authoritarian rulers).

84 Jeremy Waldron, The Dignity of Legislation 2 (1999); Waldron, Law and Disagreement 21–68 (1999).

85 Eric Posner & Adrian Vermeule, Terror in the Balance: Security, Liberty and the Courts 273–75 (2007).

86 Posner & Vermeule, *supra* note 17, at 692.

87 Waldron, *supra* note 4, at 1716.

88 *Id.* at 1695–1701, 1716. On account of such legal ambiguity, CIA and especially military officials for a time ceased their use of several methods of interrogation on terrorist suspects. Douglas Jehl & David Johnston, "C.I.A. Expands Its Inquiry into Interrogation Tactics," New York Times, Aug, 29, 2004; A. John Radsan, "The Collision between Common Article Three and the Central Intelligence Agency," 56 Cath. U.L. Rev. 959, 962, 994–95 (2007). Jack Goldsmith, The Terror Presidency 170 (2007) ("I witnessed top officials and bureaucrats in the White House and throughout the government openly worrying that investigators, acting with the benefit of hindsight in a different political environment, would impose criminal penalties on heat-of-battle judgment calls."). In 2002, the FBI opened a "war crimes file" for accumulating evidence of detainee mistreatment by the military and CIA. Eric Lictblau & Scott Shane, "Report Details Dissent on Guantánamo Tactics," New York Times, May 21, 2008.

89 Philippe Sands, Torture Team: Rumsfeld's Memo and The Betrayal of American Values 217 (2008).

90 Author's confidential interviews with JAG sources.

91 *Harlow v. Fitzgerald*, 457 U.S. 800 (1982).

92 Jaykumar Menon, "Guantánamo Torture Litigation," 6 J. Int'l Crim. Justice 323 (2008).

93 *Rasul v. Rumsfeld*, 414 F. Supp. 2d 26, 41–44 (D.D.C. 2006). The pending case is *Al Odah v. U.S.*, 127 S. Ct. 3067 (2007), granting cert.

94 Mark Osiel, Obeying Orders: Atrocity, Military Discipline, & the Law of War 71–90 (1999).

95 *See, e.g.,* Associated Press, "House Votes to Ban Harsh C.I.A. Methods," New York Times, Dec. 13, 2007 (describing a bill expressly prohibiting a variety of specifically described acts, closely resembling those uncovered in the Abu Ghraib scandal).

96 Mark Mazzetti, "'03 Memo Approved Harsh Interrogations," New York Times, April 2, 2008, at A1.

97 Stephanie Nebehay, "Top State Dept. Lawyer Seeks U.S. Clarity on Torture," Wash. Post, Nov. 27, 2007 (quoting John Bellinger).

CHAPTER 5. FAIRNESS IN TERRORIST WAR (1):
RAWLSIAN RECIPROCITY

1 Michael N. Schmitt, "Targeting and Humanitarian Law: Current Issues," 34 Israel Yearbook on Human Rights 59, 93 (2004).

2 As one author notes, rules of warfare that confine its legitimate targets to official combatants "allow for a 'fair fight' by protecting the utterly defenseless from assault." Henry Shue, "Torture," 7 Phil. & Pub. Aff. 124, 129 (1978).

3 This is the wording of Britain's reservation to the Geneva Additional Protocol I prohibition on civilian reprisals, in Art. 51(8). At http://www.icrc.org/Web/eng/siteengo.nsf/iwpList166/A06D567EA584477CC1256B66005B94B8.

4 Larry May, War Crimes and Just War 128 (2007) (quoting Alberico Gentili).

5 Hugo Grotius, *in* The Classics of International Law, trans. Francis W. Kelsey 649, 655–66 (1925).

6 *Id.* at 652.

7 This is the current formulation of the rule, from Art. 37 of the Geneva Additional Protocol I.

8 Emmerich de Vattel, Le Droit des Gens (1758), *reprinted in* The Classics of International Law, Charles Fenwick, trans. 289 (1916).

9 Military historiography and security studies long assumed that every war must have a winner and loser, an assumption that is now the focal point of much scholarly critique. *See, e.g.,* Understanding Victory and Defeat in Contemporary War, Jan Ganstrom & Isabelle Duyvesteyn, eds. (2007); William C. Martel, Victory in War: Foundations of Modern Military Policy 3–12 (2007); Elaine Scarry, The Body in Pain: The Making and Unmaking of the World 111–19 (1985). This critique is now seriously entertained even in certain elite military-intellectual circles. *See, e.g.,* J. Boone Bartholomees, "Theory of Victory," 38 Parameters 25 (Summer 2008). But if certain wars have no true victors, then several concepts central to the law of war could require considerable revision, if they could be preserved at all. Consider, for instance, the national decision to resort to force and the *jus ad bellum* governing that decision. Here, whether a particular measure of force and attendant collateral damage are "excessive" or "disproportionate" in relation to what victory requires may become a meaningless question if there is no true victory to be had. On the other hand, just as both sides may lose, in certain respects, each may also win desired concessions from the other through military force, i.e., force short of complete military "victory." In this sense, both may be winners. Bartholomees, *id.* at 36.

Yet to say that a country that has prevailed "on the battlefield" is not truly a victor may be simply to say that it has incurred disproportionate costs in relation to what it has gained, apart from the costs it has also inflicted on its adversary. This claim may be entirely compatible with the standard *jus ad bellum* proportionality analysis in which military and civilian leaders routinely engage. *See generally* A.J. Coates, The Ethics of War 167–88 (1997). Or it might require a broader conception of relevant "costs."' In either event, "victory" might legitimately have quite distinct meanings in legal versus nonlegal discourse, even if the two conceptions partly overlap. In *ex post* judicial assessment of military decisions gone awry, the law should take cognizance of such novel conceptions of victory and defeat without adopting them unreflectively.

10 One thoughtful effort to devise criteria of success in counterinsurgency warfare includes such factors as "longevity of friendly local leaders in positions of authority, number and quality of tip-offs on insurgent activity that originate spontaneously from the population, economic activity in public markets." David Kilcullen, "Twenty-Eight Articles: Fundamentals of Company-Level Counterinsurgency," March 2006, at http://www.smallwarsjournal.com/documents/28articles.pdf., at 7; on the enduring difficulties in measuring success; however, *see* James Clancy & Chuck Crossett, "Measuring Effectiveness in Irregular Warfare," 37 Parameters 88, 91 (Summer 2007); Colin Gray, "Defining and Achieving Decisive Victory," Strategic Studies Institute, U.S. Army War College (2002); Jim Baker, "Systems Thinking and Counterinsurgencies," 36 Parameters 26, 38–42 (Winter 2006–07).

11 Ken Booth, Strategy and Ethnocentrism 133 (1979).

12 For instance, the families of the four Blackwater contractors killed in Falluja, Iraq, during 2004 sued the company, alleging wrongful death. Bill Berkowitz, "Scahill's 'Blackwater' Exposes U.S. Mercenary Army," Interpress Service, Global Information Network, July 2, 2007.

13 The opposite of "unnecessary suffering" is suffering entailed by "military necessity." Despite its seemingly stringent moniker, however, this latter legal concept has been interpreted with great indulgence, as "permit[ing] a belligerent . . . to apply any amount and kind of force to compel the complete submission of the enemy with the least possible expenditures of time, life, and money." *U.S. v. List, in* Trials of War Criminals Before the Nuremberg Military Tribunals Under Control Council Law No. 10, 1253–54 (1949).

14 John Rawls, A Theory of Justice 136–42 (1971). For one effort to deduce fair rules of humanitarian law through such Rawlsian methodology, *see* Mark Osiel, Trying Tyrants: Making Sense of Mass Atrocity (2009). Rawls himself says only that "peoples are to observe certain specified restrictions in the conduct of war," listing this among several "familiar and traditional principles of justice among free and democratic peoples." John Rawls, The Law of Peoples 37 (1999). Rawls surely does not mean by this, however, that such "restrictions" should apply only in military conflicts "among free and democratic peoples," but also those involving "decent" but illiberal peoples.

15 Only recently would anyone have even thought to consider the views of the victims among noncombatants. Their participation could much affect the resulting rules. For instance, the belligerents' decision makers might select rules authorizing retaliation with weapons of mass destruction against the population centers of an adversary who first employed such methods against their own civilian population. But it is unlikely that members of either civilian population would themselves choose such a rule. Historically, the law of war concentrated on protecting combatants. Only in the 1949 version of the Geneva Conventions did civilian protections extend beyond a prohibition on their direct targeting.

16 All quotations in this paragraph and the next are from Rawls, Theory of Justice, *supra* note 14, at 494–95. Rawls even roots the inclination toward reciprocity in evolutionary biology. *Id.* at 495, citing biologists themselves. Robert Trivers, "The Evolution of Reciprocal Altruism," 46 Quart. Rev. Biology 35 (1971) (finding that several species, including bats, may be observed to reciprocate helpful

and unhelpful behavior); Robert Trivers, "Reciprocal Altruism: Thirty Years Later," *in* Cooperation in Primates and Humans, Peter Kappeler & Carel van Schaik, eds. 67 (2006); Jonathan Haidt, The Happiness Hypothesis 50 (2006) (concluding on the basis of diverse laboratory experiments by social and cognitive psychologists that "tit for tat appears to be built into human nature"); Samuel Bowles & Herbert Gintis, "Is Equality Passé? *Homo Reciprocans* and the Future of Egalitarian Politics," Boston Rev. 1, 14 (Jan. 1999) (acknowledging "the unsustainability of egalitarian programs that violate norms of reciprocity"). To be sure, membership in the moral community cannot be entirely restricted to those capable of reciprocating, insofar as we owe any duties to mentally retarded persons or to animals, a question later discussed at greater length. Allen Buchanan, "Justice as Reciprocity versus Subject-Centered Justice," 19 Phil. & Pub. Aff. 227, 230 (1990); Henry Richardson, "Rawlsian Social-Contract Theory and the Severely Disabled," 10 J. of Polit. Phil. 419, 435–30 (2006).

17 Ronald Dworkin, Law's Empire 198–99 (1986). Dworkin characteristically adds that duties of reciprocity also require "interpretation," in that within an associative relationship there may exist little accord over "what sort and level of sacrifice one may be expected to make for another."

18 John Rawls, Political Liberalism 16–17 (1993).

19 *Id.* at 49.

20 John Rawls, unpublished paper, cited in Gregory Keating, "Reasonableness and Rationality in Negligence Theory," 48 Stan. L. Rev. 311, 319 (1996).

21 Rawls, *supra* note 18, at 50.

22 Samuel Freeman, Rawls 348 (2007). Freeman calls this "reciprocity of advantage," as distinguished from mere "mutual advantage" of the Hobbesian or market-exchange varieties. *Id.* at 374–75. *See also* Brian Barry, Justice as Impartiality 59 (1995); Michael Sandel, Liberalism and the Limits of Justice 112 (1979) (showing how, in Rawls's account of justice, "there is no contradiction in a contract argument producing principles that limit the justificatory role of contract," i.e., of actual contracts as social facts). Rawls's view of reciprocity may be contrasted, in this respect, with that of David Gauthier, Morals by Agreement 187–89, 294 (1986), who views agreements as reciprocal when derived from the parties' self-interested rationality. When the latter variety of party reciprocates, it is not on account of any perceived moral obligation to do so. The difference here between Rawls and Gauthier largely mirrors that between sociologists and economists, respectively, in their understanding of reciprocity. Susana Narotzky & Paz Moreno, "Reciprocity's Dark Side: Negative Reciprocity, Morality and Social Reproduction," 2 Anthropological Theory 281, 285 (2002).

23 *Compare* John Rawls, A Theory of Justice 490–96 (1971), *with* John Rawls, Political Liberalism 16–17, 50 (1993). Whereas the first book describes reciprocity as a "psychological law" governing relations between individuals and small groups, the second is concerned largely with a more generalized reciprocity, as "a relation between the citizens of a well-ordered society expressed by its public, political conception of justice. Here . . . justice . . . formulate[s] an idea of reciprocity between citizens." For commentary on this transition in Rawls's thinking, *see* Martin Hollis, Trust within Reason 148–49 (1998). For

differing views on the importance of reciprocity in Rawls's later thought, *see* Jean Hampton, "Does Rawls Have a Social Contract Theory?" 77 J. of Phil. 315 (1980); Richardson, *supra* note 16, at 425–30. Rawls' earliest thinking on the subject is a paper from 1960 entitled "Justice as Reciprocity," *in* Collected Papers, Samuel Freeman, ed. 190 (1999).

24 Rawls, *supra* note 18, at 50 ("Reasonable persons...insist that reciprocity should hold within that world so that each benefits along with the others.").

25 John Rawls, Justice as Fairness: A Restatement 6 (2001).

26 Hollis, *supra* note 23, at 144. *See also* Thomas Franck, The Power of Legitimacy among Nations 199–200 (1990).

27 Hollis, *supra* note 23, at 144.

28 Admittedly, "returning good for good is something we generally can celebrate, whereas returning bad for bad is a dangerous and complex practice that no society can simply celebrate." David Schmidtz, Elements of Justice 80 (2007). That a practice is not "celebrated," however, need not mean that it is unfair or ineffective in restoring cooperation, as through the "forgiving" punishment of tit-for-tat. That it is also "dangerous" may simply mean that it must be employed cautiously, to avoid self-perpetuating cycles of revenge.

29 Ernst Fehr & Urs Fischbacher, "The Economics of Strong Reciprocity," *in* Moral Sentiments and Material Interests: The Foundations of Cooperation in Economic Life, Herbert Gintis et al., 151, 153 (2005).

30 Robert Delahunty, "Paper Charter: and the Failure of the United Nations Collective Security System," 56 Cath. U. L. Rev. 871, 903–08 (2007) (contending that "if . . . the failure of the Charter's collective security system entitles member states to resume at least some of their pre-Charter *jus ad bellum* rights, then states should indeed be free to develop a new customary norm of 'reasonable' reprisal").

31 There is good reason why the betrayal of the UN's promise of collective security troubles semi-authoritarian states – still a substantial portion of the world – rather less than such true constitutional democracies as the U.S. and U.K. Autocrats routinely dishonor the domestic promise, inherent in the liberal social contract, to provide personal security (and other individual rights) in exchange for the public's law-abidingness. They do so without allowing that the state's breach of its duties here absolves citizens from their side of the bargain. Reciprocity of the sort embodied in the liberal democratic state – with its standard exchange of public obedience for security in personal rights (civil, political, and social) – is simply not the manner in which highly repressive regimes sustain themselves. If one can say that there exists a social contract at all in such countries, it is a strictly Hobbesian one: unqualified subordination to the state in exchange for a life that, though by no means free or prosperous, is at least no longer "nasty, brutish and short." In the provision of collective security, however, the UN fails to perform even this core state function. This failure to provide collective security in exchange for the legal demand that UN members eschew previously permissible uses of force is just what repressive states and their citizens would have come to expect of governing institutions. This is no less true of international governance than of domestic. One should not deny that many democratic states nonetheless continue to place much hope,

if not necessarily confidence, in the UN for purposes unrelated to collective security from armed attack, though there is no strong reason why many of these functions need be performed by that particular organization.

32　Larry May, The Law of Aggression 395 (Cambridge University Press, forthcoming).

33　Many areas of domestic law, moreover, allow parties to choose the rules that will govern their relationships, including competitive relationships, and even their relations with the state, as in the alternative methods permitted for computing one's taxes.

34　Rawls, Theory of Justice, *supra* note 14, at 152–57.

35　*Id.* at 23, 137, 162, 323.

36　Al Qaeda's leaders, unlike its suicidal followers, display considerable calculation. This is true even though they also evince a "hallucinatory" side, suggesting that they are "living somewhat disconnected from reality," according to close students of their public statements. Stephen Holmes, "Al Qaeda, September 11, 2001,) *in* Making Sense of Suicide Missions, Diego Gambetta, ed. 131, 157 (2005). The worldview from which their understanding of self-interest (in salvation) is derived ultimately rests on a principled rejection of Western, secular notions of rationality itself. Roxanne L. Euben, Enemy in the Mirror: Islamic Fundamentalism and the Limits of Modern Rationalism 84–88 (1999) (parsing the works of Sayyid Qutb, who was highly influential in the intellectual formation of jihadist militance).

37　Rawls's theory has often been criticized on such grounds. Michael Sandel, *supra* note 22, at 159–161.

38　This refusal to occupy the same society with one's opponent is sometimes even described as a defining feature of terrorism. *See, e.g.,* Matthew N. Smith, "Terrorism, Shared Rules, and Trust," 16 J. of Polit. Phil. 201, 215–16 (2008).

39　Perry Anderson, "Arms and Rights: The Adjustable Center," *in* Anderson, Spectrum 140, 165 (2005) (parsing Rawls). Saudi Arabia's commitment to the Wahhabist interpretation of Islam requires its classification as traditionalist, rather than simply traditional, a distinction introduced by S. N. Eisenstadt, Tradition, Change and Modernity 156 (1973) (defining traditionalism as the selective reclamation of longstanding legitimating symbols and doctrines as protection against new cultural systems and ideas perceived as threatening). Traditionalism, thus understood, is entirely compatible with the equally selective adoption of Western technologies and organizational forms for attaining its political objectives. *See, e.g.,* Juan Cole, "The Modernity of Theocracy," *in* Cole, Sacred Space and Holy War 189–247 (2002); on Wahhabism, *see* Khaled Abou El Fadl, "9/11 and the Muslim Transformation," *in* September 11 in History, Mary Dudziak, ed. 70, 89–94 (2003).

40　Rawls, Law of Peoples, *supra* note 14, at 12–15.

41　Anderson, *supra* note 39, at 165 (parsing Rawls).

42　Jürgen Habermas, The Past as Future 119–20 (1994).

43　Rawls, Law of Peoples, *supra* note 14, at 121.

44　*See, e.g.,* Fernando Tesón, A Philosophy of International Law 109–22 (1998); Brian Barry, Theories of Justice 183–89 (1989); Charles Beitz, Political Theory and International Relations 125–53 (1979); Thomas Pogge, Realizing Rawls 211–80 (1990); David Richards, "International Distributive Justice," 24 Nomos 275 (1982).

45 Rawls, Theory of Justice, *supra* note 14, at 126–30. Rawls borrows the idea from David Hume, Enquiries Concerning Human Understanding and Concerning the Principles of Morals, §III, pt. I (1975) (1751).

46 This inference from Rawls's theory has led several theorists to explore the interdependence necessary to create circumstances of justice, as between rich and poor nation-states. *See, e.g.,* Charles Beitz, Political Theory and International Relations 150–53 (1979); A.J. Julius, "Nagel's Justice," 34 Phil. & Pub. Aff. 176, 190 (2006).

47 David Mapel, "The Contractarian Tradition and International Ethics," *in* Traditions of International Ethics, Terry Nardin & David Mapel, eds. 180, 181 (1992) ("Contractarians have viewed reliable expectations of reciprocity . . . as a necessary condition of social and political justice.").

48 Gary Bunt, Islam in the Digital Age: E-Jihād, Online Fatwās and Cyber Islamic Environments (2003).

49 This calls to mind the irresistible observation, long ascribed to Lenin, that "when it comes time to hang the capitalists, they will sell us the rope." The quotation is apocryphal, however, according to the Oxford Dictionary of Quotations, Antony Jay, ed. 254 (2001). Lenin said much the same thing, but in much more labored and turgid prose, unworthy of quotation.

50 Quoted in David Kilcullen, "Countering Global Insurgencies," at http://www.smallwarsjournal.com/documents/kilcullen.pdf, at 3. Massawi, speaking in July 2006, was here referring to the state of Israel specifically, not more generally of the United States or the West. The Hamas covenant expressly states that no peaceful solution is possible with the state of Israel.

51 *See, e.g.,* Anonymous, Imperial Hubris: Why the West is Losing the War on Terror 207 (2004); Anonymous, Through Our Enemy's Eyes: Osama bin Laden, Radical Islam and the Future of America (2001) (the author of both books is Michael Scheuer, former head of the CIA unit charged with tracking bin Laden); Ian Shapiro, Containment: Rebuilding a Strategy against Global Terror 43–44, 85 (2007); Zbigniew Brzezinski, Second Chance: Three Presidents and the Crisis of American Superpower 150–52 (2007); Chalmers Johnson, Nemesis: The Last Days of the American Republic 2 (2006); Robert Pape, Dying to Win: The Strategic Logic of Suicide Terrorism 21, 242–43 (2006).

52 Andrew F. March, "Islamic Foundations for a Social Contract in non-Muslim Liberal Democracies," 101 Amer. Polit. Sci. Rev. 235, 242 (2007)

53 As Pagden observes, for certain Muslims, "alas, often for those who are most intent on making themselves heard, all that this talk of dialogue and understanding amounts to is yet another form of westernization. Who says that tolerance, dialogue, and understanding are virtues? The answer is invariably: secular Westerners. The religion of the Prophet is not one of polite conversation. It is one of submission – that, after all, is what the words 'Islam' and 'Muslim' refer to. To believe otherwise is to fall into the same trap that Napoleon, with his blend of Islam and the Rights of Man, had hoped to set for the Egyptians. Coat your modern godless beliefs with enough Qur'anic sugar, and sooner or

later, once the poor Muslims have been persuaded to embrace equality, individual freedom, self-expression, rights and all those other shibboleths of Western society, they will come to see just how crude, brutal, and primitive their old ways always were." Anthony Pagden, Worlds at War: The 2,500 Year Struggle between East and West 517–18 (2008).

54 Cass Sunstein, "Incompletely Theorized Agreements," 108 Harv. L. Rev. 1773 (1995).

55 Rawls, Theory of Justice, *supra* note 14, at 3, 586.

56 Sandel, *supra* note 22, at 34.

57 *Id.* at 35 (parsing Rawls).

58 *Id.*

59 Rawls, Law of Peoples, *supra* note 14, at 81.

60 Immanuel Kant, "Perpetual Peace," *in* Kant: Political Writings, Hans Reiss, ed. 98 (1991); on Kant's punitiveness in this regard, *see* Jürgen Habermas, "Kant's Idea of Perpetual Peace, with the Benefit of Two Hundred Years' Hindsight," *in* Perpetual Peace: Essays in Kant's Cosmopolitan Ideal, James Bohman & Matthias Lutz-Bachmann, eds. 113, 147 (1997).

61 Bonnie Honig, Political Theory and the Displacement of Politics 137–45 (1993) (discussing the implications of Rawls's theory for practices of punishment within a just society).

62 *Id.* at 137.

63 This view of the state of nature is shared by social contract theorists as otherwise very different as Hobbes and Locke.

64 I owe most of the ideas and some formulations in this and the next two paragraphs to David Osipovich.

CHAPTER 6. FAIRNESS IN TERRORIST WAR (2): KANTIAN RECIPROCITY

1 R.A. Duff, Punishment, Communication, and Community 23 (2001); Susan Dimock, "Retribution and Trust," 16 Law & Phil. 37 (1997).

2 On how humanitarian law depends on some modicum of trust among military adversaries, *see* Matthew N. Smith, "Terrorism, Shared Rules, and Trust," 16 J. of Polit. Phil. 201 (2008).

3 Duff, *supra* note 1, at 21. In the quoted passage, Duff is describing views he himself does not hold. On the account he offers, it does not matter that the captured criminal may have failed to gain any actual advantage, as this is not a consequentialist rationale for penal sanction. "The advantage that the criminal gains in breaking the law consists not in any material consequences of the crime but in that freedom from self-restraint that is intrinsic to the crime." Conversely, then, "the removal of that advantage is not a contingent effect of punishment but intrinsic to punishment itself." *Id.* This rationale applies to punishment for certain types of wrongs much more than for others, as several have observed. The prohibition of rape, for instance, is not readily amenable to justification by way of this rationale.

4 John Gardner, Offences and Defenses: Selected Essays in the Philosophy of Criminal Law 220 (2007) (arguing "that the control of reprisal" by the victims of crime "is a central pillar of the criminal law's justification").

5 James Fitzjames Stephen, Liberty, Equality, Fraternity 10 (1993) (1873).

6 They may even be said to "consent" to punishment in that "if the criminal chooses not to sacrifice by exercising self-restraint . . . this is tantamount to choosing to sacrifice in another way – namely, by paying the prescribed penalty." Jeffrey Murphy, "Marxism and Retribution," 2 Phil. & Pub. Aff. 217, 228 (1993); *see generally* Carlos Nino, The Ethics of Human Rights 268–83 (1991).

7 Henry Shue, "Torture," 7 Phil. & Pub. Aff. 124, 136, 141 (1978).

8 Elaine Scarry, The Body in Pain: The Making and Unmaking of the World 330 (1985). She adds that "those who do confess are not dishonored by and should not be dishonored for their act." *Id.*

9 David Sussman, "What's Wrong with Torture?," 33 Phil. & Pub. Aff. 1, 18 (2005).

10 This famous statement, though universally attributed to Meir, has no authoritative source and is worded somewhat differently in several citations. For another formulation, *see* Jessica Gribetz, Wise Words: Jewish Thoughts and Stories through the Ages 182 (1997).

11 Charles Fried, An Anatomy of Values: Problems of Personal and Social Choice 183–206 (1970) (parsing and applying Kant). An influential analysis of reciprocity in terms of risk symmetry is George Fletcher, "Fairness and Utility in Tort Theory," 85 Harv. L. Rev. 537 (1972). In its focus on fairness, Kantian reciprocity differs from the sort reflected in relations of patron-client or tribal gift exchange, which are often highly inegalitarian, but to which social scientists often nonetheless apply the same term, "reciprocity." Zeba Cook, "Reciprocity: Covenantal Exchange as a Test Case," *in* Ancient Israel: The Old Testament in its Social Context, Philip Esler, ed. 78, 83–87 (2006). There is some disagreement over the extent of Kant's commitment, in his Metaphysical Elements of Justice, to reciprocity as the rationale for punishment. Prominent proponents of this reading, and defenders of this normative stance, include Herbert Morris, John Finnis, George Sher, Andrew von Hirsch, and Herbert Fingarette. *See, e.g.,* Jeffrey Murphy, Retribution, Justice, and Therapy 58–93 (1978); opponents include, *inter alia*, M. Margaret Falls, "Retribution, Reciprocity, and Respect for Persons," 6 Law & Phil. 25, 32–38 (1987).

12 Third Geneva Convention, Art. 102.

13 Jules Coleman, Risks and Wrongs 254 (1992).

14 Gregory Keating, "The Idea of Fairness in the Law of Enterprise Liability," 95 Mich. L. Rev. 1266, 1310 (1997). *See generally* Christine Korsgaard, Creating the Kingdom of Ends 188–97, 215 (1996) (discussing Kant's views on reciprocity).

15 George Kateb, The Inner Ocean: Individualism and Democratic Culture 5 (1992).

16 This interpretation is consistent with Kant's view of punishment's purpose as retributive.

17 On this key difference between Kant and Rawls, *see* Michael Sandel, Liberalism and the Limits of Justice 35–46 (1982). For Rawls, the original position encompasses "circumstances of justice" – reasonable persons displaying only limited altruism, moderate scarcity, the necessity and possibility of cooperation among all, shared desire for certain "primary goods," and so forth. John Rawls, A Theory of Justice 126–30 (1971). These same circumstances must continue to

exist in order to apply the principles of justice, derived from behind the veil of ignorance, to policy and conduct in the actual, phenomenal world. In anything that can plausibly be called a "society," this requirement is generally easy to meet; in fact, it is virtually definitional for Rawls: "A human society is *characterized by* the circumstances of justice." *Id.* at 129–30 (emphasis supplied). Kant's method and resulting moral maxims acknowledge no such limitation on their scope of application. Immanuel Kant, Groundwork of the Metaphysics of Morals, H. J. Paton, trans. 106–09 (1956) (1785).

18 I owe the ideas in this paragraph to David Osipovich.

19 Louise Richardson, What Terrorists Want: Understanding the Enemy, Containing the Threat 204–05 (2006).

20 Shue, *supra* note 7, at 124.

21 Sussman, *supra* note 9, at 6–7.

22 The severe limitations of this perennial hypothetical as a guide to legal policy are rightly stressed by David Luban, "Liberalism, Torture, and the Ticking Bomb," 91 Va. L. Rev. 1425 (2005); Kim Lane Scheppele, "Hypothetical Torture in the 'War on Terrorism,'" 1 J. National Sec. L. & Pol'cy 285 (2005). The seductive power of the hypo over the imagination of so many is disconcerting and difficult to explain, as well as frustrating, considering how rarely this situation occurs. The difficulty of moving conversation beyond this hypothetical, scarcely less in university settings than before wider audiences, ultimately led me to abandon all efforts to discuss its arguments in public, where open discussion almost immediately displaced them with demands for greater attention to the ticking bomb scenario. Still, as John Yoo rightly retorts, there is no need to rely on any imaginary thought experiment with respect to known, high-ranking Al Qaeda detainees like Khalid Sheikh Mohammed, for whom virtually every element of the "hypothetical" is, in all likelihood, straightforwardly satisfied.

23 Sussman, *supra* note 9, at 16.

24 Paul Kahn, "The Paradox of Riskless Warfare," 22 Phil. & Pub. Pol'cy Quart. 2, 3 (2002); *see also* Michael Carlino, "The Moral Limits of Strategic Attack," 32 Parameters 15, 16 (Spring 2002) ("the reason for the difference [between law's treatment of combatants and civilians] involves an exchange of rights between combatants – namely the rights to kill and be killed.")

25 H. L. A. Hart, "Are There Any Natural Rights?" 64 Philosophical Rev. 175, 191 (1955). *See also* Kent Greenawalt, Conflicts of Law and Morality 176 (1989) (noting that "the notion of reciprocation . . . lies close to a formulation of a duty of fair play").

26 *Id.* at 185. *See also* George Klosko, The Principle of Fairness and Political Obligation 34 (1992).

27 Human Rights Watch, "Russia: Three Months of War in Chechnya," HRW Index No. D706, Feb. 1995.

28 Immanuel Kant, Doctrine of Virtue: Part II of the Metaphysics of Morals, Mary Gregor, trans. 462 (1964).

29 For discussion, *see, e.g.,* Chris Downes, "'Targeted Killings' in an Age of Terror: The Legality of the Yemen Strike," 9 J. Conflict & Security L. 277, 291 (2004). Downes contends that because Ali Qaed Senyan "al-Harathi was tracked for months and was far from any . . . target when he was struck [that] alternative

action, such as arrest, was certainly conceivable." Downes nonetheless concedes that "Al-Harathi was traveling in a car carrying arms and explosives," and "was therefore engaged 'in a military operation preparatory to an attack." *Id.* at 284. He even acknowledges that "it would be possible to conceive the car itself a legitimate military objective whose destruction offered 'a definite military advantage.'" *Id.*

30 Louise Doswald-Beck, "The Right to Life in Armed Conflict: Does International Humanitarian Law Provide All the Answers?" 88 Int'l Rev. of the Red Cross 890, 903 (Dec. 2006).

31 Steven Ratner, "The War on Terrorism and International Humanitarian Law," 14 Mich. St. J. Int'l L. 19, 21–22 (2006) ("We cannot have a legal regime where only one side of combatants benefits from the protection of international humanitarian law.").

32 *Id.* at 24.

33 Jack Goldsmith, "The Self-Defeating International Criminal Court," 70 U. Chi. L. Rev. 89, 91–95 (2003).

34 Final Report To The Prosecutor By the Committee Established To Review the NATO Bombing Campaign Against The Federal Republic of Yugoslavia (2000), at http://www.un.org/icty/pressreal/nato061300.htm.

35 One scholar has nonetheless argued that, notwithstanding Art. 12(3)'s wording, the provision "should be interpreted subject to the principle of reciprocity that applies as a general rule of public international law: the complaining state cannot invoke the jurisdiction of the I.C.C. for others without subjecting the conduct of its own forces to investigation." Johan D. van der Vyver, "International Justice and the International Criminal Court: Beyond Sovereignty and the Rule of Law," 18 Emory Int'l L. Rev. 133, 139 (2004). The Vienna Convention on the Law of Treaties, in Art. 35, further provides that a treaty cannot impose an obligation on a third-party state unless that state "expressly accepts that obligation in writing."

36 Col. William Lietzau, "The U.S. and the International Criminal Court: International Criminal Law after Rome," 64 L. & Contemp. Prob. 119, 129 (2001).

37 Goldsmith, *supra* note 33, at 89.

38 *Opinions of the Lords of Appeal for Judgment in the Cause, Regina v. Bartle and the Commissioner of Police for the Metropolis and Others, Ex Parte Pinochet*, at http://www.parliament.the-stationery-office.co.uk/pa/ld199899/ldjudgmt/jd981125/pino01.htm.

39 For an argument against such jurisdiction, *see* Luc Reydams, Universal Jurisdiction: International and Municipal Perspectives 220 26 (2004).

40 This concern is vigorously raised by ICJ President M. Guillaume in his Separate Opinion in Case Concerning the Arrest Warrant of 11 April 2000 (*Democratic Republic of the Congo v. Belgium*), I.C.J. Gen List No. 121, 14 Feb. 2002, at ¶ 15 (arguing that universal jurisdiction would "risk creating judicial chaos. It would also be to encourage the arbitrary for the benefit of the powerful purportedly acting as agent for an ill-defined 'international community'").

41 In many cases, it is also the *de facto* power of apparent transgressors and the states they served, of course, which prevents their effective prosecution under the formal regime of universal jurisdiction.

42 Andrew Guzman, "The Design of International Agreements," (November 2004). U.C. Berkeley Public Law Research Paper No. 487662. At http://ssrn.com/abstract=487662; Kal Raustiala, "Form and Substance in International Agreements," 99 A.J.I.L. 581–614 (2005); Barbara Koremenos et al., "The Rational Design of International Institutions," 55 Int'l Org. 761 (2001); Scott Barrett, Environment and Statecraft: The Strategy of Environmental Treaty-Making (2003); George Downs, et al., "The Transformational Model of International Regime Design: Triumph of Hope or Experience?" 38 Colum. J. Transnat'l L. 465 (2000).

43 This is particularly true of the Basel Accord on Capital Adequacy. Daniel E. Ho, "Compliance and International Soft Law: Why Do Countries Implement the Basel Accord?" 5 J. Int'l Econ. L. 647 (2002). The Helsinki Final Act was similarly important, on many accounts, in defining common standards for galvanizing human rights advocacy within the former Soviet bloc. Erika B. Schlager, "A Hard Look at Compliance with Soft Law: The Case of the OSCE," *in* Commitment and Compliance: The Role of Non-Binding Norms in the International Legal System, Dinah Shelton, ed. 346 (2000);

44 *See supra*, Introduction, at 11.

45 Alex Wendt, Social Theory of International Politics 360–61 (1999).

46 I refer here especially to the 1949 Conventions, as some of the world's major military powers have not ratified the 1977 Protocols.

47 Oona Hathaway, "Do Human Rights Treaties Make a Difference?" 111 Yale L.J. 1935, 1951–52 (2002).

48 David Schmidtz, Elements of Justice 101 (2007).

49 Kant is the source most often invoked for this stance. For contemporary authors adopting variations of it, *see e.g.*, Ronald Dworkin, Sovereign Virtue 1–6 (2000); Allen Buchanan, "Justice as Reciprocity versus Subject-Centered Justice," 19 Phil. & Pub. Aff. 227, 231–35 (1990).

50 Allan Gibbard, Wise Choices, Apt Feelings: A Theory of Normative Judgment 267 (1990).

51 Lindsay Moir, The Law of Internal Armed Conflict 238 (2001) (observing that the asymmetry of resources and differing methods employed by state and non-state belligerents creates an "imbalance [which] inevitably renders retaliation in kind a limited possibility since comparisons between the losses and damage caused by the initial offence and reprisals will be difficult.").

52 Jonah Goldberg, "Five Minutes Well Spent: Keeping Waterboarding as an Interrogation Technique Is Not the Slippery Slope Some Say It Is," Nat. Rev. Online, Feb. 15, 2008.

53 This is what the concept entails, in fact, for the contemporary authors examined in this and the preceding chapter. *See, e.g.,* Amartya Sen, Development as Freedom 72–86, 87–110, 127–45, 285–311 (1999); Ronald Dworkin, Is Democracy Possible Here? Principles for a New Political Debate (2006).

54 Allen Buchanan, Justice, Legitimacy, and Self-Determination: Moral Foundations for International Law 469 (2004).

55 *Id.* at 470.

56 *Id.*

CHAPTER 7. HUMANITARIAN LAW AS CORRECTIVE JUSTICE:
DO TARGETED KILLING AND TORTURE "CORRECT" FOR TERROR?

1 *Cf.* Paul Kahn, "The Paradoxes of Riskless Warfare," 22 Phil. & Public Pol'cy Q. 2 (2002).

2 Though there are many variants of "realism" (including "neorealism") in international relations, virtually all view states as unitary actors concerned principally with self-preservation and often self-aggrandizement. The international arena, lacking a central government, is viewed as anarchical, "a brutal arena where states look for opportunities to take advantage of each other, and therefore have little reason to trust each other." John Mearsheimer, The False Promise of International Institutions 9 (1994).

3 Michel Foucault, Ethics: Subjectivity and Truth, Paul Rabinow, ed., Robert Hurley, trans. 257–58, 267 (2000).

4 Paul Kahn, "Lessons for International Law from the Gulf War," 45 Stan. L. Rev. 425, 436–37 (1993). The law of war, Kahn writes, "is not concerned with the disproportionality between the suffering on the Iraqi side [in 1991 and thereafter] and the minimal burden on the allied side. . . . While international law condemns Iraq's seizure of the hostages, it virtually ignores the massive numbers of Iraqi civilians – let alone a largely conscript army – that suffered the effects of the Gulf War. . . . The rules of war do not adequately reflect the reality of warfare between a third-world country and a superpower."

5 *Id.* at 437 ("One lesson of the war, therefore, might be: don't give up your hostages.").

6 *Id.* He continues, "The international law that governs the conduct of war is ultimately . . . designed to protect the self-interests of the more powerful states."

7 Richard Russell, Sharpening Strategic Intelligence 97–118 (2007); Richard Betts, "A Disciplined Defense: How to Regain Strategic Solvency," Foreign Affairs, Nov./Dec. 2007, at 47 ("With rare exceptions, the war against terrorists cannot be fought with army battalions, air force wings, or naval fleets – the large conventional forces that drive the defense budget."). An early 2008 survey of active duty and retired U.S. officers found that 73% ranked "improved intelligence" among "the two most important things . . . the U.S. government must do to win the war on terror," nearly twice the percentage of any other factor. Center for a New American Security (CNAS) and Foreign Policy Magazine, "Health and Future of the U.S. Military Survey Results," March 2008, p. 8, at http://www.foreignpolicy.com/images/mi-index/MI-2008-data.pdf.

8 As U.S. Secretary of Defense and for many years before assuming that position for a second time, Donald Rumsfeld championed the reorientation of U.S. force structure in this direction, but met considerable resistance from career military leadership.

9 *See generally* David Lonsdale, The Nature of War in the Information Age (2004).

10 Phillip Karber, "Re-constructing Global Aviation in an Era of the Civil Aircraft as Weapon of Destruction," 25 Harv. J. L. & Pub. Pol'cy 781 (2003).

11 Alan Stephens & Nicola Baker, Making Sense of War: Strategy for the 21st Century 261–62 (2007).

12 John Robb, Brave New War: The Next Stage of Terrorism and the End of Globalization ix, 31 (2007).

13 *See generally* David Jividen, "*Jus in Bello* in the Twenty-First Century: Reaping the Benefits and Facing the Challenges of Modern Weaponry and Military Strategy," *in* Yearbook of International Humanitarian Law, Timothy McCormack & Avril McDonald, eds. 113 (2007).

14 Jay Winik, April 1865: The Month That Saved America 281 (2001). Such incidents were not uncommon. *See generally* Black Flag over Dixie: Racial Atrocities and Reprisals in the Civil War, Gregory Urwin, ed. 1–18 (2004).

15 Lawrence Keeley, War Before Civilization 81 (1996).

16 Ralph Peters, Wars of Blood and Faith 15 (2007).

17 Elaine Scarry, "Rules of Engagement," in The Best American Essays 2007, David Foster Wallace, ed. 254 (2007). She writes, "We know that our terrorist opponents resort to treachery because they cannot match our military force; they must choose between accepting defeat at the outset or else opposing us through asymmetrical warfare. But given our own military prowess, why do we resort to treachery?"

18 William Polk, Violent Politics: A History of Terrorism, Insurgency, and Guerrilla War xvii (2007).

19 Gil Merom, How Democracies Lose Small Wars 24 (2003). This dynamic is particularly powerful in wars of attrition. Alexander B. Downes, "Desperate Times, Desperate Measures: The Causes of Civilian Victimization in War," 30 Int'l Security 152, 152, 155 (Spring 2006); Benjamin Valentino, Paul Huth, & Sarah Croco, "Covenants without the Sword: International Law and the Protection of Civilians in Times of War," 58 World Politics 339, 354 (2006).

20 Anatole France, The Red Lily, Frederic Chapman, ed. & trans. 95 (1914) (1894).

21 *Application of the Convention on the Prevention and Punishment of the Crime of Genocide (Bosnia and Herzegovina v. Serbia and Montenegro),* I.C.J., Feb. 26, 2007, at http://www.icj-cij.org/docket/index.php?sum=667&code=bhy&p1=3&p2=2&case=91&k=f4&p3=5.

22 The "same" legal wrong – of war crime, genocide, crimes against humanity – will often be potentially attributable both to individual officials and, through them, to the state they represent. The principle of bilateral reciprocity is more congenial, however, to a legal regime seeking to establish the civil liability of one state to another than the criminal liability of natural persons to the world. This is because criminal liability relies on the elusive but compelling notion that the wrongs it prohibits do harm not only to their immediate victim, but to – in some sense – society at large. These wrongs therefore threaten a rupture in a social contract wider than the bilateral relation between perpetrator and victim.

For this reason, the international community's increasing reliance on criminal rather than civil liability to redress and deter mass atrocity may suggest an implicit legal contraction of the reciprocity principle. But the unintended effect of this attempt may instead be simply to enlarge the scope of claims to self-defense as a legal excuse (within criminal law) for the use of force. *See generally* George Fletcher & Jens David, Defending Humanity: When Force Is Justified and Why 128–54 (2008). Self-defense, by entitling the victim to respond with force to the force first directed against him, is clearly an expression of the reciprocity principle, moreover. Arguments like Fletcher and Jens' are most compelling in how they underwrite humanitarian intervention, which trades implicitly on the notion that crimes against humanity – like all crime – are harms to society at large, with this reasoning now simply extended to international society, i.e., humanity. But this same broadened understanding of self-defense also opens up a conceptual space for more questionable invocations of the concept, indulging potentially aggressive impulses. *Id.* at 107–28, 155–76.

23 Stephen Neff, War and the Law of Nations: A General History 124 (2005).

24 Christine Gray, "The Choice between Restitution and Compensation in International Law," 10 Eur. J. Int'l L. 413 (1999); Christine Gray, Judicial Remedies in International Law (1987) (surveying available remedies for violations of public international law).

25 Neff, *supra* note 23, at 124, 226. For instance, Grotius described reprisal as "an enforcement of a right by violent means." Hugo Grotius, On the Law of War and Peace, Francis Kelsey, trans. 625 (1925) (1625). *See also* Robert Phillimore, 3 Commentaries upon International Law 18–20 (1889); Henry Wheaton, Elements of International Law 310 (1936) (1836).

26 Francisco de Vitoria, "On the Law of War," *in* Political Writings, Anthony Pagden & Jeremy Lawrance, eds. 293, 313–14 (1991).

27 As with all World Court (ICJ) litigation, both states must agree to its jurisdiction.

28 For instance, the Lieber Code, adopted by Union forces during the U.S. Civil War, provided that "military necessity does not include any act of hostility which makes the return to peace unnecessarily difficult." Francis Lieber, General Orders No. 100 to the Armies of the U.S. in the Field, Art. 15 (1863).

29 Immanuel Kant, Perpetual Peace and Other Essays, Ted Humphrey, trans. 107, 110 (1983) (1795).

30 Before that time, the closest precedent would have been the criminal prosecution of slave traders by "international" courts constituted through a multilateral alliance of leading maritime-mercantile powers. Jenny Martinez, "Antislavery Courts and the Dawn of International Human Rights Law," 117 Yale L.J. 552 (2007).

31 Influential recent interpretations of distributive justice have nonetheless sought to delimit the scope of its claims in key respects. *See e.g.,* Michael Walzer, Spheres of Justice: A Defense of Pluralism and Equality (1984) (arguing that various social goods differ in ways that require distinct principles for their just distribution); Michael Sandel, Liberalism and the Limits of Justice 31–32 (1982) (arguing that distributive justice has no bearing within certain domains of social interaction); Charles Taylor, "The Nature and Scope of Distributive Justice," *in* Justice and Equality: Here and Now, Frank Lucash, ed. 34, 46 (1986).

32 *But see* Alexander Wendt, "Why a World State is Inevitable," 9 Eur. J. Int'l Relations 491 (2003).

33 Aristotle, Nicomachaen Ethics, V, 2–5, 1130a14–33b28. *See also* Ernest Weinrib, "Corrective Justice in a Nutshell," 52 Univ. Toronto L. J. 349 (2002); Konrad Marc-Wogau, "Aristotle's Theory of Corrective Justice and Reciprocity," *in* Marc-Wogau, Philosophical Essays 26 (1967).

34 It is possible to imagine employing the reciprocity principle as a basis of distributive justice. Almost no one, however, thinks it should mean that a

national (or international) society should allocate the benefits of cooperation entirely on the basis of how much individual persons (or states) contribute. None of the thinkers here examined understand reciprocity to require that one put in just as much as one takes out, for the consequences of this arrangement would be highly regressive in economic terms (i.e., radically inegalitarian). On this point, *see* Philippe Van Parijs, "Reciprocity and the Justification of an Unconditional Basic Income," XLV Polit. Studies 327, 327 (1997). *See generally* Steven R. Smith, Defending Justice as Reciprocity 244–45 (2002); Stephen K. White, "Liberal Equality, Exploitation and the Case for an Unconditional Basic Income," 45 Polit. Studies 312 (1997); G.A. Cohen, Self-Ownership, Freedom and Equality 187–98, 224–25 (1995).

35 Weinrib, *supra* note 33, at 351–52.

36 *Id.* at 352.

37 *Id.* at 353.

38 *Id.* at 352.

39 *Id.* at 356.

40 This is true even though Weinrib's archetypes of corrective justice are tort and contract, not criminal law. Criminal law itself displays central aspects of corrective justice. Gregory Kavka, "The Costs of Crimes: Coleman Amended," 104 Ethics 582, 585–89 (1994). Like a tort award of money damages, the criminal conviction "reduces the victim's net loss at [the defendant's] own expense." *Id.* at 588. Furthermore, the costs of crime extend beyond the immediate victim and close family members, to include "the secondary cost of public fear in increased inhibition, for example, fewer people out on the streets at night because of the fear of crimes. This produces tertiary effects – lesser economic prosperity due to buyers inhibited from traveling freely, lesser social mixing because of fear of the streets. . . . These effects in turn may contribute to poverty and to antagonism among social groups and thus produce further crimes. . . . But if someone is duly convicted and punished for committing a crime, this presumably increases deterrence and the public's security against such offenses in the future, which can outweigh (or at least partly offset) the public's losses. Hence criminal punishment serves to redistribute some of the costs of crime from the public back to criminals," and so reflects a commitment to corrective justice. Kavka, *id.* at 585–86.

41 *Id.* at 585–88.

42 Jules Coleman, Risks and Wrongs 259 (1992).

43 Kahn, *supra* note 1, at 6.

44 *Id.* This view would be mistaken insofar as it suggests that Al Qaeda's decision to attack Western civilians was prompted entirely by strategic considerations. Osama bin Laden has repeatedly sought to justify such attacks independently, on theological grounds. Mary Habeck, Knowing the Enemy: Jihadist Ideology and the War on Terror 128–33 (2006) (citing primary sources to this effect).

45 Kahn, *supra* note 1, at 6.

46 *Id.*

47 Kahn, *supra* note 4 at 425, 434.

48 William T. Sherman, Memoirs 595 (1990) (1875).

49 Harold Koh, for instance, argues for a treaty and attendant enforcement mechanisms that would effectively curtail the currently lawful, multibillion

dollar annual trade in conventional weapons to poor countries. Koh, "A World Drowning in Guns," 71 Fordham L. Rev. 2333 (2003).

50 Or, more precisely, no one but a Yale Law professor or an Oxford moral philosopher. David Rodin, "The Ethics of Asymmetric War," *in* The Ethics of War: Shared Problems in Different Traditions 153, 159 (2006) (arguing that "although asymmetric tactics conflict with principles of justice in that they attack or expose non-combatants to excessive risks, they are justified by a principle of fairness to restore balance in radically unequal conflicts").

51 Kahn, *supra* note 4, at 437, emphasis supplied. Talal Asad makes a similar point about asymmetry of risk in On Suicide Bombing 35 (2007), arguing that the West's technological superiority in conventional military conflicts means that its "soldiers need no longer go to war expecting to die but only to kill," which in turn "destabilizes the conventional understanding of war as an activity in which human dying and killing are exchanged." In the interests of discretion perhaps, Asad stops just short of explicitly inferring that suicide bombing is a means of leveling the playing field. In any event, it has quite frequently been the case – think of World War I, for instance – that soldiers go off to war not expecting to die, but only to kill.

52 On the *shari'a* rejection of the killing of women and children in war, *see, e.g.,* John Kelsay, "Suicide Bombers: The 'Just War' Debate, Islamic Style," *in* Deviance across Cultures, Robert Heiner, ed. 227, 228–31 (2007); Majid Khadduri, War and Peace in the Law of Islam 87, 103–07, 115, 127–29 (1955); Suheil Laher, "Indiscriminate Killing in Light of Sacred Islamic Texts," *in* The State We Are In: Identity, Terror, and the Law of Jihad, Aftab Ahmad Malik, ed., ed. 41, 44–46 (2006); Tamara Sonn, "Irregular Warfare and Terrorism in Islam," *in* Cross, Crescent, and Sword, James T. Johnson & John Kelsey, eds. 128 (1990) (observing that "irregular warfare and terrorism, as those terms are commonly understood, are almost universally condemned in Islamic literature, both classical and contemporary"); John Kelsay, "Islam and the Distinction between Combatants and Noncombatants," *in* Johnson & Kelsay, *id.* at 197.

53 Jean Baudrillard, The Spirit of Terrorism and Other Essays, Chris Turner, trans. 9 (2003).

54 *Id.*

55 Chuck Freilich, "Six Ways Not to Deal with Hamas," Foreign Policy, March 2008, at http://www.foreignpolicy.com/story/cms.php?story_id=4225&print=1.

56 *Id.* at 17.

57 *Id.* at 17. *See also* Jean Baudrillard, "The Seismic Order," (1991), at http://www.uta.edu/english/apt/collab/texts/sedismic.html.

58 Insightfully, but not with particular originality, as many of the same points were made by Brazilian revolutionary Carlos Marighela in the 1960s, in defense of Latin American guerrilla operations. *See* his La Guerra Revolucionaria (1970). Terrorists of every ideological coloration, in fact, have long believed that the liberal state "can always be provoked by terrorism to turn itself terroristic." Giorgio Agamben, "Security and Terror," 5 Theory & Event 4 (2002). This is not to deny the genuine novelties of contemporary jihadist terror, several of which Baudrillard observes.

59 Baudrillard, *supra* note 53, at 9.

60 *Id.* at 22.

61 *Id.* at 15, 20.

62 *Id.* at 17.

63 *Id.* at 24. Baudrillard dismisses this last point as offered only in "bad faith," but does not say why.

64 George Fletcher, "Fairness and Utility in Tort Theory," 85 Harv. L. Rev. 537, 572 (1972).

65 *Id.*

66 Allan Gibbard, Wise Choices, Apt Feelings: A Theory of Normative Judgment 261, 264 (1990).

67 Deborah W. Larson, "Exchange and Reciprocity in International Negotiations," 3 Int'l Negotiation 121, 127 (1998). Nondemocratic regimes generally prove more responsive to donor pressures than do democratic states. Bruce Bueno de Mesquita & Alastair Smith, "Foreign Aid and Policy Concessions," 51 J. Conflict Resol. 251, 281 (2007).

68 Antonio Cassese, International Criminal Law 221 (2003).

69 Thomas Schelling, Arms and Influence 145–46 (1972); *see generally* D.W. Larson, "Exchange and Reciprocity in International Negotiations," 3 Int'l Negotiation 121, 121 (1998) ("It is difficult to determine whether exchanges are reciprocal without a common measure of value."); Duran Bell, "Reciprocity as a Generating Process in Social Relations," 3 J. Quantitative Anthro. 251 (1991).

70 *Id.* at 130.

71 Marc Bloch, Feudal Society, L.A. Manyon, trans. 219–40 (1989) (1961); Oxford English Dictionary, entry for "reciprocity." 1.a. Freeman, Norm. Conq. (1876) I. App. 623 ("Reciprocity of a certain kind was the essence of the feudal relation."); James Scott, The Moral Economy of the Peasant 168–69 (1976).

72 Marilyn Strathern, The Gender of the Gift: Problems with Women and Problems with Society in Melanesia 143–51, 162 (1988); Lisette Josephides, The Production of Inequality: Gender and Exchange Among the Kewa 109, 210 (1985).

73 Gibbard, *supra* note 66, at 227–30 ("Whatever the inequalities between the obligations of the respective parties, those obligations were none the less mutual: the obedience of the vassal was conditional upon the scrupulous fulfillment of his engagement by the lord. This reciprocity on unequal obligations . . . was the really distinctive feature of European vassalage. . . . This made the lord no mere master with the sole function of receiving whatever was due to him, but a partner in a genuine contract."); Patrons, Clients and Friends: Interpersonal Relations and the Structure of Trust in Society, S. N. Eisenstadt & Luis Roniger, eds. (1984). In the 1960s and 70s, even avowedly leftist historians like E. P. Thompson and anthropologists such as James C. Scott viewed premodern exchange between the powerful and powerless as nonetheless governed by traditional normative expectations, defining mutually acceptable terms of exchange, terms that would regularly be invoked by the poor (e.g., peasants, vassals, journeymen) whenever violated by their social superiors (landowners, lords, master craftsmen). Both sides accepted a norm requiring a certain amount of elite protection in exchange for a settled amount of nonelite contribution. Later scholarship by political economists and materialist sociologists (e.g., Samuel Popkin

and Theda Skocpol), however, took a harder line on such transactions, refusing them the approbative connotations of the terms "norm" and "reciprocal" (even "negative reciprocity," Sahlins's proffered compromise), viewing these characterizations as inconsistent with the measure of domination, exploitation, and/or volatility so palpable in the social structures establishing and enabling such transactions within preindustrial societies.

74 Michael Taussig, The Devil and Commodity Fetishism in South America 197 (1980).

75 Gibbard, *supra* note 66, at 262.

76 Legal systems vary greatly, for instance, in whether they accept the notion that a tort victim's physical pain and suffering, much less his or her purely mental anguish, are compensable in currency. The United States, more than virtually any other legal system, adopts the "utilitarian" view that all units of pain and pleasure are commensurable in money, fungible in this sense.

77 Baudrillard, *supra* note 53, at 74.

78 Unless captured while directly engaged in hostilities, it would be difficult to justify their detention even as unprivileged belligerents.

79 Geneva Additional Protocol I prohibits "acts or threats of violence the primary purpose of which is to spread terror among the civilian population." Art. 51(2). The Fourth Geneva Convention similarly bars "all measures of intimidation or of terrorism." Art. 33.

80 David Luban, "Liberalism, Torture, and the Ticking Bomb," 91 Val. L. Rev. 1425, 1431 (2005). He does not seek to justify torture as a reciprocal response to terrorism, however, but only to observe this resemblance. In a similar spirit, Paul Kahn writes: "Terrorism invokes torture because they are reciprocal forms of sacrifice of the most primitive kind." Paul Khan, " Who Are We? Or, The Presidential Debate Question: Are We Torturers?" Univ. of Michigan Press Blog, Sept. 29, 2008, at http://umichpress.typepad.com/university_of_ michigan_pr/2008/09/the-american-po.html.

81 Michael Taussig, "Culture of Terror – Space of Death: Roger Casement's Putumayo Report and the Explanation of Torture," *in* Interpretive Social Science: A Second Look, Paul Rabinow & William Sullivan, eds. 241, 262–77 (1987).

82 Darius Rejali, Torture and Modernity: Self, Society and State in Modern Iran (1994).

83 Mark Osiel, "Constructing Subversion in Argentina's Dirty War," 75 Representations 119 (2001).

84 Asad, *supra* note 51, at 70–71. On "learned helplessness" as a common psychological effect of sustained torture in detention, *see* Jane Mayer, "The Black Sites," New Yorker, Aug. 13, 2007, at 46, 51 (quoting CIA historian Alfred McCoy describing how extreme sensory deprivation for long periods produces "very deep breakdowns," after which detainees "bond with the interrogator like a father, or like a drowning man having a lifesaver thrown at him").

85 Charles Taylor, Sources of the Self: The Making of the Modern Identity 14 (1989).

86 *Id.* at 83.

87 Thomas Dumm, A Politics of the Ordinary 1 (1999).

88 Samuel Scheffler, "Is Terrorism Morally Distinctive?" 14 J. Polit. Phil. 1, 16 (2007).

89 The weaker version of this argument would add the qualification that procedural rules for identifying those to be detained should not be relaxed. The stronger version would authorize precisely such relaxation.

90 Marco Sassòli, "Transnational Armed Groups and International Humanitarian Law," Occasional Paper, Program on Humanitarian Policy and Conflict Research, Harvard, (Winter 2006), at 26.

91 Ernest Weinrib, "Corrective Justice," 77 Iowa L. Rev. 403, 421 (1992).

92 Ken Kress, "Introduction: Corrective Justice and Formalism," 77 Iowa L. Rev. i, ii (1992). Moreover, "if it turns out that meeting the demands of corrective justice has the effect of entrenching distributive injustice, that might well count as a reason against devoting substantial resources to meeting the demands of corrective justice." Colemen, *supra* note 42, at 305.

93 Richard Wright, "Substantive Corrective Justice," 77 Iowa L. Rev. 625, 709 (1992).

94 Raghuram Rajan & Luigi Zingales, Saving Capitalism from the Capitalists: How Open Financial Markets Challenge the Establishment and Spread Prosperity to Rich and Poor Alike 157–71, 226–74 (2003).

95 On nonideal theory, as distinguished from ideal, *see* John Rawls, A Theory of Justice, 244–48 (1971).

96 *Id.* at 176.

97 *Id.* at 145, 176, 423. Rawls derives this notion from Kant, who – in his third and most "social" formulation of the categorical imperative – contends that our basic ethical duty is to act only on principles that could win acceptance by a community of fully rational agents, each with an equal part in legislating such principles. The resulting "kingdom of ends" must at least be "possible," in both the logical sense and also in that we could imagine all members accepting it. Immanuel Kant, The Groundwork of the Metaphysics of Morals, Allen Wood, ed. 4.333–4.339 (2002).

98 Rawls, *supra* note 95, at 454.

99 *Id.* at 576.

100 Brian Barry, Justice as Impartiality 64 (1995); Barry admits that this is one among other plausible readings of Rawls on this matter. *See also* Bonnie Honig, Political Theory and the Displacement of Politics 137–45 (1993) (parsing Rawls's ideas concerning punishment).

101 David Bederman, International Law in Antiquity 255–57 (2001) (describing ancient Roman practice).

102 Rawls claims that his theory is superior to utilitarianism, in particular, because the rules he reaches can be readily justified to those who find themselves worst off under them.

103 Jeremy Waldron, Liberal Rights 262–67 (1993). In that regard, the details of current humanitarian law may offer only one among a number of morally acceptable regimes. But this possibility is well captured by Scanlon's nonrejection principle: that the particular rules under examination could not reasonably be rejected by anyone subject to them, even if one might not come up with these specific rules on one's own or repudiate all alternative ones.

104 Daniel Byman & Matthew Waxman, The Dynamics of Coercion: American Foreign Policy and the Limits of Military Might (2002) ("Success in coercive contests seldom turns on superior firepower.")

105 John Updike, Due Considerations: Essays and Criticism 413 (2007).

106 Baudrillard, *supra* note 53, at 23.

107 Mikkel Rasmussen, The Risk Society at War: Terror, Technology and Strategy in the Twenty-First Century 171 (2006).

108 Virginia Held, "Terrorism and War," 8 J. of Ethics 59, 79–80 (2004); *see also* Uwe Steinhoff, On the Ethics of War and Terrorism 125–27 (2007) (endorsing and reformulating Held's defense of terrorism's justifications); Baogang He, "Cultural Equality and Its Soft Power against Terrorism," *in* Ethics of War in a Time of Terror, Christian Enemark, ed. 80 (2006) (describing jihadist terrorism as a rational response to pervasive and recurrent Western disrespect for Muslim culture).

109 Noam Chomsky makes a similar argument in his pamphlet "9–11," 59–62, 81–84 (2001); *see also* Judith Butler, Precarious Life: The Powers of Mourning and Violence 11 (2004); Michael Mann, Incoherent Empire 167–70 (2003); Alain Badiou, Infinite Thought, Oliver Feltham & Justin Clemens, trans. 159 (2003) ("The mass crime [of 9/11] was the exact inverse of the imperial brutality. It was sewn to the latter like an inner lining and . . . came directly from the cookhouses of American hegemony.").

110 Virginia Held, The Ethics of Care: Personal, Political, and Global (2006).

111 Geoffrey Best, Humanity in War 147–79 (1980).

112 Philosophy in a Time of Terror: Dialogues with Jürgen Habermas and Jacques Derrida, Giovanna Borradori, ed. 103 (2003).

113 Keeley, *supra* note 15, at 88. "Is there any behavioral difference," Keeley feels compelled to ask, "between Caesar's extermination of the Bituriges at Bourges, the slaughter of Minnesota settlers by the Sioux in 1862, the massacres by the U.S. Army at Wounded Knee and My Lai, the Allied air strikes at Dresden and Hiroshima, the massacres committed by Japanese soldiers in Nankin and Manila, and the similar accomplishments of primitives . . . except the body counts and the assignment of our sympathies with the perpetrators or the victims?" Any honest reckoning with the law of war today must begin by acknowledging the full force of that question.

114 Osama bin Laden, interviewed by Tayseer Allouni, "The Unreleased Interview, Oct. 21, 2001, from Markaz Derasat, Muawiya ibn Abi Sufyan, trans. At http://islamicawakening.com/index.htm.

115 Koran, 2:294.

116 Sulayman Abu Ghayth, "In the Shadow of the Lances," June 2002, at http://www.memri.org, Special Dispatch Series, No. 388. For analysis, *see* John Kelsey, "Arguments concerning Resistance in Contemporary Islam," *in* The Ethics of War: Shared Problems in Different Traditions, Richard Sorabji & David Rodin, eds. 61, 79–82 (2006); Habeck, *supra* note 44, at 123.

117 Osama bin Laden, "To the Allies of the World," Nov. 12, 2002, *in* Messages to the World: The Statements of Osama bin Laden, Bruce Lawrence, ed., James Howarth, trans. 171, 171 (2005).

118 Statement by Abu Dujan al Afghani, the military spokesman for Al Qaeda in Europe, Associated Press, March 14, 2004. Shortly after 9/11, Osama bin Laden

similarly told a reporter: "We love death. The U.S. loves life. That is the big difference between us." And from Hassan Nasrallah, the Hezbollah leader: "We are going to win, because they love life and we love death."

119 Jeremy Waldron, "Is This Torture Necessary?," book review of David Cole & Jules Lobel, 54 N.Y. Rev. of Books, Oct. 25, 2007, at 40, 44.

CHAPTER 8. RECIPROCITY AS CIVILIZATION: THE TERRORIST AS SAVAGE

1 Jennifer Pitts, "Boundaries of Victorian International Law," in Victorian Visions of Global Order: Empire and International Relations in Nineteenth-Century Political Thought, Duncan Bell, ed., 67, 67–68, 71–73, 79 (2007) (parsing Sir Travers Twiss's Annuaire de L'Institut de Droit International, 1881). Alexander Orakhelashvili, "The Idea of European International Law," 17 Euro. J. Int'l L. 315, 323–27 (2006)(observing that several 19th century European legal and political thinkers, such as W. A. Heffter, John Stuart Mill, and Henry Bonfils, believed "that international law based on mutual recognition was possible only among those states for whom reciprocity of application had been established . . . The character of individual states could suffice in order to assume that one could count on reciprocal treatment and the application of norms"). They believed "that international law cannot apply to barbarians because this would imply a reciprocity of rights for which there are no conditions in relations with barbarians." *Id.* at 324. "Reciprocal observance of international law was therefore inconceivable." *Id.* at 327. In fact, however, classical Islamic jurisprudence on war actually embraced the reciprocity principle, in providing that the duty to restrain onself in the use of force was conditional on the enemy's continuing willingness to do so. Mohammad Hashim Kamali, "Jihad and the Interpretation of the Koran: Contextualizing Islamic Tradition," Third Hague Colloquium on Fundamental Principles of Law, Oct. 3, 2008.

2 Pitts, *id.* at 79 (describing the views of Antonio Gallenga).

3 Robert Pippin, Modernism as a Philosophical Problem: On the Dissatisfactions of European High Culture 153 (1991); Walter Mignolo, Local Histories/Global Designs: Coloniality, Subaltern Knowledges, and Border Thinking 297 (2000).

4 Few professional writers on military affairs today succumb to such stereotypes. *But see* Ralph Peters, Fighting for the Future: Will America Triumph? 90 (1999) (arguing that for America's adversaries, "hatred, jealousy and greed – emotion rather than strategy – will set the tone" of armed conflict in coming years); John Keegan, "In This War of Civilizations, The West Will Prevail," Daily Telegraph, Oct. 8, 2001 ("A harsh, instantaneous attack may be the response most likely to impress the Islamic mind. . . . Orientals . . . shrink from pitched battle.").

5 Joseba Zulaika & William Douglass, Terror and Taboo 150 (1996); *see also* Paul Gilroy, "Multiculturalism and Post-Colonial Theory," *in* The Oxford Handbook of Political Theory, John Dryzek, Bonnie Honig, & Anne Phillips, eds. 656, 657 (2006); Robert Young, Postcolonialism (2003).

6 Michael Taussig, Shamanism, Colonialism and the Wild Man: A Study in Terror and Healing 211 (1986).

7 Edmund Leach, Custom, Law and Terrorist Violence 36 (1977); *see also* Paolo Palladino, "On the Political Animal and the Return of Just War," 8 Theory &

Event 2 (2005) (lamenting "the dialectic of 'self' and 'other' that the figure of the 'animal' has long and problematically sustained").

8 Matthew N. Smith, "Terrorism, Shared Rules, and Trust," 16 J. Polit. Phil. 201, 215–16 (2008) (invoking John Locke's use of this metaphor).

9 Fréderic Mégret, "From 'Savages' to 'Unlawful Combatants': A Postcolonial Look at International Humanitarian Law's 'Other,'" *in* International Law and its Others, Anne Orford, ed. 265, 298–99 (2007). *See also* Antony Anghie, Imperialism, Sovereignty, and the Making of International Law 273, 298 (2005). Anghie describes the U.S. legal response to 9/11 as "law, once again initiated and animated by the invocation of the 'uncivilized' and the 'barbaric' that, in the name of security, produces a new form of imperialism." *Id.* at 302. He concludes, "My broad argument is that the War Against Terror represents a set of policies and principles that reproduces the structure of the civilizing mission." *Id.* at 309.

10 Most critics of Bush administration policy in this area view it as "the mere onslaught of power and violence against the law" (i.e., in disregarding the law's most worthy commitments); other critics, by contrast, largely acknowledge humanitarian law's moral defects and the unduly limited scope of its protections, stressing instead "the discreet exclusionary work of the law itself." Mégret, *id.* at 312. And some critics even want to have it both ways. Mégret is among these.

11 Postcolonialism's founding text, Edward Said, Orientalism (1978), is avowedly an application and extension of Michel Foucault's genealogical method. The inadequacies of the distinction between "traditional" and "modern" societies that postcolonialism emphasizes largely reiterate, in more tortured idiom, observations made by an earlier generation. *See especially* Reinhard Bendix, "Tradition and Modernity Reconsidered," 9 Comp. Stud. Soc. & Hist. 292 (1967).

12 *See, e.g.,* Michel Foucault, Discipline and Punish, Alan Sheridan, trans. 141–69 (1979). Leading postmodernist criticism of the martial conceptualization of the conflict, in particular, includes Paul Virilio, Ground Zero, Chris Turner, trans. (2002); Paul Virilio, City of Panic, Julie Rose, trans. (2002); Jean Baudrillard, The Spirit of Terrorism and Other Essays, Chris Turner, trans. (2003); Jean Baudrillard, The Intelligence of Evil or the Lucidity Pact, Chris Turner, trans. (2000); Jacques Derrida, Rogues: Two Essays on Reason, Pascale-Anne Brault & Michael Naas, trans. (2005); *see also* Julian Reid, The Biopolitics of War (2006); Daniel Pick, War Machine: The Rationalization of Slaughter in the Modern Age (1993).

13 Mégret, *supra* note 9, at 301.

14 *Id.* at 14.

15 *Id.*

16 This reflected the longstanding Western preoccupation with winning through superiority in force, technology, and organizational discipline. Geoffrey Parker, "Introduction: The Western Way of War," *in* The Cambridge History of Warfare, Geoffrey Parker, ed. 1–14 (2005); Lawrence Sondhaus, Strategic Culture and Ways of War 2 (2006); *but see* Christopher Coker, "Is There a Western Way of Warfare?" Norwegian Institute of Defense Studies (2004) (objecting

that such a notion essentializes "the West" no less than "Orientalism" does so for "the East," given the diversity of methods by which Western armies have fought throughout history).

17 Adriaan Lanni, "The Laws of War in Ancient Greece," 26 L. & Hist. Rev. 469, 485–86 (2008).

18 *Id.* at 15. Thucydides is here quoting a captured Spartan prisoner of war, when asked why he and his comrades had surrendered to a smaller, more lightly armed force of archers during the Pelopponesian War. Josiah Ober, "Classical Greek Times," *in* The Laws of War: Constraints on Warfare in the Western World, Michael Howard et al., eds., 12, 13 (1994).

19 When advised to attack the Persians by night, Alexander the Great reportedly responded, "The policy which you are suggesting is one of bandits and thieves, the only purpose of which is deception. I cannot allow my glory always to be diminished by . . . tricks of night." *Id.* at 14. The desire for glory can be counterproductive not only with regard to means of warfare but also concerning the initial resort to force. America's constitutional drafters were hence concerned that a potential presidential desire for personal glory through war would lead the country into imprudent conflicts. The constitutional requirement of congressional approval for a declaration of war has been explained on these grounds. William Treanor, "Fame, the Founding, and the Power to Declare War," 82 Cornell L. Rev. 695 (1997).

20 Victor Davis Hanson, The Western Way of War: Infantry Battle in Classical Greece 226 (1989).

21 *Id.* at 225.

22 Lanni, *supra* note 17, at 481, 486.

23 Peter Silver, Our Savage Neighbors: How Indian War Transformed Early America 56–57, 85 (2008) (quoting primary sources from Colonial New York).

24 *Id.* at 57.

25 *Id.*

26 *Id.* at 332.

27 Emmerich de Vattel, The Law of Nations, Joseph Chitty, ed. 348–49 (1852) (1758).

28 Deuteronomy 20:13–14; *see generally* Susan Niditch, War in the Hebrew Bible: A Study in the Ethics of Violence (1993).

29 Robert Edgerton, The Worldwide Practice of Torture: A Preliminary Report 91–93 (2007).

30 *See, e.g.,* Harold Selesky, "Colonial America," *in* The Laws of War: Constraints on Warfare in the Western World, Michael Howard et al., eds. 59, 67 (1994).

31 The distinction between combatants and noncombatants in advanced industrial societies has been similarly questioned on grounds of its moral coherence. A complex division of labor within such countries means that most who work in armament factories, for instance, are civilians and that the war production of belligerent states is inextricable from their foreign trade with neutral ones. Hence, the common attacks on neutral shipping during both world wars. Adam Roberts, "Land Warfare: From Hague to Nuremberg," *in* Howard, *id.* at 116, 138 (1994); Colm McKeogh, Innocent Civilians: The Morality of Killing in War 123–44 (2002).

32 Selesky, *supra* note 30, at 74.

33 Mark Grimsley, '"Rebels" and "Redskins": U.S. Military Conduct toward White Southerners and Native Americans in Comparative Perspective," *in* Civilians in the Path of War, Mark Grimsley & Clifford Rogers, eds. 137, 141 (2002).

34 Richard Slotkin, The Fatal Environment: The Myth of the Frontier in the Age of Industrialization, 1800–1890, 400 (1994) (emphasis added).

35 Silver, *supra* note 23, at 60.

36 *Id.* at 94.

37 *Id.* at 304, 303. On racism in Western imagery of Native Americans, *see, e.g.,* Helen Carr, Inventing the American Primitive 28–30 (1996); Silver, *supra* note 23, at 133, 203, 243, 264, 273, 294–96; Bernard Sheehan, Savagism and Civility: Indians and Englishmen in Colonial Virginia 48–49 (1980).

38 Mégret, *supra,* note 9, at 293–94, 297, 300–04.

39 On Jackson's Indian campaigns, *see* H.W. Brands, Andrew Jackson: His Life and Times 169–73, 309–21, 489–93 (2005).

40 The term "postcolonial" is unfortunately something of a misnomer, for its adherents seek to emphasize precisely the continuing impact of colonial domination on the territories thereby conquered, long after their formal independence. There is very little truly "post" about it. *See generally* Postcolonialism and Political Theory, Nalini Persram, ed. (2007).

41 On the sorry, sordid history of this concept, *see* Alice Conklin, A Mission to Civilize: The Republican Idea of Empire in France and West Africa, 1895–1930 1–10, 247–56 (1997).

42 Mégret, *supra* note 9, at 297.

43 Leo Lowenthal, Literature, Popular Culture, and Society xviii (1961). A more contemporary analogy would be the Taliban clergy's discouragement and later prohibition of kite-fighting, a popular and longstanding Afghan recreation, as inconsistent with Islam.

44 Patrick Brantlinger, Bread and Circuses: Theories of Mass Culture and Social Decay (1983); Hanno Hardt, Myths for the Masses (2004).

45 Dana Villa, Politics, Philosophy, Terror: Essays on the Thought of Hannah Arendt 14 (1999). Reading Villa's account of the nature of "totalitarian terror" (*id.* at 15–21, 182–85) immediately discloses, for instance, both the similarities and differences between that historical experience and contemporary militant jihadist terror. Both seek to explore "the possibility of dominating human beings entirely" through the state and its official creed (*id.* at 17), but only the former came close to succeeding, and only within its territorial home base and lands of military occupation.

46 One must at least acknowledge the possibility here that the seeming opposites in fact require one another, despite sincere protestations to the contrary by almost all concerned. In his unique brand of Hegelianism, Žižek suggests for instance that Nazism may have been necessary to defeat Communism (as many middle-class Germans plausibly believed in the early 1930s), just as the PLO may have needed to resort to terror tactics to ensure that Palestinian interests would thereafter be taken seriously in negotiations with Israel and the U.S. In the same way, Žižek continues, "good" Islam may actually require its seeming contradiction – "bad" Islamist terror – to protect itself against the secularizing social forces and

capitalist economic mentality that have so deeply weakened all other world religions in modern times, and to which Islam too would otherwise eventually succumb. In fact, he rhapsodizes, insofar as traditional Islam's commitment to social egalitarianism has inspired its unique resistance to the demands of global capitalism, this is for the best, because this principled refusal "can also be articulated into a socialist project." Slavoj Žižek, Iraq: The Borrowed Kettle 48–49 (2006).

One need not acknowledge the ultimate accuracy of any of the preceding to admit the platitude that life is full of contradictions and that it is sometimes advantageous to sharpen and capitalize on them rather than immediately resolve them harmoniously. Andrew Jackson famously seized on rumors of Indian atrocities against white settlers, for instance, to persuade President Jefferson to initiate frontier war against the indigenous peoples, with a view to acquiring their territories, a war in which U.S. forces under Jackson's command would soon perpetrate such very atrocities on a colossal scale. Michael Rogin, Fathers and Children: Andrew Jackson and the Subjugation of the American Indian 139 (1975).

47 Antony Anghie, "Finding the Peripheries: Sovereignty and Colonialism in Nineteenth-Century International Law," 40 Harv. Int'l L.J. 1, 22–80 (1999); *but see* Orakhelashvili, *supra* note 1, at 328–336 (demonstrating the ancient, non-European origins of a considerable portion of international law and the ready extension by treaty of European-made rules and rights to certain non-European peoples during the early modern period).

48 T. E. Lawrence, Seven Pillars of Wisdom (1936).

49 Lawrence Keeley, War Before Civilization 42, 79–81 (1996).

50 Adrian Greaves, Lawrence of Arabia: Mirage of a Desert War (2007); Malcolm Brown, Lawrence of Arabia: The Life, the Legend (2005).

51 Keeley, *supra* note 49, at 81; *see also* Odie Falk, Crimson Desert: Indian Wars of the American Southwest 142–57 (1974). Earlier victories by British settlers, as against the Pequot tribe, similarly depended heavily on alliances with other Indian allies (i.e., by exploiting intertribal rivalries). Harold Selesky, War and Society in Colonial Connecticut 3–11 (1990). Since the conquest of North America was protracted, several indigenous peoples themselves had time to interact with competing European groups (Dutch, French, and British) and learn to play them off against one another in bargaining for iron goods and gunpowder that would prove essential to the military longevity of the Apaches, among other tribal groups. William Polk, Violent Politics: A History of Terrorism, Insurgency, and Guerrilla War 93 (2007).

52 Bernard Brodie, War and Politics 332 (1973); David Rohde, "Army Enlists Anthropology in War Zones," New York Times, Oct. 5, 2007, at A1 (describing the U.S. army's recent employment of Western civilian anthropologists in Iraq to facilitate soldiers' understanding of, and communication with locals). Many academic anthropologists are acutely skeptical of this development. Roberto Gonzales, "Toward Mercenary Anthropology? The New U.S. Army Counterinsurgency Manual FM 3–24 and the Military-Anthropology Complex," 23 Anthro. Today 14 (June 2007).

53 An early 2008 survey of active duty and retired U.S. officers found that 38% ranked "further increase in the size of Special Operations" among "the two most important things . . . the U.S. government must do to win the war on terror," second only to "improve intelligence." Center for a New American Security (CNAS) and Foreign Policy Magazine, "Health and Future of the U.S. Military Survey Results," March 2008, p. 8, at http://www.foreignpolicy.com/images/mi-index/MI-2008-data.pdf. *See generally* Kames Kiras, Special Operations and Strategy: From World War II to the War on Terrorism (2006); Christopher Spearin, "Special Operations Forces a Strategic Resource: Public and Private Divides," 36 Parameters 58 (2007); Alastair Finlan, "Warfare by Other Means: Special Forces, Terrorism and Grand Strategy," 14 Small Wars and Insurgencies 92 (2003).

54 *See, e.g.,* David Lonsdale, The Nature of War in the Information Age (2004); Everett Dolman, Pure Strategy: Power and Principle in the Space and Information Age (2005); Jürgen Altmann, Military Nanotechnology: Potential Applications and Preventive Arms Control (2006); Charles J. Dunlap, Technology and the 21st Century Battlefield: Recomplicating Moral Life for the Statesman and the Soldier (1999).

55 Michael Hardt & Antonio Negri, Multitude: War and Democracy in the Age of Empire 58 (2004) (arguing that "it takes a network to fight a network," which "would imply a radical restructuring of the traditional military apparatuses and the forms of sovereign power they represent").

56 David Kilcullen, "Twenty-Eight Articles: Fundamentals of Company-Level Counterinsurgency," March 2006, at http://www.smallwarsjournal.com/documents/28articles.pdf.

57 *See, e.g.,* Maj. Jefferson Reynolds, "Collateral Damage on the 21st Century Battlefield," 56 Air Force L. Rev. 1, 107 (2005) ("Concealment warfare affords the most convenient, efficient, and assured means of defying a conventionally superior force by challenging strategy, technology, ideology, morality and resolve."); Col. Thomas Hammes, The Sling and the Stone: On War in the 21st Century 130–43, 208–21 (2004); Col. Harry Summers, On Strategy: A Critical Analysis of the Vietnam War 79–98, 118–21 (1982).

58 Counterinsurgency Field Manual, FM 3-24/MCWP 3-33.5 (Dec. 2006). For criticism that the manual refuses to discuss or confront the religious character of terrorist/insurgent motivations and its operational implications, *see* Lt. Col. Ralph Peters, "Politically Correct War," N.Y. Post, Oct. 18, 2006.

59 Mégret displays no awareness, however, of this considerable and serious body of writing, produced by scholars – many of them civilians – often in the U.S. war colleges, on which Defense Department planners partly rely. Perhaps he regards such scholarship as too transparently complicit in U.S. imperialism even to warrant attention and refutation. *But see, e.g.,* John Nagl, Learning to Eat Soup with a Knife: Counterinsurgency Lessons from Malaya and Vietnam (2005); Mark Moyer, Triumph Forsaken: The Vietnam War, 1954–1965 (2006). Also illustrative is the journal "Parameters: U.S. Army War College Quarterly." Many of its authors, both military and civilian, were often critical of Bush administration policy, albeit in guarded ways, as by historical allusion. *See, e.g.,*

Lou DiMarco, "Losing the Moral Compass: Torture and *Guerre Revolutionnaire* in the Algerian War," 36 Parameters 63 (2006); Gerard Fogarty, "Is Guantánamo Bay Undermining the Global War on Terror?" 35 Parameters 54 (2005); *see also* Cmdr. Syed Ahmad, "The Unconstitutional Prosecution of the Taliban Under the Military Commissions Act," 55 Naval. L. Rev. 1 (2008).

60 Said, *supra* note 11, at 92–105.

61 Robin Wright, Dreams and Shadows: The Future of the Middle East 3 (2008).

62 Juan Cole, Prof. of History, Univ. of Michigan, Lecture at Univ. of Iowa, College of Law, Spring 2007.

63 Michael Taussig, "Culture of Terror – Space of Death: Roger Casement's Putumayo Report and the Explanation of Torture," *in* Interpretive Social Science: A Second Look 241, 274, Paul Rabinow & William Sullivan, eds. (1987). Werner Herzog's cinematic evocation of this mental and moral universe, in *Aguirre: Wrath of God* (1972) is equally compelling.

64 Jack Goldsmith, The Terror Presidency (2007).

65 Michael Taussig, Mimesis and Alterity: A Particular History of the Senses 67 (1993). Practices of indigenous warfare that initially appear identical to one another have actually had quite various cultural meaning for Western adversaries in different historical periods. The inclination to discover spurious commonalities at too high a level of abstraction – as in a generic "mirroring of monsters" – should therefore be resisted. In Victorian England, for instance, British officers frequently collected the skulls of defeated native chieftains, desecrating enemy corpses to this end. Though it may at first seem a mere copying of common native conduct (originating in inter-tribal warfare), this particular practice had a very special resonance for Victorians, with their "scientific" theories of phrenology and associated ideas of racial superiority, neither of which prevailed in later or earlier periods. "On the one hand, [British officers] could appear to support the cause of universal scientific progress and, in the same breath, show they could out-savage the particular and very terrible savages whom they were fighting," writes a scholar of the subject, "outdoing them at their own primitive customs . . . " Simon Harrison, "Skulls and Scientific Collecting in the Victorian Military: Keeping the Enemy Dead in British Frontier Warfare," 50 Comp. Stud. in Soc. & Hist. 285, 300 (2008). "The skull in the retired officer's cabinet of curiosities thereby attested to a truly comprehensive defeat of the chief whose skull it once was. It confirmed its collector's superiority in intellect and culture, while proving him to have been, in his time, the more successful savage as well." *Id.* In other words, borrowing from indigenous practice here reflected a peculiarly contemporaneous, British preoccupation (i.e., craniology), rather than simply the perennial mimetic dynamic of warfare per se.

66 Robert Berkhofer, Jr., The White Man's Indian: Images of the American Indian from Columbus to the Present 83 (1978).

67 Gustav Niebuhr, "Falwell Apologizes for Saying an Angry God Allowed Attacks," New York Times, 18 September 2001, at http://www.nytimes.com/2001/09/18/national/18FALW.html.

68 Counterinsurgency, FM 3-24, MCWP 3-33.5 (Dec. 15, 2006). This new U.S. Army Field Manual makes many respectful references to insurgents' methods

and those employing them. For instance, "American ideas of what is 'normal' and 'rational' are not universal. . . . Enemy courses of action that may appear immoral or irrational to Westerners may be acceptable to extremists." *Id.* at 1–15. "In tribal- or clan-based insurgencies, . . . roles are particularly hard to define. There is no clear cadre in these movements, and people drift between combatant, auxiliary, and follower status as needed." *Id.* at 1–12. "Resolving most insurgencies requires a political solution; it is thus imperative that counterinsurgent actions do not hinder achieving that political solution." *Id.* at 1–22. "The more successful the counterinsurgency is, the less force can be used and the more risk must be accepted." *Id.* at 1–27. "Some capabilities required for conventional success – for example . . . massive firepower – may be . . . counterproductive in counterinsurgency operations." *Id.* at ix.

69 Keeley, *supra* note 49, at 83–84 ("It is extremely uncommon to find instances among nonstate groups of recognizing surrender or taking adult male prisoners . . . enemy warriors were unlikely to accept captivity without attempting violent escape or revenge; thus holding them captive required high levels of vigilance and upkeep that most tribal societies were unable or unprepared to provide.").

70 Mégret, *supra* note 9, at 303. He also laments the demise of "richly situated traditions" of restraint among tribal warriors as they faced modern armies committed only to a "decontextualized universalism." *Id.* at 314, 316. He cites no evidence of such traditions, though certain early anthropologists did claim to find them. *See, e.g.,* Helen Codere, Fighting with Property: A Study of Kwakiutl Potlaching and Warfare, 1792–1930 (1950). The single pertinent source Mégret does cite concludes, however, that "the proportion of war casualties in primitive societies almost always exceeds that suffered by even the most bellicose or war-torn modern states," on account of "the usual primitive practices of not recognizing surrender and of dispatching all male captives." Keeley, *supra* note 49, at 88, 92. "Except in geographical scale, tribal warfare," Keeley continues, "often was total war in every modern sense." *Id.* at 108; Daniel Barr, Unconquered: The Iroquois League at War in Colonial America 8, 13, 48 (2006) (describing the common Iroquois practices of "ritual torture" consisting of the pulling out of fingernails and of cannibalism in the treatment of male enemy captives). This was generally true of even the most complex tribal kingdoms. Dov Ronen, Dahomey: Between Tradition and Modernity 21–22 (1975) (describing the custom of enslaving captured soldiers when they were not used for human sacrifice); Robert Edgerton, Warrior Women: The Amazons of Dahomey and the Nature of War 20–21, 72–84 (2000) (describing the common practice of beheading enemy captives). Perhaps, then, the only "savages" actually being "recycled" here, in Mégret's terms, are Rousseau's "noble" ones, and by Mégret himself.

Historiography now suggests that early ethnographic accounting of tribal societies sometimes sought to minimize the extent of violence within and between them so as not to offer inadvertent support for the professed "civilizing mission" of Western colonial powers, which was often defended in terms of the suppression of such violence. A second reason for this decentering of war was the effort, in the disconcerting aftermath of World War I, to seek beyond the experience of Western civilization for models and methods of peaceful social order from which a morally and intellectually disoriented Europe could learn. Erik Brandt, On War and Anthropology 17–19 (2002).

It is nonetheless true that methods of tribal warfare have sometimes been ritualized in ways that had the apparently unintended effect of reducing fatalities. Brandt, *Id.* at 19, 130. Ritualization of this sort was also in evidence within early Western military history, before warfare became more instrumentally rationalized. *See, e.g.,* Guy Halsall, "Anthropology and the Study of Pre-Conquest Warfare and Society: The Ritual War in Anglo-Saxon England," *in* Weapons and Warfare in Ango-Saxon England, Sonia C. Hawkes, ed. 155 (1989).

71 On the Zulu use of such methods in fighting British forces, *see* Jonathan Sutherland & Diane Canwell, The Zulu Kings and Their Armies 2 (2004).

72 On asymmetric warfare in current U.S. strategic thought, *see, e.g.,* Jeffrey Record, "Why the Strong Lose," 35 Parameters 19 (Winter 2005); Steven J. Lambakis, "Reconsidering Asymmetric Warfare," 36 Joint Forces Quar. 21 (Feb. 2, 2005).

73 Osama bin Laden has exalted this particular feature of his strategy: "All we have to do is send two mujahidin . . . to raise a piece of cloth on which is written Al Qaeda in order to make the generals race there to cause America to suffer human, economic and political losses." Quoted in Goldsmith, *supra* note 64, at 189.

74 Martin van Creveld, The Transformation of Warfare 33–42 (1991). Clausewitz posited a harmonious "trinity," as he called it, of people, state, and army, according to which a formally organized army fights on behalf of a single state, which represents in turn a single people or national society.

75 Robert Cassidy, "The Long Small War: Indigenous Forces for Counterinsurgency," 36 Parameters 47, 50 (2006).

76 Keeley, *supra* note 49, at 12–13; Gregory Evans Dowd, War under Heaven: Pontiac, the Indian Nations, & the British Empire 115 (2002); Grimsley, *supra* note 33, at 140.

77 Keeley, *supra* note 49, at 80.

78 Brian McAllister Linn, "The Philippines: Nation-Building and Pacification," 85 Military Rev. 46, 52 (March–April, 2005); Timothy Deady, "Lessons from a Successful Counterinsurgency: The Philippines, 1899–1902," 35 Parameters 53 (Spring 2005); David Close, Greece since 1945 37–39 (2002) (describing counterinsurgency methods employed to win the Greek Civil War); Brian Jenkins, "New Modes of Conflict," Rand Series R-3009-DNA (1983), at v; Simon Romero & Anahad O'Conner, "Hostages Freed in Colombia Returning Home," New York Times, July 4, 2008. "Colombia's military appears to have drawn inspiration from one of the FARC's own most brazen actions, in which its combatants disguised themselves in 2002 as soldiers and abducted thirteen lawmakers in Cali. Six years later, Colombian agents infiltrated the FARC's ranks and persuaded a guerrilla commander . . . to allow captives held in three groups to be united for a trip by helicopter to southern Colombia." In what might be described as a ruse, the helicopter – from the Colombian armed forces – was disguised as one belonging to Venezuela, which had provided certain support to the FARC in the recent past.

The maneuver might arguably be characterized as committing the war crime of perfidy, however, insofar as it involved luring a FARC commander into enemy custody through the guise of offering him safe passage, a misrepresentation rendered credible by unlawful disguise in the white uniforms of an unspecific "international health NGO," a neutral party in relation to the armed conflict. Perfidy need not involve an effort to facilitate attack of the enemy. Pietro Verri, Dictionary of the International Law of Armed Conflict 84 (1992). But there appears no precedent for a finding of perfidy when the capture of a single enemy fighter results as an ancillary byproduct of an effort designed simply to recapture one's own POWs and civilians whom one's enemy has unlawfully detained.

If one's moral sentiments here are entirely with those rescued by the Colombian armed forces, the preceding objection to this stratagem may again reflect the inadequacy of humanitarian law in intelligently confronting belligerents who insist on intentionally mistreating civilians, whether by taking them hostages or making them the target of direct attack. Without the doctrine of reprisal for such war crimes (or a newly narrowed definition of perfidy), it would probably be impossible legally to justify the Colombian government's action.

Yet it is also likely that the tactics Colombia employed will henceforth lead belligerents to scrutinize more closely the *bona fides* of those professing to represent humanitarian NGOs, a consequence that may prejudice the needy beneficiaries of such organizations.

79 Keeley, *supra* note 49, at 80.

80 David Kilcullen, "Countering Global Insurgencies," at http://www.smallwars-journal.com/documents/kilcullen.pdf, at 8. Nagl, *supra* note 59, at 15–34; Mark Moyar, Phoenix and the Birds of Prey: The CIA's Secret Campaign to Destroy the Viet Cong 235–46, 292–94 (1997).

81 Terry Eagleton, "Amis and Post 9/11 Anti-Mulsim Hysteria," The Guardian, Oct. 11, 2007 at http://www.arabnews.com/?page=7&section=0&article=102373&d=11&m=10&y=2007.

82 On Enlightenment criticisms of empire and slavery, *see* Jonathan Israel, Enlightenment Contested: Philosophy, Modernity and the Emancipation of Man 1670–1752 590–60 (2006). On the Enlightenment origins of human rights ideas, *see* Lynn Hunt, Inventing Human Rights: A History 15–34, 60–61, 80–81, 179 (2007); Richard Tuck, "The 'Modern' Theory of Natural Law," *in* The Languages of Political Theory in Early-Modern Europe, Anthony Pagden, ed. 99–119 (1987). Some have argued, however, that Enlightenment thinking in this regard owed a great debt to the Stoics. Maurice Cranston, What Are Human Rights? 2 (1973). But though Hellenistic ethics was acutely concerned with the moral unity of the human race, as manifested in the shared emotions of its members, the Stoics gave no place to the concept of human rights. *See generally* Martha Nussbaum, The Therapy of Desire: Theory and Practice in Hellenistic Ethics (1994). For a recent effort to identify the Enlightenment's essential and distinguishing features, *see* Israel, *id.* 863–71. More credible claims for a pre-modern origin to natural rights thinking look to the 14th century. Richard Tuck, Natural Rights Theories 25–30 (1979).

83 Peter Fitzpatrick, "Magnified Features: The Underdevelopment of Law and Legitimation," *in* Morals of Legitimacy, Italo Pardo, ed. 157, 161 (2000).

84 *See generally* Matthew Craven, The Decolonization of International Law (2007) (illustrating how the international law of succession came to free itself of its historical origins in Western colonialism).

85 A long bookshelf could be assembled on this influence, of course. Notable instances include the adoption of an official civil service from China, of medieval Muslim science during the European Renaissance, and Pablo Picasso's inspiration in traditional African wood carvings. *See generally* John Hobson, The Eastern Origins of Western Civilization 283–322 (2004).

86 Gregory Evans Dowd, War under Heaven: Pontiac, the Indian Nations, & the British Empire 118 (2002).

87 Amartya Sen, "Human Rights and Asian Values," 217 New Republic, July 14, 1997, at 33; Amartya Sen, "Civilizational Imprisonments," *in* The Philosophical Challenge of September 11, Tom Rockmore et al., eds. 96, 102–06 (2005); Martha Nussbaum, The Clash Within: Democracy, Religious Violence and India's Future 80–121 (2007). The principal problem with Sen's approach is that often the currents of thought requiring restoration have been so deeply submerged for such a long time by competing interpretations of the authoritative texts that reinvigorating them uncomfortably resembles an effort simply to reinterpret the tradition in light of contemporary Western ideals.

88 Partha Chaterjee, "Empire after Globalization," Econ. & Polit. Weekly, Sept. 11, 2004, 4155, 4163 (decrying the imperialism inherent in "the liberal evangelical creed of taking democracy and human rights to backward cultures").

89 On "development" as the realization of human capabilities, *see* Amartya Sen, Development as Freedom 87–110 (1999).

90 In current usage, hybridity is a recent term referring to the adoption of ideas and practices from diverse sources, including those once deemed incompatible. Homi Bhabha, The Location of Culture 19, 240, 256, 277, 296, 322 (1994). On legal manifestations of hybridity, *see* Vernon Palmer, Mixed Jurisdictions Worldwide (2001).

91 That said, the more important traffic these days – in human rights ideas no less than in scientific medicine – is largely one way, notwithstanding the indubitable joys of Senegalese music and Afghan lamb stew. *See generally* Cross-Cultural Consumption: Global Markets, Local Realities, David Howes, ed. (1996); Tyler Cowen. Creative Destruction: How Globalization is Changing the World's Cultures (2002). To deny as much is to find oneself contending, for instance with Mignolo, that no matter how poor the material resources of universities in the "global South" (as in libraries, laboratories, Internet access, teaching assistants, research time), their scholars and intellectuals are nonetheless producing just the sort of "subaltern knowledge" most fitting and appropriate to their countries' needs, because their feet are firmly planted in local conditions, which they are therefore best placed to apprehend. Mignolo, *supra* note 3, at 4–16. Whether such an assertion is better described as ingenuous or disingenuous, readers may ponder for themselves. No one who has actually taught in such places for any length of time will ponder for long. Most refreshing in this regard was my pleasant surprise in hearing, while teaching in India for several months, learned Bengali anthropologists privately employ the term

"superstition" to describe certain traditional cultural practices of their less educated and well-off countrymen. That is a word that would never pass the lips of a Western anthropologist today, of course, except perhaps with reference to Christian evangelicals in the United States.

92 Having ventured this far into uncomfortable territory, I will graciously leave to others the task of intellectually rehabilitating the notion of "barbarism." For a promising beginning from the left, *see, e.g.*, Eric Hobsbawn, "Barbarism: A User's Guide," *in* On History 253 (1997) (tracing the return of barbarism to the methods employed in World War I, including total mobilization of a nation's material and human resources). On the concept's history, *see generally* J. G. A. Pocock, Barbarism and Religion: Barbarians, Savages, and Empire (2005). And if we are to restore that concept to discursive acceptability, then why not also its close etymological cognate "barbarian" (i.e., as a characterization of those who repudiate humanitarian law)? Anthropologist Michael Taussig is more self-conscious and circumspect than Hobsbawm about how, "in condemning [colonial] violence as savage, I endorse the very notion of the savage," a concept "drawn from that which the civilized imputed to the Indians, to their cannibal-ism especially." Yet he confesses to finding the term barbarism "a convenient term of reference." Taussig, *supra* note 65, at 65.

Such rehabilitations will surely draw inspiration from Žižek's recent charac-terization of the mid-century European conflict between Stalinism and Nazism as one "between civilization and barbarism," insofar as even political prisoners in Siberia sent birthday telegrams to Uncle Joe "wishing him all the best and the success of Socialism." Thus, "Stalinism did not sever the last thread that linked it to civilization. The lowest Gulag inmate still participated in the universal Reason: he had access to the Truth of History." Slavoj Žižek, The Parallax View 291 (2006). Of course, Žižek's distinctively dark, East European comedic edge – his sardonic authorial voice as much as his analyses themselves – is surely his most distinctive contribution to the serious discussion of history's most tragic subjects. Yet there is nothing playful or ironic in his recent characteriza-tion, while criticizing Bush administration counterterrorism policy, of torture's elimination as "arguably our civilization's greatest achievement." Slavoj Žižek, "Knight of the Living Dead," New York Times, March 24, 2007, editorial.

93 Georgia Warnke, Gadamer: Hermeneutics, Tradition and Reason 173 (1987) (parsing Alasdair MacIntyre and Hans-Georg Gadamer). Sociologists often describe this aspect of modernity as "reflexivity," in its capacity for "self-confrontation" and for resulting revision of its own presuppositions. Ulrich Beck, World Risk Society 73–75 (1999). The salience of such collective reflexivity is revealed in the frequency and earnest sincerity with which the question, "why do they hate us?," has been sincerely asked by so many Americans since 9/11.

94 Recognition of the many negative consequences of Western interaction with other parts of the world does not preclude recognition of the positive conse-quences (e.g., the rule of law, scientific medicine, many other life-improving technologies, human rights, democracy, antidiscrimination law, etc.). Critics of the West rightly accuse it of being blind to its own faults when it sometimes turned up its nose at "savage" warfare and hypocritical when it preached rea-son and enlightenment. But such critics should be careful not themselves to

descend into blindness and hypocrisy by denying the many obvious benefits of Western influence.

95 Lecture by Juan Cole, Professor of History, University of Michigan, to Iowa Law faculty, Spring 2007.

96 Such writers seek both to enlarge and contract, in different respects, the scope of the policy domain designated as concerning "security." They question the assumption that what must be secured through security policy is primarily the nation-state and its residents *qua* nationals. Such privileging of the nation-state and the status of persons as its citizens is anachronistic and ill suited to a world of global flows and diasporic attachments, it is argued. And just as we should "decenter" threats of violence originating abroad, we should enhance our concern with nonviolent sources of social insecurity, both at home and overseas. For recent surveys, *see, e.g.,* Critical Security Studies and World Politics, Ken Booth, ed. (2005); Critical Security Studies: Concepts and Cases, Keith Krause & Michael Williams, eds. (1997).

97 Jutta Weldes, et al., "Introduction," *in* Cultures of Insecurity: States, Communities, and the Production of Danger 1, 14 (1999).

98 Mary Ann Glendon, Rights Talk: The Impoverishment of Political Discourse 171–73 (1991).

99 Michael Dillon, "Governing Terror: The State of Emergency of Biopolitical Emergence," 1 Int'l Polit. Sociol. 7, 8 (2007).

100 On methods that have been successfully employed to build trust between states, *see* Aaron Hoffman, Building Trust: Overcoming Suspicion in International Conflict 136–53 (2006).

101 Husain Haqqani, "Pakistan and the Islamists," Current Hist. 147, 147 (April 2007); *see also* Carlotta Gall & Jane Perlez, "Pakistan Victors Want Dialogue with Militants," New York Times, Feb. 20, 2008, at A1. The same issue has arisen in the Phillipines. Eric Schmitt, "Experts See Gains Against Asian Terror Networks," New York Times, June 9, 2008. "Lumping the Islamic Front with Abu Sayyaf will inflame those Filipino Muslims who are seeking self-determination through a peace effort, and make it harder for the Front to cooperate in fighting terrorism," said Abhoud Syed Lingga, the executive director of the Institute of Bangsamoro Studies. "If the goal [of U.S. forces] is to defeat the Abu Sayyaf Group and its foreign, mainly Indonesian, jihadi allies, they are casting the net too widely and creating unnecessary enemies."

102 Mark Mazzetti & David Rohde, "Amid Policy Disputes, Qaeda Grows in Pakistan," New York Times, June 30, 2008, at A1 (explaining that CIA analysts believe that the ceasefire brokered between the Pakistani government and militants in 2006 enabled the latter to reestablish and enlarge their forces still more deeply in northern, Pashtun tribal areas).

103 On the increasing adoption of the most stringent forms of *shari'a* by several states in recent years, *see* Radical Islam's Rules: The Worldwide Spread of Extreme Shari'a, Paul Marshall, ed. (2005) (describing this development in Pakistan, Nigeria, the Sudan, Indonesia, Afghanistan, Malaysia, Iran, and Saudi Arabia).

104 Peter Bergen & Paul Cruickshank, "The Unraveling: Al Qaeda's Revolt against bin Laden," New Republic, June 11, 2008, at 16, 18; Lawrence Wright, "The

Rebellion Within: An Al Qaeda Mastermind Questions Terrorism," New Yorker, June 2, 2008, at 37, 44.

105 David Cole & Jules Lobel, Less Safe, Less Free: Why America Is Losing the War on Terror (2007). They write, "When we sweep away the rules [of due process and humanitarian law] in the name of preventing the next attack, we foster the conditions that make the next attack that much more likely." These authors offer no evidence or serious argument for this capacious conclusion. On the several psychological steps through which one must pass even to begin to reach the point of volunteering for a suicide mission, and the many factors affecting each such passage, *see* the work of forensic psychiatrist Marc Sageman, Leaderless Jihad: Terror Networks in the 21st Century 71–88 (2008); Daniel Benjamin & Steven Simonj, The Next Attack: The Failure of the War on Terror and a Strategy for Getting It Right 47 (2005) (distinguishing a core circle of hard-line adherents from a broader group of fellow travelers, composed of vulnerable and alienated young men, who might be convinced to enter the inner circle if changing circumstances heightened their anger and disaffection).

106 Khaled Abou El Fadl, "9/11 and the Muslim Transformation," *in* September 11 in History, Mary Dudziak, ed. 70, 95 (2003).

107 *Id.* citing Qur'an 4:135, 5:8.

108 Philip Gordon, "Can the War on Terror Be Won?" 86 Foreign Affairs 53, Nov./Dec. 2007 (summarizing survey research by Shibley Telhami); Andrew Kohut & Richard Wike, "All the World's a Stage: America's Image in the Muslim World," The National Interest, May 6, 2008, at 54 (concluding from Pew Global Attitude surveys that "fewer Muslims now consider suicide bombing justifiable, and confidence in Osama bin Laden has waned" as well as that "there is broad support for democracy, capitalism and globalization throughout the world, including Muslim nations").

109 "A Nation Challenged: President Bush Address on Terrorism before a Joint Meeting of Congress," New York Times, Sept. 21, 2001.

110 Convention (V) Respecting the Rights and Duties of Neutral Powers and Persons in Case of War on Land. The Hague, 18 October 1907, Arts. 1, 2, 10.

111 Ian Loader & Neil Walker, Civilizing Security 12 (2007); *see also* Steve Niva, "Contested Sovereignties and Postcolonial Insecurities in the Middle East," *in* Cultures of Insecurity, Jutta Weldes et al, eds. 147, 153 (1999).

112 Karl Polanyi, The Great Transformation 49 (1957) (describing how, according to Malinowski, each coastal village in the Trobriand Islands is paired with an inland village, "so that the important exchange of breadfruits and fish, though disguised as the reciprocal distribution of gifts," can maintain economic integration and social solidarity between these two geographical areas).

113 Carl Schmitt, The Concept of the Political, George Schwab, trans. 26 (1929) (2007).

114 It may then be only a slight exaggeration to contend that "seeking after security for oneself and being a cause of insecurity for others are not just closely related; they are the same thing." R. N. Berki, Security and Society: Reflections on Law, Order, and Politics 32–33 (1986).

115 Loader & Walker, *supra* note 111, at 13–14 (quoting Anthony Burke, though the citation to him is inaccurate).

116 Ciencias de La Naturaleza en al-Andalus, E. García Sánchez, ed. 3 vols. (1990–1994).

117 Noah Feldman, "War and Reason in Maimonides and Averroes," *in* The Ethics of War: Shared Problems in Different Traditions, Richard Sorabji & David Rodin, eds. 92, 104 (2006).

118 Leonard Binder, Islamic Liberalism 9, 126–27, 170–73, 274–82 (1988). *See also* Malise Ruthven, "The Rise of the Muslim Terrorists," N.Y. Rev. of Books, May 29, 2008, at 33, 34 ("Far from espousing received theological certainties in order to defend 'Muslim society' against foreign encroachments, Qutb's understanding of Islam is almost Kierkegaardian in its individualism. His 'authentic' Muslim is one who espouses a very modern kind of revolution against the deification of men, against injustice, and against political, economic, racial and religious prejudice."). Some of the Western influence on Islamist thinking is less salubrious, to be sure. Matthias Küntzel, Jihad and Jew-Hatred: Islamism, Nazism and the Roots of 9/11, Colin Meade, trans. (2007) (contending that Nazi ideas influenced Islamist thinkers like Qutb).

119 Michael Sandel, Liberalism and the Limits of Justice 151 (1979).

120 Anghie, *supra* note 9, at 311. Said writes similarly of a "dialectic of reinforcement." Said, *supra* note 11, at 94. Western colonizers relied too heavily on historical texts to interpret contemporary realities before them, Said contends: "Such texts can *create* not only knowledge but also the very reality they appear to describe" (emphasis in original).

121 Roxanne L. Euben, Enemy in the Mirror: Islamic Fundamentalism and the Limits of Modern Rationalism 123–68 (1999).

122 Sir Paul Vinogradoff, "Historical Types in International Law," *in* 1 Biblioteca Visseriana Dissertationum ius international illustrantiium 1, 14 (1923).

123 An author of more crypto-Marxist leanings like Slavoj Žižek might at least respond here that the contradictions lie not so much within his own argument as out there in the world, in the social reality he claims to explain, and that his argument hence merely registers them. The better and less flippant response, of course, is that it *is* a significant improvement, over war or other violence, to resolve disputes by way of legal argument about the relative significance of competing claims of human right. After all, resolution by legal argument – however frequently indeterminate – remains superior to resolution by violence even if such disputes would be still better resolved by reference to methods of evaluation more attentive to empirical consequences, including second-order consequences for human rights protection beyond the courtroom. This would be especially the case if the legal domain of human rights were pared to its moral essentials, stripped of its many secondary and opportunistic accretions.

124 Mikkel Rasmussen, The Risk Society at War: Terror, Technology and Strategy in the Twenty-First Century 195–96 (2006).

125 *See supra* Chapter 3 at 132–42.

126 Taussig, *supra* note 65, at 143.

127 Norbert Elias, The Civilizing Process: vol. 1, Power and Civility; vol. 2, The History of Manners, Edmund Jephcott, trans. (1982), *passim*.

128 Charles Lindholm, Culture and Identity 379 (2001) ("Working class relationships in America tend to be more volatile and confrontational.... Children

are trained to see themselves in an adversarial light and to harden themselves for the struggle against a hostile world," whereas "upper-middle-class children are socialized to imagine themselves flowering in a nurturant environment and are encouraged to seek cooperative relations with others."). *See also* Adrie Kusserow, "De-Homogenizing American Individualism: Socializing 'Hard' and 'Soft' Individualism in Manhattan and Queens," 27 Ethos 210 (1999); Paul Willis, Learning to Labor: How Working Class Kids Get Working Class Jobs (1977).

129 Several of today's human rights movements and ideas, particularly the right to self-determination of peoples, emerged from these struggles. Mary Ann Glendon, A World Made New: Eleanor Roosevelt and the Universal Declaration of Human Rights 12–13, 74, 149–50, 214 (2001). This is not to deny the intense opposition to Western imperialism among certain Enlightenment thinkers. Sankar Muthu, Enlightenment Against Empire 1–10, 259–83 (2003) (examining opposition to Western imperialism in the works of Kant, Herder, and Diderot).

130 Richard Tuck, The Rights of War and Peace: Political Thought and the International Order from Grotius to Kant 14 (1999).

131 The social philosopher I have principally in mind here is Jean Braudrillard; the military thinker, Christopher Coker.

132 National Commission on Terrorist Attacks upon the U.S. 362 (July 22, 2004).

133 Christopher Coker, Waging War without Warriors? The Changing Culture of Military Conflict 81 (2002).

134 Osama bin Laden, "A Muslim Bomb," Dec. 1998, *in* Messages to the World: The Statements of Osama bin Laden, Bruce Lawrence, ed., James Howarth, trans. 51, 72 (2005). Editorial, New York Times, Feb. 20, 2005 ("Osama bin Laden has declared acquisition of nuclear weapons to be a religious duty.").

135 Nina Tannenwald, The Nuclear Taboo: The U.S. and the Non-Use of Nuclear Weapons since 1945 (2007); Richard Price, The Chemical Weapons Taboo (1997); Thomas Schelling, "An Astonishing Sixty Years: The Legacy of Hiroshima," 96 Amer. Econ. Rev. 929 (2006).

136 This is a recurrent theme in the conversations with enlistees recorded by Robert Kaplan in his book, Imperial Grunts 14, 364 (2005).

137 Anat Berko, The Path to Paradise: The Inner World of Suicide Bombers and Their Dispatchers 74–75, 83, 86, 102–03, 115–16, 124–29, 142–46, 151, 158 (2007); Sageman, *supra* note 105, (describing the principal motives of interviewed jihadist terrorists as "love, reputation, or glory"); Ahmed Rashid, "Jihadi Suicide Bombers: The New Wave," N.Y. Rev. of Books, June 12, 2008, at 17, 17 (concluding, on the basis of two recent studies of life in the Afghan training camps during the early 1990s, that "the young men who trained in these camps were not educated in the Islamic schools called madrasas and they were inspired less by extremist Islamic ideology than by their desires to see the world, handle weapons, and have a youthful adventure").

138 Paul Lauren, Power and Prejudice: The Politics and Diplomacy of Racial Discrimination (1996); Mary Dudziak, Cold War Civil Rights: Race and the Image of American Democracy (2000).

139 Richard Schragger, "Jurisprudence: Cooler Heads: The Difference between the President's Lawyers and the Military's," Slate, Sept. 20, 2006, at http://www.slate.com/id/2150050.

140 Jon Elster, Closing the Books: Transitional Justice in Historical Perspective 235 (2005).

141 Anghie, *supra* note 9, at 311–18.

142 Anthony Burke, "Aporias of Security," 27 Alternatives 1, 7 (2002).

143 On the challenges that these new, informal cross-border processes pose for redefining the tasks and methods of social science, especially cultural anthropology, *see* George Marcus, Ethnography through Thick and Thin 57–105 (1998).

144 Michael Dillon, "Global Security in the 21st Century: Circulation, Complexity and Contingency," Chatham House, ISP/NSC Briefing Paper 05/02, Oct. 2005, at 2.

145 Taussig, *supra* note 65, at 246.

146 Barry Buzan, From International to World Society?: English School Theory and the Social Structure of Globalization (2004); Ian Clark, International Legitimacy and World Society 6–26 (2007).

147 In explaining the growth of cross-border affinities, others instead stress the importance of "top-down" processes by which states – as formal organizations – become integrated into a "world culture," enacting a "global script" that defines what modern statehood itself requires. On this view, world culture imposes expectations about desirable structures and standards of domestic governance, even if compliance with these expectations often lags far behind. In this process, collective identities and national interests are "constructed," such scholars contend. *See, e.g.,* Ryan Goodman & Derek Jinks, "Toward an Institutional Theory of Sovereignty," 55 Stanford L. Rev. 1749 (2003).

148 For recent jurisprudence on sowing terror as a war crime, *see* Alexander Zahar & Göran Sluiter, International Criminal Law: A Critical Introduction 140–45 (2007).

149 Leon Wieseltier, "The Catastrophist," New York Times, April 27, 2008.

150 On recent efforts to rethink this concept in light of contemporary intercultural experience, particularly that of the Muslim diaspora in the West, *see* Peter Mamdaville, Transnational Muslim Politics: Re-Imagining the Umma 108–51 (2001).

151 The quoted wording is from a critical review of the present book, in manuscript, written from a postcolonial perspective, for the University of Chicago Press. Many Islamic leaders, for instance in Pakistan, "insist that Al Qaeda does not exist, that it is a fictious creation of the American government as a way to control the Muslim world." Rashid, *supra* note 137, at 20. To be sure, in light of divisions among Sunni insurgent forces within Iraq alone, "it is an open question as to whether Al Qaeda is a unified operating organization at all," according to Middle East historian Ira Lapidus. Michael Cooper & Larry Rohter, "McCain, Iraq War and the Threat of 'Al Qaeda,'" New York Times, April 19, 2008 (quoting Lapidus).

152 Some Islamic scholars dispute even the designation "suicide attacks," on the view that "heroic acts of martyrdom have nothing to do with suicide" since they are "the supreme form of struggle in the path of God," as writes Shaykh Qaradhawi. Yusuf al-Qaradhawi similarly urges that "the mentality of those

who carry out martyrdom operations has nothing to do with the mentality of one who commits suicide," because suicide is often "selfish," whereas those who die killing Israeli civilians sacrifice their lives for the sake of others. Both men are quoted, without citation, by John Kelsay in his "Suicide Bombers: The 'Just War' Debate, Islamic Style," *in* Deviance across Cultures, Robert Heiner, ed. 227, 228 (2007); *but see* Hikmet Yüceoğlu, "Martyrdom – A Definition: Can a Terrorist Be a Martyr?" (answering in the negative, from a Sufi perspective) and Ergün Çapan, "Suicide Attacks and Islam," *in* Terror and Suicide Attacks: An Islamic Perspective, Egün Çapan, ed. 86, 102 (2004).

If the phenomenon in question cannot be described as suicide, then it follows that "suicide bombing" or "suicide bombers," as such, simply do not exist, and so cannot pose any danger. Presumably suicide bombers too, once properly deconstructed, are merely a fabrication of the Orientalist imagination. And if "there is nothing outside the text," as Derrida contends, then if textual references to "Islamists," "terrorists," "suicide bombers" are all foreclosed, then such are mere chimera; there can be no reason to fear them. Q.E.D. Yet it is difficult to see much point in "intercultural dialogue" – seemingly anodyne exhortations to which today abound – when one side to the discussion is apparently so quick, in this way, to pull the putative trump card of its divinely revealed text for definitions of contested concepts.

Of course, oversimplification is always a danger to be guarded against. There are fundamentalists who are not Islamists, Islamists who are not jihadists, jihadists who are not violent, violent jihadists who confine their violence to combatants, and violent jihadists who confine their attacks on noncombatants to Israeli noncombatants, etc. Through such an infinite regress, by accentuating such increasingly fine differences between this and that, one could indeed dispense with the matter entirely simply by foreclosing any textual designation of it as an overgeneralization. This is precisely the rhetorical strategy of the manuscript reviewer mentioned above.

The definitional difficulties are real, to be sure. For instance, the effort of one universally acknowledged specialist to define "Islamism" quickly descends into merely a listing of events widely agreed as manifestations of it. Gilles Kepel, The Roots of Radical Islam 20 (2005). Yet too often in postcolonial theory, if Western scholars seek to understand and respect differences between themselves and another culture, they are accused of exoticizing the Orient, whereas if they "repent" and seek out commonalities between themselves and the other culture – with its members as human beings, their longings for liberty and prosperity, in particular – they are condemned for imposing a "false universalism." For this is a second sort of misunderstanding, equally attributable to their corrupting, imperialist gaze. "Heads I win, tails you lose" is no more acceptable, however, as an intellectual strategy than in resolving a dispute by tossing a coin.

Because the "universals" are actually only self-flattering Western prejudices, within "the ethic of humanism" thus resides "the spirit of ethnocide." Pierre Clastres, "On Ethnocide," Art and Text 53, 53 (1988). It is true that, for such reasons, Britain's great nineteenth-century liberals were strikingly indifferent to the suffering their empire caused far and wide, with Bentham as a notable exception. Duncan Bell, "Empire and International Relations in Victorian

Political Thought," 49 The Historical J. 281, 285–87 (2006). Edmund Burke, with his traditionalist's respect for the infinite particularity of customs, for the limits of human reason in overcoming severe moral disagreement, and his distrust of concentrated state power, saw matters much more clearly and critically. Edmund Burke, On Empire, Liberty, and Reform: Speeches and Letters, David Bromwich, ed. 14–15, 29, 258–62, 289–91, 347 (2000).

The obstacles that the postcolonialist "discovers" to the possibility of Western understanding almost suggest that it would be better if Westerners made no effort at all, or rather more to the point, that they simply deferred uncritically to the assertions of intellectuals – often born to privileged, non-Western parents and generally educated and employed in elite Western universities – to define for the rest of us the meaning of all cultural traces left by non-Western peoples, presumably otherwise indecipherable to us. Nice career strategy, to be sure, for cleansing the Western academic labor market of domestic competitors; not much else to be said for it. For reflections in a similar spirit, informed by the sociology of ideas and intellectuals, *see* Ernest Gellner, Postmodernism, Reason and Religion 38–64, 95–96 (1992); Joseph Schumpeter, "The Sociology of the Intellectual," *in* Political Theory and Ideology, Judith Shklar, ed. 115 (1966).

This observation admittedly risks confusion with an *ad hominem*, which it is not, but it may be in any event that an *ad hominem* is exactly the fitting rejoinder – logically and morally – to what is essentially an *argumentum ad vericundiam*, the appeal to one's personal authority and position – such as, "born to the Third World, I speak for the Third World" – as grounds for others' deference and belief, rather than to evidence and reasoned argument. Surely the most pervasive *ad hominem* argument in this context, in any event, is the suggestion that because the idea of human rights is proposed to the rest by the capitalist West, it must be contaminated by everything pernicious about its native precincts, specifically by imperialism.

Another leading social theorist, equally unconvinced (as was Gellner) by postcolonialism, asks how such theory, in its rejection of the binary oppositions of "Orientalism," would define the nature of what all people, across cultural lines and historical epochs, then have in common. His answer mockingly invokes Steven Spielberg's animated children's TV series, in which several species of animals, when compelled to acknowledge their differences of size and strength, quickly reassure one another: "From and on the outside, we appear different, but inside, we are all the same – frightened individuals at a loss in the world, needing the help of others." In this way, "Hollywood meets the most radical postcolonial critique of ideological universality." We may not resist the comparison on the grounds that this "Hollywood wisdom [is] a caricature" of its more highbrow cousin"; rather, the low brow version simply "distills the ideological message out of the pseudo-sophisticated jargon" of postcolonialism, he observes. Slavoj Žižek, Welcome to the Desert of the Real! Five Essays on September 11 and Related Dates 64–66 (2002).

Even apart from such banal human commonality, the acceptance (and even embrace) as immutable of remaining cultural and civilizational variation, like that between different species of animals, is simply mistaken. Cultural traditions often encounter difficulties in solving their internal questions, problems acknowledged as such by their own standards of truth, and then venture outside of themselves to find satisfactory answers – to continue the Spielberg analogy, by consulting other animal species.

CHAPTER 9. THE INFLATIONARY RHETORIC OF TERRORIST THREAT: HUMANITARIAN LAW AS DEFLATIONARY CHECK

1 James Dawes, The Language of War: Literature and Culture in the U.S. from the Civil War through World War II 15 (2002).
2 *Id.* at 202.
3 *Id.* at 210.
4 William T. Sherman, Memoirs 602 (1990) (1875).
5 *Id.* at 601 ("War is cruelty, and you cannot refine it.").
6 Eric Posner & Alan Sykes, "Optimal War and *Jus Ad Bellum*," John M. Olin Law and Economics Working Paper No. 211 (April 2004), University of Chicago Law School.
7 Richard Posner, Becker-Posner Blog, "The costs of the war in Iraq," March 19, 2006. He writes, "I do not think a decision to go to war should be based on cost-benefit analysis. It would terrify the world if powerful nations conducted cost-benefit analyses of whether to go to war. There are 192 nations besides the United States; should we ask the Defense Department to advise us which ones we should invade because the expected benefits would exceed the expected costs?" Posner does not here specify his criteria, however, for distinguishing the situations to which cost-benefit analysis should not apply, such as this, and those – most ones, in his view – where it should.
8 This is not to deny that state-led war production has sometimes greatly increased a nation's economic activity, as in the United States during World War II. A certain strand of leftist thought has even considered war's destructiveness to be a solution to the "overproduction crisis" of modern capitalism and as therefore periodically necessary to that system's survival.
9 David Frum & Richard Perle, An End to Evil 9 (2007).
10 James Traub, "The Unrepentant," New York Times, Dec. 17, 2007, Book Review of Alan Weisman, Prince of Darkness: Richard Perle (2007).
11 Jeffrey Alexander, "From the Depths of Despair: Performance, Counterperformance, and 'September 11,'" 22 Sociological Theory 88, 103 (2004); Philip Smith, Why War? The Cultural Logic of Iraq, the Gulf War, and Suez (2005), *passim.*
12 These very features of jihadist terror actually make it confessedly appealing to at least one leading postmodernist. Jean Baudrillard, The Spirit of Terrorism and Other Essays, Chris Turner, trans. 74–76 (2003). (2003); Julian Reid, The Biopolitics of the War on Terror: Life Struggles, Liberal Modernity, and the Defense of Logistical Societies 62–81 (2006). Reid sympathetically parses Baudrillard's views in this respect, concluding that "the integrity of this Terror, [Baudrillard] argues, is to be located in its attempt to defend life against the life-governing techniques of liberal regimes." *Id.* at 67. *See also* Slavoj Žižek, Welcome to the Desert of the Real! Five Essays on September 11 and Related Dates 131 (2002) (arguing that the "reference to Western liberal tolerance . . . is the form of appearance of the neocolonialist terror of Capital; the call for

'unfreedom' (reactionary 'fundamentalism') is the form of appearance of the resistance to this terror").

13 Ian Shapiro, Containment: Rebuilding a Strategy against Global Terror 45 (2007). On the origin of the term, *see* David Frum, The Right Man: The Surprise Presidency of George W. Bush 231–39 (2003). Until the last draft of President Bush's address, the preferred wording was "axis of hatred." Speechwriter Michael Gerson switched "hatred" to "evil" because of the more theological language the president had started using publicly since 9/11.

14 Smith, *supra* note 11, at 27. The remaining quotations in this paragraph and the next are from *id.* at 27, 27, 27, 212, 221.

15 Tony Blair, Prime Minister's Address to the Labour Party Conference, cited in Mikkel Rasmussen, The Risk Society at War: Terror, Technology and Strategy in the Twenty-First Century 169 (2006).

16 Giorgio Agamben, in particular, compares the legal position of Guantánamo detainees to Jews in Nazi concentration camps. Following Walter Benjamin's observations of 1939, he also describes the "state of exception" as the paradigmatic political feature – i.e., not exceptional at all of the contemporary world. Giorgio Agamben, Homo Sacer 4 (1995).

17 Smith, *supra* note 11, at 24. The remaining quotations in this paragraph and the next are from *id.* at 24, 24, 24, 212, 21, 24, 21, 28, 29.

18 Elaine Scarry, The Body in Pain: The Making and Unmaking of the World 130, 131 (1985).

19 The deflationary effect is even greater if the situation is framed as one susceptible to resolution through enforcement of ordinary domestic criminal law, the approach adopted by the U.S. Court of Appeals for the Fourth Circuit, in *Ali Saleh Kahah Al-Marri v. Commander S.L. Wright*, U.S. Navy Commander, No. 06-7427 (June 11, 2007).

20 The Security Council may also authorize military action, under Charter Art. 42, to "maintain or restore international peace and security," as through humanitarian intervention. Prior to the Charter, widely acceptable arguments for war had included the collective of delinquent foreign debt, redress of historic injustices to the nation, the annexation of territory, and spreading a religious faith or Western "civilization."

21 *See, e.g.,* John Rawls, A Theory of Justice 379 (1971) ("Where a country's right to war is questionable and uncertain, the constraints on the means it can use are all the more severe."); Michael Walzer, Just and Unjust Wars 245–55 (1977) (defending departures from *jus in bello* rules in a "supreme emergency"); Jeff McMahan, "Précis: The Morality and Law of War," 40 Israel L. Rev. 670, 670 (2007); Thomas Hurka, "Proportionality in the Morality of War," 33 Phil. & Pub. Aff. 34, 44 (2005).

22 Another reason for treating aggressor and aggrieved alike for purposes of humanitarian law is that, as Greenwood notes, "taken to extremes, the [opposing] argument would mean that members of an aggressor's armed forces would not be entitled to prisoner of war status or be protected by other rules of the law of war." Christopher Greenwood, "The Concept of War in Modern International Law," 36 Int'l & Comp. L. Q. 283, 288 (1987).

23 Robert Pape, Dying to Win: The Strategic Logic of Suicide Terrorism (2005).

24 Those contending that Islamist distaste for the West is primarily theological and based on the spiritual condition of life in the West rather than primarily its policies toward the Middle East include Salman Rushdie, "A War That Presents Us All with a Crisis of Faith," Guardian, Nov. 3, 2001; Mary Habeck, Knowing the Enemy: Jihadist Ideology and the War on Terror 5–15, 162 (2006); Peter Berkowitz, "Vulgarizing the War Debate," Policy Rev. (Sept. 2007); Jean Bethke Elshstain, Just War against Terror 3 (2003); Roxanne Euben, Enemy in the Mirror: Islamic Fundamentalism and the Limits of Modern Rationalism (1999); Michael Mazarr, Unmodern Men in the Modern World (2007); Paul Berman, Terror and Liberalism (2003); Paul Berman, "Who's Afraid of Tariq Ramadan?," 236 New Republic, June 4, 2007, at 37; Bernard Lewis, The Crisis of Islam: Holy War and Unholy Terror (2003); and Bernard Lewis, What Went Wrong? The Conflict between Islam and Modernity in the Middle East (2003). The *Economist* magazine also adopts this view. Editorial, "The Need to Speak Up," The Economist, Oct. 13, 2001, at 14.

25 Ian Buruma & Avishai Margalit, Occidentalism: The West in the Eyes of its Enemies 8 (2004).

26 Quoted in Anthony Pagden, Worlds at War: The 2,500 Year Struggle between East and West 247 (2008); *see generally* The Sayyid Qutb Reader: Selected Writings on Politics, Religion, and Society, Albert Bergesen, ed. (2007).

27 Buruma & Margalit, *supra* note 25. This image of America has a long history in European antidemocratic thought. James Ceaser, Reconstructing America: The Symbol of America in Modern Thought (1997), *passim*; Andrei Markovits, Uncouth Nation: Why Europe Dislikes America 11–32, 142–44 (2007); Mazarr, *supra* note 24, at 163, 171.

28 On such complexities, *see generally* Cemil Aydin, The Politics of Anti-Westernism in Asia: Visions of World Order in Pan-Islamic and Pan-Asian Thought 191–203 (2007).

29 *Id.* at 196.

30 Stephen Holmes, The Matador's Cape: America's Reckless Response to Terror 7 (2007) (noting that "this sort of reciprocity cannot be expected in the war on terror"); Dennis Ross, Statecraft, and How to Restore America's Standing in the World 158 (2007); Larry May, War Crimes and Just War 302–03 (2006). *Cf.* Bryan Brophy-Baermann & John Conybeare, "Retaliating against Terrorism: Rational Expectations and the Optimality of Rules vs. Discretion," 38 Amer. J. Polit. Sci. 196, 209 (1994) (finding, from Israeli experience and data, a short-term decline in terrorism whenever groups responsible for it suffer retaliation of unanticipated magnitude; these were not episodes of suicide terrorism, however, and the groups in question sometimes held territory, making them more susceptible to deterrence).

31 Ayman al Zawahiri, for instance, criticized Abu Musab al-Zarqawi's beheading of captives as needlessly offensive to world opinion, including potential Muslim supporters. Shibley Telhami, "America in Arab Eyes," 49 Survival 107, 119 (2007). Qbu Yahya al-Libi, among other Al Qaeda leaders, prominently criticized Zarqawi for killing too many civilians. Michael Moss & Souad Mekhennet, "Rising Leader for Next Phase of Al Qaedq's War," New York Times, April 4, 2008. Other leading jihadists who once endorsed attacks on civilians have

recently renounced attacks on fellow Muslims, at least, though sometimes also on Western civilians. This reversal has been inspired in certain cases, however, no less by strategic considerations than by moral remorse; Al Qaeda's popularity in parts of the Arab world declined precipitously after its attacks on Muslims. On these developments within Al Qaeda, *see generally* Peter Bergen & Paul Cruickshank, "The Unraveling: Al Qaeda's Revolt against bin Laden," New Republic, June 11, 2008, at 16, 18; Lawrence Wright, "The Rebellion Within: An Al Qaeda Mastermind Questions Terrorism," New Yorker, June 2, 2008, at 37, 44. But there have always been certain voices among the most prominent of military jihadists, such as that of Abu Mus'ab al-Suri, contending that mass attacks on Western civilians only elicit effective U.S. retribution against jihadist forces. Brynjar Lia, Architect of Global Jihad: The Life of al-Qaida Strategist Abu Mus'ab al-Suri (2008).

32 It is not a true incorporation by reference in that the most important treaties in humanitarian law predate those specifically addressed to "human rights." The latter thus could not intend to reference the former in a literal sense.

33 Émile Durkheim, The Division of Labor in Society, G. Simpson, trans. 70–75 (1933) (1893).

34 *Id.*

35 *Id.* at 172–73. Durkheim presciently wrote, "As all the other beliefs and all the other practices take on a character less and less religious, the individual becomes the object of a sort of religion. We erect a cult on behalf of personal dignity which, as every strong cult, already has its superstitions." On the relevance of this insight for contemporary international affairs, *see* Salif Nimaga, "An International *Conscience Collective*? The Possibilities of a Durkheimian Analysis of International Criminal Law," M.A. thesis, Int'l Institute for the Sociology of Law, Antigua Universidad, Oñati, Spain, Oct. 18, 2004.

36 On the characteristic features of Western liberal society, taken as an ideal-type instantiated in different manner and measure in various countries, *see* Charles Taylor, Modern Social Imaginaries 1–22 (2004). Taylor describes these features as "individualism, personal liberty, science, industrial production, secularization, instrumental rationality, a public sphere, a market economy, a self-governing people . . . as well as alienation, meaninglessness, and a sense of impending social dissolution." *Id.* at 1–2. Taylor offers detailed accounts of all these key terms, on which the present study relies, in A Secular Age 159–81, 531–33 (2007) and Sources of the Self: The Making of Modern Identity (1989). No normative connotations need be attached to any such empirical and analytical characterizations – Taylor himself is a practicing Catholic, for that matter – though they often are, to be sure. Recent efforts by Islamic scholars to assess critically the concept of modernity and its relevance to their countries include Islam and the West: Critical Perspectives on Modernity, Michael J. Thompson, ed. (2003) and Aziz Al-Azmeh, Islams and Modernities (1996).

37 Our sense of shared humanity with the world's starving does not induce virtually any of us, for instance, to donate even 1% of our annual income to this cause. This is just as the theory of organic solidarity would have predicted. Other social thinkers have been more hopeful. But "collective compassion" of a robust variety is surely essential to any effective international promotion of

basic human rights. Bryan Turner, "Outline of a Theory of Human Rights," 27 Sociology 489, 507 (1993); Norman Fiering, "Irresistible Compassion: An Aspect of 18th-Century Sympathy and Humanitarianism," 37 J. Hist. Ideas 195 (1976).

38 On how this reality manifests itself in one region, *see, e.g.,* Curtis Doebbler, "A Human Rights Approach to Statelessness in the Middle East," 15 Leiden J. Int'l L. 527 (2002) (indicating how treaties designed to protect people rendered stateless in that region have largely failed).

39 Hannah Arendt, The Origins of Totalitarianism 336 (1973) (1951).

40 Steve Coll, The Bin Ladens: An Arabian Family in the American Century (2008); Peter Bergen, The Osama bin Laden I Know 2–19, 399–403 (2006).

41 This is essentially a sociological question about the empirical strength of felt solidarity with others. But alongside that question lies the normative one, which presently divides liberal theory into two camps. Certain liberals, such as Rawls and Thomas Nagel, believe that "the right sort of interactive interdependence" must exist in order to generate duties between particular states. Other, more "cosmopolitan" liberals reply that because justice entails impartiality toward all (i.e., regardless of one's degree of connection to particular persons) "international interdependence is flatly irrelevant to justice" and to its demands on us vis-à-vis those living in other states. A.J. Julius, "Nagel's Atlas," 34 Phil. & Pub. Aff. 176, 178 (2006); *see generally* David Miller, "The Limits of Cosmopolitan Justice," *in* International Society, David Mapel & Terry Nardin, eds. 164, 165–71 (1998); Onora O'Neill, "Justice and Boundaries," *in* Political Restructuring in Europe: Ethical Perspectives, Chris Brown, ed. 82–83 (1994) (contending that in the international arena, circumstances of justice exist with respect to certain issues, at least).

More pessimistic than even the Nagel/Rawls position is the view that interdependence, though perhaps necessary to effective cross-border humanitarianism, is woefully insufficient. World War I began, after all, at a time when international trade in Europe had reached a point greater than any before or since. Still, "however dense and intense economic exchange may be, it does not translate easily or automatically into a shared awareness of a common identity, a shared community, or a common ethos." Andrew Hurrell, "Order and Justice: What is at Stake?" in Order and Justice in International Relations, Rosemary Foot et al. 24, 37 (2003).

42 Martha Nussbaum, "Patriotism and Cosmopolitanism," *in* For Love of Country: Debating the Limits of Patriotism, Joshua Cohen, ed. 3 (1996) (describing the Stoics' worldview).

43 Christopher Coker, Waging War without Warriors? The Changing Culture of Military Conflict 63 (2002).

44 Thomas L. Haskell, "Capitalism and the Origins of Humanitarian Sensibility – Part I," 90 Amer. Hist. Rev. 339, 353–361 (1985) (describing the diffusion of humanitarian feeling and related reforms since 1750, and attributing these to enhanced awareness of connections with distant others brought about by expanding national and international markets); Joshua Cohen, "The Arc of the Moral Universe," 26 Phil. & Pub. Aff. 91 (1997) (contending that the truth of moral ideas, such as the wrongfulness of slavery, exercises a significant causal role in their ultimate success).

45 Emilie Hafner-Brown & James Ron, "Human Rights Institutions: Rhetoric and Reality," 44 J. of Peace Res. 379 (2007) (concluding that "while many case-study scholars tend to be rather optimistic about the potential for human rights change, statistically inclined researchers often lean toward greater caution and, in some cases, downright skepticism about the transformative potential of international human rights law and advocacy"); Emilie Hafner-Burton & Kiyoteru Tsutsui, "Justice Lost! The Failure of International Human Rights Law to Matter Where Needed Most," 44 J. of Peace Res. 407 (2007) (finding that "treaties may be failing to make a difference in those states most in need of reform – the world's worst abusers – even though they have been the targets of the human rights regime from the very beginning").

46 Immanuel Kant "Perpetual Peace: A Philosophical Sketch," (1795), *in* Kant: Political Writings, Hans Reiss, ed. 2nd ed , 105–08 (1991).

47 On media depictions of such distant suffering and the varieties of human response to it, including but not limited to pity, *see* Luc Boltanski, Distant Suffering: Morality, Media, and Politics (1999).

48 William James, The Principles of Psychology 692 (1891).

49 This was the language proclaimed by British Prime Minister Arthur Neville Chamberlain on returning from the Munich peace negotiations with Adolf Hitler in 1938.

50 John Rawls, "50 Years after Hiroshima," Dissent 323, 325 (Summer 1995); John Rawls, The Law of Peoples 108 (1999).

51 Rawls does say, however, "Debates about general philosophical questions cannot be the daily stuff of politics, but that does not make these questions without significance, since we think their answers will shape the underlying attitudes of the public culture and the conduct of politics. If we take for granted as common knowledge that a just and well-ordered society is impossible, then the quality and tone of those discussions will reflect that knowledge." John Rawls, Political Liberalism lxi (1996), paperback ed.

52 Charles A. Jones, "War in the 21st Century: An Institution in Crisis," *in* The Anarchical Society in a Globalized World, Richard Little & John Williams, eds. 162, 179 (2006).

53 Mary Ellen O'Connell, "The Myth of Preemptive Self-Defense," Amer. Soc. Int'l Law Task Force on Terrorism, Aug. 2002, at http://www.asil.org/taskforce/oconnell.pdf.

54 Rudolph Peters, Jihad in Classical and Modern Islam 106–28 (1996); Middle East Online, "Muslim Scholars Define 'Terrorism' as Opposed to Legitimate Jihad," Jan. 2002, at http://www. middle-east-online.com/English/?cat=main&page=1&id=174; Quintan Wiktorowicz & John Kaltner, "Killing in the Name of Islam: Al-Qaeda's Justification for September 11," 10 Middle East Policy 84 (2002); Habeck, *supra* note 24, at 110–11; Bernard Freamon, "Martyrdom, Suicide, and the Islamic Law of War," 27 Fordham Int'l L. J. 299 (2003); Shaheen S. Ali & Javaid Rehman, "The Concept of Jihad in Islamic International Law," 10 J. Conflict & Security L. 321 (2005).

55 Bin Laden declared that U.S. policies throughout the Middle East amounted to "a clear declaration of war on God, His messenger and Muslims." "*Jihad* is an Individual Duty," L.A. Times, Aug. 13, 1998, B9.

56 A leading historian writes in this regard, "With each of these [Al Qaeda] attacks the enemy has come to be conceived in broader and more general terms. Once the enemy was a religion – Christianity, Judaism – then it was a particular power – the British, the French, the Americans. Now it is merely the 'West.'" Anthony Pagden, Worlds at War: The 2,500-Year Struggle between East and West 517 (2008). I owe several of the observations in this paragraph to Neal Shuett.

57 Tim Weiner, "Iran and Allies Are Suspected in Bomb Wave," New York Times, July 29, 1994 (describing attacks in which more than 100 people were killed).

58 Osama bin Laden, interviewed by Tayseer Allouni, "The Unreleased Interview," Oct. 21, 2001, from Markaz Derasat, Muawiya ibn Abi Sufyan, trans. at http://islamicawakening.com/index.htm; *see also* Paul Berman, "Who's Afraid of Tariq Ramadan?," 236 New Republic, June 4, 2007, at 37, 54–55 (quoting Ramadan).

59 This has long been a tack in postmodernist critiques of mainstream counterterrorism analysis. Two such authors unabashedly write, for instance, "Our goal is . . . to redirect the study of terrorism into an examination of the very discourse in which it is couched. . . . The terrorist signifiers are free-floating and derive from language itself. The connections between discourse and reality therefore become open to question. The challenge is not to learn the ultimate 'truth' about terrorism," as none apparently exists or is discoverable, "but to delve into the rhetorical bases of its powerful representations . . . to dissolve the phenomenon into its ritual and imaginative bases, which are poles apart from the ongoing academic and governmental efforts to constitute it further. . . . As . . . cultural anomalies are isolated by the prohibitions of taboo, so are . . . uncompromising forms of struggle ostracized as 'terrorist.' . . . Such is the power of the terrorist bogeyman to turn even heads of state into vigilantes." Joseba Zulaika & William Douglass, Terror and Taboo xi, 154, 159 (1996). In fairness, one should perhaps observe that these words were written some years before 9/11.

60 Surely, the most candid acknowledgment of this aspiration by anyone sympathetic to it is offered by Lt. Col. Ralph Peters, a frequent writer on military affairs: In the coming years, "violent conflict will dominate the headlines, but cultural and economic struggles will be steadier and ultimately more decisive. The *de facto* role of the U.S. armed force will be to keep the world safe for our economy and open to our cultural assault. To those ends, we will do a fair amount of killing." Ralph Peters, "Constant Conflict," 27 Parameters 4, 9 Summer 1997.

61 Tony Smith, A Pact with the Devil: Washington's Bid for World Supremacy and the Betrayal of the American Promise 208 (2007); *see also* John Ikenberry, Liberal Order and Imperial Ambition: Essays on American Power and World Politics 229 (2006) (characterizing neoconservatives among Bush foreign policy advisers as the "new fundamentalists").

62 Tariq Ramadan, Islam, the West, and the Challenges of Modernity 266–67 (2001); *see also* Abdullahi Ahmed An-Na'im, "Upholding International Legality against Islamic and American Jihad," *in* Worlds in Collision: Terror and the Future of Global Order, Ken Booth & Tim Dunne, eds. 162 (2002); Bhikhu

Parekh, "Terrorism and Intercultural Dialogue," *in* Booth & Dunne, *id.* at 270, 273 (2002) ("Both claim divine blessing for their respective projects; both talk of a clash of civilizations, a long and bitter war, and a fight to the finish; both want to stand and act alone, are driven by rage and hatred, and claim absolute superiority for their respective ways of life."); Slavoj Žižek, *supra* note 12, at 52, 43 (2002) (arguing that there is a "clash of fundamentalisms" and that in the United States after 9/11, "every feature attributed to the Other is already present at the very heart of the USA," such as "murderous fanaticism"); Slavoj Žižek, Iraq: The Borrowed Kettle 33 (2006) (lamenting "the weird pact between postmodern global capitalism and premodern societies, at the expense of modernity proper.... Jihad and McWorld are two sides of the same coin; Jihad is already McJihad."); James Der Derian, "The War of Networks," 5 Theory & Event 4 (2002) ("A fearful symmetry is also at work, at an unconscious, possibly pathological level, a war of escalating and competing and imitative oppositions, a mimetic war of images."); Smith, *supra* note 61, at 228 (condemning the "phalanx of liberal internationalist jihadists" ensconced around William Kristol and Robert Kagan at The Weekly Standard and the Project for the New American Century); Giorgio Agamben, "Security and Terror," 5 Theory & Event 4 (2002) ("When politics ... reduces itself to police ... it may lead to security and terrorism forming a single deadly system in which they mutually justify and legitimate each others' actions. The risk is not merely the development of a clandestine complicity of opponents but that the hunt for security leads to a worldwide civil war which destroys all civil coexistence ... a worldwide civil war which is just the institutionalization of terror.").

63 Michael Taussig, Shamanism, Colonialism, and the Wild Man: A Study in Terror and Healing 218, 467 (1987). Taussig shows how Colombian shamans incorporated the colonizer's image of them as "wild" and "mysterious" into their own shamanic practice. He describe this "folding of the underworld of the conquering society into the culture of the conquered ... as a chamber of mirrors reflecting each stream's perception of the other." He concludes, "So it has been through the sweep of colonial history where the colonizers provided the colonized with the left-handed gift of the image of the wild man – a gift whose powers the colonizers would be blind to, were it not for the reciprocation of the colonized, bringing together in the dialogical imagination of colonization an image that wrests from civilization its demonic power."

64 Martin Shaw, The New Western Way of War: Risk-Transfer War and its Crisis in Iraq 132 (2005).

65 Jonah Goldberg & Rosa Ehrenreich Brooks, New York Times online, Dec. 10, Blogging Heads.

66 Patrick Griffin: American Leviathan: Empire, Nation, and Revolutionary Frontier 154 (2007).

67 Edward Luttwak, "Dead End: Counterinsurgency Warfare as Military Malpractice," Harper's Magazine, Feb. 2007, at 33, 42.

68 Michael Taussig, "Culture of Terror – Space of Death: Roger Casement's Putumayo Report and the Explanation of Torture," *in* Interpretive Social Science: A Second Look, Paul Rabinow & William Sullivan, eds. 241, 276–78, 245, 262 (1987). Taussig does not deny that indigenous peoples ultimately engaged in some of the violent conduct attributed to them by the colonizers, but argues

that this was largely a reaction to prior Western violation of traditional expectations that such peoples had of their rulers.

69 *Id.* at 245, 262.

70 Benjamin Valentino, Paul Huth, and Dylan Balch-Lindsay, "'Draining the Sea": Mass Killing and Guerrilla Warfare," 58 Int'l Org. 375 (2004); Benjamin Valentino, Paul Huth, & Sarah Croco, "Covenants without the Sword: International Law and the Protection of Civilians in Times of War," 58 World Politics 339, 354, 371 (2006); Adam Roberts, "Land Warfare: From Hague to Nuremberg," *in* The Laws of War: Constraints on Warfare in the Western World, Michael Howard et al., eds. 116, 136 (1994).

71 *See especially* Protocol Additional to the Geneva Conventions of 12 August 1949, and Relating to the Protection of Victims of Non-International Armed Conflicts (Protocol II), Adopted on 8 June 1977 by the Diplomatic Conference on the Reaffirmation and Development of International Humanitarian Law applicable in Armed Conflicts, entry into force 7 December 1978.

72 *See, e.g.*, Mark Neely Jr., The Civil War and The Limits of Destruction 140–42 (2008) (arguing that violence during that conflict was not uniformly unrestrained – it was greatest in the Confederate treatment of black Union soldiers and, to a much lesser degree, in the Union treatment of Confederate guerrillas); Michael Felman, "At the Nihilist Edge: Reflections on Guerrilla Warfare during the American Civil War," *in* On the Road to Total War: The American Civil War and the German Wars of Unification, 1861–1871 522, 532 (1997).

73 Apart from immediately killing Confederate partisans who had not displayed their arms openly, Union treatment of the South in the American Civil War was considerably more lenient than U.S. treatment of Native Americans in the Indian wars of the later nineteenth century. Mark Grimsley, "'Rebels" and "Redskins": U.S. Military Conduct toward White Southerners and Native Americans in Comparative Perspective," *in* Civilians in the Path of War, Mark Grimsley & Clifford Rogers, eds. 137, 139 (2002). "Although the federal government explicitly denied the Confederacy's legal existence," Grimsley observes, "it granted full belligerent rights to Southern armies and waged the Civil War largely as a contest between two nations." Native nations had better legal claim to the international status of sovereign entities, yet their warriors were accorded no such rights by U.S. forces. In contemporary legal terms, one would say that the Civil War was a noninternational armed conflict, which would mean that the federal government had no duty to afford combatant privilege to Confederate soldiers. By contrast, the wars between the U.S. government and the Indian nations laid much better claim to being "international armed conflicts," in today's terminology, with their broad scope for combatant privilege and corresponding protections, then as now. Before 1949, international treaty law provided no protections at all to rebels in civil wars.

74 René Girard, Violence and the Sacred, Patrick Gregory, trans. 71, 74, 158, 160, 164 (1977). For commentary, *see* Chris Fleming, René Girard: Violence and Mimesis 420–49 (2004). *See generally* Tara McKelvey, Monstering: Inside America's Policy of Secret Interrogations and Torture in the Terror War 161 (2007).

75 On the central place of simula in postmodernist thought and how a simulacrum differs from a mere copy, *see* Matthew Potolsky, Mimesis 152 (2006).

76 Chris Fleming, René Girard, Violence and Mimesis 42 (2004). As Fleming observes, "The more Rênal and Valenod attempt to outdo each other, the more both come to resemble each other – including the resemblance of each other with respect to their increasingly desperate attempts at differentiation."

77 Barbara Fuchs, Mimesis and Empire: The New World, Islam and European Identities 4–11 (2001).

78 On the other hand, it must be said – with the hindsight of eighteen years since the end of the Cold War, and especially the successful industrialization of China – that the U.S.-Soviet conflict was not the primary obstacle to the emergence and flourishing of an alternative model of economic development much different from that of Western capitalism.

79 A reviewer of this book in manuscript sought to insist on the surreptitiously theocratic nature of any country the president of which admits to finding moral inspiration in the Bible and whose chairman of its Joint Chiefs of Staff condemns homosexual behavior "on biblical grounds." *Cf.* Talal Asad, Formations of the Secular: Christianity, Islam and Modernity 56, 26, 201 (2003). Asad here seeks "to problematize the secular as a category" by showing how Western "liberalism is a kind of redemptive myth" on account, for instance, of its reliance on "the solemnity of state 'ritual'" and the fact that "the phrase 'separation of church and state' is not found in the Constitution." Yet if every doctrine of U.S. constitutional law had to have so express a textual footing, very little of contemporary constitutional law – including the right to abortion and to privacy more generally – would exist.

At the risk of belaboring the obvious, one must observe for such readers that, unlike in a theocracy, the personal religious views of such individuals as the Chairman of the Joint Chiefs do not establish the law of the land in the United States. The constitutional right to engage in homosexual acts, for instance, has been upheld by the U.S. Supreme Court. *Lawrence v. Texas,* 539 U.S. 558, 578 (2003). In Iran, an Islamic theocracy according to the express terms of its constitution, such acts constitute a capital offense. *Compare* Human Rights Watch, Iran: Two More Executions for Homosexual Conduct, Nov. 22, 2005, *with* Neil Macfarquhar, "Gay Muslims Find Freedom, of a Sort, in the U.S.," New York Times, Nov. 7, 2007, at A1 (describing Muslim participants in San Francisco's Gay Pride Parade who cover their faces for fear "of being ostracized at the mosque or at their local falafel stand"). To describe the U.S. state as secular is not to say anything, of course, about the degree of religiosity within the society it governs; the extent and intensity of religious enthusiasm, as in the two Great Awakenings, have varied greatly throughout U.S. history, waxing for several brief periods and waning for rather longer ones.

Moreover, a liberal democracy is still a democracy; thus, if a president can be elected who confesses to finding moral guidance in the life of Jesus and the Bible, this is because most of his fellow citizens regard this fact about him as unobjectionable. General Peter Pace, the Joint Chiefs Chairman to whom the reviewer refers, was not reappointed to a second term, despite a general practice of so doing, in a decision made shortly after his comment about gays, suggesting that his remark was objectionable to many. In any event, General Pace had expressed his disapproval of homosexuality, for which he later publicly apologized, in terms of his "personal moral views," not professedly "on biblical grounds." *See* http://rawstory.com/news/2007/General_Pace_Homosexuality_immoral_0312.html.

Asad is currently the leading intellectual exponent of the general position just described. (A Muslim educated in the United Kingdom, he is the Saudi-born son of a Jewish convert to Islam.) In his scholarship, he is circumspect about his own religious views. Yet in a less guarded moment, during a live interview, he discloses that "the Islamic tradition ought to lead us to question many of the liberal categories themselves." He then asks, "Does an exploration of Islamic traditions give us a deeper, more critical understanding of individualism, or tolerance, or pluralism?" His response: "Many of the things claimed about liberal tolerance should be questioned. . . . I think we need much more investigation of what people regard as poppycock and of what they are willing to open their minds to. Secularism has tended to regard religious traditions as . . . making nonsensical claims." This statement may first appear to be a call merely for deliberative reciprocity, as I have called it, for some variety of interfaith dialogue.

But Asad then clarifies. He offers a particularly astonishing and revealing riff regarding the effects of such misguided secularism. "Rather than thinking of power only in terms of the question of freedom of expression and its limitations," he announces, "we should also pay attention to the kinds of power that go into the formation of listening subjects, of subjects who can open their minds to something that is strange or uncomfortable." Asad here invokes Foucault – rather incongruously, in light of Foucault's antinomian, virtually anarchistic stance toward all authority – in apparent defense of keeping an open mind to the possibility of divine revelation and an attendant deference to one supreme and unquestioned authority. The obstacles that secularity creates to such openness apparently reside in how it corrupts "the formation of listening subjects," presumably because they can no longer hear the call of Allah. Q&A, Asia Source Interview, Dec. 16, 2002, at http://www.asiasource.org/news/special_reports/asad.cfm.

80 Robert Jervis, Perception and Misperception in International Politics 68–81 (1976).

81 H.H. Kelley, "Attribution Theory in Social Psychology," *in* D. Levine, ed., 15 Nebraska Symposium on Motivation 192, 222–25 (1967).

82 Jonathan Haidt, The Happiness Hypothesis 66–75 (2006) (summarizing research results).

83 Deborah Welch Larson, Anatomy of Mistrust: U.S.-Soviet Relations during the Cold War 38–49, 63–80, 91–109, 162–67 (1997); As even two scholarly admirers of Ronald Reagan and George W. Bush recently acknowledge, "What much of post-Cold War research has revealed is . . . the troubling level of mistaken beliefs and erroneous assumptions held at the time by key actors, about themselves and about their enemies." Timothy Lynch & Robert Singh, After Bush: The Case for Continuity in American Foreign Policy 13 (2008).

84 Debora Welch Larson, "The Psychology of Reciprocity in International Relations," 4 Negotiation Journal 281, 290 (1988).

85 Jacques Semelin, Purify and Destroy: The Political Uses of Massacre and Genocide, Cynthia Schoch, trans. 43–51, 145, 293 (2007).

86 Holmes, *supra* note 30 at 276–77. He writes of this "uncivilized reciprocity" that "if our enemies have renounced the laws of civilization, so will we. If they organized a sneak attack, then we will respond with a dirty war. If they terrorized us, we will terrorize them." *Id.* at 277.

87 Peter P. Ekeh, Social Exchange Theory: The Two Traditions 47 (1974) (citing Talcott Parsons, Peter Blau, and Alvin Gouldner for this view).

88 Holmes, *supra* note 30, at 7.

89 Baudrillard, *supra* note 12, at 81.

90 *Id.* at 64–65 (parsing Philippe Muray, Chers Djihadistes, 2002). Baudrillard continues, "The idea of extirpating [jihadist terrorism] as an objective evil is a total illusion since . . . it is the verdict this society passes on itself, its self-condemnation," for its own terroristic proclivities. *Id.* at 105.

91 *Id.* at 104.

92 Nietzsche himself applied his "will to power" notion only to individual persons and would never have extended it to entire nations, notwithstanding the misreading to this effect by the Nazis. The individual's free creation of his or her own character, which Nietzsche so highly valued, is inconsistent with a nation's effort to stamp its collective character uniformly on all members. Nietzsche would have found it entirely likely, however, that the "slave" who deeply identified with his nation-state would indulge his *ressentiment* by taking umbrage at its inferior place within the international order, especially at its subordination to a culturally antipathetic superpower. Several commentators have sought to explain militant jihadism in just these terms. *See, e.g.,* Thomas Friedman, "The Democracy Thing," New York Times, Oct. 30, 2002, editorial; Jean Bethke Elshtain, Just War against Terror (2003). But this is also just the kind of argument that often gives genealogy a bad name, because it either speaks powerfully to you – despite the lack of any direct evidence for it – or it does not.

There is some direct evidence, however, of resentment over social humiliation as a central motive among jihadists. One major, Moroccan-born jihadist writes, for instance, "We are totally dependent on the West – for our dishwashers, our clothes, our cars, our education, everything. It is humiliating and every Muslim feels it. . . . For centuries we ran far ahead of the West. We were the most sophisticated civilization in the world. Now we are backward. We can't even fight our wars without our enemies' weapons." Ahmed Rashid, "Jihadi Suicide Bombers: The New Wave," N.Y. Rev. of Books, June 12, 2008, at 17, 22 (quoting the pseudonymic Omar Nasiri, Inside the Jihad: My Life with Al Qaeda, A Spy's Story 2006).

93 Charles Krauthammer offers a defense of something approximating this view in "Democratic Realism: An American Foreign Policy for a Unipolar World," Feb. 12, 2004, http://www.aei.org/publications/pubID.19912,filter.all/pub_detail.asp; *see also* Richard Perle, "Thank God for the Death of the UN," The Guardian, March 21, 2003 (arguing that Bush administration foreign policy in the conflict with Al Qaeda should not be judged by predefined rules and values).

94 Friedrich Nietzsche, Beyond Good and Evil, Walter Kaufmann, trans. 136 (1966).

95 President George W. Bush, Address to Joint Session of Congress and to the American People, Sept. 20, 2001.

96 Ron Suskind, "Faith, Certainty, and the Presidency of George W. Bush," New York Times, Oct. 17, 2004, Sunday Magazine.

97 For as one philosopher writes, Nietzsche "insists that there are no kinds of actions that are good or bad in themselves, and this has . . . a fatal implication for the teaching of justice. It is justice . . . that forbids such acts as murder, torture and enslavement, and brands them as evil, whoever carries them out." Philippa Foot, "Nietzsche's Immoralism," *in* Nietzsche, Genealogy, Morality, Richard Schacht, ed. 3, 6–7 (1994).

98 Stephen Toope, "Powerful but Unpersuasive: The Role of the U.S. in the Evolution of Customary International Law," *in* U.S. Hegemony and the Foundations of International Law, Michael Byers & Georg Nolte, eds. 287, 302–18 (2003). For the prevailing U.S. account of how customary international law develops, *see* Amer. L. Institute, Restatement (Third), Foreign Relations Law of the United States, §102, Comments and Illustrations (1987).

99 Friedrich Nietzsche, The Birth of Tragedy and the Genealogy of Morals, Francis Golffing, trans. 196–97 (1956) (1887).

100 Bob Woodward, State of Denial 408 (2006).

101 Holmes, *supra* note 30, at 278.

102 *Id.* at 278–79.

103 *Id.* at 280.

104 *Id.* at 276.

105 William Shakespeare, Hamlet, Prince of Denmark, act 3, sc. 4.

106 George Fletcher, Defending Humanity: When Force is Justified and Why (2008). Fletcher is not speaking here, however, of torture as a response to an adversary's violations of humanitarian law.

107 Richard Posner, "Torture, Terrorism, and Interrogation," *in* Torture: A Collection, Sanford Levinson, ed. 291, 294 (2004) (describing this as "an apt metaphor for the use of torture . . . when nothing else will avert catastrophe").

108 Though essentially a factual argument about motivation, its claims lie largely beyond empirical assessment, because survey research has not yet asked the questions necessary to evaluate it (i.e., if that were possible).

109 Cass Sunstein, "Terrorism and Probability Neglect," 26 J. Risk & Uncertainty 121 (2003).

110 Jonathan H. Marks, "9/11+3/11+7/7=? What Counts in Counter-terrorism," 37 Colum. H.R. L. Rev. 559, 567 (2006); Jennifer S. Lerner et al., "Effects of Fear and Anger on Perceived Risks of Terrorism: A National Field Experiment," 14 Psychol. Sci. 144, 146 (2003). Certain stimuli may provoke both fear and anger, of course, and the former may be the source of the latter. *See, e.g.,* Raymond H. Johnson, Jr., "Facing the Terror of Nuclear Terrorism," 72 Occupational Health & Safety 44 (2003); Cass Sunstein, Laws of Fear: Beyond the Precautionary Principle 208 (2005) ("If indulging fear is costless, because other people face the relevant burdens, then the mere fact of 'risk' and the mere presence of fear, will seem to provide a justification" for restricting liberty.).

111 Joseba Zulaika & William Douglass, *supra* note 59, at 6, 241 (1996).

112 *See, e.g.,* Louise Richardson, What Terrorists Want: Understanding the Enemy, Containing the Threat 147 (2006) (contrasting the fewer than 3,000 killed by the 9/11 attacks with the 30,000 suicides, 16,000 homicides, and 15,000 deaths from falls in America during 2001).

113 David Hoy, "Nietzsche, Hume, and the Geneaological Method," *in* Schacht, *supra* note 97, at 251, 262 (1994) (observing that "how a Nietzschean genealogy of a particular case could be confirmed or disconfirmed is not at all clear.... Most troublesome is how the genealogist is to justify the inference that some interpretations are better than others.").

114 George Kateb, "A Life of Fear," 71 Soc. Res. (2004), at http://findarticles.com/p/articles/mi_m2267/is_4_71/ai_n14693143.

115 Alan Dershowitz, Why Terrorism Works: Understanding the Threat, Responding to the Challenge 156–60 (2003).

116 Philip Heymann & Juliette Kayyem, Protecting Liberty in an Age of Terror 35–39 (2005) (advocating a scheme for advance approval of "highly coercive interrogation techniques").

117 Aristotle, Nicomachean Ethics, Martin Ostwald, ed. and trans. 93–99 (1962).

118 Paul Rahe, "Justice and Necessity: The Conduct of the Spartans and the Athenians in the Peloponnesian War," *in* Grimsley & Rogers, *supra* note 73, at 1.

119 Peter Berger, "On the Obsolescence of the Concept of Honour," 11 Eur. J. of Sociol. 339, 342–43 (1970). Berger observes that among military officers, traditionally "honor is a direct expression of status, a source of solidarity among social equals and a demarcation line against social inferiors. Honor... also dictates certain standards of behavior in dealing with inferiors, but the full code of honor only applies among those who share the same status in the hierarchy."

120 Moreover, destruction of the enemy as an organized fighting force generally does not entail the bodily destruction of all or even most of its members.

121 Such was Nietzsche's view, in any event. Friedrich Nietzsche, "The Noble Man," *in* The Will to Power, Walter Kaufmann, ed. & trans. 493–99 (1967); Friedrich Nietzsche, Beyond Good and Evil, Walter Kaufmann, trans. 206, 215 (1966).

CHAPTER 10. RECIPROCITY AS TIT-FOR-TAT: RATIONAL RETALIATION IN MODERN WAR

1 So argue Jack Goldsmith & Eric Posner in The Limits of International Law 100–06 (2005).

2 On the inescapability of such counterfactual questions, as well as the methodological puzzles they pose for all causal inquiry, *see* Geoffrey Hawthorn, Plausible Worlds: Possibility and Understanding in History and the Social Sciences (1991).

3 Geoffrey Parker, "Early Modern Europe," *in* The Laws of War: Constraints on Warfare in the Western World, Michael Howard et al., eds. 40, 55 (1994).

4 Such patterns may be evidence merely of a "cooperation game," in the rational choice terminology. Goldsmith & Posner, *supra* note 1, at 29–32, 112–15.

5 Jon Elster, "Altruistic Behavior and Altruistic Motivations," *in* 1 Handbook of the Economics of Giving, Altruism, and Reciprocity, Serge-Christophe Kolm & Jean M. Ythier, eds. 183, 187 (2006).

6 Eric A. Posner, "A Theory of the Laws of War," 70 U. Chi. L. Rev. 297, 309 (2003).

7 Although rejecting this view, Posner apparently continues to assume that the only relevant advantage to be gained from honoring Geneva norms would follow from their possible effect in minimizing one's own immediate human losses.

8 Such work began with Stewart Macaulay, "Non-Contractual Relations in Business: A Preliminary Study," 28 Amer. Sociol. Rev. 1 (1963) and has continued vigorously apace ever since. Hugh Collins, Regulating Contracts 104–10 (1999) ("In order to overcome risks of betrayal and disappointment, trust and sanctions are vital, but within these mechanisms the legal sanction available for breach of contract appears to occupy only a marginal role.").

9 *See, e.g.,* Robert Ellickson, Order without Law: How Neighbors Settle Disputes (1991); Lisa Bernstein, "Opting out of the Legal System: Extralegal Contractual Relations in the Diamond Industry," 21 J. Leg. Stud. 115 (1992); Richard McAdams, "The Origin, Development, and Regulation of Norms," 96 Mich. L. Rev. 338 (1997).

10 Paul Robinson, Military Honour and the Conduct of War 60–82 (2006); Mark Osiel, Obeying Orders: Atrocity, Military Discipline, and the Law of War 201–04 (1999). This conception of honor may fairly be called militaristic in its welcoming of war for the opportunity thus afforded to display one's martial prowess. The later advent of the Westphalian state system extended this conception, now as national honor displayed in interstate war. This view reached its intellectual apotheosis – or nadir, we might better say – in Hegel's defense of war as a means of forging a strong sense of national identity and purpose in the lives of modern citizens. G. W. F. Hegel, Philosophy of Right, T. M. Knox, trans. 210–11 (1967).

11 Paul R. Milgrom, Douglass C. North, and Barry Weingast, "The Role of Institutions in the Revival of Trade: The Law Merchant, Private Judges, and the Champagne Fairs," 2 Econ. & Politics 1 (1990); *cf.* Afner Greif, "Contract Enforceability and Economic Institutions in Early Trade: The Maghribi Traders Coalition," 83 Amer. Econ. Rev. 525 (1993).

12 *Cf.* Kal Raustiala, "Form and Substance in International Agreements," 99 A.J.I.L. 581, 606 (2005) (comparing the informal pressures placed on rule breakers by the medieval law merchant system and by international tribunals).

13 George W. Downs, et. al, "Is The Good News about Compliance Good News about Cooperation?" 50 Int'l Org. 379, 383 (1996); Jana Von Stein, "Do Treaties Constrain or Screen? Selection Bias and Treaty Compliance," 99 Amer. Pol. Sci. Rev. 611 (2005); Alan Sykes, "International Law," *in* Handbook of Law and Economics, Mitchell Polinsky & Steven Shavell, eds. 757, 816 (2007) ("Human rights treaties in the main commit liberal states to behave as they would anyway.").

14 Clifford J. Carrubba, "Courts and Compliance in International Regulatory Regimes," 67 J. of Politics 669, 687 (2007).

15 States often have perfectly plausible legal arguments, of course, that the treaty does not actually cover the particular conduct in question.

16 Ryan Goodman & Derek Jinks, "Toward an Institutional Theory of Sovereignty," 55 Stan. L. Rev. 1749, 1757, 1786 (2005).

17 Geoffrey Parker, "Early Modern Europe," *in* Howard, *supra* note 3, at 40, 42 (observing that the law of war "reduced the danger and chaos of conflict for all combatants because creating a contractual etiquette of belligerence provided each party with a vital framework of expectations concerning the conduct of others").

18 The points made in this paragraph are developed by James D. Morrow, "The Laws of War, Common Conjectures, and Legal Systems in International Politics," 31 J. Legal. Stud. 41 (2002).

19 Several such studies have found that "the size of the population in which interactions occur must be relatively small for reciprocating strategies to survive potential errors of players." Elinor Ostrom, "Toward a Behavioral Theory Linking Trust, Reciprocity, and Reputation," *in* Trust and Reciprocity: Lessons from Experimental Research, Elinor Ostrum & James Walker, eds. 19, 42 (2003) (summarizing these studies).

20 Robert Keohane, "International Relations and International Law: Two Optics," 38 Harv. Int'l L. J. 487, 497 (1997); Benedict Kingsbury, "The Concept of Compliance as a Function of Competing Conceptions of International Law," 19 Mich. J. Int'l L. 345, 352 (1998); On the indispensability of ruthlessness in counterinsurgency warfare, in particular, *see* Martin van Creveld, "Counterinsurgency," *in* Countering Modern Terrorism, Katerina von Knop, Heinrich Neisser, & Martin van Creveld, eds. 113, 125–27 (2004) ("There should be no apologies, no kvetching about collateral damage caused by mistake, innocent lives regrettably lost, 'excesses' that will be investigated and brought to trial, and similar signs of weakness.").

21 How military adversary A treats a country B depends more on B's current power and interests than on B's "reputation for resolve." Daryl G. Press, Calculating Credibility: How Leaders Assess Military Threats 1 (2005). Investment in such a reputation also "wastes vast sums of money and, much worse, thousands of lives." *Id. See also* Jonathan Mercer, Reputation in International Politics 5 (1996) (arguing "that enormous human and material sacrifice made in the name of reputation is probably a waste of precious resources").

22 This is not to gainsay the possibility that both sides, for all intents and purposes, may "lose," in that neither achieves its initial objectives or only does so at costs greatly exceeding the perceived value of "victory."

23 Robert Scott & Paul Stephan, The Limits of Leviathan: Contract Theory and the Enforcement of International Law 69 (2007).

24 *See generally* Alexander B. Downes, "Desperate Times, Desperate Measures: The Causes of Civilian Victimization in War," 30 Int'l Security 152, 163, 171 (Spring 2006); Max Hastings, Retribution: The Battle for Japan, 1944–45 164–73, 504–51(2008) (describing how the "madness" of Japan's final fighting methods, such as *kamikaze* attacks, elicited from America a measure of ruthlessness it had not yet shown in the war, and concluding more generally that "few belligerents in any conflict are so high-minded as to offer to an enemy higher standards of treatment than that enemy extends to them").

25 The law itself no longer understands "necessity" in this manner, to be sure. Law Reports of Trials of War Criminals, Vol. VIII, (Hostages Trial of Wilhelm List and Others), Int'l Military Tribunal, 15 AD, 632, 637 (1948); Christopher

Greenwood, "The Twilight of the Law of Belligerent Reprisals," *in* Greenwood, Essays on War in International Law 295, 319 (2006).

26 These inferences are reached by deduction from realist premises, but difficult to assess empirically. They ignore important variation in how different types of states respond to similar military challenges. For instance, in conquering each city, the United States destroyed most of Fallujah no less than Russia destroyed most of Grozny. But Fallujans were warned of their city's imminent bombing, whereas Groznyans were not advised in advance of the first five months of attacks, from August through November 1999. This is a morally meaningful difference. Whether such differences in methods of warfare can be explained by self-interest alone or also by the weight of moral considerations is difficult to discern.

27 Benjamin Valentino, Paul Huth, & Sarah Croco, "Covenants without the Sword: International Law and the Protection of Civilians in Times of War," 58 World Politics 339, 354, 371 (2006); Sahr Conway-Lanz, Collateral Damage: Americans, Noncombatant Immunity, and Atrocity after World War II 20 (2006) (observing declining U.S. adherence to rules of noncombatant immunity over time in the war with North Korea).

28 *Id.* at 375 (arguing that belligerents "are more likely to resort to killing civilians in the most difficult and desperate conflicts – when conventional military means are ineffective or too costly").

29 There were several leading officers in the Army Air Force who opposed the decision to firebomb Japanese cities and had successfully resisted British promptings to adopt such measures earlier in the war. Conrad Crane, "'Contrary to Our National Ideals:' American Strategic Bombing of Civilians in World War II,' *in* Civilians in the Path of War, Mark Grimsley & Clifford Rogers, eds. 219, 232 (2002). One such officer objected until the end, complaining that the latest British proposal was "the same old baby-killing plan dressed up in a new kimono." *Id.* On changes in British thinking over the course of the war concerning strategic bombing, *see* Stephen Garrett, "Airpower and Non-Combatant Immunity: The Road to Dresden," *in* Civilian Immunity in War, Igor Primoratz, ed. 161 (2007); H.W. Koch, "The Strategic Air Offensive against Germany," 34 Historical J. 134 (1991).

30 Michael Walzer, Just and Unjust Wars 252–62 (1977).

31 Niall Ferguson, "Prisoner Taking and Prisoner Killing in the Age of Total War: Towards a Political Economy of Military Defeat," 11 War in History 148 (2004) (employing prisoners' dilemma reasoning to contrast the more frequent war crimes and less frequent surrenders of World War II, especially in the Pacific and Eastern Fronts, to the greater number of surrenders and fewer war crimes of World War I); Brian Dollery & Craig Parsons, "Prisoner Taking and Prisoner Killing: A Comment on Ferguson's Political Economy Approach," 14 War in History 499 (2007) (largely confirming Ferguson's results).

32 Mark Grimsley, "'Rebels" and "Redskins": U.S. Military Conduct toward White Southerners and Native Americans in Comparative Perspective," *in* Grimsley & Rogers, *supra* note 29, at 137, 154.

33 Helene Cooper, "Waiting for Justice," New York Times, July 27, 2008, Week in Review ("In the case of Mr. Karadzic," recently extradited to The Hague,

"Serbia's new leaders realized he was of more use to them as a way to get back into the good graces of Europe.").

34 *But see* James Kahan & Amnon Rapoport, "Test of the Bargaining Set and Kernal Models in Three-Person Games," *in* Game Theory as a Theory of Conflict Resolution, Anatol Rapoport, ed. 119 (1974); Christian Schmidt, "Rupture vs. Continuity in Game Theory," *in* Game Theory and Economic Analysis, Christian Schmidt, ed. 33, 39–40 (2002); Robert Putnam, "Diplomacy and Domestic Politics: The Logic of Two-Level Games," 42 Int'l Org. 427 (1988). Putnam's is an influential attempt to apply two-person game theory to political dynamics involving multiple actors.

35 Georg Simmel, The Sociology of Georg Simmel, Kurt Wolff, ed. & trans. 135–69 (1950).

36 *See, e.g.*, Frank Zagare, Game Theory: Concepts and Applications 64–70 (1984).

37 Thomas Schelling, "The Reciprocal Fear of Surprise Attack," *in* The Strategy of Conflict 207 (1963). He explains, "These are the 'games' in which, though the element of conflict provides the dramatic interest, mutual dependence is part of the logical structure and demands some kind of collaboration or mutual accommodation – tacit, if not explicit – even if only in the avoidance of mutual disaster. These are also games in which, though secrecy may play a strategic role, there is some essential need for the signaling of intentions and the meeting of minds." *Id.,* at 83–84.

38 In recent decades, progress in this area has come largely under the auspices of the UN Conference on Certain Conventional Weapons, in the form of several protocols, governing particular weapons technologies, some still on the drawing boards. W. Hays Parks, "Means and Methods of Warfare," 38 Geo. Wash. Int'l L. Rev. 511, 520–31 (2006) (describing post–World War II efforts to regulate land mines, incendiary weapons, small caliber arms, blinding lasers, cluster bombs, booby traps, and flechettes).

39 Posner, *supra* note 6, at 310.

40 This has been known for a long time and is by no means an insight peculiar to rational choice. Nineteenth-century diplomats, for instance, were clearly aware, in the words of James Buchanan, then Secretary of State of the United States, in speaking of the U.S. treaty of 1825 with the Federation of Central America, that some treaty provisions "though reciprocal in terms, would prove unequal in their operation." Buchanan to E. Hise, Washington, June 3, 1848 *in* W.R. Manning, ed., Diplomatic Correspondence of the United States: Inter-American Affairs, 1831–1860. III (Washington, 1933), 33–34.

41 Eric A. Posner, "Terrorism and the Laws of War," 5 Chi. J. Int'l Law 423, 429 (2005).

42 On the exploitative treatment of POWs during World War II, for labor and information extraction, *see* Richard Overy, Russia's War 297–98 (1997); A.J. Barker, Prisoners of War 99–100 (1975).

43 Omer Bartov, The Eastern Front, 1941–1945: German Troops and the Barbarisation of Warfare 118 (1985).

44 Drew Faust, This Republic of Suffering: Death and the American Civil War 44–55 (2008).

45 The statute does not prohibit admission of evidence obtained through coercion, for instance. And in employing military commissions rather than

courts-martial, it does not satisfy the Geneva requirement to prosecute war crimes in the same type of tribunal as would be used to try U.S. military personnel for like offenses.

46 Allison M. Danner, Conference on the Military Commissions Act of 2006, University of Texas, School of Law, April 11, 2007 (describing interviews with Bush administration lawyers).

47 Fourth Geneva Convention, Art 3 (prohibiting "at any time and any place . . . violence to life and person" but allowing criminal prosecution and detention in accordance with "all the judicial guarantees which are recognized as indispensable by civilized peoples").

48 *Hamdan v. Rumsfeld*, 126 S.Ct. 2749, 2795–96 (2006).

49 Posner, *supra* note 41, at 430.

50 The program is designated as R2I, short for "Resistance to Interrogation." David Leigh, "U.K. Forces Taught Torture Methods," The Guardian, May 8, 2004; Charlie Savage, Takeover: The Return of the Imperial Presidency and the Subversion of American Democracy 215–18 (2007).

51 Philip Hallie, The Paradox of Cruelty 80 (1969).

52 *See, e.g.,* Black Flag over Dixie: Racial Atrocities and Reprisals in the Civil War, Gregory Urwin, ed. (2004).

53 *See, e.g.,* Understanding Victory and Defeat in Contemporary War, Jan Ganstrom & Isabelle Duyvesteyn, eds. (2007); William C. Martel, Victory in War: Foundations of Modern Military Policy 3–12 (2007).

54 Robert Gilpin, Global Political Economy 220 (2001).

55 46 Stat. 590, June 17, 1930, 19 U.S.C. §1654. Many countries retaliated, and American exports and imports plunged by more than half. Barry Eichengreen, "The Political Economy of the Smoot-Hawley Tariff." 12 Research in Economic History 1 (1989).

56 Robert Hudec, Enforcing International Trade Law 112 (1993); Abraham Chayes & Antonia Chayes, The New Sovereignty: Compliance with International Regulatory Agreements 105 (1995). On the most recent efforts of states to employ reciprocity stratagems in inducing cooperation from trading partners, *see* Wilhelm Kohler, "The WTO Dispute Settlement Mechanism: Battlefield or Cooperation?" 4 J. Ind, Comp. & Trade 317 (2004).

57 Robert Axelrod, The Evolution of Cooperation 189 (1984).

58 *Memento*, Christopher Nolan, director (2000), at http://www.otnemem.com.

59 This is reflected in the radically different death rates for Soviet POWs (57 %, or 3.3 million people) versus American and Commonwealth POWs (3.5 %) held by Germany. S. P. Mackenzie, The Colditz Myth: British and Commonwealth Prisoners of War in Nazi Germany 267–68 (2004); Stephen Fritz, Frontsoldaten: The German Soldier in World War II 50–59 (1995).

60 In fact, in several cases where treaty standards have been widely ignored, at least one warring state had not ratified the relevant convention. During World War II, for instance, neither the Soviet Union nor Japan had ratified the 1929 Geneva Conventions. During the Korean War, neither China nor North Korea had ratified the 1949 Geneva Conventions. Another factor in explaining Germany's differential approach to the Eastern and Western fronts may have been the enemy's racial composition. On the pervasive Nazi animus against Russian POWs, *see* Mackenzie, *supra* note 59, at 267–68.

61 Vasilis Vourkoutiotis, Prisoners of War and the German High Command: The British and American Experience 200–01 (2003).

62 Press, *supra* note 21, at 1.

63 Joshua Goldstein & John Freeman, Three-Way Street: Strategic Reciprocity in World Politics (1990); Russell Leng, Interstate Crisis Behavior: Realism versus Reciprocity 122–23, 206–07 (1993) (finding that a variant of tit-for-tat, "carrot and stick initiatives and responses, offer a means of eliciting cooperation in a manner that reduces the risk of appearing irresolute"); several case studies of interstate reciprocity on diverse issues are offered in Cooperation under Anarchy, Kenneth Oye, ed. (1986).

64 Sheen Rajmaira & Michael Ward, "Evolving Foreign Policy Norms: Reciprocity in the Superpower Triad," 34 Int'l Stud. Quart. 457, 460, 473 (1990); W.J. Dixon, "Reciprocity in U.S.-Soviet Relations: Multiple Symmetry or Issue Linkage?" 30 Amer. J. Polit. Sci. 421 (1986).

65 Martin Patchen & David Bogumil, "Comparative Reciprocity during the Cold War," 3 Peace & Conflict 37, 54–55 (1997); Patrick James et al., "The Most Dangerous Game: Superpower Rivalry in International Crises, 1948–1985," 54 J. Politics 25, 33, 50 (1992).

66 In this Iraqi city, twelve American Marines caused the deaths of twenty-four noncombatants, including eleven women and children, on November 19, 2005. A U.S. military commission reviewed available evidence of the killings and found probable cause to charge the Marines with murder and manslaughter. Though two men face pending trials, six others have been acquitted or charges against them have been dropped. The Marines claimed that insurgents had situated themselves among local noncombatants to ensure civilian casualties in any potential cross-fire. Paul von Zielbauer, "At Marines' Hearing, Testament to Violence," New York Times, Sept. 1, 2007, at A1.

67 *See, e.g.,* Marc Sageman, Leaderless Jihad: Terror Networks in the Twenty-First Century (2008); Matthew Levitt, "Untangling the Terror Web: Identifying and Counteracting the Phenomenon of Crossover between Terrorist Groups," 24 SAIS Rev. 33, 42 (Winter/Spring 2004) (detailing the "network of relationships" that exist between disparate terrorist groups such as "Baathists, Sunni terrorists, Shia radicals and others opposed to [the United States]" spawning "cooperation borne of mutual interest" where none hitherto existed); Scott Peterson, "Al Qaeda among the Chechens," Christian Sci. Mon., Sept. 7, 2004 at 1 (World Section) (reporting that Chechen and Al Qaeda radicals, though autonomous groups, are "synchronized ideologically and strategically"); Rohan Gunaratran, Inside Al Qaeda: Global Network of Terror 54–70 (2002) (describing Al Qaeda's willingness to cooperate with Shia or even non-Muslim groups). Different bodies of Geneva law will also apply, depending on whether the discrete confrontation may credibly be classified as part of an "international armed conflict," rather than a noninternational one.

68 Lindsay Moir, The Law of Internal Armed Conflict 31–34 (2002). Other factors include the intensity and duration of violence, plus the belligerents' level of organization. *Id.* Prosecutor v. *Tadić,* Case No. IT-94-1-A, Decision on the Defense Motion for Interlocutory Appeal on Jurisdiction ¶ 70 (Oct. 2, 1995) (asserting that an "armed conflict exists whenever there is protracted armed violence between governmental authorities and organized armed groups").

69 The ICRC rejects every step in this analysis. ICRC, Situation of Detainees at Guantánamo Bay, E/CN.4/2006/120, ¶¶ 22–24.

70 Mary Ellen O'Connell, "The Legal Case against the Global War on Terror," 36 Case West. Res. J. Int'l L. 349, 352 (2004).

71 This conclusion and its underlying assumptions about law's purposes and interpretive goals differ from those of Kahn, criticized before, because that author tethers law's legitimate aspirations only to institutional constraints (i.e., the frequent unwillingness of weaker belligerents in asymmetrical warfare to honor extant rules of humanitarian law). By contrast, my textual passage here is more concerned with multiple normative commitments – legal duties of public office, rooted in moral principles of democratic accountability – which counter the claims of international law's anachronistically constricted definition of "armed conflict."

72 James D. Morrow, "When Do States Follow the Laws of War?" 101 Amer. Polit. Sci. Rev. 559, 562–633 (2007).

73 *The Paquete Habana*, 175 U.S. 677, 686, 708 (1900).

74 The verbal rationales offered by a state for its conduct should count only toward ascertaining *opinio juris*, not toward determining the state practice component of custom. To count such rationales twice would be redundant and logically incoherent and would give excessive weight to rhetoric over behavioral reality in the formation and preservation of custom. M. Mendleson, "The Nicaragua Case and Customary International Law," *in* The Non-Use of Force in International Law, William Butler, ed. 85, 92 (1989); Ben Chigara, Legitimacy Deficit in Customary Law 10–11 (2002).

75 Theodor Meron, "The Continuing Role of Custom in the Formation of International Humanitarian Law," 90 A.J.I.L. 238, 239 (discussing cases from the Nuremberg IMT and the ICTY); Mika N. Hayashi, "The Principle of Civilian Protection and Contemporary Armed Conflict," *in* The Law of Armed Conflict, Howard Hensel, ed. 105, 118, 120 (2005) (showing and endorsing how several international criminal tribunals, in ascertaining state practice, have come to rely entirely on what belligerents say they are doing "rather than the examination of what their armed forces actually do").

76 *Prosecutor v. Kupreskić*, Case IT-95-16-T (Judgment of Jan. 14, 2000), ¶¶ 528–30 (concluding that "opinio necessitatis, crystallizing as a result of the imperatives of humanity or public conscience, may turn out to be the decisive element heralding the emergence of a general rule or principle of humanitarian law"); Antonio Cassese, "A Follow-Up: Forcible Humanitarian Countermeasures and *Opinio Necessitatis*," 10 Euro. J. Int'l L. 791 (1991).

77 For discussion of the sources and consequences of this lack of interest, *see supra* at pages 129–32, 278, 402.

78 Vienna Convention on the Law of Treaties, Art. 31(3)(b), providing, "There shall be taken into account . . . any subsequent practice in the application of the treaty which establishes the agreement of the parties regarding its interpretation."

79 It is possible to meet the *opinio juris* requirement of customary law with evidence that a given practice is generally regarded as permissible in relevant circumstances; it need not be considered obligatory, in other words. Robert Kolb, "Selected Problems in the Theory of Customary International Law,"

Netherlands Int'l L. Rev. 119, 121–22, 138 (2003) (discussing this view and the work of several legal authorities endorsing it).

80　Morrow, *supra* note 72, at 568. Morrow acknowledges that the data set does not strongly support inferences about the strict legality of specific acts. Some of the difficulties were so pressing (and some of Morrow's solutions so innovative) that he published a lengthy article describing the data and the coding procedures. James D. Morrow & Hyeran Jo, "Compliance with the Laws of War: Dataset and Coding Rules," 23 Conflict Management & Peace Science 91 (2006). Morrow also maintains a Web site that facilitates use of his data, at http://sitemaker. umich.edu/lawsofwar/raw_data_and_documentation.

There are three central problems: First, Morrow obtains his raw data from secondary historical accounts of conflicts and codes violations only for degrees of severity, pervasiveness, centralization, etc. The CMPS article describes all this in great detail. In other words, a survey of some secondary materials is consulted to discern, in a general way, the degree to which the law of war is violated in each "dyadic" conflict. As Morrow acknowledges, the data only imprecisely track the phenomenon he aims to quantify.

Second, the data set rests on a questionable, and in some circumstances manifestly inaccurate, understanding of the law. In particular, Morrow does not adequately account for the general participation or *si omnes* clauses that are so common in pre-1949 humanitarian law treaties. Under these provisions, the treaties do not apply to any conflict in which any one of the warring states is not a party. Because of these provisions, most major humanitarian law treaties were inapplicable – as a formal matter – in most major wars (including World Wars I and II). As such, none of the acts described by Morrow are actually violations of humanitarian law. To say this is to put aside customary international law. Morrow is wise to do so, given its inevitable ambiguities.

Another example of this second problem is that Morrow does not adequately account for very real debates about the triggering and excusing conditions in pre-1949 humanitarian law. For instance, faced with allegations of mistreating civilians in violation of the laws of war, many states denied the applicability of pre-1949 rules protecting civilians on the grounds that no "military occupation" had been established, and hence no duty was owed to the foreign civilian population. These are only a few examples, but they well illustrate the potential objections. In light of these methodological difficulties, observed by an anonymous manuscript reviewer, it would be premature to base any strong conclusions about humanitarian law's efficacy on Morrow's study. It is more valuable for its claim about the efficacy of retaliatory tit-for-tat, whether or not this process occurs within the terms allowed by law at any given historical period. And it is this more modest conclusion that is especially pertinent to any theory of reciprocity in war.

Third, Morrow does not attempt to control for the conditions under which the targeting of civilians is likely in the first place (i.e., primarily in wars of attrition and guerrilla wars). If Valentino et al. are correct, however, one would expect to find a pattern that seemed to suggest "reciprocity," but not because combatants were coordinating their actions. Rather, in quick, easy wars, neither side has an incentive to kill civilians, whereas in long, difficult wars, both sides have strong incentives to do so. Valentino et al., *supra* note 27. Both interpretations are "rationalist" in theoretical spirit.

81 Morrow, *id.* at 570. Similarly, major reductions in armaments between major rivals have almost invariably been cooperative (i.e., bilateral or multilateral). Unilateral arms reductions on a major scale occur only on the complete routing or abdication of one of the states party to the terminated conflict, as when both the U.S. and Russia unilaterally disarmed many of their nuclear weapons after the end of the Cold War. As early as 1991 the U.S. Presidential Nuclear Initiatives, for instance, unilaterally eliminated all Army tactical nuclear weapons as well as most Navy nonstrategic nuclear systems. *See* http://www.acq. osd.mil/ncbdp/nm/international.html; Haralambos Athanasopulos, Nuclear Disarmament in International Law 101–27 (2000). In 1991, South Africa unilaterally disarmed its nuclear arsenal to signal the seriousness of its intention to rejoin the international community, among other possible reasons. Interview with F.W. De Klerk, Newsweek, at http://www.msnbc.msn.com/id/12758097/ site/newsweek.

82 It may sometimes be necessary to adopt a strategy slightly more forgiving of a partner's defection than tit-for-tat permits, to build a level of trust needed to reach a tipping point at which mechanisms of reciprocity set in and attain equilibrium. George Mavrodes, "Conventions and the Morality of War," 4 Phil. & Pub. Aff. 117, 130 (1975).

83 A.J. Barker, Prisoners of War 61 (1975). In the Pacific theater, U.S. policy discouraged war crime, but widespread brutality by individual GIs and Marines occurred; it was generally attributed to the particularly ferocious "dynamics of the battlefield." James Morrow, "The Institutional Features of Prisoner of War Treaties," 55 Int'l Org. 971, 977 (2001); Gerald Linderman, The World within War: America's Combat Experience in World War II 143–84 (1997).

84 Judith Gansberg, Stalag U.S.A.: The Story of German POWs in America 14–16, 37, 58–59 (1977).

85 Arnold Krammer, "American Treatment of German Generals during World War II," 54 J. Military History 27, 28–31, 37–46 (1990); Ulrich Strauss, The Anguish of Surrender: Japanese POWs of World War II 124–49 (2003); Richard Mayne, In Victory, Magnanimity, in Peace, Goodwill: A History of Wilton Park 25–26 (2003); Robert Billinger Jr., Hitler's Soldiers in the Sunshine State: German POWs in Florida 49–50 (2000).

86 Vernon E. Davis, The Long Road Home: U.S. Prisoner of War Policy and Planning in Southeast Asia 95 (2000).

87 Robert Keohane, a leading theorist of international relations, makes this point in an interview, at http://globetrotter.berkeley.edu/people4/Keohane/keohane-con2.html.

88 Morrow, *supra* note 72, at 561.

89 Eric Posner, "Apply the Golden Rule to al Qaeda?" Wall St. J., July 15, 2006, at A9.

90 René Provost, International Human Rights and Humanitarian Law 194, 227 (2002).

91 Morrow acknowledges this as a valid inference from his work, but does not make the point in his article. Correspondence with author, Jan. 2007. Legal

scholars will be understandably reluctant to accept the conclusion without careful assessment of Morrow's data and methods, for as one leading political scientist notes, "The findings produced by even the most sophisticated statistical analyses appear to be remarkably unstable and highly sensitive to changes in the cases and time periods covered, and the variables included or ignored." Fritz Scharpf, "Social Science as a Vocation – Are Max Weber's Warnings Still Valid?" at http://www.iue.it/MaxWeberProgramme/PDFs/MWLectures/Lecture_Scharpf_4Oct2006.PDF; *see also* Bernhard Kittel, "A Crazed Methodology? On the Limits of Macro-Quantitative Social Science Research," 21 Int'l Sociology 647 (2006) (same, by one of the foremost practitioners of such methods).

Several leading scholars of humanitarian law conclude that reprisals cannot be, and have not been, effectively outlawed. *See, e.g.,* Provost, *supra* note 90, at 181 (conceding that "reciprocity remains a powerful force in inducing continued compliance with humanitarian norms by belligerents, and there is some danger in proposing overly rigid rules which may remain dead letter rather than carefully crafting standards which stand a realistic chance of being applied in the field"); Rüdiger Wolfrum, "Enforcement of International Humanitarian Law," *in* The Handbook of Humanitarian Law in Armed Conflicts, Dieter Fleck, ed. 517, 527 (1995) ("Only those who themselves comply with the provisions of international humanitarian law can expect the adversary to observe the dictates of humanity in an armed conflict."); Greenwood, *supra* note 25, at 319–20 ("Where . . . military imbalance arises from the adversary's violation of certain rules of the law of armed conflict, it is unreasonable to forbid the victim of those violations to respond in kind unless other means of redress are available."); William O'Brien, Law and Morality in Israel's War with the PLO 117 (1991) (contending that a complete prohibition on reprisals "is unrealistic, based on a faulty model of the international political and legal system, and . . . manifestly unfair"); Michael Walzer, Just and Unjust Wars 220 (1977) ("Reprisals are clearly sanctioned by the practice of nations, and the (moral) reason behind the practice seems as strong as ever."); *cf.* Thomas Franck, Recourse to Force: State Action against Threats and Armed Attacks (2002) ("Like the [World] Court, the political organs of the United Nations have carefully avoided giving a broad, dogmatic answer to the issues posed by states' recourse to armed countermeasures.").

92 For a noteworthy illustration of this possibility, *see* Ze'ev Drory, Israel's Reprisal Policy 1953–1956: The Dynamics of Military Retaliation 7–39, 55 (2005). In authorizing reprisal, even the 1863 Lieber Code evinced hesitation on this ground, noting that "unjust or inconsiderate retaliation removes the belligerents farther and farther from the mitigating rules of regular war, and by rapid steps leads them nearer to the internecine wars of savages." The Lieber Code of 1863, Gen. Order 100, U.S. War Dept., Art. 28(2). *See generally* Theodor Meron, "The Humanization of Humanitarian Law," 94 A.J.I.L. 239, 251 (2000) ("As the experience of World War II suggests, one reprisal leads to another, in the long run creating a vicious circle in which the 'original sin' is often forgotten, enhancing the potential for mutual destruction.").

93 Joost Pauwelyn, "How Strongly Should We Protect and Enforce International Law," University of Chicago Law School Workshop, March 15, 2006, at 64; *see also* Greenwood, *supra* note 25, at 317 (arguing the current humanitarian

law "does very little to provide a replacement for reprisals as a sanction"); G. Draper, "The Implementation and Enforcement of the Geneva Conventions of 1949 and the Two Additional Protocols," (1979-III) 164 Hague Recueil, 1, 35 (contending that banishment of reprisals places a heavy strain on the "residual" methods of enforcing humanitarian law).

94 As one leading commentator notes, Geneva Additional Protocol I seeks to protect "civilians who may well be located in the very objectives which an army wishes to capture and thus imposes restrictions which make it markedly more difficult for a state to win a conflict in which it becomes engaged" (i.e., to win it lawfully). Greenwood, *supra* note 25, at 319.

95 Maj. W. Hays Parks, "Air War and the Law of War," 32 A.F.L. Rev. 1, 57–59 (1990); *see also* David Rivkin & Lee Casey, "Lawfare," Wall St. J. Feb. 2007, at A11 (arguing that "the criminalization of traditional warfare seems to be the goal" of recent litigation making "it exceptionally difficult – if not impossible – for a law-abiding state to wage war in anything like the traditional manner"); Glenn Sulmasy & John Yoo, "Civilian Control of the Military: A Rational Choice Approach to the War on Terror," 54 UCLA L. Rev. 1815, 1836 (2007) ("This new legalization of warfare, mostly imbued from international obligations and the realities of twenty-four hour media coverage, can prevent field commanders from achieving legitimate objectives of warfare."); Col. Kelly Wheaton, "Strategic Lawyering: Realizing the Potential of Military Lawyers at the Strategic Level," 1/998 Army Lawyer 1, 5–7 (Sept. 2006) (warning of the "use of lawfare against the U.S . . . cynically manipulating the law of armed conflict to undermine U.S. and international support for a military operation, potentially restricting or completely stopping the military effort"); *Cf.* Paul von Zielbauer, "Web Sites Rally Support for G.I.'s in Legal Trouble," New York Times, July 22, 2007, A4. The Times article describes Web sites soliciting support for U.S. military personnel pending trial for war crimes in Iraq, sites whose "organizers and contributors said they believed that many of the prosecutions were based on feeble evidence and gauzy recollections of Iraqis sympathetic to the insurgency and hostile to the American military mission in Iraq." Opponents of such prosecutions declare, "The insurgency has found a new weapon . . . and that's to accuse these young men of wrongdoing, because [it knows] we throw the book at them." *Id.* Another contributor argues, "You just can't put people under the microscope when the lines of combat are so blurred." *Id.*

96 Nicholas O. Berry, War and the Red Cross 5 (1997). ICRC Senior Representative Jean Pictet has even reportedly said, "If we cannot outlaw war, we will make it too complex for the commander to fight." Parks, *supra* note 95, at 75.

97 Belligerents may even have a "duty of care," based in the law of negligence and fiduciary duty, to avoid unnecessary civilian damage, some contend. Dakota Rudesill, "Precision War and Responsibility: Transformational Military Technology and the Duty of Care under the Laws of War," 32 Yale J. Int'l L. 517, 423–29 (2007).

98 Examples include manufacturers of football helmets, small jet aircraft, spermicides, artificial heart valves, intrauterine devices, insulation products, and breast implants. "The Serious Side-Effects of Medical Liability," The Economist, Jan. 10, 1995, at 51; "Product Liability: Silicone Valediction," The Economist, May 20, 1995, at 60.

99 David Kennedy, Of War and Law 31 (2006).

100 The effort to regulate warfare's most effective methods out of existence also somewhat resembles the effort to banish the notion of "victory" itself. Since the 1980s that concept, even as applied to conventional warfare (much less nuclear or counterinsurgency), came to be viewed with great suspicion in many respectable circles. The rationale for this skepticism, as one author then satirized it, was essentially that "if the right-thinking are to achieve their great aim of abolishing war they must first persuade us that victory is futile, or, better still, actually harmful." Edward Luttwak, On the Meaning of Victory: Essays on Strategy 289 (1986); *see also* Colin Gray, "Defining and Achieving Decisive Victory," Strategic Studies Institute, U.S. Army War College 4 (2002). This sentiment found recent expression in the widespread insistence that though the Soviet Union undeniably lost the Cold War, the United States did not "win" it. In certain quarters, it was important to establish that there had been no genuine victor, because the conflict exacted a terrible toll even on the West and might have been avoided entirely through more prudent and intelligent diplomacy. (This is a central argument of Deborah Welch Larson, Anatomy of Mistrust: U.S.-Soviet Relations during the Cold War 1997). To similar effect, in the conflict with Al Qaeda and kindred groups, some leading thinkers plausibly contend that winning must be redefined to require accepting that the terrorist threat can never be eradicated completely and that acting as though it can will only make it worse. Philip Gordon, "Can the War on Terror Be Won? How to Fight the Right War," 86 Foreign Affairs 53, 54 (Nov./Dec. 2007). The threat must instead be intelligently "managed," on this view, in much the same way modern societies manage other varieties of risk. Mikkel Rasmussen, The Risk Society at War: Terror, Technology and Strategy in the Twenty-First Century (2006).

101 On some of the difficulties in applying this doctrine, *see* Noam Neuman, "Applying the Rule of Proportionality: Force Protection and Cumulative Assessment in International Law and Morality," *in* Yearbook of International Humanitarian Law, Timothy McCormack & Avril McDonald, eds. 2004 79 (2007); David Mellow, "Counterfactuals and the Proportionality Criterion," 20 Ethics & Int'l Affairs 439 (2006); Thomas Hurka, "Proportionality in the Morality of War," 33 Phil. & Pub. Affairs 34 (2005).

102 In 2005 the ICRC issued a three-volume publication, Customary International Humanitarian Law, running to 4,411 pages, on the rules applicable to "armed conflict," which included nothing on the definition of this term, because it remains much disputed. Such terminological disputes are rife; several commentators express doubt, for instance, that attacks even by well-organized terrorist groups like Al Qaeda can constitute "armed attacks" within the meaning of UN Charter, Art. 51. *See, e.g.*, Rosa Ehrenreich Brooks, "War Everywhere: Rights, National Security Law, and the Law of Armed Conflict in the Age of Terror," 153 U. Penn. L. Rev. 675, 756 (2003); Sean Murphy, "Terrorism and the Concept of 'Armed Attack' in Article 51 of the UN Charter," 43 Harv. Int'l L. J. 41 (2002).

103 Antonio Cassese, "On Some Merits of the Israeli Judgment on Targeted Killings," 5 J. Int'l Crim. Justice 339, 341 (2007) ("It is common knowledge

that most rules of international humanitarian law on the conduct of hostilities . . . are rather broad and ambiguous; hence they do not offer great certainty in the guidance they provide to combatants."); Jack Goldsmith & Stephen D. Krasner, "The Limits of Idealism," 132 Daedalus 49, Winter 2003 (noting that much of "international criminal law is extraordinarily vague"); Sanford Levinson, "Slavery and the Phenomenology of Torture," 74 Soc. Res. 149, 161 (2007) (observing that the key language in common Art. 3 of the Geneva Conventions, prohibiting "outrages upon human dignity," would, if incorporated into an American criminal statute, be void for vagueness under U.S constitutional law).

104 The European and Inter-American Courts of Human Rights have taken this interpretive approach in several cases. Alexander Orakhelashvili, "The Interaction between Human Rights and Humanitarian Law: A Case of Fragmentation," N.Y.U. Int'l L. & Justice Colloquium, Feb. 26, 2007, at 5.

105 Scott Shane, "Waterboarding Focus of Inquiry by Justice Dept.," New York Times, Feb. 23, 2008. Even if such legal approval of waterboarding were ultimately found to have been based on faulty analysis, that analysis could well be sufficient to establish a defense of reasonable reliance on counsel for CIA interrogators. Some have suggested that providing such a "good faith" defense, however ultimately unmeritorious its legal arguments, had been the purpose of the Office of Legal Counsel torture memoranda from the beginning. David Cole, "The Man Behind the Torture," 54 N.Y. Rev. of Books, Dec. 6, 2007.

106 Presidential Order on the Treatment of Taliban and Al Qaeda Detainees, Feb. 7, 2002.

107 In a 2005 Carnegie Council panel on "The Question of Torture," journalist Mark Bowden confidently asserted of Khalid Muhammad that "he's only not a prisoner of war because we've chosen not to define him as such." At http://www.cceia.org/resources/transcripts/5207.html/:pf_printable? This is, however, actually one of the few interpretive issues on which most lawyers on both sides agree.

108 *See generally* Ivan Arreguín-Toft, "How the Weak Win Wars," 26 Int'l Security 93 (2001); Jeffrey Record, "Why the Strong Lose," 35 Parameters 16 (Winter 2005–06).

109 Kenneth Abbott, "International Relations Theory, International Law, and the Regime Governing Atrocities in Internal Conflicts," 93 A.J.I.L. 361, 369 (1999).

110 Stathis Kalyvas, The Logic of Violence in Civil War 54 (2006).

111 Provost, *supra* note 90, at 162.

112 Audrey K. Cronin, "How al-Qaida Ends: The Decline and Demise of Terrorist Groups," 31 Int'l Sec. 7, 19, 25–27; Posner, *supra* note 41, at 431.

113 Ze'ev Schiff, "Israel's War with Iran," 85 Foreign Affairs 23, 24 (Nov./Dec. 2006).

114 Human Rights Watch, War without Quarter: Colombia and International Humanitarian Law (1998). Although the FARC nonetheless largely ignored humanitarian law, the EPL generally respected it, the report concludes.

115 Adama Dieng, "La mise en oeuvre du droit international humanitaire: Les infractions et les sanctions, ou quand la pratique désavoue les textes," *in* 1 Law in Humanitarian Crises 311, 330–40, (European Commission, ed. 1995).

116 Michael Ignatieff, The Lesser Evil: Ethics in an Age of Terror 96–97 (2004). Adherence was inconsistent, however.

117 FMLN, La legitimidad de nuestros métodos de lucha (El Salvador, Secretaria de promoción y protección de los derechos humanos del FMLN, 1989), at 89; El Salvador, Informe de la Fuerza Armada de El Salvador sobre el respecto y la vigencia de las normas del derecho internacional humanitario durante el período de septiembre de 1986 a agosto de 1987 (1987). Similar unilateral undertakings by belligerents occurred during civil wars in the Congo (1964) and Nigeria (1967), as the ICTY Appeals Chamber noted in *Prosecutor v. Tadic*, Case No. IT-94-1-I, Decision on Defense Motion for Interlocutory Appeal on Jurisdiction, ¶¶ 105–06 (Oct. 2, 1995).

118 From Madness to Hope: The Twelve-Year War in El Salvador: Truth Commission 11, 20–21, 43–45 (1993); Commission for Historical Clarification, Guatemala: Memory of Silence ¶¶ 100, 129–36. (1999).

119 Posner here appears to acknowledge the importance of custom to international law making, a position he almost entirely rejects in Jack Goldsmith & Eric Posner, The Limits of International Law 23–44 (2005).

120 For instance, in 1989 the Palestine Liberation Organization gave notice to the ICRC that it would henceforth "accept and apply" all of the 1949 Geneva Conventions and their 1977 Protocols. Still, such professions of intent to comply with humanitarian law should not be dismissed categorically, as in a rule that would create "an irrebuttable presumption that the organization [once designated as "terrorist"] will act outside the law," as recommended by Michael Schmitt, "Responding to Transnational Terrorism under the *Jus ad Bellum*: a Normative Framework," *in* International Law and Armed Conflict: Exploring the Fault Lines, Michael Schmitt & Jelena Pejic, eds. 157, 174 (2007).

121 Mariane Pearl, A Mighty Heart: The Brave Life and Death of My Husband, Danny Pearl 105 (2003).

122 There is some reason for doubt, however, whether he actually committed the act. Jane Mayer, "The Black Sites," New Yorker (Aug. 13, 2007), at 46, 48.

123 "Transcript of bin Laden's October Interview," http://www.cnn.com/2002/WORLD/asiapcf/south/02/05/binladen.transcript (Nov. 18, 2003); Sohail H. Hashmi, "9/11 and the Jihad Tradition," *in* Terror, Culture, Politics, Daniel Sherman & Terry Nardin, eds. 149, 159 (2006); *see also* Interview with Tayseer Alouni, Oct. 21, 2001, *reprinted in* Al Qaeda Now, Karen Greenberg, ed. 197 (2005) ("Just as they are killing us, we have to kill them so that there will be balance of terror.").

124 Ian Shapiro, Containment: Rebuilding a Strategy against Global Terror 85 (2007).

125 Chae-Han Kim, "Reciprocity in Asymmetry: When Does Reciprocity Work?" 31 Int'l Interactions 1, 12 (2005). On how unilateral initiatives sometimes work as "starting mechanisms" in international diplomacy, *see* Daniel Druckman, "The Social Psychology of Arms Control and Reciprocation," 11 J. Polit. Psychol. 553, 561–63 (1990); William Rosek, U.S. Unilateral Arms Control Initiatives: When Do They Work? (1988); Martin Patchen, "Strategies for Eliciting Cooperation from an Adversary," 31 J. Conflict. Resol. 164 (1987).

126 Morrow, *supra* note 72, at 569. Tit-for-tat between states works best as a wartime enforcement mechanism when such doubt or noise can be minimized, ensuring

that any legal violation is attributable to decision makers at the highest levels. Noise is much greater with regard to certain kinds of humanitarian law violations than to others.

127 Provost, *supra* note 90, at 190.

128 Geoffrey Best, War and Law since 1945 335 (1994).

129 *See, e.g.*, Smart Sanctions: Targeting Economic Statecraft, David Cortright & George Lopez, eds. (2002); Daniel Byman & Matthew Waxman, Confronting Iraq: U.S. Policy and the Use of Force since the Gulf War 77–90 (2000); Jonathan Kirshner, "The Microfoundations of Economic Sanctions," 6 Security Studies 32 (1997).

130 Jonathan Schwartz, "Dealing with a 'Rogue State': The Libya Precedent," 101 A. J. I. L. 553 (2007).

131 Osiel, *supra* note 10, at 176–80.

132 For instance, in World War I, a French battery commander refused to fire on French troops who had disobeyed orders to leave their trenches for combat. The incident is described in a fictionalized account by Humphrey Cobb, Paths of Glory (1935), and in Stanley Kubrick's film of the same title (Metro-Goldwyn-Mayer 1957).

133 Mark Osiel, "The Banality of Good: Aligning Incentives against Mass Atrocity," 105 Colum. L. Rev. 175, 1773–1804 (2005) (discussing command responsibility and participation in a joint criminal enterprise, as well as complicity and conspiracy).

134 Mark Mazzetti, "New Generation of Qaeda Chiefs Is Seen on Rise," New York Times, April 2, 2007, at A1 (citing experts' views that even Al Qaeda's "leadership is now more diffuse, with several planning hubs working autonomously and not reliant on constant contact with Mr. Bin Laden"); Associated Press, "Chertoff Warns of Higher Risks of Terrorism," New York Times, July 11, 2007, at A16 (reporting that U.S intelligence analysts have concluded that Al Qaeda has rebuilt its operating capability to a level not seen since just before the 9/11 attacks); *see generally* Sageman, *supra* note 67.

135 Rohan Gunaratna, Inside Al Qaeda: Global Network of Terror 52–55, 95–101 (2002).

136 Osama bin Laden, interviewed by Hamid Mir, at http://www.dawn.com/2001/11/10/top1.htm.

137 Larry May, The Law of Aggression 414 (2008, forthcoming).

138 Talal Asad, 'Thinking about "Just War,"' July 17, 2007, http://www.huffingtonpost.com/talal-asad/thinking-about-just-warb56605.html   posted July 11 2007. "Warfare, of course, is an even greater violation of civilian 'innocence'" than terrorism, "but ideas have sedimented in us so that we regard war in principle as legitimate even when civilians are killed. . . . Deaths in war (however horrible) are necessary for the defense of 'our form of life.'"

139 Richard S. Hartigan, The Forgotten Victim: A History of the Civilian 2, 112–20, 130–31 (1982); Caleb Carr, The Lessons of Terror: A History of Warfare against Civilians 6–19, 59–62, 172–78, 190–95 (2002); *but see* Conway-Lanz, *supra* note 27, at 184, 211 (suggesting the importance to U.S. national political identity of having largely respected noncombatant immunity in the two world wars).

140 Kim Gamel, "Al-Qaeda: Captured U.S. Troops Killed," Yahoo News, June 5, 2007.

141 Posner, *supra* note 41, at 433. Posner describes this as a lack of "symmetry."
142 Robert Keohane, "Realism, Neorealism, and the Study of World Politics," *in* Neorealism and its Critics, Robert Keohane, ed. 1 (1986).
143 Posner, *supra* note 41, at 434.
144 Ralph H. Salmi, Cesar Adib Majul et al., Islam and Conflict Resolution 123–25 (1998). More generally, when governing warfare Islamic jurisprudence in the classical era embraced the reciprocity principle, providing that Muslim soldiers should abjure prohibited fighting methods as long as their enemy displayed its own continued willingness to do so. Mohammad Hashim Kamali, "Jihad and the Interpretation of the Koran: Contextualizing Islamic Tradition," Third Hague Colloquium on Fundamental Principles of Law, Oct. 3, 2008; *but see* Lena Salaymeh, "Early Islamic Legal-Historical Precedents: Prisoners of War," 26 L. & Hist. Rev. 521, 544 (2008) (showing that early Islamic jurists understood the Koran as authorizing the killing of POWs).
145 Patricia Crone, God's Rule: Government and Islam 281 (2004); Patricia Crone, Medieval Islamic Political Thought 383–84 (2004). Those contending that Islam itself, properly understood, is entirely innocent of any connection to the suicide terrorism against civilians offer a very traditional, formalist defense of their position (i.e., based on the actual text of the Koran and longstanding interpretations of it by Islamic legal scholars throughout history). This approach would be more convincing, however, if many of the same contemporary commentators did not adopt a diametrically opposed method of interpreting other Koranic passages strikingly inconsistent with the human rights concepts that have come to be embodied in international treaties of the last half-century.

   In this second context, emphasis is invariably on the mutability of meaning within any text. It is obviously true that "there is no essentialist or monolithic Islam." John Esposito, Unholy War: Terror in the Name of Islam 141 (2002). This receptivity to reinterpretation is understandably congenial to Muslims who are sympathetic to international human rights ideas, but unwilling to defend them in terms originating in secular thought from the West. These Muslims must therefore struggle to find these ideas or their functional equivalents within texts understood almost universally throughout their history, by virtually all contending schools of Islamic thought, to oppose such ideas.

   For recent examples of this heroic effort at reinterpretive transformation, *see, e.g.,* Mashood Baderin, International Human Rights and Islamic Law 219–23 (2003); Islam and Human Rights, Mashood Baderin et al., eds. (2006); Progressive Islam: On Justice, Gender and Pluralism, Omid Safi, ed. (2003); Ahmed Moussalli, The Islamic Quest for Democracy, Pluralism and Human Rights (2001); John Esposito & John Voll, Islam and Democracy (1996); Shahrought Akhavi, "Shiite Theories of Social Contract," *in* Shari'a: Islamic Law in the Contemporary Context, Abbas Amanat & Frank Griffel, eds. 137 (2007); Aziz Al-Azmeh, Islams and Modernities (1996); Scott Kugle, Sufis and Saints' Bodies: Mysticism, Corporeality, and Sacred Power in Islam (2007). Kugle, an American convert, argues, for instance, that because the primary Koranic verses employed to reject homosexuality also imply male rape, the "progressive" reading is that these passages actually repudiate sex as a form of domination. Neil Macfarquhar, "Gay Muslims Find Freedom, of a Sort, in the U.S.," New York Times, Nov. 7, 2007, at A1 (quoting Kugle). *But see* Ayatollah Ustad Muhammad Taqi Jafari, A Comparative Study of the Two Systems of Universal Human Rights: From the Viewpoints of Islam and the West 62–65, 151–58, 163–67 (1999) (observing inconsistencies between Western and prevailing Islamic understandings of human rights). On methods of legal reinterpretation within Islamic jurisprudence, *see* Felicitas Opwis, "Islamic Law and Legal Change: The Concept of Maslaha in Classical and Contemporary Islamic Legal Theory," *in* Amanat & Griffel, *id.* at 62.

If it is true that sacred texts are as malleable or mutable as this view implies, then jihadist proponents of intentional attacks on Western civilians may presumably employ the same interpretive methods. They have indeed identified several passages in the Koran and authoritative commentaries susceptible to such a reading. For that matter, all four schools of Islamic law held that male unbelievers beyond puberty could be killed outright during jihad, even those not belonging to a military organization. Mary Habeck, Knowing the Enemy: Jihadist Ideology and the War on Terror 127–28 (2006) (citing primary sources). Female captives may be enslaved. *Id.* at 129. All four schools also allowed the taking of booty from victims of jihad, a view endorsed by bin Laden. *Id.* at 131. During the Muslim conquests, soldiers were permitted to keep four-fifths of captured booty. Hugh Kennedy, The Great Arab Conquests 20–21, 64 (2007).

Accepting that both sides use the same interpretive methods would be an expression, one might say, of reciprocity in my second sense of the term (i.e., as the uniform application of a rule to all governed by it – here, a rule concerning how texts may be read). Jihadists may very well "selectively ignore a thousand years of interpretive work" on the Koran, in a way that "is a serious affront" to most Muslims' understanding of their faith. Habeck, *id.* at 54–55. The same could readily be said, however, of those claiming to discern the fundamentals of all major international human rights norms within that same text. For evidence of the common jihadist invocation of the Koran and its commentaries in defense of their martial methods, *see, e.g.,* Imam Hasan al-Banna "Explanation of Jihad," at http://www.youngmuslims. ca/articles/display.asp?ID=7;www.youngmuslims.ca/online_library/books/ jihad/; Habeck, *id.* at 3–55, 126–33; Antony Black, The History of Islamic Political Thought 155 (2005); Emmanuel Sivan, Radical Islam, Medieval Theology and Modern Politics 94–100 (1985). However, most readers of this book will have difficulty finding statements on jihadist Web sites to confirm this. Though there are many such sites and statements at any given moment, those in English, at least, are quickly removed in most cases by the Web site servers or by hackers, most employed by states. Shawn Brimley, "Tentacles of Jihad: Targeting Transnational Support Networks," 36 Parameters 30, 40 (2006); Martin Golumbic, Fighting Terror Online: The Convergence of Security, Technology, and the Law 122–24, 146–54 (2008). It is therefore better, for present purposes, to list only sites that *monitor* actual jihadist blogs and fora, such as www.freerepublic.com/focus/f-news/1870701/posts; http://www. memriiwmp.org/; www.siteinstitute.org; http://www.hizbollah.org/ar/index.

php; http://www.iaisite.net/; http://inshallahshaheed.muslimpad.com, where the reader may readily find such Koranic invocations.

In contrast, Islam's modernist potentialities were long ago emphasized by leading non-Muslim scholars of the Islamic world. *See, e.g.,* Maxime Rodinson, Islam and Capitalism 157–84 (1974); Ernest Gellner, Muslim Society 61–62, 162 (1981); Ernest Gellner, Conditions of Liberty: Civil Society and Its Rivals 15–29 (1994); Leonard Binder, Islamic Liberalism 206–92 (1988); The Public Sphere in Muslim Societies. Miriam Hoexter, Shmuel Eisenstadt, & Nehemia Levtzion, eds. (2002). Before the recent global appeal of human rights norms, an earlier generation of Arab nationalists sought to establish the compatibility of much of Islam to their political views, most of which were avowedly secular. For a recent discussion of such affinities, *see* Talal Asad, Formations of the Secular: Christianity, Islam and Modernity 195–201 (2003).

Such intellectual movements are responsive to the fact that most people wish to preserve at least a modicum of integrity over time in their sense of personal identity. It is hence perfectly intelligible that they would seek ways to reconcile the traditions in which they were raised by loved ones with ideas and foreign social practices for which they have developed a new affinity. The impulse to break entirely from past beliefs and rituals, even when one no longer fully believes in them, is rare and not strong even in most tempted by it. Hence the inclination for modern believers to "reverse engineer" historical understandings of their religious tradition in light of admiration for a competitor's "product."

A religious skeptic might here interject that if reaching modernist conclusions requires rejecting so much of the divinely revealed text and its longstanding interpretation, it is surely better to start afresh. Yet it may be a mistake to dismiss the propensity for continuity, personal and collective, as merely a psychological crutch for those unable to reinvent themselves in light of new information or unwilling to prejudice close relationships with those from whom early views and identities were acquired.

146 Salmi, *supra* note 144, at 127 (noting that enslavement of non-Muslim captives was permitted only in retaliation for the enemy's enslavement of Muslim captives); Muhammad Abu Zahra, The Concept of War in Islam (Muhammad al-Hady & Taha Omar, trans. Supreme Council for Islamic Affairs, Ministry of Waqf 1961). The Koran, at 8:61, itself admonishes, "If they incline toward peace, you incline also to it, and trust Allah."

147 Posner, *supra* note 41, at 432. Posner's IR realism here deviates curiously from the economic assumptions on which he claims to found it, because rational choice theory teaches that collective action has to be explained in terms of individuals' motivations and that it is mistaken to impute motives to collective entities, much less those as large and diverse in composition as nation-states. Mancur Olson, The Logic of Collective Action 1–3 (1971). The motivations of the individuals who lead democracies tend to differ meaningfully from those who lead dictatorships.

148 Valentino et al., *supra* note 27, at 368 (finding from a multivariate analysis of interstate wars that democratic regimes have been no more nor less likely to target civilians than other types of regimes); *but see* Alexander B. Downes, Targeting Civilians in War 246–48 (2008) (concluding from a different data set

of interstate wars between 1816 and 2003 that in wars of attrition democracies are more likely than autocracies to target civilians intentionally).

149 In response to my questioning, Morrow ran a test on his data to see if there was an interaction effect between regime type and ratification on killing of civilians. As in his published article, he again finds that joint ratification by belligerents raises law compliance (i.e., fewer violations of noncombatant immunity) for democracies, but not for nondemocracies. Correspondence with author, Feb. 18, 2008. Morrow's finding here is consistent with Oona Hathaway, "Do Human Rights Treaties Make a Difference?" 111 Yale L.J. 1935, 2019 (2002) (concluding from statistical regression that democracies are "more likely to adhere to treaty obligations" in the human rights area); Oona Hathaway, "Why Do Countries Commit to Human Rights Treaties?" 51 J. Conflict Resol. 588 (2007). Valentino et al. similarly conclude from a different data set that ratification of human-itarian law treaties, in isolation from regime type, does not much affect the incidence of state adherence to prohibitions against direct targeting of civilians. Valentino et al., *supra* note 27, at 368.

150 For assessment of this question, *see, e.g.,* Siamak Khatami, Iran, A View from within: Political Analyses 44–61, 120–43 (2004); Aserf Bayat, Making Islam Democratic: Social Movements and the Post-Islamist Turn 187–208 (2007) (examining the strength and weaknesses of democratic forces within contemporary Iran); Juan Cole, Sacred Space and Holy War 209–10 (2002) (same).

151 Michael Doyle, "Kant, Liberal Legacies, and Foreign Affairs," 12 Phil. & & Pub. Affairs 205, 213–17 (1983).

152 This is not to deny that leaders might decide on their own to moderate their methods in order to attract supporters, both personnel and financial contributors. Jarret Brachman & William McCants, "Stealing Al-Qaeda's Playbook," 29 Studies in Conflict & Terrorism 309–11 (2006); Lawrence Wright, "The Master Plan," New Yorker, Sept. 22, 2006 at 48, 53.

153 Osama bin Laden, "Letter to America," Nov. 2002, at http://www.information.clearinghouse.info/article6537.htm.

154 Downes, *supra* note 148, at 152. Downes concludes that because democratic rulers are more vulnerable than autocrats to domestic public opinion, they become less willing to incur heavy costs in war, for fear of compromising support at home. *See also* Dan Reiter & Allan Stam, Democracies at War 144–96 (2002).

155 Downes' conclusions in this regard are not supported by Valentino et al., *supra* note 27, or Morrow, *supra* note 72. In reaction to Downes' findings, Morrow writes, "While I agree . . . that democracies have often been quite willing to kill large numbers of enemy civilians, these are cases where their own populations are relatively protected, so reciprocity does not exist" (i.e., there is little prospect of retaliation against the particular democracy employing such tactics, often for geographical reasons). Correspondence with author, Feb. 18, 2008.

156 Robert Delahunty & John Yoo, "Statehood and the Third Geneva Convention," 46 Va. J. Int'l L. 131, 163 (2005).

157 W. Hays Parks, correspondence with author, Dec. 4, 2006. He adds, "This is exactly why the Army, in particular, has stumbled along so badly in counterinsurgency operations in Iraq." *See also* W. Hays Parks, "Special Forces' Wear of Non-Standard Uniforms," 4 Chi. J. Int'l L. 493, 508 (2003) (rejecting

the view that U.S. "Special Operations Forces (SOF) had to wear uniforms and treat captured al Qaeda and Taliban as enemy prisoners of war in the hope of reciprocity should any SOF fall into enemy hands" on the grounds that this view was "highly speculative at best with respect to al Qaeda and Taliban conduct"); Larry May, War Crimes and Just War 303 (2007) (asking, "If there is unlikely to be reciprocity, why should soldiers voluntarily restrain themselves in the face of terrorist violence?").

158 Edward Luttwak, "Power and Prudence," New Republic, Aug. 6, 2007 online edition (reviewing Jeane Kirkpatrick, Making War to Keep Peace).

159 May, *supra* note 157, at 419–20.

160 *Id.* For a similar view, *see* Bhikhu Parekh, "Terrorism and Intercultural Dialogue," *in* Worlds in Collision: Terror and the Future of Global Order, Ken Booth & Tim Dunne, eds. 270 (2002).

161 May, *supra* note 157, at 418.

162 Restatement 2nd, Conflicts of Law, §98, Comment (f); *Nicol v. Tanner*, 256 N.W.2d 796, 801 (Minn. 1976), citing Golomb, "Recognition of Foreign Money Judgments: A Goal-Oriented Approach," 43 St. John's L. Rev. 604, 615 ("A goal oriented approach to judgment recognition clearly indicates that reciprocity, though proper in other areas of international relations, should be excluded as a consideration in this area."). A further rationale for this approach has been that it is unfair to the party seeking the foreign judgment's enforcement to make it contingent on factors irrelevant to the claim's merits. The proper resolution of disputes between private parties should not be held hostage to the state of relations between nation-states, it has been generally thought. Susan L. Stevens, "Commanding International Judicial Respect: Reciprocity and the Recognition and Enforcement of Foreign Judgments," 26 Hastings Int'l & Comp. L. Rev. 115, 115 (2002). Courts in a few U.S. states continue to demand evidence of the other country's respect for U.S. judgments before agreeing to enforce the civil judgments of that country's courts.

163 The largely consistent practice of U.S. courts in recognizing German judgments, many believe, has caused German courts to be cooperative in interpreting the reciprocity requirement of the German civil code. *See, e.g.,* Wolfgang Wurmnest, "Recognition and Enforcement of U.S. Money Judgments in Germany," 28 Berk. J. Int'l L. 175, 186–88 (2005). Others, however, see the existing reliance on comity as insufficient. "The comity principle," write Buergenthal and Maier, "is most accurately characterized as a Golden Rule among nations – that each must give respect to the laws, policies, and interests of others that it would have others give to its own in the same or similar circumstances." Thomas Buergenthal & Harold Maier, Public International Law in a Nutshell 178, 2nd ed. (1990). The Uniform Foreign Money-Judgments Recognition Act does not demand reciprocity, and has been adopted by more than half the world's states.

164 Joel Paul, "Comity in International Law," 32 Harv. Int'l L.J. 1, 49 (1992).

165 In 2005 the American Law Institute nonetheless proposed federal statutes imposing reciprocity requirements, by treaty or a Memorandum of Understanding. *See* American Law Institute, Recognition and Enforcement of Foreign Judgments: Analysis and Proposed Federal Statute, §7, comment b ("The purpose of the reciprocity provision in this Act is not to make it more difficult to

secure recognition and enforcement of foreign judgments, but rather to create an incentive to foreign countries to commit to recognition and enforcement of judgments rendered in the U.S."), promulgated May 17, 2005.

166 *See generally* Brian Skyrms, The Stag Hunt and the Evolution of Cooperation (2004).

167 Louise Weinberg, "Against Comity," 80 Geo. L. J. 53, 54 (1991). Weinberg does not actually hold the view she here describes and is simply parsing Larry Kramer, "More Notes on Methods and Objectives in the Conflict of Laws," 24 Cornell Int'l L.J. 245 (1991).

168 In criticism of my alleged "Orientalist" stereotyping here, a reviewer of this book's manuscript sought to analogize the religiously inspired martyrdom of jihadist suicide bombers and the patriotic, avowedly secular enthusiasm with which many thousands of Americans have voluntarily joined the armed forces to serve in Afghanistan and Iraq. Both types of volunteers reinterpret seeming costs into benefits on the basis of their worldviews and personal identities. The analogies stop there, however. The reviewer goes further in apparently implying that the mental state inducing individuals to devote a couple years of public service for their country is not meaningfully distinguishable from that entailed in knowingly accepting certain death to guarantee the deaths of a maximum number of noncombatants. To thus reformulate the reviewer's question is also to answer it, of course. Not all human altruism is at once suicidal and homicidal, any more than all or even most suicide is altruistic.

169 David Cook, Martydom in Islam 135–64 (2007); Rudolf Peters, Jihad in Classical and Modern Islam 43–54 (1996); Dennis Ross, Statecraft, and How to Restore America's Standing in the World 158 (2007). This reiterates the constructivist point that one's self-interest is largely determined by one's identity, which in turn springs from one's worldview, including moral ideals.

170 Talal Asad, "On Torture, or Cruel, Inhuman, and Degrading Treatment," 63 Soc. Research 1084, 1102–04 (1996) (observing how the subjective experience of Shi'a Muslim flagellants, annually mourning the Prophet's grandson Hussain, cannot be understood in terms measurable along a single continuum of pain vs. pleasure). To be sure, there is some risk of parody here (i.e., self-parody). *See generally* Ian Hacking, The Social Construction of What? (1999).

171 Slavoj Žižek, The Parallax View 3 (2006) (describing the aesthetic inspiration behind the 1938 design, by a French anarchist, of cells and torture chambers in Barcelona for use against pro-Franco captives).

172 Seneca's Moral Epistles, Anna L. Motto, ed. XIII.3 (2001).

173 Asad applies this reasoning only to religious self-flagellation and secular sado-masochism (in its aestheticized forms), not to coercive interrogation by the infidel. Asad, *supra* note 170, at 1098–1104. But there is nothing in the logic of his argument requiring its confinement to those two cases, and there is a positive element in the subjective apprehension of physical suffering in all three situations.

174 On the other hand, one might respond that an interrogation couldn't count as much of a test of faith unless it was at least "degrading" in some significant way. In any event, Asad points out that the utilitarian perspective here described is alien to many a "religious virtuoso," a category that would include the martyr

in both early Christainity and contemporary jihad. Asad, *supra* note 170, at 1102.

175 Michel de Montaigne, "On Cowardice, the Mother of Cruelty," *in* The Essays of Michel de Montaigne, M.A. Screech, trans. 786, 795 (1991).

176 Émile Durkheim, Suicide: A Study in Sociology, trans. John Spaulding & George Simpson 152–70 (1951) (1897).

177 *Id.* at 227, 240 (considering military heroism as a subtype of altruistic suicide and religious martyrdom as "mystical suicide"); Robert Pape, Dying to Win: The Strategic Logic of Suicide Terrorism 180–98 (2005); Alan Krueger, What Makes a Terrorist: Economics and the Roots of Terrorism 48 (2007). *But see* Anat Berko, The Path to Paradise: The Inner World of Suicide Bombers and Their Dispatchers 74–75, 83, 86, 102–03, 115–16, 124–29, 142–46, 151, 158 (2007) (evidencing many other less altruistic motives, from romantic disappointment to self-hatred and financial rewards for near-starving family members); Ahmed Rashid, "Jihadi Suicide Bombers: The New Wave," N.Y. Rev. of Books, June 12, 2008, at 17, 17; *see generally* Jeffrey Reimer, "Durkheim's 'Heroic Suicide' in Military Combat," 25 Armed Forces & Soc. 113 (1998).

178 Berko, *id.* at 9, 115 (enumerating motives offered by captured suicide bombers whose vests failed to explode); Michael Mann, Incoherent Empire 176 (2003) (describing pensions to surviving family members of suicide bombers); Laurence Iannaccone, "The Market for Martyrs," Presented at the 2004 Meetings of the American Economic Association, San Diego (same); George Packer, "Knowing the Enemy: Can Social Scientists Redefine the 'War on Terror'?" 82 New Yorker, Dec. 18, 2006, at 60, 62 (quoting Australian counterinsurgency scholar/adviser David Kilcullen, contending that the appeal of violent jihadism to Muslim youth lies partly in "a sense of adventure, wanting to be part of the moment, wanting to be in the big movement of history that's happening now").

179 Deputy Secretary Wolfowitz, Interview with Sam Tannenhaus, Vanity Fair, May 9, 2003.

180 Alan Stephens & Nicola Baker, Making Sense of War: Strategy for the 21st Century 261 (2007).

181 Mikkel Rasmussen, The Risk Society at War: Terror, Technology and Strategy in the Twenty-First Century 168, 174, 193 (2006).

182 Bruno Bettelheim, "Individual and Mass Behavior in Extreme Situations," 38 J. Abnormal & Soc. Psych. 417, 425–26 (1943). *See also* Raija-Leena Punamäki, "Can Ideological Commitment Protect Children's Psychosocial Well-Being in Situations of Political Violence?" 67 Child Development 55 (1996).

183 Jean Baudrillard, The Spirit of Terrorism, Chris Turner, trans. 70 (2003).

184 Amy Zegart, Spying Blind: The CIA, the FBI, and the Origins of 9/11 (2007), *passim* (indicating how intelligence failures leading to the 9/11 attacks resulted from organizational defects and institutional obstacles to their correction).

185 Jeff W. Legro, Cooperation under Fire: Anglo-German Restraint during World War II 220 (1995); Colin Gray, Modern Strategy 146 (1999) (indicating how "strategic culture can be dysfunctional"). It is notable how readily American officers today confess to this problem. Lt. Col. George Mastroianni, "Occupations, Cultures, and Leadership in the Army and Air Force," 35 Parameters

76, 83 (Winter 2005–06) (concluding that "a paradox of Air Force culture is that it can be decidedly anti-intellectual – a circumstance perhaps not uncommon in authoritarian cultures such as the military – but nevertheless convinced of its intellectual superiority," adding that this proclivity is not confined to that branch of service); Janeen Klinger, "The Social Science of Carl von Clausewitz," 36 Parameters 79 (Spring 2006) (describing the officer corps as the "profession whose greatest occupational hazard is for doctrine to atrophy into dogmatism"); Thomas Mahnken & James Fitzsimonds, "Tread-Heads or Technophiles: Army Officer Attitudes toward Transformation," 34 Parameters 57, 71 (Summer 2004) (finding from an opinion survey that "many officers do not see the Army as open to new ideas. Instead, they see their superiors as intolerant of criticism.").

186 Legro, *id.* at 238 ("Organizational cultures can arise that distort strategic rationality and mold doctrines that do not match the demands of the external environment.").

187 On how the two organizations differed regarding the value of coercive interrogation, *see* Heather MacDonald, "How to Interrogate Terrorists," *in* The Torture Debate in America, Karen Greenberg, ed. 84, 86–90 (2006).

188 The Military Commissions Act treats evidence obtained through torture as inadmissible in commission proceedings. §948r(b). But evidence obtained by coercion short of torture may be introduced if obtained before enactment of the Dec. 2005 Detainee Treatment Act, with its bar on cruel, inhuman, and degrading treatment even by the CIA. The question of torture has compromised pending prosecutions of Al Qaeda detainees before the commissions. Jess Bravin, "The Conscience of a Colonel," Wall St. J., March 31, 2007, at A1 (noting that more than 90% of pending trials will depend on prisoner statements, and many such prisoners claim to have been tortured). Several European acquittals of terrorist suspects have resulted from the inadmissibility of evidence obtained by intelligence agencies. Craig Whitlock, "Terror Suspects Beating Charges Filed in Europe," Wash. Post, May 31, 2004, at A1.

189 Several of Eric Posner's articles on the law of armed conflict express thanks, in their acknowledgments, to John Bolton, then the U.S. Ambassador to the UN.

190 Kenneth Roth, "Human Rights and the U.S. War on Terror: Why is George Bush Reading from Al Qaeda's Playbook," Public lecture, Carr Center for Human Rights, Harvard University, April 27, 2007; *see also* Stephen Holmes, The Matador's Cape: America's Reckless Response to Terror 7 (2007).

191 Roth, *id.*

192 Philip Zelikow, "Legal Policy for a Twilight War," 5/30/07, at http://hnn.us/articles/39494.html, at 11. Zelikow focuses his criticism on lawyers and their disproportionate influence over policy formulation in the war on terrorism. This influence consisted, above all, in framing the debate in terms of what the law permitted, rather than what wise policy required. The upshot was something of an inversion of the moral philosopher's famous maxim that "ought" implies "can." The operative rule became, instead, more like "can implies ought." Whereas Zelikow blames lawyers – a perennially convenient target – for this framing of issues, he offers no account of why their nonlawyer superiors (Rumsfeld, Cheney, Rice, Bush himself) apparently accepted it. Goldsmith's

account goes deeper. He at first asserts that "the main reason that lawyers were so involved is that the war itself was encumbered with legal restrictions as never before." Jack Goldsmith, The Terror Presidency 130 (2007). He then quickly concedes, however, that "there was so much pressure to act to the edges of the law," due to a pervasive fear of failing to discover information about any planned, future attacks. *Id.* at 131. "The Administration's aim was to go right to the edge of what the torture law prohibited, to exploit every conceivable loophole in order to do everything legally possible to uncover information that might stop an attack." *Id.* at 146. Goldsmith ascribes this pressure proximately to the vice president's counsel, David Addington, but ultimately to President Bush himself.

193 Cass Sunstein, "Administrative Law Goes to War," 118 Harv. L. Rev. 2663, 2663–64 (2005).

194 Philip Tetlock, Expert Political Judgment: How Good Is It? How Can We Know? 2, 20–23, 72–86 (2005); Isaiah Berlin, The Hedgehog and the Fox: An Essay on Tolstoy's View of History (1953).

195 Cass Sunstein, "Incompletely Theorized Agreements," 108 Harv. L. Rev. 1773 (1995).

CHAPTER 11. THE "GIFT" OF HUMANITARIANISM:
SOFT POWER AND BENEVOLENT SIGNALING

1 Tom Ridge, interviewed by Associated Press, quoted in Human Rights First, Law and Security News, Jan. 25, 2008.

2 On this dispute, *see* The Right War? Conservative Debate on Iraq, Gary Rosen, ed. (2005); Stefan Halper & Jonathan Clarke, America Alone: Neo-Conservatives and the Global Order (2004); Francis Fukuyama, America at the Crossroads: Democracy, Power and the Neoconservative Legacy (2006); Jim Mann, Rise of the Vulcans: The History of Bush's War Cabinet 31–36, 90–98, 130–36 (2004); Bob Woodward, Plan of Attack 21–26, 402–27 (2004); Craig Unger, The Fall of the House of Bush 35–46, 195–214 (2007).

3 Others opposing the war on similar grounds were former national security adviser Zbigniew Brzezinski and former UN Ambassador Jeane Kirkpatrick. On debates among conservative policy elites, *see generally* Seymour Hersh, Chain of Command 249–55 (2004); James Bamford, Pretext for War: 9/11, Iraq, and the Abuse of America's Intelligence Agencies (2004); George Packer, Assassins' Gate 15–38, 59–63 (2005); Craig Unger, *supra* note 2, at 1–13, 81–99 (2007) (examining disagreements between father and son, and their respective confidants, over whether to invade Iraq).

4 Among chief U.S. leaders, "virtually no one with military experience supported or advocated the war in Iraq before the March 2003 invasion," observes one scholar of civil-military relations. "All those who supported the war ... had never served time in the military." Brandon Valeriano, book review, 33 Armed Forces & Society 647, 648 (2007). Military leaders privately opposed the size of the President's 2007 "surge" of force commitment, for instance. David Cloud, "Why Officers Differ on Troop Reduction," New York Times, Sept. 14, 2007 (noting that "among those who supported a smaller troop increase than the one Mr. Bush ordered last January were members of the Joint Chiefs of Staff").

See also Michael Mann, Incoherent Empire 9 (2003) (observing that "the notion of civilian control of the military became meaningless, since civilians were the leading militarists").

5 This raises the question of whether it was actually the American desire for access to oil that motivated the 2003 invasion of Iraq. If that thesis were correct, it would largely account for the Bush administration's ready resort to the "hard" power necessary to control Iraqi oil and the President's concomitant indifference to the decline in American "soft" power engendered by the intensely negative world reaction to that invasion and the treatment of detainees at Abu Ghraib. However, advocates of the hunger for oil thesis must overcome several compelling counterarguments, such as those of economist and Nobel Prize Laureate Gary Becker, "Why War with Iraq Is Not about the Oil," Bus. Week, March 17, 2003, at 22. Becker observes that had the U.S. been concerned with maximizing access to and minimizing the cost of Iraq's oil, it would not have sought to prevent, by way of trade sanctions, the country from exporting such oil for a decade, following the 1991 Gulf War. Restricting Iraqi oil production was a means of pressuring Saddam Hussein to dismantle his weapons of mass destruction. In 1990, the runup to the war greatly increased petroleum prices, because of heightened insecurities about continued access to Iraq's reserves. The same occurred in 2003 in anticipation of that country's invasion.

Higher prices are not in the U.S. national interest, of course, and were readily foreseeable, as leading oil executives warned at the time. In any event, since the first Gulf War, the U.S. has become much less dependent on Iraqi oil, as other reserves have been tapped in Siberia, China, and elsewhere. Moreover, the share of income spent on oil has declined by more than half in the United States and other rich countries since the last oil shock, due to technological improvements and the legal rules requiring them. Becker thus concludes, "A war with Iraq is not about oil. It is about Saddam Hussein and the threat he poses to his neighbors, his people, and to nations around the world." *Id.* Moreover, though the United States imports twice as much oil from Venezuela as from Iraq, the Bush administration made no effort to intervene militarily in the former country when its president, Hugo Chávez, blocked production. Valeria Marcel & John Mitchell, "Iraq's Oil Tomorrow," April. 8, 2003 Royal Institute of International Affairs.

For the opposing view on access to oil as a motive for the Iraq invasion, *see* Juan Cole's influential blog, particularly his entry at http://www.juancolebeta2.com/archives/2007/02/al_gore_global_warming_the_osc.html. Even if oil were the primary motivation for the invasion, it may be that it was oil for the world economy at large that policymakers had in mind, rather than for the United States alone, in which case American leaders would have been acting consistently with the country's longstanding position as guarantor of hegemonic stability. Robert Keohane, After Hegemony: Cooperation and Discord in the World Political Economy (1984); Doug Stokes, "Blood for Oil? Global Capital, Counter-Insurgency and the Dual Logic of American Energy Security," 33 Rev. Int'l Stud. 245 (2007) (contending that it was the perceived needs of the larger global market system, especially industrial societies, that prompted the invasion).

6 The decline in civil strife was partly attributable to a policy of targeted killing of leaders in extremist groups. Bob Woodward, The War Within: A Secret White House History 2006–2008 380 (2008). Also significant was a U.S. shift in strategy to allying with local Sunni leaders, as these became willing to resist Al Qaeda in Mesopotamia. Linda Robinson, Tell Me How This Ends: General David Petraeus and the Search for a Way Out of Iraq, 252–54 (2008).

7 This view was widely shared, in fact. For instance, then Secretary of State Colin Powell believed that world opinion would shift in America's favor "rather quickly . . . once we have been successful and we have prevailed and people realize that we have come to provide a better life for the people of Iraq." Quoted in Robert Kagen, "The September 12 Paradigm: America, the World, and George W. Bush," Foreign Affairs, Sept./Oct. 2008. Moreover, support for the war itself was widespread across the U.S. political spectrum, including the Congressional Democrats who voted for it by large margins and the leading media (including The Washington Post, op-ed columnists at The New York Times, and the editors of The New Yorker).

8 Joseph H. Nye, Soft Power: The Means to Success in World Politics 28, 33–72, 127–48 (2004); Joseph Nye, "Soft Power and European-American Affairs," _in_ Hard Power, Soft Power, and the Future of Transatlantic Relations, Thomas Ilgen, ed. 25 (2006).

9 Matthew Fraser, Weapons of Mass Distraction: Soft Power and American Empire (2005) (documenting the diffusion of U.S. television, popular music, and movies throughout the world); Thomas Friedman, The Lexus and the Olive Tree 379–405 (1999).

10 Paul Berman, Terror and Liberalism 193 (2003).

11 More than 80% of people in several Muslim countries believed (in June 2003) that the United States "didn't try very hard" to avoid civilian casualties in Iraq. Colin H. Kahl, "How We Fight," 85 Foreign Affairs Nov./Dec. 2006, at 83, 84.

There is uncertainty over whether the loss from resort to torture, for instance, is incurred by the U.S. government, by the ruling Republican Party, or only by President Bush himself and his closest advisers. If only the last of these, then reputation will be readily recoverable with a new chief executive, even of the same party. However thoroughly depleted for the moment, the "huge reservoirs of good will" that the United States enjoyed until recently throughout the world, as one Singaporean scholar puts it, are easily replenished. Kishore Mahbubani, Beyond the Age of Innocence: Rebuilding Trust between America and the World xvii (2005).

If it is the U.S. government or American people whose reputation has been tarnished, however, then the loss is more serious, enduring, and costly to overcome. It is also unclear how much reputational loss in the humanitarian law area carries over to other issue-areas, some quite far afield, such as trade relations or military cooperation. And presumably states with dubious human rights records themselves are less troubled by U.S. torture of terror suspects than those with spotless records, making U.S reputational loss different in measure from one audience-state to the next. Rachel Brewster, "Unpacking the State's Reputation," unpublished manuscript, Harvard Law School, Oct. 2007; _see also_ George Downs & Michael Jones, "Reputation, Compliance, and

International Law," 31 J. Leg. Stud. S95 (2002). Scott Wolford, "The Turnover Trap: New Leaders, Reputation, and International Conflict," 51 Amer. Polit. Sci. Rev. 772 (2007) (concluding that "leaders, not states, should be considered the fundamental units of analysis in international relations," where a particular country's international reputation is concerned).

12 BBC World Service poll, at http://www.bbc.uk/pressoffice/pressreleases/stories/2007/01_january/23/us.shtml. *See generally,* Peter Stearns, Global Outrage: The Impact of World Opinion on Contemporary History 191–213 (2005). Yet one resists employing here a concept like global "public opinion," for it is unclear whether that term adequately captures anything "real," much less susceptible to accurate measurement, especially but not only in nondemocratic countries. Conditions for the production of the quoted data would need to be considered, in any event. George Bishop, The Illusion of Public Opinion: Fact and Artifact in American Public Opinion Polls xiv–xv, 4–13, 35–40, 161–64 (2005) (arguing that a large portion of Americans are so poorly informed that on many public issues, especially international ones, that no such opinion can meaningfully be reported). Volatility presents another obstacle to meaningful use of the concept; the percentage of Americans ranking the threat of terrorism as a top priority for national policy, for instance, apparently fluctuates with the frequency of television news stories about terrorism. Robert Goodin, What's Wrong with Terrorism 135 (2006). Many of these problems are perennial, first raised by Walter Lippmann, Public Opinion (1922).

13 Paul von Zielbauer, "Military Cites 'Negligence' in Aftermath of Iraq Killings," New York Times, April 22, 2007, at 18 (describing results of a report by Maj. Gen. Eldon Bargewell into the deaths of twenty-four Iraqi civilians at Haditha in November 2005). Bargewell concludes, "All levels of command tended to view civilian casualties, even in significant numbers, as routine and as the natural and intended result of insurgent tactics," indeed as "just a cost of doing business." *Id.* Four U.S. officers, one a lawyer, have been criminally charged for failing to investigate the Haditha killings.

14 Kahl, *supra* note 11, at 98 (concluding that "a careful review of U.S. conduct during the Iraq war reveals no broad pattern of systematic civilian victimization by U.S. forces . . . and adherence has increased over time"); Colin Kahl, "In the Crossfire or the Crosshairs?: Norms, Civilian Casualties, and U.S. Conduct in Iraq," 32 Int'l Security 7 (2007); *but see* Human Rights Watch, "By the Numbers: Findings of the Detainee Abuse and Accountability Project," vol. 18, No. 2G (April 2006); Ryan Lenz, "Documents Show Soldiers Disregard Rules," Wash. Post, Sept. 4, 2007 online ("Newly released documents regarding crimes committed by U.S. soldiers against civilians in Iraq and Afghanistan detail a troubling pattern of troops failing to understand and follow the rules that govern interrogations and deadly actions"); Reuters, "Not All Troops Would Report Abuse," New York Times, May 5, 2007, A7 (describing results of a Pentagon study concluding that "only 40% of Marines and 55 % of soldiers in Iraq say they would report a fellow service member for killing or injuring an innocent Iraqi"); "Final Report," Mental Health Advisory Team IV, Operation Iraqi Freedom 05–07, Nov. 17, 2006, Office of the Surgeon General; Chris Hedges & Laila Al-Arian, "The Other War: Iraq Vets Bear Witness," The Nation, July

30, 2007, at 15 (relating accounts of fifty veterans who report having witnessed abuse of Iraqi civilians).

15 Andrew Abbott, Methods of Discovery: Heuristics for the Social Sciences 191 (2004) (quoting W. I. Thomas).

16 This has certainly been my experience, for instance, when addressing foreign audiences, as of Colombian law students in Bogotá and Cali, on behalf of the U.S. State Department. Sept. 2005. Several of my professional acquaintances report similar encounters elsewhere.

17 Thomas Friedman, "Swift-Boated by bin Laden," New York Times, Aug 26, 2007, editorial.

18 Craig Whitney, "Death Squad Killings of Basques: Was Spain's Government the Mastermind?" New York Times, Feb. 12, 1997, at A10; Paddy Wordsworth, Dirty War, Clean Hands: ETA, the GAL and Spanish Democracy 407–418 (2001); Antonio Vercher, Terrorism in Europe: An International Comparative Legal Analysis 231–33, 245–46, 389–90 (1992).

19 Editorial, "A Failure of Leadership at the Highest levels," Army Times, May 17, 2004, http://www.armytimes.com/print.php?f=1-292925-2903288.php. The quoted statement is too generous to Pentagon leadership (military and civilian), however, insofar as it appears to absolve such leaders and CIA personnel of any responsibility for the Abu Ghraib events. Later official investigations, beginning with the report by General Antonio Taguba, made just such attributions of responsibility to higher echelons. Dept. of the Army, Article 15–6 Investigation of the 800th Military Police Brigade 16–17 (May 27, 2004). Some evidence suggests that a significant number of American officers do not perceive great peril in the country's use of coercive interrogations. In an early 2008 survey, 44% disagreed with the proposition that "torture is never acceptable." Center for a New American Security (CNAS) and Foreign Policy Magazine, "Health and Future of the U.S. Military Survey Results," March 2008, p. 6, at http://www.foreignpolicy.com/images/mi-index/MI-2008-data.pdf. Nearly three-quarters of the officers participating in the survey, however, were more than sixty-one years old and so had retired from active duty long before 9/11. Even so, many would have been on active duty during the Vietnam War, with its counterinsurgency component. Col. John Nagl, the leading counterinsurgency expert, nonetheless goes so far as to ascribe their views in this opinion survey more to the recent influence of *24*, the television program, than to any pertinent career experience in the armed services. Video link, New York Times, March 8, 2008.

20 James Morrow, "The Institutional Features of Prisoner of War Treaties," 55 Int'l Org. 971, 990 (2001); Jonathan Vance, Objects of Concern: Canadian Prisoners of War through the 20th Century 21–22 (1994).

21 George Kennan, "Which is the Civilized Power?" 78 Outlook 515 (Sept.–Dec. 1904).

22 Tony Karon, "Muslim World Remains Cool to the U.S.," Time Mag., Feb. 26, 2002 (recounting a Gallup Poll of nine Muslim countries finding that 67% of all those polled found the attack on 9/11 "morally unjustifiable" and that Lebanon, Turkey, Kuwait, Indonesia and Morocco had less than 50% unfavorable opinion of the United States); for analysis of this data, *see* Giacomo Chiozza, "Disaggregating Anti-Americanism: An Analysis of Individual Attitudes toward the

U.S.," *in* Anti-Americanisms in World Politics, Peter Katzenstein & Robert Keohane, eds. 122–23 (2006).

23 The evidence for this proposition is necessarily anecdotal, but arises from multiple sources, some of them quite reliable. *See, e.g.,* Bruce Zagaris, "U.S. Encounters Difficulties in Europe over Extraordinary Renditions," 22/2 I Int'l Enforcement Reporter, Feb. 2006, available at http://w3.lexis.com/lawschoolreg/researchlogin04.asp (recounting European investigations into detainee abuse by the U.S. on European soil, foreseeing "grave implications for [transatlantic] intelligence and/or enforcement cooperation"); Anne Clunan, "U.S. and International Responses to Terrorist Financing," *in* Terrorism Financing and State Responses, Jeanne Giraldo & Harold Trinkunas, eds. 260, 280 (2007); "C.I.A. Affair Becoming a Sharper Thorn in Transatlantic Relations," Deutsche Welle, Sept. 5, 2006, at http://www.dw-world.de/dw/article/0,2144,1997628,00.html (noting that the U.S. detainment policies have "threatened intelligence cooperation" from European countries); The Bush Doctrine and the War on Terrorism: Global Responses, Global Consequences, Mary Buckley & Robert Singh, eds. (2006).

24 David Johnston, "C.I.A. Tells of Bush's Directive on the Handling of Detainees," New York Times, Nov. 15, 2006, at A14; R. Jeffrey Smith & Dan Eggen, "Gonzales Helped Set the Course for Detainees," Wash. Post, Jan 5, 2005, at A1.

25 Pew Global Attitudes Project, "America's Image Slips, but Allies Share US Concerns over Iran, Hamas," June 2006, http://pewglobal.org/reports/display.php?ReportID=252, and "Global Unease with Major Powers," June 2007, http://pewglobal.org/reports/display.php?ReportID=256; Shibley Telhami, "America in Arab Eyes," 49 Survival 107 (2007).

26 Commission on Security and Cooperation in Europe, U.S. Helsinki Commission, Conference, June 21, 2007. The Helsinki Commission is "an independent agency of the U.S. Government charged with monitoring and encouraging compliance with the Helsinki Final Act and other commitments of the Organization for Security and Cooperation in Europe."

27 Jack Goldsmith, The Terror Presidency 127 (2007); *see generally* Giuseppe Nesi, International Cooperation in Counter-Terrorism (2006).

28 Thomas Jefferson, A Declaration by the Representatives of the U.S. of America, in General Congress Assembled, July 4, 1776.

29 Paul Lauren, Power and Prejudice: The Politics and Diplomacy of Racial Discrimination (1996); Mary Dudziak, Cold War Civil Rights: Race and the Image of American Democracy (2000).

30 Evan Thomas & Michelle Hirsch, "The Debate over Torture," Newsweek, Nov. 21, 2005, at 26 (summarizing polling data).

31 107 James D. Fearon, "Domestic Political Audiences and the Escalation of Conflict," 88 Amer. Polit. Sci. Rev. (1994) (defining and measuring this concept).

32 Eric Posner, Law and Social Norms 28 (2002).

33 Their objection is only to the use of foreign and international sources to interpret the U.S. Constitution. When treaties are being applied, however, the prevailing stance is one of considerable sympathy to the views of courts elsewhere. *See, e.g., Olympic Airways v. Husain*, 540 U.S. 644, 659–60 (2004) (Scalia, J., dissenting); *Sanchez-Llamas v. Oregon*, 126 S.Ct. 2669, 2678–86 (2006) (J. Roberts); Melissa Waters, "Treaty Dialogue in Sanchez-Llamas: Is Chief

Justice Roberts a Transnationalist, After All?" 11 Lewis & Clark L. Rev. 89 (2007).

34 Jeff W. Legro, Cooperation under Fire: Anglo-German Restraint during World War II 123–24 (1995); Ward Thomas, The Ethics of Destruction 126–27 (2001).

35 Thomas, *id.* at 138.

36 Some scholars of the question conclude, however, that the reach of U.S. empire – if it may be so called – has actually declined since the end of the Cold War. Daniel Nexon & Thomas Wright, "What's at Stake in the American Empire Debate?" 101 Amer. Pol. Sci. Rev. 253 (2007).

37 Carla A. Robbins & Gerald Seib, "Divided at the Polls, Americans Move Closer on Role in World," Wall St. J., Nov. 2, 2004 at A1, A6 (reporting that American citizens are 87% in favor of working through international coalitions like the United Nations rather than "going it alone" in the war on terror); "Stop the World, We Want to Get Off," The Economist, Nov. 19, 2005, at 28–29 (reporting that two-thirds of Americans thought their country was less respected than in the past because of the Iraq invasion and 42% of the public thought that the United States should "mind its own business internationally and let other countries get along the best they can on their own"); "Do they Love Us?," The Economist, Oct. 2, 2004, at 33 (reporting that the American public is more concerned with national interests such as protecting jobs [78%] or preventing illegal immigration [59%] than bringing a democratic form of government to other nations [14%]).

38 Niccolò Machiavelli, The Prince, Harvey Mansfield, trans. 67–68 (1985) (1513).

39 Posner acknowledges that fear of reputational loss may influence a state's decision making in its international relations, but purports to find little evidence of this. Jack Goldsmith & Eric Posner, The Limits of International Law 90 (2005).

40 A thoughtful, journalistic comparison of the final stages of the Roman Empire with the contemporary world role of the U.S. is offered by Cullen Murphy, Are We Rome? The Fall of an Empire and the Fate of America (2007).

41 Arthur Miller, Death of a Salesman 138 (1949).

42 William Rugh, American Encounters with Arabs: The "Soft Power" of U.S. Public Diplomacy in the Middle East 158 (2006). When Beers was criticized for comparing her diplomatic duties to commercial advertising, Secretary of State Colin Powell rose to her defense. "There is nothing wrong with getting someone who knows how to sell something. We are selling a product. We need someone who can rebrand U.S. foreign policy." *Id. See generally* Carnes Lord, Losing Hearts and Minds: Public Diplomacy and Strategic Influence in the Age of Terror 54–56 (2006).

43 A useful assessment of the challenge and how it might be met is Edward Djerejian, Advisory Group on Public Diplomacy in the Arab and Muslim Worlds, "Changing Minds, Winning Peace," Oct. 2003, at http://www.bakerinstitute.org/publications/Peace.pdf. On the considerable successes of public diplomacy during the Cold War, especially by way of public radio broadcasting, *see* Kenneth Osgood, Total Cold War: Eisenhower's Secret Propaganda Battle at Home and Abroad (2006). At http://www.bakerinstitute.org/Pubs/Miscellaneous/Peace.pdf)

44 Rugh, *supra* note 42, at 158–59.

45 Anna Michalski, "The EU as a Soft Power: the Force of Persuasion," *in* The New Public Diplomacy: Soft Power in International Relations, Jan Melissen, ed. 124 (2005).

46 Jan Melissen, "The New Public Diplomacy: Between Theory and Practice, *in* Melissen, *id.* at 3, 25; *see also* Shaun Riordan, "Dialogue-based Public Diplomacy: A New Foreign Policy Paradigm," *in* Melissen, *id.* at 180.

47 Whereas "realism" refers to the state's preoccupation with its interest in self-preservation and power enhancement, "rationalism" in the study of international relations acknowledges a much broader range of state interests, many of which may be best served by adherence to international law and participation in international institutions. Oona Hathaway, "Rationalism and Revisionism in International Law," 119 Harv. L. Rev. 1404, 1422–36 (2006) (reviewing Jack Goldsmith & Eric Posner, The Limits of International Law [2005]).

48 This idea is hardly new, readily traceable as it is to Gentili, in the early seventeenth century. Gentili argued against assassination of foreign leaders on grounds of reciprocity, broadly conceived (i.e., according to one interpreter, "not only on the idea that actions taken by states against their enemies might later be taken against them, but also on a broader notion of the same idea: that the consequences of an action are not limited to immediate results but include its more generalized effects on rules governing a system of states"). Thomas, *supra* note 34, at 66; Alberico Gentile, De Iure Belli Libri, Tres 169, James Brown Scott, ed., John C. Rolfe, trans. (1933) (1612).

49 Nicholas Thompson, "A War Best Served Cold," New York Times, July 31, 2007, at A19. Counterinsurgency scholar/adviser David Kilcullen takes a similar view. George Packer, "Knowing the Enemy: Can Social Scientists Redefine the 'War on Terror'?" 82 New Yorker, Dec. 18, 2006, at 67 (quoting Kilcullen); *see also* Philip Gordon, "Can the War on Terror Be Won?" 86 Foreign Affairs 53, Nov./Dec. 2007.

50 As David Brooks wrote of the first 2007 presidential campaign debates, "Americans are having a debate about how to proceed in Iraq, but we are not having a strategic debate about retracting American power and influence. What's most important about this debate is what doesn't need to be said. No major American leader doubts that America must remain, as Dean Acheson put it, the locomotive of the world.... The two major Republican contenders are John McCain and Rudy Giuliani, the most aggressive internationalists in a party that used to have an isolationist wing. The Democrats, meanwhile, campaigned for Congress in 2006 by promising to increase the size of the military. John Edwards, the most 'leftward' Presidential contender,... castigated the Bush Administration for not being tough enough with Iran. 'To ensure that Iran never gets nuclear weapons, we need to keep all the options on the table,' Edwards warned." David Brooks, "The Iraq Syndrome, R.I.P.," New York Times, Feb. 1, 2007, at A23.

51 Editorial, "Through Others' Eyes," New York Times, July 3, 2007 (summarizing findings of a Pew opinion survey).

52 Brink Lindsey, The Age of Abundance: How Prosperity Transformed America's Politics and Culture 321 (2007) (noting, on the basis of opinion surveys, that "the typical blue state liberal is considerably redder than his predecessor when it comes to the importance of markets ... and the morality of American

geopolitical power."); Madeline Albright, U.S. Sec'y of State, Address at Rice Memorial Center, Rice University (Feb. 7, 1997) (describing the United States as "the indispensable nation in promoting international security and peace") http://secretary.state.gov/www/statements/970207.html; Former Secretary of State Colin Powell describes the United States as "the first universal nation" and "the motive force for freedom and democracy in the world." Third Annual Kahlil Gibran Spirit of Humanity Awards Gala, Arab American Institute Foundation, Washington, D.C., May 5, 2001; "Remarks at Confirmation Hearing," Senate Foreign Relations Committee, Washington, D.C., Jan. 17, 2001.

53 Barack Obama stressed the how having a "21st century military" would help the United States remain a "beacon of freedom and justice for the world." At http://my.barackobama.com/page/content/fpccga. In the April 26, 2007, debate, Hillary Clinton said of the country, "It is ready, once again, to be a leader in the world." In response to a question about what he would do during his first 100 days in office, John Edwards said, during the June 3 debate, that he would "lead in taking action that demonstrates that America is strong." In that debate, even Dennis Kucinich announced, "We certainly need to have a strong army.... We need to have a strong military."

54 John Paul Stevens, Justice Stevens Remarks, Seventh Circuit Judicial Conference Dinner (May 23, 2005).

55 John Rawls, A Theory of Justice 20, 47–51 (1971).

56 *Id.* at 48–51.

57 "Poll Finds Broad Approval of Terrorist Torture – Americas," MSNBC.com, http://www.msnbc.com/id/10345320/print/displaymode/1098.

58 Talal Asad, "Thinking about 'Just War,'" July 17, 2007, The Huffington Post, online. "Although in a formal sense state armies are subject to international humanitarian law this does not constitute as much of an obstacle to deliberate cruelty as might appear at first sight. We have learned as much from the recent conduct of Western armies of occupation."

59 John Updike, Due Considerations: Essays and Criticism 413 (2007); *see also* Susan Sontag, At the Same Time 111 (2007). "It is not the terrorists who will suffer from an all-out 'war' response [to 9/11] on the part of the U.S. and its allies," she wrote a few weeks thereafter, "but more innocent civilians – this time in Afghanistan, Iraq, and elsewhere – and these deaths can only inflame the hatred of the U.S. (and more generally of Western secularism) disseminated by radical Islamist fundamentalism."; Chris Hedges & Leila Al-Arian, Collateral Damage: America's War against Iraqi Civilians (2007), *passim.*

60 Geneva Additional Protocol I, Art. 51(5)(b), provides that attacks on military objectives are impermissible if they "may be expected to cause incidental loss of civilian life, injury to civilians, damage to civilian objects, or a combination thereof, which would be excessive in relation to the concrete and direct military advantage anticipated." Art. 57(2)(a) of that same Protocol requires military planners to "take all feasible precautions in the choice of means and methods of attack with a view to avoiding, and in any event to minimizing, incidental loss of civilian life, injury to civilians and damage to civilian objects." The term "collateral damage" does not exist within international law but has become common parlance in the U.S. armed forces since the Vietnam War, covering unintended harm to civilians and civilian objects, whether or not such harm is

anticipated. U.S. Dept. of Defense, D.O.D. Dictionary of Military and Associated Terms JP1-02, at 93 (2001). *See generally* Lt. Col. Dwight Roblyer, "Beyond Precision: Issues of Morality and Decision Making in Minimizing Collateral Casualties," Occasional Paper, Arms Control, Disarmament and International Security, Univ. of Ill., Champaign-Urbana (April 2004).

61 The word "proportionality" does not itself appear in the Geneva or Hague Conventions, but is often invoked as shorthand in legal treatises and professional discussion for the requirement, in Geneva Additional Protocol I, Art. 51(5)(b), that damage not be "excessive in relation to the concrete and direct military advantage anticipated."

62 This is known as the "lenity" rule, according to which an ambiguity in a criminal statute must be resolved in favor of lenience. Black's Law Dictionary, Bryan Garner, ed. 1332 (7th ed. 1999).

63 This is not to deny the moral soundness of the distinction itself, i.e., between intentional harm and unintentional but reasonably foreseeable harm (i.e., "side-effects"). For a brief, recent defense of the distinction and the criminal law's reliance on it, *see* John Gardner, "Introduction," *in* H.L.A. Hart, Punishment and Responsibility xxxiii–xxxiv (2008).

64 G.A. Cohen, "Casting The First Stone: Who Can, and Who Can't, Condemn the Terrorists," in Political Philosophy, Anthony O'Hear, ed. (2007).

65 Matthew Waxman, International Law and the Politics of Urban Air Operations 8 (2000). Waxman nonetheless insists on a central place for the reciprocity principle in formulating the duty to refrain from attacking civilians, observing that "targeting rules ... recogniz[e] that an attacker cannot be expected to eliminate inadvertent civilian injury while battling aggressively without reasonable reciprocal efforts by the defender to keep civilians out of harm's way." Matthew Waxman, "Detention as Targeting: Standards of Certainty and Detention of Suspected Terrorists," 108 Colum. L. Rev. 1365, 1394 (2008).

66 Michael Walzer, Just and Unjust Wars 34–37 (1977). Moral philosophers have been much less comfortable with this idea than legal and political thinkers. *See, e.g.,* Jeff McMahon, "On the Moral Equality of Combatants," 14 J. Polit. Phil. 377 (2006).

67 Talal Asad, On Suicide Bombing (2007).

68 The doctrine of double effect is the view that human actions, if done for the right reasons, are right even though they may have some bad consequences, as long as these consequences were not themselves intended. As such, the doctrine is deontological, since the reasons for action (i.e., intentions and motivations) determine the moral worth of the action, not its consequences. This stance acknowledges that some of the bad consequences that transpire will be foreseeable. But consequences ultimately do not matter to a deontologist as long as the reasons for the action are right. And consequences in the world are never fully within one's own control, in any event. We exercise much greater influence over our own motives for action than over their results. Consequentialists disagree and deny that the doctrine of double effect identifies a distinction with a moral difference. And they think we should give special weight to those consequences that we can anticipate beforehand.

69 Hart, *supra* note 63, at 124–25 (contending that there is no moral basis for the distinction between intentional killing and knowingly causing death, and

that the distinction is therefore "legalistic"). *But see* Gardner, *supra* note 63 (observing that Hart based this conclusion on his rejection of two of the most extreme and implausible illustrations of the distinction, at its outer conceptual penumbra, rather than with any core applications of the underlying principle).

70 Genesis 18:16-32.

71 Prof. Ahmed Souaiaia, Professor of Religious Studies, Adjunct Prof. of Law, Univ. of Iowa, correspondence with author, June 2008. *See also* Osama bin Laden, "The Example of Vietnam," Nov. 12, 2001, *in* Messages to the World: The Statements of Osama bin Laden, Bruce Lawrence, ed., James Howarth, trans. 139, 140 (2005) (arguing from double effect to excuse the unintended but foreseeable killing of Muslims in Al Qaeda's attacks).

72 Convention Against Torture and Other Cruel, Inhuman or Degrading Treatment or Punishment, 1465 U.N.T.S. 85 (1984), Art. 1.

73 18 U.S.C. §§2340–2340A.

74 Convention Against Torture, *supra* note 72, Art. 1 defines torture to include circumstances in which the prohibited conduct is undertaken "for such purposes as obtaining from him [i.e., the coerced person] or a third person information or a confession," among other impermissible objectives. The "understanding" that accompanied U.S. ratification and the implementing legislation did not seek to alter or exclude this language.

75 Sahr Conway-Lanz, Collateral Damage: Americans, Noncombatant Immunity, and Atrocity after World War II 230 (2006).

76 As Markovits notes, "What matters often at least as much as the visible, measurable, and manifest expressions of discontent are its silent and latent counterparts, those that set a tone, an agenda, an atmosphere, but operate stealthily to 'normal' senses of observation." Andrei Markovits, Uncouth Nation: Why Europe Dislikes America 137 (2007). Still, it must be acknowledged that political scientists have thus far discovered virtually no effects of rising anti-Americanism on other countries' policies toward the U.S. government, its companies, or citizens. Peter Katzenstein & Robert Keohane, "The Political Consequences of Anti-Americanism," *in* Katzenstein & Keohane, *supra* note 22, at 273, 287–303; John Ikenberry, Liberal Order and Imperial Ambition: Essays on American Power and World Politics 199 (2006) ("The most important characteristic of the current international order is the remarkable absence of serious strategic rivalry and competitive balancing among the great powers."). French and German armed forces have been present in both Iraq and Afghanistan, side by side with U.S. troops, even if both European governments preferred not to broadcast this fact, given the prevalence of antiwar opinion among their publics. Louise Richardson, What Terrorists Want: Understanding the Enemy, Containing the Threat 227 (2006). There is some recent evidence, however, of efforts by allies and other states informally to ally in opposition to the perceived excesses of American hegemony. Stephen M. Walt, Taming American Power: The Global Response to U.S. Primacy 109–29 (2005) (describing allies' several, subtle strategies of "soft balancing" against excessive U.S. unilateralism on a variety of issues).

77 A recent treatment is Matthew Adler & Eric Posner, New Foundations of Cost-Benefit Analysis 185, 135 (2006) (acknowledging that "the conventional

economic defense of cost-benefit analysis is not satisfactory" in normative terms, and that government "should not resolve a question of deontological rights or distributive justice – say, the use of fetal tissue in medicine – by engaging in cost-benefit analysis").

78 Eric Posner, correspondence with author, May 2007.

79 On the methodological issues, *see* John Karpoff, et al., "The Reputational Penalties for Environmental Violations: Empirical Evidence," 68 J. L. & Econ. 653, 665–68 (Oct. 2005).

80 Nira Liberman & Yaacov Trope, "The Role of Feasibility and Desirability Considerations in Near and Distant Future Decisions: A Test of Temporal Construal Theory," 75 J. Personality and Soc. Psychol. 5–18, 5 (1998) (concluding that people construe present decisions more concretely and in terms of feasibility than they do future decisions, which they construe abstractly and in terms of desirability).

81 It is illustrated in the cost-benefit analysis conducted by Ford Motor Company executives when deciding to market the Pinto without a safety device that would have saved the company many millions of dollars in punitive damage judgments. *Grimshaw v. Ford Motor Co.*, 119 Cal. App. 3d 757, 776–78 (1981) (describing the Ford management's decision to go forward with the Pinto design despite knowing that "the gas tank was vulnerable to puncture and rupture at low rear impact speeds creating a significant risk of death or injury from fire" and "knowing that 'fixes' were feasible at nominal cost").

82 Posner, *supra* note 32, at 65–67, 102–03, 157–58.

83 Eric Smith & Rebecca Bliege Bird, "Costly Signalling and Cooperative Behavior," *in* Moral Sentiments and Material Interests: The Foundations of Cooperation in Economic Life, Herbert Gintis et al., 115, 123 (2005).

84 Elasticities might be different for each foreign country and for different issue-areas, of course. Accordingly, the same measure of detainee mistreatment could have differing effects in different countries, ranging from the symbolic to the material and including lack of cooperation. One could easily model all this mathematically, if one were so inclined, but the essential idea is simple enough to convey verbally. Such a model might even disaggregate the component elements of national security, attaching a separate value of loss (or gain) to each such element, just as it does for particular issue-areas (police and military cooperation, intelligence sharing, trade relations, UN voting patterns, regulation of foreign investment, etc.) on the other side of the equation. The concept of reciprocity has been mathematically modeled, but not in the context of international relations. *See, e.g.,* Armin Falk & Urs Fischbacher, "Modelling Strong Reciprocity," *in* Gintis et al., *id.* at 193; Martin Dufwenberg & Georg Kirchsteiger, "A Theory of Sequential Reciprocity," 47 Games & Econ. Behavior 268 (2004); R. Sethi & E. Somanathan, "Understanding Reciprocity," 50 J. Econ. Behavior & Org. 1 (2003); Gary Bolton & Axel Ockenfels, "A Theory of Equity, Reciprocity, and Competition," 100 Amer. Econ. Rev. 166 (2000).

The numbers thus assembled would then enable policymakers to draw the relevant curve defining how much in security must be sacrificed for every additional increment of intelligence by torture. That curve would then be laid on top of and compared with the country's indifference curve, reflecting how much of each such variable U.S. leaders were prepared to forgo in exchange for how much of the other. Anyone genuinely committed to rational choice methods would insist on taking – quite seriously – every step in this analytical process. No one has done so.

85 This is the central proposition of a major approach to international relations called hegemonic stability theory. Charles Kindleberger, The World in Depression, 1929–1939 289 (1986); Robert Keohane, After Hegemony: Cooperation and Discord in the World Political Economy 31–39, 195–216 (2005).

86 It has even been said that NATO represented, in this respect, "the exploitation of the large by the small." James S. Coleman, "Free Riders and Zealots," *in* Social Exchange Theory, Karen Cook, ed. 59, 61 (1987).

87 Robert Boyd, Herbert Gintis, Samuel Bowles, & Peter Richerson, "The Evolution of Altruistic Punishment," *in* Gintis, *supra* note 84, at 215. "Strong reciprocity," in this sense, falls squarely within the first type of reciprocity, as that concept is typologized in this book's introduction. But it may sometimes justify more punitive response to defection, for a longer period, than would tit-for-tat, in order to vindicate the larger system of rules (i.e., even when it is unlikely that doing so will restore cooperative behavior from the defector in the immediate future). For the intended audience for this signal includes third parties who may be contemplating defection.

88 *See* http://ita.doc.gov/td/industry/otea/301alert/ for a list of current and recently closed trade disputes and sanctions between the United States and other countries.

89 John Ikenberry, Liberal Order and Imperial Ambition: Essays on American Power and World Politics 94, 118 (2006). Ikenberry here uses "reciprocity" to refer simply to the fact of participation and nontrivial contribution by many states to the process of global governance.

90 *U.S. v. Yamashita*, 327 U.S. 1, 41–42 (1945); (1946) (Rutledge, J., dissenting).

91 Mary Dudziak, Cold War Civil Rights: Race and the Image of American Democracy 79–114 (2000).

92 *Id.* at 26–31.

93 Brian A. McKenzie, Remaking France: Americanization, Public Diplomacy, and the Marshall Plan 19 (2005); The Marshall Plan Today: Model and Metaphor, John Adnew & J. Nicholas Entrikin, eds. 4–6, 171–86 (2004).

94 Marshall Sahlins, Stone Age Economics 174–75 (2004 ed.).

95 Georges Bataille, The Accursed Share: An Essay on General Economy, vol., 1, Robert Hurley, trans. 183–84 (2007) (1967).

96 Thomas Schelling, Arms and Influence 120 (1966). He writes, "One of the great advantages of international law and custom . . . is that a country may be obliged *not* to engage in some dangerous rivalry when it would actually prefer not to but might otherwise feel obliged to for the sake of bargaining reputation. . . . One of the values of laws . . . is that they provide a graceful way out." *Id.*

97 Ethan Kapstein, "Power, Fairness, and the Global Economy," in Power in Global Governance, Michael Barnett & Raymond Duvall, eds. 80, 95 (2005) (developing the analogy to insurance).

98 This term is commonly employed today by both economists and biologists, especially evolutionary and population biologists. Michael Spence, "Signaling

in Retrospect and the Informational Structure of Markets," 92 Amer. Econ. Rev. 434 (2002).

99 Boyd, *supra* note 87, at 117. *See also* Eric Smith & Rebecca Bird, "Turtle Hunting and Tombstone Opening: Public Generosity as Costly Signaling," 21 Evolution & Human Behavior 245 (2000).

100 *Id.* at 119.

101 A. Michael Spence, Market Signaling: Informational Transfer in Hiring and Related Screening Processes 5–30 (1974).

102 Marcel Mauss, The Gift: The Form and Reason for Exchange in Archaic Societies, W. D. Halls, trans. (1990) (1925). One definition of potlatch is "a ceremonial feast among certain Native American peoples of the Northwest Pacific coast, as in celebration of a marriage or an accession, at which the host distributes gifts according to each guest's rank or status. Between rival groups the potlatch could involve extravagant or competitive giving and destruction by the host of valued items as a display of superior wealth." At http://www.potlach.org; *see generally* Abraham Rosman & Paula Rubel, "The Potlach: A Structural Analysis," 74 Amer. Anthro. 658 (1972).

103 It bears emphasis here that institutions of reciprocal "gift" exchange resembling the potlatch of the Pacific Northwest have been "found to exist in every region of the world." Mary Douglas, "Forward" to Mauss, *supra* note 102, at viii.

104 Claude Lévi-Strauss, The Elementary Structures of Kinship (1969) ("There is a link, a continuity, between hostile relations and the provision of reciprocal prestations. Exchanges are peacefully resolved wars and wars are the result of unsuccessful transactions."); Mauss, *supra* note 102, at 13 ("To refuse to give, to fail to invite, just as to refuse to accept, is tantamount to declaring war; it is to reject the bond of alliance and commonality . . .").

105 Michael Taussig, The Devil and Commodity Fetishism in South America 197 (1980).

106 Thorsten Veblen, The Theory of the Leisure Class 68–101 (1979) (1899).

107 Marcel Mauss, for instance, "delighted in finding forms of behavior in the France of his day, such as competition through magnificent weddings and banquets, that resembled the potlatch or other gift performances." Natalie Zemon Davis, The Gift in Sixteenth-Century France 4 (2000).

108 William Ian Miller, Humiliation: And Other Essays on Honor, Social Discomfort, and Violence 49–50 (1993). Miller's account builds on Jonathan Parry, "*The Gift*, the Indian Gift, and the 'Indian Gift,'" 21 Man 453 (1986).

109 Limitation of Employment of Force for Recovery of Contract Debts (Hague, II); October 18, 1907; Martha Finnemore, The Purpose of Intervention: Changing Beliefs about the Use of Force 24–51 (2003).

110 Miller, *supra* note 108, at 52.

111 Pierre Bourdieu, Pascalian Meditations 193 (Richard Nice, trans. 2000); *see also* Taussig, *supra* note 105, at 195 (observing how in reciprocal "exchange with other men, festival and warfare lie close together").

112 Bataille went so far as to see a similarity between war and gift giving in how both served as an outlet for excess, for the expenditure of surplus wealth. Bataille, *supra* note 95, at 23–26. The "free gift," as Miller describes it in the text, has never been found to exist in a tribal or stateless society. Douglas, "Forward" to

Mauss, *supra* note 102, at viii. It cannot then properly be held up as yet another ennobling feature of the "savage," an intellectual stick with which to beat the capitalist West, as the occasional errant anthropologist has sought to do. *See, e.g.,* Marshall Sahlins, Stone Age Economics 162 (1972); Maurice Godelier, The Enigma of the Gift, Nora Scott, trans. 207–10 (1999). For correction, *see* Annette Weiner, "Reproduction: A Replacement for Reciprocity," 7 Amer. Ethnol. 71, 76–77 (1980). Sahlins' anticapitalism is apparent in the fact *inter alia* that he would characterize mutually beneficial exchange in a free market as a species of "negative" reciprocity, because each side is concerned only with its self-interest, even though both consider themselves better off after a voluntary exchange than before and the exchange therefore is not zero-sum. Sahlins' way of cutting up the categories thereby places market exchange within the same species of reciprocity as the patron-client relations of feudalism, because in both cases each side would have been looking out only for its own interests and largely unconcerned about the well-being of its partner.

113 Aztec rulers also sacrificed their foreign prisoners of war to the gods. Bataille, *supra* note 95, at 54.

114 Magnanimity entails a "well-founded high regard for oneself manifesting as generosity of spirit and equanimity in the face of trouble." Oxford English Dictionary Online.

115 Professional networks of the sort described in Chapter 12 provide the micro-mechanisms undergirding this macro-process.

116 Paul Veyne, Bread and Circuses: Historical Sociology and Political Pluralism, Brian Pearce, trans. 16 (1992).

117 Mary Keys, "Aquinas and the Challenge of Aristotelian Magnanimity," 1 Hist. Pol. Thought 37 (2003).

118 Hugo Grotius, Of the Rights of War and Peace, vol. 3, at 59, 80 (1715), Eighteenth Century Collections Online. Grotius did seek to distinguish magnanimity's requirements from those of justice while subsuming both under "the law of nature." *Id.*

119 Shariq Jamal, writing shortly after the fall of Saddam Hussein, that "the attitude of Bush and Rumsfeld should be magnanimous in victory." At http://news.bbc.co.uk/1/hi/talking_point/1786361.stm (last viewed 9/27/07).

120 On the difficult legal questions to which this "compromise" arrangement gives rise, *see* Samuel Issacharoff, Pamela Karlan, & Richard Pildes, The Law of Democracy: Legal Structure of the Political Process 326–457 (2007).

121 Useful analyses include Daniel Lowenstein, "Campaign Contributions and Corruption," U. Chi. Legal F. 163, 164 (1995) (summarizing the characterization of American campaign finance law by scholars David Strauss and Bruce Cain); *see also* David A. Strauss, "What is the Goal of Campaign Finance Reform?," U. Chi. Legal. F. 141 (1995); Bruce E. Cain, "Moralism and Realism in Campaign Finance Reform," U. Chi. Legal F. 111 (1995).

122 Because the terms of trade must remain tacit and private, moreover, the gift's recipient can later plausibly differ with its donor over whether those terms had been honored, whether the debt had been repaid. However, the donor cannot sue for contract breach, nor even go public with charges that the donee reneged on a private promise.

123 Deborah Welch Larson, "Exchange and Reciprocity in International Negotiations," 3 Int'l Negotiations 121, 132 (1998).

124 Seneca, "On Favors," *in* Seneca: Moral and Political Essays, John Cooper & J. F. Procopé, eds., Book I.5.2., at 201 (1995).

125 An anthropologist conveys the idea more precisely but less artfully: "What a gift transactor desires is the personal relationships that the exchange of gifts creates, and not the things themselves." Chris A. Gregory, Gifts and Commodities 19 (1982).

126 Husain Haqqani, "Pakistan and the Islamists," Current Hist. 147, 147–52 (April 2007); Craig Cohen, "When $10 Billion Isn't Enough: Rethinking U.S. Strategy and Assistance to Pakistan," Testimony before the Subcommittee on National Security and Foreign Affairs, House Committee on Oversight and Government Reform, March 30, 2007. For a Pakistani perspective (sympathetic to President Musharraf) on Pakistan's use of U.S. aid, *see* Pervaiz Iqbal Cheema, "Another Frivolous Allegation," Pakistan Observer, Islamabad Policy Research Institute, Jan. 3, 2008, at http://ipripak.org/articles/latest/frivolous.shtml. For a more independent and critical view from Pakistan, *see* Rasul Bakhsh Rais, "Democracy and American Interests," Daily Times, Lahore, June 19, 2007, at http://www.dailytimes.com.pk/default.asp?page=2007%5C06%5C19%5Cstory_19-6-2007_pg3_2.

127 Cohen, *id.* at 4. Cohen was, at the time, Deputy Chief of Staff, Office of the President.

128 For such views, *see* Ayaz Amir, "Fighting Someone Else's War," Aug. 17, 2007, Dawn: the Internet Edition, Karachi, at http://www.dawn.com/weekly/ayaz/20070817.htm.

129 Transparency Int'l, Corruption in South Asia: Insights & Benchmarks from Citizen Feedback Surveys in Five Countries, Dec. 2002, at 15–16, at 2002. http://unpan1.un.org/intradoc/groups/public/documents/APCITY/UNPAN019883.pdf; Bureau of Democracy, Human Rights, and Labor, U.S. Dept. of State, 2006 Country Reports on Human Rights Practices: Pakistan (2007), at http://www.state.gov/g/drl/rls/hrrpt/2006/78874.htm.

130 *Id.* at 5.

131 Benazir Bhutto, "Musharraf's Martial Plan," New York Times, Nov. 7, 2007, editorial.

132 *See, e.g.,* Brian Lai & Daniel Morey, "Impact of Regime Type on the Influence of U.S. Foreign Aid," 2 Foreign Policy Analysis 385 (2006); *see generally* Bruce Bueno de Mesquita & Alastair Smith, "Foreign Aid and Policy Concessions," 51 J. Conflict Resol. 251 (2007).

133 The Amarna Letters, W.L. Moran, ed. & trans. 7, 68 (1992). In modern times, Western diplomats serving in that part of the world often continue to play by local rules in this regard. For a recent example, *see* Robert Skidelsky, "Drawing a Dog in Iraq," 53 N.Y. Rev. of Books, Oct. 6, 2006. Skidelsky reports that a British diplomat assigned to the Iraqi Coalition Provisional Authority quickly learned that, to perform his job effectively, he needed to establish relations of hospitality (encompassing minor gift-giving) with tribal leaders. These courteous exchanges later enabled him "to secure the release of a British businessman" who had been taken hostage, "handed back to him as a 'present' from the uncle of the kidnapper."

134 Harold Nicolson, Diplomacy 123 (1964); Robert Jervis, The Logic of Images in International Relations 113–24 (1970); Raymond Cohen, Theatre of Power: The Art of Diplomatic Signalling 138–65 (1987).

135 *See, e.g.,* Michael Krepon et al., eds., Global Confidence Building: New Tools for Troubled Regions (1999); Aaron Hoffman, Building Trust: Overcoming Suspicion in International Conflict (2006); Pál Dunay, Open Skies: A Cooperative Approach to Military Transparency and Confidence Building (2004); Gabriella Blum, Islands of Agreement: Managing Enduring Armed Rivalries 24–26, 72–78, 103–05 (2007); *cf.* Marie-France Desjardin, Rethinking Confidence-Building Measures (1996).

136 Several thinkers stress the incompatibility of gift giving with bargaining, at least as ideal-types, often also in social reality. *See, e.g.,* Margaret Radin, Contested Commodities 93–96 (1996). *But see* Jeanne L. Schroeder, The Triumph of Venus: The Erotics of the Market 4–41 (2004) (contending that this view ignores the extent to which gifts, in practice, are "aggressive agonistic institutions in which participants attempt to attain recognition of status and prestige at the expense of others"). On the presence of negotiation within Northwestern Indian potlatch, *see* Schroeder, *id.* at 39.

137 D.W. Larson, "Exchange and Reciprocity in International Negotiations," 3 Int'l Negotiation 121, 121 (1998); *see also* James Esser & S.S. Komorita, "Reciprocity and Concession Making in Bargaining," 31 J. Personality & Soc. Psychology 864 (1975); Lloyd. Jensen, "Negotiating Strategic Arms Control, 1969–1979," 28 J. Conflict Resol. 535, 536 (1984) ("Perhaps no proposition relating to bargaining behavior has been better documented in both experimental studies and real life situations than the one suggesting that concessions tend to be reciprocated."); Richard Stoll & William McAndrew, "Negotiating Strategic Arms Control, 1969–1979," 30 J. Conflict Resol. 315, 325 (1986) (finding that "U.S.-Soviet interactions were characterized more often by cooperative reciprocity [various forms of tit-for-tat] than by inverse reciprocity [various forms of exploitation].").

138 Sergei Kan, Symbolic Immortality: The Tlingit Potlatch of the Nineteenth Century, William L. Merrill and Ivan Karp, eds. (1989); Ulli Steltzer, A Haida Potlatch (1984); Abraham Rosman, Feasting with Mine Enemy: Rank and Exchange among Northwest Coast Societies (1971).

139 Marshall Sahlins, "Exchange-Value and the Diplomacy of Primitive Trade," *in* Essays in Economic Anthropology, June Helm, ed. 95, 96 (1965).

140 This is not to deny the crucial importance of ongoing communications between military lawyers of the United States and its allies, examined in Chapter 12, beneath the more conspicuous diplomatic estrangement in high politics.

141 Mauss, *supra* note 102, at 48–53.

142 Michael Barkun, Law without Sanctions (1968); Roger Masters, "World Politics as a Primitive Political System," *in* International Politics and Foreign Policy, James Rosenau, ed. 104 (1969) (contending that tribal societies and intertribal relations resemble the modern interstate system in that, without a central government, reciprocity becomes the primary norm governing social interaction).

143 Jacques Derrida, The Gift of Death, David Wills, trans. 95–115 (1995); Jacques Derrida, Given Time: I Counterfeit Money, Peggy Kamuf, trans. 12 (1992). He writes, "For there to be a gift, there must be no reciprocity, return, exchange,

countergift or debt. If the other gives back or owes me or has to give me back what I give him or her, there will not have been a gift." The chief empirical point of reference that Derrida has in mind is the intimate, interpersonal encounters that Levinas makes the basis of his moral theorizing. *See also* Iris Marion Young, "Asymmetrical Reciprocity: On Moral Respect, Wonder, and Enlarged Thought," *in* Judgment, Imagination, and Politics: Themes from Kant and Arendt, Ronald Beiner & Jennifer Nedelsky, eds. 205, 220 (2001). Parsing and following Derrida, Young observes, "If you treat your gift to me as repayment of a debt owed, then this is too ungenerous and endangers our bond. . . . The relation of offering and acceptance is asymmetrical: I do not return, I accept."; Bataille, *supra* note 95, at 347.

    Surely, if we all acted always in the manner suggested by Derrida's conception of the gift, the resulting world would be one that all rational beings could readily endorse, to put the point in a Kantian idiom. From behind a Rawlsian veil of ignorance, we would surely choose to live in a society where gifts were given spontaneously, without duty or anxious anticipation of repayment, without any semi-conscious calculation of relative value between initial gift and responsive gift. Instead of a life experience in which most unexpected developments are unpleasant ones, everyday existence would be full of serendipitous surprise – some given, much received. The sheer mysteriousness of unsolicited giving and gracious accepting, their inexplicable effortlessness, would itself be a self-sustaining source of continuous joy. The relevance of this account of gifting to interstate relations is, however, zero – or less, if that were possible.

144 Yet the opposite concept, that of "interest" – as in "the national interest" – has occupied the very center of modern thinking about international relations. It had no acknowledged place, however, within the reciprocal gift economy of preindustrial societies. This is because the conceptual opposition of "self-interest" to the altruism of the "free gift" cannot arise in a society where virtually all exchanges are understood to combine the forms of human activity that we moderns differentiate as "the economic," "social," "moral," "affective," or "intimate," and so forth. Mauss was the first to observe, in this regard, that the concept of interest is no less distinctively modern than that of its converse, the free or altruistic gift, for they are twin sides of the same coin (i.e., modernity). The same has been observed of romantic love and disinterested friendship. Deirdre McCloskey, The Bourgeois Virtues: Ethics for an Age of Commerce 156–58 (2006); Allan Silver, "Friendship in Commercial Society: 18th Century Social Theory and Modern Sociology," 95 Amer. J. Sociol. 1474 (1990).

145 Parry, *supra* note 108, at 467; *see also* Eric Schwimmer, Exchange in the Social Structure of the Orokaiva 49 (1973).

146 Richard Posner, The Economics of Justice 138–39 (1981).

147 Moses Finlay, The World of Odysseus 64 (1978). *See also* Max Gluckman, Politics, Law and Ritual in Tribal Society 86–87 (1965) (describing gift relationships and hospitality rites as pragmatic tools for enhancing social connection, rather than altruistic).

148 The Principles of Social Order: Selected Essays of Lon L. Fuller, Kenneth Winston, ed. 242 (1981); Bronislaw Malinowski, Crime and Custom in Savage Society 22–23, 34–41, 68 (1926). Malinowski writes, "Most, if not all, economic acts are found to belong to some chain of reciprocal gifts and countergifts, which in the

long run balance, benefiting both sides. . . . The man who would persistently disobey the rulings of law in his economic dealings would soon find himself outside the social and economic order – and he is well aware of it." *Id.* at 40–41.

149 Mary Douglas, "Forward" to Mauss, *supra* note 102, at xiv. Economists and other utilitarians have often viewed archaic gift exchange in this way, as a simple, albeit imperfect form of market. But this view misses the extent to which such reciprocity is often neither voluntary nor involves exchanges of equivalent value. It ignores the extent to which it is really more "a form of war disguised as a gift." Schroeder, *supra* note 136 at 31.

150 Karl Polanyi, The Great Transformation 49 (1957). Only a genuine sacrifice can serve as evidence of one's nobility, according to theories of virtue ethics.

151 Bataille, *supra* note 95, at 179. Bataille cites no authority for this statistic.

152 Jon Elster, Sour Grapes: Studies in the Subversion of Rationality 43 (1983).

153 *Id.* at 107.

154 *Id.* at 44.

155 Linda Milm et al., "The Value of Reciprocity," 70 Soc. Psych. Q. 199 (2007).

156 Michel de Montaigne, "On Cowardice, the Mother of Cruelty," *in* The Essays of Michel de Montaigne, M.A. Screech, trans. 786, 790 (1991).

157 *Id.*

158 Claude Lévi-Strauss, "Reciprocity: The Essence of Social Life," *in* The Family: Its Structure and Functions, Lewis Coser, ed. 36, 47–48 (1964).

159 *See generally* Joel Paul, "Comity in International Law," 32 Harv. Int'l L.J. 1 (1991).

160 John B. Bellinger, "Remarks on the Military Commissions Act," 48 Harv. Int'l L.J. Online 1, 9 (2007).

CHAPTER 12. MARTIAL HONOR IN MODERN DEMOCRACY: THE JAGS AS A SOURCE OF NATIONAL RESTRAINT

1 Charlie Savage, Takeover: The Return of the Imperial Presidency and the Subversion of American Democracy 281 (2007). The information in this paragraph and the next two draw from Savage, at 279–89. *See also* Scott Horton, "Jim Haynes's Long Twilight Struggle," Harper's Magazine, Feb. 8, 2008.

2 Mark Mazzetti, "'03 Memo Approved Harsh Interrogations," New York Times, April 2, 2008, at A1.

3 To date, the best available treatment of the JAGs' resistance to torture and efforts by administration insiders to restrict their participation in decision making is Philippe Sands, Torture Team: Rumsfeld's Memo and the Betrayal of American Values 32, 90–96 134–38, 175, 212–17 (2008).

4 William Glaberson, "An Unlikely Antagonist in the Detainee's Corner," New York Times, June 19, 2008 (describing JAG resistance to implementation of the military commission system enacted by Congress in the Military Commissions Act of 2006). In still-confidential memoranda, leading JAGs also strongly resisted administration efforts to characterize U.S. and allied confrontations with Al Qaeda and related groups as a single "global war on terror." Confidential interviews, Dec. 2008.

5 Common Art. 3 to the 1949 Geneva Conventions prohibits "the passing of sentences and the carrying out of executions without previous judgment pronounced by a regularly constituted court affording all the judicial guarantees which are recognized as indispensable by civilized peoples."

6 Scott Silliman, Duke University School of Law, as quoted in Savage, *supra* note 1, at 288.

7 Author's confidential interviews with several active duty and recently retired JAGs.

8 Memorandum from Jack L. Rives, Major Gen., U.S. Air Force, Deputy Judge Advocate Gen., to Air Force Gen. Counsel 2 (Feb. 5, 2003), at http://balkin.blogspot.com/jag.memos.pdf (observing that eventual disclosure of detainee mistreatment "could have a negative impact on public perception of the U.S. military in general"); Kevin M. Sandkuhler, Brig. Gen., U.S. Marine Corps., Memorandum for General Counsel of the Air Force (Feb. 27, 2003), at 1 (expressing "the services' concerns that the authorization of aggressive counter-resistance techniques . . . will adversely impact . . . U.S. and International Public Support and Respect of the U.S. Armed Forces").

9 Forty-two percent of U.S. military officers concurred in early 2008 with the proposition that "the war in Iraq has broken the U.S. military." Center for a New American Security (CNAS) and Foreign Policy Magazine, "Health and Future of the U.S. Military Survey Results," March 2008, p. 4, at http://www.foreignpolicy.com/images/mi-index/MI-2008-data.pdf.

10 *See, e.g.,* Jack L. Rives, Maj. Gen., U.S. Air Force, Deputy Judge Advocate Gen. to Air Force Gen. Counsel (Feb. 6, 2003) (describing "the adverse effects on U.S. Armed Forces' culture and self-image, which suffered during the Vietnam conflict and . . . due to perceived law of armed conflict violations"; Sandkuhler memo, *supra* note 8, at 1 (expressing concern over the "adverse impact" to the "Pride, Discipline, and Self-Respect within the U.S. Armed Forces").

11 James Kitfield, Prodigal Soldiers: How the Generation of Officers Born of Vietnam Revolutionized the American Style of War 100–22 (1995); Andrew Bacevich, The New American Militarism 35–58 (2005).

12 The Future of the Military Commissions: Hearing before the Senate Comm. on Armed Services, 109th Cong. (July 13, 2006). On the place of "virtue ethics" in the self-understanding of professional soldiers, *see* Mark Osiel, Obeying Orders: Atrocity, Military Discipline, and the Law of War 14–37 (1999).

13 *See, e.g.,* Holly Ramer, "2008 Dems to Get Human Rights Briefings: Retired Officers to Brief Democratic Candidates on Humane Methods to Win War on Terror," ABC News, Apr. 13, 2007, at http://abcnews.go.com/Politics/wireStory?id=3038955 (quoting Marine Corps Gen. Joseph Hoar regarding detainee treatment: "This is not about our adversaries. This is about who we are.").

14 Lt. Cmdr. Charles Swift, "The American Way of Justice," 147 Esquire 192, 194–95 (March 2007).

15 Memorandum from Michael F. Lohr, Rear Admiral, U.S. Navy, Judge Advocate Gen., to General Counsel of the Air Force 1 (Feb. 6, 2003), at http://balkin.blogspot.com/jag.memos.pdf. Lohr adds that an exclusive focus on legality, at the expense of larger moral issues, invites the question, "Will

the American people find we have missed the forest for the trees in condoning such practices . . . ?" *Id.*

16 Lohr, *id.* at 1. This way of thinking about constitutive national commitments has sometimes determined results in U.S. federal courts, as when extending the constitutional duties of U.S. federal agencies extraterritorially. *See, e.g., U.S. v. Tiede,* 86 F.R.D. 227 (U.S. Ct. Berlin 1979). In that litigation, a U.S. federal court held that a foreign national accused of hijacking a Polish aircraft abroad, though tried in Berlin under German law, was constitutionally entitled to a jury trial because the court must act in accordance with the U.S. Constitution even when situated beyond national territory. *Id.* at 247–51. "It is a first principle of American life – not only life at home but life abroad – that everything American public officials do is governed by, measured against, and must be authorized by the U.S. Constitution." *Id.* at 244. The rationale for extraterritoriality was that honoring a high legal standard in American treatment of others reflects constitutive commitments, applicable regardless of what relation the beneficiaries may have to United States or of where the relevant conduct occurs.

17 Author's conversations with several leading JAGs, Washington, D.C., Nov. 2006.

18 Lt. Col. Gary Solis, correspondence with author, Jan. 2007.

19 Sharon Krause, Liberalism with Honor 2 (2002).

20 The term is Fuller's. Lon Fuller, The Morality of Law 41–44, 92–106 (1964).

21 This is not to deny that the legal profession has sometimes systematically abandoned this internal morality in the face of political pressures. *See generally* Liora Israël, Robes Noires, Années Sombres: avocats et magistrats en résistance pendant la Seconde Guerre mondiale (2006).

22 Ludwig Wittgenstein, Philosophical Investigations 243–56 (1953); Saul Kripke, Wittgenstein on Rules and Private Language (1982).

23 This paragraph draws on Michael Walzer, Spheres of Justice: A Defense of Pluralism and Equality 274 (1984).

24 *Id.* at 278.

25 Osiel, Obeying Orders, *supra* note 12, at 32.

26 Marty Lederman, "The Heroes of the Pentagon's Interrogation Scandal" (July 25, 2003), at http://balkin.blogspot.com/2005/07/heroes-of-pentagons-interrogation.html.

27 Bradley Wendel, Cornell Law School, Legal Ethics Forum, Aug. 1, 2005, at http://legalethicsforum.typepad.com/blog/2005/08/index.html.

28 To be sure, some high-ranking U.S. officers do not share this view of their profession and its duties. Some did not support official investigations into military abuses at Abu Ghraib and elsewhere. Seymour M. Hersh, "The General's Report: How Antonio Taguba, Who Investigated the Abu Ghraib Scandal, Became One of its Casualties," 83 New Yorker, June 25, 2007, at 58.

29 JAG officers Sandkulher and Romig both stressed that U.S. military personnel have for many years been trained to treat all prospective detainees as POWs, which entails a standard "far higher" than that required by Common Art. 3 of the Geneva Conventions. Military Commissions in Light of the Supreme Court Decision in *Hamdan v. Rumsfeld* Before the Senate Armed Services Comm., 109 Cong. (July–Aug. 2006).

30 Aristotle was the original and most influential defender of this view. Nichomachean Ethics, trans. Martin Ostwald 33–51 (1962).

31 *See, e.g.,* Chris Hughes, Peace Operations Training Vignettes with Possible Solutions, Call Newsletter No. 95-2 (Center for Army Lessons Learned, Fort Leavenworth, Kan.), Mar. 1995, at http://www.globalsecurity.org/military/library/report/1995/call-95-2_peace-ops-vignettes_toc.htm.

32 Paul Robinson, "Ethics Training and Development in the Military," 37 Parameters 23, 30 (Spring 2007).

33 *See generally* Nancy Sherman, Stoic Warriors: The Ancient Philosophy behind the Military Mind (2005).

34 David Luban, "Stevens's Professionalism and Ours," 38 W. & Mary L. Rev. 297 (1996). Robert Atkinson, "How the Butler Was Made to Do It: The Perverted Professionalism of *The Remains of the Day*," 105 Yale L.J. 177 (1995). It is admittedly true that virtue ethics has recently enjoyed something of a recovery, after decades of disrepute, sparked by the work of Alasdair MacIntyre.

35 U.S. Code of Mil. Just. 10 U.S.C. §933, Art. 133. The Supreme Court has upheld the military's use of such general standards against void for vagueness challenges to their constitutionality. *Parker v. Levy*, 417 U.S. 733, 737 (1974).

36 It bears emphasis that for Aristotle, habit did not mean rote, unthinking repetition, but rather a striving for excellence through continued practice of an ever-developing skill, such as the daily finger exercises of a pianist at the keyboard. To portray virtue ethics as the mindless following of one's station is to construct a straw man.

37 Rives memorandum, *supra* note 8, at 2. American armed forces have been trained for more than a generation to afford full POW (not merely Common Art. 3) protections to all persons detained in any type of armed conflict. This policy finds reflection in a number of Dept. of Defense directives and regulations. *See, e.g.,* U.S. Dep't of Army, Field Manual 2-22.3 (FM 34-52), Human Intelligence Collector Operations (Sept. 2006); U.S. Dep't of Defense, Dir. 2310.01E, The Dep't of Defense Detainee Program (5 Sept. 2006); U.S. Dept. of Defense, Dir. 2311.01E, DoD Law of War Program (9 May 2006); Chairman, Joint Chiefs of Staff, Instr. 5810.01C, Implementation of the DoD Law of War Program (31 Jan. 2007).

38 Maj. Mark S. Martins, "Rules of Engagement for Land Forces: A Matter of Training, Not Lawyering," 143 Mil. L. Rev. 1, 20–21, 82–85 (1994). Martins is currently a General, Air Force JAG.

39 Jack Goldsmith, The Terror Presidency 113 (2007).

40 Colin Kahl, "In the Crossfire or the Crosshairs? Norms, Civilian Casualties, and U.S. Conduct in Iraq," 32 Int'l Sec. 7, 8 (Summer 2007).

41 Douglas Lackey, The Ethics of War and Peace 65 (1989).

42 The most compelling, influential – and highly idiosyncratic – recent defense of virtue ethics is Alasdair MacIntyre, After Virtue: A Study in Moral Theory (1981).

43 Thomas Haskell, "Professionalism versus Capitalism: R. H. Tawney, Émile Durkheim, and C. S. Peirce on the Disinterestedness of Professional Communities," *in* The Authority of Experts: Studies in History and Theory, Thomas Haskell, ed. 180, 216 (1984).

44 Victorian critics of industrial capitalism, such as Émile Durkheim and R. H. Tawney, therefore claimed to find in professional communities a last refuge from market forces and their pressures to lower ethical and technical standards. *Id.* at 182–98.

45 Simon Weil, The Need for Roots, Arthur Wills, trans. 20 (1955).

46 It has proven difficult to conceptualize the nature of practical judgment among professionals. This has not stopped some from trying. *See, e.g.,* Donald Schön, The Reflective Practitioner: How Professionals Think in Action (1983); Donald Schön, Educating the Reflective Practitioner (1987); Eliot Freidson, Profession of Medicine: A Study of the Sociology of Applied Knowledge 158–84 (1988); Chris Argyris, Theory in Practice 158–84 (1987); Alvan Feinstein, Clinical Judgment (1967); Mark Osiel, "Lawyers as Monopolists, Aristocrats, and Entrepreneurs," 103 Harv. L. Rev. 2009, 2054–61 (1990).

47 Osiel, *supra* note 12, at 23; *see also* Kahl, *supra* note 40, at 42.

48 Seymour M. Hersh, "Manhunt," New Yorker, Dec. 23, 2002, at 66 (quotation marks omitted).

49 *Id.* at 73.

50 Robert Cooter, "Law and Unified Social Theory," 22 J. L. & Society 50, 61 (1995).

51 Michael Taylor, Rationality and the Ideology of Disconnection 81 (2006); Elizabeth Anderson, Value in Ethics and Economics 5–8 (1993).

52 Richard Posner, Overcoming Law 37–45 (1995).

53 Col. William Eckhardt, oral remarks, National Institute of Military Justice Conference, Nov. 18, 2006.

54 Tahira Khan, Beyond Honour: A Historical Materialist Explanation of Honour Related Violence 135–69 (2006) (examining "honor killings" of women in Pakistan).

55 Krause, *supra* note 19, at 184, 30.

56 The UCMJ provides, "Any commissioned officer who uses contemptuous words against the President, the Vice President, Congress, the Secretary of Defense, the Secretary of a military department, the Secretary of Transportation, or the Governor or legislature of any State, Territory, Commonwealth, or possession in which he is on duty or present shall be punished as a court-martial may direct." Uniform Code of Military Justice 1950, U.C.M.J. (2008), 10 U.S.C. §888, Art. 88. *See generally* John Loran Kiel, Jr., "When Soldiers Speak Out: A Survey of Provisions Limiting Freedom of Speech in the Military," 37 Parameters 69 (Autumn 2007). Marine Maj. Michael Mori, who represented Australian Qaeda trainee David Hicks, claims he was briefly threatened with prosecution for allegedly using contemptuous words in his criticisms of American leaders supporting the proposed military commissions. Glaberson, *supra* note 4.

57 For instance, Brig. Gen. Kevin Sandkhuler, then the leading Marine JAG, had already been designated for retirement.

58 My confidential source for this and the next five paragraphs is a high-ranking JAG officer, recently retired.

59 For a summary of these psychological studies, *see* Cass Sunstein, "The Law of Group Polarization," 10 J. Polit. Phil. 175, 176–81 (2002).

60 Author's interview, confidential informant, June 2008.

61 MacArthur wished to attack China; Truman did not. MacArthur thus sought to usurp presidential and congressional war powers under the Constitution. No one has sought to analogize closely the JAGs' opposition to the international crime of torture with MacArthur's decision to launch war against China without presidential authorization. On the latter, *see* James Matray, "Truman's Plan for Victory: National Self-Determination and the Thirty-Eighth Parallel Decision in Korea," 66 J. Amer. Hist. 314 (1979). On the general issue of military claims of expertise and professional prerogative vis-à-vis several recent American presidents, *see* Charles Stevenson, Warriors and Politicians: US Civil-Military Relations under Stress (2006); Eliot Cohen, Supreme Command: Soldiers, Statesmen, and Leadership in Wartime (2003); H.R. McMaster, Dereliction of Duty 14–31, 120–41 (1997).

62 Glenn Sulmasy & John Yoo, "Civilian Control of the Military: A Rational Choice Approach to the War on Terror," 54 UCLA L. Rev. 1815, 1824 (2007).

63 On these disagreements with Western allies and their lawyers, *see* Goldsmith, *supra* note 39, at 117.

64 Author's confidential interviews with several active duty and recently retired JAGs.

65 Rome Statute of the International Criminal Court, Art. 17. The court is thus designed to "complement" or supplement national judiciaries, not to supplant or displace their jurisdiction over the pertinent class of wrongs.

66 UCMJ, *supra* note 56. On the origins and workings of the Code, *see* Elizabeth Hillman, Defending America: Military Culture and the Cold War Court-Martial (2005); Eugene Fidell, Elizabeth Hillman, & Dwight Sullivan, Military Justice: Cases and Materials (2007).

67 Sulmasy & Yoo, *supra* note 62, at 1833. The JAGs did in fact initiate contact with the New York City Bar Association authorities to express their concerns over coercive interrogation, concerns first couched in terms of professional ethics. Lisa Hajjar, "An Army of Lawyers," The Nation, Dec. 26, 2008, at 23.

68 With the limited evidence currently available, it is admittedly difficult to arbitrate among these competing accounts.

69 Max Weber, From Max Weber: Essays in Sociology, H. H. Gerth and C. W. Mills, eds. 280 (1958).

70 Author's confidential interviews with JAG sources.

71 On the social process by which professionals with distinct claims of expertise compete for influence over public policy, *see genenerally* Yves Dezalay & Bryant Garth, The Internationalization of Palace Wars: Lawyers, Economists, and the Contest to Transform Latin American States 7 (2002).

72 Confidential JAG sources, author's interviews.

73 Quoted in Hajjar, *supra* note 67.

74 Georgetown Law, press release, "Professor Neal Katyal Named A 'Top Lawyer under 40,'" http://www.law.georgetown.edu/news/releases//may.5.2005.html. Scott Horton is another young attorney, new to humanitarian law and previously specializing in corporate transactions, who quickly gained public prominence by working on Guantánamo issues, writing about them for The Nation and The Atlantic Monthly. He now teaches the subject at Columbia Law School. On the career trajectories and strategies of those committed to the greater

juridification of war, *see* Sara Dezalay, "Trend Report: Crimes de Guerre et Politiques Impériales: L'espace Académique Américain entre Droit et Politique," 173 Actes de la Recherche en Sciences Sociales 44 (June 2008).

75 Yves Dezalay & Bryant Garth, "Law, Lawyers, and Empire," *in* The Cambridge History of Law in America, vol. 3, Christopher Tomlins & Michael Grossberg, eds., 718, 740 (2008). In explaining the elite bar's increasingly strong support for international human rights, these authors contend – in a Marxist spirit – that "the highest status in the legal profession still goes to those who embody the combination of major corporate clients and a noblesse oblige that helps create a legitimate playing field for those clients." *Id.* at 756. But the fact that those clients – Western corporations operating in the Muslim world – are some of Al Qaeda's principal targets only demonstrates the elite bar's significant measure of political independence from such clients.

76 Counterinsurgency, FM 3-24, MCWP, Appendix D, ii (Dec. 15, 2006) (concluding that "joint, inter-agency and multinational coordination is the basic foundation upon which all rule of law efforts must be built"); Col. Kenneth Watkin, "Canada/United States Military Interoperability and Humanitarian Law Issues: Land Mines, Terrorism, Military Objectives and Targeted Killings," 15 Duke J. Comp. & Int'l L. 281 (2005) (identifying obstacles to multilateral coordination arising from differing U.S. and Canadian official views on these international law issues); Charles Garraway, "The Use and Abuse of Military Manuals," *in* Yearbook of International Humanitarian Law 2004, Timothy McCormack & Avril McDonald, eds. 425, 435 (2007) (describing inconsistencies among the military manuals of several Western armed forces); European Military Law Systems, Georg Nolte, ed. v–vii (2003) (identifying obstacles to harmonization of military law across NATO countries); Maj. Christopher Jacobs, "Taking the Next Step: An Analysis of the Effects the Ottawa Convention May Have on the Interoperability of U.S. Forces with the Armed Forces of Australia, Great Britain, and Canada," 180 Mil. L. Rev 49 (2004) (examining obstacles to joint operations arising from differences between American and allies' views on the legitimacy of anti-personnel landmines).

77 Counterinsurgency, FM 3-24, *id.*

78 *Id.* at i.

79 Kal Raustiala, "The Architecture of International Cooperation: Transgovernmental Networks and the Future of International Law," 43 Va. J. Int'l L. 1, 9, 28, 91 (2002).

80 *Id.* at 91.

81 Gary Solis, The Law of Armed Conflict (Cambridge University Press, forthcoming 2009).

82 Rule of Law Handbook: A Practitioner's Guide for Judge Advocates, Center for Law and Military Operations, Judge Advocate General Legal Center, July 2007. This document, which received no major media attention when issued (unlike the new Counterinsurgency Field Manual issued contemporaneously), was drafted by the Center for Law and Military Operations at the Judge Advocate General's Legal Center and School, in conjunction with the Joint Force Judge Advocate, U.S. Joint Forces Command.

83 *Id.* at 45.

84 *Id.*
85 *Id.* at 46.
86 *Id.* at 49–50, 65–66.
87 *Id.* at 65 (noting, "For these reasons, U.S. armed forces have given comparatively little attention to human rights law as such").
88 *Id.* at 66.
89 Counterinsurgency, FM 3-24, MCWP, Appendix D, ii (Dec. 15, 2006).
90 *Id.*, at 251, 352.
91 David Fidler, "Counterinsurgency, Rule of Law Operations, and International Law," ASIL Insight, Sept. 19, 2007, Amer. Soc. Int'l L. at 2. Fidler reads rather more into the Manual here than I would, however.
92 Talcott Parsons, "The Professions and the Social Structure," *in* Essays in Sociological Theory 185, 194 (1954); A. M. Carr-Saunders & P. A. Wilson, The Professions 477–504 (1933); Eliot Freidson, Professionalism: The Third Logic 220–22 (2001); Harold Wilensky, Intellectuals in Labor Unions: Organizational Pressures on Professional Roles 129–31, 163–70 (1956); Steven Brint, In an Age of Experts: Professionals in Politics and Public Life 81–103 (1994); Alvin Gouldner, The Future of Intellectuals and the Rise of a New Class (1982); Barbara Ehrenreich & John Ehrenreich, "The Professional-Managerial Class," 11 Radical America 7 (1977). Such hopes were mostly abandoned in recent years, however. *See, e.g.,* Magali Sarfati-Larson, The Rise of Professionalism: A Sociological Analysis (1977); Richard Abel, "The Decline of Professionalism?" 49 Mod. L. Rev. 1, 41 (English lawyers increasingly faced with "employment in large bureaucracies, dependence on a public paymaster, or competition within an increasingly free market").
93 Freidson, *id.* at 221 (emphasis in original).
94 Krause, *supra* note 19, at xi, 29.
95 *See, e.g.,* Robert Gordon, "The Independence of Lawyers," 68 B.U. L. Rev. 1 (1988); Robert Gordon & William Simon, "The Redemption of Professionalism," in Lawyers' Ideals/Lawyers' Practices, Robert Nelson et al., eds. 230 (1992).
96 Alexis de Tocqueville, Democracy in America, J. Mayer & M. Lerner, eds. G. Lawrence, trans. 243 (1966); *See also* Louis Brandeis, "The Opportunity in the Law," *in* Brandeis, Business: A Profession 329, 337–39 (1914).
97 Thomas Haskell, "The New Aristocracy," 44 N.Y. Rev. of Books, Dec. 4, 1997, at 47.
98 A physician was reportedly on hand during every coercive interrogation of a major terror suspect. Scott Shane, "Inside a 9/11 Mastermind's Interrogation," New York Times, June 21, 2008. *See generally* Associated Press, "Doctors Decry Guantanamo Treatment," New York Times, Sept. 7, 2007, at A1 ("The U.S. medical establishment appears to have turned a blind eye to the abuses of military medicine at . . . Guantanamo . . . , doctors from around the world said in a letter published Friday in a prestigious British medical journal," The Lancet.); Benedict Carey, "Psychologists Clash on Aiding Interrogations," New York Times, Aug. 15, 2008 (reporting that American psychologists "have closely studied [detained, terrorist] suspects, looking for mental quirks [and] have suggested lines of questioning. They have helped decide when a confrontation is too intense, or when to push harder.")

99 Charles A. Jones, "War in the 21st Century: An Institution in Crisis," *in* The Anarchical Society in a Globalized World, Richard Little & John Williams, eds. 162, 180 (2006).

100 William H. Eckhardt, oral remarks, National Institute of Military Justice Conference, Washington, D.C., Nov. 18, 2006.

101 Rives Memo, *supra* note 10, at 1 (noting how "the DoD Law of War Program in 1979 and subsequent service regulations, greatly restored the culture and self-image of U.S. Armed Forces by establishing high benchmarks of compliance with the principles and spirit of the law of war, and humane treatment of all persons in U.S. Armed Forces custody").

102 Senate Armed Services Hearings, *supra* note 29, at 25.

103 Lt. Cmdr. Charles Swift, Keynote Address, Conference on the Military Commissions Act of 2006, University of Texas, School of Law, April 1, 2007.

104 Author's interviews, Air War College, Sept. 2003.

105 Michel de Montaigne, "On Apology," *in* The Essays of Montaigne, E.J. Trechman, trans, vol. 1, 466 (1946). He also writes, however, "The only, essential, proper form of nobility in France is the profession of arms ... from which derive our terms of honour and dignity." Montaigne, "On Rewards for Honour," *in* The Essays of Michel de Montaigne, M.A. Screech, trans. 428, 431 (1991). Toqueville similarly observed that the European nobility regarded military courage as "foremost among virtues and in lieu of many of them." Alexis de Toqueville, II Democracy in America, Henry Reeves, trans. 245 (1952).

106 MacIntyre, *supra* note 42, at 119.

107 Gilles Deleuze & Felix Guattari, A Thousand Plateaus: Capitalism & Schizophrenia 351–423 (1999); Julian Reid, The Biopolitics of the War on Terror: Life Struggles, Liberal Modernity, and the Defense of Logistical Societies 61 (2006). Reid analyzes how Deleuze and Guattari, in their celebration of "nomadic life," give pride of place to "the life of the warrior." He writes, "Not the soldierly life of uniformity and docility with which liberal regimes stamp their armies of subjects in the name of liberal peace, but another, utterly disordered form of life ... which resists the imposition of the terms of such a peace through the use of tactics and strategies deriving from its own peculiar traditions of war."

108 Charles Taylor, Sources of the Self: The Making of the Modern Identity 215 (1989).

109 The JAGs' refusal to grant legal approval to military use of several coercive methods of interrogation proved ineffective insofar as it prompted the Bush administration to turn to private contractors and the Central Intelligence Agency (neither of whose members are generally subject to prosecution under the UCMJ or Military Commissions Act), without much altering policy.

110 To be sure, even efforts to prohibit new weapons technologies, though usually couched in humanitarian terms, are sometimes demonstrably inspired by national interests in selling a competing product in the international arms market. W. Hays Parks, "Special Forces' Wear of Non-Standard Uniforms," 4 Chi. J. Int'l L. 493, 513 (2003) (explaining Sweden's opposition in the 1970s to NATO adoption of the U.S.-made M16 rifle to Sweden's promotion of its own, competing MKR assault rifle); Sahr Conway-Lanz, Collateral Damage:

Americans, Noncombatant Immunity, and Atrocity after World War II 30–55 (2006) (partly attributing the U.S. Navy's opposition in the late 1940s and early 1950s to a national security strategy of reliance on nuclear strategic bombing, opposition cast in terms of respecting noncombatant immunity, and to rivalry with the Air Force for scarce resources).

111 A notable example of recent European theorizing about international law and relations, rejecting American-style realism, is Jürgen Habermas, The Divided West 116–18, C. Cronin, trans. (2006) (arguing for a thorough constitutional-ization of international relations).

112 Peter Beinart, The Good Fight: Why Liberals – and Only Liberals – Can Win the War on Terror and Make America Great Again xiii (2006).

113 Editorial, "Looking at America," New York Times, Dec. 31, 2007.

114 *Id.*

115 Christopher Kutz, "Torture, Necessity and Existential Politics," 95 Cal. L. Rev. 235. 266 (2007); *cf.* Jack Balkin, "In Giving Up Our Rights, We'd Lose the War," New Orleans Times-Picayune, Sept. 11, 2002 ("The War on Terrorism is a war to defend our country's way of life . . . including a commitment to . . . the rule of law. It would be ironic indeed if in our zeal to preserve our way of life we destroyed it.").

116 The first of these three formulations is the one most consistent with virtue ethics, the last most congruent with Kantian/deontological views.

117 Samuel Huntington, Who Are We? The Challenges to America's National Identity 9 (2004).

118 *Id.* at xvi. Huntington is not speaking here of military elites in particu-lar and would surely be particularly chagrined to suspect that JAG leader-ship might be answering to any 'master' other than the U.S. Commander in Chief.

119 Sulmasy & Yoo, *supra* note 62, at 1826–39. For evidence of the JAGs' self-aggrandizement, the authors cite the observations of Richard Betts, "Com-promised Command," 80 Foreign Affairs 126 July–Aug. 2001) (commenting on Gen. Wesley Clark's account of JAG contributions to targeting decisions in NATO's 1999 Kosovo campaign). Sulmasy & Yoo contend that "the JAGs have been influenced in part by nongovernmental organizations in the human rights area" that "characterize U.S. strategic and tactical decisions as violating moral as well as legal principles." *Id.* at 1844.

120 *Id.* at 1832.

121 Maj. Gen. Charles Dunlap, "Lawfare Today: A Perspective," 33 Yale J. Int'l L. 146, 151 (Winter 2008) (citing Department of the Air Force, the Judge Advocate General (JAG) Policy Memorandum, TJAGC Standards-2, Air Force Rules of Professional Conduct and Standards for Civility in Professional Conduct, attachment 1, Rule 2.1, Advisor, Aug 2005).

122 Sulmasy & Yoo, *supra* note 62, at 1844–45. An early, influential formulation of the theory was Steven Calabresi & Kevin Rhodes, "The Structural Constitution: Unitary Executive, Plural Judiciary," 105 Harv. L. Rev. 1165 (1992); for criticism, *see* Cass Sunstein, "The Myth of the Unitary Executive," 7 Am. U. Admin. L. J. 299 (1993); Robert Percival, "Presidential Management of the Administrative State: The Not-So-Unitary Executive," 51 Duke L. J. 963 (2001).

123 Correspondence with author, Dec. 7, 2007. The Detainee Treatment Act in §1005 (f) provides, "Nothing in this section shall be construed to confer any constitutional right on an alien detained as an enemy combatant outside the U.S." Department of Defense Appropriations Act of 2006 (Title X, H.R. 2863).

124 Linda Greenhouse, "Justices Come under Election-Year Spotlight," New York Times, June 14, 2008 (quoting Senator John McCain).

125 John McCain, "Respecting the Geneva Conventions," in Torture, Kenneth Roth et al., eds 155–56 (2005).

126 Oona Hathaway, "*Hamdan v. Rumsfeld*: Domestic Enforcement of International Law," *in* International Law Stories, John Noyes et al., eds. 229, 249 (2007).

127 Honor, heroism, and excellence – individual and, to a lesser extent, collective – are consistent themes in McCain's memoirs and his other recent books. John McCain, Hard Calls: Great Decisions and the Extraordinary People Who Made Them (2007); McCain, Character is Destiny (2005); McCain, Why Courage Matters (2004); McCain, Worth the Fighting For: A Memoir (2002); *see also* Benjamin Storey & Jenna Silber Storey, "No Substitute for Virtue: Why Conservatives Should be Open to John McCain," Weekly Standard, Jan. 24, 2008, at 18.

128 David Stout, "Bush Nominee Is Questioned over Torture," New York Times, Oct. 17, 2007, at A1 (quoting Mukasey).

129 Morris Davis, "Unforgivable Behavior, Inadmissible Evidence," New York Times, Feb. 17, 2008, editorial.

130 Quoted in Sands, *supra* note 3, at 208.

131 One might almost say that the desire to be honored for acting above and beyond duty's call induces a certain, *sub rosa* reserve in officers about others' efforts at raising the legal standards to which humanitarian law will hold professional soldiers.

132 Michel de Montaigne, "On Cruelty," *in* The Essays of Michel de Montaigne, M. A. Screech, trans. 472, 472 (1991).

133 On the European and especially German origins of this notion – the right of all nationals and citizens, at least, to be treated honorably – *see* James Whitman, "On Nazi 'Honour' and the New European 'Dignity,'" *in* Darker Legacies of Law in Europe, Christian Joerges & Mavraj Singh Ghaleigh, eds. 243 (2003).

134 Gary Shapiro, Alcyone: Nietzsche on Gifts, Noise, and Women 30 (1991) (parsing Nietzsche and Mauss).

135 A poll in mid-November 2001 found that 32% of surveyed Americans favored torturing such detainees. Abraham McLaughlin, "How Far Americans Would Go to Fight Terror," Christian Sci. Monitor, Nov. 14, 2001, at 1.

136 Mark Danner, "We Are All Torturers Now," Int'l Herald Trib., Jan. 7, 2005, at 6; Joseph Lelyveld, "Interrogating Ourselves," New York Times Magazine, June 12, 2005, at 36.

137 Deborah Pearlstein, Princeton University, former Legal Director of Human Rights First, Military Commissions Act Conference, University of Texas, Austin, April 11, 2007. However, coercive interrogation of such important Al Qaeda members as Mohammed Al-Qahtani – who was to have been among those who hijacked United Flight 93 – did not diminish. Sands, *supra* note 3, at 126–27.

138 Jane Mayer, "The Black Sites," New Yorker, Aug. 13, 2007 at 49, 55.
139 Editorial, "On Torture and American Values," New York Times, Oct. 7, 2007. The Times editorialist asks, regarding torture, "Is this really who we are? . . . Is this a nation that tortures human beings and then concocts legal sophistries to confuse the world and avoid accountability before American voters?" Mukasey himself, in the testimony just quoted, refused to say whether the practice of waterboarding constitutes torture. True, his is a legally sustainable viewpoint, though the practice is undoubtedly degrading. Yet his statement surely displays an unfortunate similarity to such definitional dodges as President Bush's "this government does not torture," or Waldron's "the law is not brutal."
140 Judith Shklar, "Introduction," *in* Political Theory and Ideology, Judith Shklar, ed. 1, 14 (1966) (parsing Erich Fromm's Escape from Freedom (1941), at 277); *see also* Hans H. Gerth & C. Wright Mills, Character and Social Structure: The Psychology of Social Institutions (1953).
141 The only intellectually serious effort that comes readily to mind, within legal scholarship of recent years, to employ notions of national culture and character to explain interstate difference is James Whitman, Harsh Justice: Criminal Punishment and the Widening Divide between America and Europe (2003). But it has been rightly criticized on precisely this account. David Garland, "Concepts of Culture in the Sociology of Punishment," 10 Theoretical Criminology 419, 431 (2006). Before Whitman's study, one might have to go back to the work of Alex Inkeles, National Character: A Psycho-Social Perspective vii (1997) (summarizing work done mostly in the 1960s and 70s, and acknowledging in his first sentence that "this book is about a subject that some people believe does not exist"); Robert A. LeVine, Culture, Behavior and Personality 1 (2nd ed. 1982) ("The dominant theoretical positions in the 'institutional' social sciences . . . do not favor acceptance of the basic assumptions on which the study of culture and personality is based."). The notion of national character has nonetheless exercised considerable appeal to many since the eighteenth century, especially in French thought, most convincingly in de Tocqueville and Montesquieu. Henry Vyverberg, Human Nature, Cultural Diversity, and the French Enlightenment 64–97 (1989).
142 Campbell Gibson and Kay Jung, "Historical Census Statistics on the Foreign-Born Population of the United States: 1850 to 2000," Working Paper No. 81, U.S. Census Bureau, 2006; Statistical Abstract of the U.S., 2007: The National Data Book 47 (2006).
143 On this issue, an early, influential account was David Riesman, The Lonely Crowd: A Study of the Changing American Character (1961).
144 Richard E. Nisbett, The Geography of Thought: How Asians and Westerners Think Differently – and Why xx, 79–190 (2003) (finding from laboratory experiments that Asians tend to think differently about social causation and moral responsibility, i.e., more "wholistically" than Westerners, whose thought patterns are more "linear," and less "relational"); Rethinking Comparative Cultural Sociology: Repertoires of Evaluation in France and the United States, Michèle Lamont & Laurent Thévenot, eds. 1, 2 (2000) (finding from detailed opinion surveys that, compared to the French, Americans rely more on market criteria and less on aesthetics in making moral and other judgments).

145 Kennedy School Immigration Study, Sept. 2004, at http://www.npr.org/news/specials/polls/2004/Immigration/summary.pdf.

146 Michael Kammen, People of Paradox: An Inquiry concerning the Origins of American Civilization 4 (1980).

147 Will Kymlicka, "Territorial Boundaries: A Liberal Egalitarian Perspective," *in* Boundaries and Justice: Diverse Ethical Perspectives David Miller & Sohail Hashmi, eds. 249, 258–62 (2001).

148 Inkeles, *supra* note 141, at 169–71; Geoffrey Gorer, The American People: A Study in National Character 40 (1948).

149 *Id.* at 171–75; Robert D'Andrade, The Development of Cognitive Anthropology 88 (1995).

150 The idea of performativity, derived from John Austin's speech act theory, refers to an "illocutionary" utterance, one that performs an act rather than describing a fact or even communicating an idea. From this insight, developed further by John Searle, Butler infers "the reiterative power of discourse to produce the phenomena that it regulates and constrains." Judith Butler, "Critically Queer," *in* Identity: a Reader, Paul Du Gay et al., eds. 108, 110 (2000). Yet "who we are" is not confined to what we say and encompasses many other types of acts.

151 David Campbell, Writing Security: U.S. Foreign Policy and the Politics of Identity 143 (1992) (describing foreign policy as "constituting the identity in whose name it operates"); *cf.* Jean Bethke Elshtain, Just War against Terror: The Burden of American Power in a Violent World 1 (2004) (criticizing those who reject the necessity for a war on terrorism as "unwilling or unable to peer into the heart of darkness and recognize the reality of evil").

152 Campbell, *id.* at 153.

153 Michael Dillon, The Politics of Security: Towards a Political Philosophy of Continental Thought 16 (1996).

154 Anne Norton, Reflections on Political Identity 55–56 (1988).

155 Eric Hobsbawn, "Introduction: Inventing Tradition," *in* The Invention of Tradition, Eric Hobsbawm & Terence Ranger, eds. 1, 2 (1983) ("Insofar as there is a reference to a historic past, the peculiarity of 'invented' traditions is that the continuity with it is largely factitious").

156 To be sure, these texts do not wholly constrain what counts as an appeal to the American political tradition, of course, for some of the most important events in the national past, like the Civil War, are not textual at all, even if the intergenerational transmission of their memory is partly text dependent.

157 The insight might even take an almost Kantian form: With so much freedom and responsibility for what one becomes, one should not act in such a way that, if others so acted, would create a world in which one could not or would not wish to live.

158 The concern with preserving secrecy regarding the methods used to elicit information from particular detainees continued long thereafter. Mark Mazzetti, "C.I.A. Destroyed Tapes of Interrogations," New York Times, Dec. 6, 2007, at A1 (reporting that the agency "in 2005 destroyed at least two videotapes documenting the interrogation of two Al Qaeda operatives in the agency's custody, a step it took in the midst of congressional and legal scrutiny about the CIA's secret detention program, according to current and former government officials").

159 Press Release, President George W. Bush, President Discusses Creation of Military Commissions to Try Suspected Terrorists (Sept. 6, 2006), at http://www.whitehouse.gov/news/releases/2006/09/20060906-3.html.

160 President Bush declared in February 2002 that the Geneva Conventions, including Common Art. 3, did not apply to the conflict against Al Qaeda. As a matter of policy, the armed forces were to treat detainees consistently with the "principles" of Geneva, but only "to the extent appropriate and consistent with military necessity." The reference to U.S. "armed forces" was apparently intended to exclude the CIA from even the humane treatment requirement. The CIA is not subject to the UCMJ, but only to federal antiterror statutes, which the early OLC memoranda therefore sought to interpret in the narrowest manner possible, according to Martin Lederman, a lawyer for the OLC at the time. Even the CIA is subject to the Geneva Conventions when operating within Iraq, however, as that country ratified them without limiting their application to members of the country's "armed forces." Since 2005, it is also subject to a provision of the Detainee Treatment Act barring "cruel, inhuman, or degrading treatment" of anyone "in the custody or under the physical control of the U.S. Government . . . regardless of nationality or physical location." Pub. L. No. 109–48, §1003(a).

161 François Duc de La Rouchefoucauld, Moral Maxims, Irwin Primer, trans. 105 (2003).

162 Merriam-Webster Online Dictionary.

163 Slavoj Žižek, "Knight of the Living Dead," New York Times, March 24, 2007, editorial. On the legitimate place of hypocrisy in democratic politics, *see* Ruth Grant, Hypocrisy and Integrity, Machiavelli, Rousseau, and the Ethics of Politics 16 (1997).

164 In September 2006, only a month before President Bush's declaration on national character, he had been compelled to admit the existence of secret CIA prisons.

165 At http://www.whitehouse.gov/news/releases/2006/10/20061013-17.html.

166 "World View of U.S. Role Goes from Bad to Worse," World Public Opinion, Jan. 22, 2007, at http://www.worldpublicopinion.org/pipa/articles/home_page/306 (showing that 50% of surveyed Americans disapprove of U.S. handling of detainees at Guantánamo and other foreign prisons); "World Citizens Reject Torture Global Poll Reveals," BBC World Service Poll, Oct. 19, 2006, at 3 & 6, at http://www.globescan.com/news_archives/bbctorture06/BBCTorture06.pdf (showing that 58% of Americans agree that clear rules against torture should be maintained).

167 *See, e.g.,* Thomas Berger, Cultures of Antimilitarism: National Security in Germany and Japan 7–12, 42, 56, 60, 72, 84–5 (1998); Peter Katzenstein, Cultural Norms and National Security: Police and Military in Postwar Japan 29–31, 100–118, 150–151 (1996).

168 Alastair Iain Johnston, "Conclusions and Extensions: Toward Mid-Range Theorizing and Beyond Europe," 59 Int'l Org. 1013, 1014, 1040–41 (2005) (suggesting that social constructivist theories poorly specify when this norm-socialization process of identity formation will succeed and when it will not).

169 *But see* Alexander Wendt, Social Theory of International Politics 78–83, 113–35, 165–78, 287, 327–33 (1999); Martha Finnemore & Kathryn Sikkink,

"International Norm Dynamics and Political Change," 52 Int'l Org. 887, 888 (1998). Sociological work on the varieties of "legal consciousness," particularly on law's contribution to the constitution of individual "subjectivity," is also pertinent here. *See, e.g.,* Susan Silbey, "After Legal Consciousness," 1 Ann. Rev. L. & Soc. Sci. 231 (2005).

170 Rawls describes self-respect as "perhaps the most important primary good" and contends that "therefore the parties in the original position would wish to avoid at almost any cost the social conditions that undermine self-respect." John Rawls, A Theory of Justice 440 (1971). He discusses shame immediately thereafter, as the emotion naturally issuing from a lack of self-respect. *Id.* at 442–46.

171 Bernard Williams, "The Idea of Equality," *in* Philosophy, Politics, and Society, P. Laslett & W.G. Runciman, eds. 110, 114 (1962).

172 Sandkuhler memo, *supra* note 8, at 1.

173 Stanley Benn, Political Participation 3 (1978) (parsing Weber); Max Weber, 1 Wirtschaft und Gesellschaft, 12–13 (1921/1972).

174 Walzer, *supra* note 23, at 279, quoting William Shakespeare, Antony and Cleopatra, III:4.

175 Walzer, *supra* note 23, at 289.

176 *Id.* at 276.

177 Among early twentieth-century social thinkers, both Weber and Simmel emphasized this point. *See, e.g.,* Georg Simmel, "The Persistence of Social Groups," 3 Amer. J. Sociol. 662, 681 (1897) (noting that "honor is originally a class standard (*Standesehre*)").

178 Tocqueville, *supra* note 96, at 599.

179 Stanley Fish, "Condemnation without Absolutes," New York Times, Oct. 15, 2001, editorial at 19.

180 Eric Posner, "Human Welfare, Not Human Rights," Human Rights and the New Global Order: An Interdisciplinary Conference, Harvard University, April 18, 2008.

181 This paragraph and the next are inspired by Taylor, *supra* note 51, at xiv, 14, 39, 53, 148, 153, 167. On the incommensurability of value (i.e., the absence of a common metric for comparing gains in self-respect against losses in personal security), for instance, *see* Joseph Raz, "Incommensurability and Agency," *in* Incommensurability, Incomparability, and Practical Reason, Ruth Chang, ed. 110 (1997).

182 Posner would surely respond that what motivates the first and seemingly more affectionate statement is merely the speaker's self-interest in signaling his abiding loyalty; his desire to do so really just means, when translated into economic terms, that he assesses the costs of exiting the relationship as high. (Costs of entry to a more desirable relationship are part of the same calculation.) Or perhaps he merely wishes his "loved" one to *believe* his exit costs high, so that she will place more trust in him and reciprocate his high valuation of the relationship; for that result would, in turn, reduce the odds that she will leave him before he decides to leave her. Hence Posner writes, in connection with personal relationships, "One way to signal loyalty is to *say* that the relationship is incommensurable with other options." Eric Posner, Law and Social Norms 197 (2000) (emphasis supplied). Perhaps. But one hopes, if he is married, that

his spouse has not read the next sentence: "Few people really believe this, but no one can express this skepticism openly without risking the end of the relationship." As he offers no evidence whatever about what "few people really believe" – a proposition presented in the language of rigorous science – one may read it more persuasively (and more generously) simply as social satire, in the literary genre running from Jonathan Swift through H. L. Mencken to Tom Wolfe. Posner would assuredly not see himself in this unscientific company. On the vicissitudes and flagrant failure of economics' efforts to theorize romantic love, *see* Deirdre McCloskey, The Bourgeois Virtues: Ethics for an Age of Commerce 108–50 (2006).

183 Émile Durkheim, The Elementary Forms of Religious Life, J. W. Swain, trans. 40, 85 (1915) (1912).

184 Matthew Adler, "Incommensurability and Cost-Benefit Analysis," 146 U. Penn. L. Rev. 1169, 1175–76 (1998); Kip Viscusi, "The Generational Divide in Support for Climate Change Policies: European Evidence," 77 Climate Change 121 (2006).

185 Michel Foucault, Discipline and Punish: The Birth of the Prison, Alan Sheridan, trans. 7–8, 39, 56–57 (1977).

186 UN Convention Against Torture and Other Cruel, Inhuman or Degrading Treatment or Punishment, 1465 U.N.T.S. 85 (1984), Art. 2(2). "No exceptional circumstances whatsoever, whether a state of war or a threat of war, internal political instability or any other public emergency, may be invoked as a justification of torture." The U.S. implementing legislation did not adopt this language, however. 18 U.S.C. §§2340–2340A (2000).

187 Joseph Raz, Practical Reason and Norms 35–45 (1975).

188 On the rationality of such "taboos," *see* Herbert Tetlock, "Thinking the Unthinkable: Sacred Values and Taboo Cognitions," 7 Trends in Cognitive Sciences 320 (2003), *passim.*

189 On the antitorture rule as an expression of precommitment, *see* Sanford Levinson, "'Precommitment and Postcommitment': The Ban on Torture in the Wake of September 11,' 81 Tex. L. Rev. 2013 (2003).

190 On the frequency of such precommitments within liberal law and political institutions, *see* Jon Elster, Ulysses and the Sirens: Studies in Rationality and Irrationality viii (1984). One author observes that panic may occur in exaggerating not only to threats to national security but also to threats to civil liberty. Adrian Vermeule, "Libertarian Panics," 36 Rutgers L.J. 871 (2005).

191 *See, e.g.,* William Shakespeare, Much Ado about Nothing, Act 5, II, 35–36 (1993) (1600).

192 Michel de Montaigne, "On Fear," *in* The Essays of Michel de Montaigne, M.A. Screech, trans. 81, 83 (1991).

CHAPTER 13. ROOTS OF ANTIRECIPROCITY: TRANSNATIONAL IDENTITY AND NATIONAL SELF-RESPECT

1 Ruth Wisse, Jews and Power ix (2007).

2 Joshua Goldstein & Jon Pevehouse, "Reciprocity, Bullying, and International Cooperation: Time-series Analysis of the Bosnia Conflict," 91 Amer. Polit. Sci. Rev. 515, 528 (1997) ("In eliciting cooperation from a bully, the relatively cheap

options of the accommodation approach, such as mediation and peacekeeping, are unlikely to succeed.").

3 Emmanuel Levinas, Ethics and Infinity: Conversations with Philippe Nemo, Richard Cohen, trans. 94–95 (1985).

4 Kristen Renwick Monroe, The Hand of Compassion xii (2004) (finding, in studies of Holocaust resisters, "the tremendous power of identity to constrain choice" through its impact on "cognitive frameworks").

5 Thomas Scanlon, What We Owe to Each Other 154 (1998). This notion is sometimes described as a form of reciprocity, a usage occasionally employed in Rawls's last works and developed by Amy Gutmann & Dennis Thompson, Why Deliberative Democracy? 98–110 (2004).

6 *See* the opinion surveys summarized in Colin H. Kahl, "How We Fight," 85 Foreign Affairs 83, 84 (Nov./Dec. 2006). According to Pew Charitable Trust surveys, between 2002 and 2007, favorable views of the United States fell from 60 to 30% in Germany, from 61 to 29% in Indonesia, and from 30 to 9% in Turkey. James Traub, "Persuading Them," New York Times, Nov. 25, 2008, at A13.

7 Jinks implicitly relies on a similar idea in arguing for humane treatment of Al Qaeda detainees on grounds that this "might form part of a more generalized reciprocity – one that aims to promote cooperation and fair play with states not party to the instant conflict and perhaps even in issue areas not related to the laws of war." Derek Jinks, "The Applicability of the Geneva Conventions to the 'Global War on Terrorism,'" 46 Va. J. Int'l L. 165, 191 (2005). Robert Keohane, "Reciprocity in International Relations," 40 Int'l Org. 1, 4 (1986), René Provost, International Human Rights and Humanitarian Law (2002), and Kahan similarly distinguish wider reciprocity of this sort from tit-for-tat. Dan Kahan, "The Logic of Reciprocity: Trust, Collective Action, and the Law," 102 Mich. L. Rev. 71 (2003).

8 Dan Kahan, "Signaling or Reciprocating? A Response to Eric Posner's Law and Social Norms," 36 U. Richmond L. Rev. 367, 368-69 (2002) (summarizing the results of several laboratory experiments by social and cognitive psychologists). *See, e.g.,* Trust and Reciprocity: Lessons from Experimental Research, Elinor Ostrom & James Walker, eds. Part IV (2003); Margaret Levi, Consent, Dissent and Patriotism 19–26, 150–60 (1997) (finding from comparative, historical evidence that compliance with military conscription has been greatest where conscripts believe that fellow citizens are similarly complying and trust the state to ensure this result).

9 This is the fallacy in drawing a conclusion about a "whole" based on features of its constituent elements. The entity as a whole often displays processes and dynamics of its own, not apparent at the level of its component parts. (This is often true of the international system, in distinction from the states largely constituting it. J. D. Singer, "The Level-of-Analysis Problem in International Relations," *in* The International System: Theoretical Essays, Klaus Knorr & Sidney Verba, eds. 77 [1961]). The factual disparities at each level often have important moral implications. For instance, natural persons, possessing a single ego, have an inherent capacity for rationality, in a sense that does not pertain to states. Because a state is not a moral being, moreover, it does not have precisely

the same sort of interest in sovereignty that a natural person has in autonomy, despite the longstanding analogy. Some go so far as to question whether the moral right of self-defense possessed by natural persons directly extends to nation-states (i.e., without revisions and qualifications that transform the initial right almost beyond recognition). David Rodin, War and Self-Defense 127–41 (2002). The present study seeks to remain attentive to both differences and similarities in the dynamics at both levels.

It may be a mistake to equate individual survival with national survival, and hence to transfer arguments for individual self-defense – well established and accepted within domestic criminal law – without qualification to the realm of interstate relations, as Rodin contends. Yet entirely rejecting the notion of national self-defense by force of arms all but requires embracing the historic "strategy" of Tibet, as Bataille characterizes it: "In a humanity everywhere prepared to start a war, Tibet is paradoxically an enclave of peaceful civilization, incapable of attacking others or defending itself. Poverty, immensity, topography, and cold are in this case the only defenders of a country with no military force." The Dalai Lama and the Buddhist monks always remained "at the mercy of outside forces," but nevertheless ensured, through the sheer force of their faith, that "the world of prayers . . . prevailed over that of arms," in that successive waves of conquest passed over them with minimal impact on their culture, leaving their form of life substantially unaltered. George Bataille, 1 The Accursed Share, Robert Hurley, trans. 93, 102 (1991) (1967). This is not a survival strategy to which most Americans or other Westerners, however, would likely prove receptive, even if our topography, etc., equally facilitated it.

10 Robert Scott & Paul Stephan, The Limits of Leviathan: Contract Theory and the Enforcement of International Law 122 (2007). In summarizing results across several areas of international law, particularly foreign trade, the authors conclude that "this preference [for reciprocity] does not disappear when individuals act collectively, whether through firms or political organizations. It manifests itself in some risk of harm from opportunism, a willingness to absorb some costs to signal a preference for cooperation, and a propensity to engage in costly retaliation against opportunists."

11 Maj. Gen. Thomas Romig, U.S. Army JAG, Memorandum for General Counsel of the Department of the Air Force (March 3, 2003), at 1; *see also* Kevin M. Sandkuhler, Brig. Gen., U.S. Marine Corps., Memorandum for General Counsel of the Air Force (Feb. 27, 2003), at 1 (noting the likely "adverse impact" of detainee mistreatment on the "Cooperation and Support of Friendly Nations"); Jack L. Rives, Maj. Gen., U.S. Air Force, Deputy Judge Advocate Gen. to Air Force Gen. Counsel (Feb. 6, 2003), at 1 (noting that "other nations are unlikely to agree with DoJ/OLC's interpretation of the law" and "other nations may disagree with the President's status determinations" regarding detainee entitlement to POW treatment.); JAG Memorandum, Comments on Draft Working Group Report on Detainee Interrogations, (Oct. 11, 2002) (noting "possible perception by other nations that the United States is lowering standards relating to the treatment of prisoners, generally").

12 On the provision of global public goods, *see* Scott Barrett, Why Cooperate? The Incentive to Supply Global Public Goods (2007); International Public Goods:

Incentives, Measurements, and Financing, Ashoka Mody & Marco Ferroni, eds. (2002); Providing Global Public Goods, Inge Kaul et al., eds. (2003).

13 Kahan defends this view, in connection with domestic law and policy; *supra* note 7, at 71. *See also* John Rawls, A Theory of Justice 499 (1971) (noting that "persons tend to develop friendly feelings toward those who with evident intention do their part in cooperative schemes"). Even some economists have acknowledged the point. An early contribution was Robert Sugden, "Reciprocity: The Supply of Public Goods through Voluntary Contributions," 94 Econ. J. 772, 775–76 (1984) (observing that in some societies it is widely believed that "you must not take a free ride when other people are contributing"). The best current economic work is summarized in Ernst Fehr & Urs Fischbacher, "The Economics of Strong Reciprocity," *in* Moral Sentiments and Material Interests: The Foundations of Cooperation in Economic Life, Herbert Gintis et al., eds. 15 (2005); Armin Falk & Urs Fischbacher, "Modelling Strong Reciprocity," *in id.* at 193; Serge-Christophe Kolm, "The Theory of Reciprocity," *in* The Economics of Reciprocity, Giving and Altruism, L.-A. Gérard-Varet et al., eds. 115 (2000).

14 On the importance of such networks in linking national judges and civil servants throughout the world, *see* Anne-Marie Slaughter, The Real New World Order 3–11, 135–44 (2004).

15 The reinterpretation of humanitarian law here at issue involves the infusion of principles from the international law of human rights, along the lines described at some length in Chapter 3.

16 Mark Osiel, Obeying Orders: Atrocity, Military Discipline & the Law of War 201–06 (1999).

17 Ulysses S. Grant, Personal Memoirs 489 (1886).

18 Robin Wagner-Pacifici, The Art of Surrender: Decomposing Sovereignty at Conflict's End 152 (2005).

19 Ryan Goodman & Derek Jinks, "Colloquy – How to Influence States: International Law and State Socialization," 54 Duke L. J. 983, 984 (2005). On the processes by which this occurs, especially the increasing sensitivity of national policy elites to their country's international image, *see* Alastair Iain Johnston, "Socialization in International Institutions: The ASEAN Way and International Relations Theory," *in* The Emerging International Relations of the Asia-Pacific Region, Michael Mastanduno & G. John Ikenberry, eds. 107 (2003) (offering several East Asian illustrations).

20 Theodor Meron, "Reflections on the Prosecution of War Crimes by International Tribunals," 100 A. J. I. L. 551, 566 (2006); Provost, *supra* note 7, at 3–10.

21 The JAGs are particularly vehement in their defense of international humanitarian law against what they view as its defective interpretation by Office of Legal Counsel lawyers. JAG Admiral Romig, for instance, takes issue with the view that the president, as Commander in Chief, may by his executive "automatically displace any contrary provision of customary international law," regarding this view as "contrary to the historic position taken by the U.S. Government concerning such laws." He also questions whether the OLC's broad view of the "necessity" defense in international law "would ultimately prevail in either the U.S. courts or in any international forum." Romig memorandum, *supra* note 11, at 2.

JAG Admiral Lohr reports that "the working group believes that [confidential interrogation] technique 36 would constitute torture under international law and . . . accordingly, should not be utilized." He concludes that technique 26 is similarly prohibited, as "threatening the detainee with death or injury (by the transfer [to another country]) may be considered torture under international law." Memorandum for the Air Force General Counsel (March 13, 2002), at 3. Admiral Lohr adds that "the protections of the Fourth Geneva Convention may apply to the detainees."

JAG General Rives argues that "other nations are likely to view the exceptional interrogation techniques as violative of international law." Rives memo, *supra* note 11, at 2. JAG General Sandkuhler adds that the OLC memoranda fail to consider "foreign views of international law," particularly "foreign interpretations of Geneva Convention IV (Civilians) and customary international law." Sandkuhler memo, *supra* note 11, at 1.

22 Jon Elster, Alchemies of the Mind 155 (1999).

23 The Merrian-Webster Dictionary defines the term as "a gnawing distress arising from a sense of guilt for past wrongs." Webster's Third New Int'l Dictionary of the English Language Unabridged 1921 (1993).

24 Alexander Pope, "Eloisa to Abelard," *in* Alexander Pope: Selections, Pat Rogers, ed., 137, 143 (1993).

25 Thomas Ricks & Ann Scott Tyson, "Troops at Odds with Ethics Standards," Wash. Post, May 5, 2007, at A1. The article describes results of opinion surveys among U.S. soldiers finding that more than one-third believe that interrogators should be allowed to employ torture if it helps gather important information about insurgents. Forty percent approve of such abusive treatment if necessary to save the life of a fellow soldier. The survey did not distinguish between the opinions of officers and enlisted personnel.

26 Chalmers Johnson, The Sorrows of Empire: Militarism, Secrecy, and the End of the Republic 13, 284–85, 310 (2004).

27 This third type of reciprocity originates in the social contract tradition of Hobbes, Locke, and Rousseau, just as the first and second types arise from J. S. Mill and Kant, respectively.

28 Claude Lévi-Strauss, "The Principle of Reciprocity," *in* Sociological Theory: A Book of Readings, Lewis Coser & Bernard Rosenberg, eds. 84 (1957). *See generally* Peter P. Ekeh, Social Exchange Theory: The Two Traditions 205 (1974).

29 Jean Piaget, The Moral Judgment of the Child 232 (1962). Schelling quotes these words in his Arms and Influence 149 (1972). Rawls, too, draws on Piaget's account of the child's moral development in constructing a theory of justice that, like Schelling's account of military strategy, assumes self-interest to be a central feature of human nature – here, behind the veil of ignorance. Rawls, *supra* note 13, at 460–61.

30 Robert Jervis, The Logic of Images in International Relations 124, 137 (1970). Jervis explains interstate relations in the way Goffman describes how individuals get to know one another; they often disclose information about themselves little by little, with intentionally ambiguous statements. Ambiguity allows the speaker to keep open a number of paths, including disavowal and retreat, if the listener does not adopt the speaker's preferred meaning. Jervis finds that the strategic utility of this practice accounts for much in diplomatic

communication between states, especially those not already on congenial terms or closely connected to each other through shared interpretation of a common history.

31 Schelling, *supra* note 29.

32 *Id.*

33 *Id.*

34 Garrett Hardin, "The Tragedy of the Commons," 162 Science 1243 (1968).

35 This is not to suggest, of course, that the JAGs provided the only significant check on the Bush administration's attempted deviations from Geneva norms. Also of significance, increasingly over time at least, was the litigation initiated by several human rights NGOs, staffed in part by many major private law firms. Deborah N. Pearlstein, "Finding Effective Constraints on Executive Power: Interrogation, Detention, and Torture," 81 Ind. L.J. 1255, 1257 (2005).

36 Jon Elster offers a convincing critique of functionalism in social science in Explaining Social Behavior: More Nuts and Bolts for the Social Sciences 271–86 (2007); Jon Elster, The Cement of Society 147–49 (1989).

37 Even when institutions *do* seek to serve the purpose for which they were created, they often simply prove ineffective. The Bush administration simply shifted responsibility from the military to the CIA and civilian contractors, for instance, for interrogations involving highly coercive methods. On the legal training that U.S. JAGs provide to military interrogators, *see* Maj. Thomas Barnard, "Preparing Interrogators to Conduct Operations Lawfully," Army Lawyer 3 (Feb. 2007), at http://www.encyclopedia.com/doc/1G1-165235907.html; Lt. Col. Paul Kantwill et al., "'Improving the Fighting Position: A Practitioner's Guide to Operational Law Support to the Interrogation Process," Army Lawyer 12, 23–24 (July 2005).

38 There is much great scholarship on the nature and implications of social networks within particular national societies. *See, e.g.,* Fernando Vega-Redondo, Complex Social Networks (2007); John Heinz et al., The Hollow Core: Private Interests in National Policy Making (1993); Networks in the Knowledge Economy, Robert Cross et al., eds. (2003); Harrison White, Markets from Networks (2002).

39 For a survey of recent studies in this regard, *see* Anne-Marie Slaughter & David Zaring, "Networking Goes International: An Update," 2 Ann. Rev. L. & Soc. Sci. 211 (2006).

40 The U.S. officer corps has a high measure of self-recruitment; that is, many officers are recruited from military families, though more than half do have other origins. This pattern showed no sign of changing over the twentieth century. Morris Janowitz, The Professional Soldier xxv–xxvi (1971); G. W. Thomas, "Military Parental Effects and Career Orientation under the AVF," 10 Armed Forces & Society 293 (1984); J. H. Faris, "The All Volunteer Force: Recruitment from Military Families," 7 Armed Forces & Society 545 (1981); Michel Martin, "Like Father, like Son: Career Succession among the Saint-Cyrients," 7 Armed Forces & Society 561 (1981). One researcher in the field believes that the degree of self-recruitment is currently increasing. Prof. Morten Ender, Sociology Program Director, Dept. of Behavioral Sciences and Leadership, U.S. Military Academy, correspondence with author, Oct. 2007.

41 Many have questioned Aristotle's favorable treatment of magnanimity on the grounds that it implies "the social type of a rich noble," as Veyne observes. Paul Veyne, Bread and Circuses: Historical Sociology and Political Pluralism, Brian Pearce, trans. 16 (1992). St. Thomas Acquinas, for instance, prominently raised this objection. Summa Theologica, Secunda secundae, qu. 134, ct. 129.

42 It may be no coincidence in this regard that, within Britain, despite their more limited powers, the House of Lords – many of whose members were still hereditary peers – proved considerably more resistant than the House of Commons to the Prime Minister's repeated efforts to enact legislation restricting the movement of British subjects suspected of involvement in terrorist groups. Louise Richardson, What Terrorists Want: Understanding the Enemy, Containing the Threat 68–71(2006).

43 Among the many theorists defending the importance of public deliberation within democratic polities are Amy Gutmann & Dennis Thompson, Why Deliberative Democracy? (2004); Amy Gutmann & Dennis Thompson, Democracy and Disagreement (1996).

44 Howard Rhodes, correspondence with author, April 29, 2008.

45 Sharon Krause, Liberalism with Honor 16–17 (2002). One military thinker defends a similar view with regard to martial honor as a source of moral restraint in the conflict with Al Qaeda. "In the Long War . . . the 'warrior's honour' still matters. . . . We need warriors precisely because the state cannot always be trusted to act in accordance with its own honour." Christopher Coker, The Warrior Ethos: Military Culture and the War on Terror 146 (2007).

46 John Keegan, "If You Won't, We Won't: Honour and the Decencies of Battle," 24 Times Lit. Supp. 11, Nov. 1995.

47 Adam Roberts, "Land Warfare: From Hague to Nuremberg," *in* The Laws of War: Constraints on Warfare in the Western World, Michael Howard et al., eds. 116 (1994).

48 Anthony Dworkin, "The Laws of War and the Age of Asymmetric Conflict," *in* The Barbarisation of Warfare, George Kassimeris, ed. 220, 232 (2006).

49 Human rights standards may also become increasingly efficacious in some respects, in some places, albeit often in subtle and circuitous ways, even if this is not yet true in warfare. *Compare* Kathryn Sikkink & Carrie B. Walling, "Errors about Trials: The Political Reality of the Justice Cascade," American Political Science Association conference paper (2005); Kathryn Sikkink & Carrie B. Walling, "The Impact of Human Rights Trials in Latin America," 44 J. Peace Res. 427 (2007), *with* Emilie Hafner-Brown & Kiyo Tsutsui, "Human Rights Practices in a Globalizing World: The Paradox of Empty Promises," 110 Amer. J. Sociol. 1373 (2005); Emilie Hafner-Brown & James Ron, "Human Rights Institutions: Rhetoric and Reality," 44 J. Peace Res. 379 (2007); Eric Neumayer, "Do International Human Rights Treaties Improve Respect for Human Rights?" 49 J. Conflict Resol. 922 (2005).

50 The most telling evidence of this is the fact that the U.S. armed forces now award medals of honor for the decision *not* to employ force where initial indications suggested its necessity, but where patience disclosed the possibility of forbearance, enabling civilian lives to be saved.

51 On the role of military lawyers in infusing human rights norms into armed services, *see* Peter Rowe, The Impact of Human Rights Law on Armed Forces (2007), *passim.*

52 Military Commissions in Light of the Supreme Court Decision in *Hamdan v. Rumsfeld* Before the Senate Armed Services Comm., 109 Cong. (2006), at 26.

53 *Id.* Senator McCain has similarly remarked, "It's not about the terrorists, it's about us. It's about what kind of country we are." Adam Nagourney & Marc Santora, "G.O.P. Hopefuls Differ on Response to Terror Attack," New York Times, May 16, 2007, at A17 (quoting Senator McCain). Senator Graham's views on these issues are more complex than the quoted exchange would suggest, as he introduced a successful legislative amendment limiting federal court jurisdiction over Guantánamo detainees.

54 Alexander Wendt, Social Theory of International Politics 92–138 (1999)

55 President George W. Bush, Inaugural Address for Second Term, Jan. 20, 2005, Wash., D.C., paragraph 6.

56 Robert Keohane, "Empathy and International Regimes," *in* Beyond Self-Interest, Jane Mansbridge, ed. 227, 236 (1990).

57 It may be, however, that the Iraq war's critics have not fully assessed the likely costs of losing, particularly the probable increase in terrorist access to petrodollars. Losing the Vietnam War put nothing so prejudicial to U.S. interests at stake. Jeffrey Herf, "New Liberalism, Radical Islam, and the War in Iraq," *in* New American Liberalism, at http://www.newamericanliberalism.org/. *See also* Michael Janofsky, "Saudis Aiding in Cutting off Terrorism Funds, Panel Is Told," New York Times, (March 25, 2004), at A5 (reporting that Saudi cooperation with U.S. banking authorities, in freezing assets of institutions suspected of financing terrorist organizations, increased significantly in the months immediately following the U.S. invasion of Iraq).

58 Richard Tuck, The Rights of War and Peace 109–39 (1999) (parsing Thomas Hobbes's view of international relations).

59 Adam Smith, The Wealth of Nations 689 (1979) (1776) ("The first duty of the sovereign, that of protecting the society from the violence and invasion of other independent societies, can be performed only by means of a military force."); Robert Nozick, Anarchy, State, and Utopia ix, 28, 113–18 (1974).

60 *A and Others v. Sec'y of State for the Home Dep't* (2005), UKHL 71, 2 A.C. 221 (U.K.).

61 *Cf.* D. Dwyer, "Closed Evidence, Reasonable Suspicion, and Torture," 9 Int'l J. Evidence & Proof 126, 131 (2005) (discussing how the Appellate Court in this same case even authorized admission of evidence obtained by torture of a third party (i.e., not the defendant) conducted abroad by a foreign state); Dimitrios Giannoulopoulos, "Torture, Evidence and Criminal Procedure in the Age of Terrorism: A Barbarization of the Criminal Justice System?" *in* Warrior's Dishonour: Barbarity, Morality and Torture in Modern Warfare, George Kassimeris, ed. 223, 228–29 (2006) (same).

62 Even the United States, the implicit object of British criticism here, has long upheld – in its constitutional law rule on the "fruit of the poisonous tree" – a somewhat more stringent position against torture for police purposes. *But see Chavez v. Martinez* 538 U.S. 760, 773 (2003). Three of the Justices in this

case appeared to countenance a high level of coercion short of torture, and three other Justices conspicuously refrained from addressing this question at all. Thus, only three Justices specifically objected to the interrogation practices employed by police in this case. Some have therefore interpreted the result to mean that "the Fifth Amendment right to remain silent is violated only when the information is used against the individual in a criminal case." Geoffrey Stone, "Series Editor's Note," *in* Alan Dershowitz, Is There a Right to Remain Silent? Coercive Interrogation and the Fifth Amendment After 9/11 vii, xiv (2008).

63 Michael Moss & Souad Mekhennet, "Jailed 2 Years, Iraqi Tells of Abuse by Americans," New York Times (Feb. 18, 2007), at A1. Mark Denbeaux & Joshua Denbeaux. "Report on Guantánamo Detainees: A Profile of 517 Detainees through Analysis of Department of Defense Data," Seton Hall University School of Law, 11 at http://law.shu.edu/aaafinal.pdf. The report found that only 45% of detainees were found to have committed a "hostile act" against the U.S. using a broad definition of "hostile act" to include persons who "fled, along with others, when the U.S. forces bombed their camp" or were "captured in Pakistan, along with other Uighur fighters." *Id.* at 11. The report noted that 40% of detainees were not affiliated with al Qaeda and 18% were not affiliated with either al Qaeda or the Taliban. *Id.* at 8. Of those detainees who were identified with either al Qaeda or the Taliban, only a small minority (9% and 16%, respectively) fought for the groups, whereas a significant number (57% and 38%, respectively) were only "associated with" the groups. *Id.* at 10. A great deal depends, however, on how narrowly such terms are interpreted and applied. Even the Chinese Uighurs, for instance, admitted that they had undergone weapons training – for reasons not disclosed – in parts of Afghanistan controlled by the Taliban, though the Bush administration ultimately declined to classify them as enemy combatants. William Glaberson, "In Blow to Bush, Judge Order 17 Guantánamo Detainees Freed," New York Times, Oct. 8, 2006.

64 John Mintz, "Released Detainees Rejoining the Fight," Wash. Post, Oct. 22, 2004, at A1 (reporting that several Guantánamo detainees, released after officials concluded that they "posed little threat," had been recaptured or killed, after reenlisting with Al Qaeda and fighting in Pakistan and Afghanistan).

65 John B. Bellinger, "Remarks on the Military Commissions Act," 48 Harv. Int'l L. J. Online 1, 9 (2007); The Defense Department has recently withdrawn the number of "recidivists" initially claimed in this regard. Anthony Lewis, "Official American Sadism," N.Y. Rev. of Books, Sept. 25, 2008.

66 Benjamin Wittes, "Detention Retention," New Republic, Dec. 7, 2007, at 33. Wittes concludes that the Bush administration itself became "another victim of the inadequate process it set up for reviewing the detainees – which lost in the public arena no matter what those reviews found. . . . When detainees openly admitted their affiliations, validating the government's claims, the secrecy associated with the hearings and records meant that the public never learned about it."

It may be that the very experience of unjust confinement radicalizes the innocent detainees, however few these may have been, so that they will enter the conflict, for the first time, on release. This point is vigorously raised by

Bush administration critics in response to the number of former detainees who have been recaptured. Yet those who may initially find this scenario plausible, in explaining such recaptures, should ask themselves how many of those wrongfully convicted by ordinary courts of murder, and later exonerated on discovery of the error, have responded to the injustice by committing themselves to a life of murder on release from prison.

This argument that wrongful incarceration creates criminals may take two forms. In one version, the very indignity inflicted on the inmate, when perceived as unjust, would elicit a resentment inducing him to rebel further against the authority responsible for it. Lawrence W. Sherman, "Defiance, Deviance, and Irrelevance: A Theory of the Criminal Sanction," 30 J. Research in Crime & Delinquency 445 (1993). The motivation of suicide bombers reflects this process, according to those captured before the deed or after their vests failed to explode. Anat Berko, The Path to Paradise: The Inner World of Suicide Bombers and Their Dispatchers 33–44, 83, 102–03, 109–16, 127–28, 133, 139, 157, 166 (2007). Also plausible is the possibility that the innocent detainee might simply be resocialized by several years of shared habitation with more numerous, genuinely jihadist fellow prisoners, on whose good will his welfare partly depended, and who could capitalize on his understandable indignation over his wrongful captivity, arguing that it was no mere accident but reflected deeper corruption in the society of his captors. It is demonstrably true, moreover, that the felt experience of having been treated unjustly by legal authorities makes many people less inclined to obey the law, even where it continues to threaten real punishment. Tom R. Tyler, Why People Obey the Law 269–88 (2006, 2nd ed.)

67 *See, e.g.,* Philip Heymann, Protecting Liberty in an Age of Terror 15 (2005); Bruce Ackerman, Before the Next Attack: Preserving Liberty in an Age of Terrorism 51–55 (2006). A failure of public international law here is that it provides no civil remedies whatever against individual persons.

68 United Nations Convention Against Torture and Other Cruel, Inhuman or Degrading Treatment or Punishment, 1465 U.N.T.S. 85 (1984), Art. 14.

69 Eric Lichtblau, Bush's Law: The Remaking of American Justice 73 (2008) (describing the U.S. government's payment of $2 million in compensation to the family of Brandon Mayfield for his misidentification and mistreatment by the FBI).

70 Solomon Moore, "DNA Exoneration Brings Change in Legal System," New York Times, Oct. 1, 2007, at A1.

71 Reuters, "British Terror Bill Divides Labor," New York Times, June 11, 2008, at A2.

72 David Cole, "The Priority of Morality: The Emergency Constitution's Blind Spot," 113 Yale L. J. 1753, 1781 (2004).

73 *Id.* at 1783. Cole further notes some perverse incentives here (i.e., the "effect of encouraging unnecessary detentions by legitimating them – 'Yes, we locked you up despite your innocence and despite lacking any evidence to establish that you were suspicious, but we paid you for it'"). *Id.* at 1784.

74 For an argument to this effect regarding U.S. attitudes to terrorism, *see* John Mueller, Overblown: How Politicians and the Terrorism Industry Inflate

National Security Threats, and Why We Believe Them (2006); in economic terms, the matter does not technically concern "risk," but rather "uncertainty," in that it is impossible to attach any credible statistical probabilities. Frank Knight, Risk, Uncertainty, and Profit 19 (1921).

75 Mueller, *id.* (contending that Republican politicians exploit Americans' fear of "another 9/11"); Joanna Bourke, Fear: A Cultural History 61–67, 233–34, 385–86 (2005); Peter Stearns, American Fear: The Causes and Consequences of High Anxiety ix–xi (2005).

76 Richard Ericson & Aaron Doyle, "Introduction," *in* Risk and Morality, Richard Ericson & Aaron Doyle, eds. 13, 16 (2003); *see also* Jutta Weldes et al., "Introduction: Constructing Insecurity," *in* Cultures of Insecurity: States, Communities, and the Production of Danger, Jutta Weldes et al., eds. 1, 10 (1999) (arguing that national "insecurity is itself the product of processes of identity construction in which the self and the other, or multiple others, are constituted").

77 Cass Sunstein, Worst-Case Scenarios 9 (2007).

78 Franklin D. Roosevelt, "First Inaugural Address," *in* II The Public Papers and Addresses of Franklin D. Roosevelt 11 (1950).

79 Editorial, "The Fear of Fear Itself," New York Times, Aug. 7, 2007, at A22.

80 Stanley Hoffman, "Thoughts of Fear in Global Society," 71Soc. Res. (2004), at http://findarticles.com/p/articles/mi_m2267/is_4_71/ai_n13807485.

81 Dan Kahan, Donald Braman et al., "Second National Risk and Culture Study: Making Sense of – and Making Progress in – the American Culture War of Fact," 2008, at http://papers.ssrn.com/sol3/papers.cfm?abstract_id=1017189 (concluding that the activities individuals view as dangerous and the policies they view as effective embody coherent visions of social justice and individual virtue).

82 *Id.* This is not what any reader of Kahan's prior research would have led one to anticipate. *See, e.g.,* Sunstein, *supra* note 77, at 67. It is true, however, that people displaying these disparate cultural orientations differ greatly over what they see as the *sources* of terror risk (e.g., over whether the U.S. invasion of Iraq increased or decreased such risk). They disagree in their perceptions of many other risks as well, from environmental pollution to the eating of red meat, these authors find.

83 Kahan, *supra* note 81, at 49.

84 Pew Research Center, http://pollingreport.com/prioriti.htm (2006).

85 Scott Plous, The Psychology of Judgment and Decision Making 125–26, 178–80 (1993) (discussing the salience heuristic and the closely related heuristics of vividness and availability). *Cf.* Robert M. Reycs, William C. Thompson & Gordon H. Bower, "Judgmental Biases Resulting from Differing Availabilities of Arguments," 39 J. Personality & Soc. Psychol 2, 5-12 (1980); Jonathan Baron, "Heuristics and Biases in Equity Judgments: A Utilitarian Approach," *in* Psychological Perspectives on Justice, Barbara Mellers & Jonathan Baron, eds. (1993).

86 Lisa Heinzerling, "The Rights of Statistical People," 24 Harv. Env. L. Rev. 189, 189 (2000).

87 Barbara Whitaker, "Ready for Anything (That's Their Job)," New York Times, Sept. 9, 2007, at A17.

88 Poems from Guantánamo: The Detainees Speak, Marc Falkoff, ed. (2007).

89 Roger G. Noll & James E. Krier, "Some Implications of Cognitive Psychology for Risk Regulation," 19 J. Legal Stud. 747, 777 (1990); Howard Margolis, Dealing with Risk: Why the Public and the Experts Disagree on Environmental Issues (1996).

90 To characterize this cost as "inconvenience" is not to trivialize it, and the word is entirely inapplicable to the experience of those killed or tortured during interrogation.

91 Denbeaux & Denbeaux, *supra* note 63; Mark Bowden, "The Dark Art of Interrogation," 292 Atlantic Monthly, Oct. 2003, 18, 56, 58, 60, 70 (citing Marine Lt. Col. William Cowan, who conducted many interrogations during the Vietnam War).

92 Stathis Kalyvas, The Logic of Violence in Civil War 176–83, 336–63 (2006) (analyzing the high incidence of denunciation of intimates to political authorities during civil wars).

93 Kenneth Roth, "Human Rights and the U.S. War on Terror: Why is George Bush Reading from Al Qaeda's Playbook," Public Lecture, Carr Center for Human Rights, Harvard University, April 27, 2007; Denbaux & Denbeaux, *supra* note 63.

94 We do know, however, that at least five, and maybe more than twenty detainees have been beaten to death during U.S. interrogations. David Luban, "Liberalism, Torture, and the Ticking Bomb," 91 Va. L. Rev. 1425, 1437 (2005) (summarizing the findings of several official reports to this effect).

95 *See, e.g.,* Amos Guiora, Constitutional Limits on Coercive Interrogation 89 (2008) (announcing, without supportive citation of any kind: "Torture is illegal, immoral, and does not lead to actionable intelligence."); Philippe Sands, Torture Team: Rumsfeld's Memo and The Betrayal of American Values 224 (2008) ("There was never any possibility that his [Al-Qahtani's abusive] treatment would produce any meaningful material.").

96 John A. Wahlquist, "Educing Information: Interrogation – Science and Art," in National Defense Intelligence College, Educing Information, xxi (2006) (drawing this conclusion after surveying existing studies); Philip Rumney, "The Effectiveness of Coercive Interrogation: Scholarly and Judicial Responses," 44 Crime, Law & Soc. Change 465 (2005) (same). It must be conceded nonetheless that there is abundant anecdotal evidence of torture's occasional efficacy in eliciting vital information. Alissa J. Rubin, "After Iraqi Troops Do Dirty Work, Three Detainees Talk," New York Times, April 22, 2007, at A1 (describing how U.S. interrogation of three suspected Al Qaeda detainees elicited important life-saving and demonstrably accurate information after one detainee was first tortured by Iraqi troops), at A1; Bowden, *supra* note 91, at 18 (describing several successful coercive interrogations of terrorist suspects, where coercion was resorted to only after less draconian methods had failed); *but see* Tony Lagouranis, Fear up Harsh: An Army Interrogator's Dark Journey Through Iraq 242 (2007) ("I never got intelligence using torture, but it is possible that I was a bad torturer and perhaps a bad interrogator."). Once one adopts consequentialism of any sort as a moral guide, moreover, the decision about

what to do must ultimately depend on empirical questions like those posed by such social scientists as Morrow and Valentino et al.

97 One tries in vain to imagine what the wording would look like on the relevant "human subjects" application to the Institutional Review Board of any U.S. university. The type of laboratory experiments that Milgram conducted in the early 1970s, in which participants were asked to administer (apparent) electric shocks to other participants, are no longer permitted. Stanley Milgram, Obedience to Authority: An Experimental View (1974). This is likely for the best. A leading moral and legal theorist, who would surely wish to remain nameless, nonetheless laments this state of affairs: "The kids get over it," he says of the deleterious effects on participants, "and we learn such incredibly interesting things from this research!"

98 Richard A. Leo, "Miranda's Revenge: Police Interrogation as a Confidence Game," 30 L. & Soc. Rev. 259, 260-61 (1996).

99 *See, e.g.,* Stephen Budiansky, "Truth Extraction," 295 Atlantic Monthly, June 2005, 32, 35; Lt. Col. Paul Kantwill et al., "'Improving the Fighting Position': A Practitioner's Guide to Operational Law Support to the Interrogation Process," Army Lawyer 12, 23–24 (July 2005) ("Interrogators should be skilled in the art of manipulating the subject of an interrogation into providing information that he may have been initially determined to withhold. . . . The instinct of interrogators to develop creative manipulation techniques should be encouraged, so long as such techniques are monitored to ensure that they remain within the bounds of humane treatment. . . . No detainee has a right to be protected against trickery, deception, . . . incentives . . . nonviolent or noncoercive ruses."). Even such deception is forbidden to police in some Western European states, including Germany, according to Prof. Jacqueline Ross, a specialist in the subject. Correspondence with author, May 2008.

100 Philip Zelikow, for instance, argues that in a "professional, objective analysis" of interrogation successes and failures "the elementary question would not be: Did you get information that proved useful? Instead it would be: Did you get information that could have been usefully gained only from these methods?" Philip Zelikow, "Legal Policy for a Twilight War," 5/30/07, at http://hnn. us/articles/39494.html, at 11; *see also* Stephen Bottomley & Simon Bronitt, Law in Context 414 (2006) (observing that "there is little compelling evidence that requiring higher standards of due process and protection of human rights impedes effective law enforcement or counter-terrorism activity"); David Cole & Jules Lobel, Less Safe, Less Free: Why America is Losing the War on Terror 254 (2007) ("Bush cannot show that any useful information obtained through coercive interrogation could not have been obtained through lawful methods.").

101 Mark Bowden, "The Ploy," 299 The Atlantic Monthly, May 2007, at 54, 54 (describing the successful use of noncoercive interrogation, including positive rather than negative incentives, to elicit information leading to the discovery and killing of Al Qaeda leader Abu Musab al-Zarqawi).

102 Aristotle, Nicomachean Ethics, Christopher Rowe, trans. 96 (2002).

103 This literature is sympathetically examined by Michel Foucault in his last lectures. The Hermeneutics of the Subject: Lectures at the Collège de France, Graham Burchell, trans. 1981–1982 355–70, 409–11 (2004).

104 For a contemporary articulation of this ideal, *see* Susan Verducci, "The Ability to Respond," *in* Responsibility at Work: How Leading Professionals Act (or Don't Act) Responsibly, Howard Gardner, ed. 43, 47–50 (2007).

105 David Brooks, "Center First Gives Way to Center Last," New York Times, Sept. 4, 2007, A23 (describing efforts by U.S. military commanders to form relationships with tribal leaders in Iraqi localities, in alliance against more sectarian leaders at the national level). *See also* David Kilcullen, "Anatomy of a Tribal Revolt," Small Wars Journal (Aug. 31, 2007), at http://smallwarsjournal. com/blog/2007/08/anatomy-of-a-tribal-revolt/; David Sanger, "News Analysis: Bush Shifts Terms for Measuring Progress in Iraq," New York Times, Sept. 5, 2007.

106 Michael Walzer, Arguing About War 45 (2004).

107 Carl Von Clausewitz, On War 117, Michael Howard & Peter Paret, eds. & trans. (1976) (1832).

108 Mirko Bagaric & Julie Clarke, Torture: When the Unthinkable is Morally Permissible 61 (2007).

109 Mary Ellen O'Connell, "Affirming the Ban on Harsh Interrogation," 66 Ohio St. L. J. 1231, 1263 (2005).

110 On the arguably *jus cogens* status of common Art. 3 of the Geneva Conventions, *see* Stefanie Schmahl, "An Example of *Jus Cogens*: The Status of Prisoners of War," *in* The Fundamental Rules of the International Order, Christian Tomuschat et al., eds. 41, 56 (2006).

111 The evidentiary burden ought not to be as high, however, as in a legal proceeding, much less a criminal one. Frederick Schauer, "Slightly Guilty," U. Chi. Leg. F. 83, 88–92 (1993) (arguing that the severity of evidentiary burdens in public policy deliberation should not be as high as in criminal prosecutions).

112 Michael N. Schmitt, "Targeting and Humanitarian Law: Current Issues," 34 Israel Yearbook on Human Rights 59, 84 (2004).

113 Tara McKelvey, "Washingtonians," New York Times, Feb. 9, 2008.

114 Timur Kuran, Private Truths, Public Lies: The Social Consequences of Preference Falsification 3–9 (1995).

115 Such public-private opinion disparities are common on a number of controversial social policy issues. Phillip Jelson & Kenneth Greene, Signaling Goodness: Social Rules and Public Choice 117 (2003); Kuran, *supra* note 114, at 139–41, 145–50, 233–38. The distorted communication here at issue may be attributable merely to the not-so-subtle incentives within more elite American universities to signal colleagues that one is a "good type," loyal to the group, meriting its esteem. Eric Posner, Law and Social Norms 18–31 (2000). The most reliable way to send this signal has been to dissociate oneself conspicuously from Bush administration policies of any sort, whatever one's true and more ambivalent views, apparently shared only in more intimate interactions. Rational choice theory defines a "good type" not in normative terms, but simply as a person who values future returns in relations with others more than does a "bad type."

116 The entire subject is only beginning to receive sustained and thoughtful attention. Such reticence surely cannot be unequivocally condemned, moreover, for "the difference between what we actually notice and what we publicly acknowledge having noticed is at the very heart of what it means to be tactful,"

as notes one sociologist. Eviatar Zerubavel, The Elephant in the Room: Silence and Denial in Everyday Life 29 (2006).

117 *Id.*

118 Bernard Williams, "The Idea of Equality," *in* Philosophy, Politics, and Society, P. Laslett & W.G. Runciman, eds. 90 (1962).

119 *See, e.g.,* Thomas Nagel, "Autonomy and Deontology," *in* Consequentialism and Its Critics 142, 156–67 (Samuel Scheffler, ed. 1988); David Sussman, "What's Wrong with Torture?" 33 Phil. & Pub. Aff. 1, 2–3 (2005); Jeremy Waldron, "Torture and Positive Law: Jurisprudence for the White House," 105 Colum. L. Rev. 1681 (2005) (arguing for an absolute legal prohibition on torture, but not on the basis of a moral absolutism against it); Yuval Shany, "The Prohibition against Torture and Cruel, Inhuman, and Degrading Treatment and Punishment: Can the Absolute Be Relativized under Existing International Law?" 56 Cath. U. L. Rev. 837, 868 (2007) (same).

120 Eduard Brandstatter, Gaer Gigerenzer & Ralph Hertwig, "The Priority Heuristic: Making Choices without Trade-Offs," 113 Psychological Rev. 409 (2006) (describing the cognitive shortcuts by which people semi-consciously conduct cost-benefit analyses in their daily lives).

121 *U.S. vs. Carroll Towing Co.*, 159 F.2d 169 (2d Cir. 1947). The Hand formula finds negligence whenever the defendant's burden (B) is less than the probability (p) of harm, multiplied by the degree of loss (L). In short, $B < p \times L$. Thus, by multiplying outcomes by their probability, we discover the expected value of alternative courses of action.

122 Sunstein, *supra* note 77, at 3.

123 Seth F. Kreimer, "Too Close to the Rack and the Screw: Constitutional Constraints on Torture in the War on Terror," 6 U. Penn. J. Const. L. 278, 306 (2003).

124 Ron Suskind, The One Percent Doctrine 61–62 (2006).

125 Timothy Lynch & Robert Singh, After Bush: The Case for Continuity in American Foreign Policy 11–15 (2008).

126 Cass Sunstein, The Laws of Fear: Beyond the Precautionary Principle 14 (2005).

127 Jonathan Simon, "Risk and Reflexivity: What Socio-Legal Studies Add to the Study of Risk and the Law," 57 Ala. L. Rev. 119, 138 (2006).

128 Richard Tuck, "The Dangers of Natural Rights," 20 Harv. J.L. & Pub. Pol'y 683, 692 (1997).

129 President Bush claimed in 2007 that the secret interrogation program "has given us information that has saved innocent lives, by helping us stop new attacks." He asserted, in particular, that at least ten serious Al Qaeda plots since September 11, three of them inside the United States, had been thereby averted. Jane Mayer, "The Black Sites," 83 New Yorker, Aug. 13, 2007, at 46, 48.

130 George Tenet, At the Center of the Storm 242 (2007). Former CIA officer John Kiriakou, who witnessed the interrogation of Abu Zubaydah, reports that "the threat information he provided disrupted a number of attacks, maybe dozens of attacks." This information reportedly included Al-Qaeda's leadership structure. Jonah Goldberg, "Five Minutes Well Spent: Keeping Waterboarding as an Interrogation Technique Is Not the Slippery Slope Some Say It Is," Nat. Rev. Online, Feb. 15, 2008.

131 Quoted in Jack Goldsmith, The Terror Presidency 151 (2007).

132 CIA sources also claim that it was only by recourse to waterboarding that Khalid Sheik Mohammed, the prime plotter of the 9/11 attacks, was induced to provide useful information. Walter Pincus, "Waterboarding Historically Controversial," Wash. Post, Oct. 5, 2006, at A17.

133 General James T. Hill, Chief Commander of U.S. Southern Command, similarly contends that coercive methods of interrogation, adopted after softer techniques had failed, succeded in producing useful new information from Al Qaeda and Al Wafa al Igatha al Islamia operative Mohammed Al-Qahtani. Quoted in Sands, *supra* note 95, at 145. Others familiar with the case report the same. *See, e.g.,* Drew Brown, "Coercive Methods Prompted Sept. 11 Figure to Talk, General Testifies," Knight Ridder, July 14, 2005, at http://www.commondreams.org/headlines05/0714-05.htm (quoting Air Force Lt. General Randall Schmidt). The CIA also claims that it was only by recourse to waterboarding that Khalid Sheik Mohammed, the prime plotter of the 9/11 attacks, was induced to provide useful information. Walter Pincus, "Waterboarding Historically Controversial," Wash. Post, Oct. 5, 2006, at A17. At sixty places within its text, the 9/11 Commission Report credits the interrogation of Khalid Shaikh Mohammed for yielding significant facts about Al Qaeda. *See also* Scott Shane, "Inside a 9/11 Mastermind's Interrogation," New York Times, June 21, 2008, at A13 (quoting former CIA counterterrorism officer John Kiriakou, the first to question Abu Zubaydah on his capture, describing the effect of later waterboarding as "like flipping a switch" in shifting detainee response from resistance to active cooperation).

134 "Informant Key to Plot: In JFK Airport Case, Drug Dealer Posed as Wannabe Terrorist," Detroit Free Press, June 4, 2007, at 6.

135 David Cole, Terrorism and the Constitution 240 (2002).

136 When fundamental liberties are in issue, the Constitution generally requires "strict scrutiny" of restrictions on their exercise. *Korematsu v. United States,* 323 U.S. 214, 215 (1944); *Roe v. Wade,* 410 U.S. 113 (1973). This means that the "state interest" must be "compelling" and the means employed to attaining it no more liberty restrictive than necessary.

137 Richard Betts, "Intelligence Warning: Old Problems, New Agendas," 28 Parameters 26, 30 (Spring 1998).

138 The True Cost of Conflict: Seven Recent Wars and Their Effects on Society, Michael Cranna, ed. (1994) (showing how far afield these costs can run, over time and space, beyond the most immediate and most readily measurable casualties).

139 Realist approaches to international relations do not do so, however, and so are untrue to any putative moral foundations in utilitarianism.

140 Walzer, *supra* note 106, at 39.

141 Most criticisms of Posner's cost-benefit defenses of current U.S. policy adopt these approaches. *See, e.g.,* Paul Schiff Berman, "Seeing beyond the Limits of International Law," 84 Tex. L. Rev. 1265, 1267 (2006) (arguing that the notion of a state's having a unitary interest is conceptually incoherent and empirically inaccurate).

142 A deeper skeptic of rational choice would admittedly contend that whenever a method is consistently misapplied in a given way, this is unlikely to be

coincidental. It is no accident that its disinterested and more careful application would give greater attention to other, neglected considerations, fully cognizable within its terms, if the method were employed in this more careful fashion. For then it could not advance the power-knowledge purposes for which it is more routinely invoked and for which it was developed. For instance, one scholar contends – albeit quite unconvincingly – that rational choice thinking arose from the peculiar geopolitical configuration of the Cold War and U.S. concerns within it. S. M. Amadae, Rationalizing Capitalist Democracy: The Cold War Origins of Rational Choice Liberalism (2003). Yet recent uses of rational choice methods in service of more "critical" politics reveal their underutilized potential to quite different ends. *See, e.g.,* Bernard Harcourt, Against Prediction: Profiling, Policing, and Punishing in an Actuarial Age 31–35 (2007). Cost-benefit analysis was highly influential in inducing President Ronald Reagan to lead the world toward aggressive efforts to protect the ozone layer. Cass Sunstein, *supra* note 77.

143 Robert Goodin, Political Theory and Public Policy 97 (1982). *See also* Linda Molm et al, "Building Solidarity through Generalized Exchange: A Theory of Reciprocity," 113 Amer. J. Sociol. 205 (2007).

144 Keohane, *supra* note 56, at 233 (emphasis supplied).

145 Robert Gilpin, Global Political Economy 192 (2001). Such contractual "countertrade," if made between two private parties, closely resembles what American antitrust law prohibits as a type of "reciprocal dealing" or "tying" arrangement.

146 Will Bardenwerper, "Party Here, Sacrifice over There," New York Times, Oct. 20, 2007, editorial (by an Army infantry officer, noting "the disparity between the lives of the few who are fighting and being killed, and the many who have been asked for nothing more than to continue shopping"). For such veterans, the social contract appears to read: Toward a common end as important as the national defense, all must meaningfully contribute, even if not in identical currency. This is not to say that the entire country need be mobilized for war – a position taken by only certain of the most extreme Christian evangelicals – but simply that the burdens of whatever measure of mobilization does occur should be shared more evenly. From the vets' recent observations, some in turn argue for a public duty to increase the range of postservice benefits accorded to recent veterans. Senators Jim Webb & Chuck Hagel, "A Post-Iraq G.I. Bill," New York Times, Nov. 9, 2007, editorial.

A further implication of the vets' criticism is that, as a commercial republic, we may have come to adore luxury in ways that sap the sterner, more stoic virtues necessary to collective self-preservation in a harsh world. This suspicion, in fact, embodies a longstanding criticism of modern liberalism. Peter Berkowitz, Virtue and the Making of Modern Liberalism 177 (1999) (noting the inattention of classical liberal thought to this problem).

147 Most of the common objections to social contract theory, especially to its lack of historical realism, are thus irrelevant here.

148 The limited nature of international economic interdependence in the early eighteenth century (other than empire, an involuntary variety) drew classical theorists of the social contract to a skeptical "realism" on international relations. David Mapel, "The Contractarian Tradition and International Ethics," *in* Traditions of International Ethics, Terry Nardin & David Mapel, eds. 180, 191

(1992). The only exception here is Kant, who thought that the moral basis for cosmopolitan duty lay simply in reason itself. International morality was no different from domestic morality in this respect, for the categorical imperative applied equally to both. Thomas Donaldson, "Kant's Global Rationalism,' *in* Nardin & Mapel, *Id.* at 136, 142–44. However, Kant does imply in places that the fact of interstate cooperation creates an additional basis for international morality, according to Charles Beitz, Political Theory and International Relations 144 (1979) (parsing passages from Kant's The Metaphysical Elements of Justice and his Perpetual Peace).

149 On Kant as a "virtue ethicist" in this regard, *see* Christine Korsgaard, The Sources of Normativity 90–130 (1996) (interpreting Kant to hold that all practical identities, including those of particular professions and their codes of honor, are relative to our identity as human beings, because it is on the basis of this primary identity that we are able to acquire any others); Robert Louden, "Kant's Virtue Ethics," 61 Philosophy 473, 485 (1986) (arguing that in Kant's ideal "one strives for a way of life in which all of one's acts are a manifestation of a character which is in harmony with moral law"); Onora O'Neill, Constructions of Reason: Explorations of Kant's Practical Philosophy 150–61 (1989).

150 John Stuart Mill, "Utilitarianism," Samuel Gorovitz ed. 38 (1971) (1863) ("Virtue, according to the utilitarian doctrine, is not naturally and originally part of the end [of happiness], but it is capable of becoming so; and in those who love it disinterestedly it has become so, and is desired and cherished, not as a means to happiness, but as a part of their happiness."). Thus, even arch consequentialists like Mill do not deny that virtue can become an end in itself; they only deny that it is originally so. They would say that virtue becomes an end in itself once being virtuous has become a source of one's pleasure. Once the two are so tied, one then values virtue even if one doesn't obtain any immediate pleasure from particular acts of virtue.

151 Daniel Bell, The Cultural Contradictions of Capitalism 76 (1976); Irving Kristol, Two Cheers for Capitalism 139–40 (1978); *but see* Deirdre McCloskey, The Bourgeois Virtues: Ethics for an Age of Commerce 74–78 (2006) (arguing that a bourgeois ethic of honorable work robustly endures and pervades most of American society).

152 Max Weber, The Protestant Ethic and the Spirit of Capitalism, Talcott Parsons, trans. 16–17, 54, 62–68, 79 (1958) (1905).

153 Author's confidential interviews with several active-duty JAGs.

154 On the relevance of this consideration, *see* Nils Melzer, Targeted Killing in International Law (2008) (discussing the scholarship of M. Kremnitzer).

155 Schauer, *supra* note 111, at 84.

CONCLUSION

1 Elaine Scarry, The Body in Pain: The Making and Unmaking of the World 139 (1985).

2 In such political discourse, one more often encounters the opposite – essentially contested concepts, over which there may be widespread agreement concerning

an abstract core notion (e.g., "fairness"), but endless argument about what its proper realization would entail. W.B. Gallie, "Essentially Contested Concepts," 56 Proceedings of the Aristotelian Society 167 (1956). As noted earlier, European colonial powers continued to practice torture well into the mid-twentieth century.

3 In 1911, the article on torture in the Encyclopaedia Britannica stated that "the whole subject is now one of only historical interest as far as Europe is concerned." 27 Encyclopaedia Britannica 72, 72 (11th ed. 1911); *see also* Judith Shklar, "The Liberalism of Fear," *in* Liberalism and the Moral Life, Nancy Rosenblum, ed. 27 (1989).

4 Long before the Bush administration's counterterrorism policies, the scope of torture's legal meaning had been subject to some disagreement because of ambiguities in statutory and treaty definitions. International tribunals had made some genuine progress toward its clarification, however. *See, e.g., Ireland v. United Kingdom,* 2 Eur. Ct. H.R. (ser. A) 25, 79–80 (1979–80); *Selmouni v. France,* 29 Eur. Ct. H.R. 403, 440–43 (2000).

5 Amnesty Int'l, The Pain Merchants: Security Equipment and Its Use in Torture and Other Ill-Treatment, AI Index ACT 40/008/2003, Dec. 2, 2003. During 2002 Amnesty International reported torture or ill treatment by security forces, police, or other state authorities in 106 countries. A study of Amnesty documentation for the years 1997–2000 showed that torture was reported in more than 150 countries. In more than seventy of them, reports of torture were widespread or persistent. In more than eighty countries, people reportedly died as a result. Most of the documented torturers were police officers. In its latest annual report, Amnesty reported that 102 countries had practiced torture or ill treatment in 2006. Amnesty Int'l, Amnesty International Report 2007: Facts and Figures, AI Index POL 10/007/2007, May 23, 2007.

6 This would be a reasonable inference from, *inter alia*, the March 2008 presidential veto of legislation that would have outlawed "waterboarding" of terror suspects by the CIA (i.e., assuming that this practice may be fairly characterized as torture). Steven Lee Myers, "Bush Uses Veto on C.I.A. Tactics to Affirm Legacy," New York Times, March 9, 2008.

7 Slavoj Žižek, "Knight of the Living Dead," New York Times, March 24, 2007, editorial.

8 Jonathan Alter, "Time to Think about Torture," Newsweek, Nov. 5, 2001, at 45; Alan Dershowitz, Why Terrorism Works 139–41 (2002); David Cole & Jules Lobel, Less Safe, Less Free: Why American Is Losing the War on Terror 198 (2007) (quoting Richard Posner).

9 Amy Gutmann & Dennis Thompson, Democracy and Disagreement 53, 55 (1996).

10 Slavoj Žižek, Welcome to the Desert of the Real! Five Essays on September 11 and Related Dates 104 (2002) (satirizing the quoted statement).

11 The present argument resembles in this respect that of George Norman & Joel Trachtman, "The Customary International Law Game," 99 A.J.I.L. 541 (2005), who contend that rational choice theory, properly understood and applied, does not support Posner's and Goldsmith's conclusion that custom has no significant impact on states' conduct. *See also* Jean Maria Arrigo, "A

Utilitarian Argument against Torture Interrogation of Terrorists," 10 Science & Engineering Ethics 543 (2007). Even *realpolitik* often counsels caution if not opposition to the use of force, after all, as its leading adherents wisely did regarding the 2003 decision to invade Iraq. John Mearsheimer & Stephen Walt, "An Unnecessary War," Foreign Policy, Jan./Feb. 2003, at 4. The Vietnam War was similarly opposed by the leading realist of the day, Hans Morgenthau. *See* his Vietnam and the United States. 19–20, 604–06 (1965).

12 This is not to suggest that detention and interrogation policy are the only grievances that America's closest allies have against it, but rather that they are among the more compelling ones. Andrei Markovits, Uncouth Nation: Why Europe Dislikes America 139 (2007) (summarizing survey data suggesting that a major source of anti-Americanism in many countries, particularly in the Arab world, is the view that American women are sexually immoral).

13 Moreover, there is no need to accept that entire nation-states may make constitutive commitments as a collectivity – whatever that might turn out to mean – to acknowledge that most citizens may individually do so (i.e., may commit themselves to common principles and associated prohibitions because they believe that they share a civic identity with other Americans).

14 James Whitman, Harsh Justice: Criminal Punishment and the Widening Divide between America and Europe 150 (2003).

15 James Whitman, "On Nazi 'Honour' and the New European 'Dignity,'" *in* Darker Legacies of Law in Europe, Christian Joerges & Mavraj Singh Ghaleigh, eds. 243 (2003).

16 *See* Albert Hirschman, The Rhetoric of Reaction: Perversity, Futility, Jeopardy 148–63 (1991) (describing liberal and leftist usages of reactionary rhetorical moves). The current antiglobalization movement, for instance, certainly defines itself more in terms of what it opposes (i.e., reacts against) than by way of any detailed, alternative social vision. And there is surely nothing pernicious or even "merely derivative" in the common tendency to work out one's own views partly in reaction to more extreme ones, and events inspired by them.

17 To be sure, "reaction" is a central feature of political life in the aftermath of virtually every large-scale effort at transformative change, from the French Revolution to the American New Left of the 1960s.

18 As Ikenberry observes, "Throughout the West, the dominant form of political identity is based on a set of abstract and juridical rights and responsibilities which coexist with private and semi-public ethnic and religious associations. Just as warring states and nationalism reinforce each other, so too do Western civil identity and Western political structures and institutions reinforce each other. Political order – domestic and international – is strengthened when there exists a substantial sense of community and shared identity." John Ikenberry, Liberal Order and Imperial Ambition: Essays on American Power and World Politics 102, 163 (2006).

19 On the psychological dynamics of this process, *see* Jon Elster, Explaining Social Behavior: More Nuts and Bolts for the Social Sciences 102–03 (2007).

20 *See also* Husain Haqqani, "Pakistan and the Islamists," Current Hist. 147 (April 2007); Stephen P. Cohen, "America and Pakistan: Is the Worst Case Avoidable?" 104 Current Hist. 131 (2005).

21 This is not to deny the desirabilitly of an administrative system of sustained detention, encompassing due process protections different from, and probably less demanding than those required by criminal prosecution for terrorism-related offenses.

22 "Polemics, Politics, and Problematizations," *in* Ethics: Essential Works of Foucault 1954–1984, vol. 1, Paul Rabinow, ed. 111, 111–12 (1997).

23 Martha Nussbaum, The Therapy of Desire: Theory and Practice in Hellenistic Ethics 403 (1994). She adds, "In circumstances where evil prevails, anger is an assertion of concern for human well-being and human dignity; and the failure to become angry seems at best "slavish" (as Aristotle put it), at worst a collaboration with evil."

24 For two particularly intemperate and careless statements from leading political thinkers on the right and left, respectively, *see* Jean Bethke Elshtain, Just War against Terror: The Burden of American Power in a Violent World (2003); Iris Marion Young, Global Challenges: War, Self-Determination and Responsibility for Justice 105–39 (2007).

25 Claude Lévi-Strauss, "Reciprocity: The Essence of Social Life," *in* The Family: Its Structure and Functions, Lewis Coser, ed. 36 (1964).

26 This raises the question, beyond this book's scope, of whether the continued practice of bilateral "gift" reciprocity between states impedes a global social contract, which is necessarily multilateral, from attaining greater breadth and depth over time. Within a given nation-state, it is often the case that ethnic or tribal bonds and associated duties to kin limit the capacity of state officials, such as judges and police, to implement the rule of law (i.e., impartially). This is a developmental drawback to the gift economy within a national society. Similarly in the international arena, a gift economy enables wealthier states – as through their foreign aid programs and bilateral investment treaties – to exercise greater influence than they would have under a more centralized, rule of law/social contract regime at the global level. Generous bilateral foreign aid by states here sits uneasily with the provision of such assistance through a regime of multilateral organizations, much as national reprisals for humanitarian law violations fit only very uncomfortably with the early postwar aspiration to providing collective security against such wrongs through the UN Security Council and an international criminal tribunal. Gifts and violence may here, at least, indeed run in the same grooves.

These potential problems with bilateral reciprocity do not pertain to intersocietal gifting in the present case, however. For the world considers humane treatment of terror suspects to be required by international law, and hence views the ensuing melioration of conditions through the lens of the global contract, even if the United States may view it only as a gesture of magnanimity, a way to signal the benevolence of American hegemony. This is not a stable arrangement for the long term, to be sure, because each side to the interaction understands it differently and hence is likely to draw contrary lessons from it. Nor is such an overlapping consensus – here, on the desirability of more humane detainee treatment – so easily obtained in other issue-areas of U.S. foreign relations. Scholars would do well to consider more seriously both the complementarities and tensions between nonmarket gift reciprocity and the legal/social contract as bases of order and solidarity in international relations.

States are unequal in their donative capacity, even if they enjoy a formal legal equality – the moral basis of which is dubious, in any event. Thomas H. Lee, "International Law, International Relations Theory, and Preemptive War: The Vitality of Sovereign Equality Today," 67 L. & Contemp. Prob. 147, 154–57 (2004). Lee effectively dispatches all arguments for treating sovereign states as legal equals, thereby rejecting the analogy to individual persons before domestic law, but then concedes the pragmatic utility of this fiction for keeping hegemonic states like the United States better apprised of actual threats to world order (i.e., to help them accurately assess the nature and extent of such dangers). The legal equality of sovereign states may contribute to this end. It is not obviously necessary, however, because the views of key allies, plus a few other trustworthy states most concerned with the given issue, would likely suffice to serve this epistemic function. The equality of sovereign states long upheld by public international law may be morally defensible only within a Kantian league or concert of democratic republics, where respect for national sovereignty could be treated as a reasonable proxy for popular sovereignty. The international law produced by such a league, including its humanitarian law, would deserve more deference than the law generated by UN-related organs in current form.

But democracies almost never fight one another, so the law they adopted for governing war among themselves would be largely irrelevant. And a league of democracies could not presume to apply its law to nonmembers, whether states or nonstate actors, without purporting to act as a "world state." A democractic league could nonetheless condition trade with, and aid from its members on adherence to such law, thereby incentivizing other states (albeit doubtfully non-state actors) to respect such norms. The EU's persistent pressure on Serbia to extradict war criminals for prosecution in The Hague offers the most pertinent experience and model here. Steven Blockmans, Tough Love: The European Union's Relations with the Western Balkans (2007). And since a league of democracies would at least be legitimate among member states, it would not require their unanimous consent to every major enactment, the situation approximated by most international law today.

To be sure, this lovely scenario – though partly realized on a geographically limited scope in the EU and occasionally broached on a broader scale by American leaders in both politial parties – is not exactly at the center of anyone's immediate global agenda. For the time being, then, within a global zone of law and peace there will likely continue to develop an increasingly multilateral and issue-diverse reciprocity approximating a social contract. Beyond that zone, however, there will remain possible only an immediate, bilateral and more contingent variety of reciprocity. And where even that becomes impossible, as in conflicts with most terrorist networks, hopes for restraint will rest entirely on considerations of identity and interest, i.e., on collective self-understandings concerning martial/national virtue and on enlightened calculations of how best to advance America's influence.

Index